Readings in Comparative Health Law and Bioethics

Readings in Comparative Health Law and Bioethics

THIRD EDITION

Edited by

Nathan Cortez
Adelfa Botello Callejo Endowed Professor of Law
SMU Dedman School of Law

I. Glenn Cohen
James A. Attwood and Leslie Williams Professor of Law and
Faculty Director of the Petrie-Flom Center for
Health Law Policy, Biotechnology, and Bioethics
Harvard Law School

Timothy Stoltzfus Jost
Robert L. Willett Family Professor of Law Emeritus
Washington and Lee University School of Law

Carolina Academic Press
Durham, North Carolina

Library of Congress Cataloging-in-Publication Data

Names: Cortez, Nathan, editor. | Cohen, I. Glenn, editor. | Jost, Timothy S., editor.
Title: Readings in comparative health law and bioethics / by Nathan Cortez, I. Glenn Cohen, Timothy Stoltzfus Jost.
Description: Third edition. | Durham, North Carolina : Carolina Academic Press, [2019] | Includes bibliographical references and index.
Identifiers: LCCN 2019032692 | ISBN 9781531002459 (paperback) | ISBN 9781531002466 (ebook)
Subjects: LCSH: Medical care--Law and legislation. | Medical laws and legislation. | Bioethics.
Classification: LCC K3601 .R415 2019 | DDC 344.04/1--dc23
LC record available at https://lccn.loc.gov/2019032692

Carolina Academic Press
700 Kent Street
Durham, North Carolina 27701
Telephone (919) 489-7486
Fax (919) 493-5668
www.cap-press.com

Printed in the United States of America

For N.S.C., H.A.C., and M.S.C.
—Nathan Cortez

For J.A.
—I. Glenn Cohen

Contents

Introduction

This book is a collection of annotated readings to be used for teaching comparative health law and bioethics.

Since the Second Edition was published in 2007, comparative health law has become a much more mature, substantial field. Legions of academic books and articles have been written about comparative health systems, comparative law, and/or comparative policy in health care over the last decade. Indeed, these topics have caught the attention of popular audiences in recent years. For example, immediately after the Second Edition was published, the PBS Frontline documentary *Sick Around the World* (2008) and T.R. Reid's popular book *The Healing of America: A Global Quest for Better, Cheaper, and Fairer Health Care* (2009) highlighted for lay audiences how unique America's health care system is, particularly when viewed in comparative context.

Like the Second Edition, the Third Edition is located within the discipline of comparative law. The traditional concerns of comparative law have been to analyze, classify, and (to the extent possible) understand a foreign legal system as a whole. Traditionally, comparative law has concentrated on comparing continental European civil law systems with common law systems. It has also focused on private law. More recently, comparative law has attempted to apply new tools to comparative analysis—law and economics, feminist legal theory, critical legal theory, or postcolonial theory—to craft metatheories for understanding legal systems.

The task of understanding a foreign legal system as a whole is hard work, whatever approach one takes. One must be grounded in the culture and society of that country, which usually requires a knowledge of the country's language and some time spent on the ground. One must master procedural as well as substantive law. One must also distance oneself from one's own legal system and begin to see that system as a foreign system.

This book stands in the tradition of micro, rather than macro, comparative law. It does not offer an understanding of other legal systems as a whole, but focuses rather on understanding how a wide variety of disparate legal systems deal with issues in a particular field—health care. While this book attempts from time to time to describe the legal or societal context in which health care law is located in various countries, it does not pretend to present a complete picture of the legal systems of these countries. It also does not offer a metatheory that would make sense of the similarities and differences observed in health law in different legal systems.

The goals of this book are instead fairly pragmatic. It is our hope that readers will come to a better understanding of the health care law of their own jurisdiction through absorbing these materials. Our assumption is that many (indeed likely most) users of these materials will be from the United States. We assume that many of these students will take an American health law course at some point. We also realize, however, that many students using this book will either be in American summer programs between their first and second year of law school, or in non-law school settings, and will not have taken an American health law course prior to using these materials. We do not see this as an impediment, as the textual notes (supplemented, of course, by the teacher's knowledge) should provide enough information about American health law to orient the novice.

We also hope that the book proves helpful for non-American readers to understand how unusual American health law is, but also draw important comparisons between their own health care system and those of a myriad of other countries. These countries cross divides between common and civil law, between countries with strong versus weaker rule of law traditions, and conservative or progressive issues on some of the most hot button topics (all covered in this book) such as abortion, end of life decision-making, and reproductive technologies.

We hope that every reader will come to see how contingent; how culturally, politically, and historically-determined; and how dependent on the substantive, procedural, and evidentiary law of particular legal systems domestic approaches to various health law issues are. We hope that readers will better understand the possibility that there are very different solutions to the very difficult health law problems we face than the ones we commonly imagine. Finally, we hope that at those points in the reader's later career when an opportunity arises to influence health law or policy, the reader will remember the wealth of alternatives available beyond those that are obvious in the reader's particular system.

While this book is in part intended to inform health policy and bioethics, it is not a book about comparative health policy and bioethics. Many excellent books are available, both in the United States and elsewhere, about comparative health policy, health economics, and health politics. Though the first chapter of this book contains a rather lengthy section describing and analyzing health care systems, it is not the intent of this book to duplicate these sources. Rather, this book focuses on how law, legal systems, and legal institutions influence health care recipients, professionals, institutions, and systems. Thus, for example, this book is not so much concerned with how various health care systems ration care as it is with the role of the courts or of administrative agencies in health care rationing.

Because this is a book about health law and bioethics, it is organized, not surprisingly, around the notion of rights. Whatever else law may be, it is generally understood as an attempt to articulate and protect rights. This book's four chapters deal with legal rights in different settings. The first chapter examines the concept of a human right to health care, established by international law, national constitutions, and domestic legislation. As a context for this discussion, and indeed for most of the rest of the book, this chapter also includes readings describing generally how health care systems are organized and function.

The second chapter deals with the rights of patients in their relationships with health care professionals and institutions. After a brief section introducing the notion of patients' rights, the topics of malpractice, alternatives to malpractice litigation, informed consent, confidentiality and rights to access medical records are examined.

The third chapter addresses core questions of bioethics about the rights claims of patients and others at the beginning and end of life. This chapter examines abortion, assisted reproduction, and the right to die.

The fourth chapter examines the interface between the rights of individuals and the interests of society in four contexts. First, it looks at the role of public health law in reconciling the rights of the individual and of the public in the context of the worldwide HIV-AIDS crisis. Second, it looks at the role of public health law in infectious disease emergencies—focusing on SARS and Ebola. Third, it examines the attempts of various nations to limit tobacco use. Finally, it looks at issues that arise in health care research, where the interests of society in advancing knowledge sometimes come in conflict with the rights of the individual research subject.

Five final comments may be useful to understand this book. First, throughout the book we generally use the word "patient" to refer to recipients of health care. The word "patient" has increasingly become only one of many words used to describe persons who receive health care in the United States—including also consumer, beneficiary, member, resident, or recipient, to name a few. Patient has, indeed, sometimes taken on a negative connotation, describing one who passively receives health care as opposed to an active participant in the health care enterprise. The word is used here, however, for two reasons. First, it is still, even in the United States, the most specific word used to describe the person who receives health care from health care professionals and institutions. Second, it is the word that is used most widely throughout the world to describe recipients of health care. Given the international scope of this book, deference to international usage is perhaps appropriate.

Second, readers of the Second Edition may notice that the Third Edition is broader in geographic scope. Our goal with this edition was to expand discussions beyond the traditional focus of comparative health law, which tends to linger on North American, European, British, and English-speaking jurisdictions like Australia and New Zealand, with occasional focus on Japan. This edition adds materials from jurisdictions in Africa, Asia, Latin America, and the Middle East to provide a more varied picture of the already-varied approaches to common legal and ethical challenges in health care. It also adds more material from supranational bodies. Comparative lessons can be more difficult to draw the more the jurisdictions being compared differ along social, economic, cultural, and religious dimensions. But we think the effort to be more expansive is worthwhile.

Third, the reader will surely notice that, although this book resembles in many respects a traditional American law school casebook, the excerpts are much longer than would be found in most contemporary casebooks. It is for this reason that the book is entitled "*Readings* in Comparative Law and Bioethics." These lengthy excerpts are used for a reason. At the outset, it was noted that to do comparative law properly one should really know the language of the country one is studying, and spend time there observing the cultural context. While most readers of these materials will not have yet had the opportunity to do this for the range of the countries whose law is examined here, this book attempts at least to let the reader stay with one court or one scholar long enough to not simply catch a snippet of black-letter law, but also to observe how the particular author or country thinks about health law. For example, with respect to courts like the British House of Lords or Australian High Court, where multiple opinions are customary, a range of these are reproduced to give the reader a sense of the debate that characterizes these courts.

Fourth, the reader may observe that some of the writing deviates from standard American English. While we are very fortunate that English has become the world language, the English that others speak and write is not always that with which we are most comfortable. We can also learn, therefore, from seeing how others use the English language. This experience may also help us to remember a very important fact: just because others are speaking English does not mean that we can understand them (or they us). Often, really understanding what another is saying is hard work for us, even when the other seems to be speaking our language.

Fifth, some explanation of editing conventions may be helpful. First, cites, which were appropriately numerous in all sources, were in most instances omitted. Second, internal section titles and paragraph numbers were omitted from many sources. Third, ellipses (* * *) are inserted where text was omitted by the editor. Ellipses within a paragraph (or at its beginning or end) show that text was omitted from that paragraph. Centered ellipses between paragraphs show that a full paragraph or more of text was omitted. Brackets indicate additional explanatory text that has been added.

We are very grateful to the many authors and publishers who graciously allowed us to reprint their works in this text, often with no charge or at a reduced charge. The permissions table that follows lists their names. We are also grateful to Herman Nys, who contributed an original article on assisted suicide and the right to die that was adapted from his prior work; Colleen Flood, who patiently explained the last decade's worth of important developments in Canada; Alain Garay, who assisted us in locating French sources; and Robert Leflar, Pierrick LeGoff, Konstantin Tretyakov, and Martine Jean who translated source materials for us. Finally, we would like to thank all of those who helped bring this work to fruition—our Deans, Jennifer Collins and John Manning, our research liaisons and assistants, including Taylor Custer, Cassie DuBay, Victoria Hall-Palerm, Ellora Israni, Megan Jones, Jessica Ljustina, Michelle Melton, Colin Metcalf, Dana Paikowsky, Haley Penan, Shaiba Rather. Ross Slaughter, Priya Sundaresan, and our assistants, Sharon Magill Tabbert and Jennifer Minnich. Finally, Nathan and Glenn would like to thank our co-author Tim Jost for trusting us with this wonderful project. This edition tries to build on the significant contributions of the first and second editions, for which we thank

Mark Hall, Barry Furrow, Rob Leflar, Norio Higuchi, Eleanor Kinney, Colleen Flood, Ted Marmor, Herman Nys, Eric Feldman, Margaret Lock, Kevin Outterson, Chris Newdick, Hank Greely, Andre den Exter, Larry Gostin, Naoki Ikegami, Fran Miller, Brian Murchison, the Frances Lewis Law Center, and Vera Mencer.

Acknowledgments

Chapter 1: The Right to Health and Its Implementation

Eleanor D. Kinney, The International Human Right to Health: What Does This Mean for Our Nation and the World, 34 Indiana Law Review 1457, 1459–62, 1467–71 (2001), copyright © 2001, The Trustees of Indiana University. Reproduced with permission from the Indiana Law Review.

Karen Noelia Llantoy Huamán v. Peru, Human Rights Committee, Communication No. 1153/2003, 24 October 2005. Copyright © 2005 United Nations Publications Board. Used with permission.

Eleanor D. Kinney and Brian Alexander Clark, Provisions for Health and Health Care in the Constitutions of the Countries of the World, Cornell International Law Journal, vol. 37, pp. 285, 287, 289–90, 292–96, 298–301 (2004). Copyright © Cornell International Law Journal, 2004. Used with permission.

WHO, World Health Report 2000, pp. 11–13 (2000). Reprinted with Permission.

Timothy Jost, Why Can't We Do What They Do? National Health Reform Abroad, Journal of Law, Medicine and Ethics 432, 432–35 (2004). Copyright © 1999, American Society of Law, Medicine and Ethics. Reprinted with permission.

Theodore R. Marmor, Comparative Studies and the Drawing of Policy Lessons: Describing, Explaining, Evaluating, and Predicting, Journal of Comparative Policy Analysis, 1–4, 8–9, 12–13 (2017). Copyright © 2017, Taylor and Francis, Ltd. Reprinted with the kind permission of Ted Marmor and Taylor and Francis.

Nathan Cortez, The Elusive Ideal of Market Competition in United States' Health Care, from Health Care and EU Law, 359–69. Copyright © 2011, Springer. Reprinted with permission.

Uwe E. Reinhardt, Reforming the Health Care System: The Universal Dilemma, 19 Am.J.L. & Med. 21, 21–27, 29, 31–36 (1994). Copyright © 1994, American Society of Law, Medicine and Ethics and Boston University School of Law. Reprinted with permission.

Carolyn Hughes Tuohy, Dynamics of a Changing Health Sphere: The United States, Britain, and Canada, 18 Health Affairs 114, 115–16, 118–120, 129–131 (May/June 1999). Copyright © 1999, Health Affairs, Published by Project Hope. Reprinted with permission.

George J. Annas & Frances H. Miller, The Empire of Death: How Culture and Economics Affect Informed Consent in the U.S., The U.K., and Japan, 20 Am.J.L. & Med. 357, 360–62, 377–81, 387–90 (1994). Copyright © 1994, American Society of Law, Medicine and Ethics, Boston University School of Law, Frances Miller and George Annas. Reprinted with permission.

Jenna Wright and Jeanna Holtz, Essential Packages of Health Services in 24 Countries: Findings from a Cross-Country Analysis, 1–2, 9, 12–13, 19. Copyright © 2017 U.S. Agency for International Development (USAID). Reprinted with permission.

Timothy Jost, ed. Health Care Coverage Determinations: An International Comparative Study. 240–44, 251–53. Copyright © 2005 Open University Press. Used with the kind permission of Open University Press.

Colleen Flood, Mark Stabile and Carolyn Tuohy, What is In and Out of Medicare? Who Decides, from Just Medicare, 15, 16–17, 23–30. Copyright © University of Toronto Press, 2005. Used with the permission of the University of Toronto Press.

Christopher Newdick, Rebalancing the Rationing Debate: Tackling the Tensions Between Individual and Community Rights, in Prioritization in Medicine: An International Dialogue. 123–29, 132–35. Copyright © 2015 Springer Nature. Reprinted with permission.

Nathan Cortez, Patients Without Borders: The Emerging Global Market for Patients and the Evolution of Modern Health Care[10]. 71–73, 77–82. Copyright © 2008, Indiana Law Journal. Reprinted with permission.

I. Glenn Cohen, Patients With Passports: Medical Tourism, Law and Ethics. 169–73, 186–87, 191, 194–96, 204–05. Copyright © 2014 I. Glenn Cohen and Oxford University Press. Reprinted with permission.

Chapter 2: The Rights of Patients in Relationship with Health Care Professionals and Institutions

World Health Organization, Regional Office for Europe, Copenhagen, European Health Reforms: Citizens' Choice and Patients' Rights, 11, 12–15, 17–19 (1996). Reprinted with permission.

World Medical Association, World Medical Association Declaration on the Rights of the Patient, 2015. Reprinted with permission.

World Health Organization, European Office, A Declaration on the Promotion of Patients' Right in Europe, 1994. Reprinted with permission.

Tamara K. Hervey and Jean V. McHale, Rights: Mobile Patients' Rights as Human Rights, in European Union Health Law: Themes and Implications, 185–89. Copyright © 2015, Cambridge University Press. Reprinted with permission.

Nathan Cortez, Recalibrating the Legal Risks of Cross-Border Health Care, Yale Journal of Health Policy, Law, and Ethics, vol. 10, 58–62. Copyright © 2010, Yale Journal of Health Policy, Law, and Ethics. Reprinted with permission.

Ken Oliphant, Medical Malpractice and Compensation: Comparative Observations, in Medical Malpractice and Compensation in Global Perspective, 514–20. Copyright © 2013, Walter de Gruyter GmbH. Reprinted with permission.

Zhu Wang and Ken Oliphant, Yangge Dance: The Rhythm of Liability for Medical Malpractice in the People's Republic of China, in Medical Malpractice and Compensation in Global Perspective, 97–99, 117–18, 120–25, 127–28. Copyright © 2013, Walter de Gruyter GmbH. Reprinted with permission.

Nathan Cortez, A Medical Malpractice Model for Developing Countries? Drexel Law Review, vol. 4, 217–18. Copyright © 2011, Drexel Law Review. Reprinted with permission.

Robert B. Leflar, The Law of Medical Misadventure in Japan. Chicago-Kent Law Review, vol. 87, 80–85, 88–89. Copyright © 2012, Chicago-Kent Law Review. Reprinted with permission.

Michelle M. Mello, Allen Kachalia, and David M. Studdert, Administrative Compensation for Medical Injuries: Lessons from Three Foreign Systems. Issues in International Health Policy. 1–9. Copyright © 2011, the Commonwealth Fund. Reprinted with the kind permission of the Commonwealth Fund.

John G. Culhane, King-Jean Wu, Oluyomi Faparusi, and Eric J. Juray, Toward a Mature Doctrine of Informed Consent: Lessons from a Comparative Law Analysis. British Journal of American Legal Studies, vol. 1, 551, 552–55, 572–79. Copyright © 2012, British Journal of American Legal Studies. Reprinted with permission.

Colin J. Bennett, The European General Data Protection Regulation: An Instrument for the Globalization of Policy Standards? Information Polity, vol. 23, 239–40, 243–45. Copyright © 2018, Information Policy, IOS Press. Reprinted with the kind permission of Colin J. Bennett.

Peter Carey, Data Protection: A Practical Guide to UK and EU Law, xxxiii–xxxv. Copyright © 2018, Oxford University Press. Reprinted with permission.

Chen-Hung Chang, Controversy over Information Privacy Arising from the Taiwan National Health Insurance Database Examining the Taiwan Taipei High Administrative Court Judgment No. 102-SU-36 (*Tsai v. NHIA*). Pace International Law Review, vol. 28, 27. Copyright © 2016, Pace International Law Review. Reprinted with permission.

Luca Marelli and Giuseppe Testa, Scrutinizing the General Data Protection Regulation. Science, vol. 360, 496–98. Copyright © 2018, Science. Reprinted with permission.

Mohammad Hossein Yarmohammadian, Ahmad Reza Raeisi, Navid Tavakoli, & Leila Ghaderi Nansa, Medical Record Information Disclosure Laws and Policies Among Selected Countries: A Comparative Study. Journal of Research in Medical Sciences, vol. 15, 140–49. Copyright © 2010. Reprinted with permission.

Chapter 3. The Patient's Right to Self-Determination and Competing Considerations.

Abortion Policies: A Global Review, United Nations, 1–2, 4–7 (2003). Copyright © United Nations Publications Board. Used with permission.[11]

Reva Siegal, the Constitutionalization of Abortion The Constitutionalization of Abortion. 1071–1075, in Abortion Law in Transnational Perspective: Cases and Controversies (ed. Rebecca Cook, Joanna Erdman & Bernard Dickens). Copyright © 2014[12], Oxford University Press. Reprinted with permission.

Rebecca Cook & Women's Link Worldwide, Excerpts of the Constitutional Court's Ruling That Liberalized Abortion in Colombia, vol. 15, Reproductive Health Matters, 160–62 (2007[13]). Reprinted with permission.

Dov Fox, Reproductive Negligence, Columbia Law Review, vol. 117, 163–65 (2017). Copyright © 2017, Columbia Law Review. Reprinted with permission.

Marsha Garrison, Regulating Reproduction, George Washington Law Review, vol. 75, 1623–24. Copyright © 2008, George Washington Law Review. Reprinted with permission.

Doron Dorfman, The Inaccessible Road To Motherhood—The Tragic Consequence Of Not Having Reproductive Policies For Israelis With Disabilities, Columbia Journal of Gender & Law, vol. 30, 55–59. Copyright © 2015, Columbia Journal of Gender & Law. Reprinted with permission.

Martin Hevia and Carlos Herrera Vacaflor, The Legal Status of In Vitro Fertilization in Latin America and the American Convention on Human Rights, Suffolk Transnational Law Review, vol. 36, 58–62. Copyright © 2013, Suffolk Transnational Law Review. Reprinted with permission.

Rosario M. Isasi, Bartha M. Knoppers, Peter A. Singer, and Abdallah S. Daar, Legal and Ethical Approaches to Stem Cell and Cloning Research: A Comparative Analysis of Policies in Latin America, Asia, and Africa, Journal of Law, Medicine & Ethics, vol. 32, 626. Copyright © 2004, American Society of Law, Medicine & Ethics. Reprinted with permission.

Regina (Quintavalle) v. Human Fertilisation and Embryology Authority, [2005]. Reprinted with permission of the Controller of Her Majesty's Stationary Office.[14]

Katherine Voskoboynik, Clipping the Stork's Wings: Commercial Surrogacy Regulation and Its Impact on Fertility Tourism, Indiana International & Comparative Law Review, vol. 26, 341–352. Copyright © 2016, Indiana International & Comparative Law Review. Reprinted with permission.

Lisa C. Ikemoto, Reproductive Tourism: Equality Concerns in the Global Market for Fertility Services, Law & Inequality, vol. 27, 277. Copyright © 2009, Law & Inequality. Reprinted with permission.

I. Giesen, Of Wrongful Birth, Wrongful life, Comparative Law, and the Politics of Tort Law Systems, Tydskrif vir Heedendaagse Romeins-Hollandse Reg (THRHR), vol. 72, 257. Copyright © 2009, THRHR. Reprinted with permission.

Herman Nys, Physician Involvement in a Patient's Death: A Continental European Perspective, Medical Law Review, vol. 7. Copyright © 1999, Oxford University Press, and update, copyright ©2007, Herman Nys. Reprinted with permission.

Konstantin Tretyakov, The Right to Die in the United States, Canada, and China: Legal Fictions and Their Utility in a Comparative Perspective, University of Pennsylvania Journal of Law & Social Change, vol. 21, 108–113. Copyright © 2018, University of Pennsylvania Journal of Law & Social Change. Reprinted with permission.

Chabot, Supreme Court of the Netherlands, Criminal Chamber, 21 June 1994, no. 96.972, from John Griffiths, Alex Bood, and Haleen Weyers, Euthansia and the Law in the Netherlands, 329–38. Copyright © 1998, Amsterdam University Press. Reprinted with permission.

Chapter 4: The Rights of the Individual and the Interests of Society

John A. Harrington, AIDS, Public Health and the Law: A Case of Structural Coupling? European J. Health Law, vol. 6, 213, 213–26. Copyright © 1999, Kluwer Law International. Reprinted with permission.

Maya Berinzon, Copy and Paste: Transplanting International HIV/AIDS Model Laws into African Countries, Cardozo Journal of International and Comparative Law, vol. 23, 296–297, 308–313. Copyright © 2015, Cardozo Journal of International and Comparative Law. Reprinted with permission.

Chenglin Liu, Regulating Sars in China: Law as an Antidote?, Washington University Global Studies Review, vol. 4, 81, 82–101, 103–09, 115–17, Copyright © 2005, Washington University Global Studies Review. Reprinted with permission.

Jason W. Sapsin, Lawrence O. Gostin, Jon S. Vernick, Scott Burris, and Stephen P. Teret SARS and International Legal Preparedness. Temple Law Review, vol. 77, 155, 155–165, 167–68. Copyright © 2004, Temple Law Review. Reprinted with permission.

Mark A. Rothstein, From SARS to Ebola: Legal and Ethical Considerations for Modern Quarantine, Indiana Health Law Review, vol. 12, 228, 250–51, 252–54, 254–57, 263–67, 267–68, 271–73, 273–76. Copyright © 2015, Indiana Health Law Review. Reprinted with permission.

Mark J. Siedner, Lawrence O. Gostin, Hilarie H. Cranmer, John D. Kraemer, Strengthening the Detection of and Early Response to Public Health Emergencies: Lessons from the West African Ebola Epidemic, PLoS Medicine, vol. 12, e1001804 (2015[15])

Emily A. Largent, EBOLA and FDA: Reviewing the Response to the 2014 Outbreak, to Find Lessons for the Future, Journal of Law and the Biosciences, vol. 3, 489, 499–501. Copyright © 2016, Oxford University Press. Reprinted with permission.

J. Benton Heath, Global Emergency Power in the Age of Ebola, Harvard International Law Journal, vol. 57, 26–27, 28, 29–30, 32–33, 35. Copyright © 2016, Harvard International Law Journal. Reprinted with permission.

Roseann B. Termini, The "Why" of Tobacco Products Regulation, Food and Drug Law: Federal Regulation of Drugs, Biologics, Medical Devices, Foods, Dietary Supplements, Personal Care, Veterinary and Tobacco Products, vol. 12, 481–491, 497, 504, 509–511. Copyright © 2019, Roseann B. Termini. Reprinted with permission.

William Tilburg, Kathleen Hoke & Melissa Sager, FDA Regulation of Electronic Nicotine Delivery Systems and the "Deeming" Rule: What's Left for States?, Journal of Health Care Law and Policy, vol. 20, 28–29, 56–63. Copyright © 2017, Journal of Health Care Law and Policy. Reprinted with permission.

Leslie Zellers, Global Tobacco Control: What the U.S. Can Learn from Other Countries, Tobacco Control Legal Consortium. Copyright © 2013, Tobacco Control Legal Consortium. Reprinted with permission.

World Medical Association, Declaration of Helsinki, Ethical Principles for Medical Research Involving Human Subjects, adopted by the 18th WMA General Assembly, Helsinki, Finland, June 1964, as revised 1975, 1983, 1989, 1996, 2000, 2002, 2004, 2008, 2013. Copyright © 2013, World Medical Association, Inc. Reprinted with permission[16].

Solomon R. Benatar, Towards Progress in Resolving Dilemmas In International Research Ethics, Journal of Law, Medicine and Ethics, vol. 32, 574, 574–75, 579–81 Winter 2004. Copyright © 2004, American Society of Law, Medicine and Ethics. Reprinted with Permission.

Readings in Comparative Health Law and Bioethics

Chapter 1

The Right to Health and Its Implementation

A. The Right to Health in International Law

Is there a right to health? If so, is it a fundamental right? Would it best be characterized as a right to *health*, a right to health *care*, or a right to health *protection*? What difference does it make? And if there is a right to health, what does such a right entail? Is it a meaningful right? Is it enforceable? Against whom would it be? To what extent should a right to health guarantee equal access to health care for all? What disparities, if any, might be tolerable?

International law—as expressed through treaty conventions, customs, and general principles—has long grappled with these questions. The right to health, and to access health care, is supported by international law and by regional conventions. Article 25 of the Universal Declaration on Human Rights, adopted by the United Nations (UN) General Assembly in 1948, provides that:

> Everyone has the right to a standard of living adequate for the health and well-being of himself and of his family, including food, clothing, housing and medical care and necessary social services, and the right to security in the event of unemployment, sickness, disability, widowhood, old age or other lack of livelihood in circumstances beyond his control.

Although the Universal Declaration does not have the legal force of a treaty—it is a resolution by the UN General Assembly—it is generally regarded as constituting customary international law.

Related treaties also contemplate a right to health. Perhaps the most definitive statement is in the International Covenant on Economic, Social, and Cultural Rights (ICESCR), adopted by the UN General Assembly in 1966 and implemented by dozens of signatories since 1976. Article 12 provides that "[t]he States Parties ... recognize the right of everyone to the enjoyment of the highest attainable standard of physical and mental health." In signing the Covenant, countries commit themselves to take several steps to implement it, including public health measures and "[t]he creation of conditions which would assure to all medical service and medical attention in the event of sickness."

The Covenant has been ratified by nearly two hundred countries (the United States has signed but not ratified it). The Covenant does not, however, create clear and immediately binding legal obligations, as does the companion Covenant on Civil and Political Rights. Instead, it obligates each State Party "to take steps ... to the maximum of its available resources, with a view to achieving progressively the full realization of the rights ... by all appropriate means, including legislative measures." Art 2.(1). Compliance with the Covenant is monitored by the UN Committee on Economic, Social and Cultural Rights, which receives periodic reports from signatory states. But the monitoring effort is under-resourced and largely ineffective. Noncompliance results not in fines or other sanctions, but in a request by the Committee to comply. As Lawrence Gostin observes more broadly, "[t]he overriding principle of sovereignty has driven the international system toward 'law' that is essentially voluntary ... There is often no supranational authority to monitor, adjudicate, and enforce international law against states." Lawrence O. Gostin, *Global Health Law* 64 (Harvard 2014). Others call state sovereignty "a type of universal trump card" often played against health rights. Colleen M. Flood & Aeyal Gross, *The Right to Health at the Public/Private Divide: A Global Comparative Study* 9 (Cambridge 2014). Nevertheless, in 2008, the UN General Assembly incorporated into the ICESCR an "Optional Protocol" to monitor and enforce compliance, including formal procedures for filing and investigating complaints, after the complainant exhausts domestic remedies. UN General Assembly, Resolution 63/117, "Optional Protocol to the International Covenant on Economic, Social and Cultural Rights," (Dec. 10, 2008), arts. 10–11. But the new procedures still cannot impose economic penalties or other sanctions.

Nevertheless, the language of the ICESCR is echoed in regional human rights covenants, such as the American Declaration of the Rights and Duties of Man (Art. XI), the American Convention on Human Rights (Optional Protocol of San Salvador), the European Social Charter (Arts. 11 & 13), the European Convention on Human Rights and Biomedicine (Art. 3), and the African Charter on Human Rights (Art. 16).

A right that creates a conditional obligation, to be progressively achieved contingent upon the availability of resources, can be somewhat ephemeral. States fulfill their duty by taking initial steps, even if they have not fully realized the goal yet. The Covenant, then, "is to a large extent a declaration of intent." Paul Schoukens, *The Right to Access Health Care: Health Care According to International and European Social Security Law Instruments, in International Health Law: Solidarity and Justice in Health Care* 24 (Maklu, Antwerp, 2008) (den Exter ed.). Thus, the legal enforceability and lexical primacy that is commonly thought to attend human rights does not seem to apply here. Neither does such a right seem to focus exclusively on the relationship between individuals and states, as do most human rights. The right is even more problematic if it is articulated as a right to health, rather than health care. There are, of course, many factors that contribute to poor health that states can do little to influence. Thus, "one would be hard pressed to find a more controversial or nebulous human right than the right to health." Jennifer Prah Ruger, *Health and Social Justice* 119 (Oxford, 2010).

The mere fact that a right requires positive action, rather than merely negative restraint, on the part of the state, however, does not render it less valid, or even less important. Many well-established rights require the state to take positive protective actions. Recognizing that a human right has a special claim on resources and legislative prerogatives gives it a special dignity, and at least a rhetorical primacy. A conference convened to establish principles for implementing the ICESCR concluded that it should be interpreted to mean that "State parties must at all times act in good faith to fulfill" their obligations, being "accountable both to the international community and to their own people for their compliance." The Limburg Principles on the Implementation of the International Covenant on Economic, Social and Cultural Rights, 9 *Human Rights Quarterly* 122 (1987).

Whatever else a right to health may mean, it should require that insofar as a state provides health protection or health care services, it should do so on a nondiscriminatory basis. For example, Article 2 of the Universal Declaration of Human Rights, discussed above, prohibits states from discriminating when protecting the rights provided by the Declaration. Similarly, Article 2(2) of the ICESCR recognizes that the rights will be "exercised without discrimination." Thus, the UN's monitoring committee for the ICESCR expects that states will not discriminate when organizing access to health care facilities, goods, or services—meaning that there is adequate physical, economic, and informational access to such things, and that none discriminate. Committee on Economic, Social and Cultural Rights, *Substantive Issues Arising in the Implementation of the International Covenant on Economic, Social and Cultural Rights, General Comment No. 14*, 3, E/C.12/2000/4, II/08/2000. Similarly, the 1978 Declaration of Alma-Ata called disparities in access to care "unacceptable." WHO, Declaration of Alma-Ata (Sep. 1978), at http://www.who.int/publications/almaata_declaration_en.pdf. Although it is widely accepted that the right to health precludes unjust discrimination, it does not entail absolute equality of access. André den Exter, *International Health Law: Solidarity and Justice in Health Care* 7 (Maklu, Antwerp 2008).

A number of international covenants protecting special populations or addressing specific human rights issues reinforce this right to equal access to health protection and health care. For example, the International Convention on Rights of the Child recognizes "the right of the child to the enjoyment of the highest attainable standard of health and to facilities for treatment of illness and rehabilitation of health," Art. 24(1), and the Convention on the Rights of Persons with Disabilities (2006) also speaks to access to health care services. Discrimination in health care is also prohibited by the conventions on the Elimination of All Forms of Racial Discrimination (Art. 5(e)(iv)); on Elimination of all Forms of Discrimination Against Women (Arts. 11(1)(f) and 12); and on the Protection of Migrant Workers and Their Families (Art. 28). Moreover, minimum standard-setting instruments, such as those promulgated by the UN's International Labor Organization (ILO), articulate various standards related to health care access and benefits. Schouckens at 33. In particular, ILO Convention 102 specifies minimum standards for "social security," including medical care, sickness benefits, unemployment benefits, old-age benefits, employment injury benefits, family benefits, maternity benefits, "invalidity" benefits, and survivors' benefits, with special provisions for "non-national residents." ILO, C102—Social Security

(Minimum Standards) Convention, 1952 (No. 102). Finally, there is growing recognition that the human security and global public goods frameworks "join the human rights framework in recognizing global health as a shared responsibility, a partnership, and a priority that requires international cooperation." Lawrence O. Gostin, Global Health Law 21–22 (Harvard 2014).

At the same time, other international frameworks, including bilateral and regional free trade agreements, can detract from the ideal of health care as a human right. In particular, international trade and intellectual property instruments create barriers to health care access and equity. For example, the three multilateral agreements implemented by the World Trade Organization (WTO, 1995), including the General Agreement on Tariffs and Trade (GATT, 1947/1994), General Agreement on Trade in Services (GATS, 1995), and Trade-Related Aspects of Intellectual Property Rights (TRIPS, 1995) are criticized for rendering health care priorities subservient to free trade or patent protection, to the systematic disadvantage of patients in the global south. Moreover, the Technical Barriers to Trade (TBT) Agreement (1995) and the Sanitary and Phytosanitary Measures (SPS) Agreement (1995) specifically restrain domestic public health and safety regulation, on the idea that such regulations sometimes mask protectionism. TRIPS in particular has created barriers to accessing essential medicines in developing countries. But observers worry that regional and bilateral free trade agreements, such as the Trans-Pacific Partnership (TPP), can impose even more onerous obligations on less-developed countries than would be possible through WTO agreements. Office of the U.S. Trade Representative, "Free Trade Agreements," at http://www.ustr.gov/trade-agreements/free-trade-agreements.

Nevertheless, the most important influence toward promoting access to health care at the international level may not be human rights covenants, but rather the primary international institution concerned with the promotion of health and health care, the World Health Organization (WHO). The WHO, a successor to the Parisian Office Internationale d'Hygiène Publique and the Health Organization of the League of Nations, was founded in 1946 as a specialized international organization to work together with the UN to promote health. Its Constitution states:

> The enjoyment of the highest attainable standard of health is one of the fundamental rights of every human being without distinction of race, religion, political belief, economic or social condition. The objective of the World Health Organization shall be the attainment by all peoples of the highest possible level of health.

The WHO, however, pursues this objective through education and exhortation, and has no authority to compel compliance with this objective by member states. See, David P. Fidler, Examining the World Health Organization in the Context of International Law, *in* The Future of the World Health Organization: What Role for International Law?, 31 *Vand. J. Transnat'l L.* 1079 (1998). The WHO Constitution grants the WHO authority to adopt conventions (Article 19) and promulgate quasi-legislative health regulations (Article 21), but it rarely exercises either power. The WHO also can influence international customs and practices through Article 23 by promulgating soft, nonbinding recommendations, which often contain detailed standards and metrics for compliance. Although the WHO's recommendations, guidelines, and action plans are non-enforceable, they often help build consensus, and can be used to pressure domestic governments into compliance. Still, critics observe that such norms are often flouted, without the ability to formally compel sovereign states.

The following article explores the ramifications of a right to health, as does the opinion of the Human Rights Committee which follows it:

Eleanor D. Kinney, *The International Human Right to Health: What Does This Mean for Our Nation and World?*

Indiana Law Review, vol. 34, pp. 1457, 1459–62, 1467–71 (2001)

* * *

In the 1960s, the UN sponsored the development of two international covenants that articulate the human rights recognized in the UN Universal Declaration of Human Rights. These two covenants are the International Covenant on Civil and Political Rights (ICCPR) and the International Covenant on Economic, Social and Cultural Rights (ICESCR).

The ICESCR—the so-called Economic Covenant—is the most important in terms of the right to health. Article 12 of ICESCR states that the right to health includes "the enjoyment of the highest attainable standard of physical and mental health." * * *

The UN Committee on Economic, Social and Cultural Rights has responsibility for the promotion, implementation and enforcement of this covenant. A human right to health is also recognized in numerous other international human rights authorities that establish prohibitions against government conduct that is detrimental to health. Such treaties include the International Convention on the Elimination of All Forms of Racial Discrimination of 1965, the Convention on the Elimination of All Forms of Discrimination against Women of 1979, and the Convention on the Rights of the Child of 1989.

The UN also has established several international agencies to promote economic and social development world wide. The World Health Organization (WHO) has a legislative capacity to make international health regulations in addition to its health promotion functions. The WHO constitution states a right to the "highest attainable standard of health" and defines health broadly as "a state of complete physical, mental and social well-being and not merely the absence of disease or infirmity."

In addition, regional international organizations have treaties and implementation bodies. The Inter-American system for the protection of human rights of the Organization of American States (OAS) is based on the OAS American Declaration of the Rights and Duties of Man and the OAS American Convention on Human Rights, among other instruments. Specifically, Article 11 of the American Declaration of the Rights and Duties of Man states "[e]very person has the right to the preservation of his health through sanitary and social measures relating to food, clothing, housing and medical care, to the extent permitted by public and community resources." The more recent Protocol of San Salvador specifies a human right to health in its interpretation of the OAS Convention on Human Rights. * * *

The Pan-American Health Organization (PAHO), located within WHO, promotes health in the Americas and implementation of these OAS instruments that recognize an international human right to health.

Also of interest, the 1993 Vienna Declaration and Programme of Action emphasizes the fundamental inter-relatedness of political and civil human rights and economic social and cultural human rights. The Vienna Declaration specifically provides:

> All human rights are universal, indivisible and interdependent and interrelated. The international community must treat human rights globally in a fair and equal manner, on the same footing, and with the same emphasis. While the significance of national and regional particularities and various historical, cultural and religious backgrounds must be borne in mind, it is the duty of States, regardless of their political, economic and cultural systems, to promote and protect all human rights and fundamental freedoms.

The Vienna Declaration has become a crucial principle in international human rights law recognizing the irreducible truth that all human rights must be recognized if specific human rights are to have concrete meaning. A look to the body of international treaties that comprise the corpus of human rights law at first glance seems promising. However, these treaties bind only those nations that ratify them. This situation is immediately disappointing with respect to the United States as the United States has not ratified many UN or OAS human rights treaties. Most importantly, the United States has signed but not ratified ICESCR and the two conventions on the rights of women and children. * * *

* * *

If there is a binding international human right to health, then how would it be defined and implemented? This is a challenge. In this effort, we should be imaginative. As lawyers, we tend to think of administrative regulation and enforcement as well as judicial recourse as the primary mechanisms for assuring the implementation of rights. However, these models may not be particularly appropriate or effective when we are talking about what, at least in the United States and many other nations, is essentially a right to health under international customary law.

Such legalistic visions of the right to health may also not be appropriate or effective as there is still some uncertainty about the content of the international human right to health. Indeed, getting a handle on the content of the right to health is a necessary first step to effective implementation. But this is no easy task. To have meaning, the content of the right to health must be essentially the same for all nations and people. Yet implementation is dependent on the resources, as well as cultures, of individual countries. How do we articulate the right to health in countries with vastly different economic resources and cultural traditions?

The UN Committee on International Economic, Social and Cultural Rights—the treaty body responsible for implementing and monitoring ICESCR—has published a General Comment 14 to ICESCR that outlines the content to the international right to health. This General Comment is extensive and quite specific and intended to apply to nations that have ratified the ICESCR. It addresses the content of the right to health and the implementation and enforcement of the right to health. It also provides remedies for individual parties who have been denied the human right to health.

General Comment 14 begins with some observations about the normative content of the right to health. Specifically, General Comment 14 states that "[t]he right to health is not to be understood as a right to be healthy" and that "[t]he right to health contains both freedoms and entitlements." The General Comment 14 specifies the freedoms and entitlements as follows:

> The freedoms include the right to control one's health and body, including sexual and reproductive freedom, and the right to be free from interference, such as the right to be free from torture, non-consensual medical treatment and experimentation. By contrast, the entitlements include the right to a system of health protection which provides equality of opportunity for people to enjoy the highest attainable level of health.

General Comment 14 then observes that the right to health extends

> not only to timely and appropriate health care but also to the underlying determinants of health, such as access to safe and potable water and adequate sanitation, an adequate supply of safe food, nutrition and housing, healthy occupational and environmental conditions, and access to health-related education and information, including on sexual and reproductive health.

These provisions of General Comment 14 indeed prescribe a broad and inclusive conception of the content of the human right to health.

General Comment 14 also provides that the health care system of a states party must have certain institutional characteristics to realize the right to health. These include the availability, accessibility, acceptability and quality of needed health care services and facilities. "Availability" means that the states party has sufficient facilities and services for the population given the country's state of development. Services include those that affect the underlying determinants of health, such as safe and potable drinking water. "Accessibility" to health care facilities and services include[s] the four dimensions: non-discrimination, physical accessibility, economic accessibility (affordability), and information accessibility. "Acceptability" means that services and facilities must be respectful of medical ethics and culturally appropriate as well as being designed to respect confidentiality and improve the health status of those served. "Quality" means that services must also be scientifically and medically appropriate and of good quality.

General Comment 14 imposes three types or levels of obligations: the obligations to respect, protect and fulfill. The obligation to respect requires states parties to refrain from interfering directly or indirectly with the enjoyment of the right to health.

The obligation to protect requires states parties to take measures that prevent third parties from interfering with article 12 guarantees. The obligation to fulfill requires states parties to adopt appropriate legislative, administrative, budgetary, judicial, promotional and other measures towards the full realization of the right to health. General Comment 14 also reaffirms that several "core" obligations have been established in prior international human rights instruments * * *.

General Comment 14 clearly addresses implementation. It imposes a duty on each states party "to take whatever steps are necessary to ensure that everyone has access to health facilities, goods and services so that they can enjoy, as soon as possible, the highest attainable standard of physical and mental health." Implementation requires adoption of "a national strategy to ensure to all the enjoyment of the right to health, based on human rights principles which define the objectives of that strategy, and the formulation of policies and corresponding right to health indicators and benchmarks." The national health strategy should also "identify the resources available to attain defined objectives, as well as the most cost-effective way of using those resources." The national health strategy and plan of action should "be based on the principles of accountability, transparency and independence of the judiciary, since good governance is essential to the effective implementation of all human rights, including the realization of the right to health."

General Comment 14 has extensive enforcement provisions and specifies violations of the right to health. The Comment explicitly provides that a states party which "is unwilling to use the maximum of its available resources for the realization of the right to health is in violation of its obligations under Article 12." Further, if resource constraints make compliance impossible, the states party "has the burden of justifying that every effort has nevertheless been made to use all available resources at its disposal in order to satisfy, as a matter of priority, the obligations outlined above."

General Comment 14 also specifies violations. For example, violations of the obligation to respect include "state actions, policies or laws that contravene the standards set out in Article 12 of the Covenant and are likely to result in bodily harm, unnecessary morbidity and preventable mortality." Violations of the obligation to protect include "failure of a State to take all necessary measures to safeguard persons within their jurisdiction from infringements of the right to health by third parties." Finally, violations of the obligation to fulfill include "failure of States parties to take all necessary steps to ensure the realization of the right to health."

Finally, General Comment 14 accords remedies to individual parties. Specifically, any person or group victim of a violation of the right to health should have access to effective judicial or other appropriate remedies at both national and international levels. All victims of such violations should be entitled to adequate reparation, which may take the form of restitution, compensation, satisfaction or guarantees of non-repetition. National ombudsmen, human rights commissions, consumer forums, patients' rights associations or similar institutions should address violations of the right to health.

General Comment 14 represents a significant step in delineating the international human right to state parties to the ICESCR. Yet, despite General Comment's specificity, as well as flexibility, the issue of how General Comment 14 will be interpreted, implemented and enforced in states parties at different stages of economic development and with markedly different cultures and values will still be a challenge. In sum, the content of the international right to health remains a tough issue.

* * *

Notes

Americans with legal training sometimes criticize international law for its vague and weak norms, inadequate implementation, and lack of enforceability. Lawrence O. Gostin, *Global Health Law* 64 (Harvard 2014). Moreover, they often feel uncomfortable with the notion of rights that are, on the one hand, absolute human rights, and on the other, that are to be implemented "progressively" as resources permit. Because positive rights (*i.e.* rights that support a claim for resources against the state) are almost invariably resource-dependent, they present this problem. This is not to say that we do not recognize positive rights in the United States. Prisoners, for example, have a positive right to health care under the Eighth Amendment (*Estelle v. Gamble*, 492 U.S. 97 (1976)). Also, even negative rights, such as the freedoms of expression or religion, are not absolute under the United States' constitutional system. And some rights, such as school desegregation, have been "progressively" realized. (Recall the "with all deliberate speed" language of the second *Brown v. Board of Education* decision, 349 U.S. 294 at 300 (1955)).

The notion of a "right" to health has been controversial in the United States. In 2008, for example, the U.S. State Department under President George W. Bush called the right to health an "ultimate goal, not an immediate entitlement," articulating its disagreement with how the WHO and the Office of the UN High Commissioner for Human Rights characterized the "right to health" in a publication discussing the ICESCR, among other treaties. U.S. Department of State, Observations by the United States of America on "The Right to Health, Fact Sheet No. 31," https://www.state.gov/documents/organization/138850.pdf. But the notion that access to health care is a "right" has gained some traction in the United States as a result of intense debates regarding the potential repeal of the Affordable Care Act of 2010 and the likelihood that such a repeal would cause millions to lose health insurance—though such notions have not generally been grounded in international law.

It may be, however, that the notion of rights familiar to American law students is bound up with the way in which rights are customarily enforced in the United States. In the United States, the primary institution for enforcing rights is the court system. Further, under the constitutional system of the United States, the courts, and in particular the Supreme Court, have final responsibility for interpreting the Constitution and the laws, and therefore can hold legislation or executive action to be unconstitutional as a violation of basic rights. While this model of judicial review is seen in many other countries, it is far from universal. In France, for example, laws passed by the National Assembly can be reviewed by a Constitutional Council, but only at the time the legislation is passed, and only at the request of the executive or a certain proportion of members of the legislature. England, on the other hand, has no written constitution as such and a strong tradition of legislative supremacy, though the courts tend to interpret legislation so as not to conflict with human rights, and England recognizes European human rights law. See Diana Brahams, UK: The Impact of European Human Rights Law, 356 *Lancet* 1433 (2000). Rights in other nations are often effectuated through means other than a court system—through complaint mechanisms, through human rights commissions, or through monitoring mechanisms (such as the United Nations Committee on Economic, Social and Cultural Rights which oversees compliance with the ICESCR). These mechanisms offer far more flexibility in procedure and remedies, as well as the ability to conduct more wide-ranging fact-finding inquiries than are possible for a court. They may thus be better suited for enforcing progressively realized, resource-dependent positive rights.

This is not to say, however, that health rights are never enforceable through litigation or proceedings that resemble litigation. The following decision of Human Rights Committee, the body of experts created under the International Covenant on Civil and Political Rights to enforce the terms of that Convention, represents one example of such proceedings.

Karen Noelia Llantoy Huamán v. Peru

Human Rights Committee,
Communication No. 1153/2003, 24 October 2005

1. The author of the communication is Karen Noelia Llantoy Huamán, born in 1984, who claims to be a victim of a violation by Peru of articles 2, 3, 6, 7, 17, 24 and 26 of the International Covenant on Civil and Political Rights. She is represented by the organizations DEMUS, CLADEM and Center for Reproductive Law and Policy. * * *

2.1 The author became pregnant in March 2001, when she was aged 17. On 27 June 2001 she was given a scan at the Archbishop Loayza National Hospital in Lima, part of the Ministry of Health. The scan showed that she was carrying an anencephalic foetus.

2.2 On 3 July 2001, Dr. Ygor Pérez Solf, a gynaecologist and obstetrician in the Archbishop Loayza National Hospital in Lima, informed the author of the foetal abnormality and the risks to her life if the pregnancy continued. Dr. Pérez said that she had two options: to continue the pregnancy or to terminate it. He advised termination by means of uterine curettage. The author decided to terminate the pregnancy, and the necessary clinical studies were carried out, confirming the foetal abnormality.

2.3 On 19 July 2001, when the author reported to the hospital together with her mother for admission preparatory to the operation, Dr. Pérez informed her that she needed to obtain written authorization from the hospital director. Since she was under age, her mother, Ms. Elena Huamán Lara, requested the authorization. On 24 July 2001, Dr. Maximiliano Cárdenas Díaz, the hospital director, replied in writing that the termination could not be carried out as to do so would be unlawful, since under article 120 of the Criminal Code, abortion was punishable by a prison term of no more than three months when it was likely that at birth the child would suffer serious physical or mental defects, while under article 119, therapeutic abortion was permitted only when termination of the pregnancy was the only way of saving the life of the pregnant woman or avoiding serious and permanent damage to her health.

* * *

2.5 On 20 August 2001, Dr. Marta B. Rondón, a psychiatrist and member of the Peruvian Medical Association, drew up a psychiatric report on the author, concluding that "the so-called principle of the welfare of the unborn child has caused serious harm to the mother, since she has unnecessarily been made to carry to term a pregnancy whose fatal outcome was known in advance, and this has substantially contributed to triggering the symptoms of depression, with its severe impact on the development of an adolescent and the patient's future mental health".

2.6 On 13 January 2002, three weeks late with respect to the anticipated date of birth, the author gave birth to an anencephalic baby girl, who survived for four days, during which the mother had to breastfeed her. Following her daughter's death, the author fell into a state of deep depression. * * *

2.7 The author has submitted to the Committee a statement made by Dr. Annibal Faúdes and Dr. Luis Tavara, who * * * stated that anencephaly is a condition which is fatal to the foetus in all cases. Death immediately follows birth in most cases. It also endangers the mother's life. * * *

2.8 Regarding the exhaustion of domestic remedies, the author claims that this requirement is waived when judicial remedies available domestically are ineffective in the case in question, and she points out that the Committee has laid down on several occasions that the author has no obligation to exhaust a remedy which would prove ineffective. She adds that in Peru there is no administrative remedy which would enable a pregnancy to be terminated on therapeutic grounds, nor any judicial remedy functioning with the speed and efficiency required to enable a woman to require the authorities to guarantee her right to a lawful abortion within the limited period, by virtue of the special circumstances obtaining in such cases. She also states that her financial circumstances and those of her family prevented her from obtaining legal advice.

* * *

3.2 The author claims to have suffered discrimination in breach of article 3 of the Covenant [ensuring equal rights], in the following forms:

(a) In access to the health services, since her different and special needs were ignored because of her sex. In the view of the author, the fact that the State lacked any means to prevent a violation of her right to a legal abortion on therapeutic grounds, which is applicable only to women, together with the arbitrary conduct of the medical personnel, resulted in a discriminatory practice that violated her rights—a breach which was all the more serious since the victim was a minor.

(b) Discrimination in the exercise of her rights, since although the author was entitled to a therapeutic abortion, none was carried out because of social attitudes and prejudices, thus preventing her from enjoying her right to life, to health, to privacy and to freedom from cruel, inhuman and degrading treatment on an equal footing with men.

(c) Discrimination in access to the courts, bearing in mind the prejudices of officials in the health system and the judicial system where women are concerned and the lack of appropriate legal means of enforcing respect for the right to obtain a legal abortion when the temporal and other conditions laid down in the law are met.

3.3 The author claims a violation of article 6 of the Covenant [right to life]. She states that her experience had a serious impact on her mental health from which she has still not recovered. She points out that the Committee has stated that the right to life cannot be interpreted in a restrictive manner, but requires States to take positive steps to protect it, including the measures necessary to ensure that women do not resort to clandestine abortions which endanger their life and health, especially in the case of poor women. She adds that the Committee has viewed lack of access for women to reproductive health services, including abortion, as a violation of women's right to life, and that this has been reiterated by other committees such as the Committee on the Elimination of Discrimination against Women and the Committee on Economic, Social and Cultural Rights. The author claims that in the present case, the violation of the right to life lay in the fact that Peru did not take steps to ensure that the author secured a safe termination of pregnancy on the grounds that the foetus was not viable. She states that the refusal to provide a legal abortion service left her with two options which posed an equal risk to her health and safety: to seek clandestine (and hence highly risky) abortion services, or to continue a dangerous and traumatic pregnancy which put her life at risk.

3.4 The author claims a violation of article 7 of the Covenant. The fact that she was obliged to continue with the pregnancy amounts to cruel and inhuman treatment, in her view, since she had to endure the distress of seeing her daughter's marked deformities and knowing that her life expectancy was short. She states that this was an awful experience which added further pain and distress to that which she had already borne during the period when she was obliged to continue with the pregnancy, since she was subjected to an "extended funeral" for her daughter, and sank into a deep depression after her death.

* * *

3.6 The author claims a violation of article 17 [right to privacy], arguing that this article protects women from interference in decisions which affect their bodies and their lives, and offers them the opportunity to exercise their right to make independent decisions on their reproductive lives. The author points out that the State party interfered arbitrarily in her private life, taking on her behalf a decision relating to her life and reproductive health which obliged her to carry a pregnancy to term, and thereby breaching her right to privacy. She adds that the service was available, and that if it had not been for the interference of State officials in her decision, which enjoyed the protection of the law, she would have been able to terminate the pregnancy. * * *

3.7 The author claims a violation of article 24 [protecting the rights of children], since she did not receive the special care she needed from the health authorities, as an adolescent girl. Neither her welfare nor her state of health were objectives pursued by the authorities which refused to carry out an abortion on her. * * *

3.8 The author claims a violation of article 26 [equal protection], arguing that the Peruvian authorities' position that hers was not a case of therapeutic abortion, which is not punishable under the Criminal Code, left her in an unprotected state incompatible with the assurance of the protection of the law set out in article 26. The guarantee of the equal protection of the law implies that special protection will be given to certain categories of situation in which specific treatment is required. In the present case, as a result of a highly restrictive interpretation of the criminal law, the health authorities failed to protect the author and neglected the special protection which her situation required.

3.9 The author claims that the administration of the health centre left her without protection as a result of a restrictive interpretation of article 119 of the Criminal Code. She adds that the text of the law contains nothing to indicate that the exception relating to therapeutic abortion should apply only in cases of danger to physical health. But the hospital authorities had drawn a distinction and divided up the concept of health, and had thus violated the legal principle that no distinction should be drawn where there is none in the law. She points out that health is "a state of complete physical, mental and social well-being and not merely the absence of disease or infirmity", so that when the Peruvian Criminal Code refers to health, it does so in the broad and all-embracing sense, protecting both the physical and the mental health of the mother.

4. * * * The Committee * * * regrets that the State party has not supplied any information concerning the admissibility or the merits of the author's allegations. It points out that it is implicit in the Optional Protocol that States parties make available to the Committee all information at their disposal. In the absence of a reply from the State party, due weight must be given to the author's allegations, to the extent that these have been properly substantiated.

* * *

5.3 The Committee considers that the author's claims of alleged violations of articles 3 and 26 of the Covenant have not been properly substantiated, since the author has not placed before the Committee any evidence relating to the events which might confirm any type of discrimination under the article in question. * * *

* * *

6.2 The Committee notes that the author attached a doctor's statement confirming that her pregnancy exposed her to a life-threatening risk. She also suffered severe psychological consequences exacerbated by her status as a minor, as the psychiatric report of 20 August 2001 confirmed. The Committee notes that the State party has not provided any evidence to challenge the above. It notes that the authorities were aware of the risk to the author's life, since a gynaecologist and obstetrician in the same hospital had advised her to terminate the pregnancy, with the operation to be carried out in the same hospital. The subsequent refusal of the competent medical authorities to provide the service may have endangered the author's life. The author states that no effective remedy was available to her to oppose that decision. In the absence of any information from the State party, due weight must be given to the author's claims.

6.3 The author also claims that, owing to the refusal of the medical authorities to carry out the therapeutic abortion, she had to endure the distress of seeing her daughter's marked deformities and knowing that she would die very soon. This was an experience which added further pain and distress to that which she had already borne during the period when she was obliged to continue with the pregnancy. * * * The omission on the part of the State in not enabling the author to benefit from a therapeutic abortion was, in the Committee's view, the cause of the suffering she experienced. * * * Consequently, the Committee considers that the facts before it reveal a violation of article 7 of the Covenant [cruel and inhumane treatment]. In the light of this finding the Committee does not consider it necessary in the circumstances to made a finding on article 6 of the Covenant [right to life].

6.4 The author states that the State party, in denying her the opportunity to secure medical intervention to terminate the pregnancy, interfered arbitrarily in her private life. The Committee notes that a public-sector doctor told the author that she could either continue with the pregnancy or terminate it in accordance with domestic legislation allowing abortions in cases of risk to the life of the mother. * * * In the circumstances of the case, the refusal to act in accordance with the author's decision to terminate her pregnancy was not justified and amounted to a violation of article 17 of the Covenant.

6.5 The author claims a violation of article 24 of the Covenant, since she did not receive from the State party the special care she needed as a minor. The Committee notes the special vulnerability of the author as a minor girl. It further notes that, in the absence of any information from the State party, due weight must be given to the author's claim that she did not receive, during and after her pregnancy, the medical and psychological support necessary in the specific circumstances of her case. Consequently, the Committee considers that the facts before it reveal a violation of article 24 of the Covenant.

* * *

7. The Human Rights Committee, acting under article 5, paragraph 4, of the Optional Protocol to the Covenant, is of the view that the facts before it disclose a vio-

lation of articles 2 [which gives a right to enforce other rights], 7, 17 and 24 of the Covenant.

8. In accordance with article 2, paragraph 3 (a), of the Covenant, the State party is required to furnish the author with an effective remedy, including compensation. The State party has an obligation to take steps to ensure that similar violations do not occur in the future.

9. Bearing in mind that, as a party to the Optional Protocol, the State party recognizes the competence of the Committee to determine whether there has been a violation of the Covenant, and that, under article 2 of the Covenant, the State party has undertaken to ensure to all individuals within its territory and subject to its jurisdiction the rights recognized in the Covenant and to offer an effective and enforceable remedy when a violation is found to have occurred, the Committee wishes to receive from the State party, within 90 days, information about the measures taken to give effect to the present Views. The State party is also requested to publish the Committee's Views.

Note

What is the nature of the Human Rights Committee's opinion here? Does it legally bind the Peruvian government? Note that although Peru had ratified both the ICCPR and the Optional Protocol, the Committee's opinion is not binding and the state party is not required to comply. In fact, the state party did not respond in a meaningful way to the allegations in the *Huamán* case. But the final paragraph makes clear that Peru recognizes the Committee's jurisdiction to decide the matter, and calls for the government to respond within 90 days. Nevertheless, the right to health, animated by human rights principles, has succeeded in ensuring access to AIDS medications in India, Latin American, and South Africa, mental health care reform in Paraguay, access to abortion procedures in Colombia, and a ban on public smoking in India. Lawrence O. Gostin, *Global Health Law* 243 (Harvard 2014).

Several excellent sources are available discussing international law obligations, including: Lawrence O. Gostin, *Global Health Law* (Harvard, 2014); Colleen M. Flood & Aeyal Gross, *The Right to Health at the Public/Private Divide* (Cambridge, 2014); John Tobin, *The Right to Health in International Law* (Oxford, 2012); André den Exter ed., *International Health Care Law: Solidarity and Justice in Health Care* (Maklu, Antwerp, 2008); Gunilla Backman et al., Health Systems and the Right to Health: An Assessment of 194 Countries, 372 *The Lancet* 13 2047 (Dec. 2008); Judith Asher, *The Right to Health: A Resource Manual for NGOs* (2004); Rebecca Cook, Bernard Dickens and Mahmoud Fathalla, *Reproductive Health and Human Rights* (Clarendon Press, Oxford, 2003); Brigit C.A. Toebes, *The Right to Health as a Human Right in International Law* (Intersentia, Antwerp, 1999); Aart Hendriks, The Right to Health in National and International Jurisprudence, 5 *European J. Health L.* 389 (1998); Steven Jamar, The International Human Right to Health, 22 *So.U. L. Rev.* 1 (1994); and Virginia A. Leary, The Right to Health in International Human Rights Law, 1 *Health & Hum. Rts.* 25 (1995).

B. The Right to Health in Constitutional Law

The constitutions of many countries also recognize a right to health or to health care. Note the different treatment in the constitutions of Spain, Switzerland and Brazil that follow:

Spanish Constitution, 1978

(last amended in 2011)

Article 43 [Health Protection, Promotion of Sports]

1. The right to health protection is recognized.

2. It is incumbent upon the public authorities to organize and safeguard public health by means of preventive measures and the necessary benefits and services. The law shall establish the rights and duties of all concerned in this respect.

* * *

Swiss Constitution, 1999

(last amended in 2017)

Article 41 [Social Objectives]

1. The Confederation and the Cantons shall, as a complement to personal responsibility and private initiative, endeavor to ensure that:

* * *

b. every person has access to the health care that they require;

* * *

2. The Confederation and Cantons shall endeavor to ensure that every person is protected against the economic consequences of old-age, invalidity, illness, accident, unemployment, maternity, being orphaned and being widowed.

3. They shall endeavor to achieve these social objectives within the scope of their constitutional powers and the resources available to them.

4. No direct right to state benefits may be established on the basis of these social objectives.

Brazilian Constitution, 1998

(last amended in 2017)

Chapter II. Social Rights

Article 6

Education, health, nutrition, labor, housing, transport, leisure, security, social security, protection of motherhood and childhood and assistance to the destitute, are social rights, as set forth in this Constitution.

Section II. Health

Article 196

Health is the right of all and the duty of the National Government and shall be guaranteed by social and economic policies aimed at reducing the risk of illness and other maladies and by universal and equal access to all activities and services for its promotion, protection and recovery.

Article 197

Health activities and services are of public importance, and it is the Government's responsibility to provide, in accordance with the law, for their regulation, supervision and control. Such activities and services shall be carried out directly or through third parties and also by individuals or legal entities of private law.

Article 198

Public health activities and services are part of a regionalized and hierarchical network and constitute a unified system, organized in accordance with the following directives:

I. decentralization, with a single management in each sphere of government;

II. full service, giving priority to preventive activities, without prejudice to treatment services;

III. community participation.

(1) The unified health system shall be financed * * * with funds from the social security budget of the Union, States, Federal District, and Counties, as well as other sources. * * *

Article 199

Health care is open to private enterprise.

§ 1. Private institutions may participate on a supplementary basis in the unified health system, according to its directives, by means of contracts or agreements of public law, with a preference for philanthropic and non-profit entities.

§ 2. Allocation of public funds to aid or to subsidize for-profit private institutions is prohibited.

§ 3. Direct or indirect participation of foreign firms or capital in health assistance in the Country is prohibited, except for cases provided by law.

§ 4. The law shall provide for the conditions and requirements to facilitate removal of human organs, tissues, and substances for transplants, research and treatment, as well as collection, processing and transfusion of blood and its byproducts, forbidding all types of commercialization.

What difference does the approach of these three constitutions make? The following excerpt analyzes constitutional approaches to guaranteeing health care.

Eleanor D. Kinney & Brian Alexander Clark, *Provisions for Health and Health Care in the Constitutions of the Countries of the World*

Cornell International Law Journal,
vol. 37, pp. 285, 287, 289–90, 292–96, 298–301 (2004)

* * *

This Article reports findings of an empirical analysis of the provisions of the constitutions of the world that address health and health care. * * * The Article concludes that the national commitment to health and health care is not highly related to whether or not a nation's constitution specifically addresses health or health care * * *

* * * [W]e identified five types of constitutional provisions that addressed health and health care in national constitutions:

1. A statement of aspiration, stating a goal in relation to the health of its citizens.
2. A statement of entitlement, stating a right to health or health care or public health services.
3. A statement of duty, imposing a duty to provide health care or public health services.
4. A programmatic statement, specifying approaches for the financing, delivery or regulation of health care and public health services.
5. A referential statement, incorporating by specific reference any international or regional human rights treaties recognizing a human right to health or health care.

* * *

According to our criteria, 67.5% of the constitutions of the world have a provision addressing health or health care. In almost all of these constitutions, the provisions regarding health and health care are universal, rather than limited to particular groups. * * *

The fact that countries adopted their constitutions during different historical periods is a critical factor in determining whether the constitution addresses health or health care. Constitutions reflect the period of their formation as well as the level of the constitutional law development in other countries and international law at the time. Constitution making has occurred in specific periods of history—generally spawned by cataclysmic events affecting groups of nations in a particular geographic territory.

For purposes of this analysis, the basic periods of constitution making have been as follows: (1) England and its common law progeny, 1660s–present, including the United States; (2) European democratic states and constitutional monarchies, 1887–1960, including liberated nations after World War II in both the democratic West and the Communist Eastern Bloc; (3) emergence of new nations from former colonies in Africa, Asia, and the Middle East, 1945–1960; (4) the Latin American constitutional revolution, 1983–1994, replacing constitutions adopted in the 19th and 20th centuries following liberation from colonial rule; and (5) emergence of new democracies from the former Communist Bloc, 1989–present. During the last two periods, constitution making became something of a cottage industry among academics with the constitutions of many countries written in consultation with the same experts. Most of the constitutions were adopted after World War II. Indeed, only twenty-one constitutions adopted before World War II are currently in place and, of these, nine countries have substantially revised their constitutions since World War II. Of the twenty-one states, nine have provisions regarding health and health care in their constitutions, many of which were added when constitutions were revised after World War II.

It is clear that not all of the countries that have provisions regarding health and health care in their constitutions have in practice lived up to these mandates. Some of the most resounding constitutional commitments to health and health care are in poor countries with tenuous democracies. Haiti's constitution is exemplary of this phenomenon:

> Strengthen national unity by eliminating all discrimination between the urban and rural populations ... and by recognizing the right to progress, information, education, health, employment and leisure for all citizens.
>
> The State has the absolute obligation to guarantee the right to life, health, and respect of the human person for all citizens without distinction, in conformity with the Universal Declaration of the Rights of Man.
>
> The State has the obligation to ensure for all citizens in all territorial divisions appropriate means to ensure protection, maintenance and restoration of their health by establishing hospitals, health centers and dispensaries.

Many countries that devote extensive resources to assuring the health of and providing health care to their populations have no relevant provisions in their constitutions regarding health or health care. * * * Only three of the [twenty countries with highest per capita government expenditures for health care] * * * have provisions conferring an entitlement to health and/or imposing a duty on the state to provide health care. Thirteen countries have no provisions regarding health and health care in their constitutions.

* * *

The number or strength of constitutional provisions does not appear to have a determinative role in the amount of resources that countries spend for the health care of their populations. Specifically, countries that expressed the greatest constitutional commitment to health—evidenced by inclusion of both a statement of entitlement and duty]—had an average government per capita expenditure for health care of $308 in 2000. However, the same average for countries that had no provision regarding health or health care was $716.95. * * *

This finding is not surprising. There are many factors influencing governments' decisions to finance programs promoting health and providing health care services. In addition, constitutions' national legal frameworks vary tremendously in at least three important ways. First, the general attitude toward the constitution influences the degree to which a population and the representative advocacy groups look to the constitution for resources and remedies for the promotion of health and health care. In some countries, the constitution is part of the political culture and is viewed as a source of protections, whereas in other countries, the population has little knowledge of the constitution and its potential for advancing legal and social protections. Second, the degree of legal remedies, such as judicial review, private rights of action and access to courts, and the opportunity to challenge policymakers who fail to implement or enforce constitutional provisions regarding health and health care, vary between the countries. Finally, many countries, particularly in the southern hemisphere and in other parts of the developing world, do not have the financial resources to devote to improving health or providing health care services.

* * *

The question of constitutional provisions' meaning is complex and has at least two dimensions. First is the actual content of the concepts of "health" and "health care." * * *

The second dimension of meaning refers to enforceability of the individual interest in health and health care. Customarily, lawyers and legal scholars think of the interests that constitute enforceable "rights" as the only interests with legal meaning. This view of rights as "trumps" in the Dworkian sense exposes the problematic distinction between social and economic rights on the one hand and civil and political rights on the other. Often these two groups of rights are characterized, respectively, as positive rights requiring affirmative state action and as negative rights requiring state abstention from specific conduct. This distinction quickly disappears when one considers that proper enforcement of so-called negative rights often implicates affirmative state action and that substantial implementation of positive rights may well result when the state refrains from conduct limiting access to existing services.

To be recognized and implemented, economic and social rights require affirmative state action, which creates the problem with their designation as "rights." The conventional understanding of rights is that, if violated, they assure legal remedies from courts or other authoritative adjudicative tribunals. Extant legal remedies are often tailored to addressing the denial of civil and political rights by governments or even private actors within the governments' jurisdiction. Under this more conventional understanding, if rights are without legal remedies, they are simply aspirational statements. Such rights, some argue, water down the concept of rights and rob it of its meaning and effectiveness.

There is a significant difference between remedies designed to prevent a government or regulated private party from acting in a certain way, such as curtailing civil rights, and a remedy intended to force a government or regulated party to provide a particular service. Specifically, the latter remedy implicitly asks the government or regulated private party to allocate resources as the legal remedy. Thus, in the act of granting the remedy, the adjudicator invariably steps into the role of policymaker regarding the allocation of resources, which is quintessentially a legislative function. This phenomenon poses the dilemma of who is best charged with making the policy call in this instance—the activist judge witnessing the deficiency, or the reluctant legislature facing the full panoply of national needs and state obligations.

* * *

A more useful observation about individual enforcement of economic and social rights is that the determination of their content involves facts and issues that are not appropriate for courts or other adjudicative tribunals to decide. * * *

Lon Fuller also addresses the use of adjudication in deciding policy issues. Policy concerns, such as the appropriate content of government programs to assure health care services and the allocation of budgetary resources, are "polycentric" issues that are least amenable to satisfactory adjudication. The resolution of polycentric issues inevitably involves multiple implications and trade-offs to accommodate various exigencies and constituencies. Their resolution involves making decisions about * * * "legislative facts," the accuracy or persuasiveness of which are not easily determined through adjudicative techniques.

However, conceiving of rights as only those interests that are enforceable in a court or adjudicative tribunal is a very narrow concept. Why do rights have to be legally enforceable in that manner for validation? A right might also include a policy imperative established by authoritative law such as a constitution, treaty, or other legal mandate. As such, the right as policy imperative requires bound states to take legislative action and array national budgetary priorities in ways that fulfill that policy imperative. * * * This idea is captured in the thoughtful observation of an Eastern European scholar, commenting on economic and social rights as human rights:

> To call social and economic rights "human rights" is not to make them automatically enforceable. Human rights should set standards and provide justification for moral claims to decent treatment, and should guide legislators in the implementation of legal rights.

* * *

Note

Reviews differ on the precise number of constitutions that recognize a right to health. For example, a 2008 study of 194 countries found that only 63 had formally recognized the right to health in a domestic constitution, bill of rights, or statute. Gunilla Backman et al., Health Systems and the Right to Health: An Assessment of 194 Countries, 372 *The Lancet* 2047, 2062–71 (2008). The authors of *The Lancet* study noted that only 56 of the countries that had ratified the ICESCR, discussed above, had taken the next step of including the right to health in domestic constitutions or statutes, speculating that international recognition of the right to health is much more widespread than domestic recognition, "probably because international accountability is weaker than national accountability." *Id.* But other reviews, such as the Kinney and Clark article above, found higher levels of adoption, reporting that more than 130 of the world's constitutions guarantee the right to health. Similarly, in 2008, the Office of the UN High Commission for Human Rights found 115 constitutions around the world that incorporated a right to health. Fact Sheet No. 31, *The Right to Health* (2008).

Regardless of the precise number, there is a clear long-term trend toward formally recognizing the right to health in domestic law. In the last decade, for example, several Latin American countries ratified new constitutions that did so. The Constitution of Ecuador (2008) requires free, universal state care for all. The Constitution of Bolivia (2009) requires a unified health system with free and universal access to health services. And the Constitution of the Dominican Republic (2010) requires the state to protect the health of all persons, including access to hospital care, medical care, medications, and to better food and sanitation. These efforts were preceded in the 1990s by countries like Argentina, which in 1994 granted constitutional status to international treaties such as the ICESCR, the formal recognition of which was embraced by Argentine courts. Paola Bergallo, Argentina: Courts and the Right to Health: Achieving Fairness Despite "Routinization" in Individual Coverage Cases?, in *Litigating Health Rights: Can Courts Bring More Justice to Health?* 43, 45 (Alicia Ely Yamin & Siri Gloppen eds., 2011). In 1999, Venezuela adopted a constitution recognizing a fundamental right to health as part of the right to life. But the Supreme Tribunal of Justice has interpreted the right very narrowly, holding that broad public policies involving social and economic rights were not subject to judicial review, contrary to earlier precedents. Thus, Venezuela's "disintegrating and poorly coordinated" system is not subject to much law, despite the constitution and despite Venezuela's ratification of the ICESCR. Oscar A. Cabrera & Fanny Gómez, Litigating the Right to Health in Venezuela, in *The Right to Health at the Public/Private Divide: A Global Comparative Study* 394–96, 406 (Colleen M. Flood & Aeyal Gross eds., 2011). The Brazilian constitution, excerpted above, establishes a clear right to health, but without notions of progressive realization or resource constraints. As a result, Brazilian judges have interpreted articles 6 and 196 as "entitlements" to health care services, without regard to cost. Octávio Luiz Motta Ferraz, The Right to Health in the Courts of Brazil: Worsening Health Inequities?, 11(2) *Health & Human Rights Journal* 33, 40 (2009). Not surprisingly, the number of cases in Brazil invoking these articles rose dramatically after the early 1990s, although litigants sometimes also rely on the right to life in Article 5. Mariana Mota Prado, Provision of Health Care Services and the Right to Health in Brazil, in *The Right to Health at the Public/Private Divide: A Global Comparative Study* 337–38 (Colleen M. Flood & Aeyal Gross eds., 2011). There remains significant debate in Brazil regarding how well entrenched the right to health is, and whether courts should construe it as an entitlement or more of a programmatic goal to be progressively realized, despite the lack of express language to that effect. *Id.* at 337–39; Octavio L. Motta-Ferraz, Brazil: Health Inequalities, Rights, and Courts: The Social Impact of the Judicialization of Health, in *Litigating Health Rights: Can Courts Bring More Justice to Health?* 76 (Alicia Ely Yamin & Siri Gloppen eds., 2011).

Likewise, African nations such as South Africa (1996), Nigeria (1999), and Kenya (2009) have incorporated a right to health into their constitutions. Nigeria's constitution guarantees "adequate medical and health facilities for all persons," but this guarantee is non-justiciable unless made so by federal legislation. Remigius N. Nwabueze, The Legal Protection and Enforcement of Health Rights in Nigeria, in *The Right to Health at the Public/Private Divide: A Global Comparative Study* 380–82 (Colleen M. Flood & Aeyal Gross, eds. 2011). South Africa's post-apartheid constitution has significant attention. It includes a "right to have access to health care services, including reproductive health care" and a guarantee that "[n]o one may be refused emergency medical treatment," which are credited for motivating a number of enduring statutory reforms. Lisa Foreman & Jerome Amir Singh, The Role of Rights and Litigation in Assuring More Equitable Access to Health Care in South Africa, in *The Right to Health at the Public/Private Divide: A Global Comparative Study* 317 (Colleen M. Flood & Aeyal Gross, eds. 2011).

Asian countries likewise display a range of approaches. In Japan, Article 25 of the Constitution calls for the state to "use its endeavors for the promotion and extension of social welfare and security, and of public health," but Japanese courts have yet to formally recognize a right to health from this language. Nevertheless, by statute Japan's population is automatically enrolled in its universal health insurance system. Tokuko Munesue, The Right to Health in Japan: Its Implications and Challenges, in *The Right to Health: A Multi-Country Study of Law, Policy and Practice* 123 (Brigit Toebes et al. eds., 2014). Meanwhile, China has ratified the ICESCR, which in China gives it the same legal force as domestic law. Shengnan Qiu, Equality and the Right to Health: A Preliminary Assessment of China, in *The Right to Health: A Multi-Country Study of Law, Policy and Practice* 97 (Brigit Toebes et al. eds., 2014). Moreover, China's "Constitution mentions health and medicine in fairly prominent ways," including the call for "material assistance" from the state in the event of illness, which traces back through several constitutions adopted since the 1949 Communist Revolution. Christina S. Ho, Health Rights at the Juncture between State and Market, in *The Right to Health at the Public/Private Divide: A Global Comparative Study* 270 (Colleen M. Flood & Aeyal Gross, eds. 2011). But constitutional and statutory rights to health in China generally are not realized through litigation, which "is a relatively weak tool in China" due to the reluctance of courts to interfere in socioeconomic disputes, the fact that judicial decisions are not recognized as a source of law in the Chinese legal system, and the reality that courts are compromised both by corruption and by direct political oversight. *Id.* at 273. Thus, non-judicial methods such as arbitration, mediation, and political protests seem to be more effective in China in pursuing health claims.

In the Middle East and North Africa, a study of the right to health in the "Arab world" found that only 5 of 23 countries did not incorporate health or health care into their constitutions (Jordan, Lebanon, Mauritania, Morocco, Somalia). Salman Rawaf and Sondus Hassounah, Codification and Implementation of the "Right to Health" in the Arab World, *The Right to Health: A Multi-Country Study of Law, Policy and Practice* 135, 148 (Table 5.3) (Brigit Toebes et al. eds., 2014). In Israel, although lacking a "full, comprehensive constitution," its Basic Law on Human Dignity and Liberty has been interpreted to include very minimal "access to rudimentary medical services," and its courts sometimes interpret domestic statutes with health rights in mind, including Israel's ratification of the ICESCR. Aeyal Gross, The Right to Health in Israel between Solidarity and Neoliberalism, in *The Right to Health at the Public/Private Divide: A Global Comparative Study* 165 (Colleen M. Flood & Aeyal Gross eds. 2011). Saudi Arabia is not a party to many international treaties recognizing a right to health, and its governing Islamic law ("sharia," deriving from the Koran and Sunna) is uncodified and thus unclear on the matter. Lara Walker, The Right to Health and Access to Health Care in Saudi Arabia with a Particular Focus on the Women and Migrants, in *The Right to Health: A Multi-Country Study of Law, Policy and Practice* 165, 170–71 (Brigit Toebes et al. eds., 2014). Nevertheless, a Royal Decree in 1992 declared it to be Saudi basic law that "The state shall look after public health and provide health care for every citizen." Rawaf & Hassounah, at 150 (Table 5.3).

Without relying on international treaty or domestic constitutional obligations, can courts effectuate a right to health? The following case from the Indian Supreme Court represents one of the few instances in which a national supreme court has done so.

Paschim Banga Khet Mazdoor Samity v. State of West Bengal

Supreme Court of India, AIR 1996 Supreme Court 2426

S.C. Agrawal and G.T. Nanavati, JJ.

S.C. Agrawal, J.:—In Pt Parmanand Katara v. Union of India (1989), this Court in the context of medico-legal cases, has emphasised the need for rendering immediate medical aid to injured persons to preserve life and the obligations of the State as well as doctors in that regard. This petition, filed under Article 32 of the Constitution raises this issue in the context of availability of facilities in Government hospitals for treatment of persons sustaining serious injuries.

Hakim Seikh [Petitioner No. 2] who is a member of Paschim Banga Khet Mazdoor Samity [Petitioner No. 1], an organisation of agricultural labourers, fell off a train at Mathurapur Station in West Bengal at about 7.45 P.M. on July 8, 1992. As a result of the said fall Hakim Seikh suffered serious head injuries and brain haemorrhage. He was taken to the Primary Health Centre at Mathurapur. Since necessary facilities for treatment were not available at the Primary Health Centre, the medical officer in charge of the Centre referred him to the Diamond Harbour Sub-Divisional Hospital or any other State hospital for better treatment. Hakim Seikh was taken to N.R.S. Medical College Hospital near Sealdah Railway Station, Calcutta at about 11.45 P.M. on July 8, 1992. The Emergency Medical Officer in the said Hospital, after examining him and after taking two X-ray prints of his skull recommended immediate admission for further treatment. But Hakim Seikh could not be admitted in the said hospital as no vacant bed was available in the Surgical Emergency ward and the regular Surgery Ward was also full. He was thereafter taken to Calcutta Medical College Hospital at about 12.20 A.M. on July 9, 1992 but there also he was not admitted on the ground that no vacant bed was available. He was then taken to Shambhu Nath Pandit Hospital at about 1.00

A.M. on July 9, 1992. He was not admitted in that hospital and referred to a teaching hospital in the ENT, Neuro Surgeon Department on the ground that the hospital has no ENT Emergency or Neuro Emergency Department. At about 2.00 A.M. on July 9, 1992 he was taken to the Calcutta National Medical College Hospital but there also he was not admitted on account of non-availability of bed. At about 8.00 A.M. on July 9, 1992 he was taken to the Bangur Institute of Neurology but on seeing the CT Scan (which was done at a private hospital on payment of Rs.1310/-) it was found that there was haemorrhage condition in the frontal region of the head and that it was an emergency case which could not be handled in the said Institute. At about 10.00 A.M. on July 9, 1992 he was taken to SSKM Hospital but there also he was not admitted on the ground that the hospital has no facility of neuro surgery. Ultimately he was admitted in Calcutta Medical Research Institute, a private hospital, where he received treatment as an indoor patient from July 9, 1992 to July 22, 1992 and he had incurred an expenditure of approximately Rs 17,000/- in his treatment.

Feeling aggrieved by the indifferent and callous attitude on the part of the medical authorities at the various State run hospitals in Calcutta in providing treatment for the serious injuries sustained by Hamik Seikh the petitioners have filed this writ petition.

* * *

The Constitution envisages the establishment of a welfare State at the federal level as well as at the State level. In a welfare State the primary duty of the Government is to secure the welfare of the people. Providing adequate medical facilities for the people is an essential part of the obligations undertaken by the Government in a welfare State. The Government discharges this obligation by running hospitals and health centres which provide medical care to the person seeking to avail those facilities. Article 21 imposes an obligation on the State to safeguard the right to life of every person. Preservation of human life is thus of paramount importance. The Government hospitals run by the State and the Medical Officers employed therein are duty bound to extend medical assistance for preserving human life. Failure on the part of a Government hospital to provide timely medical treatment to a person in need of such treatment results in violation of his right to life guaranteed under Article 21. In the present case there was breach of the said right of Hakim Seikh guaranteed under Article 21 when he was denied treatment at the various Governmental hospitals which were approached even though his condition was very serious at that time and he was in need of immediate medical attention. Since the said denial of the right of Hakim Seikh guaranteed under Article 21 was by officers of the State in hospitals run by the State, the State cannot avoid its responsibility for such denial of the constitutional right of Hakim Seikh. In respect of deprivation of the constitutional rights guaranteed under Part III of the Constitution the position is well settled that adequate compensation can be awarded by the court for such violation by way of redress in proceedings under Articles 32 and 226 of the Constitution. Hakim Seikh should, therefore, be suitably compensated for the breach of his right guaranteed under Article 21 of the Constitution. Having regard to the facts and circumstances of the case, we fix the amount of such compensation at Rs 25,000/-. A sum of Rs. 15,000/- was directed to be paid to Hakim Seikh as interim compensation under the orders of this Court dated April 22, 1994. The balance amount should be paid by respondent No. 1 to Hakim Seikh within one month.

We may now come to the remedial measures to rule out recurrence of such incidents in future and to ensure immediate medical attention and treatment to persons in real need.

* * *

[W]e are of the view that in order that proper medical facilities are available for dealing with emergency cases it must be that:

1. Adequate facilities are available at the Primary Health Centres where the patient can be given immediate primary treatment so as to stabilize his condition;

2. Hospitals at the district level and Sub-Division level are upgraded so that serious cases can be treated there;

3. Facilities for giving Specialist treatment are increased and are available at the hospitals at District level and Sub-Division level having regard to the growing needs;

4. In order to ensure availability of bed in an emergency at State level hospitals there is a centralised communication system so that the patient can be sent immediately to the hospital where bed is available in respect of the treatment which is required;

5. Proper arrangement of ambulance is made for transport of a patient from the Primary Health Centre to the District Hospital or Sub-Division hospital to the State hospital;

6. The ambulance is adequately provided with necessary equipment and medical personnel;

7. The Health Centres and the hospitals and the medical personnel attached to these Centres and hospitals are geared to deal with larger number of patients needed emergency treatment on account of higher risk of accidents on certain occasions and in certain seasons.

It is no doubt true that financial resources are needed for providing these facilities. But at the same time it cannot be ignored that it is the constitutional obligation of the State to provide adequate medical services to the people. Whatever is necessary for this purpose has to be done. In the context of the constitutional obligations to provide free legal aid to a poor accused this Court has held that the State cannot avoid its constitutional obligation in that regard on account of financial constraints. The said observations would apply with equal, if not greater, force in the matter of discharge of constitutional obligation of the State to provide medical aid to preserve human life. In the matter of allocation of funds for medical services the said constitutional obligation of the State has to be kept in view. It is necessary that a time-bound plan for providing these services should be chalked out keeping in view the recommendations of the Committee as well as the requirements for ensuring availability of proper medical services in this regard as indicated by us and steps should be taken to implement the same.

The Union of India is a party to these proceedings. Since it is the joint obligation of the Centre as well as the States to provide medical services it is expected that the Union of India would render the necessary assistance in the improvement of the medical services in the country on these lines.

As regards the medical officers who have been found to be responsible for the lapse resulting in denial of immediate medical aid to Hakim Seikh it is expected that the State Government will take appropriate administrative action against those officers.

* * *

Notes

1. India has ratified the ICESCR but does not provide a fundamental right to health in its constitution; rather, the Indian Constitution classifies socioeconomic rights as "Directive Principles" that are not judicially enforceable. Nonetheless, Indian courts have been particularly active in attempting to operationalize a right to health via the fundamental right to life, thus creating positive obligations on the part of the state, as the *Samity* case above demonstrates. After the *Samity* decision, the Indian Supreme Court affirmed that "it is now settled law that right to health is integral to right to life." *State of Punjab v. Mohinder Singh Chawla*, (1997) 2 S.C.C. 83. Per the Indian Constitution, health care is the primary responsibility of state governments, and thus state courts have been a key source of law. K. Srinath Reddy, India's Aspirations for Universal Coverage, 373 *New England Journal of Medicine* 1 (Jul. 2, 2015). In one case, the High Court of Orissa ordered the state government to open a primary care center in a rural area to provide preventive services (*Mahendra Pratap Singh v. State of Orissa*, A.I.R. 1997 Ori. 37), while in another the Allahabad High Court held that hospital patients had the right to have access to medicine at night and at reasonable prices (*Prayag Vyapar Mandal v. State of Uttar Pradesh*, A.I.R. 1991, All. 1). Indian courts have also invoked the right to life in the context of states subsidizing private hospitals (*Social Jurist, A Lawyer's Group v. Government of NCT*, (2007) 140 D.L.T. 698) and providing access to pharmaceuticals (*KS Gopinath v. Union of India*, (2003) 1 K.C.C. R. 269). Notwithstanding these court decisions, practical access to health care in India is undermined by poor planning and lack of resources. See Anand Grover et al., Right to Health: Addressing Inequities through Litigation in India, in *The Right to Health at the Public/Private Divide: A Global Comparative Study* 423 (Colleen M. Flood & Aeyal Gross, eds. 2011); Sheetel B. Shah, Illuminating the Possible in the Developing World: Guaranteeing the Human Right to Health in India, 32 *Vand. J. Transnat'l L.* 435 (1999).

2. Other countries in which the Supreme or Constitutional Court has recognized an enforceable right to health care, including treatment for AIDS, include South Africa and Venezuela. See Lisa Forman, Ensuring Reasonable Health: Health Rights,

the Judiciary, and South African HIV/AIDS Policy, 33 *J. L. Med. & Ethics* 711 (2005); Mary Ann Torres, The Human Right to Health, National Courts, and Access to HIV/AIDS Treatment: A Case Study from Venezuela, 3 *Chi. J Int'l L.* 105 (2002).

3. The experience of Colombia is worth noting. In 1991, it adopted a new constitution declaring that "Every person has guaranteed access to services that promote, protect, and improve health," making the state responsible for ensuring that services are provided "according to the principles of efficiency, universality, and solidarity." Constitution of Colombia, Article 49. Importantly, the drafters chose to frame health as a public service rather than a right. *See* Everaldo Lamprea, Colombia's Right-to-Health Litigation in a Context of Health Care Reform, in *The Right to Health at the Public/Private Divide: A Global Comparative Study* 138 (Colleen M. Flood & Aeyal Gross, eds. 2011). But Colombia's courts gradually transformed health into a right. The 1991 constitution introduced a "Tutela claim," which allows any citizen to seek an injunction in court when their basic rights are threatened by the government or by a third party. Article 85 of the constitution gives the judge or court hearing the case less than ten days to decide the claim, thus eliminating legal formalities and expenses associated with most litigation. The 1991 constitution also created a Constitutional Court that could reject or accept Tutela rulings. Early cases established important precedents that would later be used as foundations for recognizing a right to health in Colombia. These decisions also brought into sharp relief underperformance by the Ministry of Health and other agencies in implementing the country's 1993 health system reforms. Ultimately, a landmark decision by the Colombian Constitutional Court in 2008 relied explicitly on the right to health in ordering that the country's health system be restructured. Constitutional Court, Sentencia T-760/08 (Colom.), at http://www.corteconstitucional.gov.co/relatoria/2008/T-760-08.htm. The 2008 decision relied on an early 1992 Constitutional Court decision that itself looked to jurisprudence from the German Constitutional Court in deriving a right to health from the right to life. Constitutional Court, Sentencia T-484/92, at http://www.corteconstitucional.gov.co/relatoria/1992/T-484-92.htm. Thus, since 1991 Colombia has experienced a "dramatic escalation of right-to-health litigation," which "is unparalleled among middle-income countries." Ottar Moestad et al., Assessing the Impact of Health Rights Litigation: A Comparative Analysis of Argentina, Brazil, Colombia, Costa Rica, India, and South Africa, in *Litigating Health Rights: Can Courts Bring More Justice to Health?* 273 (Alicia Yamin & Siri Gloppen eds., 2011). Between 2006 and 2012, residents filed roughly 100,000 Tutela claims each year relating to the right to health—mostly for medical goods and services denied by health insurance companies, despite being included in the "basket" of covered services. Health-related claims constituted between 23–41% of all Tutela claims. In these cases, plaintiffs prevailed in 85% of rulings. Defensorí del Pueblo [Human Rights Obmudsman Office], Colombia, La Tutela y el Derecho a la Salud [The Tutela and the Right to Health] (2013); Lamprea, Colombia's Right-to-Health Litigation at 144, 145 Table 5.1. In response to the structural reforms required by the 2008 ruling, and to the fiscal burdens imposed by frequent Tutela litigation, President Uribe issued emergency decrees to

undermine Tutela claims, but the Constitutional Court ruled that most of the decrees were unconstitutional. Later, President Santos rejuvenated some of these efforts, successfully creating a Peer Scientific Committee to review certain services excluded from the "basket" of covered treatments, in theory rendering Tutela decisions moot. Thus, Colombia continues to grapple with the tension between fiscal pressures and the right to health recognized in constitutional law. For a comprehensive review of this tension, see Lamprea, *supra*.

4. Some courts also use international agreements as a sort of canon of construction for interpreting domestic laws, thus reading them in a way that assumes they intend to comply with international agreements. As Gostin emphasizes, domestic litigation "demonstrates the justiciability of health rights despite their progressive nature and budgetary implications," which can "help break the second-class status of socioeconomic rights" and "catalyze policy reform." Gostin, *Global Health Law*, at 264–65.

At the same time, observers worry that litigation driven by health rights can inflate medical spending and shift control from legislators and central planners to courts without the competence or expertise to balance conflicting priorities. For example, one study found that litigation in Colombia generated $750 million in expenditures for services not included in the national health plan in 2009, which comprised 5.4% of the total health budget. Alicia Ely Yamin et al., Colombia: Judicial Protection of the Right to Health: An Elusive Promise?, *in Litigating Health Rights: Can Courts Bring More Justice to Health?* 103 (Alicia Ely Yamin and Siri Gloppen, eds., 2011). And in São Paolo, Brazil's largest state, a separate study found that pharmaceuticals provided in response to litigation constituted 25% of the medicines budget in 2008. Ottar Mæstad et al., Assessing the Impact of Health Rights Litigation: A Comparative Analysis of Argentina, Brazil, Colombia, Costa Rica, India, and South Africa, in *Litigating Health Rights: Can Courts Bring More Justice to Health?* 290 (Alicia Ely Yamin and Siri Gloppen, eds., 2011).

Constitutional law need not only expand positive government obligations to provide health care, however. Human rights charters might also provide negative rights to be free from government interference in seeking private health care, as the following recent Canadian Supreme Court case illustrates.

Chaoulli v. Quebec (Attorney General)

2005 SCC 35 (Canada 2005)

1. Deschamps J.—Quebeckers are prohibited from taking out insurance to obtain in the private sector services that are available under Quebec's public health care plan. Is this prohibition justified by the need to preserve the integrity of the plan?

2. As we enter the 21st century, health care is a constant concern. The public health care system, once a source of national pride, has become the subject of frequent and sometimes bitter criticism. This appeal does not question the appropriateness of the state making health care available to all Quebeckers. On the contrary, all the parties stated that they support this kind of role for the government. Only the state can make

available to all Quebeckers the social safety net consisting of universal and accessible health care. The demand for health care is constantly increasing, and one of the tools used by governments to control this increase has been the management of waiting lists. The choice of waiting lists as a management tool falls within the authority of the state and not of the courts. The appellants do not claim to have a solution that will eliminate waiting lists. Rather, they submit that the delays resulting from waiting lists violate their rights under the Charter of Human Rights and Freedoms ("Quebec Charter"), and the Canadian Charter of Rights and Freedoms ("Canadian Charter"). They contest the validity of the prohibition * * * on private insurance for health care services that are available in the public system. * * *

* * *

4. In essence, the question is whether Quebeckers who are prepared to spend money to get access to health care that is, in practice, not accessible in the public sector because of waiting lists may be validly prevented from doing so by the state. For the reasons that follow, I find that the prohibition infringes the right to personal inviolability and that it is not justified by a proper regard for democratic values, public order and the general well being of the citizens of Quebec.

5. The validity of the prohibition is contested by the appellants, George Zeliotis and Jacques Chaoulli. Over the years, Mr. Zeliotis has experienced a number of health problems and has used medical services that were available in the public system, including heart surgery and a number of operations on his hip. The difficulties he encountered prompted him to speak out against waiting times in the public health care system. Mr. Chaoulli is a physician who has tried unsuccessfully to have his home delivered medical activities recognized and to obtain a licence to operate an independent private hospital.* * *

6. The Superior Court dismissed the motion for a declaratory judgment * * *.

7. On the subject of s. 7 of the Canadian Charter, * * * Piché J.* * * was of the opinion that the purpose of the [the prohibition of private insurance contained in] the Hospital Insurance Act (HOIA) and the Health Insurance Act (HEIA) is to establish a public health system that is available to all residents of Quebec. The purpose of s. 11 HOIA and s. 15 HEIA [prohibiting the purchase of private medical insurance] is to guarantee that virtually all of Quebec's existing health care resources will be available to all residents of Quebec. In her opinion, the enactment of these provisions was motivated by considerations of equality and human dignity. She found no conflict with the general values expressed in the Canadian Charter or in the Quebec Charter. She did find that waiting lists are long and the health care system must be improved and transformed. In her opinion, however, the expert testimony could not serve to establish with certainty that a parallel health care system would solve all the current problems of waiting times and access.

* * *

11. The Court of Appeal dismissed the appeal * * *. According to Delisle J.A., the right affected by s. 11 HOIA and s. 15 HEIA is an economic right and is not funda-

mental to an individual's life. In addition, in his opinion, the appellants had not demonstrated a real, imminent or foreseeable deprivation. He was also of the view that s. 7 of the Canadian Charter may not be raised to challenge a societal choice in court. * * *

* * *

27. In the instant case, s. 7 of the Canadian Charter and s. 1 of the Quebec Charter have numerous points in common:

> Canadian Charter 7. Everyone has the right to life, liberty and security of the person and the right not to be deprived thereof except in accordance with the principles of fundamental justice.
>
> Quebec Charter 1. Every human being has a right to life, and to personal security, inviolability and freedom.

* * *

37. The appellant Zeliotis argues that the prohibition infringes Quebeckers' right to life. Some patients die as a result of long waits for treatment in the public system when they could have gained prompt access to care in the private sector. Were it not for s. 11 HOIA and s. 15 HEIA, they could buy private insurance and receive care in the private sector.

38. The Superior Court judge stated "that there [are] serious problems in certain sectors of the health care system." The evidence supports that assertion. After meticulously analysing the evidence, she found that the right to life and liberty protected by s. 7 of the Canadian Charter had been infringed. * * *

* * *

40. Dr. Daniel Doyle, a cardiovascular surgeon, testified that when a person is diagnosed with cardiovascular disease, he or she is "always sitting on a bomb" and can die at any moment. In such cases, it is inevitable that some patients will die if they have to wait for an operation. Dr. Doyle testified that the risk of mortality rises by 0.45 percent per month. The right to life is therefore affected by the delays that are the necessary result of waiting lists.

* * *

44. In the opinion of my colleagues Binnie and LeBel JJ., there is an internal mechanism that safeguards the public health system. According to them, Quebeckers may go outside the province for treatment where services are not available in Quebec. This possibility is clearly not a solution for the system's deficiencies. The evidence did not bring to light any administrative mechanism that would permit Quebeckers suffering as a result of waiting times to obtain care outside the province. The possibility of obtaining care outside Quebec is case specific and is limited to crisis situations.

* * *

46. Section 9.1 of the Quebec Charter sets out the standard for justification. It reads as follows:

> "9.1. In exercising his fundamental freedoms and rights, a person shall maintain a proper regard for democratic values, public order and the general well being of the citizens of Québec.
>
> In this respect, the scope of the freedoms and rights, and limits to their exercise, may be fixed by law."

* * *

48. * * * First, the court must determine whether the objective of the legislation is pressing and substantial. Next, it must determine whether the means chosen to attain this legislative end are reasonable and demonstrably justifiable in a free and democratic society. For this second part of the analysis, three tests must be met: (1) the existence of a rational connection between the measure and the aim of the legislation; (2) minimal impairment of the protected right by the measure; and (3) proportionality between the effect of the measure and its objective. * * *

* * *

74. Even if it were assumed that the prohibition on private insurance could contribute to preserving the integrity of the system, * * * prohibiting insurance contracts is by no means the only measure a state can adopt to protect the system's integrity. * * * The regimes of the provinces where a private system is authorized demonstrate that public health services are not threatened by private insurance. It can therefore be concluded that the prohibition is not necessary to guarantee the integrity of the public plan.

* * *

78. In a number of European countries, there is no insurance paid for directly out of public funds. In Austria, services are funded through decentralized agencies that collect the necessary funds from salaries. People who want to obtain health care in the private sector in addition to the services covered by the mandatory social insurance are free to do so, but private insurance may cover no more than 80 percent of the cost billed by professionals practising in the public sector. The same type of plan exists in Germany and the Netherlands, but people who opt for private insurance are not required to pay for the public plan. Only nine percent of Germans opt for private insurance.

* * *

83. As can be seen from the evolution of public plans in the few OECD countries that have been examined in studies produced in the record, there are a wide range of measures that are less drastic, and also less intrusive in relation to the protected rights * * * A measure as drastic as prohibiting private insurance contracts appears to be neither essential nor determinative.

* * *

101. For these reasons, I would allow the appeal with costs throughout and would answer the questions relating to the Quebec Charter as follows:

Question 1: Does s. 11 of the Hospital Insurance Act, R.S.Q., c. A-28, infringe the rights guaranteed by s. 1 of the Quebec Charter? Answer: Yes.

Question 2: If so, is the infringement a reasonable limit prescribed by law as can be demonstrably justified in a free and democratic society under s. 9.1 of the Quebec Charter? Answer: No.

Question 3: Does s. 15 of the Health Insurance Act, R.S.Q., c. A-29, infringe the rights guaranteed by s. 1 of the Quebec Charter? Answer: Yes.

Question 4: If so, is the infringement a reasonable limit prescribed by law as can be demonstrably justified in a free and democratic society under s. 9.1 of the Quebec Charter? Answer: No.

McLachlin C. J.C. The Chief Justice, Major J.:

1102. We concur in the conclusion of our colleague Deschamps J. that the prohibition against contracting for private health insurance violates the Quebec Charter of Human Rights and Freedoms. On the argument that the anti-insurance provision also violates s. 7 of the Canadian Charter of Rights and Freedoms ("Charter"), we conclude that the provision impermissibly limits the right to life, liberty and security of the person protected by s. 7 of the Charter and has not been shown to be justified as a reasonable limit under s. 1 of the Charter.

103. The appellants do not seek an order that the government spend more money on health care, nor do they seek an order that waiting times for treatment under the public health care scheme be reduced. They only seek a ruling that because delays in the public system place their health and security at risk, they should be allowed to take out insurance to permit them to access private services.

104. The Charter does not confer a freestanding constitutional right to health care. However, where the government puts in place a scheme to provide health care, that scheme must comply with the Charter. * * *

* * *

106. The Canada Health Act, the Health Insurance Act, and the Hospital Insurance Act do not expressly prohibit private health services. However, they limit access to private health services by removing the ability to contract for private health care insurance to cover the same services covered by public insurance. The result is a virtual monopoly for the public health scheme. The state has effectively limited access to private health care except for the very rich, who can afford private care without need of insurance. This virtual monopoly, on the evidence, results in delays in treatment that adversely affect the citizen's security of the person. Where a law adversely affects life, liberty or security of the person, it must conform to the principles of fundamental justice. This law, in our view, fails to do so.

* * *

108. The government defends the prohibition on medical insurance on the ground that the existing system is the only approach to adequate universal health care for all Canadians. The question in this case, however, is not whether single-tier health care is preferable to two-tier health care. Even if one accepts the government's goal, the legal question raised by the appellants must be addressed: is it a violation of s. 7 of

the Charter to prohibit private insurance for health care, when the result is to subject Canadians to long delays with resultant risk of physical and psychological harm? The mere fact that this question may have policy ramifications does not permit us to avoid answering it....

Binnier, Lebel JJ. (Dissenting):

* * *

166. The Quebec government views the prohibition against private insurance as essential to preventing the current single tier health system from disintegrating into a de facto two-tier system. The trial judge found, and the evidence demonstrated, that there is good reason for this fear. * * *

* * *

176. It would be open to Quebec to adopt a U.S.-style health care system. No one suggests that there is anything in our Constitution to prevent it. But to do so would be contrary to the policy of the Quebec National Assembly, and its policy in that respect is shared by the other provinces and the federal Parliament. As stated, Quebec further takes the view that significant growth in the private health care system (which the appellants advocate) would inevitably damage the public system. Our colleagues the Chief Justice and Major J. disagree with this assessment, but governments are entitled to act on a reasonable apprehension of risk of such damage. * * *

* * *

242. * * * We now propose to review briefly some of the evidence supporting the findings of the trial judge. * * *

* * *

248. The experience in other OECD countries shows that an increase in private funding typically leads to a decrease in government funding. At trial, Dr. Bergman explained that a service designed purely for members of society with less socio-economic power would probably lead to a decline in quality of services, a loss of political support and a decline in the quality of management.

* * *

249. The evidence suggests that parallel private insurers prefer to siphon off high income patients while shying away from patient populations that constitute a higher financial risk, a phenomenon known as "cream skimming". The public system would therefore carry a disproportionate burden of patients who are considered "bad risks" by the private market by reason of age, socio-economic conditions, or geographic location.

* * *

251. Reference has already been made to the U.S. health care system, which is the most expensive in the world, even though by some measures Americans are less healthy than Canadians. The existence of a private system has not eliminated waiting times. The availability, extent and timeliness of health care is rationed by private in-

surers, who may determine according to cost, not need, what is "medically necessary" health care and where and when it is to occur. Whether or not the private system in the U.S. is better managed is a matter of debate amongst policy analysts. The point here is simply that the appellants' faith in the curative power of private insurance is not borne out by the evidence put before the Court.

* * *

Note

Importantly, Justice Deschamps' majority decision held that the Quebec statute violated only the Quebec Charter, without ruling on whether it also violated the Canadian Charter (the court split 3–3 on that question). Thus, the *Chaoulli* decision applies only in Quebec, and not to other provinces. In the aftermath of *Chaoulli*, the Quebec government both loosened restrictions on private health insurance and committed itself to reducing waiting times in the public system. But the latter provisions targeted only three services: hip, knee, and cataract surgery. Bill 33: *An Act to amend the Act respecting health services and social services and other legislative provisions*, R.S.Q., ch. 43. The *Chaoulli* decision did, however, inspire different types of legal claims in other provinces: claims for greater access to publicly-financed care; claims as in *Chaoulli* to loosen restrictions on privately-financed care; and challenges to limits on publicly-financed care based on tort and other private law claims. Colleen Flood & Sujith Xavier, *Health Care Rights in Canada: The Chaoulli Legacy, in International Health Law: Solidarity and Justice in Health Care* 98 (Maklu, Antwerp, 2008). But litigation pushing for the right to access private services has been more successful than litigation pushing for increased access to public services, "even though the latter would arguably improve overall equity and be far more in keeping with [Canadian Charter] values." Colleen M. Flood, Litigating Health Rights in Canada: A White Knight for Equity?, in *The Right to Health at the Public/Private Divide: A Global Comparative Study* 79 (Colleen M. Flood & Aeyal Gross, eds. 2011). Moreover, even in the rare case when a plaintiff succeeds in arguing for a positive right to health care (*Eldridge v. British Columbia* (Att'y Gen.), [1997] 3 S.C.R. 624 (Can.)), they "see that right go unenforced on the ground." *Id.* at 86. For a thorough review and critique of the *Chaoulli* case in a national and international context, see *id*; Colleen Flood, Lorne Sossin and Kent Roach, eds., *Access to Care, Access to Justice: The Legal Debate Over Private Health Insurance in Canada* (2005).

Did fears of a two-tiered system in Canada materialize? Although the *Chaoulli* decision "legitimized" a two-tiered health system, it did not usher in a genuine two-tiered public-private system across the country. First, because the decision relied on the Quebec Charter rather than the Canadian Charter, similar prohibitions on private insurance in other provinces remain untouched. Moreover, no real two-tiered health system emerged even in the four provinces that did not ban private health insurance (New Brunswick, Newfoundland, Nova Scotia, and Saskatchewan). Nonetheless, *Chaoulli* has inspired similar litigation in Alberta, Ontario, and British Columbia, not to mention the de facto spread of privatization through user fees, extra billing, and reliance on goods and services not covered by Medicare Canada, such as pharmaceuticals. Flood, *Litigating Health Rights in Canada*, at 96–98.

In summary, there is a clear trend toward more frequent and assertive judicial review of national health care policies. As Gostin notes, "at some point, government's failure to provide essential health services must be actionable if the right to health is to have meaning." Yet, questions remain regarding the competence, jurisdiction, and legitimacy of court decisions that require certain allocations of scarce health care resources, particularly when they contradict the decisions of democratically accountable branches of government, like the legislature. The fact remains that "the right to health requires the cooperation of all branches of government." Gostin, *Global Health Law*, at 268.

C. The Organization of National Health Care Systems

While nations widely recognize the right to health, the manner in which they implement it varies dramatically. All nations, including the United States, have adopted some form of public insurance for at least a portion of their population. At the same time, most nations also have some form of private market for health care, including private health insurance. All nations also, obviously, have a delivery system to provide health care to residents. The variety of approaches to delivering and financing health care is endless. Still, as this section shows, a few models for delivery and finance emerged early and then became dominant.

This book is not primarily concerned with comparative health care organization and finance. A wealth of excellent books and articles written by experts in health policy, politics, and economics thoroughly explore this territory. Our focus is rather health law. Of course, it is difficult to understand health law without some understanding of the systems in which health law operates. This section and the one that follows provide a basic background in health care systems, and offer some basic tools of health policy analysis.

We use two primary sources here to introduce health systems. The first is a nice summary from the WHO's *World Health Report 2000*, which ranked the world's health care systems with three variables in mind: (i) the extent to which the system contributed to improving its residents' health status; (ii) how fairly the system distributes health care resources and costs; and (iii) how responsive the system is to standards for respecting dignity, autonomy, and confidentiality. Measured by these variables, the United States ranked 37, in company with Costa Rica at 36 and Slovenia at 38. The low U.S. score was largely due to poor performance on health status and fairness, adjusted for available resources. France ranked first among all nations in overall performance. Although the methodology of the *Report* has been controversial, it is useful insofar as it takes a truly global view of health systems, both in its worldwide focus and in its emphasis on preventive and public health measures, as well as on curative care. The excerpt from the *Report* included here explores the history of how different models of health care systems emerged, illustrating their historical contingence and rich variety. The second article by Tim Jost describes the major models used for organizing health care delivery and provides some information as to the comparative performance of these systems. Although both sources are over a decade old, and though many system reforms have occurred since then, they still provide excellent foundations for comparing health systems.

World Health Report 2000

World Health Organization, pp. 11–13 (2000)

* * *

With rare exceptions, even in industrialized countries, organized health systems in the modern sense, intended to benefit the population at large, barely existed a century ago. Although hospitals have a much longer history than complete systems in many countries, few people living 100 years ago would ever visit one—and that remains true for many millions of the poor today. Until well into the 19th century they were for the most part run by charitable organizations, and often were little more than refuges for the orphaned, the crippled, the destitute or the insane. And there was nothing like the modern practice of referrals from one level of the system to another, and little protection from financial risk apart from that offered by charity or by small-scale pooling of contributions among workers in the same occupation.

Towards the close of the 19th century, the industrial revolution was transforming the lives of people worldwide. At the same time societies began to recognize the huge toll of death, illness and disability occurring among workforces, whether from infectious diseases which killed many thousands during the construction of the Panama Canal or from industrial accidents and exposures. Once it was realized that mosquitoes transmitted malaria and yellow fever, control of the insects' breeding-sites became part of prevention efforts that also translated into benefits for surrounding communities. In addition to the human costs, the toll of illness and death meant great losses in productivity. In response, company owners began providing medical services to treat their workers. * * *

About the same time, workers' health was becoming a political issue in some European countries, but for quite different reasons. Bismarck, Chancellor of Germany, reasoned that government take-over of labour unions' sickness funds would remove a source of their support at a moment when socialist workers' movements were gaining strength, and also increase workers' economic security. Thus, in 1883, Germany enacted a law requiring employer contributions to health coverage for low-wage workers in certain occupations, adding other classes of workers in subsequent years. This was the first example of a state-mandated social insurance model. The popularity of this law among workers led to the adoption of similar legislation in Belgium in 1894 and Norway in 1909. Until Britain followed suit in 1911, medical care for British wage earners tended to be paid for by their subscriptions to trade unions or friendly societies, which in turn paid the providers. But only the worker, and not his family, had such coverage.

In the late 1800s, Russia had begun setting up a huge network of provincial medical stations and hospitals where treatment was free and supported by tax funds. After the Bolshevik revolution in 1917, it was decreed that free medical care should be provided for the entire population, and the resulting system was largely maintained for almost eight decades. This was the earliest example of a completely centralized and state-controlled model.

The influence of the German model began to spread outside Europe after the First World War. In 1922, Japan added health benefits to the other benefits for which workers were eligible, building on its tradition of managerial paternalism. In 1924, Chile brought all covered workers under the umbrella of a Ministry of Labour scheme. By 1935, a total of 90% of Denmark's population was covered by work-related health insurance. Social insurance was introduced in the Netherlands during the country's occupation in the Second World War.

Not least among its effects, the Second World War damaged or virtually destroyed health infrastructures in many countries and delayed their health system plans. Paradoxically, it also paved the way for the introduction of some others. Wartime Britain's national emergency service to deal with casualties was helpful in the construction of what became, in 1948, the National Health Service, perhaps the most widely influential model of a health system. The Beveridge Report of 1942 had identified health care as one of the three basic prerequisites for a viable social security system. The government's White Paper of 1944 stated the policy that "Everybody, irrespective of means, age, sex or occupation shall have equal opportunity to benefit from the best and most up-to-date medical and allied services available," adding that those services should be comprehensive and free of charge and should promote good health, as well as treating sickness and disease. New Zealand had already become, in 1938, the first country to introduce a national health service. Almost simultaneously, Costa Rica laid the foundation for universal health insurance in 1941. In Mexico, the Institute of Social Security and the Ministry of Health were both founded in 1943.

In the immediate post-war period, Japan and the Soviet Union also extended their limited national systems to cover most or all of the population, as did Norway and Sweden, Hungary and other communist states in Europe, and Chile. As former colonies gained independence, they also tried to adopt modern, comprehensive systems with heavy state participation. India developed ambitious five-year development plans for a health system, based on the Bhore Report of 1946. The factors which made this period of system-building and expansion possible included realization of the power of the modern state, post-war movements towards reconciliation, stability and reconstruction, and collective solidarity stemming from the war effort. Newly acquired citizenship and the belief in a relatively effective and benevolent state which could promote development of all kinds led to a social and political environment in which "classical universalism," the concept of free access to all kinds of health care for all, could take root.

Today's health systems are modelled to varying degrees on one or more of a few basic designs that emerged and have been refined since the late 19th century. One of these aims to cover all or most citizens through mandated employer and employee payments to insurance or sickness funds, while providing care through both public and private providers. The earliest such social insurance systems usually evolved from small, initially voluntary, associations; later versions have sometimes been created *ex nihilo* by public action. Another, slightly more recent, model centralizes planning and financing, relying primarily on tax revenues and on public provision. Resources are traditionally distributed by budgets, sometimes on the basis of fixed ratios between populations and health workers or facilities. In a third model, state involvement is more limited but still substantial, sometimes providing coverage only for certain population groups and giving way for the rest of the populace to largely private finance, provision and ownership of facilities. Relatively pure examples, in which one or another model accounts for the bulk of resources or provision, are found mostly in rich countries; health systems in middle income countries, notably in Latin America, tend to be a mixture of two or even all three types.

* * *

Timothy Stoltzfus Jost, *Why Can't We Do What They Do? National Health Reform Abroad*

Journal of Law, Medicine and Ethics,
vol. 32, pp. 432–35 (2004)

* * *

All other developed nations of the world [other than the United States], including developed countries in Western Europe, Asia, North and South America, and on the Pacific Rim, provide health care for all or most of their residents. Although private health insurance products are available for purchase on a voluntary basis in virtually every country, no other developed country relies on private insurance as does the United State to provide primary coverage for its population. All developed nations have recognized that voluntary private insurance cannot cover everyone, (as it does not in the U.S.) and have developed some form of public health insurance.

Two primary models can be found in the world: social insurance and national health insurance. Each term refers to a specific approach to the task of financing and organizing a nation's system for providing personal health care. The first, and older, model is social insurance, often called the Bismarck model after the German leader who established the first social health insurance system. The second, more recent, is the national health insurance model, often called the Beveridge model after Lord Beveridge who proposed this approach for the U.K. during World War II.

Chancellor Bismarck established the German social insurance system in 1883 in an attempt to turn back the tide of socialism that he feared would engulf Germany. Under the German system as it has developed, most citizens have an obligation to secure health insurance coverage, which in turn is paid for, usually by a deduction from earnings, on the basis of the insured's income rather than the insured's risk status or family size, in order to ensure affordability. In Germany the conceptual foundation of health insurance lies in a belief that members of a society have obligations to each other, a concept referred to as "solidarity," rather than in the belief that individuals are responsible only for themselves. This insurance obligation is effectuated through a system that collects the necessary revenues needed to sustain health care. Employers and employees each contribute a percentage of wages to social insurance funds; in turn, these funds provide health insurance for employees and their families. Most persons in Germany whose income falls below a certain level (46,350 Euros in 2004) must participate in this social health insurance program. Persons with incomes above this level are not required to participate, and many buy private insurance instead. However, about 60 percent of all of these upper income persons in fact participate in the public system because family coverage costs extra in the private system but not in the public, private insurance rates are risk-adjusted while social insurance rates are not, and persons who opt out of the social insurance system may not in most instances ever return.

Social insurance funds in Germany are not administered by the government, but rather by non-profit organizations, which are accountable to their members (and their members' employers). There are many of these funds, some tied to a particular employer, others occupation based, and still others locally-based. Thus employees of Mercedes or BMW would be insured through a company fund; farmers, miners or seamen are covered by special funds, and many people are insured through a general locally-based fund or through special funds that used to only cover white collar workers. All social insurance funds operate within a framework of laws, and all cover essentially the same services and charge similar (though not identical) premiums. In order to ensure the stability of the health funds—and thus the effectuation of a truly nationwide system—health plans that have younger and less costly members must transfer money through a risk-equalization scheme to the plans that have older and more expensive patients, but the plans also compete with each other for members and thus have some incentive to keep their premiums down.

Health insurers have traditionally paid hospitals on the basis of negotiated budgets, though Germany is moving toward payment on a diagnosis related group (DRG) basis. Physicians and dentists in Germany who furnish health care to plan members are organized into corporate bodies that resemble unions. In other words, while physicians and dentists are private businessmen, they negotiate with the health insurers collectively, much like an independent practice association would do in the U.S. In recent years these corporate entities have negotiated with social insurers for a fixed budget, which they have allocated among their members on a fee-for-service basis.

* * *

For each component of the health care sector (physician services, hospitals, pharmaceuticals, etc.) and in each region, budgets in Germany are established globally within a framework of "premium stability." This framework limits the rate of increase in social insurance premiums to the rate of increase in inflation generally and tends to ensure that practice style and practice choices evolve within a fundamental environment of overall health care spending control. * * *

The social insurance model created in Germany has been adopted in much of the world. Other central European countries, including Austria, Switzerland, France, Belgium, and the Netherlands have social insurance systems, as do many South American and Asian countries for at least part of their workforce. Many of the emerging democracies of Eastern Europe have also embraced the social insurance model. Part A of the U.S. Medicare program in most respects resembles a social insurance system. Though these systems vary in many important respects, in each one health insurance is financed primarily by payroll taxes or wage-based premiums, and services are purchased from independent health care providers who often are in private practice.

If the social insurance model was adopted by conservative governments to suppress the growth of socialism in the late 19th and early 20th century, the national health insurance model emerged from the triumph of socialism in Europe after World War II. The United Kingdom had adopted a limited social insurance system in 1911, but many people were excluded from it, and the U.K. emerged from WWII determined to provide health care as a right to its entire population. Access to health care would no longer depend on belonging to a social insurance plan (which was usually, in some sense, employment-related), but rather would be free at point-of-service to all residents. Thus, universal coverage was created independent of the economic or employment status of any individual.

The English NHS is financed through general revenue taxation. These funds are administered by local units called primary care trusts. These units purchase services from NHS hospital trusts, which are currently public corporations, as well as from general practitioners, who are private businessmen. These services are then provided to the general public, in most instances without cost, although co-payments are imposed for some things like drugs, and a few services—like most dental care—are provided mainly in the private sector.

The U.K., like many European countries, has a strong gatekeeper system. Every Briton has a general practitioner (GP), and a patient's first contact with the health care system is almost always with the GP. GPs still make house calls in the U.K., and the level of satisfaction with primary care in the U.K. is very high. Specialist services, including surgery, are only provided through hospitals and upon referral from a GP.

Many nations have adopted the national health insurance model of public health insurance in the past half century, although, again, in each nation the model looks somewhat different. Canada, Australia, the Scandinavian countries, Spain, Portugal, Italy, and some Latin American and Asian countries have national health insurance systems. Other countries, particularly less developed countries, provide services through public hospitals and clinics without necessarily developing a full and comprehensive national system of health care finance that would be essential to make such a network of services accessible to all persons. Our own Medicaid program, as well as our veterans', military, and Indian health services, resemble the "national health insurance" model, in that all use general revenue funds to pay for health services, but they are different in that their coverage is limited to certain narrowly delineated populations, which may even, as with Medicaid, vary from state to state.

In virtually all countries, voluntary private health insurance of the sort sold in the U.S. to both groups and individuals continues to exist, although it serves different functions in different countries. In some, such as Germany and the Netherlands, it covers wealthy people who are not covered by social insurance. In others, such as Canada, it covers services such as pharmaceuticals, which are not universally covered by public insurance. In yet others, such as France, it covers cost-sharing obligations, much like our own Medigap policies. In still others, such as the U.K. or Australia, it allows privately insured persons to jump the queue and get services faster or more conveniently than publicly insured patients.

Countries that have national health insurance programs cover all of their citizens and long-term residents, although in most countries individuals can choose to carry private insurance and obtain services privately. Some countries with social insurance funds, such as France or Austria, cover their entire populations as well. Others, however, such as Germany and the Netherlands, only require people whose income falls below a certain level to be part of the social insurance program. Although people with higher incomes can choose to be uninsured, few make this choice. In Australia, government subsidies are available that cover 30 percent of the cost of hospital care, while tax penalties are imposed on higher income persons who choose not to purchase private insurance. This results in about 43 percent of the population being privately insured for hospital care. In several of the southern European nations, many people choose to purchase care privately, even though everyone is covered by national health insurance, because they believe that they will get better care or more attention from their providers.

A number of countries apply means tests for determining coverage for certain services or for determining the applicability or level of cost-sharing. The Irish health care system is partially means tested: only low income holders of medical cards (about a third of the population) have free access to general practitioner services, and higher income people without medical cards must pay a co-payment for hospital and pharmacy services under some circumstances. In the U.K. where long-term nursing home care is primarily regarded as a social service, nursing homes are publicly funded only for those who do not have the means to pay privately. Pharmaceutical coverage in the U.K. is also means tested to the extent that the system waives required co-payments for low-income persons, although the government also waives co-payment for children, the elderly, and persons with certain chronic conditions. No developed nation other than the U.S., however, makes access to public health insurance depend totally on economic "medical dependency" (Medicaid), or on age and disability status (Medicare). And no other developed country has nearly as high a proportion of its population uninsured.

Social insurance and national health insurance programs vary somewhat in the benefits they offer. The Canadian health insurance program, for example, only requires the provinces to cover hospital, physician, and surgical dental services, though most provinces also cover pharmaceutical costs for at least some of their residents. Coverage in Australia is limited to hospital, physician, and pharmaceutical care. Most countries do not cover nursing home care or cover it as a social service rather than a health care service. In some countries some benefits that are nominally covered are in fact not generally available because of high cost sharing obligations, limited coverage, or lack of provider participation.

Though public finance of health care services is quite common in other countries, public provision of health care services is less universal. In most national health insurance countries, many health care services are furnished by private entities and health professionals in private practice. In few countries, for example, does the government directly employ primary care physicians or dentists. Pharmaceuticals and medical devices are generally produced by private manufacturers and sold through private pharmacies or medical equipment suppliers. In most national health insurance countries public hospitals are dominant, but in some countries private nonprofit or private hospitals also exist. Private hospitals are even more common in social insurance countries.

* * *

Notes

1. The health care systems of other nations continue to evolve. In 2006, the Netherlands passed major insurance reforms, merging its public and private insurance systems into a single system based on "managed" or "regulated" competition among private insurers. All Dutch residents are required to purchase plans from private insurers, who must offer a basic package of benefits and may not deny coverage or charge more based on individuals' health status. Premiums are paid in part by a social insurance fund and in part by the insured, with additional assistance for lower income residents. Dutch residents either renew or change insurance plans yearly, with insurers competing on premiums, the quality of their service, and the quality of care offered. In 2007, Germany passed major reforms that largely took effect by 2009, including a health insurance mandate, reorganization of the sickness funds, and new risk-sharing and premium contribution arrangements. In 2012, England passed the Health and Social Care Act, perhaps the most significant and controversial NHS legislation since 1946. The Act, building on years of pro-market reforms dating back to the 1980s, reorganized the NHS by abolishing primary care trusts (PCTs) and shifting local management to roughly 200 "Clinical Commissioning Groups" led by general practitioners (GPs). More recently, scholars have focused on how European health systems are changing due to fiscal austerity measures. *See, e.g.*, *Health Care Systems in Europe under Austerity* (Emmanuele Pavolini & Ana M. Guillén, eds., 2013). For example, between 2009 and 2013, public health spending in Greece fell by 32% ($5.2 billion). And the portion of Greeks covered by public insurance fell from 100% in 2008 to 86% in 2015. *See* OECD Health Policy Overview: Health

Policy in Greece, at http://www.oecd.org/greece/Health-Policy-in-Greece-January-2016.pdf. Comprehensive information on the health care systems of European nations is available from the European Observatory on Health Systems and Policies. The Observatory's Health Systems in Transition (HiT) profiles currently cover about 60 countries, including "honorary European" countries like Australia, Canada, New Zealand, and Israel. See http://www.euro.who.int/en/about-us/partners/observatory/publications/health-system-reviews-hits/full-list-of-country-hits.

Perhaps the most active region since 2000 has been Latin America. Several countries passed laws to strengthen their ministries of health in managing their health systems, including Ecuador (2006), Argentina (2007), and Costa Rica (2008). Others focused on enhancing access to care, including Colombia (2007), Uruguay (2007), El Salvador (2007), and Peru (2009). In 2010, Bolivia adopted a national health system and universal insurance. For a survey of recent system reforms in Latin America, see Pan American Health Organization (PAHO), *Health in the Americas* (2012), Ch. 5: Health Systems and Social Protection in Health, at http://www.paho.org/salud-en-las-americas-2012/index.php?. PAHO, a regional arm of the WHO, observes in a 2012 report that:

> Several of the Region's countries have embarked on an important shift in how they approach the financing of the health system, the organization of health-system resources, and the role of the various stakeholders in these processes, by replacing the individual risk approach that prevailed in the 1990s with the concept of the right to health. The fact that this change has occurred in both high- and middle-income countries (*e.g.*, Brazil, Chile, Colombia, Ecuador, Mexico, Peru, the United States, and Uruguay) with highly developed health institutions, in one lower middle-income country (El Salvador), and one very low-income country (Haiti) whose health institutions are in an incipient stage of development is significant.

2. How might the role of legal institutions vary depending on whether health care systems are organized around a social insurance or national health service model? How will the role differ depending on whether services are provided by salaried or contracted providers? Are legal rights more important in systems that depend on private provision and finance, as in the United States, or on public finance or provision, as in Europe and much of the rest of the world?

3. In 2010, the United States adopted its most significant health reforms since creating the Medicare and Medicaid programs in 1965. The Patient Protection and Affordable Care Act, known as the "Affordable Care Act" (ACA) or "Obamacare," did not abandon the country's unique heavy reliance on private, employer-sponsored insurance. The United States is quite unusual on the world stage because of the extent to which it relies on private insurance. Virtually every other nation has private health insurance, but usually it only allows persons wealthy enough to opt out of public insurance, insures services not covered by the social insurance program, or permits the insured person to "queue jump," *i.e.* to avoid the waiting lists found in the public system. In the United States, by contrast, private insurance is the primary means of financing health care for non-indigent, non-elderly persons. It is important to realize,

however, that we also have public health care systems in the United States, which today in fact fund nearly half of the nation's health care. Medicare, our program for the elderly and long-term disabled, is a traditional social insurance program, funded through payroll taxes. Medicaid, our program for the poor, is financed through general revenues, and thus resembles more closely national health insurance programs of other countries. The ACA reforms in 2010 sought to reduce the number of uninsured through insurance mandates for individuals and employers, a complex web of tax credits and subsidies to make insurance more affordable, and market reforms to protect access to private insurance. But perhaps the most ambitious reform was dramatically expanding eligibility for Medicaid, the joint federal-state program for low-income populations. Although thwarted in part by a Supreme Court decision (*National Federation of Independent Businesses v. Sebelius*, 567 U.S. 519 (2012)) and the subsequent refusal of several Republican-led states to expand their Medicaid programs, the ACA still reduced the number of uninsured from roughly 49 million in 2010 (16% of the population) to roughly 27 million in 2016 (9%). In 2017, however, Republican proposals under President Trump would dramatically scale back reforms under the ACA and increase the uninsured by 22–26 million, depending on the bill. Thus, the long, contentious debate over health reform in the United States continues unabated.

D. Perspectives on Health Care Systems

As we see throughout this book, differences (and similarities) in the law between countries often can be explained by some combination of political, economic, and cultural factors. This section, then, opens the discussion by offering such perspectives on how and why countries diverge (or converge) in how they approach similar problems in health care. The first excerpt, from a distinguished scholar in health politics, discusses the possibilities and pitfalls of learning from comparative experience.

Theodore R. Marmor, *Comparative Studies and the Drawing of Policy Lessons: Describing, Explaining, Evaluating, and Predicting*

Journal of Comparative Policy Analysis,
1–4, 8–9, 12–13 (May 25, 2017)

Introduction

The world of public policy is no stranger to cross-national commentary[…]. It has been particularly evident in the arena of medical care and public health. Claims about new drugs, devices, and procedures fly around the world with electronic speed. Professionals regularly jet off to conferences, and cross-national dialogue takes place in seminars, journals, email exchanges, and study tours. No one, as Rudolf Klein (1995) once remarked, can "escape the bombardment of information about what is happening in other countries." Yet there is a large gap between promise and performance in comparative policy commentary. Superficiality and mistaken description are all too common. Caricatures, rhetorical distortion, and unwarranted inferences all show up regularly.

The question this article—and much of my scholarship—raises is how to assess the burgeoning field of comparative policy analysis and to separate learning from mis-learning, myth from fact, theoretical concern from theoretical posturing. What ground rules make sense to apply? And can they be applied in any policy field? If so, the comparative discussion of health policy can be a window on any policy field.

Different Purposes and Defensible Rules for International Comparison

What purposes, then, can be usefully served by cross-national policy analysis and what are the basic rules of that game? [...] One can enumerate five guiding rules—three positive, two cautionary. The first positive rule is simple but powerful: cross-national investigation permits one to understand one's own circumstances more clearly by comparison. So, for example, it can clarify the policy problems, options, or evaluations in setting A by placing them against those of another context B. Such knowledge offers perspective, not direct lessons. It illuminates subtle differences among nations that are quite similar, and sharper differences when applied to very different national arrangements. We might term this "illumination without [policy] transplantation."

Second, cross-national inquiry can help one assess the adequacy of nation-specific accounts of policy development. We can label that a "defense against explanatory provincialism." Canada, Australia, and the USA, for example, all debated whether to adopt national health insurance in the decades after the Second World War. All faced heated struggles over this deeply divisive moral and economic issue. In the 1970s both Australia and Canada had enacted such programs while the US had not. The American result was separate health financing programs for the elderly, the disabled, veterans, and some groups of the poor. Only careful comparative analysis can separate the fundamental causal differences from the many developments that accompanied this policy differentiation among broadly similar welfare states. The answer comparative analysis suggests is this: the distinctive institutional character of American politics and, most particularly, its dispersed structure of authority, provides many more veto points than the parliamentary structure of the other two federal states (Marmor and Klein 2012).

Treating cross-national experiences as quasi-experiments is a third option. In this instance, the more similar the countries compared the more reliable are the inferences one can draw from the quasi-experiment. But, as Rose (1991) cautioned, with that comes limits. The range of options will be narrower as the set of comparative examples is smaller (but allowing more in-depth analysis). Relationships that hold over many very different national experiences are likely to be few in number but powerful and thus important. For instance, across the industrial democracies in the past four decades there has been a general trend to mixed systems of payments of physicians. At one time, it would have been possible to categorize nations as devoted to fee-for-service, capitation, or salary models, but that is no longer the case. Why that is so, and what it suggests, is a promising topic for comparative analysis.

The cautionary remarks apply to two misleading approaches to cross-national inquiry. The most familiar is the "naïve transplantation" conception. The idea is simple: search for best practices and, if found, assume that they can be imported. There are many examples of this in the professional literature, but no social science support for the claim that a practice in site A or country A can be transplanted without adaptation to site B or country B with the same effects. The opposite vice is what can be termed the "fallacy of comparative difference." The major contention is that nations differing in any respect cannot learn from another's policy experience. The factual premise is that countries always differ in some respect. The conclusion of the syllogism is that no cross-national policy learning is possible. This is a form of intellectual nihilism, but it is not uncommon in policy debates.

Sources of Confusion in Cross-Border Research and Policy Debate: Health Care Illustrations

Why do so many of the cross-border studies of health policy muddle rather than clarify the debates? Is that really so? I hope to convince you that the problems cited in comparative health policy work are serious (and not in that field alone). The very place of "health" in the field of social policy is itself unclear. There is no generally agreed upon vocabulary to describe the issues at hand, itself a barrier to scholarly understanding, let alone cumulative knowledge. Public discussion of medical care issues is replete with misleading labels […]. Time pressure on policy makers looking elsewhere for promising reforms produces many cycles of naïve enthusiasm and regrettable neglect.

These are bold claims. They call for good examples of inaccurate and misleading reporting on experiences abroad, with special reference to North American and Western European experience, my area of expertise.

The public portrait of Canada's experience with national health insurance is one striking example of uneven comparative treatment, typically inaccurate. In the last three decades of the twentieth century, the US media paid attention intermittently to Canada's version of national health insurance known as Medicare. When covering Canada's experience, they did so mostly in negative terms. Commentators used the vocabulary of "socialized medicine" when, in fact, Canada's Medicare is a form of social health insurance in which nongovernmental hospitals and physicians provide the services that are publicly financed. There were repeated references to a government run system, with long waiting lists and inaccessible general practitioners, with numerous patients and physicians fleeing to the United States to seek care and earn higher incomes unencumbered by government. All of those characterizations are highly exaggerated and overwhelmingly misleading, as some specialist scholars have documented. But confusion arises from the conflict among accounts, not all of which can be true. Note also that European health commentators regularly label American health care as a "private, consumer driven" market system (Lubbers 1997; Rothgang et al. 2005). Yet the obvious and central fact is that more than 50 per cent of America's $3 trillion medical economy is publicly financed—by social insurance contributions, public taxes, or tax expenditures. Factual accuracy, a necessary prerequisite for useful comparative work, is regularly absent in the health policy field, and, I would suggest, in many other fields of public policy.

A different but equally misleading area is published reports of how the use of electronic medical records can improve the quality of health care and reduce its costs. These reports typically fail to describe accurately the actual use, and the financial realities of that use. They conflate policy intentions and promises with implementation and outcomes (e.g. the reports of the Commonwealth Fund). As for broader health reform, note that European commentators had high expectations for the Patient Protection and Affordable Care Act (PPACA) in 2010. But they paid little attention to the barriers to change in America's political institutions, barriers that severely limited the Obama administration's capacity either to restrain medical costs or to reach most of the 50 million uninsured Americans. That the reform expanded coverage somewhat is true—by about 20 million. But it did so in ways that are not easy for most Americans to understand, let alone commentators new to American politics. The obvious inference is that cross-national policy comparison is hard because factual accuracy is itself demanding when one is dealing with the experiences of multiple countries. It also implies that collaborators with special expertise in the national experiences being compared is a promising remedy, but still difficult to arrange.

Another source of confusion is the very conceptual location of health care and health policy making. Carolyn Tuohy (1993) has rightly argued that there are now "two worlds of welfare" in most Organization for Economic Co-operation and Development (OECD) nations: health care separate from other social welfare programs. This divergence had taken place almost everywhere in the OECD world by the late 1980s. In the Canadian case, the separation illustrates how complicated the descriptions of a welfare state can become. Canada's Medicare is similar to the health care arrangements in Western Europe—universal health insurance based on principles of solidarity and equal treatment. In contrast, Canada's unemployment and disability programs are more similar to those of the United States, more parsimonious, with comparatively low levels of benefits and restrictive eligibility criteria. So, what kind of welfare state does Canada exhibit? To what model is it an approximation?

During the 1970s, several industrial democracies established independent departments or organizations to administer (public) health care and appointed cabinet ministers of separate health departments. Universities followed, with independent schools of public health and health policy departments, with their own niche of health policy analysis. Such developments cut the umbilical cord between health care and the income protection schemes of the modern welfare state such as old age pensions, unemployment insurance and sickness payment (Okma 2002). Governments and academics active in the health care field increasingly left behind their roots in the domain of social welfare policy. They developed "epistemic communities," or networks of experts, focused on health care organization, finance and provision, and their associated issues of governance. Attention shifted away from the general policy goal of protecting family income against the financial risks of illness or disability. Inspired by the rise of "new public management" ideas, some commentators came to regard health care as a conventional industry—and with that came a change in language. Patients became "consumers," department heads and medical directors became managers and CEOs, and hospital departments became profit centers (Marmor 1998).

* * *

A fourth source of confusion, as noted before, is time pressure. Policy makers are under pressure to come up quickly with seeming solutions for (or at least responses to) policy problems (Klein 1995). Looking abroad for new policy ideas is one way to do so, even if those ideas have not been evaluated properly. Politicians are engaged in political struggles, after all, not academic debates. They have little time to distinguish policy goals and proposals sharply from implemented programs or policy results. They regularly use cross-national information as "warfare ammunition" for policies they support on other grounds (Marmor et al. 2005, Introduction). There has been a rapid growth of "health policy tourism"—quick trips to study policy experiences abroad. For example, several delegations of European experts visited California's Kaiser Permanente (KP) in the 2000s. They saw KP as the ultimate role model for "integrated care." Such visits are typically very short, sometimes only one day. Most pay little attention to the question of why and how KP came to be successful. As a result, commentary typically ignores selection bias, the fact that both the providers contracted by Kaiser and its patients are quite distinct from modal physicians and nonmembers in several important ways. Since KP's organizational innovation emerged through self selection of both patients and professionals, the transferability of its model is open to serious question. But that, unfortunately, has not been the focus of most external evaluations of this distinctive organization.

Understanding the broader political context in which health policy debates take place is enormously important and too often neglected. Failing to do so commonly produces both unwarranted generalizations and misleading policy recommendations. Health care systems across the world do have much in common. On the funding side, they all collect taxes, contributions for social insurance, premiums for private insurance and direct patient payments for medical care. All systems combine to some degree the public and private provision of health care services. The announced policy goals in most industrialized nations and emerging economies are broadly similar: to safeguard access to a good quality of health care for all. But there are major differences in how the funding, contracting, payment, and management of health care takes place. The mix of public and private funding differs as well as the ownership of hospitals and other health facilities. Country specific cultural and institutional features shape national policy making. Policy makers and policy analysts alike pay too little attention to the transferability of policy. So the question worth posing is this: under what conditions can we expect that measures which worked abroad will also work at home? The sciences of medicine or economics are "landless theories," as Richard Rose (1991) has powerfully argued. They largely ignore the country specific policy context that enables reforms or creates barriers to change. Political science—understood as discipline studying the shaping and results of public policy—should do better than that. But it is not at all clear that comparative policy studies are fulfilling that role.

* * *

Conclusion

[...] The striking feature of this body of writing is highlighting the very variety of concerns and work that mark cross-national policy analysis. The optimistic view is that the variety will prompt searches for analytic improvement, and will winnow out the less useful approaches and leave the superior work like boats at low tide, revealed and obvious. The less optimistic view is that we have had a huge increase in crossnational communication, travel, familiarity, and commentary, but that the amount of accurate, incisive, and helpful policy analysis from scholarly studies has hardly been an illustration of cumulative advance.

Notes

1. Canada has been an obvious object of study for Americans considering comparative health policy—not only because it is so accessible geographically, but also because Canada and the United States resemble each other in so many other respects. Indeed, the fact that the health care systems of the United States and Canada were so similar prior to the implementation of the Canadian Medicare system in 1966 makes the subsequent history of the two countries look almost like a controlled experiment. During the U.S. health reform debates of the early 1990s and again surrounding the Affordable Care Act, the Canadian health system was used by both those who favored and opposed the Clinton and Obama health reform proposals. Among many excellent sources comparing the U.S. and Canadian experiences, see June E. O'Neill & Dave M. O'Neill, *Health Status, Health Care and Inequality: Canada vs. the U.S.*, 10 Forum for Health Economics & Policy 1 (2008); Gerard W. Boychuk, *National Health Insurance in the United States and Canada: Race, Territory, and the Roots of Difference* (2008); Carolyn Tuohy, *Accidental Logics: The Dynamics of Change in the Health Care Arena in the United States, Britain, and Canada* (1999).

2. In the wake of rather rancorous health reform debates in the United States, some U.S. scholars also have examined how the U.S. system performs in relation to its counterparts in the EU.

Nathan Cortez, *The Elusive Ideal of Market Competition in United States' Health Care*

Health Care and EU Law, ch. 15, 359–69
(van de Gronden et al. eds., 2011)

* * *

15.1 Introduction

What role does market competition play in the United States' health care system, and what might the United States (US) and the European Union (EU) learn from each other's experiences? Market competition remains a persistent but elusive ideal in American health care. More than its peers, the US health care system looks to market-inspired theories and policy instruments to solve its problems. But decades of policies promoting this ideal have not given Americans the health system they desire. Most recognize that equity is not what markets provide, yet markets have also failed to produce a more efficient US health care system. Ironically, the ideal of market competition has both driven and undermined contemporary health reform efforts in the United States. Even reforms designed to stimulate more competitive markets have faced considerable resistance because the political branches could not agree how to balance the public and private sectors.

Markets versus government remains the "basic dividing line and dominant theme in American health policy." Academics and policymakers have long struggled to identify the appropriate role for markets in health care. And there remains "deep social ambivalence about whether health care should be considered a public good or a commodity."

Of course, the United States is not alone in this struggle. Because there has never been a purely public or private health care system, every country must determine the appropriate relationship between markets and government in health care. Even countries with robust public health care systems are trying to use markets to squeeze more efficiency out of their systems without jeopardizing other priorities, such as universal coverage or solidarity. * * * Most countries labor to find the appropriate role for market competition in health care.

* * *

15.2 American Exceptionalism in Health Care

The US health care system is exceptional. So-called "American exceptionalism," the idea that the United States is unique in the world, has been controversial since Alexis de Tocqueville published his observations in the 1830s. But the health policy world generally agrees that the US health care system is singular. Among developed countries, the United States is the only one without a single health care system organized around "a common philosophy about coverage, access, and cost." Ours is a fragmented pastiche of health insurers, providers, and facilities, each of which is regulated primarily by states rather than the federal government. Indeed, calling ours a "system" is charitable; its defining feature may be its extreme decentralization.

So precisely how is the US health care system exceptional? Health care systems are generally evaluated along three dimensions: cost, quality, and access. As [David Hyman and Charlie Silver] note[], "enhancing quality, lowering cost, and broadening access" is the "holy grail" or "holy trinity" of health care policy. Compared to its peers, the US health care system does not fare particularly well along any of these three dimensions.

The first and increasingly central criterion is cost. How expensive is the health care system? What does it spend per capita, and what percentage of the economy does health spending occupy? The US health care system is by far the most expensive in the world, both in aggregate and per capita terms. In aggregate terms, the United States spends as much on health care as every other nation in the world combined. In 2007, worldwide health care spending reached around $4.1 trillion, and the United States alone accounted for over half of that amount ($2.3 trillion). Moreover, most predict that US spending will continue to rise, potentially to as much $4.3 trillion by 2018—equal to total worldwide health spending today. Unsurprisingly, the United States spends a much larger portion of its gross domestic product (GDP) on health care than other countries. In 2008, health care spending accounted for 16.2% of the US economy, and experts predict it could reach 20.4% by 2018. By contrast, health spending occupies significant but much more modest portions of the economies in Germany (10.6% of its GDP), Canada (10.1%), the Netherlands (9.8%), Denmark (9.8%), Spain (8.5%), and the United Kingdom (8.4%). Moreover, US health care is exceptionally expensive in per capita terms. In 2007, US residents spent an average of $7,290 on health care, roughly twice what their counterparts spent in Canada ($3,895), Germany ($3,588), the Netherlands ($3,837), Denmark ($3,512), the United Kingdom ($2,992), and Spain ($2,671). Again, experts largely project US spending to rise, though other countries certainly also struggle with rising costs.

The second criterion for evaluating health systems is quality: Does the health care system provide necessary, appropriate, and high quality care? Does it ensure that health care professionals, facilities, and products meet minimum quality standards? What results does the system generate, and how healthy are residents? The US system does not provide high quality care commensurate with its spending. Although the "quality" of health care is notoriously difficult to measure, most metrics show that the United States lags behind its peers. For example, in 2000 the World Health Organization (WHO) famously and somewhat controversially ranked 193 countries by the quality and performance of their health systems. The United States ranked 37th in overall performance and 24th in the overall health of its population. More specific comparisons show that the United States does not score well compared to other developed countries on several health-related metrics, such as life expectancy and infant mortality rates, which are admittedly imperfect barometers of quality. Yet, virtually every comparison of "quality" shines an unfavorable light on the US health care system. The US system does certain things very well. It is good at providing innovative, extraordinary, life-saving treatments. But it struggles to provide basic care and prevent common illnesses. As two notable scholars [David Cutler and Patricia Keenan] conclude, "there is precious little evidence that the United States does better than other countries in any material outcome."

The third criterion is access to care: How difficult is it for people of ordinary means to access health care goods and services? What percentage of the public has health insurance, and what percentage can obtain basic care? How long must patients wait for care? Does the system make care reasonably available to those who need it? Again, despite ample spending, access to health care in the United States is exceptionally erratic. In 2008, 46.3 million people lacked health insurance in the United States, and undoubtedly more have lost insurance during the recent recession. Another 25 million Americans are "underinsured," defined as those with insurance that requires relatively high cost-sharing obligations (such as premiums, deductibles, and other out-of-pocket spending) relative to income. Although some argue that the uninsured can always get care somewhere, the uninsured do face consequences—in 2002 the Institute of Medicine estimated that 18,000 adults aged 25–64 die each year from treatable conditions because they lack insurance. The United States is the only modern industrialized democracy that relies primarily on private, voluntary health insurance; every other such country approximates universal coverage. United States' residents who are not offered or cannot afford health insurance typically go uninsured. Although it is true that the uninsured do not lack access to all necessary care, they must rely on an unorganized patchwork of "safety net" providers with precarious funding. Moreover, there are significant disparities in access to care and the quality of care received depending on one's race, ethnicity, and socioeconomic status. Even among the insured, there is significant variation in health care costs, quality, and access. Although no country's health care system is completely equitable—wealthier residents tend to access higher quality care more quickly than non-wealthy residents virtually everywhere, the United States is alone among developed countries in allocating health care primarily based on one's ability to pay. For decades, US policymakers have tried unsuccessfully to approximate universal insurance coverage.

The US health care system is exceptional in countless other ways. It spends markedly more on administrative costs than any other system. Its medical malpractice compensation system is notorious for being excessive and punitive. And it uses "one of the most regressive approaches to financing of any country in the world."

In sum, the US health care system is exceptional: exceptionally expensive, exceptionally inefficient, and exceptionally uneven in distributing care to its population. As [Timothy] Jost concludes, other countries demonstrate that they can "provide universal access at much lower cost without sacrificing quality." Indeed, the experience of other countries "tends to show that in this one particular corner of the economy, government often outperforms the private sector." Yet the US health care system still clings to the ideal that market competition can solve its problems.

15.3 Market Competition in Europe: Proceeding from a Different Baseline

Despite its exceptional nature, the US health care system is far from the only one to embrace market competition. Virtually every health care system in the EU relies on at least some market-based tools and incentives, typically to reduce costs, enhance efficiency, and give patients greater choice. Indeed, health reforms in [EU] Member States have generally converged around the common trend of introducing market-based incentives.

Of course, some Member States embrace market incentives in health care more than others. For example, [Daniel] Callahan and [Angela] Wasunna have identified certain States as "market rejectors" (Denmark, France, Ireland, Italy, Sweden, and the United Kingdom), and others as "market accommodators" (Belgium, Germany, Israel, the Netherlands, and Switzerland), with others falling in between. Market "accommodators" generally try to utilize market instruments without sacrificing principles of solidarity or universal coverage. But even the market "rejectors" (States that historically reject broader, more invasive market mechanisms in health care) generally "accept some limited role for the market."

The "accommodators" have embraced market instruments in several ways. Most notably, the Dutch health care system relies on individual insurance mandates and competition between private insurers (often referred to as "regulated competition"), building on theories of managed competition developed originally by American economist Enthoven. The Dutch Health Insurance Act, which entered into force on 1 January 2006, requires private managed care organizations to compete annually for individual patients, implementing concepts like selective contracting, using general practitioners as gatekeepers, and vertically integrating with providers. The Dutch system is also notable for the government's efforts to provide objective price and quality information to consumers. Likewise, reforms in Germany, with one of the most expensive health care systems in the world, have tried to encourage competition among both providers and the sickness funds that pay for them. Switzerland, another expensive system, has also encouraged competition among its insurance funds. In fact, the Dutch and Swiss health care systems both have inspired US reform discussions. Thus, although only the Dutch system relies primarily on private insurers, other systems in the EU implement market-inspired policies.

Even the market "rejectors" have experimented with market instruments in health care. Sweden—with its robust welfare state and general wariness of market influences in health care—has tried easing cost pressures by (i) encouraging hospitals to compete with one another, (ii) utilizing private providers, and (iii) shifting costs to patients via co-payments. Italy has tried to encourage equal competition among public and private providers and, like other countries, has tried to use copayments to contain costs. Denmark, which has one of the most comprehensive health systems in Europe, increasingly relies on private supplemental insurance. Likewise, 80% of the population in France relies on supplemental private health insurance. Even the United Kingdom's National Health Service (NHS), a wellknown paradigm for public, centralized health care, has implemented market-based reforms. Prime Ministers Thatcher and Major both encouraged "internal competition" among NHS hospitals. The NHS has also tried to encourage managed competition by introducing primary care trusts to pay for care.

Despite these examples, and there are many more, the United States and EU Member States have implemented market-based tools from very different baselines. While the United States is alone among developed countries in relying primarily on private, voluntary health insurance, Member States generally cover everyone, usually through national or social health insurance. Historically, the arguments for more competition in European health care systems "overwhelmingly took for granted that universal entitlement to health insurance was a given." Even the Netherlands, with its entrepreneurial traditions and reliance on private insurers, operates from the baseline of solidarity. In contrast, there has been significant disagreement in the United States whether universal coverage is "desirable and implementable."

These baselines derive from different priorities. Although every country generally aims to provide quality care to everyone for a reasonable price, the US health care system places a higher priority on independence and entrepreneurship than its peers. Patients are responsible for themselves. Americans generally trust private industry and distrust the government to solve problems. Unsurprisingly, our health care system reflects these values.

In contrast, health systems in the EU are generally based on social solidarity, the belief that citizens are responsible to each other, not just themselves, and that all citizens should have equal access to care, regardless of their ability to pay. There is less distrust of government and less faith that the market can solve all problems. Indeed, "[s]olidarity is fundamentally a rejection of markets as the best means to distributing health care goods and services." Logically, EU health systems reflect these values.

* * *

Thus, although health care systems in the United States and EU both rely on market instruments, these jurisdictions generally proceed from very different baselines. In Europe, market competition enhances more cohesive, comprehensive systems; in the United States, it forms the philosophical foundation. Nevertheless, the United States need not look to Europe or even Canada for examples of efficient, "government-run" health care. The US Veterans Health Administration has been hailed as our most successful health care system after major reforms over the past 10–15 years, providing perhaps the most recent domestic example of how non-market alternatives can outperform market instruments in health care.

* * *

Notes

1. As the excerpt above suggests, the EU and its Member States have struggled to determine whether health care is a public good or a private good. Moreover, Member States have had to grapple with EU treaties, directives, regulations, and decisions by the European Court of Justice (ECJ) that severely limit the extent to which domestic laws restrict the free movement of goods, services, persons, and capital within the EU common market, thus opening up their health systems to competition and potentially undermining domestic health policy priorities. An excellent source examining these tensions is the book *Health Care and EU Law* (Johan Willem van de Gronden, Erika Szyszczak, Ulla Neergaard, & Markus Krajewski, eds. 2011), in which the above chapter appears. Another excellent look at the tension between public and private goods in health care markets across jurisdictions, including developing countries less often studied by scholars, is Daniel Callahan and Angela A. Wasunna, *Medicine and the Market: Equity v. Choice* (2006).

2. In addition to comparisons by academics, recent comparisons by journalists emphasize for lay audiences how different health care systems can approach common challenges of cost, quality, and access to health care. For example, longtime *Washington Post* correspondent T.R. Reid visited physicians and hospitals in Canada, France, Germany, India, Japan, Taiwan, the U.K., and the U.S. to evaluate his injured shoulder. He found foreign systems that provided high-quality coverage to virtually all residents while spending far less than the United States, debunking various myths that "socialized medicine" necessarily means less patient choice and longer waits. *See* T.R. Reid, *The Healing of America: A Global Quest for Better, Cheaper, and Fairer Health Care* (2009).

3. Economics is a prominent lens through which health care systems can be viewed comparatively. Indeed, much of the literature on comparative health systems focuses on economic aspects. See, e.g. Elias Mossialos et al., *Funding Health Care: Options for Europe* (2002); A. J. Culyer & J.P. Newhouse, *Handbook of Health Economics*, vols. 1A & 1B (2000); *Markets and Health Care: A Comparative Analysis,* (Wendy Ranade, ed., 1998); *Health Care and its Financing in the Single European Market* (R. Leidl, ed. 1998); *Fixing Health Budgets: Experience from Europe and North America* (Friedrich Wilhelm Schwartz, Howard Glennerster, Richard B. Saltman, eds., 1996); and *Implementing Planned Markets in Health Care: Balancing Social and Economic Responsibilities* (Richard B. Saltman and Casten von Otter, eds. 1995). The American law and economics movement has also championed the use of economics as a means of understanding law in other countries. See, for example, J. Mark Ramseyer and Minora Nakazato, *Japanese Law: An Economic Approach*, 66–74 (1999), attempting to explain Japanese malpractice law from a law and economics perspective.

The excerpt that follows, from a preeminent scholar of health economics, Uwe Reinhardt, brings an economic perspective to the study of health care systems:

Uwe E. Reinhardt, *Reforming the Health Care System: The Universal Dilemma*

19 Am. J. L. & Med. 21, 21–27, 29, 31–36 (1994)

The human condition surrounding the delivery of health care is the same everywhere in the world: the providers of health care seek to give their patients the maximum feasible degree of physical relief, but they also aspire to a healthy slice of the gross national product ("GNP") as a reward for their efforts. Patients seek from health care providers the maximum feasible degree of physical relief, but, collectively, they also seek to minimize the slice of the GNP that they must cede to providers as the price for that care.

In other words, while there typically is a meeting of the minds between patients and providers on the clinical side of the health care transaction, there very often is conflict on the economic front. * * *

* * *

II. Controlling the Transfer of GNP to Providers

Society can control the total annual transfer of GNP to health care providers through the demand side of the health care market, the supply side, or both. Nations differ substantially in the mix of approaches they use. Their choice of cost-control policies hinges crucially on the social role that they ascribe to health care. The two extremes of the spectrum of views on this issue are:

1. Health care is essentially a private consumption good, whose financing is the responsibility of its individual recipient.

2. Health care is a social good that should be collectively financed and available to all citizens who need health care, regardless of the individual recipient's ability to pay for that care.

Canadians and Europeans have long since reached a broad social consensus that health care is a social good. Although their health systems exhibit distinct, national idiosyncracies, they share an obedience to that overarching, ethical precept.

Americans have never been able to reach a similarly broad political consensus regarding the point at which they would like their health care system to sit on the ideological spectrum that is defined by these two extreme views. Instead, American health policy has meandered back and forth between the two views, in step with the ideological temper of the time. During the 1960s and 1970s, the American health care system moved toward the social good end of the spectrum. On the other hand, during the 1980s, a concerted effort was made to move the system in the opposite direction. * * * This meandering between distinct, ethical precepts has produced contradictions between professed principles and actual practice that confuse and frustrate even the initiated in the United States.

Table 1 presents a menu of alternative approaches to financing and organizing health care. It makes explicit distinctions between the ownership of the health insurance mechanism and the production of health care. Almost all health care systems in the world fit into his grid, and most extend over more than one cell in the grid.

For example, the health systems of the United Kingdom and Sweden occupy primarily Cell A in Table 1, though private medical practices in the United Kingdom occupy Cell C. One may think of Cell A as socialized medicine in its purest sense because the production of health care is substantially owned by the government. Clearly, the health care system of the United States Department of Veterans Affairs also resides in Cell A, as does the bulk of the health care system for the United States armed forces.

Table 1 Alternative Mixes of Health Insurance and Health Care Delivery

	Collectivized (Socialized) Financing of Health Care			Direct Financing
		Private Health Insurance		
Production and Delivery	Government Financed Insurance	within a statutory framework	within an unregulated market	Out-of-pocket by Patients at Point of Service
Purely Government-Owned	A	D	G	J
Private Not-for-Profit Entities	B	E	H	K
Private For-Profit Entities	C	F	I	L
	The Canadian health system	The West German health system	The private portion of the American system	

The Canadian health care system occupies primarily Cells A, B, and C, as does the American federal Medicare program and the federal-state Medicaid program. Systems falling into Cells B and C represent government-run health insurance, not socialized medicine, because the delivery system is largely in private hands. This distinction between socialized insurance and socialized medicine is often lost on American critics of foreign health care systems.

Germany's health care system is best described by Cells D, E, and F. Health insurance in Germany is provided by a structured system of not-for-profit sickness funds that are privately administered, albeit within a federal statute that tightly regulates their conduct. This statutory health insurance system has evolved gradually over the span of 100 years and now covers eighty-eight percent of the population. The remainder is covered by private, commercial insurers more akin to commercial insurers in the United States. On the other hand, Germany's health care delivery system is a mixture of private and public, for-profit and not-for-profit, providers that is similar to the mix of providers found in the United States. In other words, the German health care system also does not represent socialized medicine, but socialized insurance.

As noted above, parts of the American health system fall squarely into Cell A. Others fall into Cells A, B, and C. Together, Cells A through C accounted for about forty-four percent of national health care spending in 1991. The rest of the system, its private sector, is spread from Cells G to L. * * *

A. The Approaches Used in Canada and Europe

As noted, Canadians and Europeans typically view health care as a social good. In these countries, it is anathema to link an individual household's health care financing contribution to the health status of that household's members. Health care in these countries is collectively financed, with taxes or premiums based on the individual household's ability to pay. Only a small, well-to-do minority—so far, less than ten percent of the population—opts out of collective social insurance in favor of privately insured or privately financed health care. Nevertheless, nearly ninety percent of the population typically shares one common level of quality and amenities in health care.

Control of health care costs in these countries is exercised partly by controlling the physical capacity of the supply side. The chief instrument for this purpose is formal regional health planning. Planning enables policymakers to limit the number of hospital beds, big-ticket technology (such as CT scanners or lithotripters), and sometimes even the number of physicians who are issued billing numbers under these nations' health insurance systems.

However, regulatory limits on the capacity of the health care system inevitably create monopolies on the supply side. To make sure that these artificially created monopolies do not exploit their economic power, these countries generally couple health planning on the supply side with stiff price and budgetary controls imposed on the demand side. Sometimes, price controls alone are deemed sufficient to control overall health spending. However, where the intent of price controls has been thwarted through rapid increases in the volume of health services rendered, these countries have imposed strictly limited global budgets on the health care systems as a whole, or upon particular segments (e.g., hospitals and doctors). Canada, for example, has long compensated its hospitals through pre-set global budgets. Similarly, West Germany now operates strict, state-wide expenditure caps for all physicians who practice within a state under the nation's Statutory Health Insurance system. The United Kingdom and the Nordic countries budget virtually their entire health systems.

To implement their price and budget controls, Canada and the European countries tend to structure their health insurance systems so that money flows from third-party payers to health care providers through only one or a few large money-pipes. The "money-pipe" throughput is then controlled through formal negotiations between regional or national associations of third-party payers and associations of providers. The negotiated prices in these countries are usually binding on providers, who may not bill patients for extra charges above these prices. Although France permits extra billing within limits, most of these countries perceive unrestrained extra billing as a violation of the spirit of health insurance.

Remarkably, and in sharp contrast with the United States, Canada and Europe typically do not look to the individual patient as an agent of cost control. Usually, there is no significant flow of money from patient to provider at the time health services are received. Instead, most of these countries provide patients with comprehensive, universal first-dollar coverage for a wide range of services, including drugs (Canada covers drugs only for the poor). France does have co-payments at the point of service for all ambulatory care and hospital care, but not for certain high-cost illnesses. Furthermore, many French patients have supplemental private insurance to cover any co-payments.

One should not assume that Canada and the European nations eclipse patients from cost control because these nations' health policy analysts and policymakers lack the savvy of their American colleagues. American debates on health policy tend to characterize patients as "consumers" who are expected to shop around for cost-effective health care. One suspects that Canadians and Europeans are inclined to perceive patients as, for the most part, "sick persons" who should be treated as such. * * * [T]he distribution of health expenditures across a population tends to be highly skewed. In the United States, for example, only five percent of the population accounts for about half of all national health expenditures in any given year, and ten percent account for about seventy percent. The distribution of health expenditures in other countries is apt to present a similar pattern.

One must wonder whether the few individuals who account for the bulk of health care expenditures in any given year can actually act like regular "consumers" who shop around for cost-effective health care. Although cost sharing by patients can be shown to have some constraining effect on utilization for mild to semi-serious illness, it is unlikely to play a major role in the serious cases that appear to account for the bulk of national health care expenditures.

Where price and ability to pay cannot ration health care, something else must. Usually, in Canada and Europe, that non-price rationing device is a queue for elective medical procedures. At the extreme, some high-tech medical interventions, such as renal dialysis or certain organ transplantations, are simply unavailable to particular patients if the attending physician judges the likely benefits of intervention to be low. High-tech innovations are introduced rather cautiously in these nations, and only after intensive benefit-cost analysis. Therefore, at any given time, these nations' health care systems are likely to lag behind that in the United States in the degree to which a new medical technology has been adopted.

Finally, the tight control on overall outlays for health care tends to preclude the often luxurious settings in which health care is dispensed to well-insured patients in the United States. Atriums and gourmet dining in hospitals, or physician offices with plush carpets, are not common in Canada or Europe.

* * *

III. The Economic Footprints of These Approaches

It is generally agreed, both here and abroad, that the American entrepreneurial approach to health care has begotten one of the most luxurious, dynamic, clinically and organizationally innovative, and technically sophisticated health care systems in the world. At its best, the system has few rivals anywhere, though many health care systems abroad also have facets of genuine excellence. At its worst, however, it has few rivals as well.

A. The Cost of Health Care

Unfortunately, but perfectly predictably, the open-ended supply side of the American health care system, coupled with a financing system that looks to sick human beings (patients) as major agents of cost control, has led to perennial excess capacity in most parts of the country, and to large and rapidly growing costs. * * *

* * *

C. Styles of Rationing

The myth that, unlike other nations, America does not ration health care is just that, a myth. Americans do ration health care by price and ability to pay, sometimes in rather disturbing ways. Nations differ from one another not in whether they ration health care—all of them do somehow and in varying degrees—but in their style of rationing and their definition of that very term.

One rationing style is to limit physical capacity and use triage, based on medical judgment and the queue, to determine the allocation of artificially scarce resources among the population. That style of rationing is sometimes referred to as implicit rationing. The other style is to ration explicitly by price and ability to pay. It is the natural by-product of the so-called "market approach" to health care.

Implicit rationing predominates outside of the United States. In principle, the approach is thought to allocate health care strictly on the basis of medical need, as perceived and ranked by physicians. It is not known whether other variables, such as the patient's social status, ultimately enter the allocation decision as well. * * *

Many Americans believe that health care is not currently rationed in the United States. That belief seems warranted for well-insured patients who are covered by traditional, open-ended indemnity insurance and living in areas with excess capacity. For many of these patients, there seems to be virtually no limit to the use of real resources in attempts to preserve life or gain certainty in diagnosis.

On the other hand, persons who are less well-insured, uninsured, or covered by managed-care plans (including HMOs) do occasionally experience the withholding of health care resources strictly for economic reasons. In fact, in a recent cross-national survey, some 7.5 percent of the American respondents (the equivalent of eighteen million Americans) claimed that they had been denied health care for financial reasons. In Canada and the United Kingdom, fewer than one percent of the survey respondents made that claim.

Remarkably, the defenders of the American system, who are typically also vehement detractors of all foreign health systems, generally define rationing as only the withholding of health care from people who would have been able and willing to pay for such care with their own money. It is the nightmare of the well-to-do. Apparently, denial of health care to needy, uninsured patients who are unable to pay for that care is not viewed as rationing by these commentators because they have long countenanced it. How else can one explain these commentators' warnings that health care in, for example, the Canadian model would lead to rationing of health care, as if no American were ever denied needed or wanted health care?

* * *

IV. The Convergence of Health Care Systems

If one wished to paint with a very broad brush the evolution of health care policy during the past four decades in the industrialized world, one might describe it as a gradual shift from expenditure-driven financing of health care to budget-driven delivery of health care.

Under expenditure-driven financing, health care providers were allowed to do for patients whatever they saw fit and send the rest of society a bill at prices that seemed "reasonable." Typically, those presented with that bill paid without reservation. If they had reservations, they paid the bill nevertheless because they lacked the countervailing power present in normal markets without third-party payment. Naturally, under this open-ended approach, the supply side of the health sector became a rich economic frontier that attracted both the genius of private entrepreneurship and its relentless search for revenues.

Technological innovation flourished under this approach as the health sector stood an old adage on its head: instead of necessity being the mother of invention, invention became the mother of necessity. Once a technological innovation was at hand, its application was quickly deemed a "medical necessity" as long as it promised any additional benefits at all to the patient. * * *

Under the second approach, budget-driven health care delivery, society establishes some sort of prospective budget for health care and tells providers to do the best they can within that budget. Typically, the establishment of the overall budget has been rather arbitrary in practice, in the sense that the budget is tied to some arbitrary criterion—such as a fixed percentage of the GNP or a fixed annual growth rate. Ideally, this approach should lead policymakers to explore what additional benefits might be gained through incremental budget expansions, and to set the ultimate budget limits accordingly. In any event, however, the application of new medical technologies in this world will typically be subjected to rigorous benefit-cost analysis before payment for such technologies will be made out of the fixed budget. Merely demonstrating promised benefits is no longer sufficient and will not be accepted by those who would stand to lose from applications of novel technology within the given budget constraints.

As noted earlier, most of the industrialized world has already gone a long way toward budget-driven health care delivery, some (England and Sweden, for example) completely. The United States is the odd one out because it is only just beginning to move in that direction. * * *

* * *

At this time, the contrast between the current Canadian/European approach to resource allocation in health care and this newly emerging American approach is stark. Canadians and Europeans still appear to believe that the best way to control overall health spending is to: (1) constrain the physical capacity of the health system, (2) control prices, and, for good measure, (3) impose something as close as possible to global monetary budgets on the entire system. Within these constraints, however, they allow doctors and their patients considerable clinical freedom. In this way, the system will tend to maximize the benefits that are wrung out of the constrained set of real and financial resources. In other words, there is considerable trust in the medical establishment's willingness and ability to use the resources made available to it properly, without the need for day-to-day supervision. Direct comanaging of an on going patient-doctor relationship in the American model is still rather rare in Canada and Europe.

In contrast, the American proponents of managed competition believe that, by paying for everything that is beneficial, but denying payment for everything else, the nation can avoid setting an arbitrary global budget and will, in the end, devote the "right" percentage of GNP to health care. These proponents have considerable faith in the ability of ordinary consumers to choose wisely among the alternative cost-quality combinations that competing managed-care systems in the health care market offer. On the other hand, they have little faith in the ability or willingness of the individual physician to use scarce resources wisely in the treatment of patients; therefore, they would subject each doctor to constant statistical monitoring and hands-on supervision.

* * *

Notes

1. Uwe Reinhardt is one of the best known American health economists, though not perhaps the most conventional. Dr. Reinhardt was born and raised in Germany, and lived in Canada before moving to the United States. It is not surprising, therefore, that he sees the American health care system in a comparative perspective. This article was written in the context of the American debate on the Clinton health plan proposal in the early 1990s, so the data are somewhat dated. The issues, however, remain very current.

2. One striking impression that emerges from comparative health policy studies is the difference in the perspective of most American health economists and that of most health economists from other countries. Although Americans represent a wide range of interests and approaches, most begin with the position that market competition is good for society and government interference in markets—be it through regulation, tax subsidies, or social welfare programs—is on the whole not. Professor Reinhardt is in fact atypical in the extent to which he accepts government intervention in health care markets. More typical would be Mark Pauly (*Health Reform Without Side Effects: Making Markets Work for Individual Health Insurance*, 2010), John Cogan, R. Glenn Hubbard, and Daniel Kessler (*Healthy, Wealthy, and Wise: Five Steps to a Better Health Care System,* 2005); or John Goodman, Gerald Musgrave and Devon Herrick (*Lives at Risk: Single-Payer National Health Insurance Around the World*, 2004). British, Canadian, and most continental European health economists, on the other hand, are more likely to accept (even embrace) an active government role in health care purchasing or delivery. See, e.g. Robert Evans, A Casualty in the Class War: Canada's Medicare, 7 *Healthcare Policy/Politiques de Santé* 14 (2012); Robert Evans, *An Undisciplined Economist: Robert G. Evans on Health Economics, Health Care Policy, and Population Health* (Morris L. Barer et al. eds, 2016). They are also more interested in making government programs work efficiently than in abolishing them. See, e.g., Cam Donaldson et al., *Economics of Health Care Financing: The Visible Hand* (2004); Anthony J. Culyer & Adam Wagstaff, Equity and Equality in Health and Health Care, 12 *Journal of Health Economics* 431 (1993); Gavin Mooney, *Challenging Health Economics* (2009) (a well-respected Australian health economist).

3. In the excerpt above, Reinhardt discusses the "convergence" of health systems that shifted away from "expenditure-driven financing of health care to budget-driven delivery of health care." There has been significant attention in the health policy community looking for evidence of policy "convergence" among health care systems—reforms that gradually make health care systems around the world more similar than dissimilar over time. See, e.g., David Mechanic, The Comparative Study of Health Care Delivery Systems, 1 *Ann. Rev. Soc.* 43 (1975). In 1994, the Organization for Economic Cooperation and Development (OECD) examined health system reforms in 17 countries, finding "remarkable" the extent to which later reforms borrowed ideas pioneered in other countries. OECD, The Reform of Health Care Systems: A Review of Seventeen OECD Countries, *Health Policy Stud. No. 5*, 61 (1994). For the argument that health care convergence is being driven by

markets and private actors, see Nathan Cortez, International Health Care Convergence: The Benefits and Burdens of Market-Driven Standardization, 26 *Wisconsin Int'l L.J.* 646 (2009); Nathan Cortez, Globalization, *in The Oxford Handbook of U.S. Healthcare Law* 1075–96 (I. Glenn Cohen, Allison K. Hoffman, & William M. Sage eds., 2017).

Economic explanations of legal phenomena have been very influential in American legal scholarship over the past three decades. Other factors, however, such as politics and culture should not be ignored in understanding legal systems. The following excerpt of an article written by a prominent Canadian political scientist analyzes developments in the United States, Canada, and Britain from a political perspective:

Carolyn Hughes Tuohy, *Dynamics of a Changing Health Sphere: The United States, Britain, and Canada*

18 Health Affairs 114, 115–16, 118–120, 129–131 (May/June 1999)

* * *

Framework for Analysis

This paper highlights two key dimensions of the decision-making system. The first relates to the balance of influence across key components of the politicoeconomic structure of interests—state actors, private finance, and health care professionals (principally the medical profession)—representing the key bases of power in the arena: authority, wealth, and skill, respectively. The second relates to the mix of mechanisms of social control that systematize and legitimize the relationships among these actors. In health care such mechanisms are typically threefold: the market, based on voluntary exchange; hierarchy, based on obedience to rules within a chain of command; and collegiality, based on subscription to a set of norms of behavior derived from a common knowledge base.

Different balances of influence imply the predominance of different lines of accountability. State actors, private financial interests, and professionals derive their influence from different sources and, accordingly, respond to different demands. In very broad terms, state actors function within systems in which those in command ultimately are dependent upon political support and therefore seek to accommodate a range of interests and opinions sufficient to maintain a coalition of support. Actors whose influence is based on access to private finance must respond to the demands of owners of private capital to realize rates of return comparable with those in other areas of investment. And professionals, who derive their influence from membership in the professional group, must maintain standing in the group by continuing to meet its evolving standards and norms.

* * *

The Distinctive Logic of the Three Systems

* * *

Britain's largely state financed system was founded upon an "implicit bargain" between the state and the medical profession under which the profession retained clinical autonomy to allocate resources within budgetary parameters established by the state. Collegial mechanisms of decision making were incorporated within structures of "hierarchical corporatism." The distinctive blend of hierarchy and collegiality that constituted NHS-style corporatism comprised two fundamental elements. First, it involved defined spheres of authority based on functional expertise, creating a set of parallel authority structures—some hierarchical, some collegial. Second, it brought these spheres together in hierarchical structures of "consensus management," which gave effective veto powers to the key functional groups (most notably, physicians) at each level of the hierarchy. These essential features persisted through two major NHS reorganizations, in 1974 and again in 1982.

Expectations regarding the roles of the various participants within these structures were fairly clear. Doctors, both general practitioners (GPs) and specialists, were to exercise their clinical judgment as independent professionals. GPs contracted independently with local "executive councils" and later with family practitioner committees to provide services on a modified capitation basis. Hospital consultants were salaried employees of the NHS, but their employment contracts were regional, not at the level of the operational unit (the hospital) in which they practiced. Consultants did not "report," then, to local managers, but rather formed self-governing, hospital-based medical staffs. Professional networks, not administrative rules, determined referral patterns from the "gatekeeper" GPs to the specialist consultants. Nurses performed within a hospital-based functional hierarchy dominated by the hospital matron. Here the administrative manager played the role of "diplomat" mediating across the various functional NHS authority centers and was always seen as being in service to, not in authority over, clinicians. Even when "general management" structures replaced "consensus management" following the Griffiths Report of 1983, these relationships remained essentially unchanged.

In Canada, more than perhaps any other nation in the late twentieth century, the health care system functioned according to the logic of an accommodation between the medical profession and the state. It was, in economic terms, the logic of an agency relationship in a bilateral monopoly. Under the terms of Canadian Medicare, provincial governments were the "single payers" for most medical and hospital services within a framework established by federal legislation: A single government plan in each province covered a comprehensive range of medical and hospital services, and no private insurance alternatives existed for coverage of those services. But provincial governments exercised their monopsony power in very gross terms. Decisions about the allocation of resources were made through negotiations with the monopoly providers of services, particularly with the medical profession. Those negotiating relationships left great discretion in the hands of the organized profession to govern the behavior of its members. The collegial mechanisms that permeated the system before Medicare, including independently constituted hospital medical staffs, were left in place. Medicare, moreover, was established on generous terms: The state provided universal coverage of medical and hospital services by essentially underwriting the costs of an existing system based on independent fee-for-service (FFS) medical practice and voluntary hospitals. * * *

As in Britain, the state developed a "second-level" agency relationship with the profession, which acknowledged the primacy of professional judgment in making decisions about the allocation of resources at the level of the clinical case, the professional practice, and the institution, within overall budgetary parameters established by the state. In Canada, however, because the state was a monopsonist but not an employer or even a contractor, the profession enjoyed even more formal autonomy. Medical fee schedules were negotiated at the provincial level between governments and medical associations. In all provinces but one these negotiations concerned only the aggregate percentage level of increase in fees, leaving the value of individual items in the schedule to be determined by the association itself. * * *

These arrangements made sense for both sides. The profession retained broad clinical autonomy and influence over the system as a whole, and the state kept budgetary control without incurring the transaction costs (or developing the capacity) to manage a very diffuse system. Furthermore, this accommodation retained the structures of health care delivery—private medical practices, free choice of physicians—to which Canadians were long accustomed and that were features of an extraordinarily popular system.

* * *

[The author proceeds to describe the health care system of the United States, and then discusses developments in all three systems during the 1990s.]

Lessons Drawn From the Three Systems

A review of the experience of the health care arenas of the United States, Britain, and Canada in the 1990s gives credence to the argument that each health care decision-making system has its own powerful logic, born of the intersection between the balance of influence and the mix of instruments in the system—a logic with particular implications for the pattern and the pace of change. In Britain the internal-market initiative [introduced by Margaret Thatcher in the 1990s] constituted an attempt to introduce a model with very high information costs (as necessary for writing specific contracts between independent units where various contingencies were possible) into a system with well-developed hierarchical and collegial networks for the exchange of information as deemed necessary. Within a budget-limited system, it is not surprising that actors would seek to economize on information costs by continuing to rely on established networks and relationships. Although the internal-market reforms of the NHS did bring about substantial change in the decision-making system, that change amounted largely to the introduction of explicit bargaining relationships between organized bodies of purchasers and providers—a form of voluntary exchange, but far from a competitive market.

In the United States the increasing price-consciousness of purchasers—which occurred somewhat later in the diffuse and heterogeneous U.S. mixed-market system than in state-financed systems in which costs were concentrated—ultimately limited the potential for cost shifting, required providers to minimize costs per case, broke the "alignment of incentives" between providers as professionals and providers as entrepreneurs, and led to the rise of for-profit, investor-owned entities in the entrepreneurial role. And in Canada provincial-level accommodations between the medical profession and the state that had served the purposes of both sides for two decades—affording physicians a high degree of individual and collective autonomy and allowing governments to maintain a highly popular system and to exercise broad budgetary control—persisted uneasily through the 1990s, even as they were threatened by the progressive tightening of their fiscal underpinnings.

These individual system logics are enlightening, and they remind us that the dynamics of systems need to be understood on their own terms. But two-way comparisons of these three cases also can generate some more generalizable propositions. Consider first the Canada/U.S. comparison. Two systems, almost identical in the 1960s, were set on different paths when Canada adopted universal hospital and medical care insurance and the United States adopted a program confined to the elderly and the poor. In particular, the collegial mechanisms that had permeated both systems prior to the adoption of governmental health insurance fared very differently. These mechanisms were elaborated in Canada as vehicles of profession/state collaboration but were supplanted in the United States by increasingly explicit forms of contracting (and, in some cases, hierarchical integration) with the rise of private MCOs.

The suggestion of this comparison—that collegial mechanisms and medical influence are better preserved in the context of a profession-state accommodation than in private markets—is reinforced by a comparison of Britain and Canada. Both of those nations, despite the very different organization of their publicly financed systems, were characterized by an "implicit bargain," a "second-level agency relationship" between the state and the medical profession with broadly similar terms: The state established broad budgetary parameters, and physicians were free to exercise clinical judgment in the allocation of resources within those parameters.

Finally, a comparison between Britain and the United States throws light on the implications of the "state/market" distinction in health care. The import of this paper has been to argue that "state" and "market" belong in fact to different dimensions of decision-making systems: The state is a set of actors; the market is a set of instruments. Placing "market-oriented" contracting instruments in the hands of state actors in Britain did not change those actors' lines of accountability. This meant that partisan and electoral considerations brought about direct political intervention. Even more importantly, it meant that the implementation of the reforms had to respect the need for state actors to maintain coalitions of support—coalitions that accorded a central role for the medical profession. In the United States, in contrast, private entrepreneurs in for-profit enterprises had to meet the demands of highly mobile investors for competitive rates of return, and their behavior drove the competitive dynamic of the system.

These differences between systems of public and private finance have at least two important corollaries. First, they explain the central role for the medical profession and for collegial mechanisms that is observed in systems of public finance.

The foundational bargain between the state and the medical profession that characterizes systems of public finance can be seen as a logical component of such systems: An accommodation with the medical profession has been a significant component of the political coalitions of support that characterize state-financed systems.

A second implication of the fundamental difference between systems of public and private finance concerns the pace of change. The ease of exit for private investors, their quest for more profitable forms of organization in which to invest, and their attraction to entities that can demonstrate growth and expanding market share have driven rapid and volatile change in the industrial structure of health care delivery and financing in the United States and have given rise to a range of organizational innovation that is without parallel in systems dominated by public finance. In contrast, the need to maintain coalitions of political support moderated the pace and nature of change initiated by state actors in Britain and kept the basic features of the Canadian system remarkably constant, in an international perspective.

Notes

1. These themes are explored further in Tuohy's book, *Accidental Logics* (1999). In later work, Tuohy has examined the politics of how more recent reforms in Britain and the Netherlands created "hybrid" systems with features from both national health systems and social insurance. Canada's health system, in contrast, largely resisted this "politics of redesign." See Carolyn Hughes Tuohy, Reform and the Politics of Hybridization in Mature Health Care States, 37 *Journal of Health Politics, Policy, and Law* 611 (2012).

2. Politics is always an important consideration in health care policy. Political dysfunctions, for example, undoubtedly explain the rancorous health reform debates in the United States. The fear of socialism undoubtedly contributed to the extension of health coverage to workers in central Europe in the nineteenth century, while the triumph of socialism explains the creation of national health insurance systems in the middle of the twentieth. Politics, as Tuohy illustrates, involves not only national politics, but also politics within and among the professions, and between the professions and the state.

3. An important part of understanding the politics of health care in many countries is considering domestic race relations and views on immigration. Racial inequality in the American health care system is relatively well-documented, though undoubtedly not given sufficient attention by policymakers. See Dayna Bowen Matthew, *Just Medicine: A Cure for Racial Inequality in American Health Care* (2015). However, even more toxic from a political standpoint—at least in the United States—is tackling immigrants' access to health care. Thus, most U.S. policymakers avoid addressing the problems immigrants face in accessing health care in the United States, lest the attention derail broader efforts at reform. See Patricia Illingworth and Wendy E. Parmet, *The Health of Newcomers: Immigration, Health Policy, and the Case for Global Solidarity* (2017). One notable effort to link race to the politics of health care in mul-

tiple countries is Gerard W. Boychuk, *National Health Insurance in the United States and Canada: Race, Territory, and the Roots of Difference* (2008).

4. Though political positions often are based on economic considerations, they also often reflect cultural influences as well. The next excerpt discusses these influences.

George J. Annas & Frances H. Miller, *The Empire of Death: How Culture and Economics Affect Informed Consent in the U.S., the U.K., and Japan*

20 Am. J. L. & Med. 357, 360–62, 377–81, 387–90 (1994)

* * *

II. Culture and Medical Science

The definition of good medical care varies enormously from country to country. For example, German and French physicians for decades routinely prescribed government-financed "spa cures" for their patients. Such therapy choices would invite professional scorn, not to mention malpractice litigation, and would not be covered by insurance if prescribed by U.S. doctors. The international medical community often disagrees significantly about appropriate diagnosis and treatment. Most physicians are relatively ignorant, if not openly skeptical, about scientific findings reported from foreign countries.

At a more fundamental level, medical experts often frankly disagree about what constitutes disease. Many physical states defined and treated as worthy of medical intervention in the U.S., such as moderately elevated blood pressure, are considered unremarkable variations of the human condition elsewhere in the world. By way of contrast, low blood pressure is treated as a medical disorder in Germany while at the same time it is welcomed as a longevity indicator in both the U.S. and the U.K. American travelers becoming ill in foreign countries are often surprised to learn that 98.6° is not necessarily the gold standard for normal body temperature, notwithstanding what they have been led since childhood to believe. Far from being an "exact" science with commonly acknowledged definitional, diagnostic, and treatment principles, scientific uncertainty permeates medicine.

Professional cultural values also both overtly and subliminally prejudice medical practice, as do the cultural values imbedded in the particular society in which physicians practice their skills. Moreover, patients have culturally influenced attitudes of their own that affect their willingness to accept—as well as their response to receiving—medical therapy. * * *

The U.S. public has always been culturally predisposed toward action in the face of threatened adversity, medical or otherwise. Lynn Payer's masterful book *Medicine & Culture* * * * links the aggressive American approach toward medicine to the frontier spirit, and to Americans' deeply ingrained belief that "the main purpose of a man's life is to solve problems." For decades Americans have tolerated—if not encouraged—the delivery of superfluous medical services under the rubric of medical necessity, financed by cost-pass-through health insurance. * * *

Cost containment pressures are bringing home the lesson that medical necessity is actually a fluid notion, continually reconceived as scientific understanding, payment incentives, and culture evolve. Containing costs necessarily implies setting limits on health care expenditures, and cultural values are critical to determining where those limits will lie. * * *

[The authors use the example of informed consent doctrine to illustrate their theme of cultural differences, describing first the situation in the United States, where patient-centered informed consent is accepted in theory, if not always in practice; then the United Kingdom, where, as is demonstrated in chapter 2, medical custom dictates the extent of disclosure in informed consent cases; and Japan (also discussed in chapter 2), where doctors have until recently resisted disclosing information to their patients and often sought consent from the patient's family.]

IV. Culture, Choice and Health Resource Allocation

Patient knowledge advances personal autonomy; it elevates consent to medical treatment from a flak jacket merely protecting doctors from battery liability to an enhancement of patient sovereignty. * * *[N]ot all cultures place the same value on truth-telling and on an individual's ability to make fully informed choices, nor do they share the same fear of death. Informed consent legal doctrine reflects and shapes societal value choices, and thus it varies from country to country, and from time to time within countries.

* * *

Different cultures take differing official approaches to health resource allocation. Some countries rely primarily on governmental price and spending controls that affect everything from technology acquisition to hospital and physician reimbursement rates. For example, in the circumstances of tightly managed supply that exist in the U.K., primary care physicians assume powerful gatekeeping functions. These general practitioners must filter patient demand for medical services from clinical "need" for limited specialist and high technology care. This filter entails correspondingly narrower scope for individual choice. When medical choice is constrained by supply limitations, telling patients about potentially beneficial but economically unattainable therapy can be criticized as inhumane. However, such disclosure can also mobilize public opinion to challenge resource allocation inconsistent with societal values.

* * *

In countries officially dependent on gatekeeping like the U.K., informed consent doctrine not unsurprisingly favors professional rather than patient-oriented standards of disclosure, particularly with regard to treatment alternatives. Other cultures—most prominently the U.S.—prefer to let a more entrepreneurial market set the basic dimensions for health sector investment. U.S. informed consent law generally reflects support for market allocation mechanisms, and thus tends to expand the possibilities for patient choice through more thoroughgoing informed consent requirements.

But how can we explain Japan, where physicians are highly entrepreneurial and most hospitals and all clinics are privately owned, yet where the law supports keeping patients in the dark about diagnoses of serious illness? First, Japan does not impose the same budgetary controls that cap total health care spending in the U.K., although it regulates physician fees tightly and capped the number of hospital beds in 1985. It is dangerous for outsiders to generalize about any society, but cultural analysts from both Japan and America agree that in Japan individuality is deemed subservient to group needs and ideals. As a consequence, the proper role of the patient is to follow the instructions of the physician, who presumably has a superior understanding of the patient's illness and its significance.

Regardless of official government policy concerning health sector resource allocation, more or less flexibility concerning that policy usually exists within any society in practice. This flexibility is strongly influenced by the general cultural attitude toward death, and by what patients, health policy experts, and financiers actually know or believe about the availability and efficacy of medical services. * * *

* * *

Any country's health policy must continuously grapple with economic scarcity and with scientific, political, and cultural change. The successes and failures of other systems can be illuminating, but cultural attitudes toward medical information and other medical issues as well must be unearthed and understood if reform imported from other countries can succeed in new environments. Of course, societies and medical practitioners must grapple with the role of malpractice litigation in setting standards of care.

Customary medical practice, the standard against which a doctor's conduct is usually measured in a medical malpractice action, reflects the way resources are spent on care for individual patients in every culture. Since patients rarely refuse their doctors' recommendations for therapy, physician treatment preferences strongly influence the way societies allocate total health resources. But the concept of customary medical practice defies precise definition. What doctors actually do develops gradually over time as physicians adapt treatment to scientific advance, economic rewards and penalties, and more generalized legal and cultural incentives, especially a society's attitude toward death. * * *

* * *

V. Culture and Death

* * *

Ultimately a culture's view of death, and the role of medicine in preventing or postponing it, is at work when unpleasant or uncertain medical facts are not communicated to patients. In the U.S., for example, we usually seem to accept that prolonging life (at virtually any price) is a reasonable goal for medicine. Thus, procedures are introduced and utilized that offer hope of extending life without regard to cost, or even to the quality of the life prolonged. * * *

Our seemingly automatic use of technology to protract the dying process has spawned development of a clearly articulated legal right to refuse treatment. More than fifty state appeals court decisions and an opinion of the U.S. Supreme Court have affirmed this patient prerogative. In a country where still no right of access to basic health services exists, and where the major problem for approximately forty million Americans is obtaining any medical care outside hospital emergency departments, the development of such a right seems remarkable. The rallying cry of U.S. medical ethics has been focused more on the "right to die" than on the right to health care. We continue to debate physician-assisted suicide and euthanasia far more passionately than we debate the appropriate minimum benefit package. Americans rightly fear that doctors often ignore their wishes to refuse treatment, and to have proper medication for pain control near the end of life. Physician surveys consistently indicate that doctors routinely ignore patient wishes to end treatment, undermedicate for pain, and continue to see death as professional failure.

* * *

In countries like Japan and the U.K., which do not spend inordinate amounts of money on health care at the end of life, failure to discuss prognosis seems to be societally acceptable because death is not viewed as professional defeat. It is accepted as both natural and necessary by physicians and their patients alike. As Rihito Kamura has explained of Japan, "Death is an integral part of the Japanese cultural tradition. Most Japanese people resist the modern, technological death in which machines can supplant important rituals surrounding death and dying." Because members of these relatively more homogeneous societies share common perceptions about how much medical intervention is appropriate at the end of life, comprehensive discussion of treatment alternatives between doctor and patient seems less necessary.

In the more pluralistic U.S. society, however, there is less social consensus on the role of medicine toward the end of life, and physician biases toward more aggressive treatment may offend the value systems of many Americans. These people are going to great lengths, such as executing living wills, petitioning courts to terminate treatment, and committing suicide, to assert that merely prolonging the dying process is unacceptable to them.

* * *

Notes

1. Japanese culture helps explain how the country approaches not only medical research, resource allocation, and death and dying—the issues flagged by Annas and Miller above—but also medical malpractice liability, a focus in Chapter 2. Of course, to fully comprehend how the law is constructed and operates in practice, it is useful to understand the Japan's legal culture, procedures, and educational system, as well as key trends in a variety of fields related to health law, such as administrative law, constitutional law, contracts, and criminal law. For an excellent contemporary review of these topics in Japan, see *Law in Japan: A Turning Point* (Daniel H. Foote ed., 2007).

2. Cuba has drawn significant interest from American scholars given its close proximity to the United States, its socialist government, and its historical emphasis on

health care. In addition to the politics of health care in Cuba, scholars offer important insights into the Cuban system by using the methods of ethnography, history, and medical anthropology. See, e.g., Katherine Hirschfeld, *Health, Politics, and Revolution in Cuba Since 1898* (2007).

3. The excerpt above raises themes that will recur throughout this book. One of these is the tension between paternalism and autonomy. Whether a doctor decides what medical care a patient needs or the patient is able to choose what care he or she wants is to a considerable degree culturally determined. The choices that either or both may make are also influenced by cultural factors. The relationship between the individual and society, which in turn may influence the health care resources available to any individual, is also a cultural artifact. Perceptions of life, death, and even of tolerable pain, are also affected by culture. All of these factors are in turn reflected in the laws of particular jurisdictions. It is to law that we now again turn.

E. The Role of Legal Institutions in Allocating and Rationing Health Care Resources

As noted above, virtually all of the world's nations have recognized some sort of a right to health by maintaining public systems for financing or delivering health care. These systems are established by legislation. Although such legislation typically creates a framework for administering the public system, the laws are not always clear on who is eligible, what technologies or services are covered, and how much the government will pay for them. In many cases, these decisions are made by administrative agencies, and may be reviewable by courts, or in rarer cases by international tribunals. This section examines the role of legal institutions in determining what services get covered by government health programs.

The first selection discusses the rationale for creating official lists of covered health products and services, sometimes called essential health "packages" or "baskets." This task can differ greatly between low-, middle-, and high-income countries. In wealthier countries, the task has been described as follows:

> [A] serious challenge is how to deal with new health technology, for example, an innovative hip prosthesis, a computerized prosthetic leg, robot-assisted cardiac surgery, non-invasive prenatal testing and new cancer medicines and orphan drugs. While mandatory health insurance generally covers a broad range of health technology, new technology may not be—readily—covered because of budgetary reasons or because there is no unanimity (yet) about the evidence-based character or the medical necessity. In case of doubt, national health authorities can decide not to cover a new health technology, even if the technology has been acknowledged by health technology assessment centres and/or is covered by health insurers in other countries.

Piet Calcoen, Albert Boer, and Wynand P.M.M. van de Ven, Should New Health Technology Be Available Only for Patients Able and Willing to Pay?, 5 *Journal of Market*

Access & Health Policy 1 (2017). The study below, in contrast, focuses on what animates coverage choices in low- and middle-income countries. After that, the excerpt by Jost evaluates health care coverage determinations in wealthier countries.

Jenna Wright & Jeanna Holtz, *Essential Packages of Health Services in 24 Countries: Findings from a Cross-Country Analysis*

U.S. Agency for International Development (USAID)
1–2, 9, 12–13, 19 (June 2017)

* * *

Every country has finite resources for providing health care to its citizens. Policy makers are faced with a need to determine where to target limited resources.

Explicitly priorizing certain health care services and technologies can enable low- and middle-income countries to reach key development and public health goals []. Certain health care interventions generate greater positive outcomes than others, which in turn lead to improvements in a country's poverty, disease, or inequity burden. Such interventions may be prioritized because they are highly cost-effective or of moral importance, as is generally the case for maternal, newborn, and child health care interventions, among others.

* * *

According to the World Health Organization (WHO 2008), EPHSs [essential packages of health services] "aim to concentrate scarce resources on interventions which provide the best 'value for money.' [Later in the document, USAID explains that "[a]n EPHS is a package of health care services that the government is providing or is aspiring to provide to its citizens in an equitable manner. An EPHS, published by a national government, can be an important and in some cases bellwether policy document and governance tool for the health sector."] By doing this, [essential packages of health services] are often expected to achieve multiple goals: improved efficiency; equity; political empowerment; accountability; and altogether more effective care." * * * No single EPHS is appropriate for every country. Countries vary with respect to disease burden, level of poverty and inequality, moral code, social preferences, operational challenges, financial challenges, and so on.

* * *

We found that 23 of the 24 [low- and middle-income] countries in the review have defined an EPHS. The one exception is the Government of Mozambique, which does not have an EPHS that fits our definition but recently committed to developing one. Also, only one of Pakistan's four provinces (Punjab) has defined an EPHS * * *. Eighteen of the 24 governments have adopted an official name for their EPHS and the names vary. For example, Ethiopia's government refers to its EPHS as "Essential Health Services Package for Ethiopia," while Mali calls its EPHS the "*Paquet Minimum d'Activité*" (Minimum Package of Activities)."

Several countries—Ghana, Madagascar, Senegal, Yemen, and Zambia—define essential services in multiple policy documents rather than packaging them under one umbrella term.

* * *

Governments use the EPHS for a range of practical governance applications.

Our review of policy documents showed that different governments appear to use the EPHS for different health sector governance purposes. * * *

Some governments use the EPHS for health sector stewardship or for guiding private sector service delivery. For example, in Afghanistan, health service provision is through non-governmental organization facilities.

The government intends to use the EPHS as a means of setting standards for provision of care across all providers. Similarly, in Zambia, the government signed agreements with Churches Health Association of Zambia facilities to provide the services in the EPHS in areas not adequately covered by a public facility, and uses the EPHS as a means of setting standards.

Governments use the EPHS to promote accountability among health care facilities and facility staff by specifying which services should be available across the system. India's government, for example, uses its EPHS (also known as the Indian Public Health Standards) in this way.

Other governments use the EPHS as a planning tool for improving population coverage, increasing financial protection or improving certain factors that affect service delivery. The Liberian government's EPHS is an example of an EPHS that serves a planning and implementation function.

* * *

Timothy Stoltzfus Jost ed., *Health Care Coverage Determinations: An International Comparative Study*

pp. 240–44, 251–53 (2005)

* * *

The answer to the question of who has standing to initiate a [technology] assessment [for determining coverage by public insurance programs] varies from country to country. In those countries where technology assessment is a necessary prerequisite to coverage, technology manufacturers or other sponsors usually have the opportunity to apply for coverage. This is true in the United States, Switzerland, Australia, and the Netherlands. Indeed, in the Netherlands, only manufacturers have standing to request coverage. In Spain, Canada, the US, Australia, and England, requests for appraisals can come from other sources as well, including patients, providers or insurers. * * *

In Germany and Switzerland (and in Ontario, Canada, as to medical procedures), however, the corporatist institutions serve as gatekeepers to the technology assessment process. In Germany, a new technology cannot be covered out of hospital without a coverage determination, and the determination process can only be initiated by the sickness [health insurance] funds or by the insurance doctor's organizations. In Switzerland, by contrast, a new technology will be covered unless the application for coverage is contested by either the insurance fund or medical association. * * *

In most of our countries coverage determinations are usually reactive—appraisal bodies respond to a request for an assessment. Only in a few places, England, some of the Spanish regions, and to some extent in the US, is "horizon scanning" conducted proactively to identify new technologies that merit assessment.

The procedures followed by the various appraisal groups vary from highly structured to quite informal. The US Medicare process, for example, is a multistage process with time limits (not always strictly observed) at each step. * * * The Australian MSAC [Medical Services Advisory Committee] and Spanish regional committee processes, by contrast, appear quite flexible. Most countries contemplate a multistep process, that usually involves a screening process to make sure the application is complete, review of the application by commission staff, review and recommendation by an expert committee, and preliminary and final coverage determinations. The process also sometimes involves the commissioning or acquisition of an external technology assessment. Provision may be made during the process for comments by the technology sponsor, or, in a few instances, as in the US or England, by the public.

* * *

Coverage processes in general seem to be investigational as opposed to adversarial in nature. An attempt is made, that is, to assess scientifically the proposed technology without a predisposition toward coverage or noncoverage, rather than requiring the proponent of a technology to meet a particular burden of proof in the face of opposition from a party contesting coverage. In some countries, notably Australia, the procedure is viewed as somewhat more adversarial, though the process is described in our Australian chapter as really more a process of bargaining.

Opportunities for appeal vary from country to country. The United States is most generous, offering several paths for appeal, and allowing challenges to the substance of coverage decisions, and not just to the procedures through which they were formulated. In Germany appeals to the Ministry are only available for procedural errors, while in the Netherlands an appeal can only be brought if there is new information with respect to the therapeutic value of the drug. Appeals in England are available only if NICE [the National Institute for Clinical Excellence] failed to act fairly or in accordance with its own procedures, the decision is perverse, or NICE exceeded its powers. Patients who are denied services in Ontario, or who face extraordinarily long waits, can appeal to an independent tribunal, the Health Services Appeal and Review Board.

In most countries coverage denials can be contested in court. In some countries these challenges can be brought by the applicant denied coverage, but in most countries a patient who needs a product or service has the right to appeal a coverage denial as well. In Germany and Switzerland cases involving coverage are quite common, though in Switzerland they rarely involve new technologies. In Australia and the Netherlands such litigation is apparently unusual and rarely successful. In the US Medicare system, appeals of individual technology coverage decisions are very common, but there are many layers of administrative review through which an appeal must wend its way before judicial review becomes available, and thus judicial review is quite uncommon. There is no appellate review of the decisions of the Spanish regional technology assessment bodies. Even when formal judicial processes for appeal are not available, however, technology sponsors may still find a way to challenge a decision in court, as is demonstrated in the Canadian situation where Bristol-Myers Squibb sued (unsuccessfully) to block release of a report from the Canadian Coordinating Office for Health Technology Assessment arguing "negligent misstatement."

On the whole, the processes reviewed here are not very transparent. The most transparent is the American system, where assessment processes are tracked at each stage on the web, and opportunities for public comment are offered at several stages. England also seems to be moving toward a more transparent process, though comments are only accepted from invited participants in the process, who are often interested parties, such as technology sponsors, providers, or patient groups. By contrast, the German, Dutch, and Swiss processes take place largely behind closed doors. Reports are published, and comments are accepted at points in the process, but the decision making processes are not visible to the public. If anyone has access to information regarding an assessment process, it is usually the proponent. In Australia, the proponent of a technology, and only the proponent, has the right to comment on draft assessment papers. Similarly in Switzerland, only the applicant receives a written summary of the reasons supporting the Federal Department of Home Affairs coverage decision.

* * *

Most countries base coverage decisions on the criteria of efficacy, effectiveness, and medical necessity. These terms may be defined comparatively; *i.e.* a product or service may only be approved for coverage if it is as or more effective than existing technologies. In several countries there is a conscious effort to avoid the appearance of rationing, however, and all effective technologies will be covered. The authors of our German report, for example, report the findings of their own research which demonstrates that only effectiveness, and not cost, is considered in the German process. The United States has also been reluctant to embrace cost as a concern in coverage policy, though more expensive technologies get closer attention than less expensive technologies.

In some countries, however, there is more openness to consideration of economic concerns. This is clearly true in Australia, and will soon be true in the Netherlands. Even in Australia, however, imatinib (or GLIVEC® or GLEEVAC®) has been covered despite its high cost per case and a comparatively high cost-effectiveness ratio because it was the only drug available for treating CML [chronic myeloid leukemia] for some patients, * * * NICE in England also takes cost per QALY [quality-adjusted life year] into account in making coverage policy, though the experience in imatinib in England also demonstrates that cost is far from the only consideration taken into account in approving technologies for coverage. The purpose of a drug and distributional concerns are also important. * * *

* * *

When we look for overall lessons that can be drawn, then, from our comparative study of institutions and procedures and of how they have dealt with specific technologies, several emerge. First, despite widespread fears that technology assessment will lead to rationing, most countries still focus primarily on questions of effectiveness rather than on cost considerations. Only in Australia and England does cost seem to play a major and explicit role in making coverage determinations. Moreover, in England NICE only has authority to require coverage, its jurisdiction with respect to noncoverage decisions is strictly advisory, thus primary care trusts [which purchase health care in England] may be required to cover cost-effective technologies, but are not barred from covering technologies that are not cost effective. The drug approval process in the Netherlands is moving toward consideration of cost-effectiveness data, but it is not there yet. * * * Coverage evaluation in other countries focuses on effectiveness, or at most, on effectiveness in comparison to existing technologies.

Moreover, coverage assessment organizations seem quite willing to approve coverage for life-threatening, or even serious non-life-threatening, conditions, when there is some evidence of effectiveness of a breakthrough technology and no other technology adequate to treating the condition is otherwise available, as our case studies of imatinib and HBOT [hyperbaric oxygen therapy] demonstrate. The "rule of rescue" still plays a major role in technology approval. Finally, political considerations, independent of science, can play a role in coverage processes, as is demonstrated by the Swiss experience with in vitro fertilisation.

Second, each of the technologies that were the subjects of our case studies are approved only for limited, specific indications. In some programs, like the US, technologies are also explicitly not covered for other specific indications. In other countries, technologies are implicitly not covered for indications for which they are not explicitly covered. Because technologies are only covered for particular indications, and sometimes when provided in particular settings by particular providers, however, coverage determination based on HTA [health technology assessment], which was supposed to result in macro-rationing, has in fact become micro-rationing. Coverage policy decisions often, that is, increasingly take the form of cost-effectiveness guidelines that resemble practice guidelines, rather than up or down determinations of what a public insurer will pay for.

Third, partial coverage tends to expand over time. Technology proponents denied tend to return with applications for coverage for additional indications, and thus coverage tends to expand to new indications. * * * Moreover, in several of our countries coverage expansion can take place de facto, without explicit approval, through doctors prescribing outside of approved indications, or through the use of existing codes to cover new technologies, albeit at a reduced price. In the end coverage assessment often has the effect of delaying rather than ultimately denying coverage.

Fourth, lack of hard scientific coverage does not necessarily block coverage expansion (but different countries reach different results). Indeed, on the whole, the results of the technology assessments from the various countries were quite consistent. The responses of the coverage assessment organizations, however, were not. * * * The fact that different countries reach different conclusions based on the same evidence suggests, of course, that the process is not wholly driven by scientific evidence, or, at least, that where evidence is open to varying interpretations, different countries place different weight of various aspects of that evidence reflecting different values.

Of course, in each of our countries coverage has also continued for existing technologies despite lack of hard scientific evidence supporting effectiveness. It is always easier to block expansion of coverage to new technologies than to remove existing technologies from coverage, a [phenomenon] referred to by our Canadian authors as the "stickiness" of coverage.

Fifth, where agency procedures afford opportunity for public participation in the process, participants uniformly press for coverage. Where outsiders are permitted to apply for coverage, applications usually come from technology manufacturers, groups of providers or professionals who offer a new technology in their institutions or practices, or patient groups. When public hearings are held or public comments are solicited regarding technologies under consideration for coverage, these are also the groups that testify and comment. * * *

It is rare, on the other hand, that pressure is brought directly to bear on assessment agencies opposing coverage of any particular technology. Cost is, of course, a major consideration affecting all public insurance systems, and coverage organizations cannot help but be aware of it. Also, competitors may on occasion show up to contest exclusive coverage of one product to the exclusion of their products. * * * But except in rare instances, pressure is rarely directed at any particular product. * * *

* * *

Colleen Flood, Mark Stabile & Carolyn Tuohy, *What Is In and Out of Medicare? Who Decides?*

in Colleen Flood, ed., Just Medicare, pp. 15, 16–17, 23–30 (2005)

* * *

A Decision-Making Framework Grounded in the Canadian System

There have been many models put forward to guide decision-making about what should and should not be publicly funded both in Canada and internationally. However, these theoretical models have not been implemented in Canada or particularly successfully in any jurisdiction. In our view they suffer from being too general, too abstract, and divorced from messy local details. In particular, the existing models fail to take into account the political economy of particular systems. In any system of decision-making, considerations of values, resources, and information about costs and benefits are filtered through local structures and processes. As we discuss further below, in Canada, these structures and processes are characterized by accidents of history and by long-held accommodations between governments and the medical profession, inflexible and inadequate regulations and law, and the interaction of different stakeholders and interest groups.

Thus, before we can theorize about what processes and principles should be adopted we must understand how decisions are made now. The existing system will constrain what reforms are possible. For example, starting from the top, the overarching normative framework that governs it, the *Canada Health Act* (CHA), drives decision-making about what is in and what is out of Canadian Medicare. The CHA requires that provinces publicly fund all "medically necessary" hospital services and "medically required" physician services in order to receive federal funding. But, the CHA does not provide definitions of "medically necessary" or "medically required." Nor, in turn, does provincial legislation provide such definitions. How, then, do provinces determine which particular health care services to fund?

* * *

[The authors proceed to describe the role of the Physician Services Committee, a joint committee of the Ontario government and the Ontario Medical Association, which, among other things, recommends the listing and delisting of services to meet financial targets in Ontario, and of the medical directors of the provincial ministries of health, who decide which services to cover. They then proceed to discuss review of these decisions.]

The Health Services Appeal and Review Board

* * * [I]n most provinces, the only recourse from a decision not to fund a particular treatment or service is to seek relief in the general courts, either through judicial review or through a *Charter* challenge. Some relief may be obtained from appeal to an Ombudsman in the case of decisions made by the government or government-owned institutions (i.e., some psychiatric hospitals). The Ombudsman, however, intervenes as a last recourse; complainants have to first use all other complaints processes or means of appeal available to them before the Ombudsman will conduct an investigation. Quebec has a more generous system in that there is a Patient Ombudsman, charged with specifically investigating health complaints.

Three provinces (Ontario, Alberta, and British Columbia) have administrative tribunals to which the citizens thereof can bring (on limited grounds) an application to review a decision not to publicly fund a service or treatment. In Quebec, the Tribunal administrative du Québec hears appeals concerning health treatment or service coverage in Quebec as well as appeals from all administrative bodies in the province. Of all the specific tribunals Ontario's is the most active and has a broader mandate to review decisions but, as we discuss below, its discretion nonetheless remains limited.

* * *

The ability [in Ontario] to seek relief before an administrative tribunal rather than having to apply to the general courts offers the prospect of quicker, easier and cheaper recourse to justice. However, many who do appeal to the Ontario Board are disappointed to find that its discretion to review delisting or failure to list decisions is significantly constrained by the terms of the act and the regulations. For example, section 24 of the relevant regulations lists medical services that are specifically excluded from OHIP [Ontario Health Insurance Plan] coverage. These include: in subsection 24(1); services solely for the purposes of altering or restoring appearance (para. 10); treatment for a medical condition that is generally considered experimental (para. 17); in vitro fertilization, except in limited circumstances (para. 23); reversal of sterilization (para. 22); and the fitting and evaluation of hearing aids (para. 27). These services are not insured services (and thus, by a process of reverse engineering, are considered not "medically necessary" under the *Canada Health Act*). The Board has almost no discretion to reverse a decision not to publicly fund these services.

The Board does have some discretion with respect to access to out-of-country services. This occurs in two circumstances: when a citizen of Ontario requires unanticipated, emergency treatment while traveling, and/or when a citizen of Ontario secures prior approval to obtain treatment that is unavailable, or unavailable without significant delay, in the province. Most of the Board's discretion, and the most interesting decisions, revolve around the issue of pre-approved treatment.

* * *

The Courts

The role of the courts in determining the boundaries of Medicare is often overstated in the media and/or assumed to be much more significant than is actually the case. There are two main mechanisms by which the courts play a role in determining what is in and what is out of Medicare: judicial review through general administrative law and through *Charter* challenges. In general, plaintiffs are unsuccessful.

Faced with a challenge in administrative law, courts demonstrate their deference for determining what is in and out of Medicare, by reviewing decisions on the standard of "patent unreasonableness." This is the most deferential standard of review possible in administrative law, with the other possibilities being "reasonableness simpliciter" and "correctness" (the latter being the least deferential). For example, the only successful judicial review claim before the courts with regard to waiting times has been *Stein v. Québec (Régie de l'Assurance-maladie)*. In this case Mr. Stein waited months for surgery, even though his doctors warned that his life was in danger if he was not operated on within four to eight weeks. He was successful before the Quebec Superior Court in overturning the Quebec health insurance board officials' refusal to pay for his treatment in a New York hospital on the grounds that, given the facts of the case, the decision was patently unreasonable. Thus, the court was prepared to be very deferential to the Board's decision making; however, even allowing for this very high standard of deference the court felt compelled to overturn the Board's decision. The courts will check the *rationality* of governmental decisions about what is in and out of Medicare, but to date have not held the government or other institutions to any higher standard.

* * *

With respect to *Charter* challenges, applicants have met with a similar lack of success. For example, the courts to date (with one exception) have not found that section 7 of the *Charter*, which guarantees life, liberty, and security of the person, entitles Canadians to publicly funded health care.

* * *

Most of the *Charter* challenges to limits on publicly funded health care are brought arguing section 15, the equality provision. Despite the absence of a *Charter* right to publicly funded health care, once a government elects to provide some publicly funded health care services, it must do so in compliance with the equality provisions of the *Charter*. Section 15(1) provides that "[E]very individual is equal before and under the law and has the right to the equal protection and equal benefit of the law without discrimination and, in particular, without discrimination based on race, national or ethnic origin, colour, religion, sex, age or mental or physical disability." However, even if discrimination is found under section 15(1), it may be "saved" by section 1 of the *Charter*, which provides that "the *Canadian Charter of Rights and Freedoms* guarantees the rights and freedoms set out in it subject only to such reasonable limits prescribed by law as can be demonstrably justified in a free and democratic society." Thus, a government may defend a finding that a particular policy or decision is discriminatory by pointing to the principles and processes that were followed in making it and arguing that although the needs of those discriminated against were considered, there were other countervailing needs or considerations that outweighed these concerns.

There have been a number of section 15 challenges that have grabbed attention. But between 1985 and 2002 of the thirty-three cases that have challenged health care policy, only eleven have been successful. More specifically, of the cases that have challenged policies limiting insured medical services only one has been upheld at the Supreme Court level. The successful case was in 1997, *Eidridge v. British Columbia* which was a claim by a deaf couple that they were discriminated against in contravention of theft section 15 rights by the failure of the British Columbian government (and more specifically a hospital) to fund interpretation services. The facts of this case were very compelling. The deaf woman was giving birth to twins and there were problems at the time of delivery. A nurse communicated to the mother through gestures that the heart rate of one of the babies had gone down. The twins were whisked away from the distressed women who did not know what was going on apart from a note being flashed at her with the word "fine" written thereon.

* * *

There are many issues that are raised by the court's review on *Charter* grounds of decisions not to publicly fund treatments. The first point to note is that only a very few patients have been successful. The expense and delay inherent in *Charter* litigation means that recourse to the *Charter* remains an unsatisfactory way to deal with *most* grievances and concerns that citizens have regarding access to health care services. Also, although the *Charter* can, in certain circumstances, address explicit rationing decisions by governments (for example, failing to fund a particular service or delisting a particular service), it has far less capacity to challenge the multitude of resource allocation decisions that are made in the health care system every day. In other words, although the *Charter* can protect against explicit governmental decisions that openly deny or prevent access to a particular treatment, most decisions are not explicit and have an indirect effect on access. Governments can eviscerate a health care system through underfunding so that services are available in theory although not in practice, and it is much harder to launch legal challenge against such methods of dilution. Second, it is important to note that *Charter* challenges are a one-way street, and they do nothing to counter the difficulty of *delisting* treatments and may, indeed, exacerbate the existing reluctance of decision-makers to formally delist treatments that are of relatively less benefit. However, given that the *Charter* as part of the *Constitution* is as clear a statement of agreed-upon public values as one is likely to find, the courts play a critical role in checking governmental decision-making, which increasingly emphasizes cost-effectiveness analysis and the objective of restraining government spending, that may unlawfully discriminate against marginalized and vulnerable groups of people. * * *

* * *

The Role of Law and Legal Institutions

Law and legal institutions can be both barriers and facilitators to an equitable and efficient health care system. For example, in Canada, the *Canada Health Act* gives primacy to hospital and physician services. Although the CHA has protected Canadians well through the years, it has skewed public resources towards hospital and physician services rather than community care, home care, public health, preventive care, drugs, and new technologies. Thus, while law can be a powerful force, entrenching values and protecting entitlements, it can also result in inflexibility and present barriers to reform if it fails to keep pace with changing technology, expectations, and health care needs.

* * *

Notes

1. Health care coverage and "rationing" decisions can be very contentious for governments. "To ration health care means to deny claims to treatment and to remove services that formerly would have been covered ..." Claudia Landwehr & Katharina Böhm, Delegation and Institutional Design in Health-Care Rationing, 24 (4) *Governance: An International Journal of Policy, Administration, and Institutions* 665 (2011). It can be particularly problematic when the decisions are made by "nonmajoritarian, more or less independent agencies." *Id.* at 665. However, an agency's expertise and specialized medical knowledge can be crucial in evaluating how effective new products

and treatments are likely to be—decisions that, in their complexity and volume, are likely to "overtax" legislatures that lack the time, expertise, and often inclination to make such decisions themselves. Not surprisingly, then, a number of scholars have evaluated who is allowed to influence or appeal coverage decisions in various countries, particularly in jurisdictions experimenting with new institutions making these decisions. *See, e.g.*, Adun Mohara et al., Using Health Technology Assessment for Informing Coverage Decisions in Thailand, 1 (2) *Journal of Comparative Effectiveness Research* (Mar. 2012) (special report). Despite the risk of coverage decisions being dominated by manufacturers, providers, and patients with acute interests in coverage, the involvement of such groups is often viewed as essential for ensuring the process is open and legitimate. *Id.* For example, one study of coverage decisions for expensive drugs in Australia, Canada, England and Wales, Israel, and the United States found that "the stakeholders that were most often involved in the deliberative process were health care professionals, academics and the public," with significant variation in who is allowed to lodge formal appeals (*e.g.*, drug manufacturers, patient groups, or professional groups). Zahava R.S. Rosenberg-Yunger et al., Stakeholder Involvement in Expensive Drug Recommendation Decisions: An International Perspective, 105 *Health Policy* 226 (2011).

2. Most nations provide some forum for review of improper administrative actions. The courts are usually available for this purpose, though in some nations a special forum exists that takes the place of, or supplements, the courts. France, for example, has a special tribunal, the Conseil d'Etat, for reviewing executive action—a function forbidden the courts. Other nations have complaint systems within the administrative agency, or health care ombudsmen with various jurisdictions. Where judicial review is available, courts are usually quite deferential to administrative agencies. This is especially true in England.

3. In the United States, private health insurers and managed care organizations often provide internal appeal procedures. Most states by statute also provide external reviews of coverage decisions. It is also possible for beneficiaries to sue their insurer or managed care organization for breach of contract if services or payment for services is denied. Under the law of several of the states, moreover, a beneficiary may sue in tort for bad faith breach of an insurance contract if the insurer or managed care organizations refusal was egregious. For years, however, the federal Employee Retirement Income Security Act of 1974 (ERISA), preempted these remedies with respect to employee benefit plans. 29 U.S.C.A. §§1132(a), 1144(a). Since most Americans obtain health insurance through their employer, ERISA effectively preempted state court remedies when employees were denied care or payment. The Supreme Court, however, has held that ERISA permits states to provide binding external review procedures for ERISA plans that are not self-insured. See *Rush Prudential HMO, Inc. v. Moran*, 536 U.S. 355 (2002). ERISA permits the recovery of benefits denied in federal court, but it does not permit recovery of extra-contractual damages or tort damages. See *Aetna Health, Inc. v. Davila*, 542 U.S. 200 (2004). Finally, the Affordable Care Act of 2010 requires employee health plans, including

self-insured plans, to provide both internal appeal procedures and external review. ACA § 2719, 42 U.S.C. § 300gg-19.

4. The reading notes that one means of challenging health care allocation decisions is through raising claims of discriminatory treatment. In the United States, denials of access to health care are occasionally challenged on the grounds of discrimination. A few lawsuits have brought under Title VI, claiming race discrimination, and more recently under the Americans with Disabilities Act on the basis of disability discrimination. Another statute, the Emergency Medical Treatment and Active Labor Act, 42 U.S.C.A. § 1395dd, more directly prohibits denial of emergency medical care to those who present at hospital emergency rooms requiring emergent care or in active labor, regardless of ability to pay. This statute also provides administrative means of enforcement. How effective has the strategy of prohibiting discrimination in the delivery of health care in the United States proved as a strategy for expanding access to health care?

The following excerpt, by an eminent scholar of the law of the UK's National Health Service (NHS), describes the roles courts and local health commissioners play in rationing within the NHS. The description highlights the tension between accommodating individuals' interests in obtaining specific treatments and broader, community interests when making difficult line-drawing decisions regarding what treatments the NHS will and will not cover.

Christopher Newdick, *Rebalancing the Rationing Debate: Tackling the Tensions between Individual and Community Rights*

in Eckhard Nagel & Michael Lauerer, eds.,
Prioritization in Medicine: An International Dialogue
123–29, 132–35 (2015)

1 Introduction

Health care is not just about the rights of individuals. It is part of a larger endeavour to secure optimum performance from finite funds for a community of patients and to do so fairly, safely and effectively. At a time of economic austerity, questions arise about affordability. Health economists refer to this as "opportunity cost" because choices to commit finite funds to particular purposes prevent those funds being available for other purposes. Inevitably, choices that favour the needs of individuals (what I call the "individualist" approach) tend to disfavour the needs of communities (what I call the "community" approach). * * * By itself, the individualist approach is not equipped to respond to the challenges presented by scarce resources, especially in the light of the increase in chronic, "lifestyle" diseases. I do not deny the importance of the individual perspective but argue that we need to rebalance the debate.

Therefore, we should be more explicit about the public dimension of health care. However, the community-based approach presents problems of its own, and there is a risk that it may undermine the legitimate clinical rights of individuals. Unless we get the balance right, the forces acting on health-care costs will make the individualist approach unsustainable. By looking through a telescope, instead of a microscope, we highlight broader concerns and different objectives. This chapter considers examples from the English National Health Service (NHS), but the issues it raises are international in scope. * * *

2 The Individual Rights Model of Substantive and Procedural Rights

In the NHS, two systems emphasise individual rights, i.e. *substantive* rights and *procedural* rights. Substantive rights guarantee access to the treatment itself. In the English NHS, substantive rights have been created by the National Institute for Health and Care Excellence (NICE). NICE is a national authority which makes recommendations to commissioners of health care. NICE exists because about 200 clinical commissioning groups are responsible for commissioning patient care in England.[1] The Secretary of State is subject to a legal duty to "promote a comprehensive health service," but this duty is delegated by regulations to each of them to perform on his behalf. There is clearly a risk of unacceptable variations in local decision-making which, in a *national* health service, is unattractive. NICE introduces greater consistency between commissioners. Thus, recommendations in its *technology appraisal guidance* (TAG) have mandatory legal effect so that the treatment must be made available by commissioners provided a doctor prescribes it. This substantive duty is confirmed by the NHS Constitution, and the duty upon commissioners to support funding is enforceable by individuals against "health care commissioners" in judicial review. Conscious of opportunity costs, NICE becomes more critical of the clinical evidence of effectiveness for drugs which cost more than £20,000 per quality-adjusted life-year (QALY) and is unlikely to support treatments costing more than £30,000 per QALY. Thus, a number of expensive treatments for cancer have not been recommended because their costs are not justified by their limited therapeutic benefits.

This encourages consistency throughout the NHS, and it can respond to general concerns about particular illness, such as cancer (treatments for which are frequently considered by NICE). However, with the exception of NICE, the NHS does not use a national list of approved treatments. Instead (as we have seen), it delegates to commissioners the duty to promote a "comprehensive" health service subject to their own discretion. One of the benefits of delegating this duty to local health commissioners is their ability to respond to local needs in consultation with their local communities. Clearly, decisions made at national level tend to be detached from the concerns of local health commissioners and the stresses on their resources. Each of NICE's mandatory (i.e. substantive) recommendations carries opportunity costs which have consequences for other patients, and there is a balance between consistency at national level and local responsiveness. Put another way, within finite resources, the greater the number of treatments subject to substantive rights, the smaller the discretion

1. Clinical commissioning groups replaced primary care trusts as the commissioners of NHS care from April 2013. See the Health and Social Care Act 2012. For convenience, the word "commissioner" is used to describe the public function of purchasing health care on behalf of a community.

that remains to local decision-makers. This brings us to the alternative mechanism for rationing health care: the procedural rights approach.

Procedural rights are promoted at national level by the English *NHS Constitution*. Procedural rights do not guarantee access to treatment. Instead, they guarantee a fair and transparent procedure by which the decision-makers are required to justify decisions. After years of denying that rationing was really necessary, the government promoted the NHS Constitution in the form of a statutory bill of rights for patients in 2010. The ideas promoted by the NHS Constitution reflect over 10 years of principles developed by judicial review cases. Thus (other than the substantive rights supported by NICE), in allocating health resources, local commissioners must adhere to the procedural rights approach promoted by the NHS Constitution. The procedural approach recognises that hard choices are inevitable and accommodate broader, community interests alongside the needs of individuals. Equally, it is heavily accountable to the individual. Actually, the Constitution is not wholly candid about the need for hard choices in health care. It says only: "The NHS is committed to providing best value for taxpayers' money and the most effective use of finite resources." However, documentation which explains the Constitution confirms: "Like all public authorities, [commissioners] are required to operate within finite budgets and, therefore, have to prioritise some treatments over others according to the needs of local communities … [] Disinvestments should be considered along with investments." "Disinvestment" recognises that, as in any system working within fixed financial allocations, choices that favour some may disfavour others. The NHS Constitution describes how decisions should be made according to transparent procedures. Promoting the principle of transparency, it says:

> … each [commissioner] must have in place arrangements for making decisions and adopting policies on whether particular healthcare interventions are to be made available for patients for which the [commissioner] is responsible … Each [commissioner] must compile and publish clear written information outlining the arrangements specified. …

Promoting accountability to individuals, it says that patients are entitled to know how those arrangements have been applied in their individual case:

> You have the right to expect local decisions on funding of … drugs and treatments to be made rationally following a proper consideration of the evidence. If the local NHS decides not to fund a drug or treatment you and your doctor feel would be right for you, they will explain that decision to you.

This means that: "Where a [commissioner] makes a decision to refuse a request for the funding of a health-care intervention, where the [commissioner's] general policy is not to fund that intervention, the [commissioner] must provide that individual with a written statement of its reasons for that decision." In addition, the right of explanation is supplemented by a further right of appeal because "[commissioners] should establish an appeals process for decisions made on individual funding requests, including clearly defined grounds of appeal, independent of the original process and open to patients and the public."

Therefore, health service commissioners must have fair, reasonable and accountable systems for setting health priorities and be prepared to explain to individual patients the reasons for their decisions. Procedural rights insist that rationing decisions are taken within a fair and consistent framework of values capable of explaining why a particular treatment cannot be funded. Although they are procedural only, they are certainly enforceable by individual patients. The legal power of procedural rights enables judicial review courts to "overturn" (but not reverse) a decision and to return it to the commissioner to be reconsidered in the light of the court's criticisms. In legal theory, the decision-maker may come to the same conclusion in respect of a particular case, provided the reasoning is defensible, but political and media pressure often mean that the decision is reversed. However, it stops short of creating substantive rights to particular treatment.

These generic procedural rights are given effect by local commissioners of health care (other than treatments subject to mandatory NICE guidance). Local commissioners may combine in consortia to use ethical frameworks to make decisions about treatments consistent with the NHS Constitution. For example, such a framework exists in the South Central region of the English NHS where nine health care commissioners have combined to adopt a single ethical framework which forms the basis of its advice to its commissioners. The ethical framework is applied to specific treatments to determine which should be recommended to local commissioners and which should be considered "low priority." Low priority means that the treatment will not normally be purchased by the commissioner unless the patient is judged to have exceptional circumstances which merit an exceptional response. To preserve consistency in its approach, it considers the following criteria for decisionmaking: (a) evidence of clinical and cost-effectiveness of the treatment, (b) equity and the principle of equal access for equal need, (c) the health-care needs of the patient and their capacity to benefit from the treatment, (d) the cost of the treatment and its opportunity costs, (e) the sometimes countervailing needs of the community and (f) guidance from national institutions such as NICE or the government. This "procedural-individual" rights approach puts individual claims into a community context and, with proper procedural safeguards in place, can do so fairly and consistently.

Whether they are procedural, or substantive, decisions about affordability involve judgments which are not uniquely clinical. They involve distributive ethics which also engage a range of other views, including those of the public. Although one can attempt to put numbers against criteria to produce (what is called) a "balanced scorecard" which enables comparisons to be made, in reality, this is often no more than a guide because each numerical assessment requires judgment. Therefore, it is difficult to use a single scoring system to compare, for example, a need for mental health care as opposed to palliative care or orthopaedic care and paediatric care. Different assessors may give different scores to identical situations. It is important that this system is not used as a crude utilitarian calculation which promotes aggregates of health benefit by ignoring individual need. Clinicians must be prominent amongst commissioning decision-makers to represent the patient-centred perspective as a counterbalance to broader, economic and managerial considerations. In this way, individual needs can properly be weighed against those of the community. The transparency of the NHS Constitution and local ethical frameworks recognise that we could spend more on the NHS but choose not to. We prefer to value health care in a way that provides extensive but not infinite access to treatment because we also value other non-health "priorities." These structures promote fairness, consistency and equality in the NHS in the hard choices created by this balance. Although the underlying purpose of making choices is to promote community interests, individual claimants are entitled to proper recognition as an expression of the humanity and compassion inherent in the health-care system. * * *

3 The Community Dimension of Health Care

Why is it important to keep the community dimension in health care in mind? Once we acknowledge that demand for care will exceed the resources we make available, the answer is obvious. Unless we engage fair and consistent systems for allocating scarce resources, the process is likely to become inconsistent and unfair and respond to patients unequally. The question is more urgent than ever. For the past 20 years, the response of government to increased demand has been additional investment; the funds invested in the NHS in the UK have increased steadily from about £24 billion in 1990 to about £110 billion today. Now all that has changed. Additional investment is no longer available as a solution. * * *

* * *

The individual rights approach (whether substantive or procedural) is not designed to respond to this challenge. It is good at articulating the patient's voice, but it is not intended to address community interests or redress social inequalities in health status. Courts are not equipped to perform such a role. Public health certainly promotes sanitation, clean air and water, nutrition and tackling infectious diseases. But it also has an *ethical* dimension. * * * In any public health system committed to social solidarity, the presumption of equality is axiomatic. Whilst inequalities in *private* income are largely acceptable, rights of access to *public* health funds to which we have all contributed are a different matter. Public health policy is committed to ensuring that all those it serves have equal access to health. As WHO recommends in *Closing the Gap in a Generation*, "In any country, economic inequality—including inequity in public financing—needs to be addressed to make progress towards health equity." This commitment to social solidarity has a redistributive element which is no part of the "individual rights" approach.

* * *

4 Community Interests and the Politics of Individualism

* * *

Although in theory the courts endorse the procedural rights approach to rationing, similar pressure is imposed by litigation. By their nature, rationing cases highlight the rights of individuals. And by *their* nature, lawyers are probably better at comprehending individual rights than more recondite "public" or "community" interests. Indeed, modern legal theory lauds individual and human rights as a bulwark *against* the state. This preconception in favour of individual patients is demonstrated by the principle of "exceptional circumstances." Judicial review requires decision-making to be based on all the relevant considerations, which include the *exceptional* needs of the patient. For example, a last-chance, life-saving treatment for a terminal illness may be refused under the general ethical framework because its cost is not justified by its benefits. However, in response to this general policy, individual patients are entitled to argue that their circumstances are so "exceptional" that they should be given exceptional access to funding. The difficulty is in knowing how readily the court should concede such claims. Too much willingness and *litigants* will tend to get special consideration over others, and this would be unfair. But if there is too little, the sense of compassion for individuals will be undermined. The strength and weakness of the judicial forum in these cases are that it focuses on the tragedy the individual is facing, but can it also give adequate weight to the interests of others whose interests are unknown to the court?

* * *

The community side of the rationing debate has also been undermined by litigation in the European Court of Justice (ECJ). Applying the principle protecting free movement of services between member states, it has developed a theory of *substantive* rights of access to treatment. Thus, it says if a patient requires "normal" treatment which cannot be provided in the "home" state within a "reasonable time," the treatment may be obtained from a "host" member state, paid for by the patient and its cost reimbursed by the local health system. This individualistic approach favours those who are robust and wealthy enough to travel but ignores those who are too frail or poor to do so. It also ignores those denied care because younger, fitter and stronger patients who can travel may take priority in respect of funding. The only exception to this principle is when there is a risk of "undermining the balance of a social security system." But whilst this may focus on economic stability, it has little to do with fairness, democracy or equality, i.e. the ethical integrity of the system. Until recently, it appeared that the ECJ had simply not understood the implications for resource allocation of its individualistic approach to patients' rights. However, in October 2010, in *Commission v France*, the ECJ accepted the argument for balance between individual and community choices. Rejecting the Commission's claim that free movement principles protected individuals' right of access to expensive diagnostic testing in another member state, it said:

> If persons insured under the French system could, freely and in any circumstances, obtain at the expense of the competent institution, from service providers established in other Member States, treatment involving the use of major medical equipment corresponding to that listed exhaustively in the Public Health Code [i.e. Scintillation camera, magnetic resonance imaging, medical scanner, hyperbaric chamber, cyclotron], the planning endeavours

> of the national authorities and the financial balance of the supply of up-to-date treatment would as a result be jeopardised. That possibility could lead to under-use of the major medical equipment installed in the Member State of affiliation and subscribed by it or yet a disproportionate burden on the Member State's social security budget.

This community-sensitive approach has also been endorsed by the European Directive on Cross-border Access to Healthcare which concerns the rights of EU citizens to obtain treatment in a "host" member state and to have the costs reimbursed by the "home" health system. Despite strong opposition from the European Parliament (which argued for individual-substantive rights), the final version of the Directive created *procedural* rights. Thus, Directive 2011/24 of 9 March 2011 on the Application of Patients' Rights in Cross-Border Healthcare confirms that subject to the principles of non-discrimination * * * public health insurers may impose on patients wishing to obtain hospital treatment elsewhere in the EU

> … the same conditions, criteria of eligibility and regulatory and administrative formalities, whether set at a local, regional or national level, as it would impose if this healthcare were provided in its territory. This may include an assessment by a health professional or healthcare administrator providing services for the statutory social security system or national health system of the Member State of affiliation … if this is necessary for determining the individual patient's entitlement to healthcare.

Accordingly, member states "may provide for a system of prior authorisation for reimbursement of the costs of cross-border healthcare."

Thus, procedural rights systems are preferable for providing a fair, consistent and objective mechanism for balancing individual and community interests. Put another way, individual needs cannot be considered in isolation from the wider context of community interests. The precise balance between the two is a matter for effective political participation by all socio-economic groups, assisted by the "procedural" approach discussed above. In truth, the NHS has had limited success in engaging public opinion, and this important subject deserves considerably more attention.

* * *

Note

Among a number of excellent sources on NHS law are Professor Newdick's book, *Who Should we Treat?—Rights, Rationing and Resources in the N.H.S.* (2005); John Carrier & Ian Kendall, *Health and the National Health Service* (2015); and Margaret Brazier & Emma Cave, *Medicine, Patients, and the Law* (6th ed. 2016).

F. Traveling to Pursue Health: Patient Mobility and Medical Tourism

Despite domestic and international legal commitments to provide health care, sometimes patients find themselves unable to access certain care where they live and thus decide to travel to a foreign jurisdiction. This phenomenon (known variously as "medical tourism," "patient mobility," or "cross-border health care") not only brings to the forefront differences in law between jurisdictions, but also forces those involved in such cross-border transactions to evaluate and weigh those differences.

Patients, for example, sometimes engage in what lawyers would call "forum shopping" to find foreign jurisdictions with more favorable laws, regulations, and/or ethical standards regarding what medical treatments are available. Medical professionals and facilities may have to consider whether they will refer patients abroad for a treatment not available for one reason or another domestically, or whether to market their own services to a global clientele. Public and private payors facing immense cost pressures may consider "outsourcing" certain expensive treatments to reputable providers in developing countries that can offer treatment of comparable quality for a fraction of the domestic price. Lawyers, judges, and policymakers may agonize over the legal (and medical) risks of patients being treated in foreign jurisdictions with dramatically different laws, regulations, and ethical standards. *See, e.g.*, I. Glenn Cohen, *Protecting Patients with Passports: Medical Tourism and the Patient-Protective Argument*, 95 Iowa Law Review 1467 (2010); Nathan Cortez, *Recalibrating the Risks of Cross-Border Health Care*, 10 Yale Journal of Health Policy, Law, and Ethics 1 (2010); Leigh Turner, *Patient Mortality in Medical Tourism: Examining News Media Reports of Deaths following Travel for Cosmetic Surgery or for Bariatric Surgery*, *in* The Globalization of Health Care: Legal and Ethical Issues 3 (I. Glenn Cohen ed., 2013).

In each instance, both differences and similarities in law between jurisdictions are brought into sharp relief. This section, then, is a case study in how globalization is forcing some patients, providers, payors, and policymakers to confront comparative health law in practice.

Nathan Cortez, *Patients Without Borders: The Emerging Global Market for Patients and the Evolution of Modern Health Care*

83 Indiana Law Journal 71–73, 77–82 (2008)

Introduction

A growing number of patients are leaving the United States for medical care. They are traveling to developing countries like India and Thailand for a variety of sophisticated treatments, such as heart surgeries, joint replacements, and fertility treatments. In the process, they are choosing to forego the legal and regulatory protections—and perhaps even insurance coverage—they receive in the United States. Essentially, patients are waiving the rights, benefits, and protections offered by our health care regulatory system to seek medical care in countries that may not grant them remotely similar rights or protections.

"Medical tourism" is the latest response to a familiar trend. Each year, the United States spends more on health care, but insures fewer people. Health care spending is predicted to account for one of every five dollars spent in the United States by 2015, and the United States by itself spends roughly half of the $4 trillion spent on health care each year worldwide. Meanwhile, nearly 47 million Americans had no health insurance in 2005, up from 31 million in 1987. The Institute of Medicine recently estimated that 18,000 uninsured adults in the United States die each year from treatable conditions.

In the face of this widening gap, U.S. patients are beginning to leave our health care system, joining a growing international population of patients that are seeking medical treatments outside of their own countries. * * *

To complicate matters further, though many policy organizations are aware of this trend, it is developing almost entirely independently of lawmakers and regulators. This is more than a little troubling for a phenomenon that confronts us with such profound legal and policy questions. It is not simply a matter of patients seeking less expensive medical care elsewhere; patients are opting out of our health care system and the delicate equilibrium of policy choices that it represents. For example, our health care financing system reflects who we think should pay for health care and how much. Our systems for licensing, accreditation, malpractice, and regulatory approval of medical technologies reflect the quality standards we desire. Our public and private health insurance systems reflect the risks we can tolerate.

By choosing other health care systems, patients force us to reevaluate the policy equilibria we have set. Medical tourism compels us to think more broadly about how globalization may alter our health policy calculations, and even the underlying principles upon which we calculate. For such a long time, health care has been "peculiarly and tenaciously local in its character." But for a growing number of patients, this is no longer the case. * * *

A. Why Do Patients Travel Abroad for Medical Care?

Patients generally seek medical care abroad for one of two reasons: either they do not have access to a particular treatment, or they cannot afford it, in their own country.

1. Access to Medical Procedures

Historically, patients have traveled overseas when a particular medical treatment is not available where they live. First, local laws may prohibit a medical procedure as immoral or unethical, which occurs most often with reproductive medicine. For example, patients in Europe flock to Belgium and Italy for in vitro fertilization (IVF) treatments because these two countries "have no or very little legislation concerning medically assisted reproduction." Many patients visit from France, Germany, or the Netherlands, whose governments impose various restrictions on IVF treatments. Every year, 7,000 women from Ireland travel to England for abortions because abortion is illegal in Ireland. In the United States, we can imagine women seeking abortions in Canada if the Supreme Court overturned *Roe v. Wade*. Thus, restrictive laws can encourage patients to travel to more permissive jurisdictions.

Second, certain treatments may not be available when they have not been approved by regulators. In the United States, the Food and Drug Administration (FDA) must approve most medical technologies before they can be marketed. Many believe that a strict, lengthy FDA approval process delays the availability of cutting-edge medical technologies that are widely used overseas. American patients obtained a hip resurfacing surgery in Europe, Asia, and India that FDA had not approved until recently. Patients are keenly aware that foreign regulators have approved certain procedures that FDA has not. A patient that traveled to India for heart surgery testified to the U.S. Senate that "[p]rocedures are often available in developing countries years before the FDA approves them in the U.S." Whether it is wise or not, patients travel overseas for procedures that have not been approved by their domestic regulators.

Third, even in the absence of restrictive laws or regulations, non-governmental actors may ban certain medical procedures not as a matter of law, but as a matter of fact. Physicians, hospitals, and particularly insurers can decide to make a procedure unavailable. For example, in countries that do not legislate reproductive treatments, "each doctor and clinic decides autonomously whether to provide a certain type of treatment and whether to offer a service to a certain type of patient." In Mississippi, only one clinic is willing to perform abortions, even though decisions by the U.S. Supreme Court currently prohibit states from banning all abortion procedures outright. Perhaps more common is where a health insurer refuses to cover a particular treatment, whether because the insurer deems the procedure to be immoral, experimental (despite FDA approval), or not worth the expense compared to more established treatments. Thus, an insurer's decision to not cover a particular fertility treatment could lead those with insurance to travel overseas. The absence of laws and regulations leaves a void that non-governmental actors can fill at their discretion. Their decisions may drive patients to forum shop.

Fourth, certain procedures may be unavailable in certain countries that lack the requisite medical technology, expertise, or infrastructure. For example, patients from Bolivia, Peru, and Ecuador travel to Chile for its superior medical care. Indian hospitals attract 50,000 patients each year from Bangladesh. Jordanian hospitals attract medical tourists from Yemen, Sudan, Libya, Algeria, Tunisia, and Iraq. Since the 1970s, the EU recognized that some member states may have medical capabilities that other states lack, and has required states to permit their citizens to travel to other states for medical care when the treatment cannot be given domestically in a medically appropriate timeframe. Thus, variations in medical sophistication between countries can encourage medical tourism.

Finally, foreign doctors provide an outlet to patients in countries with socialized medicine that may have to wait several months for certain medical treatments. In the United Kingdom in 2004, the National Health Service (NHS) expected 41,000 patients to wait at least six months for various surgeries. In response, the NHS began sending patients to France, Spain, and Germany for orthopedic, eye, and other surgeries. As noted above, EU regulations require member states to reimburse for the medical treatments their citizens receive in other states if there is an "undue delay" in the patient's home country, given the patient's medical condition. Based on these regulations, the European Court of Justice recently required the NHS to reimburse a U.K. resident for a hip replacement she obtained in France, even though she failed to obtain prior authorization from the NHS. Thus, patients in countries with socialized medicine may travel to bypass long waiting lists.

2. Cost Discrepancies

Although most patients have traveled overseas for procedures that were not available, for one reason or another, where they resided, a new breed of patients is traveling to take advantage of the significant cost discrepancies between countries. In effect, these patients are engaging in international health care arbitrage.

Unsurprisingly, Americans can easily find less expensive medical care overseas. A World Bank study found that the costs of health care and insurance "are significantly higher in the U.S. than in a number of other countries." We spend far more on health care than even our peer countries. In 2000, we spent 44% more per capita on health care than the next highest spending country, Switzerland. That year, we spent 13% of our GDP on health care, significantly higher than Australia (8.3%), Canada (9.1%), Japan (7.8%), and the United Kingdom (7.3%).

These discrepancies are driven in substantial part by the cost of individual medical procedures. For example, the World Bank found that inpatient knee surgery costs over $10,000 on average in the United States, but is only $1,500 at the top hospitals in Hungary and India. A coronary artery bypass graft costs over $35,000 in the United States but is less than $9,000 (including travel expenses) at the top hospitals in India and Thailand. The WHO found that the cost of medical treatment in developing countries such as India can be 3–10% of the cost in the United States.

The World Bank compared the costs of the most common surgical procedures in the United States and in 20 developing countries. The authors used several criteria to identify medical procedures that patients could easily obtain overseas. For example, they searched for low-risk, non-emergency treatments with quick recovery periods. The authors applied these criteria to a list of 230 of the most commonly performed surgeries in U.S. hospitals and compared the mean and median prices for fifteen procedures in twenty countries. Factoring in the cost of round-trip airfare, the World Bank concluded that the United States could save $1.4 billion if only 10% of patients traveled for these fifteen procedures. Half of these savings ($690 million per year) would accrue to the Medicare program.

* * *

* * * For many patients, treatment overseas is the best option, and for some patients, it is the only option. A medical tourist testified to the U.S. Senate that he paid $6,700 for life-saving heart surgery in India because he could not afford the estimated $200,000 it would have cost in the United States. Similar stories abound. Put

simply, a growing number of patients are prepared to travel abroad for medical treatments. * * *

The following excerpt, from the most thorough treatment of the legal and ethical issues raised by medical tourism, highlights how various strains of patient travel require patients, providers, insurers, and policymakers to consider differences in law between jurisdictions. The excerpt below focuses on how the EU, as a supranational authority, has tried to manage patient mobility among member states, which largely involves patients traveling for treatment that would be legally provided in their home country (as opposed to traveling for treatment that is prohibited in the home country but permitted in the destination country, including variations such as "reproductive tourism," "stem cell tourism," and patients traveling for abortion or assisted suicide procedures, which raise a host of separate legal questions). One theme to keep in mind is how EU policy tries to balance the autonomy interests of Member States in managing their own domestic health care systems with the broader interests of the European community in harmonizing divergent local laws to ensure the free movement of persons, goods, and capital among Member States, as required by EU treaties.

I. Glenn Cohen, *Patients with Passports: Medical Tourism, Law and Ethics*

169–73, 186–87, 191, 194–96, 204–05 (2014)

Ch. 5: Medical Tourism through Public Health Insurance: The EU Model and Beyond

* * * In this chapter, we ... examine what happens when public health care systems deal with medical tourism. I will focus on the European Union (EU), which, for the last three decades, has struggled in setting the rules that dictate when Member States should reimburse their citizens for health care services obtained in another Member State: for example, when a citizen of Luxembourg seeks dental surgery in Germany.

* * *

I. A Brief Primer on Cross-Border Health Care in the European Union

A. The EU System

* * * The European Union has a number of EU level institutions, of which the Commission, the Council, the Parliament, and the European Court of Justice [ECJ] are the most important for our purposes. The Commission is responsible for promoting the general interests of the European Union, and can take appropriate initiatives to do so. It also oversees the application of the Treaties and the application of EU law under the control of the ECJ, and proposes the legislative acts of the EU. The Council and the Parliament are bodies that jointly adopt (or decline to adopt) legislation proposed by the Commission.

The EU Treaties are the primary law of the European Union, but the EU institutions have been granted certain competencies to enact secondary legislation. There are three main types of "secondary legislation" that the Council and Parliament can enact: Regulations, Directives, and Decisions. *Regulations* have general application and are immediately binding in their entirety upon all Member States of the European Union. *Directives*, by contrast, are only binding as to the result to be achieved, and leave to the Member States' discretion as to how the Directives' objectives are to be achieved. In other words, Member States must adopt appropriate domestic legislation to give effect to these directives within a specific time frame provided by the Directive in question, but the particular legislation they adopt will not be uniform. *Decisions* are immediately binding in their entirety upon Member States to whom they have been addressed.

The ECJ has the duty and jurisdiction to ensure "that in the interpretation and application of the Treaties the law is observed." The ECJ is also responsible for the issuance of preliminary rulings on the interpretation of the EU law and the validity of EU legislative acts. Among the key features of the ECJ system are a noncompliance procedure that authorizes the European Commission to challenge national policies that conflict with community rules, and a preliminary reference mechanism that sometimes permits or requires national courts to suspend legal proceedings and send questions of interpretation of community law to the ECJ.

B. EU Health Care Systems

The European Union has no single health care system. Instead, the Member States that make up the European Union retain competency in this area, and each provides health care to its nationals. * * *

* * * Providers can and do offer a vastly different array of services and technologies from one Member States to another, much more so than between U.S. states, for example. Because patients can move from one kind of system to another in seeking cross-border care, the interactions between these systems for EU medical tourism are potentially quite complex.

It is important to emphasize that nationals of Member States are free to obtain health care in another Member State if paid for privately. Therefore, the key question I will focus on in this chapter is when a patient's Member State of Affiliation is required to provide reimbursement for medical tourism to another Member State.

At the highest level, the problem medical tourism presses on the EU system is one of mediating between the sovereignty of Member States to organize their own social security systems—and in particular their conception of a right to health care access—with the EU's commitment to the free movement of persons, goods, and capital between the Member States and the freedom to provide and receive services. * * *

[The chapter proceeds to discuss in depth various EU treaties, secondary legislation, and opinions by the ECJ regarding emergency treatment and scheduled treatment in other Member States. These all preceded the EU Directive on Cross-Border Healthcare, Directive 2011/24/EU of the European Parliament and of the Council of 9 March 2011 on the Application of Patients' Rights in Cross Border Healthcare 2011 O.J. (L 88) 45, Art 3(c).]

III. The Post-2011 Landscape: The New EU Directive

The new EU Directive 2011/24 [...] purports to facilitate cross-border health care in the European Union, primarily in regard to the "scheduled care" case rather than the "emergency care" one. * * *

The Directive recognizes that Member States have exclusive responsibility for the organization and delivery of health care, and on the definition of social security benefits. The Directive takes into consideration the "operating principles" that are shared by health systems throughout the Union, and are necessary to ensure patients' trust in cross-border health care and to achieving patient mobility.

* * *

The Directive focuses on four topics. The first three are familiar from the EU case law: Prior Authorization, Reimbursement, and Patient Rights. It also provides a number of new initiatives that I group under the heading "Cooperation." * * *

A. Prior Authorization

At the threshold, the Directive answers one of the questions left open by the ECJ case law regarding the ability to impose pretreatment requirements, such as assessment by a health professional or health care administrator. The Member State of Affiliation is permitted to impose a pretreatment requirement as a condition of reimbursement for medical tourism if it would require the same pretreatment procedure to reimburse the same patient within its territory.

* * *

The Directive recognizes that the Member State "of Affiliation may provide for a system of prior authorization," but in accord with the ECJ case law [...], also recognizes that such a prior authorization system can serve as a barrier to the freedom to provide medical services. Therefore, following the ECJ case law, the Directive requires that prior authorization must be justified and restricted to what is necessary and proportionate to the objective to be achieved (e.g., financial balance of social security budget, needs for planning, etc.), and may not constitute a means of arbitrary discrimination or unjustified obstacle to the free movement of patients. * * *

B. Reimbursement

On the question of reimbursement (Article 7 of the Directive), the Directive again mostly accepts and reflects the ECJ case law [...].

The costs of the service provided in the Member State of Treatment will be reimbursed or paid directly by the home Member State of Affiliation "up to the level of costs that would have been assumed by the [home] state, had this healthcare been provided in its territory." * * * Under the Directive, in cases "[w]here the full cost of cross-border healthcare exceeds the level of costs that would have been assumed had the health care been provided in its territory," the Member State of Affiliation retains discretion to "top up" its reimbursement to make up the difference, but is not required to do so. Similarly, it is permitted, but not required, to decide to "reimburse other related costs, such as accommodation and travel costs, or extra costs which persons with disabilities might incur due to one or more disabilities when receiving" care in the destination country [...].

* * *

C. New Rights for Patients

The Directive quite self-consciously purports to take what has been called a patient-centered and needs-based approach, which the ECJ, as well as the European Commission, has consistently supported. Specifically, the Directive provides patients a number of new rights. Among these, it requires "healthcare providers [to] provide relevant information to help individual patients to make an informed choice, including on treatment options, on the availability, quality, and safety of the healthcare they provide in the Member State of treatment," as well as "provide clear invoices and clear information on prices, as well as on their authorisation or registration status, their insurance cover or other means of personal or collective protection with regard to professional liability." * * *

Second, it requires that Member States of Treatment provide "transparent complaints procedures and mechanisms in place for patients, in order for them to seek remedies in accordance with the legislation of the Member State of Treatment if they suffer harm arising from the healthcare they receive." * * *

Third, it requires that Member States of Treatment provide that "[s]ystems of professional liability insurance, or a guarantee or similar arrangement that is equivalent or essentially comparable as regards its purpose and which is appropriate to the nature and the extent of the risk, are in place for treatment provided on its territory."

Fourth, it guarantees some amount of data privacy, indicating that "the fundamental right to privacy with respect to the processing of personal data is protected in conformity with national measures implementing Union provisions on the protection of personal data."

Fifth, the Member State of Affiliation has a responsibility to ensure that, for individuals who seek treatment in another Member State, if "medical follow-up [care] proves necessary, the same medical follow-up is available as would have been if that healthcare had been provided on its territory," such that they will not be disadvantaged in that follow-up care as compared to those who were not medical tourists. * * *

In theory, these rights could mean a lot for patients. They could require changes in patient safety requirements, transparency on morbidity and mortality outcome data as well as pricing, alternative dispute or other means of settling malpractice and other disputes, and ways of facilitating the interoperability of health records and follow-up care. * * *

D. Cooperation

Finally, the Directive initiates a number of additional initiatives to foster cooperative links between Member States on cross-border health care. These include the following:

The Member States must render mutual assistance, as it is necessary for the implementation of the Directive (including standards and guideline formation); Member States are obliged to recognize prescriptions issued in another Member State for medicinal products when their products are authorized to be marketed in their territory; the Directive enables the voluntary development of European reference networks between health care providers and centers of expertise in the Member States; the Commission will support Member States in cooperating in the development of diagnosis and treatment capacity of rare diseases; the European Union will support cooperation and exchange of information among Member States working within a voluntary network connecting national authorities responsible for "eHealth."

* * *

VI. Conclusion

In this period of economic recession, the United States and many other countries are looking for ways to trim the costs of their social welfare programs, and, given demographic trends, publicly subsidized health insurance plans present a clear target of opportunity. * * *

Although publicly insured medical tourism [is] in its very nascent stages in the United States, Europe has had more than three decades of experience with patients traveling from one EU Member State to another for health care. * * *

Notes

1. Lisa Ikemoto, among others, discusses the inequality concerns with reproductive tourism, including its effect on access to health care in destination countries, the unique risks to women and racial minorities, and potential exploitative practices. *See, e.g.*, Lisa Ikemoto, *Reproductive Tourism: Equality Concerns in the Global Market for Fertility Services*, 27 Law & Inequality 277 (2009), excerpted in Chapter 3 at [[add page # ref]]. Other scholars similarly explore the ethical implications of leaving one jurisdiction for another that permits dramatically different treatments. *See, e.g.*, I. Glenn Cohen, *Circumvention Tourism*, 97 Cornell Law Review 1309 (2012); I. Glenn Cohen, *Transplant Tourism: The Ethics and Regulation of International Markets for Organs*, 41 Journal of Law, Medicine, and Ethics 269 (2013); Kimberly M. Mutcherson, *Welcome to the Wild West: Protecting Access to Cross Border Fertility Care in the United States*, 22 Cornell Journal of Law and Public Policy 349 (2012).

2. Other excellent and expansive evaluations of the legal and ethical implications of cross-border health care include *Dialogue on Cross-Border Health Care*, 26(3) Wisconsin International Law Journal (2008) (symposium); *The Globalization of Health Care: Legal and Ethical Issues* (I. Glenn Cohen ed., 2013); I. Glenn Cohen, *Patients with Passports: Medical Tourism, Law, and Ethics* (2015).

Chapter 2

The Rights of Patients in Relationship with Health Care Professionals and Institutions

A. Patients' Rights

Although historically the relationship between health care professionals and patients has been paternalistic, most western countries now recognize at least in principle the notion of patients' rights. This chapter explores the most important of these rights: the right to receive competent care; the right to consent to treatment; the right to confidentiality; and the right to access one's own medical information. We begin with a comparative discussion of how various European countries formally recognize patients' rights, followed by the articulation of patients' rights formulated by two international bodies: the World Health Organization's European Region and the World Medical Association.

Lars Fallberg, *Citizens' Choice and Patients' Rights*

World Health Organization, Regional Office for Europe, Copenhagen,
European Health Care Reforms,
Chapter One, Patients' Rights, 11, 12–15 (1996)

* * *

The rights of patients and patient-centred care are concepts which are now stressed in almost every European country. Some have come farther than others. This status has to do with new factors such as culture, organization of health care, financing, legal traditions, power of actors, etc. The use of "push" principles are of interest in the sense that laws and normative rules have to influence and change a traditional, well-rooted health care system. This is influenced to a large extent by "paternalistic" views. The other side of the change process is that of patients. They have been, and are to a large extent obedient. In order to change this attitude, terminology such as "health consumers" and "users" are being used as an alternative for "patients." The use of such terminology is, however, criticized by some patient organizations as well as by groups of health care personnel.

Patient organizations are somewhat afraid that "strong" groups and individuals will gain more from such a change in terminology. It is reminiscent of market terminology, with negative connotations. This is partly supported by an analysis of Norwegian health care legislation where persons with certain diagnoses have legal entitlements to care within six months. It seems natural that the more severe diagnosis a patient has, the earlier he or she will receive treatment, provided the treatment is likely to succeed. An analysis of patients waiting for treatments of various kinds illustrates that psychiatric patients were "parked" on the lowest level without any entitlements whatsoever. A conclusion is that "patients' rights" have to be closely and continuously monitored and altered. A risk is that weak groups will tend to be forgotten in relation to more articulate citizens with well defined diagnoses.

In order to describe the development of patients' rights, it is necessary to have a "common language." For some people, patients' rights are related to legal rights where the key question is whether the right is enforceable in court or not. * * * In general, it is fair to say that patient rights are a combination of legislation and principles including ethical guidelines for different professional groups. The judicial part of the term includes civil rights for patients, material procedural as well as and duties for health care personnel, often interpreted as "rights" for patients. Principles on patients' rights are based on general agreements, consensus and the will to live up to agreed principles.

Depending on tradition and culture, the two patients' rights tools are used differently in various countries. The idea of general principles related to more defined forms of care guarantee is used in the Nordic countries. The principles are often national and improved in the County Council or municipality depending on regional conditions. Similar to the Nordic approach is that of the national patient charter, used in the UK. The Patient Charter, however, contains more defined principles, partly replacing similar legal provisions. The aim is to set a national minimum level of care and treatment.

Patient Charters are also used by East European countries as an effective way to promote the rights of patients. Civil legislation is perhaps most commonly used in the northern European countries. The general principle is to let patients choose and provide legal provisions in order to safe keep rights. Regardless of whether legislation, guidelines or principles are used to promote the situation of patients, it has to be used in consensus with all parties involved in providing health services.

* * *

The Nordic countries (Denmark, Finland, Iceland, Norway and Sweden) are characterized by administrative legislation which emphasizes the duties of the physicians and other professional groups rather than the rights of patients. Even if they are two sides of the same coin, there is a fundamental difference in that professional legal duties can not be enforced by patients, contrary to legal rights. The rights of various kinds which are expressed in health legislation are largely related to patient autonomy and access to information. There is no tradition of any considerable extent of civil court procedures. However, it is possible to seek compensation via the tort system. In all Nordic countries except Iceland there is some kind of "No fault patient insurance scheme" where patients are financially compensated for injuries received through health care services. The schemes are implemented in law or as an agreement between care providers and the state. The investigation regarding injuries is free of charge to the patient and is made by a patient insurance association. * * * Special legal (civil) entitlements to care are not to be found in Scandinavia. However, there is a tradition to use "principal documents" or "care guarantees" quasi rights. They give patients access to health care within a set time frame under certain circumstances, for defined illnesses and within the frame of available government resources. There are usually no sanctions when the obligation is not fulfilled, but the time limits are generally respected by health care providers and hospitals. Some Swedish County Councils have additional "rights" which compensate the patient when, for example, the doctor is more than 30 minutes late for an appointment.

Scandinavian medical associations are traditionally powerful in health policy. Their declared ambition is to work in favour of empowered patients. The influence of the many hundred patients organizations is acknowledged by the governments from which they receive considerable financial support. The major organizations are often heard when there is a patient related bill in the Parliament. There is no tradition of private fund-raising in Scandinavian patient organizations, * * *.

Northern Europe except the Nordic countries (Netherlands, Germany, Belgium, Luxembourg) have a similar organization for health care: as various forms of competing sickness funds and a choice of hospital organizations. This means a market influenced health care system where what in Germany is called *Krankenkasse* acts as purchaser and financier of health services. The legislation empowers patients somewhat differently in these countries. In the Netherlands patients' rights are implemented by legislation as well as by principal documents. In the Act on Medical Treatment Contracts from 1995 the objective is to strengthen the legal position of patients and the law compares to an ordinary tenancy agreement or employment contract. In Germany the rights of patients are not emphasized in the same way, which to some extent may depend on a strong medical profession with, as it seems, a relatively paternalistic view. The most active patient organizations are to be found in the Netherlands where patient perspectives play an important role, based on a strong consumer organizations representing over two million consumers.

In the United Kingdom the national Patients' Charter has had a major impact on public awareness of the performance of health care providers. It was launched in 1991 as a management tool for improving standards. It is described as part of an overall trend to improve the quality of health services and give more value to the views of patients and carers. The charter does not include any entitlements to health care and can be described as a statement of fundamental principles. The national Patients' Charter outlined ten "rights" and nine national standards such as the right to register with a general practitioner, to information, to be treated with dignity, etc. As an effect of this "charterism," several care providers have adopted local charters with various kinds of principles, originating, however, from the national charter. Yet the legal right of individuals to health care service, enforceable in court, is not emphasized in the United Kingdom. In general, the objective is to set a minimum standard throughout the country with local improvements.

Patient organizations and self-help groups in the United Kingdom receive little financial support from the government. Fund-raising is necessary and the financial frames of these organizations' activities are often narrow. The day-to-day work in the organizations is active and several of them provide a range of services to members as well as non-members. The hot-lines are popular and some organizations, such as the British Diabetic Association, help its members to get cheap insurance etc.

In southern Europe (Portugal, Italy, Greece, Spain) patients and consumers have a broad range of rights and principles. Health care providers and national authorities are active in developing and promoting various charters for patients rights. Legislation also explicitly provides citizens with certain rights. However, due to financial reasons, culture etc. these rights are not linked to sanctions if not fulfilled. The consequence of this is that existing rights are not fully taken advantage of by patients, nor are they respected by care providers and others.

Former socialist block countries (Hungary, Rumania, Russia, Lithuania) had for decades organized their health care services in a centralized way with practically no regard for the rights of patients. If there were any in the previous systems, they existed on paper and were rarely implemented in practice. However, recent developments have made these countries aware of the importance of patient centred care and the empowerment of patients. In order to keep pace with other European countries, several former East European countries are working on patients' right legislation and patients' rights charters, etc. Characteristic of this development is that the ambitions of politicians and legislators do not fit together economic resources and health services practice. One illustrative example is Lithuania. In 1994 the Health System Law was adopted. It contained a few citizens' rights such as a right to choose health care facility and health care provider, a right to information about ones' health status, a right to certain medical services, etc. Because of a wide gap between ambitions and primary conditions, the law had to be altered and the ambitions lowered one year later.

In other cases, ambitious declarations on the rights of patients have been made but have not reached the individual citizen. Behind these high ambitions is the pressure from other European countries to hasten the process of democratisation.

* * *

World Medical Association Declaration on the Rights of the Patient

Adopted by the 34th World Medical Assembly, Lisbon, Portugal, September/October 1981, amended by the 47th General Assembly, Bali, Indonesia, September 1995, editorially revised by the 171st WMA Council Session, Santiago, Chile, October 2005, and reaffirmed by the 200th WMA Council Session, Oslo, Norway, April 2015

Preamble

The relationship between physicians, their patients and broader society has undergone significant changes in recent times. While a physician should always act according to his/her conscience, and always in the best interests of the patient, equal effort must be made to guarantee patient autonomy and justice. The following Declaration represents some of the principal rights of the patient that the medical profession endorses and promotes. Physicians and other persons or bodies involved in the provision of health care have a joint responsibility to recognize and uphold these rights. Whenever legislation, government action or any other administration or institution denies patients these rights, physicians should pursue appropriate means to assure or to restore them.

Principles

1. Right to medical care of good quality
   a. Every person is entitled without discrimination to appropriate medical care.
   b. Every patient has the right to be cared for by a physician whom he/she knows to be free to make clinical and ethical judgements without any outside interference.
   c. The patient shall always be treated in accordance with his/her best interests. The treatment applied shall be in accordance with generally approved medical principles.
   d. Quality assurance should always be a part of health care. Physicians, in particular, should accept responsibility for being guardians of the quality of medical services.
   e. In circumstances where a choice must be made between potential patients for a particular treatment that is in limited supply, all such patients are entitled to a fair selection procedure for that treatment. That choice must be based on medical criteria and made without discrimination.
   f. The patient has the right to continuity of health care. The physician has an obligation to cooperate in the coordination of medically indicated care with other health care providers treating the patient. The physician may not discontinue treatment of a patient as long as further treatment is medically indicated, without giving the patient reasonable assistance and sufficient opportunity to make alternative arrangements for care.

2. Right to freedom of choice
   a. The patient has the right to choose freely and change his/her physician and hospital or health service institution, regardless of whether they are based in the private or public sector.
   b. The patient has the right to ask for the opinion of another physician at any stage.
3. Right to self-determination
   a. The patient has the right to self-determination, to make free decisions regarding himself/herself. The physician will inform the patient of the consequences of his/her decisions.
   b. A mentally competent adult patient has the right to give or withhold consent to any diagnostic procedure or therapy. The patient has the right to the information necessary to make his/her decisions. The patient should understand clearly what is the purpose of any test or treatment, what the results would imply, and what would be the implications of withholding consent.
   c. The patient has the right to refuse to participate in research or the teaching of medicine.

* * *

6. Procedures against the patient's will

   Diagnostic procedures or treatment against the patient's will can be carried out only in exceptional cases, if specifically permitted by law and conforming to the principles of medical ethics.
7. Right to information
   a. The patient has the right to receive information about himself/herself recorded in any of his/her medical records, and to be fully informed about his/her health status including the medical facts about his/her condition. However, confidential information in the patient's records about a third party should not be given to the patient without the consent of that third party.
   b. Exceptionally, information may be withheld from the patient when there is good reason to believe that this information would create a serious hazard to his/her life or health.
   c. Information should be given in a way appropriate to the patient's culture and in such a way that the patient can understand. * * *

* * *

8. Right to confidentiality
   a. All identifiable information about a patient's health status, medical condition, diagnosis, prognosis and treatment and all other information of a personal kind must be kept confidential, even after death. Exceptionally, descendants may have a right of access to information that would inform them of their health risks.

b. Confidential information can only be disclosed if the patient gives explicit consent or if expressly provided for in the law. Information can be disclosed to other health care providers only on a strictly "need to know" basis unless the patient has given explicit consent.

c. All identifiable patient data must be protected. The protection of the data must be appropriate to the manner of its storage. Human substances from which identifiable data can be derived must be likewise protected.

9. Right to health education

Every person has the right to health education that will assist him/her in making informed choices about personal health and about the available health services. The education should include information about healthy lifestyles and about methods of prevention and early detection of illnesses. The personal responsibility of everybody for his/her own health should be stressed. Physicians have an obligation to participate actively in educational efforts.

10. Right to dignity

a. The patient's dignity and right to privacy shall be respected at all times in medical care and teaching, as shall his/her culture and values.

b. The patient is entitled to relief of his/her suffering according to the current state of knowledge.

c. The patient is entitled to humane terminal care and to be provided with all available assistance in making dying as dignified and comfortable as possible.

* * *

A Declaration on the Promotion of Patients' Rights in Europe, 1994

World Health Organization, European Office

* * *

In the treatment of patients' rights, a distinction should be made between social and individual rights. Social rights in health care relate to the societal obligation undertaken or otherwise enforced by government and other public or private bodies to make reasonable provision of health care for the whole population. What is reasonable in terms of the volume and range of services available and the degree of sophistication of technology and specialization will be dependent on political, social, cultural and economic factors. Social rights also relate to equal access to health care for all those living in a country or other geopolitical area and the elimination of unjustified discriminatory barriers, whether financial, geographical, cultural or social and psychological.

Social rights are enjoyed collectively and are relative to the level of development of the particular society; they are also in some measure subject to political judgement regarding priorities for development in a society.

In contrast, individual rights in patient care are more readily expressed in absolute terms and when made operational can be made enforceable on behalf of an individual patient. These rights cover such areas as the integrity of the person, privacy and religious convictions. Although this text does address social rights, the main focus is on individual rights. * * * The intention is not to create new rights but to apply them in one coherent, comprehensive statement to the field of patients and health care. For similar reasons the text does not address general rights, obligations and liabilities, which are covered by the statutes and case law of each country.

The Rights of Patients

1. *Human rights and values in health care*

The instruments cited in the Introduction [i.e. the international conventions listed in Chapter 1 Section A above] should be understood as applying also specifically in the health care setting, and it should therefore be noted that the human values expressed in the instruments shall be reflected in the health care system. It should also be noted that where exceptional limitations are imposed on the rights of patients, these must be in accordance with human rights instruments and have a legal base in the law of the country. It may be further observed that the rights specified below carry a matching responsibility to act with due concern for the health of others and for their same rights.

1.1 Everyone has the right to respect of his or her person as a human being.

1.2 Everyone has the right to self-determination.

1.3 Everyone has the right to physical and mental integrity and to the security of his or her person.

1.4 Everyone has the right to respect for his or her privacy.

1.5 Everyone has the right to have his or her moral and cultural values and religious and philosophical convictions respected.

1.6 Everyone has the right to such protection of health as is afforded by appropriate measures for disease prevention and health care, and to the opportunity to pursue his or her own highest attainable level of health.

2. *Information*

2.1 Information about health services and how best to use them is to be made available to the public in order to benefit all those concerned.

2.2 Patients have the right to be fully informed about their health status, including the medical facts about their condition; about the proposed medical procedures, together with the potential risks and benefits of each procedure; about alternatives to the proposed procedures, including the effect of non-treatment; and about the diagnosis, prognosis and progress of treatment.

2.3 Information may only be withheld from patients exceptionally when there is good reason to believe that this information would without any expectation of obvious positive effects cause them serious harm.

2.4 Information must be communicated to the patient in a way appropriate to the latter's capacity for understanding, minimizing the use of unfamiliar technical terminology. If the patient does not speak the common language, some form of interpreting should be available.

2.5 Patients have the right not to be informed, at their explicit request.

2.6 Patients have the right to choose who, if anyone, should be informed on their behalf.

2.7 Patients should have the possibility of obtaining a second opinion.

2.8 When admitted to a health care establishment, patients should be informed of the identity and professional status of the health care providers taking care of them and of any rules and routines which would bear on their stay and care.

2.9 Patients should be able to request and be given a written summary of their diagnosis, treatment and care on discharge from a health care establishment.

3. *Consent*

3.1 The informed consent of the patient is a prerequisite for any medical intervention.

3.2 A patient has the right to refuse or to halt a medical intervention. The implications of refusing or halting such an intervention must be carefully explained to the patient.

3.3 When a patient is unable to express his or her will and a medical intervention is urgently needed, the consent of the patient may be presumed, unless it is obvious from a previous declared expression of will that consent would be refused in the situation.

* * *

3.7 In all other situations where the patient is unable to give informed consent and where there is no legal representative or representative designated by the patient for this purpose, appropriate measures should be taken to provide for a substitute decision making process, taking into account what is known and, to the greatest extent possible, what may be presumed about the wishes of the patient.

3.8 The consent of the patient is required for the preservation and use of all substances of the human body. Consent may be presumed when the substances are to be used in the current course of diagnosis, treatment and care of that patient.

3.9 The informed consent of the patient is needed for participation in clinical teaching.

3.10 The informed consent of the patient is a prerequisite for participation in scientific research. All protocols must be submitted to proper ethical review procedures. Such research should not be carried out on those who are unable to express their will, unless the consent of a legal representative has been obtained and the research would likely be in the interest of the patient.

* * *

4. *Confidentiality and Privacy*

4.1 All information about a patient's health status, medical condition, diagnosis, prognosis and treatment and all other information of a personal kind must be kept confidential, even after death.

4.2 Confidential information can only be disclosed if the patient gives explicit consent or if the law expressly provides for this. Consent may be presumed where disclosure is to other health care providers involved in that patient's treatment.

4.3 All identifiable patient data must be protected. The protection of the data must be appropriate to the manner of their storage. Human substances from which identifiable data can be derived must be likewise protected.

4.4 Patients have the right to access to their medical files and technical records and to any other files and records pertaining to their diagnosis, treatment and care and to receive a copy of their own files and records or parts thereof. Such access excludes data concerning third parties.

4.5 Patients have the right to require the correction, completion, deletion, clarification and/or updating of personal and medical data concerning them which are inaccurate, incomplete, ambiguous or outdated, or which are not relevant to the purposes of diagnosis, treatment and care.

4.6 There can be no intrusion into a patient's private and family life unless and only if, in addition to the patient consenting to it, it can be justified as necessary to the patient's diagnosis, treatment and care.

4.7 Medical interventions may only be carried out when there is proper respect shown for the privacy of the individual. This means that a given intervention may be carried out only in the presence of those persons who are necessary for the intervention unless the patient consents or requests otherwise.

4.8 Patients admitted to health care establishments have the right to expect physical facilities which ensure privacy, particularly when health care providers are offering them personal care or carrying out examinations and treatment.

5. *Care and Treatment*

5.1 Everyone has the right to receive such health care as is appropriate to his or her health needs, including preventive care and activities aimed at health promotion. Services should be continuously available and accessible to all equitably, without discrimination and according to the financial, human and material resources which can be made available in a given society.

5.2 Patients have a collective right to some form of representation at each level of the health care system in matters pertaining to the planning and evaluation of services, including the range, quality and functioning of the care provided.

5.3 Patients have the right to a quality of care which is marked both by high technical standards and by a humane relationship between the patient and health care providers.

5.4 Patients have the right to continuity of care, including cooperation between all health care providers and/or establishments which may be involved in their diagnosis, treatment and care.

5.5 In circumstances where a choice must be made by providers between potential patients for a particular treatment which is in limited supply, all such patients are entitled to a fair selection procedure for that treatment. That choice must be based on medical criteria and made without discrimination.

5.6 Patients have the right to choose and change their own physician or other health care provider and health care establishment, provided that it is compatible with the functioning of the health care system.

5.7 Patients for whom there are no longer medical grounds for continued stay in a health care establishment are entitled to a full explanation before they can be transferred to another establishment or sent home. Transfer can only take place after another health care establishment has agreed to accept the patient. Where the patient is discharged to home and when his or her condition so requires, community and domiciliary services should be available.

5.8 Patients have the right to be treated with dignity in relation to their diagnosis, treatment and care, which should be rendered with respect for their culture and values.

5.9 Patients have the right to enjoy support from family, relatives and friends during the course of care and treatment and to receive spiritual support and guidance at all times.

5.10 Patients have the right to relief of their suffering according to the current state of knowledge.

5.11 Patients have the right to humane terminal care and to die in dignity.

6. *Application*

6.1 The exercise of the rights set forth in this document implies that appropriate means are established for this purpose.

6.2 The enjoyment of these rights shall be secured without discrimination.

6.3 In the exercise of these rights, patients shall be subjected only to such limitations as are compatible with human rights instruments and in accordance with a procedure prescribed by law.

6.4 If patients cannot avail themselves of the rights set forth in this document, these rights should be exercised by their legal representative or by a person designated by the patient for that purpose; where neither a legal representative nor a personal surrogate has been appointed, other measures for representation of those patients should be taken.

6.5 Patients must have access to such information and advice as will enable them to exercise the rights set forth in this document. Where patients feel that their rights have not been respected they should be enabled to lodge a complaint. In addition to recourse to the courts, there should be independent mechanisms at institutional and other levels to facilitate the processes of lodging, mediating and adjudicating complaints. These mechanisms would, inter alia, ensure that information relating to complaints procedures was available to patients and that an independent person was available and accessible to them for consultation regarding the most appropriate course of action to take. These mechanisms should further ensure that, where necessary, assistance and advocacy on behalf of the patient would be made available. Patients have the right to have their complaints examined and dealt with in a thorough, just, effective and prompt way and to be informed about their outcome.

Tamara K. Hervey & Jean V. McHale, *Rights: Mobile Patients' Rights as Human Rights*

European Union Health Law: Themes and Implications, 185–89, (2015)

* * *

Patients' Rights in International and Comparative Contexts

The EU legislature adopted the Patients' Rights Directive 2011/24/EU in response to the uncertainty engendered by decisions of the [Court of Justice of the European Union] concerning the rights of patients to receive cross-border health care services, under EU law on free movement of services. * * *

* * *

The notion of patients' rights had already appeared in some EU policy documentation before 2008. For instance, the important 2006 Council Conclusions on Common values and principles in European Union Health Systems noted that some Member States had expressed the value of equity (equal access to healthcare according to need, regardless of ethnicity, gender, age, social status, or ability to pay) in terms of patients' rights. The Council Conclusions note that rights to redress if things go wrong and rights to privacy and confidentiality are important "operating principles," shared across the EU's Member States. In 2008, the European Economic and Social Committee (an EU institution that advises the EU legislature) adopted its opinion on patients' rights. This opinion refers to the work of the umbrella NGO, the "Active Citizenship Network," which brings together national citizens' NGOs, which had adopted a "European Charter of Patients' Rights" in 2002. In turn, this document refers to the work of the Council of Europe and the WHO on patients' rights, undertaken during the 1990s.

Following a quite extensive consultation and data gathering exercise, WHO (Europe) adopted a Declaration on the Promotion of Patients' Rights in Europe in 1994. The Declaration was supposed to inspire national patients' rights policies, in the context of emergent healthcare system reforms. The Declaration explicitly calls for cooperation between WHO (Europe), the Council of Europe and the EU, in the area of patients' rights. The Council of Europe's Convention on Human Rights and Biomedicine in 1997 echoes many of the patients' rights found in WHO (Europe's) Declaration.

Feeding into and flowing from the work of the WHO and Council of Europe, several Member States of the EU have developed patients' rights instruments. Finland adopted a Patients' Rights Law in 1992, the Netherlands in 1995, Lithuania in 1996, Denmark in 1998, Belgium in 2002, France in 2002, Bulgaria in 2004, Cyprus in 2005, and Slovenia in 2008. Hungary's Law on Rights and Obligations of Healthcare Workers, Estonia's Law of Obligations Act 2001 and the Scottish Government's consultation on patients' rights and responsibilities mainly express patients' rights in terms of duties of healthcare professionals, but contain many of the same ideas. Many of the relevant national instruments, such as the Netherlands Medical Checks Law 1997, the Danish Order no. 665 of 14 September 1998 on Information and Consent and the Communication of Information Relating to Health, Finland's Personal Data Law 1999, Italy's 1999 Decree-Law on Health-related Personal Data, and Spain's Patients' Autonomy and Rights Law 2002, implement the EU's Data Protection Directive, and focus primarily on rights to health information privacy.

All of these international and policy strands converge around a consensus of three basic types of patients' rights: to privacy and confidentiality; to dignity, especially to consent to or refuse treatment; and to be informed (or choose not to be informed) about risk. Notably, none of these types of patients' rights reflects the collectively enjoyed social right to health care; on the contrary, all are expressions of individual rights, to be enjoyed and enforced by individual patients. This aspect of patients' rights is reflected in the Patients' Rights Directive. The Directive sets out responsibilities of the Member States with regard to cross-border health care, distinguishing between the obligations of the Member State of treatment (where the cross-border healthcare takes place) and those of the Member State of affiliation (where the patient is "insured" or part of a national health system). Member States of affiliation must reimburse the cost of cross-border healthcare, giving individual patients a (limited) right to such healthcare. * * * Patients' rights to information feature strongly. Member States of affiliation must provide information about rights and entitlements to reimbursement for cross-border healthcare, and mechanisms for enforcement of those rights. Member States of treatment must set up "national contact points" to provide information on patients' rights, treatment options, quality and safety standards in healthcare, prices, authorization systems, and system of professional liability. This information is supposed to "help individual patients make an informed choice." The right to privacy also features strongly, with multiple references to the protection of personal data, as found in the EU Charter of Fundamental Rights, Article 8, and Directive 95/46/EC. Patients have the right to access their medical records (an obligation of the Member State of affiliation); and to access the record of their cross-border treatment (an obligation of the Member State of treatment). To stress the individual nature of these rights, the Directive requires that patients be given information on dispute settlement procedures, complaints procedures and remedies.

The version of patients' rights reflected in this strand of EU law and policy is thus strongly individuated, focused on the central value of patient choice (instrumentalized through the requirement to give patients information), and concerned with enforcement of individual rights. Rights in the sense of human rights are presented as individual civil and political rights, in particular the right to privacy and to human dignity (consent). There is very little attention to patients' rights as a collective phenomenon, as part of national health systems, which are themselves part of national welfare or social security systems. This latter aspect of patients' rights is, however, reflected in the second strand that feeds into EU law and policy on patients' rights, that of coordination of social security entitlements.

* * *

Notes

1. The World Medical Association is an association of the world's doctors, represented by the medical associations of the various nations. The World Health Organization is the official organ of the United Nations that focuses on health issues. The European Regional Office in Copenhagen has been a leader in promoting patients' rights.

2. Compare and contrast the WHO's and WMA's statements on patients' rights. On the surface they are very similar. Compare, however, their different specifications of the information necessary for informed consent, of rights to medical records, of abandonment or discharge. Look at the order in which rights are presented. Who are the audiences to which these statements are addressed? Who are the constituents whom these statements serve?

3. How should patients' rights be enforced? What form of enforcement is contemplated by the WMA patients' rights statement? What form of enforcement do the WHO guidelines suggest? Statements of patients' rights are found both in legislation and professional codes. The former emphasizes the rights of patients, the latter the duties of professionals. What difference does it make which approach is taken? Several countries, most notably the United Kingdom, have adopted "Patient Charters"— statements of patient rights that are not specifically subject to judicial enforcement. What would be the benefit of this approach?

4. The EU has been active in expanding patients' rights in light of new developments, such as technological advances in the biosciences and patient travel between Member States. In 1997, the Council of Europe adopted the Convention on Human Rights and Biomedicine, with the stated goal of preventing the "misuse of biological and medical advances." Council of Europe, Convention for the Protection of Human Rights and Dignity of the Human Being with regard to the Application of Biology and Medicine, Oviedo 4.IV.97, ETS 164. And in 2011, the EU adopted a Directive on Patients' Rights in Cross-Border Health Care, though it focuses primarily on the right to receive health care in other Member States without overly restrictive rules on prior authorization by the home state. See Directive 2011/24/EU [2011] OJ L88/45. For an explanation of the complex interplay between the case law, regulations, and directives here, see Tamara K. Hervey & Jean V. McHale, *European Union Health Law: Themes and Implications* 73–97 (Cambridge 2015). Other gestures, like the United Nations Educational, Scientific, and Cultural Organization's (UNESCO's) *International Declaration on Human Genetic Data* (2003) and its *Universal Declaration on Bioethics and Human Rights* (2005), also tackle patients' rights in more specific contexts.

5. In many countries, patient advocacy and self-help groups, often disease specific, play an important role in realizing rights. In some countries, such as the Scandinavian countries, these groups receive public support. In other countries, such as the U.K., they engage extensively in fund-raising activities (most conspicuously operating used clothing stores). A coalition of patients' rights organizations, the Active Citizenship Network, has drafted a European Charter of Patients' Rights (2002) and monitors compliance by European countries with this charter. See Allessandro Lamanna, Giovanni Moro and Melody Ross, *Citizens' Report on the Implementation of the European Charter of Patients' Rights* (2005), http://www.activecitizenship.net/documenti/patients_rights/ACN%20Working%20Paper.pdf. The rights included in this charter include the

- right to prevention,
- right to access (including financial and physical access),
- right to information,
- right to free choice,
- right to consent,
- right to privacy and confidentiality,
- right to respect of patients' time,
- right to the observance of quality standards,
- right to safety,
- right to innovation,
- right to avoid unnecessary suffering and pain,
- right to personalized treatment (with attention to diversity),

- right to complain, and
- right to compensation.

How and why does this list of rights differ from those set out above?

6. Many countries (and in particular countries with national health services) have ombudspersons or special administrative bodies charged with receiving, investigating, and resolving patient complaints. What advantages might administrative complaint mechanisms provide over compensation systems, usually administered through the courts? What weaknesses might they have compared to judicial remedies?

7. In the United States, federal patients' rights legislation exists only for nursing home residents (See 42 U.S.C.A. §§ 1395i-3(d); 1396r(d)). However, the Affordable Care Act of 2010 (ACA) created various statutory rights vis-à-vis private health insurers. Moreover, the Joint Commission, which accredits virtually all hospitals in the United States, includes patients' rights requirements among its accreditation requirements. Many hospitals have patients' rights statements as well. Some states also have patients' rights statutes or regulations. Unless a breach of patients' rights by an institution amounts to malpractice and results in serious injury, however, enforcement of patients' rights is difficult.

8. In a number of nations, recipients of medical care are increasingly referred to as "consumers" rather than patients. "Consumer-driven" health care has been a longstanding fad in the United States, particularly among conservatives. See Timothy Jost, *Health Care at Risk: A Critique of the Consumer-Driven Movement* (2007). What difference does it make whether patients are considered to be patients or consumers? Many EU countries have enacted reforms intended to give patients more economic incentives to economize, such as co-payments and cost-sharing obligations, sometimes inspired by countries like the United States. Ironically, efforts to promote health care consumerism and market competition have both driven and undermined broader reforms in the United States. *See* Nathan Cortez, The Elusive Ideal of Market Competition in United States Health Care, *Health Care and EU Law* 359–83 (2011); Daniel Callahan & Angela A. Wasunna, *Medicine and the Market: Equity v. Choice* (2006).

B. The Right to Be Free from Medical Negligence

1. Civil Liability

In most countries of the world, medical professionals and institutions can face civil liability for injuring their patients through negligence. But causes of action can differ significantly between common law and civil code countries. Common law jurisdictions typically impose liability through the common law of tort, with judicial opinions establishing legal duties and tests for identifying a standard of care. Civil code countries, by contrast, typically impose liability through contract law, often called the law of "obligations."

Cour de Cassation of France

1st Civil Chamber, Decision of 25 February 1997
(translated by Pierrick LeGoff)

On the motion to overrule the decision of the Court of Appeals, the following was decided:

Whereas, according to the facts established in the judgment rendered by the judges of the Court of First Instance, Mr. Mazoyer, surgeon, performed surgery at the Engene Andre clinic on September 15, 1987, on Mr. Goenvic, a civil servant working for the city of Lyon. The surgery was performed under local anesthesia and was intended to eliminate a carotid fistula by the use of an inflatable and releasable balloon. While the balloon was being put in place, it became evident that it was necessary to modify the position of the balloon by deflating it. This could only be done by piercing the balloon; therefore the surgeon attempted to retrieve the balloon.

During this procedure, the deflated balloon detached itself from the carrying catheter and entered into the internal carotid artery. From there, it entered into the mid cerebral artery which became obstructed. This resulted in an emiplegia (paralysis of the right side of the body) even though the patient was immediately transported to a neurological hospital and underwent surgery intended to unblock the artery. M. Goenvic and his employer have initiated litigation against Mr. Mazoyer, the clinic, and the clinic's insurer to recover compensation for the damage suffered. Based on the report issued by two medical experts and the contrary report issued by three other medical experts, the Court of Appeals of Lyon (decision of 10 November 1994) rejected the compensation claim on the ground that neither medical malpractice nor defective medical equipment were present, and that the incident suffered by Mr. Goenvic was to be viewed as the materialization of a risk inherent in any surgery.

Whereas, the city of Lyon and Mr. Goenvic have filed a motion to overrule the decision rendered by the Court of Appeals of Lyon arguing (i) that the surgeon who uses a device to be placed inside the body of the patient is bound by an "obligation of result" as far as the safety of the patient is concerned and (ii) that having concluded that there was a problem with the balloon used by the surgeon, since it could not be deflated during the normal course of the surgery and had detached itself from the carrying catheter, the Court of Appeals should have decided that Mr. Mazoyer did not comply with the "obligation of result" concerning the safety of his patient, and did not need to investigate further whether the balloon was affected by a defect. According to the plaintiffs, it would follow therefrom that the Court did not draw the conclusions it should have in the light of article 1147 of the Civil Code.

Whereas, however, a surgeon who places a device in a patient is only bound by an "obligation of means." Whereas, further, the Court of Appeals, having due regard to the reports of the medical experts, concluded (i) that in view of the pathology of the patient, the medical procedure used was not only justified but also was the best one under the current state of medical knowledge, (ii) that the equipment used was free from any defect, and (iii) that the surgeon had checked the equipment prior to its use in the particular case by testing the balloon. The surgeon therefore took all standard precautions recommended in the medical field for such situations. Based again on the experts' views, the Court of Appeals concluded further that no medical malpractice was committed at the time of placing the balloon or during its retrieval. The Court of Appeals added further (i) that the medical treatment had been performed in a conscientious manner and in compliance with the current state of knowledge of medical science and (ii) that the method used for the retrieval of the balloon was sensible. As a result, the Court of Appeals, by concluding that no mistake had been made in the preparation, performance, and follow-up of the surgery, gave a proper legal justification for its decision. The motion to overrule this decision is therefore rejected.

Notes

1. Article 1147 referred to in the decision is part of the Civil Code section on damages imposed for failure to comply with an obligation. This article has been the basis for developing the distinction between an "obligation of result" and an "obligation of means." Article 1147 states: "Even if he acted in good faith, the obligor is liable to pay damages if there is either a failure to perform or a delay in the performance of the obligation, unless the obligor is able to prove that such failure or delay was due to a reason beyond his control."

2. Whether the obligation owed the patient is based on tort or contract, however, in most jurisdictions professionals and institutions are held to a standard of reasonable conduct, defined as what a professional of similar training and experience would have done in similar circumstances. Courts, then, must turn to medical experts for evidence of the appropriate standard of care.

3. The following famous case involves an injury sustained by a patient, John Bolam, who received electro-convulsive therapy ("E.C.T.") at Friern Hospital, a mental facility in London. E.C.T. is administered by placing electrodes on each side of the patient's head, using an electrical current to pass through the brain. Bolam, who was being treated for depression, suffered fractures in his pelvis from violent muscular spasms and convulsions generated by the current. Because spasms and convulsions are expected, Bolam alleged that defendants were negligent for administering the therapy without also administering a relaxant or anaesthetic, or otherwise physically restraining his movements.

Bolam v. Friern Hospital Management Committee

1956 B. No. 507, Queen's Bench Division
[1957] 1 W.L.R. 1957

MCNAIR J.

Members of the jury, it is now my task to try to help you to reach a true verdict, bearing in mind that you take the law from me and that the facts are entirely a matter for your consideration. You will only give damages if you are satisfied that the defendants have been proved to be guilty of negligence. * * *

* * * Another general comment which I would make is this: on the evidence it is clear, is it not, that the use of E.C.T. is a progressive science. You have had it traced for you historically over the quite few years in which it has been used in this country, and you may think on the evidence that even today there is no standard settled technique upon all points, to which all competent doctors will agree. The doctors called before you have mentioned in turn different variants of the technique they use. Some use restraining sheets, some use relaxants, some use manual control; but the final question you have got to make up your minds about is this, whether Dr. Allfrey, following upon the practice he had learnt at Friern and following upon the technique which he had shown to him by Dr. Bastarrechea, was negligent in failing to use relaxant drugs or, if he decided not to use relaxant drugs, that he was negligent in failing to exercise any manual control over the patient beyond merely arranging for his shoulders to be held, the chin supported, a gag used, and a pillow put under his back. No one suggests that there was any negligence in the diagnosis or in the decision to use E.C.T. * * * The only question is really a question of professional skill.

Before I turn to that, I must tell you what in law we mean by "negligence." In the ordinary case which does not involve any special skill, negligence in law means a failure to do some act which a reasonable man in the circumstances would do, or the doing of some act which a reasonable man in the circumstances would not do; and if that failure or the doing of that act results in injury, then there is a cause of action. How do you test whether this act or failure is negligent? In an ordinary case it is generally said you judge it by the action of the man in the street. He is the ordinary man. * * * But where you get a situation which involves the use of some special skill or competence, then the test * * * is the standard of the ordinary skilled man exercising and professing to have that special skill. A man need not possess the highest expert skill; it is well established law that it is sufficient if he exercises the ordinary skill of an ordinary competent man exercising that particular art. * * * [I]n the case of a medical man, negligence means failure to act in accordance with the standards of reasonably competent medical men at the time. That is a perfectly accurate statement, as long as it is remembered that there may be one or more perfectly proper standards; and if he conforms with one of those proper standards, then he is not negligent. * * * [A] mere personal belief that a particular technique is best is no defence unless that belief is based on reasonable grounds. * * * In a recent Scottish case, *Hunter v. Hanley*, Lord President Clyde said:

> In the realm of diagnosis and treatment there is ample scope for genuine difference of opinion and one man clearly is not negligent merely because his conclusion differs from that of other professional men, nor because he has displayed less skill or knowledge than others would have shown. The true test for establishing negligence in diagnosis or treatment on the part of a doctor is whether he has been proved to be guilty of such failure as no doctor of ordinary skill would be guilty of, if acting with ordinary care.

* * * [H]e is not guilty of negligence if he has acted in accordance with a practice accepted as proper by a responsible body of medical men skilled in that particular art. * * * Putting it the other way round, a man is not negligent, if he is acting in accordance with such a practice, merely because there is a body of opinion who would take a contrary view. At the same time, that does not mean that a medical man can obstinately and pig-headedly carry on with some old technique if it has been proved to be contrary to what is really substantially the whole of informed medical opinion. * * *

The *Bolam* decision has been controversial because courts have used it to grant extreme deference in many cases to the judgment of medical professionals in identifying the standard of care, even if the judgment represents a minority view. Moreover, *Bolam*'s legacy extends to former territories like India and Singapore that have incorporated British precedents. The following article, evaluating the options for legal remedies that foreign patients might have in certain jurisdictions, explains how *Bolam* serves as a barrier to meaningful redress in Singapore.

Nathan Cortez, *Recalibrating the Legal Risks of Cross-Border Health Care*

10 Yale Journal of Health Policy, Law, and Ethics
pp. 58–62 (2010)

* * *

Physicians in Singapore may be civilly liable for medical malpractice under theories of both contract and tort—though the most common allegation is simple negligence in tort.

As a foundational matter, Singapore inherits its common law from England, and to this day, Singaporean courts often apply judicial precedents from English courts. Courts tend to treat English decisions as "highly persuasive if not practically binding," although the Singapore High Court has held that courts need not follow English common law. In addition, a 1993 statute allows courts to reject English precedents if applying them would be inappropriate. Thus, courts in Singapore have shown increased willingness to depart from English common law and follow more patient-friendly precedents from Australian or Canadian courts (though Singaporean courts remain reluctant to adopt U.S. precedents). The Parliament of Singapore has grown more assertive in regulating medical professionals, but medical practice remains governed almost exclusively by the common law of contract and tort.

Courts in Singapore continue to adhere to the infamous *Bolam* rule, the standard for finding medical negligence that has been widely criticized for unduly favoring physicians. In *Bolam v. Friern Hospital Management Committee*, the court explained that it would not find medical professionals to be negligent if they "acted in accordance with a practice accepted by a responsible body of medical men skilled in that particular art." This famous test simply states that the standard of care for physicians is not that of the ubiquitous "reasonable man," but of a reasonable physician possessing roughly the same special skills and competencies.

On its face, the *Bolam* rule seems to be innocuous, even bland. But most courts have interpreted *Bolam* to create almost insurmountable hurdles for patients. First, if the standard of care is that of "a responsible body of medical men skilled in that particular art," who else but those same "medical men" could identify what practices were appropriate in each case? *Bolam* requires courts to refer to expert testimony to help determine the standard of care—as do courts in most common law jurisdictions—but courts in Singapore rely overwhelmingly on such testimony with very little independent, critical assessment. In fact, courts applying *Bolam* do not grant themselves much leeway to decide between conflicting medical experts. Most courts applying *Bolam* prohibit non-experts like judges from independently determining whether the physician was negligent as long as some evidence supports the defendant's conduct. Courts have even held that the testimony of a single expert defense witness can represent a "responsible body" of medical opinion, even if it contradicts a larger body of opinion. Thus, courts applying *Bolam* often refrain from finding negligence if only one expert finds the defendant's conduct reasonable—even if multiple competent experts find it unreasonable.

As a practical matter, therefore, medical negligence under *Bolam* is often "determined by the lowest standard of care (accepted by the medical profession) rather than reasonable contemporary standards." One lawyer notes that "barring a truly exceptional case, there will invariably be a body of medical opinion that supports the allegedly negligent physician's practice." Essentially, courts in Singapore enforce standards that the medical profession set for itself without independently assessing those standards. Scholars in Singapore bemoan that courts have forgotten the normative interpretation required when determining whether a physician acted in accordance with a "responsible body" of professional medical opinion. Indeed, courts in Singapore seem quicker to chastise themselves than physicians. For example, in one highly-publicized case, the Singapore Court of Appeal fumed that:

> It would be pure humbug for a judge, in the rarified atmosphere of the courtroom and with the benefit of hindsight, to substitute his opinion for that of the doctor in the consultation room or operating chamber. We often enough tell doctors not to play God; it seems only fair that, similarly, judges and lawyers should not play at being doctors.

A recent trend suggested that courts might retreat from *Bolam* or at least domesticate it, but this proved not to be much of a revolution. In 1998, the English House of Lords left room for courts to depart from *Bolam* in its well-known *Bolitho* opinion, where it held that courts should depart from *Bolam* when the professional medical opinion "is not capable of withstanding logical analysis." *Bolitho* seemed to give judges an opportunity—albeit a narrow one—to reassert themselves and critically weigh expert opinions in medical negligence cases. Although several courts did use *Bolitho* to appraise expert medical testimony more critically, Lord Browne-Wilkinson warned lower courts in his House of Lords opinion in *Bolitho* to apply the case only in exceptional circumstances. Thus, many observers view *Bolitho* as only slightly altering *Bolam*'s status quo.

In 2002, in the case of *Dr. Khoo James v. Gunapathy d/o Muniandy*, the Singapore Court of Appeal systematically reviewed the common law in this area. Reacting to public backlash against a S$1.4 million trial court award, the Court of Appeals announced that judges should not determine the reasonableness of medical opinions but should merely determine whether the expert medical testimony is logically defensible. Indeed, the Singapore High Court noted in a 2002 case predating *Gunapathy* that *Bolam* and its progeny prevent courts from finding negligence "even if the diagnosis or treatment were wrong." As such, the *Gunapathy* opinion represents the current law in Singapore, cementing the near sacrosanct status of the *Bolam* rule. One scholar has interpreted *Gunapathy* as rendering malpractice cases more hostile to plaintiffs in Singapore than in England.

Professor Amirthalingam has called for courts to "reassert their role as the final arbiters in determining medical negligence." He criticizes *Bolam* for allowing the medical profession to self-regulate and for allowing judges to abdicate their responsibility to determine the legal standards of care and negligence. Professor Amirthalingam also recommends that Singaporean courts abandon the English approach in *Bolam* and embrace the more neutral Australian approach enunciated in *Rogers v. Whitaker*, which reasserted the role of courts in determining the standard of care. As it is under *Bolam* in India and Thailand, expert medical testimony in Singapore enjoys almost talismanic power, which of course lowers the chance that patients will successfully recover damages.

* * *

Just as *Bolam* has influenced the law in several jurisdictions, so too has the relatively unique medical malpractice system of the United States, which has served as both a model and cautionary tale for other countries. Over the last few decades, countries all around the world have grappled with how best to handle medical malpractice complaints. The following two excerpts, from a volume that examines the law of medical malpractice in 14 countries (treating the Scandinavian countries as one), demonstrate at once both the diversity of approaches and the common challenges involving burdens of proof, standards of care, etc. *See Medical Malpractice and Compensation in Global Perspective* (Ken Oliphant & Richard W. Wright, eds.) (2013).

Ken Oliphant, *Medical Malpractice and Compensation: Comparative Observations*

Medical Malpractice and Compensation in Global Perspective
(Ken Oliphant and Richard W. Wright, eds.)
pp. 514–20 (2013)

* * *

For better or worse, medical malpractice law in the United States has acted as a yardstick in debates about the topic throughout the world, both as a source of ideas and inspiration and as the perceived embodiment of how things can go wrong. But it must be remembered that liability law in the United States has a number of special features that make it somewhat untypical, and limit its utility as a comparator in a cross-jurisdictional investigation, amongst them the role of the jury in deciding upon liability and assessing the damages, the availability of punitive damages, the rule that each party should bear its own legal costs, win or lose, the large role played by contingency fees, and the availability of extensive pre-trial procedures to require the disclosure of documents and the taking of witness statements.

The inclusion of New Zealand, on the other hand, is significant inasmuch as it presents a polar opposite approach to medical malpractice and compensation for medical injuries, centred around a no-fault accident compensation scheme introduced in 1974. This goes even further than the Nordic systems of first-party insurance through its absolute exclusion of the award of compensatory damages in respect of personal injuries covered by the no-fault system. Because the latter focuses almost exclusively on the compensation of injuries, other mechanisms have to be found for the performance of tasks such as prevention and accountability that liability law purports to accomplish elsewhere.

A comparative survey cannot be expected to provide final answers to the intractable questions of policy and principle that surround the issues of medical malpractice and compensation. Nevertheless, taking a comparative approach to this subject matter can serve a number of useful purposes. First, comparative legal research provides an aid to critical reflection of one's own legal system and the development of a better understanding of its distinctive traits. A comparative perspective can call into question the existence of institutions that are taken for granted, and serves to highlight alternatives that might otherwise be dismissed out of hand. Secondly, knowledge of how other legal systems solve universal problems provides a source of ideas and mechanisms that help in the search for creative solutions to practical problems in one's own jurisdiction. Thirdly, a comparative approach enables one to identify international developments that may evolve further and spread more widely in years to come, and thus performs a predictive function, allowing future trends to be anticipated and prepared for. * * *

1. Liability systems

The law of civil liability is the principal mechanism employed in most countries to regulate liability for medical malpractice and the corresponding compensation entitlements of its victims. However, there are divergent views as to whether the liability is properly classified as contractual or tortious, or as concurrently contractual *and* tortious, or even as falling in an intermediate category between contract and tort. A further option, at least insofar as public health care is concerned, is to apply principles of administrative law, but the trend has been away from the application of separate liability regimes depending on the public or private nature of the health care provision and towards the adoption of a uniform system based on established principles of civil liability.

Liability for medical malpractice is seen as primarily, though not exclusively, tortious throughout the Common Law world, as well as in Poland, Scandinavia and China. The latter is unique in that, since 2009, liability for medical malpractice has rested on explicit provisions in legislation governing tortious liability in general. In France, where a separate statutory liability has applied to treatment errors since 2002, claims based on a lack of informed consent are still founded on tort law because this analysis allows reliance upon the constitutional principle requiring the protection of human dignity. In at least some of the countries mentioned, the tortious analysis has been preferred because of (current or past) difficulties in establishing liability in contract law. There may be doubts, for example, whether public health care rendered under a statutory obligation is properly regarded as pursuant to a contract, or whether the patient provides adequate "consideration" for the treatment received, and hence whether the relationship between patient and care-provider is contractual at all. Contract claims are possible where private health care is at issue, but even in that context the tort analysis generally prevails. In the United States, most health care is private, but the tort analysis is still routinely applied. The same applies in China, even though a large portion of expenditure on medical care is paid directly out of the patient's pocket. Another factor favoring a tortious basis for the liability, even in claims against private health care providers, is that many legal systems in the Civil Law (or mixed) tradition are or have been unwilling to award damages for non-pecuniary loss in respect of a breach of contract. This accounts, for example, for the substantial role previously played by tort law in malpractice cases in Germany, but the balance between the two causes of action was shifted once the former restrictions on such awards were relaxed.

Conversely, the contractual analysis has generally been preferred in Austria, Germany (in recent times) and Italy. In these systems, it provides the patient with a number of potential advantages over the available remedies in tort, for example, a presumption of fault, more favorable statutes of limitation, or the easier imposition of vicarious liability on health care institutions, especially for harm caused by individual practitioners who are not employees. In Brazil, the contractual analysis is adapted in a rather interesting way through the application of consumer law to the doctor-patient relationship. The relationship is no longer merely a private matter but instead is heavily regulated, providing the patient with a particularly favorable set of legal tools for use in malpractice litigation. Amongst these may be highlighted the doctor's obligation to disclose information to the patient, which provides the context for the acceptance in Brazil of ideas of informed consent, and a judicial discretion to reverse the burden of proof in cases where the patient does not have the means (either financially or technically) to prove the elements of the claim.

* * *

Zhu Wang & Ken Oliphant, *Yangge Dance: The Rhythm of Liability for Medical Malpractice in the People's Republic of China*

Medical Malpractice and Compensation in Global Perspective
(Ken Oliphant and Richard W. Wright, eds.)
pp. 97–99, 117–18, 120–25, 127–28 (2013)

Introduction

Yangge Dance is a popular folk dance in rural China. Its basic pattern is three paces forwards, followed by two paces back; then a step to the right, followed by a step to the left. In our view, Yangge Dance is an apt simile for the process of legal development relating to liability for medical malpractice in the People's Republic of China (P.R. China). The three paces forward refer to successive reforms furthering the interests of patients, following an initial period—dating from the foundation of P.R. China in 1949 until 1987—during which medical malpractice was handled by an administrative system without formal liability rules. The first of these advances came in 1987, when the existing administrative system was formalized by an administrative regulation, the Rules on the Handling of Medical Accidents, which provided not only for administrative sanctions in the event of malpractice, but also for a (limited) liability to pay compensation for resultant injury. A further advance came in 2002 with the amendment of this system of administrative liability by the Regulations on the Handling of Medical Accidents. The third and final advance, consolidated by rulings of the Supreme People's Court (SPC) in 2002–2003, was to recognize that liability could be established—independently of the administrative system—under the ordinary rules of tort liability, then embodied in the General Principles of the Civil Law of the People's Republic of China (GPCL). Conversely, the enactment of the new Tort Liability Law (TLL) in 2009, taking effect on July 1, 2010, arguably marks a step backwards, subordinating the interests of patients in favor of the interests of the medical community. A second backwards step, through the prospective enactment of additional rules relating to liability to medical malpractice that further advantage healthcare providers, may also be anticipated in the future.

The sideways steps of the Yangge Dance—first to the right, then to the left—may be taken to refer to the constant interplay (at least since 1992) between the two concurrent systems of liability for medical malpractice—one administrative, broadly favoring the interests of the medical community, and the other tortious, broadly favoring the interests of patients.

* * *

V. Reform of Medical Liability under the Tort Liability Law of 2009

* * *

According to a survey by the Chinese Medical Association in 2003, among 326 medical institutions investigated, 321 (98 percent) were involved in medical disputes of one type or another. A further survey in 2005 by the China Hospital Management Association looked at the incidence of disputes in 270 hospitals. Even in high-rated (Grade 3-A) hospitals, there were on average over thirty lawsuits every year, and more than one million RMB was paid as compensation in them. Doctors were assaulted, threatened, and abused in 73 percent of all hospitals; in 60 percent of hospitals patients besieged and threatened hospital superintendents of out dissatisfaction with the outcomes of their treatment; in 77 percent of hospitals patients and their families refused to leave the premises or to pay their bill after treatment; in 62 percent of hospitals patients' families laid wreaths and created mourning halls on the premises following the patient's death. Increasing numbers of these disputes resulted in litigation. Taking the Haidan district court in Beijing as an example, eighty-nine medical disputes were tried in 2003, 103 in 2004, 124 in 2005, 138 in 2006, and 160 in 2007.

* * *

The [Tort Liability Law] was the outcome of a long history of unsuccessful attempts at codification in P.R. China. Following previous failed attempts to introduce a Civil Code, it was decided to proceed incrementally by way of a series of enactments dealing with particular areas of civil law. The first draft of the TLL was actually the title on tort liability (Title VIII) in a new draft Civil Code of 2002. This made no specific provision for medical liability. It was in the second draft of December 21, 2008, that a new chapter on Liability for Injury in Medical Treatment was added, reflecting the legislature's conclusion that a specific provision was necessary in view of the chaos that had arisen in practice. * * *

* * *

The relevant chapter of the TLL begins with a general statement of the responsibility of the medical institution both for its own fault and for that of its medical staff. Article 54 of the TLL provides "If a patient suffers injury in the course of medical diagnosis or treatment, and the medical institution or medical personnel are at fault, the medical institution shall bear compensatory liability."

This umbrella clause subsumes two specific liabilities for medical fault that the Law goes on to specify, dealing respectively with the breach of medical ethical duties and the breach of medical technical duties. As the provision makes clear, the medical institution's liability in each case may be either personal (i.e., for its own fault) or vicarious. Additionally, the same chapter of the TLL specifies a separate strict liability for the medical institution as the supplier of medical products. In all, then, the TLL provides for three basic types of liability for injury resulting from medical treatment * * *.

* * *

Article 57 of the TLL is about liability for breaching medical technical duties: "[i]f, in the course of diagnosis or medical treatment, medical personnel fail to fulfill the duty of diagnosis and medical treatment then and there, and cause injury to the patient, their medical institution shall bear compensatory liability." As the content of the applicable standard of care * * * is not specified in the TLL or in other legislation, it becomes a further question for the courts to decide.

* * *

The new law does not explicitly deal with proof of causation, but makes significant changes in the principles applicable to the proof of fault. The burden of proving fault, or (as the case may be) the absence of fault, on the part of the medical institution is no longer on the hospital or doctor (as it was under the SPC Stipulations on Evidence in Civil Litigation) but primarily on the patient. According to the new law, if a patient suffers injury in the course of diagnosis or medical treatment, and the medical institution or its medical personnel are at fault, the medical institution shall bear compensatory liability. On the other hand, fault on the part of the medical institution is presumed in special circumstances. If a patient is injured, and any of the following circumstances apply, fault on the part of the medical institution is taken to be established unless the medical institution proves the contrary: (1) violation of provisions of laws, administrative regulations, ministerial rules, or other standards regarding diagnosis and medical treatment; (2) concealing or refusing to provide medical record materials related to the dispute; and (3) falsifying, distorting, or destroying medical record materials.

* * *

VI. Another Step Backwards on Its Way?

* * * [I]n considering the basis of the cause of action, it seems likely that clarification will be required of the standard of care to which doctors are held in performing their technical duties. The "then and there" medical standard adopted as the criterion to judge medical misconduct is arguably too imprecise, and should be supplemented with a list of specific factors. In fact, [an earlier version of the TLL] contained a provision (deleted in the final version) which expressly required the court to consider the location of the medical institution, its accreditation, and the qualifications of its medical personnel. An almost identical provision has now found its way into guidance issued to the local courts in Beijing by the city's Higher People's Court. In a country so large and with such substantial differences in healthcare delivery between different areas—especially between urban and rural areas—it is easy to see that such a provision might be considered desirable. However, insofar as it rubber-stamps local practice even if it fails to attain reasonable quality standards, such reform could well be seen as contrary to the interests of patients.

* * *

---

2. Administrative and Specialized Tribunals

Most countries also have disciplinary tribunals that can hear complaints against health care professionals for improper or unethical conduct. But in most jurisdictions, these tribunals rarely address issues of competency or sub-standard care. An exception may be the Netherlands, which established disciplinary courts for various health care professions. Initial complaints are heard by a regional disciplinary tribunal, composed of both lawyers and colleagues with the same professional registration as the defendant. These tribunals investigate complaints and hold hearings at which the complainant and doctor may appear. They then issue decisions, which must impose a sanction if they find the professional is guilty. These decisions often remain private, though they can be made public if the proceeding was open to the public, or if the court otherwise decides that the decision should be made public. Sanctions ranging from warning to loss of license to practice are possible. These decisions may be appealed to a Central Medical Disciplinary Court in the Hague, composed of three lawyers and three licensed professionals. Some consider these tribunals an inadequate substitute for civil or criminal proceedings, as they permit doctors to pass on their colleagues in secrecy, though others believe that the confidentiality of these proceedings leads to greater candor. See Professions in Individual Health Care Act (BIG Act, or *Wet op de beroepen in de individuele gezondheidszorg*) of 1993; André den Exter & Martin Buijsen, *The Netherlands*, in *International Encyclopedia of Laws: Medical Law*, vol. 4, pp. 61–62 (2013).

Like the Netherlands, some countries have created tribunals that serve as an alternative for adjudicating medical malpractice claims, though they exist outside of formal disciplinary systems. The next excerpt evaluates two such examples: the Consumer Dispute Redressal Agencies (CDRAs) of India, and the National Commission for Medical Arbitrarion (Comisión Nacional de Arbitraje Médico, or "Conamed") in Mexico.

Nathan Cortez, *A Medical Malpractice Model for Developing Countries?*

4 Drexel Law Review, 217–18, 229–40 (2011)

* * *

Introduction

For all the angst over medical malpractice litigation in developed countries like the United States, very little has been written about it in the developing world. Developing countries account for more than 80% of the world's population, but they are often an after-thought in comparative health law literature. Noteworthy comparative compilations include either very few developing countries or none at all. For example, the iconic treatise *International Medical Malpractice Law* by Dieter Giesen focuses mostly on wealthy, developed countries like our own. And the more recent corpus of comparative health literature published in American law reviews focuses mainly on the usual suspects—Canada, the United Kingdom, France, Germany, Japan, and Australia.

* * *

* * * [T]his Article explores two contemporary examples of how developing countries have reformed their medical malpractice redressal systems. Both India, a common

law jurisdiction, and Mexico, a civil code jurisdiction, have reformed their systems in recent years. India now uses quasi-judicial consumer forums that feature streamlined procedures, allowing patients to bypass India's cumbersome civil courts. Mexico now uses a public medical arbitration system that allows parties to avoid litigating an archaic body of law in its outmoded civil and criminal courts. * * *

A. India

Patients injured by medical malpractice in India can seek redress in one of two venues—sue in a consumer forum or sue in civil court. The latter is not much of an option. Plaintiffs can sue for malpractice in India's civil courts under the Fatal Accidents Act, which compensates the families of those killed by an "actionable wrong," defined as death caused by a "wrongful act, neglect, or default."

Those lucky enough to survive can sue in civil court for common law negligence. India inherited its common law system from the English, so it uses a familiar formula that requires tort plaintiffs to establish duty, breach, causation, and damages. Unfortunately for medical malpractice plaintiffs, Indian courts also follow English precedents, including the infamous *Bolam* decision that helps courts determine the standard of care. * * *

Civil litigation in India is also known for its interminable delays. Plaintiffs may wait ten, twenty, or even twenty-five years for cases to conclude. Such delays undoubtedly deter many would-be plaintiffs. Authors have documented other reasons why India's civil courts are inhospitable to medical malpractice claims, and in aggregate, these obstacles make it difficult for plaintiffs to recover in civil courts.

The second avenue for redressing medical malpractice in India is to file a complaint in its consumer forums, also known as Consumer Disputes Redressal Agencies (CDRAs). India originally created its consumer forums as an alternative to civil courts in general, not as a venue for resolving medical malpractice claims. India's 1986 Consumer Protection Act implemented the United Nation's 1985 Consumer Protection Resolution, which called for signatories to strengthen their consumer protection laws and enact "measures enabling consumers to obtain redress." * * *

* * * [A]t first it was unclear whether the consumer forums even had jurisdiction to hear medical malpractice cases. The forums began hearing general consumer complaints in 1987, but it was not until 1992 that the National Consumer Disputes Redressal Commission declared that the Act covered medical services. It took another three years for the Indian Supreme Court to confirm this interpretation. Since then, the medical community in India has become intimately familiar with the Act, frequently citing it as a "source of anxiety."

India's Parliament designed the consumer forums to be a quicker, more economical, and more accessible alternative to civil courts. To achieve these goals, India structured the consumer forums as quasi-judicial forums, vested with the imprimatur of the government, along with various judicial powers—but without the full panoply of powers that civil or criminal courts enjoy. For example, forums may summon witnesses and receive documentary evidence, including affidavits and laboratory results, but the forums seem reluctant to handle more complex cases. The forums use panels of professional adjudicators rather than juries, and the members can have judicial or non-judicial training and experience.

The Consumer Protection Act created district, state, and national consumer forums. Each forum has primary jurisdiction to hear complaints, and the state and national forums also have appellate jurisdiction to hear appeals from below. Original jurisdiction depends on the amount of compensation the plaintiff seeks: the roughly 600 District Forums have jurisdiction over matters involving up to two million rupees in claimed compensation (roughly $44,300), 34 State Commissions have jurisdiction over matters involving up to ten million rupees (roughly $221,400); and the National Commission has jurisdiction to hear matters involving more than ten million rupees.

The Consumer Protection Act itself created causes of action for consumer forums to resolve. Medical malpractice plaintiffs typically file complaints for "deficient" medical services, defined as "any fault, imperfection, shortcoming or inadequacy in the quality, nature and manner of performance." Legal scholars in India interpret this to require simple negligence, though it seems redundant with section 14 of the Act, which awards compensation for negligence as well.

The forums may award different types of compensation, including compensatory damages, punitive damages (where appropriate), and costs, but they generally do not award noneconomic damages like pain and suffering. During my prior research, I did not find evidence that courts award punitive damages or costs very often.

The Act creates streamlined adjudications, calling for forums to resolve complaints within five to six months after being filed. Plaintiffs have two years to file a complaint after the cause of action arises, though forums can waive that requirement if the plaintiff shows cause. After receiving the defendant's response, the forum must resolve the case within three months, bringing the adjudication to the five or six month total.

Of course, these statutory deadlines are infrequently met in practice, despite national regulations calling for forums to clear a certain percentage of cases each month. Thus, consumer forum cases typically take two to three years to be resolved. Although this still compares very favorably to civil courts, it is not the quick six-month adjudication that the Act contemplates.

India's use of consumer forums certainly has been an antidote to its notoriously inefficient civil courts, but the forums are not ideal venues for resolving medical malpractice claims. Plaintiffs must overcome two significant, if not insurmountable, obstacles.

First, patients in India often struggle to find a medical expert willing to testify that another physician was negligent. Whether this is a matter of physician scarcity in India—there are only 0.6 physicians per thousand residents in India, and the WHO listed India as one of the fifty-seven countries facing crisis-level shortages of health care professionals—or the "conspiracy of silence," this is likely a major problem in many other developing countries as well. In India, most plaintiffs ultimately fail to present any kind of expert testimony. Conversely, defendants seem to have no problem finding colleagues to testify. These realities combine to make it very difficult for plaintiffs to carry their burden of proving that a physician was negligent and thus provided "deficient" services under the Act.

The scarcity of plaintiff-friendly medical experts is not necessarily a design problem with India's consumer forums. Virtually any adversarial system that relies on experts to set the standard of care in tort cases will pivot on the ability of adversaries to find experts willing to testify. For that reason, some in India have proposed solutions, such as using independent advisory panels on medical negligence cases, using special panels staffed with medical experts to hear all malpractice cases once a month, or requiring each panel in these cases to have at least one medical expert on staff. Nevertheless, my research on India's consumer forums has not found any major movement to address this problem.

The second obstacle for malpractice plaintiffs in India's consumer forums is obtaining medical records. Physicians and hospitals in India often refuse to hand over documents to patients suing them, including even basic information about their course of treatment or the medications they receive. For a long time, no laws in India required providers to maintain such records or disclose them to patients. A 1996 opinion by the Bombay High Court held that medical providers must give records to patients or their families, but this opinion did not ignite a revolution. In 2002, the Indian Medical Council finally created regulations that require practitioners to keep records for at least three years and disclose them to patients, but my research did not find evidence that the Council enforces them. Finally, the National Commission has held that a hospital is not required to maintain or disclose medical records under the Consumer Protection Act. There have been various calls to require hospitals and physicians to disclose medical records to patients, but not always for the benefit of patients. Thus, malpractice plaintiffs in India struggle to document what happened to them.

For these reasons, plaintiffs rarely succeed in bringing complaints against physicians under the Consumer Protection Act. Various sources report that plaintiffs lose between 70 and 90% of malpractice cases in the consumer forums. A physician described the medical malpractice atmosphere as "absolute chaos." Given these shortcomings, is there a better model for developing countries to follow?

B. Mexico

* * *

Unlike India, Mexico is a civil code jurisdiction. Mexican courts do not use familiar common law staples like juries or stare decisis. Judges decide cases and are not really bound by any common law precedents.

Traditional U.S.-style tort litigation is alien to Mexico and, as a subset, medical malpractice litigation is exceedingly rare. Personal injury cases in Mexico are governed by the Federal Civil Code, or one of the thirty-one state codes that largely track it. These codes remedy personal injuries and deaths through "extra-contractual liability" that arises from illegal acts based on duties and obligations owed to one another.

As a civil code jurisdiction, Mexico's legislature, the Congress of the Union, is responsible for developing the law in the area of personal injury. However, as Mexican law expert Jorge Vargas has emphasized, the legislature has largely neglected personal injury law. Only 35 of the over 3000 sections in the civil code address what we would think of as tort law. Moreover, "the legal principles that control personal bodily injuries and wrongful deaths in [Mexico] have been kept in isolation and virtually untouched in a legal time capsule that is today legally obsolete and completely out of sync with Mexico's economic and industrial realities." The Mexican Congress "has not clarified when courts should find fault, negligence, or causation," leaving significant discretion to the court in each case. And Mexican courts cannot fill the void in the same way that common law courts can. Thus, Mexican law governing personal injuries remains severely underdeveloped and outdated.

The way Mexican law calculates compensation also deters plaintiffs from using civil courts to redress medical malpractice claims. As in India, laws in Mexico do not grant damages for noneconomic injuries like pain and suffering. Rather, the Civil Code requires Mexican courts to calculate compensatory damages by using a statutory workers' compensation formula. This formula, found in the Federal Labor Act, compensates injured plaintiffs as if they were employees injured on the job. This allows courts to award the costs of medical care incurred after the injury, for example, but limits economic losses to four-times the minimum wage in that state for the duration allowed for the corresponding disability in the Federal Labor Act.

For all these reasons, patients rarely bring malpractice cases in Mexico's civil courts. In fact, Professor Vargas has found that U.S. courts actually hear more personal injury cases arising from Mexico than Mexican courts. Culturally, there is widespread distrust of courts and an aversion to litigation. Parties tend to settle personal injury cases informally, and medical providers generally offer to treat whatever harms they might have caused.

But as in India, an alternative emerged. In 1996, then-President Ernesto Zedillo declared that a new national arbitration agency would be formed within Mexico's Ministry of Health. Thus, the National Commission for Medical Arbitration (Comisión Nacional de Arbitraje Médico, or "Conamed") was born.

Like India's consumer forums, Conamed was designed as a more accessible, efficient, and less costly alternative to civil courts. But unlike India's consumer forums, Conamed was designed specifically to handle disputes over medical care—a feature that developing countries might emulate.

Conamed's primary charge is to mediate disputes between patients and providers, saving the parties from litigating in civil, criminal, or administrative venues. Conamed can resolve cases at any one of these three stages.

Roughly 73% of cases are resolved at the first stage, within two days of a conflict being submitted to Conamed. The first stage involves an immediate, somewhat informal intervention that opens the lines of communication between the patient and provider, sometimes involving one of Conamed's specialized consultants. This relatively quick and informal initial intervention might be particularly attractive to both patients and providers in developing countries that have a low tolerance—and few resources—for adversarial litigation.

If the parties do not resolve their dispute during this initial intervention, a complaint is filed with Conamed, and the case proceeds to conciliation. Conamed's experts will screen complaints before formally accepting them for conciliation, separating medical malpractice cases from disputes over other matters, like a physician refusing to treat a patient. Conamed will advise the parties on the latter, but will not admit complaints formally unless the dispute involves allegations of malpractice. This second, conciliatory phase introduces a medical review by both Conamed's experts and the treating physician(s). At this phase, the parties can sign a conciliatory agreement, opt out of the Conamed process and file a lawsuit, or proceed to the last stage, arbitration. Between 2001 and 2003, roughly 27% of cases proceeded to conciliation, over half of which were resolved at this second stage, typically within three to six months.

To arbitrate, the parties must sign an agreement that precludes them from taking the case to court. The arbitrators are independent physicians or attorneys trained to handle these cases. Conamed supports the arbitrators by peer-selecting expert consultants based on the medical issues in each case. Conamed thus enjoys credibility both with the judicial and medical communities in Mexico—it provides expert opinions for courts and consults with hospitals about medical errors. This is a key component to its success, and one that might be difficult to replicate for developing countries with weaker pools of medical and legal experts.

If arbitrators conclude that the physician committed malpractice—typically through "negligence or inexperience"—it can award compensation, including damages, medical expenses, or cancelling the patient's debt to the provider. Conamed arbitrators calculate damages based on the same workers' compensation formula used in the Civil Code, though arbitration awards are usually less than those awarded by a court. Conamed may not sanction physicians and cannot award "moral damages" like civil courts can. As a counterbalance, patients avoid the costs of litigation.

Of the roughly 15,000 cases filed with Conamed between 2001 and 2003, only 81 (0.05%) were resolved by arbitration, taking an average of fifteen months to resolve. Over 10% of all cases filed during that period were not resolved. Of those, Conamed estimates that a third of complainants simply left the process, and "the remaining unresolved cases probably went to court."

Conamed certainly is not perfect. Providers still win roughly two-thirds of the cases surveyed. The remaining third receives somewhat modest compensation—free treatment, costs, or financial compensation (averaging only $4841 per patient). And it is not clear whether or to what extent patients and physicians are represented by counsel and if there is any discrepancy between the parties. In that vein, Conamed is markedly less judicial than India's consumer forums. Indeed, they are entirely different phenotypes, with Conamed sharing much more in common with other arbitration systems.

Overall, the parties before Conamed report high levels of satisfaction with the process—Conamed received ratings of "good" or "excellent" by 97% of roughly 5500 patients and providers surveyed anonymously by Conamed. I have never seen a similar survey of U.S. medical malpractice plaintiffs and defendants, but it is probably safe to say that those numbers might be the inverse of Conamed's.

* * *

---

3. Criminal Liability

While civil liability is the standard legal approach to addressing medical negligence in the United States, other countries rely more on criminal sanctions, as is illustrated by the following excerpt on Japan. Japan is notable for its use of criminal law to answer the medical profession's weak self-policing mechanisms, such as medical licensure, discipline, and hospital peer-review. As Robert Leflar, the foremost comparative expert on Japanese medical malpractice law, has observed, accountability for malpractice in the United States derives from civil liability, while in Japan "the chief accountability mechanisms are the media and the criminal justice system. It is not so much the plaintiff's attorney as the whistleblower, the reporter, and the police that Japanese hospitals fear." Robert B. Leflar, "Medical Error, Deception, Self-Critical Analysis, and the Law's Impact: A Comparative Examination," *Law in Japan: A Turning Point* 404 (2007).

Robert B. Leflar, *The Law of Medical Misadventure in Japan*

87 Chicago-Kent Law Review 80–85, 88–89 (2012)

* * *

* * * [I]atrogenic harm-injury resulting from medical care has long been a simmering concern. The number of civil malpractice claims, though relatively small, rose steadily through the 1980s and 1990s. During the same period, dissatisfaction with physicians' paternalistic attitudes, a scandal over HIV-contaminated blood supply, a national debate over brain death issues, and concern over excessive and irrational drug prescriptions combined to undercut the public's previously almost unquestioned faith in medicine's beneficence. These developments fed a growing current of public opinion favoring transparency in medicine, reflecting movements toward greater openness in other spheres of society. * * *

Beginning in 1999, reports of a series of errors at hospitals of high repute filled the headlines and newscasts. The first notorious case arose from switched-patient surgeries in Yokohama. Under the eyes of the nation's media, subsequent cases occurred in quick succession in Tokyo itself. A nurse accidentally injected a toxic agent, killing her patient. An inexperienced team of young doctors bungled delicate laparoscopic surgery while insufficiently trained on the equipment, having also neglected to secure an adequate supply of the patient's rare blood type. A child died after an operation at a major pediatric cardiovascular surgery center, one among a series of children's deaths at the center. In each of these cases, physicians and hospital personnel altered medical records, gave misleading accounts of events to bereaved families or investigating officials, or engaged in other untrustworthy acts. Many other cases of alleged malpractice surfaced around the country.

* * *

I. Prosecutions and Their Consequences

* * *

Prosecutors have typically brought charges against health care personnel on any of three grounds. The first, and most common, is "professional negligence causing death or injury." This crime is derived, like most of Japan's Criminal Code, from the German penal code. The *mens rea* required for conviction, as a formal matter, is simple negligence, although as a practical matter the cases in which prosecutors obtain convictions typically involve acts or omissions amounting to gross negligence or recklessness.

A second ground for prosecution is concealment or destruction of evidence. Physicians and nurses attempting to cover up medical mistakes by altering patients' medical charts have been found criminally liable for this offense.

The third basis for recent prosecutions of physicians is failure to notify police in a timely fashion of "unnatural deaths." Physicians once assumed that this notification requirement, found in Article 21 of the Medical Practitioners' Law, applied only to violent deaths, suicides, infectious diseases threatening public health, and the like. However, when the CEO of Tokyo's Hirō Hospital in 2000 submitted a falsified death certificate for a patient killed by an accidental toxic injection and delayed reporting the death to police, prosecutors—fully aware of intensified public concern over medical errors—charged the CEO with violating Article 21. The Supreme Court, affirming his conviction in 2004, confirmed that the "unnatural death" notification requirement may encompass deaths causally related to medical management.

The Hirō Hospital CEO's arrest and subsequent conviction placed hospital administrators in a dilemma. For purposes of medical care, no clear definition of "unnatural death" exists. When a patient dies following less-than-optimal care, should the hospital routinely notify police, inviting criminal investigation disruptive of hospital routine and patient care, or avoid notification and risk public condemnation for a cover-up and possible criminal prosecution? * * *

Critics of the criminal justice system's involvement in monitoring medical mistakes raise concerns relating to police lack of medical expertise, disruption of patient care by criminal investigations, disproportionality of criminal sanctions to the inadvertence typical of lapses in care, and criminal law's tendency to focus on individual blame rather than addressing more significant problems of system failure. Even granting the substantial merit of these criticisms, criminal law's prominence in regulating medical quality in the early years of this century is understandable in light of these factors: (1) public expectation that the criminal justice system's protective reach does not stop at the hospital doors; (2) police and prosecutors' commitment to professional duty in enforcing the criminal code, applicable by its terms to medical personnel as to everyone else; and (3) the need in a democratic society for public accountability of the medical profession for its errors, a need not adequately fulfilled in Japan by professional self-regulation, administrative oversight, the death inquest system, or civil litigation.

* * *

C. One Prosecution Too Many: The Medical Professionals' Counterattack and the String of Acquittals

Police led obstetrician Katsuhiko Katō in handcuffs out of Ohno Hospital in rural Fukushima prefecture in 2006, after belatedly learning of the 2004 death of one of his patients subsequent to a particularly difficult childbirth. The reaction against Dr. Katō's humiliating arrest (broadcast on national news), detention, and prosecution was intense: petitions and remonstrances poured into the National Police Agency from medical organizations across the country. The fervor of this reaction launched a movement led by physicians employing the slogan "*iryō hōkai*"—"the collapsing health care system."

The "*iryō hōkai*" movement has engineered a significant shift in public opinion. The movement's proponents have called editorial and political attention to the shortage of physicians willing to attend childbirths, particularly in rural areas, and to repeated instances of hospital emergency rooms turning away ambulances for fear of liability exposure. As one chief cause of these problems, the movement has targeted alleged abuses of the criminal justice system, much as medical "tort reformers" attack the civil justice system in the United States. To be sure, other factors have contributed to Japan's shortages in obstetrical care, such as the adoption of a residency matching system undercutting traditional hierarchical job placement practices that once ensured a supply of young physicians to smaller hospitals. Nevertheless, the Ohno Hospital prosecution served as an effective rallying point for critics of the criminal justice system's medical oversight role. The "*iryō hōkai*" movement offers sympathetic portrayals of the plight of overworked, harassed, underappreciated physicians and the importance of protecting them from overreaching prosecutors. The movement appears to have turned media and public attention away, to a considerable extent, from concerns over medical error.

The "*iryō hōkai*" movement's efforts have borne fruit not only on the editorial pages, but also perhaps in the minds of some of the nation's judges. Acquittals in criminal trials are extremely rare in Japan; more than 99 percent of criminal trials result in convictions. But in four successive recent cases, including Dr. Katō's prosecution, medical personnel were acquitted of all charges, and in the two cases that prosecutors appealed, the acquittals were affirmed.

This series of acquittals, in the wake of medical society protests against physicians' arrests, constitutes a major public embarrassment for Japan's procuracy. Police and prosecutors have been further embarrassed by the recent arrests for unprofessional conduct of a top detective in the medical investigation unit of the Tokyo police force and of a top prosecutor for altering evidence in the unsuccessful prosecution of a health ministry official for alleged corruption. These acquittals and scandals, in the author's view, mark a watershed point in Japanese medical jurisprudence. Henceforth, police and prosecutors will be considerably more cautious in targeting health care personnel. Pressures for medical quality improvement must come chiefly from other directions.

* * *

Notes

1. In other work, Professor Leflar has examined why Japanese patients seem to bring medical injury claims much less frequently than their U.S. counterparts. He points to "institutional, social, and cultural factors," including historically more deferential relationships with physicians in Japan (*jōge kankei*), a dearth of malpractice attorneys able to handle cases there, more plaintiff-friendly fee arrangements in the United States (particularly contingency fees that do not require substantial up-front retainers, or *chakushukin*), and greater access to medical records in the United States. See Robert B. Leflar, "Law and Patient Safety in the United States and Japan," (published as *Iryō anzen to hō no Nichibei hikaku*), 1323 *Jurist* 8, 14–18 (2006) (Tomoko Mise, trans.).

2. Although criminal liability for medical error is certainly possible in common law jurisdictions, (see Alexander McCall Smith, "Criminal Negligence and the Incompetent Doctor," 1 *Med. L. Rev.* 336 (1993)), it is much more common in civil law countries. In a number of civil law countries, a criminal prosecution may be brought in tandem with a civil action, the criminal prosecution being initiated by the civil plaintiff. A civil plaintiff may want to initiate a criminal complaint for a variety of reasons. It may provide the plaintiff easier access to the medical records (via subpoena) or to an expert opinion on the case. It may put additional pressure on the defendant to settle. A favorable criminal judgment may also effectively be *res judicata* in the civil proceeding, precluding the defendant from claiming he or she was not negligent (though this may also mean that a finding of innocence in a criminal proceeding may bar a civil proceeding). The criminal law of civil law countries generally recognizes criminal liability for medical professionals who cause bodily harm to their patients under certain circumstances. These include treatment without consent, treatment by personnel who are not properly licensed, treatment lacking a therapeutic justification, or treatment that is not medically indicated. In some jurisdictions (Austria for example), the conduct must also cause a serious injury to the patient.

3. Under French law, for example, the conduct that a physician undertakes with respect to a patient is considered to be interference with a human being, which can only be justified if it is within the scope of the physician's duties as prescribed by the state. The physician's duty is to undertake only therapeutic actions, including diagnosis, treatment and prevention. Moreover, a physician's actions can be considered criminal if they are done without consent. This understanding of the obligation of

the physician to act therapeutically has led to special legislation to justify research, in vitro fertilization, abortions, and other conduct that is not strictly speaking therapeutic. Anne-Marie Duguet, *International Encyclopedia of Laws: Medical Law*, France para. 141–64.

4. "No Fault" Alternatives to Negligence Litigation

Americans frustrated with the current medical malpractice scheme often fantasize about experimenting with a "no-fault" scheme. In such schemes, injured patients can file claims with a compensation fund instead of suing a health care professional or facility—regardless of whether the care was faulty or negligent. New Zealand pioneered the first comprehensive no-fault scheme in 1974, followed by the Scandinavian countries; Sweden in 1975; Finland in 1984; Norway in 1988; and Denmark in 1992. Later, Austria (2001), France (2002), Belgium (2007), and Poland (2011) adopted no-fault schemes to varying degrees, often inspired by other countries' experiences.

Michelle M. Mello, Allen Kachalia & David M. Studdert, *Administrative Compensation for Medical Injuries: Lessons from Three Foreign Systems*

Issues in International Health Policy (Commonwealth Fund), pp. 1–9 (July 2011)

Medical malpractice reform is a perennial issue for state legislatures and, more recently, for the U.S. Congress. The American medical liability system is widely acknowledged to perform poorly in several important respects. Few patients with injuries due to negligence file claims, in part because of the difficulty of obtaining attorney representation and the arduousness of the litigation process. Many meritorious cases do not result in compensation to the patient, while many non-meritorious cases do lead to settlements or jury awards. * * *

Conversations about medical liability reform in the U.S. increasingly reflect an acknowledgment that traditional tort reform measures, such as caps on noneconomic damages, have limited effectiveness in solving the system's fundamental problems. * * *

Among the liability reform options that have recently received attention is administrative compensation of medical injuries. * * * Administrative compensation proposals are often labeled "no-fault" proposals, but in fact, they rarely suggest that compensation should be awarded on a true no-fault basis (meaning that the claimant need only show that the injury was causally related to medical care). Most would require that the injury also have been avoidable—a standard that is easier to meet than the negligence standard but still requires an evaluation of the quality of care that was provided.

Policymakers in the U.S. have raised many questions about how an administrative compensation system would operate here. The American experience with administrative compensation for medical injuries is quite limited. The federal Vaccine Injury Compensation Program provides compensation on a no-fault basis for a defined set of injuries related to vaccine administration, and Florida and Virginia have long operated no-fault compensation funds for serious birth-related neurological injuries. There are no precedents, however, for the types of broader schemes operated by Denmark, Finland, Norway, and New Zealand.

* * *

Administrative Compensation Systems Abroad

New Zealand

In 1974, New Zealand introduced a comprehensive accidental injury compensation scheme that was not limited to medical injuries. The system, which is managed by the Accident Compensation Corporation (ACC), replaced injured individuals' right to file personal injury lawsuits with an entitlement to rehabilitation and compensation via an administrative process. The change was motivated by a 1967 Report by the Woodhouse Commission that strongly criticized the tort system as an ineffective mechanism for compensating and deterring injuries. There was also a perception that the concept of compensation based on individual fault no longer enjoyed broad support and should be replaced by a principle of community responsibility for accidental injuries.

The ACC is tax funded, government operated, and accountable to a parliamentary minister * * *. It functions alongside a national health care system that provides care to all New Zealanders. Most hospital care is provided through public sector hospitals, although there are many smaller, private facilities as well. Most specialist physicians are employed by hospitals, while general practitioners operate private practices and are merely paid by the government. Hospital care is provided free of charge, while primary care is available with small copayments. About a third of New Zealanders have supplementary private health insurance. * * *

Sweden

In 1975, Sweden established a voluntary scheme in which public and private health care providers assumed responsibility for compensating injured patients through a consortium of insurers. The impetus for reform was a perception that compensation was too difficult for patients to obtain in the tort system, which required plaintiffs to meet a higher standard of proof than the "preponderance of the evidence" standard used in personal injury litigation in the U.S. The process was protracted and expensive. As a result, very few claims were brought and even fewer resulted in compensation.

The objective of the new system was to channel compensation more efficiently to injured patients. Disciplining health care providers and deterring medical errors were not among its missions. On the contrary, system designers eschewed these goals because they were regarded as potentially corrosive to the compensation objective.

In 1995, the voluntary system was restructured and a mutual insurance company (Landstingens Ömsesidiga Försäkringsbolag, or LOF) owned by the regional hospital authorities began insuring all public hospitals and physicians, as well as private providers who have a contract with the government. From 1995 to 2009, LOF delegated responsibility for investigating and evaluating injury claims to a private claims handling company (Personskadereglering AB, or PSR), but these functions were integrated into LOF's operations in 2010.

Legislation in 1997 made it mandatory for all health care providers to carry liability insurance, with most insuring through the LOF as described above. A provider's insurer pays for claims that arise out of the provider's care and meet the criteria for compensation. Because some providers do not comply with the requirement to carry insurance, the insurance companies formed the Patient Insurance Association (Patientförsäkringsföreningen, or PFF) for the purpose of making compensation available to patients injured by uninsured providers. The PFF also finances and operates a Patient Claims Panel to which patients can appeal compensation decisions regardless of whether or not the provider was insured.

As in New Zealand, the compensation system in Sweden is part of a larger, tax-funded system of social insurance, including a national health care system with universal access. The National Insurance Act of 1962 set up a system that covers basic medical expenses and wage loss due to illness of injury, regardless of cause, as well as disability and old age pensions. Sweden's single-payer health care system provides comprehensive medical coverage, with modest cost-sharing by patients. About 5 percent of Swedes carry supplemental private health insurance. Nearly all hospital care is provided through public sector hospitals and specialist physicians are generally salaried employees of the national health system. Primary care physicians may be either government employees working in public clinics or private practitioners.

Denmark

Denmark's medical injury compensation system, adopted in the Patient Insurance Act of 1992, is very similar to Sweden's. It was modeled after Sweden's 1975 voluntary scheme and motivated by similar concerns about patient access to compensation.

By law, Danish regional hospital authorities are required to pay the costs of malpractice claims. Although they have the option to purchase insurance through a private insurance company, in practice, it has been more cost-effective to self-insure. The insurance companies and self-insuring authorities formed a joint association, the Patient Insurance Association (Patientforsikringen, or PIA) to evaluate all claims in accordance with the law. The PIA is an independent association governed by a board of directors made up primarily of regional council members. Compensation payments to patients are made by the self-insured county councils.

Denmark has a tax-funded national health care system with universal, free access. The counties are legally and financially responsible for all treatment, from primary to tertiary care. There is no cost-sharing by patients for hospital or primary care services, but there is modest cost-sharing for prescription drugs and certain other services. About 30 percent of Danes carry supplemental private health insurance to cover these costs. Most hospitals are publicly operated, while most health professionals are self-employed and reimbursed by the government. Denmark also maintains social insurance schemes for sickness and disability, unemployment, and retirement income.

FINDINGS

1. The systems have rejected the notion that compensation should be available only to patients who are injured by negligence.

New Zealand has experimented with several alternatives to a negligence standard. Originally, it compensated all medical "misadventures," a term that was interpreted by claims handlers, the courts, and eventually a statute to include two kinds of injuries: "medical error" and "medical mishap." A medical error was an injury due to negligence, defined as it is in tort law. A medical mishap was a rare and severe adverse consequence of treatment given properly by a registered health professional.

Legislation enacted in 2005 eliminated fault-based negligence determinations from the system, adopting a single "treatment injury" standard. Under this standard, there must be a physical injury causally related to treatment by a registered health professional that is not a necessary part or ordinary consequence of the treatment. This standard comes closest to a true no-fault standard in any of the foreign schemes, although questions of appropriateness still arise in determining the eligibility for compensation of claims relating to failures to provide timely treatment or failures to obtain informed consent.

The 2005 change was motivated by several concerns: the sense that the medical error standard adversely affected physician-patient relationships and reduced physicians' willingness to participate in the claims process; a desire to put medical injuries on equal footing with other kinds of accidental injuries, which were eligible for ACC compensation without regard to fault; the sense that learning opportunities were lost by focusing on individual error rather than systems of care; and a dissatisfaction with the cost of investigating medical injury cases to determine whether an error occurred.

In Sweden and Denmark, a standard of "avoidability" is applied. Injuries are compensable if they would not have occurred in the hands of a highly skilled and experienced physician in the relevant specialty—a standard quite different from negligence, which compensates only those injuries resulting from care that fell below the customary standard of care that would be rendered by a reasonable practitioner. The avoidability inquiry * * * examines not only the skill and conscientiousness of the physician in rendering the treatment but also whether an alternative technique or treatment would have met the patient's needs and been less dangerous. The Danes evaluate avoidability based on what was known at the time care decisions were made, while the Swedes evaluate it retrospectively, incorporating all information available at the time the question of compensation is decided (which is a more permissive standard for patients than Denmark's known-at-the-time standard). Although the avoidability standard governs the payment of most claims, the Swedish and Danish schemes also apply other criteria to compensate certain unavoidable injuries. For example, a wide range of treatment-related injuries that are more rare and severe in nature than what a patient should reasonably be expected to endure are compensated in Denmark; Sweden covers a narrower group of unavoidable injuries caused by equipment failures or severe hospital-acquired infections.

These compensation criteria tend to lead to similar compensation outcomes for the same injury, but through different reasoning. * * * All are more likely to result in compensation to injured patients than is the U.S. standard of negligence. System administrators in each of the three countries reported that their compensation criteria were workable in practice and, in their opinion, were preferable to a negligence standard.

2. The systems have been able to provide a simple, fast, accessible process for obtaining compensation that preserves physician-patient relationships.

In all three systems, claims can be filed free of charge without the need for assistance of legal counsel, although lawyers do participate in filing about 10 percent of claims in Denmark * * *. Sweden allows only patients to submit claims, while Denmark also permits hospitals to file claims on behalf of patients. New Zealand requires that patients initiate a claim through a physician or other recognized health care provider, who need not be the clinician involved in the injury. In Sweden, an estimated 60 percent to 80 percent of claims are facilitated by health care providers on behalf of patients—sometimes by the physician involved in the incident, and sometimes by a primary care physician. In Denmark, physicians file about 15 percent of claims and assist in most other cases. In New Zealand, 46 percent of treatment injury claims are lodged by patients' primary care providers, who receive reimbursement for the time they spent filing the claim if the claim is accepted. Of the remaining claims, 44 percent are filed by public or private hospital staff, and 10 percent by other providers, on behalf of patients.

All of the systems report that jettisoning negligence determinations has been effective in enabling clinicians and patients to maintain their therapeutic relationship and cooperate in the pursuit of compensation. Moreover, although the easier claiming process has resulted in higher rates of claims than are seen in the U.S., * * * it has not opened the floodgates to an unmanageable number of claims. System administrators estimate that about 10 percent of injured patients file claims, as compared with 2 percent to 3 percent in the U.S. Finally, the systems are able to process claims expeditiously. Whereas in the U.S., the average time from injury to disposition of a malpractice claim is five years, in Sweden and Denmark it is eight months. In New Zealand it is 16 days, although where there are allegations of failure to treat or delayed treatment, claims may take longer to investigate. Patients infrequently appeal the initial decision and, when they do, generally are not successful.

3. The systems have been able to effectively use neutral medical experts as well as information on previous, similar cases to help render consistent compensation decisions.

In Sweden and Denmark, the frontline claims handlers in the systems typically do not have clinical backgrounds, but are in all cases assisted by a panel of senior physicians in a range of specialties. These physicians are retained by the compensation system through standing contracts, with most serving for an extended period of time and accumulating substantial experience and institutional memory. For decisions that are not clear-cut, the claims handlers and medical experts may also examine past decisions in similar cases, which are available in a searchable database. In addition to fostering consistency in decision-making, review of prior decisions has proved effective in reducing the time and labor necessary to decide cases, as reviewers are not reinventing the appropriate methodology with each new case.

In New Zealand, the claims assessors have clinical backgrounds (often in nursing) and do not necessarily consult specialist clinicians in every case. Approximately two-thirds of claims are decided in house by a peer-review panel comprising these assessors and team managers. Advice may also be sought from one of the in-house medical advisors. Independent experts with the relevant scope of practice are, however, typically consulted in complex cases or where the claim alleges failure to treat or delayed treatment. In such cases, the causal connection between the medical management and the injury tends to be less clear, necessitating greater investigation and expertise to reach a judgment about eligibility for compensation.

4. Although they compensate a broader range of injuries than the U.S. tort system, the foreign systems' costs have not been exorbitant.

Based on medical injury studies conducted in the U.S., about twice as many injuries are eligible for compensation under an avoidability standard than under a negligence standard, and three to four times as many are eligible under a true no-fault standard. However, several factors have kept costs manageable in the systems that employ these alternative standards. First, the availability of other social insurance programs obviates the need for some injured individuals to file injury compensation claims, keeping claiming rates relatively low in comparison to the estimated prevalence of medical injuries. For example, a New Zealand patient who sustained a disabling injury could receive free or very low-cost care through the national health care system as well as disability and unemployment benefits that are generous by U.S. standards. The availability of other sources of support also keeps average claims costs lower because "collateral-source offset" rules stipulate that the medical injury systems need not pay for lost wages, medical expenses, and other expenses that are covered by the national insurance system.

Second, these systems have low overhead costs—around 17 percent of the total cost of the system, compared to an estimated 55 percent to 60 percent in the U.S. Third, Sweden and Denmark impose a cap on the total compensation a patient may receive * * *. Fourth, payments for noneconomic losses are much smaller than is typically the case in the U.S.

Because of these features, the average total award size in these systems is much lower than in the U.S. In 2009, the average compensation per paid claim was approximately US$20,000 in Sweden and US$40,000 in Denmark, compared to approximately $324,000 in the U.S. In New Zealand, it was even lower, around US$4,450.

5. The systems use fixed award amounts, schedules, and caps to make payments for noneconomic loss, provoking controversy about the adequacy of awards.

New Zealand provides lump sum payments for noneconomic loss associated with permanent impairment (the loss, or loss of use, of a bodily part, system, or function).

However, the payments historically have generated some controversy because they are relatively modest (currently capped at US$85,500), have been adjusted only infrequently, and are conditional on permanent impairment, meaning that individuals whose impairment is temporary or whose injuries involve pain but not impairment do not have their noneconomic loss compensated. Sweden and Denmark calculate noneconomic damages in accordance with pre-established tables, or schedules, which are adjusted annually for inflation. In these systems, pain and disfigurement is compensated even if not disabling, but there are sometimes complaints of inadequate compensation for severe injuries, particularly in Denmark, where maximum total awards are capped at about US$1.7 million.

6. The systems are complemented by strong, independent, parallel systems of physician discipline.

Each of the countries has chosen to delink its patient compensation system from its system of policing physician competence to assure health care quality. Since 1994, New Zealand's Office of the Health and Disability Commissioner has provided a mechanism for patients to complain about the quality of health care and disability services. By law, all patients who file a compensation claim with ACC must be informed of the availability of the complaints process. The commissioner investigates patient complaints and may pursue a variety of remedies where complaints are found to have merit. These remedies range from facilitating mediation and apology to referring the case to a prosecutorial authority for disciplinary action to recommending that a health care organization improve its care processes. Sweden and Denmark also operate separate systems of physician discipline, with boards for patients' complaints empowered to investigate complaints and refer cases to disciplinary authorities.

None of these countries currently permits routine information sharing between the discipline system and the compensation system, although this has only been the case in New Zealand since 2005. New Zealand also requires the ACC to make a report to the Director General of Health if, based on a pattern of claims, conditions in a facility appear to pose a threat to the public. In rare cases, ACC may make a similar report regarding an individual health professional to the relevant registration authority.

A perceived advantage of the information firewall is that it encourages physicians to make patients aware of their right to seek compensation and to assist them in claiming, which physicians might be reluctant to do if they feared a compensation claim could trigger or facilitate disciplinary action. On the other hand, operating completely separate systems of discipline and compensation has some disadvantages: health care providers may feel besieged by multiple investigations and the lack of information sharing contributes to inefficiency and redundancy in the investigation process. Some have also criticized the New Zealand and Scandinavian systems for eliminating any possible deterrent effect of the injury compensation system on medical negligence, while others argue that there is little evidence that deterrence occurs in the U.S. system.

* * *

CONCLUSIONS

* * *

The available research indicates that, despite differences in health care systems and cultures, most features of these country models are readily applicable to the U.S. system. A private financing scheme, similar to the Swedish model, is likely to be the most feasible for the U.S. The responsibility for initial investigation of an incident would presumably remain where it currently lies, with private insurers, although it should be expedited and take a much less defensive approach—similar to the approach taken in the U.S. in the emerging "disclosure-and-offer" model of early settlement. Because of insurers' financial interest in cost control, it would be important to provide a neutral, external panel to investigate and adjudicate claims in the event that the insurer and patient do not reach a satisfactory agreement about compensation. In some states, constitutional barriers may make it difficult to make an administrative compensation system the exclusive remedy available to injured patients, but there are still possibilities for voluntary systems even in those jurisdictions.

Cost control in an injury compensation system would be more of a challenge in the U.S. than in foreign countries. It would be feasible to cap awards, as half of U.S. states currently do. However, it is unlikely that Americans would accept a system that awarded the relatively modest compensation amounts provided in the foreign systems. Average awards would likely be much higher in the U.S. because of public expectations and because private insurance would likely cover a smaller share of medical expenses than the single-payer health systems abroad. The proportion of injured patients who file claims may also be higher in the U.S. There is a strong tradition of seeking compensation for injuries in the U.S., and the skimpier social insurance safety net in the U.S. creates a greater financial necessity for filing claims. * * *

* * *

Notes

1. In 2002, France created a kind of "no-fault" compensation system. People who are seriously injured in medical accidents can file a claim with a compensation board. This board then compensates the injured party. The board next determines fault, and if the provider is found at fault it (or, as a practical matter, its insurer) must pay. Otherwise, the patient is paid from a compensation fund. The system is thus fault-based from the perspective of the provider, no-fault from the perspective of the patient. The system only applies, however, to serious injuries. For a helpful evaluation of the French system, including its benefits and limitations, particularly in light of other countries' experiences, see, Janine Barbot, Isabelle Parizot, Myriam Winance, "No-Fault" Compensation for Victims of Medical Injuries: Ten Years of Implementing the French Model, 114 *Health Policy* 236 (2014).

2. Many believe that the United States is not well served by its medical malpractice system. Health care professionals hate it because they view it as random and devas-

tating in its effects. They also fear the shame and psychological stress that malpractice litigation brings and the career consequences that can follow from even nuisance settlements being reported to the National Practitioner Data Bank. Injured patients, on the other hand, are unlikely to recover except for the most severe injuries, and then must share much of the recovery with their attorneys. Transaction costs are very high, with considerably less than half of the money paid in malpractice insurance premiums ending up with injured patients. Our fault-based system also does not seem to have been very effective in deterring medical error.

For all of these reasons, the idea of a no-fault compensation system has long interested American legal academics, leading to a considerable volume of comparative scholarship considering the Scandinavian and New Zealand approaches. See, e.g. Stephen Todd, Privatization of Accident Compensation: Policy and Politics in New Zealand, 39 *Washburn L.J.* 404 (2000); David M. Studdert, et al., Can the United States Afford a "No-Fault" System of Compensation for Medical Injury? 60 *Law & Contemp. Probs.* 1 (1997); Patricia M. Danzon, The Swedish Patient Compensation System: Myths and Realities, 14 *Int'l Rev. L. & Econ.* 453 (1994).

These readings, however, illustrate the difficulty of establishing a no-fault system. If fault is not the basis of recovery, what is? It is difficult to define otherwise the event that precipitates compensation, unless one is prepared to compensate all adverse events related to health care, a very expensive proposition. Other problems have also deterred the adoption of no-fault to deal with medical error in the United States, not the least of which is the likelihood that many more iatrogenic injuries would be compensated under a no-fault system than are now compensated under our fault-based system, leading to much higher costs. To date, only Virginia and Florida have adopted limited no-fault system for dealing with babies who are brain damaged at birth. See David M. Studdert, Lori A. Fritz, Troyen A. Brennan, The Jury is Still In: Florida's Birth-Related Neurological Injury Compensation Plan After a Decade, 25 *J. Health Pol. Pol'y & L.* 499 (2000); Randall R. Bovbjerg & Frank A. Sloan, No-Fault for Medical Injury, Theory and Evidence, 67 *U. Cin. L. Rev.* 53 (1998).

C. The Right to Consent to Treatment

Prior to the twentieth century, medical professionals did not feel much obligation to ask patients for consent before providing medical treatment. The dominant attitude was that "patients ought not to be needlessly upset with worrisome news about their medical condition." *See* Trudo Lemmens, Informed Consent, in *Routledge Handbook of Medical Law and Ethics* 27, 28 (Yann Joly & Bartha Maria Knoppers eds. 2015). Indeed, an influential 1803 book, *Medical Ethics* by Thomas Percival, as well as versions of the Hippocratic Oath circulating in the early 20th century recommended hiding any information from patients that might trouble them. Although a 1914 judicial opinion by Benjamin Cardozo first articulated the idea of "informed consent" in Anglo-American law (*Schloendorff v. New York Hospital*, 211 N.Y. 125 (1914)), it was not extended in a meaningful way to research subjects until the Nuremberg Code in 1947, written in response to horrific experiments conducted by German doctors on concentration camp prisoners.

1. The Standard of Disclosure

Today, it is long accepted law virtually everywhere that providing medical treatment without consent is a battery, resulting in civil damages. And in most of the world, the law goes further, declaring that consent to a medical procedure is not effective unless the medical professional has provided the patient with information about the nature of the procedure, its risks, and alternatives. But this doctrine of "informed consent" has developed quite differently from country to country.

The first case below discusses the standard applied in informed consent cases for determining the scope of disclosure. The initial case, *Sidaway*, represents the long-standing approach, still applied in many United States jurisdictions, that defines the duty to disclose by referring to professional practice—what a reasonable practitioner would disclose under similar circumstances. The second case, *Rogers v. Whitaker*, an Australian High Court case, represents the position taken by Australia, Canada, many U.S. states, and most civil law jurisdictions, that the physician's obligation to disclose is measured by the patient's need to know. The third case, *Montgomery v. Lanarkshire Health Board*, overturned *Sidaway*, opting for the patient-centered standard of disclosure. A fourth excerpt discusses the approach to informed consent in Taiwan, a country with very different medical and legal traditions.

Sidaway v. Bethlem Royal Hospital Governors and Others

[1985] 1 AC 871, [1985] 1 All ER 643, [1985] 2 WLR 480,
1 BMLR 132 (House of Lords, 1985)

Panel: Lord Scarman, Lord Diplock, Lord Keith of Kinkel, Lord Bridge of Harwich, and Lord Templeman.

Lord Scarman [Some commentators characterize Lord Scarman's opinion as a dissent. Although he agrees with the other Lords as to the result, his reasoning is very different.]

My Lords, the state of the evidence in this case compels me to the conclusion that the appellant has not made out a case of negligence against her surgeon, the late Mr Murray A Falconer. * * *

* * * The issue is whether Mr Falconer failed to exercise due care (his skill was not challenged) in the advice which he gave his patient when recommending an operation. * * * Whatever be the correct formulation of the applicable law, the issue cannot be settled positively for or against the doctor without knowing what advice, including any warning of inherent risk in the operation, he gave his patient before she decided to undergo it and what was his assessment of the mental, emotional and physical state of his patient. The trial judge derived no help on these two vital matters from the evidence of the appellant. Mr Falconer was not an available witness, having died

before trial, and the medical records afforded no sure guide on either matter. Regrettable though a "non-proven" verdict is, it is not, therefore, surprising. Where the court lacks direct evidence as to the nature and extent of the advice and warning (if any) given by the doctor and as to his assessment of his patient the court may well have to conclude that the patient has failed to prove her case.

* * *

This is an appeal by the plaintiff, Mrs Sidaway, from the dismissal by the Court of Appeal of her appeal from the judgment of Skinner J given on 19 February 1982 whereby he dismissed her action for damages in respect of the personal injuries which she suffered as a result of a surgical operation performed on her by a neurosurgeon on 29 October 1974. * * * Mrs Sidaway does not allege negligence in the performance of the operation. Her case is that she was not informed of a risk inherent in the operation, that the risk materialised with the result that she suffered, and continues to suffer, serious personal injury, and that, had she been warned, she would not have consented to the operation. Damages are agreed at £67,500 subject to liability.

The case is plainly of great importance. It raises a question which has never before been considered by your Lordships' House: has the patient a legal right to know, and is the doctor under a legal duty to disclose, the risks inherent in the treatment which the doctor recommends? If the law recognises the right and the obligation, is it a right to full disclosure or has the doctor a discretion as to the nature and extent of his disclosure? And, if the right be qualified, where does the law look for the criterion by which the court is to judge the extent of the disclosure required to satisfy the right? Does the law seek guidance in medical opinion or does it lay down a rule which doctors must follow, whatever may be the views of the profession? There is further a question of law as to the nature of the cause of action. Is it a cause of action in negligence, i.e. a breach of the duty of care, or is it based on a breach of a specific duty to inform the patient which arises not from any failure on the part of the doctor to exercise the due care and skill of his profession but directly from the patient's right to know?

Before attempting to answer these questions it is necessary to set out the facts of the case. At once a formidable difficulty arises. Mr Falconer was dead before the trial. The judge was not prepared to accept Mrs Sidaway's evidence that he gave no warning. The judge was, therefore, without any direct evidence as to the extent of the warning given. * * *

Mrs Sidaway was 71 years of age at the time of the trial in 1982. She was severely disabled by a partial paralysis resulting from her operation. The relationship of doctor and patient between Mr Falconer and herself had been long-standing prior to the operation. * * *

Mr Falconer annually reviewed his patient's progress between 1960 and 1970. In 1973 he wrote to Mrs Sidaway asking how she was. She replied, complaining of very persistent pain "in the right arm and shoulder," which was the same area as before, and now also of pain in the left forearm. Mr Falconer saw her in the early months of 1974. After some delays, she was admitted to hospital on 11 October 1974. Her pain in the mean time had got progressively worse.

On admission Mrs Sidaway was thoroughly examined by Dr Goudarzi, a junior member of Mr Falconer's team. On 17 October she underwent a myelogram which revealed a partial block at the level of the C4/5 disc space, a posterior ridge in the same area which appeared to have, at least in part, a bony structure, and a narrowing of the subarachnoid space in the same area. Mr Falconer diagnosed that pressure on a nerve root was the cause of her pain and decided to operate. * * *

* * *

The two specific risks of injury were (1) damage to a nerve root in the area of the operation and (2) damage to the spinal cord either by direct contact or by some interference, which might be slight and of short duration or very much more serious, of the radicular arteries running through a foramen. The risk of either sort of damage occurring was not great: one surgeon estimated the degree of risk at between 1% and 2%. But, if either risk materialised, the injury could be severe. Mr Uttley, the distinguished surgeon called on behalf of Mrs Sidaway, said that the possible effects of the damage ranged from a sensation of pins and needles in the hand to paraplegia, i.e. a partial paralysis. * * * [The witnesses] distinguished between the two categories of specific risk, the effect of damage to a nerve root being in all probability that the operation would fail to relieve and might increase pain, while damage to the spinal cord might cause a partial paralysis. The risk of damage to the spinal cord was, however, in their opinion less than 1%.

* * *

Mrs Sidaway consented to the operation. She signed the usual consent form, in which she declared that the nature and purpose of the operation had been explained to her by Dr Goudarzi. Dr Goudarzi confirmed that he had given her this explanation but he made it clear in his evidence that he would have left warning of the risks to Mr Falconer. And we know from the hospital records that Mr Falconer saw his patient before he operated. It would have been his practice to give a warning but a finding as to what warning he gave faces the formidable difficulty to which I have already referred, that Mr Falconer was not available to give evidence. Nevertheless, the judge, while refusing to accept Mrs Sidaway's evidence that she was given no warning, made the following findings on the balance of probabilities. He said:

> On the evidence ... the probabilities are that ... on the day before the operation he [Mr Falconer] followed his usual practice ... it is probable that he explained the nature of the operation [to his patient] in simple terms ... As to the risks, I think it is probable that he mentioned the possibility of disturbing a nerve root and the consequences of doing so, but I am satisfied that he did not refer to the danger of cord damage or to the fact that this was an operation of choice rather than necessity.

The medical witnesses were agreed that they would give a patient some warning of the specific risks involved before performing an operation of this kind. They would explain the nature and purpose of the operation, and that there was a small risk of untoward consequences and of an increase of pain instead of relief. Mr Uttley would go further: he would warn of the possible risk of some weakness of the legs resulting from the operation. Two answers in his cross-examination were of great importance. When asked whether he would question the judgment of a surgeon that it was not in his patient's interest to frighten her by talking about death or paralysis, he replied, "Not at all" and he agreed that such a judgment would be in accordance with a practice accepted as proper by a responsible body of competent neuro-surgeons. * * *

This being the state of the evidence, the question for the House is whether the omission by Mr Falconer to warn his patient of the risk inherent in the operation of damage to the spinal cord with the possible result of a partial paralysis was a breach of duty owed by him to his patient. The duty of a doctor to warn was considered in *Bolam v Friern Hospital Management Committee.* * * *

* * *

The *Bolam* principle may be formulated as a rule that a doctor is not negligent if he acts in accordance with a practice accepted at the time as proper by a responsible body of medical opinion even though other doctors adopt a different practice. In short, the law imposes the duty of care but the standard of care is a matter of medical judgment. * * *

But was the judge correct in treating the "standard of competent professional opinion" as the criterion in determining whether a doctor is under a duty to warn his patient of the risk, or risks, inherent in the treatment which he recommends? * * * The implications of this view of the law are disturbing. It leaves the determination of a legal duty to the judgment of doctors. Responsible medical judgment may, indeed, provide the law with an acceptable standard in determining whether a doctor in diagnosis or treatment has complied with his duty. But is it right that medical judgment should determine whether there exists a duty to warn of risk and its scope? It would be a strange conclusion if the courts should be led to conclude that our law, which undoubtedly recognises a right in the patient to decide whether he will accept or reject the treatment proposed, should permit the doctors to determine whether and in what circumstances a duty arises requiring the doctor to warn his patient of the risks inherent in the treatment which he proposes.

The right of "self-determination," the description applied by some to what is no more and no less than the right of a patient to determine for himself whether he will or will not accept the doctor's advice, is vividly illustrated where the treatment recommended is surgery. A doctor who operates without the consent of his patient is, save in cases of emergency or mental disability, guilty of the civil wrong of trespass to the person. He is also guilty of the criminal offence of assault. The existence of the patient's right to make his own decision, which may be seen as a basic human right protected by the common law, is the reason why a doctrine embodying a right of the patient to be informed of the risks of surgical treatment has been developed in some jurisdictions in the United States of America and has found favour with the Supreme

Court of Canada. Known as the "doctrine of informed consent," it amounts to this: where there is a "real" or a "material" risk inherent in the proposed operation (however competently and skillfully performed) the question whether and to what extent a patient should be warned before he gives his consent is to be answered not by reference to medical practice but by accepting as a matter of law that, subject to all proper exceptions (of which the court, not the profession, is the judge), a patient has a right to be informed of the risks inherent in the treatment which is proposed. * * *

* * *

* * * [T]he *Bolam* principle does not cover the situation. The facts of this very case expose its limitation. Mr Falconer lacked neither care for his patient's health and well-being nor professional skill in the advice and treatment which he offered. But did he overlook or disregard his patient's right to determine for herself whether or not to have the operation? Did he fail to provide her with the information necessary for her to make a prudent decision? There is, in truth, no evidence to answer these questions. Mrs Sidaway's evidence was not accepted and Mr Falconer was dead. Assume, however, that he did overlook this aspect of his patient's situation. Since neither his advice nor his treatment could be faulted on the *Bolam* test, his patient may have been deprived of the opportunity to exercise her right of decision in the light of information which she, had she received it, might reasonably have considered to be of importance in making up her mind. On the *Bolam* view of the law, therefore, even if she established that she was so deprived by the lack of a warning, she would have no remedy in negligence unless she could also prove that there was no competent and respected body of medical opinion which was in favour of no warning. Moreover, the tort of trespass to the person would not provide her with a remedy, for Mrs Sidaway did consent to the operation. Her complaint is that her consent resulted from ignorance of a risk, known by the doctor but not made known by him to her, inherent in the operation. Nor would the law of contract offer her a sure way forward. Medical treatment, as in her case, is frequently given today under arrangements outside the control of the law of contract.

* * *

It is, I suggest, a sound and reasonable proposition that the doctor should be required to exercise care in respecting the patient's right of decision. He must acknowledge that in very many cases factors other than the purely medical will play a significant part in his patient's decision-making process. The doctor's concern is with health and the relief of pain. These are the medical objectives. But a patient may well have in mind circumstances, objectives and values which he may reasonably not make known to the doctor but which may lead him to a different decision from that suggested by a purely medical opinion. The doctor's duty can be seen, therefore, to be one which requires him not only to advise as to medical treatment but also to provide his patient with the information needed to enable the patient to consider and balance the medical advantages and risks alongside other relevant matters, such as, for example, his family, business or social responsibilities of which the doctor may be only partially, if at all, informed.

* * *

My conclusion as to the law is therefore this. To the extent that I have indicated, I think that English law must recognise a duty of the doctor to warn his patient of risk inherent in the treatment which he is proposing and especially so if the treatment be surgery. The critical limitation is that the duty is confined to material risk. The test of materiality is whether in the circumstances of the particular case the court is satisfied that a reasonable person in the patient's position would be likely to attach significance to the risk. Even if the risk be material, the doctor will not be liable if on a reasonable assessment of his patient's condition he takes the view that a warning would be detrimental to his patient's health.

Applying these principles to the present case, I ask first: has the appellant shown the risk of damage to the spinal cord to have been a material risk? The risk was slight, less than 1% but, if it were to materialise, it could result in severe injury. It was for the appellant, as plaintiff, to establish that the risk was so great that the doctor should have appreciated that it would be considered a significant factor by a prudent patient in the appellant's situation deciding whether or not to have the operation. * * * After an anxious consideration of the evidence I do not find it possible to say that it has been proved that Mr Falconer failed in his duty when he omitted, as we must assume that he did, to warn his patient of the risk of injury to the spinal cord.

* * *

Lord Diplock

* * * Inevitably all treatment, medical or surgical, involves some degree of risk that the patient's condition will be worse rather than better for undergoing it. Statistically, the chances of any risk of the proposed treatment going awry at all may be small, but, particularly if surgery is involved * * * it is never totally absent and the degree of possible worsening involved may cover a whole spectrum of disabilities from mild occasional discomfort to what might justify the epithet "catastrophic." * * *

There is no evidence in the instant case that the patient asked the neuro-surgeon a single question about whether there were any risks involved in undergoing the operation that he was proposing for her, or, if there were, what were the consequences of those risks or the chances of their occurring. * * *

* * *

What we do know, however, and this is in my view determinative of this appeal, is that all the expert witnesses specialising in neurology (including the patient's own expert witness, Mr Uttley, who would not himself have undertaken a similar operation without waiting a period of time, after October 1974, to see what developed as to the persistence of the patient's pain) agreed that there was a responsible body of medical opinion which would have undertaken the operation at the time the neuro-surgeon did and would have warned the patient of the risk involved in the operation in substantially the same terms as the trial judge found on the balance of probabilities the neuro-surgeon had done, i.e. without specific reference to risk of injuring the spinal cord.

My Lords, it is the very paucity of facts in evidence that makes it possible, in my view, to treat this appeal as raising a naked question of legal principle. * * * For the last quarter of a century the test applied in English law whether a doctor has fulfilled his duty of care owed to his patient has been that set out in the summing up to the jury by McNair J in *Bolam v Friern Hospital Management Committee.* * * *

* * *

My Lords, no convincing reason has in my view been advanced before your Lordships that would justify treating the *Bolam* test as doing anything less than laying down a principle of English law that is comprehensive and applicable to every aspect of the duty of care owed by a doctor to his patient in the exercise of his healing functions as respects that patient. What your Lordships have been asked to do, and it is within your power to do so, is to substitute a new and different rule for that part only of the well-established test as comprises a doctor's duty to advise and warn the patient of risks of something going wrong in the surgical or other treatment that he is recommending.

The juristic basis of the proposed substitution, which originates in certain state court jurisdictions of the United States of America and has found some favour in modified form by the Supreme Court of Canada, appears to me, with great respect, to be contrary to English law. Its foundation is the doctrine of "informed consent" which was originally based on the assumption made in the United States Court of Appeals, District of Columbia Circuit, in *Canterbury v Spence* * * * that prima facie the cause of action in a case of surgery was trespass to the person unless "informed consent" to the particular battery involved in the surgical operation could be proved. From a period long before American independence this, as I have pointed out, has never been so in English law. The relevant form of action has been based in negligence, i.e. in assumpsit, alone.

The Supreme Court of Canada, after some initial vacillation, rejected trespass to the person, i.e. battery, as the cause of action in cases of surgery but endeavoured to transfer the concept of "informed consent" to a patient's cause of action in negligence, into which, in my opinion, it simply cannot be made to fit. Consent to battery is a state of mind personal to the victim of the battery and any information required to make his consent qualify as informed must be relevant information either actually possessed by him or which he is estopped from denying he possessed, because he so acted towards the defendant as to lead to the latter reasonably to assume the relevant information was known to him. There is no room in the concept of informed consent for the "objective" patient (as he is referred to at one point by the Supreme Court of Canada) to whom the doctor is entitled, without making any inquiry whether it is the fact or not, to attribute knowledge of some risks but not of others. * * *

* * *

I agree with your Lordships that this appeal should be dismissed.

Lord Bridge of Harlock

* * *

Broadly, a doctor's professional functions may be divided into three phases: diagnosis, advice and treatment. In performing his functions of diagnosis and treatment, the standard by which English law measures the doctor's duty of care to his patient is not open to doubt. "The test is the standard of the ordinary skilled man exercising and professing to have that special skill." * * * The test is conveniently referred to as the *Bolam* test. * * *

* * *

The important question which this appeal raises is whether the law imposes any, and if so what, different criterion as the measure of the medical man's duty of care to his patient when giving advice with respect to a proposed course of treatment. It is clearly right to recognise that a conscious adult patient of sound mind is entitled to decide for himself whether or not he will submit to a particular course of treatment proposed by the doctor, most significantly surgical treatment under general anaesthesia. This entitlement is the foundation of the doctrine of "informed consent" which has led in certain American jurisdictions to decisions and, in the Supreme Court of Canada, to dicta on which the appellant relies, which would oust the *Bolam* test and substitute an "objective" test of a doctor's duty to advise the patient of the advantages and disadvantages of undergoing the treatment proposed and more particularly to advise the patient of the risks involved.

There are, it appears to me, at least theoretically, two extreme positions which could be taken. It could be argued that, if the patient's consent is to be fully informed, the doctor must specifically warn him of all risks involved in the treatment offered, unless he has some sound clinical reason not to do so.

* * *

At the other extreme it could be argued that, once the doctor has decided what treatment is, on balance of advantages and disadvantages, in the patient's best interest, he should not alarm the patient by volunteering a warning of any risk involved, however grave and substantial, unless specifically asked by the patient. I cannot believe that contemporary medical opinion would support this view, which would effectively exclude the patient's right to decide in the very type of case where it is most important that he should be in a position to exercise that right and, perhaps even more significantly, to seek a second opinion whether he should submit himself to the significant risk which has been drawn to his attention. * * *

* * *

* * * [T]he question remains whether that right is sufficiently safeguarded by the application of the *Bolam* test without qualification to the determination of the question what risks inherent in a proposed treatment should be disclosed. The case against a simple application of the *Bolam* test is cogently stated by Laskin CJC, giving the judgment of the Supreme Court of Canada in *Reibl v Hughes*:

> To allow expert medical evidence to determine what risks are material and, hence, should be disclosed and, correlatively, what risks are not material is to hand over to the medical profession the entire question of the scope of

> the duty of disclosure, including the question whether there has been a breach of that duty. * * *

I fully appreciate the force of this reasoning, but can only accept it subject to the important qualification that a decision what degree of disclosure of risks is best calculated to assist a particular patient to make a rational choice whether or not to undergo a particular treatment must primarily be a matter of clinical judgment. It would follow from this that the issue whether non-disclosure in a particular case should be condemned as a breach of the doctor's duty of care is an issue to be decided primarily on the basis of expert medical evidence, applying the *Bolam* test. But I do not see that this approach involves the necessity "to hand over to the medical profession the entire question of the scope of the duty of disclosure, including the question whether there has been a breach of that duty." * * * But, even in a case where, as here, no expert witness in the relevant medical field condemns the non-disclosure as being in conflict with accepted and responsible medical practice, I am of opinion that the judge might in certain circumstances come to the conclusion that disclosure of a particular risk was so obviously necessary to an informed choice on the part of the patient that no reasonably prudent medical man would fail to make it. The kind of case I have in mind would be an operation involving a substantial risk of grave adverse consequences, as for example the 10% risk of a stroke from the operation which was the subject of the Canadian case of *Reibl v Hughes*. In such a case, in the absence of some cogent clinical reason why the patient should not be informed, a doctor, recognising and respecting his patient's right of decision, could hardly fail to appreciate the necessity for an appropriate warning.

* * *

I would dismiss the appeal.

Lord Templeman

* * *

In my opinion a simple and general explanation of the nature of the operation should have been sufficient to alert Mrs Sidaway to the fact that a major operation was to be performed and to the possibility that something might go wrong at or near the site of the spinal cord or the site of the nerve root causing serious injury. If, as the judge held, Mr Falconer probably referred expressly to the possibility of damage to a nerve root and to the consequences of such damage, this warning could only have reinforced the possibility of something going wrong in the course of a delicate operation performed in a vital area with resultant damage. In view of the fact that Mr Falconer recommended the operation, Mrs Sidaway must have been told or could have assumed that Mr Falconer considered that the possibilities of damage were sufficiently remote to be ignored. Mrs Sidaway could have asked questions. If she had done so, she could and should have been informed that there was an aggregate risk of between 1% and 2% of some damage either to the spinal cord or to a nerve root resulting in injury which might vary from irritation to paralysis. But to my mind this further information would only have reinforced the obvious, with the assurance that the maximum risk of damage, slight or serious, did not exceed 2%. Mr Falconer may reasonably have taken the view that Mrs Sidaway might be confused, frightened or misled by more detailed information which she was unable to evaluate at a time when she was suffering from stress, pain and anxiety. A patient may prefer that the doctor should not thrust too much detail at the patient. * * *

* * *

In my opinion, if a patient knows that a major operation may entail serious consequences, the patient cannot complain of lack of information unless the patient asks in vain for more information or unless there is some danger which by its nature or magnitude or for some other reason requires to be separately taken into account by the patient in order to reach a balanced judgment in deciding whether or not to submit to the operation.

* * *

I do not subscribe to the theory that the patient is entitled to know everything or to the theory that the doctor is entitled to decide everything. The relationship between doctor and patient is contractual in origin, the doctor performing services in consideration for fees payable by the patient. The doctor, obedient to the high standards set by the medical profession, impliedly contracts to act at all times in the best interests of the patient. No doctor in his senses would impliedly contract at the same time to give to the patient all the information available to the doctor as a result of the doctor's training and experience and as a result of the doctor's diagnosis of the patient. An obligation to give a patient all the information available to the doctor would often be inconsistent with the doctor's contractual obligation to have regard to the patient's best interests. Some information might confuse, other information might alarm a particular patient. * * * At the same time the doctor is not entitled to make the final decision with regard to treatment which may have disadvantages or dangers. Where the patient's health and future are at stake, the patient must make the final decision. The patient is free to decide whether or not to submit to treatment recommended by the doctor and therefore the doctor impliedly contracts to provide information which is adequate to enable the patient to reach a balanced judgment, subject always to the doctor's own obligation to say and do nothing which the doctor is satisfied will be harmful to the patient. * * * If the doctor making a balanced judgment advises the patient to submit to the operation, the patient is entitled to reject that advice for reasons which are rational or irrational or for no reason. The duty of the doctor in these circumstances, subject to his overriding duty to have regard to the best interests of the patient, is to provide the patient with information which will enable the patient to make a balanced judgment if the patient chooses to make a balanced judgment. A patient may make an unbalanced judgment because he is deprived of adequate information. A patient may also make an unbalanced judgment if he is provided with too much information and is made aware of possibilities which he is not capable of assessing because of his lack of medical training, his prejudices or his personality. Thus the provision of too much information may prejudice the attainment of the objective of restoring the patient's health. * * * At the end of the day, the doctor, bearing in mind the best interests of the patient and bearing in mind the patient's right to information which will enable the patient to make a balanced judgment, must decide what information should be given to the patient and in what terms that information should be couched. The court will award damages against the doctor if the court is satisfied that the doctor blundered and that the patient was deprived of information which was necessary for the purposes I have outlined. In the present case on the judge's findings I am satisfied that adequate information was made available to Mrs Sidaway and that the appeal should therefore be dismissed.

Appeal dismissed.

Notes

1. Until 2009, the Appellate Committee of the House of Lords was the United Kingdom's highest court. House of Lords opinions look unfamiliar to American law students because there is no opinion of the Court. Rather, each Lord issues his or her own written opinion, speaking only for him or herself. One can, of course, determine who won a case, but there is often no single *ratio decidendi* for a decision. In 2005, Parliament passed the Constitutional Reform Act, establishing a Supreme Court of the United Kingdom, which formally assumed the remaining judicial functions of the House of Lords on October 1, 2009.

2. Does the House of Lords in *Sidaway* consider recipients of medical care to be patients or consumers? How complete is its faith in the competency of medical science? Is this decision simply attributable to a primitive medical paternalism, or might there be more going on here? See Frances H. Miller, Denial of Health Care and Informed Consent in English and American Law, 18 *Am. J. L. & Med.* 37 (1992).

Rogers v. Whitaker

109 A.L.R. 625, 67 A.L.J.R. 47 (1992)
(High Court of Australia)

Judgment: Mason CJ, Brennan, Dawson, Toohey and McHugh JJ.

The appellant, Christopher Rogers, is an ophthalmic surgeon. The respondent, Maree Lynette Whitaker, was a patient of the appellant who became almost totally blind after he had conducted surgery upon her right eye. The respondent commenced proceedings against the appellant for negligence in the Supreme Court of New South Wales and obtained judgment in the amount of $808,564.38. After an unsuccessful appeal to the Court of Appeal of New South Wales, the appellant now appeals to this court.

There is no question that the appellant conducted the operation with the required skill and care. The basis upon which the trial judge, Campbell J, found the appellant liable was that he had failed to warn the respondent that, as a result of surgery on her right eye, she might develop a condition known as sympathetic ophthalmia in her left eye. The development of this condition after the operation and the consequent loss of sight in her left eye were particularly devastating for the respondent as she had been almost totally blind in her right eye since a penetrating injury to it at the age of nine. Despite this early misfortune, she had continued to lead a substantially normal life: completing her schooling, entering the workforce, marrying and raising a family. In 1983, nearly 40 years after the initial injury to her right eye and in preparation for a return to the paid workforce after a three year period during which she had looked after her injured son, the respondent decided to have an eye examination. Her general practitioner referred her to Dr Cohen, an ophthalmic surgeon, who prescribed reading glasses and referred her to the appellant for possible surgery on her right eye.

The respondent did not follow up the referral until 22 May 1984 when she was examined by the appellant for the first time. The appellant advised her that an operation on the right eye would not only improve its appearance, by removing scar tissue, but would probably restore significant sight to that eye. At a second consultation approximately three weeks later, the respondent agreed to submit to surgery. The surgical procedure was carried out on 1 August 1984. After the operation, it appeared that there had been no improvement in the right eye but, more importantly, the respondent developed inflammation in the left eye as an element of sympathetic ophthalmia. Evidence at the trial was that this condition occurred once in approximately 14,000 such procedures, although there was also evidence that the chance of occurrence was slightly greater when, as here, there had been an earlier penetrating injury to the eye operated upon. The condition does not always lead to loss of vision but, in this case, the respondent ultimately lost all sight in the left eye. As the sight in her right eye had not been restored in any degree by the surgery, the respondent was thus almost totally blind.

In the proceedings commenced by the respondent, numerous heads of negligence were alleged. Campbell J rejected all save the allegation that the appellant's failure to warn of the risk of sympathetic ophthalmia was negligent and resulted in the respondent's condition. While his Honour was not satisfied that proper medical practice required that the appellant warn the respondent of the risk of sympathetic ophthalmia if she expressed no desire for information, he concluded that a warning was necessary in the light of her desire for such relevant information. The Court of Appeal dismissed all grounds of the appellant's appeal from the judgment of $808,564.38 on both liability and damages * * *.

Neither before the Court of Appeal nor before this court was there any dispute as to the existence of a duty of care on the part of the appellant to the respondent. The law imposes on a medical practitioner a duty to exercise reasonable care and skill in the provision of professional advice and treatment. That duty is a "single comprehensive duty covering all the ways in which a doctor is called upon to exercise his skill and judgment" * * *.

The standard of reasonable care and skill required is that of the ordinary skilled person exercising and professing to have that special skill, in this case the skill of an ophthalmic surgeon specialising in corneal and anterior segment surgery. As we have stated, the failure of the appellant to observe this standard, which the respondent successfully alleged before the primary judge, consisted of the appellant's failure to acquaint the respondent with the danger of sympathetic ophthalmia as a possible result of the surgical procedure to be carried out. The appellant's evidence was that "sympathetic ophthalmia was not something that came to my mind to mention to her."

The principal issue in this case relates to the scope and content of the appellant's duty of care: did the appellant's failure to advise and warn the respondent of the risks inherent in the operation constitute a breach of this duty? The appellant argues that this issue should be resolved by application of the so-called *Bolam* principle * * *.

* * *

One consequence of the application of the *Bolam* principle to cases involving the provision of advice or information is that, even if a patient asks a direct question about the possible risks or complications, the making of that inquiry would logically be of little or no significance; medical opinion determines whether the risk should or should not be disclosed and the express desire of a particular patient for information or advice does not alter that opinion or the legal significance of that opinion. The fact that the various majority opinions in *Sidaway*, for example, suggest that, over and above the opinion of a respectable body of medical practitioners, the questions of a patient should truthfully be answered (subject to the therapeutic privilege) indicates a shortcoming in the *Bolam* approach. The existence of the shortcoming suggests that an acceptable approach in point of principle should recognise and attach significance to the relevance of a patient's questions. Even if a court were satisfied that a reasonable person in the patient's position would be unlikely to attach significance to a particular risk, the fact that the patient asked questions revealing concern about the risk would make the doctor aware that this patient did in fact attach significance to the risk. Subject to the therapeutic privilege, the question would therefore require a truthful answer.

In Australia, it has been accepted that the standard of care to be observed by a person with some special skill or competence is that of the ordinary skilled person exercising and professing to have that special skill. But, that standard is not determined solely or even primarily by reference to the practice followed or supported by a responsible body of opinion in the relevant profession or trade. Even in the sphere of diagnosis and treatment, the heartland of the skilled medical practitioner, the *Bolam* principle has not always been applied. Further, and more importantly, particularly in the field of non-disclosure of risk and the provision of advice and information, the *Bolam* principle has been discarded and, instead, the courts have adopted the principle that, while evidence of acceptable medical practice is a useful guide for the courts, it is for the courts to adjudicate on what is the appropriate standard of care after giving weight to "the paramount consideration that a person is entitled to make his own decisions about his life."

In *F v R*, which was decided by the Full Court of the Supreme Court of South Australia two years before *Sidaway* in the House of Lords, a woman who had become pregnant after an unsuccessful tubal ligation brought an action in negligence alleging failure by the medical practitioner to warn her of the failure rate of the procedure. The failure rate was assessed at less than 1% for that particular form of sterilisation. The court refused to apply the *Bolam* principle. King CJ said:

> The ultimate question, however, is not whether the defendant's conduct accords with the practices of his profession or some part of it, but whether it conforms to the standard of reasonable care demanded by the law. That is a question for the court and the duty of deciding it cannot be delegated to any profession or group in the community.

King CJ considered that the amount of information or advice which a careful and responsible doctor would disclose depended upon a complex of factors: the nature of the matter to be disclosed; the nature of the treatment; the desire of the patient for information; the temperament and health of the patient; and the general surrounding circumstances. His Honour agreed with the following passage from the judgment of the Supreme Court of Canada in *Reibl v Hughes* :

> To allow expert medical evidence to determine what risks are material and, hence, should be disclosed and, correlatively, what risks are not material is to hand over to the medical profession the entire question of the scope of the duty of disclosure, including the question whether there has been a breach of that duty. * * *

The approach adopted by King CJ is similar to that subsequently taken by Lord Scarman in *Sidaway* and has been followed in subsequent cases. In our view, it is correct.

Acceptance of this approach does not entail an artificial division or itemisation of specific, individual duties, carved out of the overall duty of care. The duty of a medical practitioner to exercise reasonable care and skill in the provision of professional advice and treatment is a single comprehensive duty. However, the factors according to which a court determines whether a medical practitioner is in breach of the requisite standard of care will vary according to whether it is a case involving diagnosis, treatment or the provision of information or advice; the different cases raise varying difficulties which require consideration of different factors. * * * In diagnosis and treatment, the patient's contribution is limited to the narration of symptoms and relevant history; the medical practitioner provides diagnosis and treatment according to his or her level of skill. However, except in cases of emergency or necessity, all medical treatment is preceded by the patient's choice to undergo it. In legal terms, the patient's consent to the treatment may be valid once he or she is informed in broad terms of the nature of the procedure which is intended. But the choice is, in reality, meaningless unless it is made on the basis of relevant information and advice. Because the choice to be made calls for a decision by the patient on information known to the medical practitioner but not to the patient, it would be illogical to hold that the amount of information to be provided by the medical practitioner can be determined from the perspective of the practitioner alone or, for that matter, of the medical profession. Whether a medical practitioner carries out a particular form of treatment in accordance with the appropriate standard of care is a question in the resolution of which responsible professional opinion will have an influential, often a decisive, role to play; whether the patient has been given all the relevant information to choose between undergoing and not undergoing the treatment is a question of a different order. Generally speaking, it is not a question the answer to which depends upon medical standards or practices. Except in those cases where there is a particular danger that the provision of all relevant information will harm an unusually nervous, disturbed or volatile patient, no special medical skill is involved in disclosing the information, including the risks attending the proposed treatment. Rather, the skill is in communicating the relevant information to the patient in terms which are reasonably adequate for that purpose having regard to the patient's apprehended capacity to understand that information

In this context, nothing is to be gained by reiterating the expressions used in American authorities, such as "the patient's right of self-determination" or even the oft-used and somewhat amorphous phrase "informed consent." The right of self-determination is an expression which is, perhaps, suitable to cases where the issue is whether a person has agreed to the general surgical procedure or treatment, but is of little assistance in the balancing process that is involved in the determination of whether there has been a breach of the duty of disclosure. Likewise, the phrase "informed consent" is apt to mislead as it suggests a test of the validity of a patient's consent. Moreover, consent is relevant to actions framed in trespass, not in negligence. Anglo-Australian law has rightly taken the view that an allegation that the risks inherent in a medical procedure have not been disclosed to the patient can only found an action in negligence and not in trespass; the consent necessary to negative the offence of battery is satisfied by the patient being advised in broad terms of the nature of the procedure to be performed.

* * * The law should recognise that a doctor has a duty to warn a patient of a material risk inherent in the proposed treatment; a risk is material if, in the circumstances of the particular case, a reasonable person in the patient's position, if warned of the risk, would be likely to attach significance to it or if the medical practitioner is or should reasonably be aware that the particular patient, if warned of the risk, would be likely to attach significance to it. This duty is subject to the therapeutic privilege.

The appellant in this case was treating and advising a woman who was almost totally blind in one eye. As with all surgical procedures, the operation recommended by the appellant to the respondent involved various risks, such as retinal detachment and haemorrhage infection, both of which are more common than sympathetic ophthalmia, but sympathetic ophthalmia was the only danger whereby both eyes might be rendered sightless. Experts for both parties described it as a devastating disability, the appellant acknowledging that, except for death under anaesthetic, it was the worst possible outcome for the respondent. According to the findings of the trial judge, the respondent "incessantly" questioned the appellant as to, amongst other things, possible complications. She was, to the appellant's knowledge, keenly interested in the outcome of the suggested procedure, including the danger of unintended or accidental interference with her "good," left eye. * * * She did not, however, ask a specific question as to whether the operation on her right eye could affect her left eye.

The evidence established that there was a body of opinion in the medical profession at the time which considered that an inquiry should only have elicited a reply dealing with sympathetic ophthalmia if specifically directed to the possibility of the left eye being affected by the operation on the right eye. While the opinion that the respondent should have been told of the dangers of sympathetic ophthalmia only if she had been sufficiently learned to ask the precise question seems curious, it is unnecessary for us to examine it further, save to say that it demonstrates vividly the dangers of applying the *Bolam* principle in the area of advice and information. The respondent may not have asked the right question, yet she made clear her great concern that no injury should befall her one good eye. * * *

For these reasons, we would reject the appellant's argument on the issue of breach of duty.

* * *

For the foregoing reasons, we would dismiss the appeal.

Notes

1. Notice how the Australian High Court draws on British and Canadian, as well as Australian, precedents in reaching its decision. In notes edited out, it also cited repeatedly *Canterbury v. Spence*, 464 F.2d 772 (D.C.Cir. 1972), a leading American authority. What vision of the common law does this evidence? Is this vision shared by courts in the United States? Is it appropriate, given the different histories and cultural contexts of the various common law countries?

2. Does the British House of Lords in *Sidaway* seem to focus on the doctor's duty while the Australian High Court in *Rogers* focuses on the patient's rights? What difference does this make? What different vision of the professional-patient relationship does it evidence? Does the following House of Lords opinion veer more towards *Sidaway* or *Rogers*?

Montgomery v. Lanarkshire Health Board

[2015] UKSC 11 (House of Lords, 2015)

Panel: Lord Neuberger, Lady Hale, Lord Kerr, Lord Clarke, Lord Wilson, Lord Reed, Lord Hodge

Lord Kerr and Lord Reed

Introduction

1. Nadine Montgomery gave birth to a baby boy on 1 October 1999 at Bellshill Maternity Hospital, Lanarkshire. As a result of complications during the delivery, the baby was born with severe disabilities. In these proceedings Mrs Montgomery seeks damages on behalf of her son for the injuries which he sustained. She attributes those injuries to negligence on the part of Dr Dina McLellan, a consultant obstetrician and gynaecologist employed by Lanarkshire Health Board, who was responsible for Mrs Montgomery's care during her pregnancy and labour. She also delivered the baby.

2. Before the Court of Session, two distinct grounds of negligence were advanced on behalf of Mrs Montgomery. The first concerned her ante-natal care. It was contended

that she ought to have been given advice about the risk of shoulder dystocia (the inability of the baby's shoulders to pass through the pelvis) which would be involved in vaginal birth, and of the alternative possibility of delivery by elective caesarean section. The second branch of the case concerned the management of labour. It was contended that Dr McLellan had negligently failed to perform a caesarean section in response to abnormalities indicated by cardiotocograph ("CTG") traces.

3. The Lord Ordinary, Lord Bannatyne, rejected both grounds of fault: [2010] CSOH 104. In relation to the first ground, he based his decision primarily on expert evidence of medical practice, following the approach laid down by the majority in *Sidaway v Board of Governors of the Bethlem Royal Hospital and the Maudsley Hospital* [1985] AC 871. He also concluded that, even if Mrs Montgomery had been given advice about the risk of serious harm to her baby as a consequence of shoulder dystocia, it would have made no difference in any event, since she would not have elected to have her baby delivered by caesarean section. That decision was upheld by the Inner House (Lord Eassie, Lord Hardie and Lord Emslie): [2013] CSIH 3; 2013 SC 245.

4. The appeal to this court has focused on the first ground of fault. The court has been invited to depart from the decision of the House of Lords in *Sidaway* and to re-consider the duty of a doctor towards a patient in relation to advice about treatment. * * *

* * *

The facts

* * *

7. In 1999 Mrs Montgomery was expecting her first baby. She is of small stature, being just over five feet in height. She suffers from insulin dependent diabetes mellitus. Women suffering from diabetes are likely to have babies that are larger than normal, and there can be a particular concentration of weight on the babies' shoulders. Because of her diabetes, Mrs Montgomery's was regarded as a high risk pregnancy requiring intensive monitoring. She therefore attended the combined obstetric and diabetic clinic at Bellshill Maternity Hospital, under the care of Dr McLellan, throughout her pregnancy.

* * *

11. According to Dr McLellan's evidence, in some cases the mother may be entirely unaware that shoulder dystocia has occurred. It is clear, however, that when shoulder dystocia happens and the mother knows of it, dealing with it is, at least, an unpleasant and frightening experience for her. It also gives rise to a variety of risks to her health.

12. Shoulder dystocia also presents risks to the baby. The physical manoeuvres and manipulations required to free the baby can cause it to suffer a broken shoulder or an avulsion of the brachial plexus—the nerve roots which connect the baby's arm to the spinal cord. An injury of the latter type may be transient or it may, as in the present case, result in permanent disability, leaving the child with a useless arm. The risk of a brachial plexus injury, in cases of shoulder dystocia involving diabetic mothers, is about 0.2%. In a very small percentage of cases of shoulder dystocia, the umbilical cord becomes trapped against the mother's pelvis. If, in consequence, the cord

becomes occluded, this can cause the baby to suffer from prolonged hypoxia, resulting in cerebral palsy or death. The risk of this happening is less than 0.1%.

13. Mrs Montgomery was told that she was having a larger than usual baby. But she was not told about the risks of her experiencing mechanical problems during labour. In particular she was not told about the risk of shoulder dystocia. It is agreed that that risk was 9–10% in the case of diabetic mothers. Unsurprisingly, Dr McLellan accepted that this was a high risk. But, despite the risk, she said that her practice was not to spend a lot of time, or indeed any time at all, discussing potential risks of shoulder dystocia. She explained that this was because, in her estimation, the risk of a grave problem for the baby resulting from shoulder dystocia was very small. She considered, therefore, that if the condition was mentioned, "most women will actually say, 'I'd rather have a caesarean section'". She went on to say that "if you were to mention shoulder dystocia to every [diabetic] patient, if you were to mention to any mother who faces labour that there is a very small risk of the baby dying in labour, then everyone would ask for a caesarean section, and it's not in the maternal interests for women to have caesarean sections".

* * *

17. At the 36-week appointment, Dr McLellan noted that Mrs Montgomery was "worried about [the] size of [the] baby". In her evidence, she accepted that Mrs Montgomery had expressed concern at that appointment about the size of the foetus and about the risk that the baby might be too big to be delivered vaginally. Dr McLellan also accepted that it was possible that Mrs Montgomery had expressed similar concerns previously. Certainly, she said, such concerns had been mentioned more than once. She stated that Mrs Montgomery had not asked her "specifically about exact risks". Had Mrs Montgomery done so, Dr McLellan said that she would have advised her about the risk of shoulder dystocia, and also about the risk of cephalopelvic disproportion (the baby's head becoming stuck). * * * In accordance with her practice in cases where she felt (in her words) that it was "fair to allow somebody to deliver vaginally", Dr McLellan advised Mrs Montgomery that she would be able to deliver vaginally, and that if difficulties were encountered during labour then recourse would be had to a caesarean section. Mrs Montgomery accepted that advice. But if she had requested an elective caesarean section, she would have been given one.

* * *

20. Mrs Montgomery's labour was induced by the administration of hormones, as Dr McLellan had planned. After several hours, labour became arrested. The strength of the contractions was then augmented by the administration of further hormones over a further period of several hours, so as to overcome whatever was delaying progress towards vaginal delivery. When the baby's head nevertheless failed to descend naturally, Dr McLellan used forceps. At 5.45 pm the baby's shoulder became impacted at a point when half of his head was outside the perineum.

21. Dr McLellan had never dealt with that situation before. She described it as very stressful for Mrs Montgomery and for all the staff in theatre, including herself. Mr

Peter Stewart, an expert witness led in support of Mrs Montgomery's case, described the situation as every obstetrician's nightmare. An anaesthetist gave Mrs Montgomery a general anaesthetic so as to enable the Zavanelli manoeuvre (i.e. pushing the baby back into the uterus, in order to perform an emergency caesarean section) to be attempted. Dr McLellan decided however that she had no other option but to try to complete the delivery. She pulled the baby's head with "significant traction" to complete the delivery of the head. In order to release the shoulders, she attempted to perform a symphysiotomy, and succeeded to some extent in cutting through the joint. No scalpels with fixed blades were available, however, and the blades she used became detached before the division of the joint had been completed. Eventually, "with just a huge adrenalin surge", Dr McLellan succeeded in pulling the baby free, and delivery was achieved at 5.57 pm.

22. During the 12 minutes between the baby's head appearing and the delivery, the umbilical cord was completely or partially occluded, depriving him of oxygen. After his birth, he was diagnosed as suffering from cerebral palsy of a dyskinetic type, which had been caused by the deprivation of oxygen. He also suffered a brachial plexus injury resulting in Erb's palsy (i.e. paralysis of the arm). All four of his limbs are affected by the cerebral palsy. If Mrs Montgomery had had an elective caesarean section her son would have been born uninjured.

* * *

Sidaway

* * *

40. * * * The question whether the same approach should be applied (as it had been, in *Bolam* itself) in relation to a failure to advise a patient of risks involved in treatment was considered by the House of Lords in *Sidaway v Board of Governors of the Bethlem Royal Hospital and the Maudsley Hospital* * * *.

41. In *Sidaway's* case this question was approached by the members of the House in different ways, but with a measure of overlap. At one end of the spectrum was Lord Diplock, who considered that any alleged breach of a doctor's duty of care towards his patient, whether it related to diagnosis, treatment or advice, should be determined by applying the *Bolam* test * * *.

* * *

43. At the other end of the spectrum was the speech of Lord Scarman, who took as his starting point "the patient's right to make his own decision, which may be seen as a basic human right protected by the common law" (p 882). * * *

44. In other words, if (1) the patient suffers damage, (2) as a result of an undisclosed risk, (3) which would have been disclosed by a doctor exercising reasonable care to respect her patient's right to decide whether to incur the risk, and (4) the patient would have avoided the injury if the risk had been disclosed, then the patient will in principle have a cause of action based on negligence.

* * *

50. Lord Bridge of Harwich, with whom Lord Keith of Kinkel agreed, accepted that a conscious adult patient of sound mind is entitled to decide for herself whether or not she will submit to a particular course of treatment proposed by the doctor. He recognised the logical force of the North American doctrine of informed consent, but regarded it as impractical in application. Like Lord Diplock, he emphasised patients' lack of medical knowledge, their vulnerability to making irrational judgments, and the role of "clinical judgment" in assessing how best to communicate to the patient the significant factors necessary to enable the patient to make an informed decision (p 899).

51. Lord Bridge was also unwilling to accept without qualification the distinction drawn by the Supreme Court of Canada, in *Reibl v Hughes* [1980] 2 SCR 880, between cases where the question is whether the doctor treated the patient in accordance with acceptable professional standards and cases concerned with the patient's right to know what risks are involved in undergoing treatment. In Lord Bridge's view, "a decision what degree of disclosure of risks is best calculated to assist a particular patient to make a rational choice as to whether or not to undergo a particular treatment must primarily be a matter of clinical judgment" (p 900). It followed that the question whether non-disclosure of risks was a breach of the doctor's duty of care was an issue "to be decided *primarily* on the basis of expert medical evidence, applying the *Bolam* test" (p 900; emphasis supplied).

* * *

55. Lord Templeman implicitly rejected the *Bolam* test, and approached the issue on the basis of an orthodox common law analysis. He noted, like Lord Diplock and Lord Bridge, the imbalance between the knowledge and objectivity of the doctor and the ignorance and subjectivity of the patient, but accepted that it was the right of the patient to decide whether or not to submit to treatment recommended by the doctor, and even to make an unbalanced and irrational judgment (p 904). In contract, it followed from the patient's right to decide whether to accept proposed treatment that "the doctor impliedly contracts to provide information which is adequate to enable the patient to reach a balanced judgment, subject always to the doctor's own obligation to say and do nothing which the doctor is satisfied will be harmful to the patient" (p 904). The obligation of the doctor "to have regard to the best interests of the patient but at the same time to make available to the patient sufficient information to enable the patient to reach a balanced judgment" (pp 904–905) also arose as a matter of a duty of care. Lord Templeman's formulation of the doctor's duty was, like Lord Scarman's, not confined to the disclosure of risks: the discussion of "the possible methods of treatment" (p 904), and therefore of reasonable alternatives to the treatment recommended, is also necessary if the patient is to reach a balanced judgment.

56. Lord Templeman thus arrived, by a different route, at an outcome not very different from that of Lord Scarman. Although Lord Scarman drew on the language of human rights, his reasoning was in substance the same as Lord Templeman's: the doctor's duty of care followed from the patient's right to decide whether to undergo the treatment recommended.

57. It would therefore be wrong to regard *Sidaway* as an unqualified endorsement of the application of the *Bolam* test to the giving of advice about treatment. Only Lord Diplock adopted that position. On his approach, the only situation, other than one covered by the *Bolam* test, in which a doctor would be under a duty to provide information to a patient would be in response to questioning by the patient.

* * *

59. There is also a logical difficulty inherent in this exception to the *Bolam* test, as the High Court of Australia pointed out in *Rogers v Whitaker* (1992) 175 CLR 479, 486–487. Why should the patient's asking a question make any difference in negligence, if medical opinion determines whether the duty of care requires that the risk should be disclosed? The patient's desire for the information, even if made known to the doctor, does not alter medical opinion. The exception, in other words, is logically destructive of the supposed rule. Medical opinion might of course accept that the information should be disclosed in response to questioning, but there would then be no exception to the *Bolam* test.

* * *

Comparative law

70. The court has been referred to case law from a number of other major common law jurisdictions. It is unnecessary to discuss it in detail. It is sufficient to note that the Supreme Court of Canada has adhered in its more recent case law to the approach adopted in *Reibl v Hughes*, and that its approach to the duty of care has been followed elsewhere, for example by the High Court of Australia in *Rogers v Whitaker* (1992) 175 CLR 479 and subsequent cases.

* * *

72. The High Court of Australia in *Rogers* also reformulated the test of the materiality of a risk so as to encompass the situation in which, as the doctor knows or ought to know, the actual patient would be likely to attach greater significance to a risk than the hypothetical reasonable patient might do:

> "a risk is material if, in the circumstances of the particular case, a reasonable person in the patient's position, if warned of the risk, would be likely to attach significance to it or if the medical practitioner is or should reasonably be aware that the particular patient, if warned of the risk, would be likely to attach significance to it." (p 490)

73. That is undoubtedly right: the doctor's duty of care takes its precise content from the needs, concerns and circumstances of the individual patient, to the extent that they are or ought to be known to the doctor. * * *

Conclusions on the duty of disclosure

74. The Hippocratic Corpus advises physicians to reveal nothing to the patient of her present or future condition, "for many patients through this cause have taken a turn for the worse" (*Decorum*, XVI). Around two millennia later, in *Sidaway's* case Lord Templeman said that "the provision of too much information may prejudice

the attainment of the objective of restoring the patient's health" (p 904); and similar observations were made by Lord Diplock and Lord Bridge. On that view, if the optimisation of the patient's health is treated as an overriding objective, then it is unsurprising that the disclosure of information to a patient should be regarded as an aspect of medical care, and that the extent to which disclosure is appropriate should therefore be treated as a matter of clinical judgment, the appropriate standards being set by the medical profession.

75. Since *Sidaway*, however, it has become increasingly clear that the paradigm of the doctor-patient relationship implicit in the speeches in that case has ceased to reflect the reality and complexity of the way in which healthcare services are provided, or the way in which the providers and recipients of such services view their relationship. One development which is particularly significant in the present context is that patients are now widely regarded as persons holding rights, rather than as the passive recipients of the care of the medical profession. They are also widely treated as consumers exercising choices: a viewpoint which has underpinned some of the developments in the provision of healthcare services. In addition, a wider range of healthcare professionals now provide treatment and advice of one kind or another to members of the public * * *. The treatment which they can offer is now understood to depend not only upon their clinical judgment, but upon bureaucratic decisions as to such matters as resource allocation, cost-containment and hospital administration: decisions which are taken by non-medical professionals. Such decisions are generally understood within a framework of institutional rather than personal responsibilities, and are in principle susceptible to challenge under public law rather than, or in addition to, the law of delict or tort.

76. Other changes in society, and in the provision of healthcare services, should also be borne in mind. One which is particularly relevant in the present context is that it has become far easier, and far more common, for members of the public to obtain information about symptoms, investigations, treatment options, risks and side-effects via such media as the internet (where, although the information available is of variable quality, reliable sources of information can readily be found), patient support groups, and leaflets issued by healthcare institutions. The labelling of pharmaceutical products and the provision of information sheets is a further example, which is of particular significance because it is required by laws premised on the ability of the citizen to comprehend the information provided. It would therefore be a mistake to view patients as uninformed, incapable of understanding medical matters, or wholly dependent upon a flow of information from doctors. The idea that patients were medically uninformed and incapable of understanding medical matters was always a questionable generalisation, as Lord Diplock implicitly acknowledged by making an exception for highly educated men of experience. To make it the default assumption on which the law is to be based is now manifestly untenable.

* * *

80. In addition to these developments in society and in medical practice, there have also been developments in the law. Under the stimulus of the Human Rights Act

1998, the courts have become increasingly conscious of the extent to which the common law reflects fundamental values. As Lord Scarman pointed out in *Sidaway's* case, these include the value of self-determination * * *. As well as underlying aspects of the common law, that value also underlies the right to respect for private life protected by article 8 of the European Convention on Human Rights. The resulting duty to involve the patient in decisions relating to her treatment has been recognised in judgments of the European Court of Human Rights * * *, as well as in a number of decisions of courts in the United Kingdom. The same value is also reflected more specifically in other international instruments: see, in particular, article 5 of the Convention for the Protection of Human Rights and Dignity of the Human Being with regard to the Application of Biology and Medicine: Convention on Human Rights and Biomedicine, concluded by the member states of the Council of Europe, other states and the European Community at Oviedo on 4 April 1997.

81. The social and legal developments which we have mentioned point away from a model of the relationship between the doctor and the patient based upon medical paternalism. They also point away from a model based upon a view of the patient as being entirely dependent on information provided by the doctor. What they point towards is an approach to the law which, instead of treating patients as placing themselves in the hands of their doctors (and then being prone to sue their doctors in the event of a disappointing outcome), treats them so far as possible as adults who are capable of understanding that medical treatment is uncertain of success and may involve risks, accepting responsibility for the taking of risks affecting their own lives, and living with the consequences of their choices.

82. In the law of negligence, this approach entails a duty on the part of doctors to take reasonable care to ensure that a patient is aware of material risks of injury that are inherent in treatment. This can be understood, within the traditional framework of negligence, as a duty of care to avoid exposing a person to a risk of injury which she would otherwise have avoided, but it is also the counterpart of the patient's entitlement to decide whether or not to incur that risk. The existence of that entitlement, and the fact that its exercise does not depend exclusively on medical considerations, are important. They point to a fundamental distinction between, on the one hand, the doctor's role when considering possible investigatory or treatment options and, on the other, her role in discussing with the patient any recommended treatment and possible alternatives, and the risks of injury which may be involved.

83. The former role is an exercise of professional skill and judgment * * *. But it is a *non sequitur* to conclude that the question whether a risk of injury, or the availability of an alternative form of treatment, ought to be discussed with the patient is also a matter of purely professional judgment. The doctor's advisory role cannot be regarded as solely an exercise of medical skill without leaving out of account the patient's entitlement to decide on the risks to her health which she is willing to run (a decision which may be influenced by non-medical considerations). Responsibility for determining the nature and extent of a person's rights rests with the courts, not with the medical professions.

84. Furthermore, because the extent to which a doctor may be inclined to discuss risks with a patient is not determined by medical learning or experience, the application of the *Bolam* test to this question is liable to result in the sanctioning of differences in practice which are attributable not to divergent schools of thought in medical science, but merely to divergent attitudes among doctors as to the degree of respect owed to their patients.

* * *

86. It follows that the analysis of the law by the majority in *Sidaway* is unsatisfactory, in so far as it treated the doctor's duty to advise her patient of the risks of proposed treatment as falling within the scope of the *Bolam* test, subject to two qualifications of that general principle, neither of which is fundamentally consistent with that test. It is unsurprising that courts have found difficulty in the subsequent application of *Sidaway*, and that the courts in England and Wales have in reality departed from it * * *.

87. The correct position, in relation to the risks of injury involved in treatment, can now be seen to be substantially that adopted in *Sidaway* by Lord Scarman * * *. An adult person of sound mind is entitled to decide which, if any, of the available forms of treatment to undergo, and her consent must be obtained before treatment interfering with her bodily integrity is undertaken. The doctor is therefore under a duty to take reasonable care to ensure that the patient is aware of any material risks involved in any recommended treatment, and of any reasonable alternative or variant treatments. The test of materiality is whether, in the circumstances of the particular case, a reasonable person in the patient's position would be likely to attach significance to the risk, or the doctor is or should reasonably be aware that the particular patient would be likely to attach significance to it.

88. The doctor is however entitled to withhold from the patient information as to a risk if he reasonably considers that its disclosure would be seriously detrimental to the patient's health. The doctor is also excused from conferring with the patient in circumstances of necessity, as for example where the patient requires treatment urgently but is unconscious or otherwise unable to make a decision. It is unnecessary for the purposes of this case to consider in detail the scope of those exceptions.

* * *

The disclosure of risks in the present case

94. Approaching the present case on this basis, there can be no doubt that it was incumbent on Dr McLellan to advise Mrs Montgomery of the risk of shoulder dystocia if she were to have her baby by vaginal delivery, and to discuss with her the alternative of delivery by caesarean section. * * *

95. There is no question in this case of Dr McLellan's being entitled to withhold information about the risk because its disclosure would be harmful to her patient's health. Although her evidence indicates that it was her policy to withhold information about the risk of shoulder dystocia from her patients because they would otherwise

request caesarean sections, the "therapeutic exception" is not intended to enable doctors to prevent their patients from taking an informed decision. Rather, it is the doctor's responsibility to explain to her patient why she considers that one of the available treatment options is medically preferable to the others, having taken care to ensure that her patient is aware of the considerations for and against each of them.

* * *

Conclusion

106. For these reasons, we would allow the appeal.

Lady Hale

107. In the third (2010) edition of their leading work on *Principles of Medical Law*, Andrew Grubb, Judith Laing and Jean McHale confidently announced that a detailed analysis of the different speeches of the House of Lords in *Sidaway v Board of Governors of the Bethlem Royal Hospital and the Maudsley Hospital* [1985] AC 871 was no longer necessary. A combination of the 2008 Guidance provided by the General Medical Council, the decision of the Court of Appeal in *Pearce v United Bristol Healthcare NHS Trust* [1999] PIQR P 53 and the decision of the House of Lords in *Chester v Afshar* [2005] 1 AC 134 meant that it could now be stated "with a reasonable degree of confidence" that the need for informed consent was firmly part of English law (para 8.70). This case has provided us with the opportunity, not only to confirm that confident statement, but also to make it clear that the same principles apply in Scotland.

* * *

114. We do not have a full transcript of the evidence, but in the extracts we do have Dr McLellan referred to explaining to a mother who requested a caesarean section "why it may not be in the mother's best interest" and later expressed the view that "it's not in the maternal interests for women to have caesarean sections". Whatever Dr McLellan may have had in mind, this does not look like a purely medical judgment. It looks like a judgment that vaginal delivery is in some way morally preferable to a caesarean section: so much so that it justifies depriving the pregnant woman of the information needed for her to make a free choice in the matter. Giving birth vaginally is indeed a unique and wonderful experience, but it has not been suggested that it inevitably leads to a closer and better relationship between mother and child than does a caesarean section.

115. In any event, once the argument departs from purely medical considerations and involves value judgments of this sort, it becomes clear, as Lord Kerr and Lord Reed conclude at para 85, that the *Bolam* test, of conduct supported by a responsible body of medical opinion, becomes quite inapposite. A patient is entitled to take into account her own values, her own assessment of the comparative merits of giving birth in the "natural" and traditional way and of giving birth by caesarean section, whatever medical opinion may say, alongside the medical evaluation of the risks to herself and her baby. She may place great value on giving birth in the natural way and be prepared to take the risks to herself and her baby which this entails. The medical profession must respect her choice, unless she lacks the legal capacity to decide (*St George's Healthcare NHS Trust v S* [1999] Fam 26). There is no good reason why

the same should not apply in reverse, if she is prepared to forgo the joys of natural childbirth in order to avoid some not insignificant risks to herself or her baby. She cannot force her doctor to offer treatment which he or she considers futile or inappropriate. But she is at least entitled to the information which will enable her to take a proper part in that decision.

116. As NICE (2011) puts it, "Pregnant women should be offered evidence-based information and support to enable them to make informed decisions about their care and treatment" (para 1.1.1.1). Gone are the days when it was thought that, on becoming pregnant, a woman lost, not only her capacity, but also her right to act as a genuinely autonomous human being.

117. These additional observations, dealing with the specific example of pregnancy and childbirth, are merely a footnote to the comprehensive judgment of Lord Kerr and Lord Reed, with which I entirely agree. Were anyone to be able to detect a difference between us, I would instantly defer to their way of putting it. I would allow this appeal.

Notes

1. Commentators have noted that *Montgomery* represents not only an evolution in informed consent doctrine, but also in the doctor-patient relationship, which today involves more "nuanced negotiation of information" and "a more cooperative approach in the consultation room." Sarah W. Chan et al., *Montgomery* and Informed Consent: Where Are We Now?, 357 *British Medical Journal* (May 12, 2017). Others echo the sentiment that *Montgomery* is a product of increasingly sophisticated patients and increasingly accessible medical information. Luke Sizer & Philip Arnold, The Changing Paradigm of the Doctor-Patient Relationship: *Montgomery v Lanarkshire Health Board* and Developments in the "Duty to Warn," 129 (1429) *New Zealand Medical Journal* (Jan. 29, 2016).

2. Today, many jurisdictions have codified informed consent standards by statute or regulation. Indeed, most U.S. states and Canadian provinces have codified the rules for informed consent. For example, the *Civil Code of Quebec* includes several sections that grant decisionmaking authority to patients. Likewise, New Zealand addresses informed consent in its *Code of Health and Disability Services Consumers' Rights*, reflecting the broader trend of codifying patients' rights in general.

3. Despite the *Nuremberg Code* and *Declaration of Helsinki*, there have been several major scandals involving breaches of informed consent in research — from the infamous multi-decade Tuskegee experiment that exposed African American men to untreated syphilis, not uncovered until 1972, to syphilis research sponsored by the United States and the Pan American Health Organization (PAHO) in Guatemala, for which the U.S. government formally apologized in 2010. Later incidents include observational studies of women suffering from cervical cancer in New Zealand, to nutritional studies of native school children in Canada, to Pfizer conducting clinical

trials of Trovan on children in Nigeria. *See* Trudo Lemmens, Informed Consent, *Routledge Handbook of Medical Law and Ethics* 27–48 (Yann Joly & Bartha Maria Knoppers eds., 2015); Jacqui Wise, Pfizer Accused of Testing New Drug Without Ethical Approval, 322 *British Medical Journal* 194 (Jan. 27, 2001); Jacob Schuman, Beyond Nuremberg: A Critique of "Informed Consent" in Third World Human Subject Research, 25 *Journal of Law and Health* 123 (2012).

4. The next reading compares informed consent reforms in Taiwan—a country in which doctors previously had no duty to inform patients—to the more well-established standards in the United States, United Kingdom, and Canada.

John G. Culhane, King-Jean Wu, Oluyomi Faparusi & Eric J. Juray, *Toward a Mature Doctrine of Informed Consent: Lessons from a Comparative Law Analysis*

1(2) *British Journal of American Legal Studies*
551, 552–55, 572–79 (Fall 2012)

Today the doctrine of informed consent is generally well accepted in the United States and other common law countries. Deriving from the principle of patient autonomy, the doctrine places the force of law behind the common-sense notion that every medical patient "of sound mind" has the right to be armed with all of the information that might be relevant to the decision-making process. Thus, the material risks of the proposed treatment (and of non-treatment) and the availability of alternatives are to be disclosed. When such disclosure is not made, the physician can be liable when the undisclosed risk materializes. In recognizing the doctrine, courts have (at least conceptually) come down on the side of injured patients and the legal system through which they seek redress rather than in favor of the medical profession. In so doing, courts abolished the regime in which doctors had enjoyed the benefits of a rule that allowed their judgment to dictate what was best for the patient.

* * *

* * * This article brings a comparative law analysis to bear on the doctrine of informed consent. In doing so, we search for a standard that would be more faithful to the animating principles of the doctrine, while taking seriously concerns about extensive physician liability and the related issue of judicial management of such liability. We draw on the law of the United States, the United Kingdom, Taiwan, and finally Canada. We focus on the various standards and tests courts have developed to adjudicate negligence claims stemming from lack of informed consent in those countries. * * *

* * *

[This article] describes and analyzes the law of informed consent as it has developed in Taiwan. We praise the law as a significant advance over the previous legal regime, under which physicians were under no legal obligation to arm their patients with information sufficient to enable informed decision making. However, meaningful as these advances have been, Taiwanese doctors still rely in large part on a signed consent waiver. Yet courts have begun to see that forms, however comprehensive, are no substitute for a truly informed discussion between health care providers and their patients.

* * *

IV. INFORMED CONSENT LAW IN TAIWAN: FROM FORMS TO REALITY

A. History and the Rise of Forms

The concept of informed consent is relatively new to Taiwan. Before 2003, patients in Taiwan generally lacked sufficient information about the nature, risks and alternatives of contemplated procedure, let alone their rights. While there was typically a requirement for consent to the procedure itself—thereby precluding a claim based on battery—such consent was not required to be informed. This problem became more serious as the number of needless surgeries performed in Taiwan continued to increase. Generally speaking, these increases were caused by insurance payments and for cultural reasons.

From the insurance perspective, the reimbursement system of National Health Insurance (NHI) plays a factor in therapeutic decision-making. Sometimes, it encourages surgeons to perform surgeries, because generally the insurance will pay more reimbursements (benefits) than the alternate conservative managements. Further exacerbating the problem are the medical cultural norms at play in Taiwan. Historically, the physician-patient relationship has been very one-sided, with very few patients questioning the decision-making of the physician. Therefore, the default model has been that the patient generally accepts the risks of the suggested surgeries while the surgeon enjoys the benefits of enhanced reimbursements.

There are several cases that addressed the issue of lack of informed consent. As the cases increased dramatically, the government felt compelled to solve the underlying problems giving rise to them. In August 2003, the Department of Health (DOH), which governs medical care in Taiwan, introduced a medical consent form. This new medical consent form requires a detailed explanation of the nature of the disease, the surgical site and how the operation will be carried out, the success rate of the operation, the possibility of transfusion, the possible risks and their managements, the possible outcomes of refusing the treatment or procedure, the alternatives, and the possible temporal and permanent complications. At the end, there are declarations from both the patient and physician to ensure that the physician has fully described the operation, and that the patient was fully aware of the nature of the operation and agreed to undergo the surgery.

In 2004, the commitment to informed consent represented by this form was strengthened by the issuance of a document by the DOH entitled *Guiding Principles for Medical Care Institutions in Informing Patients and Obtaining Surgery and Anesthesia Informed Consent from Patient when Performing Surgery* (Guiding Principles). These principles begin with procedures: The consent forms are both to be filled out in duplicate. The physician/anesthesiologist shall explain all information relevant to the operation to be performed. After the informing process is completed, the physician/anesthesiologist in charge of the operation/anesthesia shall answer the patient's questions and discuss the procedure, and then sign the appropriate consent forms and record the time and date of notification.

The Guiding Principles next discuss the notification guidelines. Before information is provided to the patient, the patient's level of receptivity should be assessed. In principle, information shall be given directly to the patient. In the event that the patient is unable to give informed consent, the physician must receive informed consent from the patient's guardian or agent. Physicians should respect patients' decision-making power, present information in simple, easy-to-understand language and a calm manner, and avoid exaggerated or threatening words. Similar to the first section of the Guiding Principles, this section further imposes stringent requirements on the physician to fully inform the patients. Finally, the section strongly encourages all members of the medical team to participate in these discussions with the patients, and instructs them to direct all necessary questions to higher authorities. This is a particularly important provision, because as we will discuss, the imposition of more demanding informed consent standards should naturally include more members of the medical profession. This allows patients to receive more information without overburdening the physicians.

The third section refers to signing the surgery consent form. The surgery consent form must [be] signed personally by the patient, except under the following circumstances: if the patient is a minor, or for any reason is unable to express consent, the form may be signed by a person specified under the Medical Care Act (legal agent, spouse, relative or related party). After a consent form is signed and verified, the medical care institution must file one copy with the patient's medical records, and provide the other copy to the patient.

The legislators also created new articles relating to surgery consent (article 63) and invasive examination consent (article 64) in [the] Act of Medical Care in 2004. According to article 63:

> Before a surgical intervention, a patient or his/her legal representative, spouse, relative or interested person should be informed, by the medical care organization, of the reasons, success rate or possible complications and risks of an operation which may be incurred. Unless in an emergency, no surgery can be performed without the written consents on anesthesia and surgery, which should be signed by the patient or his/her legal representative, spouse, relatives or interested persons. In case the patient is a minor or unable to sign the written consents by himself/herself, it could be signed by his/her legal representative, spouse, relatives or interested persons.

Analogous language appears in article 64. The goal, of course, is to help the patient to determine whether to consent to or to reject an invasive examination.

B. Cases Claiming Failure to Provide Informed Consent

In Taiwan, patients seeking redress under a medical malpractice claim can resort to either civil or criminal procedures. In a civil lawsuit, plaintiffs need to demonstrate the fault, injury, and proximate causation of fault and injury for torts compensation. But in a situation that will surely perplex the American audience, most patients (79%)

choose to proceed through criminal law channels by filing the case with prosecutors. In the criminal procedures, plaintiffs do not have to pay fees for litigation and can get medical history or any related records by prosecutors. The court is required to investigate, and the sentence can include monetary recovery to the patient or imprisonment of the medical practitioners.

In addition to the consent forms, the doctrine of informed consent in Taiwan can also be understood through criminal and civil case law that has developed. In *Kuo v. Yang*, the Supreme Court held that, if the physician asked the patient to sign the consent form (before a cardiac catheterization) but did not explain the essence of this procedure to the patient, it would be difficult to know whether the patient understood what he or she was consenting to. The Court held that the doctor had not properly obtained informed consent from the patient. Theoretically, the physician could not know the patient's apprehensions about surgery if there was no discussion.

On this vital question of what the patient understood, another important case is *Hong v. Huang* where a gynecologist injured a young female during an examination. The patient chose to seek redress via criminal procedures under an informed consent theory, alleging that the doctor did not inform her about the nature, modality, and the risk of this invasive examination. The court agreed that there was a lack of communication and that injuries had occurred, despite the fact that a witness nurse proved the doctor did inform the patient about the examination briefly and the additional difficulty that proximate causation between the fault and the injuries were hard to define. These cases suggest that the judiciary is leading the effort in Taiwan to encourage physicians to disclose all material risks in going beyond the standard consent form.

C. Is the Law Working in Taiwan?

Six months after the implementation of the consent forms, a survey was conducted for evaluation of the effectiveness of the forms and the new articles in the Act of Medical Care. Out of a total of 500 issued questionnaires, 444 were returned and collected, a returns ratio of 88.8%. Disappointingly, the results showed that only 65.09% of patients agreed that doctors had mentioned the possible complications of the surgery, 89.77% knew the reasons for surgery, 86.57% realized the success rate and risks of the surgery, and 88.04% understood the prognosis of this scheduled management. While 87.39% of the patients were satisfied with the new consent form, only 61.0% of them received it before they were admitted.

These results and the cases discussed suggest that the law is not working as effectively as was hoped/intended. It was argued that most physicians still lacked awareness about the concept of patient's autonomy and the intent of informed consent. Most of the doctors only focused on practicing medicine; they paid little attention on the paperwork, and simply lacked sufficient time to explain and discuss the full extent of the operation and other alternatives with the patients. In order to improve the unfavorable situation, the DOH announced that the proper implementation of informed consent would be an item in the regular review of hospitals, and that the NHI would not reimburse the costs of operation to hospitals without completed informed consent procedures.

Requirements are in place to encourage hospitals to help doctors conduct the consent procedures with patients. In addition to the efforts of government, Taiwan Healthcare Reform Foundation (THRF) also suggests that patients should try to ask important questions before accepting the operation: *Should I undergo this operation? What kind of operation it is? Is there any alternative to the operation? What might happen after the operation?* These questions will help the patients understand the reason, method and possible achievement of this operation, and at the same time prevent them from falling victim to the questionable procedures set up for additional reimbursements. While ultimate responsibility for informing patient consent must remain with health care professionals—because lay patients will not be able to formulate all the questions that must be asked in order to inform themselves—the THRF's list of questions is nonetheless an important acknowledgment that communication is a back-and-forth process, and that patients might be more attuned to physician disclosures where they actively participate in the discussion.

The problem with using consent forms has been raised in other jurisdictions, and the deficiencies with this approach are apparent. The primary problem, as discussed above, is the tendency of over-extended health care providers to rely on forms without properly apprising the patients of the risks associated with surgery. They believe that the form includes most of the relevant information, the patient will sign it, and consent will be deemed informed. As a Canadian court recently stated, reliance on a form is "absurd and contrary to the guiding principles of the informed consent process." This approach completely ignores the successes of informed consent—subjective patient autonomy. As we argue in Part V, the Canadian approach is desirable because it requires subjective factors to be taken into consideration in every case. The Taiwanese form is a standard document that fills in certain blanks related to the procedure. While it is personalized with the name, treatment, and risks, this approach is not a substitute for the meaningful discussion required to give the patient the opportunity to make an informed decision.

Conversely, consent forms can be beneficial to both the patient and the physician if utilized appropriately. While they have too often been used as ends in themselves, rather than a means towards the goal of truly informed consent, they can also be used as a starting point to a more informed discussion. If the subsequent discussion does not in fact take place, the problem might be cultural boundaries that sometimes prevent the patient from comfortably asking questions of the physician's decisions. Therefore, if the form provides answers to the patient's questions, that result will in some cases be an improvement over the situation that existed before the forms were created.

Likewise, the consent form may assist the physician in avoiding criminal punishment in informed consent cases. The form may therefore have been an appropriate step for Taiwan to have taken in 2003. The country was working to move past the problem of excessive patient deference to physicians that had existed for too long. The form has likely helped patients understand more information while shielding the physicians from excess civil and criminal liability. Further, the DOH has provided directives seeking to impose even greater responsibilities on physicians.

The question then is whether this would be an effective system to implement in the United States, in the on-going struggle to expand the boundaries of informed consent law to cover medical procedures beyond surgical care. Experience with consent forms in the U.S. suggests otherwise. Too often, such forms are filled in by rote, and summon little if any discussion between patient and health care provider. Thus, the forms sometimes have the unintended consequence of compromising the very principles of informed consent they are supposed to be furthering.

Further, the doctrine of informed consent evolved in drastically different ways in the United States and Taiwan, and for very different reasons. In Taiwan, the change was statutorily driven to escape the cultural norms that had dominated the culture. In the United States, the change was judicially driven because of an emerging view of autonomy over one's body. Fidelity to that principle can be achieved only by legal rules that encourage the physician to speak with the patient and disclose all of the material risks to that patient. If the stock form is used, it typically will not be tailored to the particular patient nor, as stated above, will it usually encourage the patient to ask more questions.

Yet the American approach is itself flawed, too often sacrificing patient autonomy to the perceived need for an objective standard that will further both judicial management of the cases and, overall, more just outcomes. A better accommodation of these competing values can, and must, be achieved. It happens that a successful model already exists—just to our north. It turns out that the Canadian approach—referred to by the shorthand description of the "modified objective" test—safeguards patient autonomy without creating unmanageable physician liability. * * *

* * *

Note

One of the pleasures of comparative law is to experience the exotic in other legal cultures. The *Sidaway* decision and the traditional Taiwanese practice of informed consent certainly seem exotic to the American observer. Likewise, Robert Leflar has written extensively on the Japanese system, and his evaluation of informed consent law there shows how different the traditional Japanese approach was. *See* Robert B. Leflar, *Law and Health Care in Japan: The Renaissance of Informed Consent,* published as *Nihon no iryō to hō: Infōmudo konsento runessansu* (2002), pp. 125–146 (Michiyuki Nagasawa, trans.). What are the benefits, and risks, of experiencing the exotic in other legal cultures? See Nathaniel Berman, Aftershocks: Exoticization, Normalization, and the Hermeneutic Compulsion, 1997 *Utah L. Rev.* 281

2. The Problem of Causation

In the United States, plaintiffs rarely succeed in pressing informed consent complaints because many courts have followed the D.C. Circuit's opinion in *Canterbury v. Spence*, 464 F.2d 772 (D.C. Cir. 1972) on causation. Under *Canterbury*, a plaintiff has not suffered from a failure to disclose unless the patient would have declined the treatment that resulted in harm had the withheld information been disclosed. The *Canterbury* court, however, worried about the doctor falling victim to patient hindsight, held that causation could be shown only if a prudent person in the patient's position would have declined treatment if suitably informed. 464 F.2d at 790–91. *Canterbury* applied, that is, an objective test for determining causation. A moment's reflection, however, suggests that it will rarely be possible to prove that a reasonable patient would have declined treatment unless the treatment itself was unreasonable (or experimental). Thus, a patient who undergoes a procedure without sufficient information will rarely be able to recover for lack of informed consent unless the proposed treatment was itself unreasonable.

As the following excerpt from Dieter Giesen's monumental treatise on medical negligence shows, this position is rejected by continental legal systems, which apply a subjective test, looking to what the particular patient would have done. Many courts go even further, moreover, requiring the defendant to show that the patient would have accepted treatment were the information provided. The case of *Chappel v. Hart,* which follows, represents a common law court applying a subjective standard.

Dieter Giesen, *International Medical Malpractice Law*

341–355 (1980)

* * *

According to the Civil Law, causation between the physician's failure to discharge his duty of disclosure and the resulting damage is sufficient to establish both contractual and/or delictual liability. Where personal injury is caused by unconsented-to medical procedures, the physician causing the damage has the burden of proving that his acts were legal and covered by a valid consent based on a proper exercise of his duty of disclosure. Consent is a defence throughout the law of delict, and, like all other defences in that branch of the law, must always be raised and substantiated by the defendant. However, by implication, before a defendant can obtain a legally acceptable consent, he must first have rendered to his patient such information as to enable him to appreciate the nature and significance of the proposed procedure, available alternatives, anticipated results, and the risks that may ensure, and if called upon, show to the satisfaction of the court that he did so. As usual, courts will be the final arbiter. Where it is established that the disclosure malpractice did not cause the injury because the patient would in any case have submitted to it, then at least according to German and Swiss law, the plaintiff's case comes to a quick end. Since the basis of the physician's liability is his negligent failure properly to discharge his duty of care and disclosure, there is no need for the patient to go on to establish that the physician reckoned with or negligently disregarded the damage thereby caused.

At Common Law, the position is somewhat different. As far as the tort of battery is concerned, the patient does not have to prove either causation or damage in order to establish a cause of action (although causation is, however, relevant to the recovery of compensatory damages). But actions in trespass are now rather restricted and, after cases such as *Cobbs v. Grant*, *Canterbury v. Spence*, *Reibl v. Hughes*, or *Chatterton v. Gerson* and *Hills v. Potter* are, except for the more extreme cases of an invalid (vitiated) consent, probably beyond recall outside this narrowly confined area. In both the law of contract and the remainder of the law of torts, it normally is the patient who must prove both causation and damage, especially in negligence actions.

In the tort of negligence, where substandard disclosure practices and the question of the patient's consent are at issue, Common Law courts apply different tests of causation. They may apply a subjective test, as in England or New Zealand, and ask what *this* plaintiff patient would have decided had he been informed of the risk which was in fact concealed. Alternatively, as in Canada and the United States, they may apply an "objective" test of "what a prudent [or reasonable] person in the patient's position would have decided if suitably informed of all perils bearing significance." Finally, they may apply a "combined test," now slowly emerging in Canada in what could be called the post-*Reibl* case law, consisting of considerations both of what this particular patient, and a reasonable patient in that patient's position, would have decided.

In all these cases, the causal relationship between the physician's failure of disclosure and the injury to the patient's health "arises only if it is established that, had revelation been made, consent to treatment would not have been given." Much will, of course, depend on which "test" is being used; if treatment turns out to be unsuccessful, the patient certainly will sometimes be sorely tempted to say that, had he been told of the risks, he would not have chosen to undergo the treatment proposed, or, as in cases like *Thake v. Maurice* or a similar German decision, would have taken the necessary precautions or steps to avoid the damage now incurred.

a) Where an objective test of causation is applied, "it is not enough ... for the Court to be convinced that the plaintiff would have refused the treatment if he had been fully informed; the Court must *also* be satisfied that a reasonable patient, in the same situation, would have done so." This astonishing proposition apparently arises from the fear "that every patient who becomes a plaintiff will insist that he would have foregone the operation if he had been properly warned." The objective test can thus be interpreted "as a method of protecting doctors from unwarranted claims." Several important North American decisions have firmly rejected the subjective test on this basis.

But it is "unclear how justice is advanced by wilfully closing your eyes to evidence of what the patient actually would have done in those cases where the reasonable patient test fails." Courts which apply a subjective test have had to come to grips with the problem of embittered patients; patients must not be modeled to fit the law but the law must rather be organized in a way which sufficiently protects the patient's right of self-determination, including his or her idiosyncracies.

According to Professors Hart and Honoré, the adoption of an "objective" test can also be seen "as a *pis aller* resorted to because direct evidence of the patient's probable reaction is unlikely to be reliable." It may be questioned, however, why an assessment of what the "reasonable" patient might have done in the real patient's position should in any way be more reliable as a test, than what a patient with hindsight knowledge of subsequent events and developments, says he would have done. At least the *real* patient's credibility can be evaluated by sensitive courts whereas that of "this excellent but odious character" the prudent reasonable but imaginary model of near-perfection on the Clapham omnibus cannot or, at least, adds to the problems of evaluating a hypothetical case those of evaluating a hypothetical fellow and his hypothetical reactions.

As has been said with apposite irony by Lord Diplock in the *Sidaway* case, courts which measure a patient's right of self-determination by the yardstick of "reasonableness," pay no more than lip service to the concept. In the words of the German Federal Supreme Court, "no one has the right to set himself up as judge and decide in what circumstances another person would reasonably be prepared to sacrifice his bodily integrity in order to recover from illness." As has been stated by the New Zealand Court of Appeal in a well-known case, every patient has "[a] right to decline operative investigation or treatment however unreasonable or foolish this may appear in the eyes of his medical advisers."

This right of self-determination is not legally protected only to the extent and standards of what *others* think is reasonable. Every adult patient of sound mind is legally free to decide for *any* reason that appeals to him and has a right to be taken seriously; he also "has a right to be wrong." The causation hurdle for the plaintiff in informed consent or substandard disclosure cases remains formidable enough, but it would indeed be ironical if the courts, by applying a fallacious "objective" patient test, were to take away with one hand the greater fairness given to the patient with the other in abandoning the medical professional standard of disclosure in favour of a principally patient-based informational needs test. This should itself be sufficient to exclude "objective" tests from any further consideration as a test of causation.

b) Furthermore, it is submitted that the "objective" test is, quite apart from what the late Chief Justice of Canada propounded in *Reibl v. Hughes*, *not* in itself a test of causation at all.

First, there is the serious problem inherent in the "objective" test of "causation," that there can be more than just one "reasonable" decision in any given situation. Each of two mutually exclusive choices can be regarded as reasonable in the sense that a reasonable man might equally choose either. Thus, the *post Canterbury* and *Reibl* cases fail to allow for the possibility of a decision to decline and a decision to accept being equally reasonable.

Secondly, as has been convincingly argued by Professor Robertson,

> [t]he only way in which the objective test can operate as a test of causation is if there is added to it the presumption that the plaintiff would have acted in the same way as a reasonable person. By applying this presumption, a causal link is established between the defendant's negligence and the plaintiff's injury. Moreover, for the objective test to apply as the sole test of causation in informed consent cases, this presumption must be regarded as irrebuttable. Thus, evidence that the plaintiff, if properly informed, would still have agreed to the treatment, even though a reasonable person would not have done so, must be regarded as irrelevant.

Accordingly, it has been concluded that the "objective" test is in fact not operating as a test of causation; rather, it is performing primarily "an evidentiary function in that it provides a test of the credibility and reliability of the plaintiff's own testimony that he would have declined the treatment if he had been informed of the risks." Thus, it operates to dispose of altogether unreasonable claims. Professor Robertson concludes, therefore, that "to satisfy the objective test the plaintiff does not have to establish that a reasonable man *would have* declined the treatment. Instead, it is sufficient if the plaintiff establishes that his decision to forego the treatment would have been reasonable in the sense that it is a decision which a reasonable man might well have reached in similar circumstances."

However, it is submitted that the "reasonable" man still figures too prominently in this proposition for it to work as a test of causation. As was aptly emphasized by Cox J in the recent South Australian case of *Gover v. State of South Australia*: "At any rate the basic causation principle governing actions in negligence plainly supports, in my opinion, the subjective test."

It should be noted that English, New Zealand and also perhaps Australian courts and judges still adhere to a subjective test, as do some American jurisdictions and most courts in Civil Law countries. It is significant that, in evidential circumstances much more favourable to the plaintiff patient than at Common Law outside the field of trespass, the German Federal Supreme Court, although it has similarly warned of the dangers of hindsight, still adheres to a subjective test which accepts that a patient may be as unreasonable to himself as he wishes as long as he is an adult person and of sound mind. Even the most unreasonable conduct is protected by the law as the right of self-determination also includes, within the boundaries of *boni mores*, the right to be what others may look upon as "objectively" unreasonable.

In a more recent summary, the German Federal Supreme Court spoke once again in favour of a clearly subjective test of causality:

> First, since every bodily invasion not validly consented to was *a priori* illegal, the onus was on the defendant physician to justify his intervention by proving a valid consent and, as a logical precondition to the consent's validity, a legally acceptable discharge of his duty of disclosure and information. The facts to prove this were peculiarly within the knowledge of the health care providers whose duty it was to doc-

ument such consent appropriately and to satisfy a court of law that a legally acceptable consent had in fact been obtained from the patient as alleged by the defendant. To prove negligence (and by implication also a substandard disclosure practice) would actually also at Civil Law be for a plaintiff to establish, but as an indispensable precondition which determines whether the *consent* of an adult person of sound mind allegedly obtained really was valid, and not vitiated by unacceptable disclosure practices (or practices to keep silent), it had to be established by the defendant who wants to avail himself of the *defence* of consent. * * * As the German Federal Supreme Court re-emphasized, it was up to the defendant physician to prove that there had been acceptable consent, not on the patient to show there had been none.

Secondly, it was admissible, both according to German and Swiss law, to allow the defendant physician to show that, alternatively, this particular patient would have undergone the procedure proposed even if he had been properly informed.

But thirdly, the onus was again on the defendant physician to show this, and courts, as a general rule had to apply very strict standards for this proof to succeed "lest the right of the patient to receive proper disclosure is being undermined."

Fourthly,

> most importantly, it is not sufficient for a physician to show that disclosure of the inherent risks would not have deterred a reasonable patient from submitting to the operation. The patient's right of self-determination, which is meant to be protected by the physician's legal duty of disclosure, extends to decisions which according to medical judgment appear to be indefensible. However, this Court has repeatedly emphasized that patients, when claiming damages for breach of duty of disclosure, may also have their own obligation to substantiate their allegation [that they would not have consented had they been informed]. Such obligations exist at least where the reasons adduced for refusing treatment are not altogether comprehensible in the light of the specific facts of the case, where the patient is suffering from a serious condition which could be treated by an established therapy with favourable prospects of success and at low risk. In such cases it is for the patient to furnish some plausible reason why he would have refused to be treated had he known the risks in advance. It is true, again, that the patient's personal reasons for this refusal must be respected. No generalizing yardstick is allowed: not that of a reasonable patient, and even less so that of medical judgment. But the reasons to be adduced by the patient must be such as to enable the court to be satisfied that the patient, had he received proper disclosure as to the risks, would have been faced—from his *own* perspective—with a real conflict which now makes his hypothetical refusal at *that* time appear to be plausible and not simply dictated by hindsight. Only in this way can the patient's right to receive appropriate disclosure be shielded against arising from forensic considerations.

If the patient is required by the court to substantiate or make plausible why he would not have submitted to the treatment had he been properly informed, he need not do so by reference to a total refusal of treatment. The patient may, for instance, allege that, had he been properly informed, he would not have submitted to the treatment at all, or not at that particular time, or without first obtaining a second opinion, or that he would have chosen to undergo the procedure not by that particular physician or surgeon but a more specialized one, or would have opted for a better equipped or more highly specialized hospital, such as a university clinic with all its additional facilities. Once the court finds that *from the patient's point of view* a decision not to undergo treatment would have been plausible *at the time*, it is again incumbent on the defendant physician to prove the contrary. He may do so, for instance, by showing that the same incident or accident resulting in the damage now complained of would have occurred in any event at a later time, or even had the patient been treated by a more specialized physician, or in a better equipped or more specialized university institution. But "lest the patient's right of self-determination be undermined," Civil Law has only rarely accepted this proof.

Further, various courts have made it clear beyond doubt that the physician's onus of proof cannot be met by proving that the procedure proposed was medically indicated and that the patient would therefore have consented to it. It is also inadmissible to allege that the patient would nevertheless have consented on the basis of medical experience with the average patient, or because the greater number of patients would have done so. * * *

In view of the widely-accepted difficulties of proof facing the plaintiff patient in a Common Law medical malpractice action, it is hardly helpful to confine his recourse to the action of battery (where at least he is relieved of the onus of proving causation and damage in establishing a cause of action) to cases where consent is totally absent or where treatment is extended beyond the scope of consent given. If a trespass to the patient's body is committed by medical intervention not covered by valid consent, then to refer any failure to disclose material risks, however serious, to negligence rather than battery, is to assert that the quality of disclosure can never affect the validity of consent outside the narrow field of misrepresentation and actual fraud.

If it is true that the patient's interest in bodily integrity, self-determination and patient choice commands protection not only against intentional invasions by an unauthorized operation or treatment but also against a negligent invasion by his physician's dereliction or substandard discharge of his duty to adequately disclose, then the true test is whether the procedure proposed was validly consented to or not. If the protectional needs of the patient are the same, namely freedom from non-consensual bodily invasion, then it appears quite unreasonable to maintain artificial procedural differences which can only be explained in terms of legal history. Judicial efforts in medical malpractice law to make sense of the old distinctions between battery and negligence once again highlight the difficulties experienced by some Common Law countries in adapting their traditional range of torts to modern exigencies and in avoiding entrapment in conflicting strains of authority.

Instead of emphasizing the important role of the tort of battery in the vindication of constitutional rights, some courts have obstructed use of the action by the patient in need of such protection, on the basis that the moral opprobrium which "battery" connotes, renders it an undesirable remedy in this context. Such decisions, however, fail to recognize that outside the battery action evidential problems may defeat the broad justice of the patient's general case. The patient has come out the loser from the changes in the law effected by decisions such as *Cobbs v. Grant*, *Hopp v. Lepp*, *Reibl v. Hughes*, or *Chatterton v. Gerson*, *Hills v. Potter*, *Freeman v. Home Office* and the like, and impressive scholarly efforts at restructuring the issues of consent in medical malpractice cases show clearly how much additional light needs to be shed in the dark of the re-opened graves from which the old forms of action, buried long ago, continue to rule.

It should also be noted in this context that it is rather problematic to create new and extremely doubtful judicial distinctions in the medical malpractice field between consent to the basic nature and character of the treatment on the one hand (battery issue) and to "collateral risks" (negligence issue). This amounts to a distortion of an ordinary understanding of consent as covering the procedure in its entirety, and will often "defeat our normal, reasonable expectations." Untenable distinctions at war with a natural usage of language should give way to an example set by the uniform law of delict which comprizes both intentional and unintentional infringements of the right of bodily integrity and, at least in this context, has no difficulties in applying to all delictual and contractual actions the same definitions and principles.

* * *

In other words, this time from the Swiss Federal Court, the risks normally borne by the patient as to what happens to him if he submits to medical treatment, *shift* to the physician who negligently fails to discharge a duty of disclosure which would have enabled the patient to make his own final decision either to accept the risks or to forego the treatment proposed. It is submitted here that this legal reasoning can and should also be applied to Common Law medical malpractice actions for substandard disclosure practices.

a) Encouraging cases from England and elsewhere hold that the plaintiff discharges his burden of proof by showing that the defendant's conduct has materially contributed to the risk to which he is exposed. The leading case, *McGhee v. National Coal Board*, can further be interpreted to hold that in cases of negligent omission (and this includes all cases of negligent disclosure practices when in the court's view more should have been disclosed than actually was), causation can be established, and compensation awarded, for the loss of a chance. In this case, the House of Lords held that it was sufficient for a plaintiff to show that the defendant's breach of duty made the risk of injury more probable, even though it was uncertain whether it was the actual cause. As was emphasized by an English writer in this context, Michael A. Jones, this case is indeed remarkable since, "logically, it appears as though the plaintiff has succeeded without actually proving that the defendants caused him any injury—what the defendants did merely increased the risk of injury." But the reasoning would appear to be sound enough, as will be seen from the following statement from Lord Wilberforce in the *McGhee* case:

> From the evidential point of view, one may ask, why should a man who is able to show that his employer should have taken certain precautions, because without them there is a risk, or an added risk of injury or disease, and who in fact sustains exactly that injury or disease, have to assume the burden of proving more: namely, that it was the addition to the risk, caused by the breach of duty, which caused or materially contributed to the injury? In many cases, of which the present is typical, this is impossible to prove, just because honest medical opinion cannot segregate the causes of an illness between compound causes. And if one asks which of the parties, the workman or the employers, should suffer from this inherent evidential difficulty, the answer as a matter of policy or justice should be that it is the creator of that risk who, *ex hypothesi*, must be taken to have foreseen the possibility of damage, who should bear its consequences.

b) On this basis it appears to be clear that negligent failure to disclose a material risk of proposed treatment necessarily increases the likelihood of the patient's deciding to undergo the treatment and thus of losing a chance to decline it, and it is an impressive argument that the fundamental nature of the patient's right to make his own decision in the full or appropriate knowledge of all relevant facts and risks justifies applying the *McGhee* principle with regard to medical liability for loss of a chance to decline treatment.

This principle, now elaborated in two more recent English cases of medical negligence, *MacLennan* and *Hotson*, and praised by a distinguished Canadian authority on the law of torts as having much to commend it, would enable the plaintiff patient to succeed in cases where the nondisclosure substantially reduced the likelihood of his declining the treatment and thus avoiding the ensuing injury.

* * *

In other words, where a physician falls below the legally acceptable standard of disclosure, and injury occurs which that duty to disclosure was designed to prevent, he will have the burden of proving that he was not in fact negligent. The plaintiff's lost chance of making his own informed and final decision would be regarded as an injury *per se* giving rise to liability under *McGhee* or, alternatively, the violation of the patient's right to make an informed decision could be regarded as an injury in itself which would permit a court to view the loss of the chance to decline the proposed treatment simply as an item of damage flowing from that injury, and thus to award damages in accordance with well-settled general principles in personal injury actions. As was stated by Mr. Justice Bayda (now CJ) of the Saskatchewan Court of Appeal, when embracing the *McGhee* decision of the House of Lords, "if causation is overwhelmingly difficult to prove or impossible to prove then it is a matter of public policy or justice that it is the creator of the risk who should be put to the trouble of hurdling the difficulty or bearing the consequences," and not the victim.

Notes

1. Dieter Giesen had appointments both at the Free University of Berlin and at Oxford and had a thorough understanding of both the civil and common law. Is his observation correct that the problems common law countries experience in dealing with causation in informed consent cases stem from the common law writs, in particular from the relationship between trespass and trespass on the case; between battery and negligence? If we think of the right to consent to medical treatment as a basic human right, then why would we ever apply an objective, reasonable-patient, rather than a subjective, this-patient, test in determining whether proper consent had been given? Do we rely on negligence law because accusing a doctor of battery seems too extreme? Once we start thinking in terms of negligence, can we escape the application of "reasonableness" in evaluating behavior? Does the civil law escape this quandary?

2. Note the role of allocation of the burden of proof in the German law of informed consent. It is far easier to win an informed consent case in Germany than in the United States, in large part because the burden rests largely on the defendant medical professional to establish proper consent. The fact, of course, that the patient can win if it is established that the withheld information could have caused a "real conflict" in the patient as to which course of action to pursue, also makes it much easier for the patient to win than in many jurisdictions in the United States, where it must be proved that a reasonable patient would have declined the proffered treatment.

Chappel v. Hart

195 CLR 232, [1998] HCA 55,156 A.L.R. 517 [2 September 1998]
(High Court of Australia)

Judges: Gaudron, McHugh, Gummow, Kirby & Hayne, JJ

[The opinion of Gaudron J. is omitted.]

McHugh J. [dissenting].

* * *

The plaintiff's claim must fail. This follows from her failure to prove that there was open to her an alternative course of action which would have reduced the inherent chance of a perforation and consequent onset of mediastinitis and damage to the recurrent laryngeal nerve. The highest that her case can be put is that the defendant's failure to warn her resulted in her having the procedure at an earlier date and no doubt at a different place with a different surgeon than would have been the case if the defendant had carried out his duty and warned her. On the evidence, the carrying out of the procedure by the defendant on the day and at the place did not increase the risk of injury involved in the procedure. That being so, the defendant's failure to warn did not materially contribute to the plaintiff's injury. Her claim that a causal connection existed between that failure and her injury must be rejected.

On the view that I take of the case, it is of no relevance that, if she had been warned, another surgeon would have performed the procedure and that the chance of her suffering damage to the laryngeal nerve in that procedure was very remote. Perforation of the oesophagus with consequential mediastinitis and inflammation resulting in damage to the laryngeal nerve is such a rare event that it is close to a certainty that the plaintiff would have avoided mediastinitis and consequential damage to the laryngeal nerve if another surgeon had performed the procedure.

* * *

However, it is also close to a certainty that neither mediastinitis nor damage to the laryngeal nerve would have occurred if the defendant had performed the operation on some other day or even at some different hour on that day. * * *

To hold the defendant liable on the basis that if the plaintiff had been given a warning of the risk of mediastinitis occurring she would have avoided that condition is simply to apply the "but for" test, * * *. If, as the result of the defendant warning the plaintiff about the risk of perforation, the plaintiff had sought out another surgeon who had operated and accidentally perforated the plaintiff's oesophagus with consequent mediastinitis, only the most faithful adherents to the "but for" test would argue that the defendant's warning had caused the perforation and mediastinitis. To so argue would seem an affront to common sense. Similarly, with great respect to the learned judges in the courts below, it seems contrary to common sense to conclude that the defendant's failure to warn caused or materially contributed to him perforating the plaintiff's oesophagus on this occasion. From a common sense point of view, the cause of the perforation and the consequent mediastinitis was the examination of the oesophagus with a rigid endscope, an examination which carried with it an inherent risk of perforation.

The plaintiff also sought to rely on an alternative case that she lost the chance of having the procedure performed without a perforation occurring. However, this is not a case concerned with "loss of a chance". * * * Her relationship with the defendant gave her a legal right to have her condition examined, diagnosed and treated with reasonable care and skill by the defendant and to be informed and advised by him of any material risk inherent in the proposed procedure. But nothing in that relationship required the defendant to provide opportunities of the kind to which I have just referred. The damage that the plaintiff suffered was physical injury, not loss of a chance or opportunity. That being so, her claim stands or falls according to whether the physical injury that she suffered was causally connected for legal purposes with the defendant's failure to warn.

The appeal must be allowed.

Gummow J.

* * *

In the present case, the obtaining of adequate advice as to the risks involved was a central concern of Mrs Hart in seeking and agreeing to undergo the surgical procedure in question. It would, in the circumstances of the case, be unjust to absolve the medical practitioner from legal responsibility for her injuries by allowing decisive weight to hypothetical and problematic considerations of what could have happened to Mrs Hart at the hands of some other practitioner at some unspecified later date and in conditions of great variability.

* * *

The appeal should be dismissed with costs.

Kirby J.

This is yet another appeal concerned with the difficult topic of causation.

Establishing a causal connection between an alleged wrongdoer's conduct or default and the harm complained of is a pre-condition to the legal liability to pay damages. But, as Professor Dieter Giesen has observed, establishing a causal connection between medical negligence and the damage alleged is often the most difficult task for a plaintiff in medical malpractice litigation (as, indeed, in other negligence actions). Judges in common law countries can take only the smallest comfort from the fact that determining what caused an injury, for the purposes of legal liability, is also regarded as a most difficult task by the courts of civil law countries. Like courts of the common law, those courts have searched for principles to provide a "filter to eliminate those consequences of the defendant's conduct for which he [or she] should not be held liable". The search sets one on a path of reasoning which is inescapably "complex, difficult and controversial". * * *

There are no easy solutions to these problems. This is apparent from the many cases concerned with causation in the context of medical negligence coming before final and other courts of appeal in England, Canada, the United States of America, and Australia. It is further illustrated by the division of opinions in this case, Gaudron J and Gummow J favouring the dismissal of the appeal, McHugh J and Hayne J being in favour of allowing it. * * *

* * * Mrs Beryl Hart [the respondent] underwent an operation performed by Dr Clive Chappel [the appellant]. He was, and is, a medical practitioner and an ear, nose and throat specialist. The purpose of the operation, from Mrs Hart's point of view, was to relieve a long period of difficulty she had experienced in swallowing, eating and digestion, as well as with soreness of the throat. Radiological examination revealed pharyngeal diverticular and associated narrowing of the adjacent oesophagus. Dr Chappel suspected the presence of a pharyngeal pouch in which food could become caught. He proposed a procedure known as a Dohlman's operation.

Unfortunately, the operative procedure perforated Mrs Hart's oesophagus. This set in train the escape of an infection (mediastinitis) which, in turn, compromised one of her laryngeal nerves. This, in its turn, severely affected her voice. It resulted in her premature retirement from a position as principal education officer. Mrs Hart sued Dr Chappel for negligence and breach of contract. At the trial in the Supreme Court of New South Wales, Donovan AJ upheld her claim. He awarded her $172,500.61 damages. Dr Chappel and Mrs Hart both appealed to the Court of Appeal. He contended that no damages should have been awarded. She argued that the damages were inadequate. The Court of Appeal dismissed both appeals. Dr Chappel now appeals to this court. * * *

* * *

Mrs Hart's claim against Dr Chappel was limited to a complaint that he had failed to warn her adequately, or at all, of the dangers involved in the operation: specifically, that there was a danger that her voice could be compromised by the complications which, in fact, occurred. A claim that Dr Chappel had conducted the operation negligently, although initially pleaded, was not supported by evidence and was abandoned at the trial.

* * *

The aetiology of the damage to Mrs Hart's laryngeal nerve was not in doubt. It required the coincidence of three events: (1) the operative tear to the oesophagus; (2) an escape of bacteria from the oesophagus; and (3) consequential impingement of the resulting infection upon the nearby right vocal cord causing paralysis and damage. Each of these preconditions was accepted to be very rare. A tear could occur * * * once in every 20, 30 or 40 operations. Usually, it resulted in nothing more than the "escape of a few bubbles of air". The complication of mediastinitis that occurred in this case was "very rare indeed".* * * However, it was a recognised possibility. Once a patient asked a question about that possibility, he or she was entitled to have an accurate and candid answer so that the patient could make an informed decision about the surgery. For Mrs Hart, the consequences were important and they were large.

The condition which originally took Mrs Hart to Dr Chappel was "relentlessly progressive". Surgery was the "only relief" for it. Without surgery there would not only be soreness and difficulty in swallowing but the danger that food might become caught in the throat needing emergency attention. It was therefore accepted that, even if Mrs Hart had been warned of the danger of damage to her voice, she would eventually have undergone an operation on her throat. In any such operation the slight risk would exist of the kind that followed Dr Chappel's procedure. Mrs Hart did not dispute this. Dr Chappel conceded that, if the surgery had in fact been postponed and carried out at a different time, "[i]n all likelihood [Mrs Hart] would not have suffered the random chance of injury" to her vocal cord. This represented nothing more than acceptance that such injury was an extremely rare occurrence. * * *

Mrs Hart swore that if she had been told by Dr Chappel of the risks to her voice she would not have gone ahead with the operation by him. She would have sought further advice. She would have wanted the operation performed by the most experienced person available. * * * The primary judge accepted that Mrs Hart was a witness of truth. Her claim must therefore be assessed on the footing that, with the warning that the law required Dr Chappel to give her, she would not have gone ahead with the operation when she did. She would thus not in fact have suffered the damage which ensued.

Dr Chappel contended that, in the foregoing facts, Mrs Hart was not entitled to recovery. The random chance of complications could just as easily have struck during an operation at a later time and place and conducted by a different surgeon. In the absence of proof of negligence in the performance of the operation, his accepted failure to warn Mrs Hart had not caused her damage. Mrs Hart, armed with the decisions below, contended that she had established sufficient facts to demonstrate a causal connection and to retain her damages.

To answer the problem presented by the appeal, it is useful to collect a number of propositions, established by authority, relevant to a case such as the present:

A practical question: The starting point is to remember the purpose for which causation is being explored. It is a legal purpose for the assignment of liability to one person to pay damages to another. It is not to engage in philosophical or scientific debate, still less casuistry.

* * *

The law allocates responsibility by a process which at once determines the entitlement of the particular plaintiff and sets the standards of conduct that may be expected of other persons in positions analogous to the defendant. The law's concern is entirely practical. * * * Where a breach of duty and loss are proved, it is natural enough for a court to feel reluctant to send the person harmed (in this case a patient) away empty handed. However, such reluctance must be overcome where legal principle requires it. It must be so not only out of fairness to the defendant but also because, otherwise, a false standard of liability will be fixed which may have undesirable professional and social consequences.

A common sense approach: Causation is essentially a question of fact. It is to be resolved as a matter of common sense. This means that there is usually a large element of intuition in deciding such questions which may be insusceptible to detailed and analytical justification. * * * Yet, a losing party has a right to know why it has lost and should not have its objections brushed aside with a reference to "common sense", at best an uncertain guide involving "subjective, unexpressed and undefined extra-legal values" varying from one decision-maker to another. Nevertheless, despite its obvious defects, the common sense test has been embraced by this court as a reminder that a "robust and pragmatic approach" to such questions is the one most congenial to the common law.

The "but for" consideration: If, but for the negligent act or omission, the actual damage suffered by a plaintiff would not have occurred, it will often be possible, as a practical matter, to conclude the issue of causation in the plaintiff's favour. Similarly, where the damage would probably have happened anyway, it will often be possible to conclude that the act or omission was not the cause for legal purposes. In this sense, the "but for" test, so qualified, remains a relevant criterion for determining whether the breach of duty demonstrated is a cause of the plaintiff's damage. However, it is not the exclusive test. Nor is it sufficient on its own to demonstrate the causal link for legal purposes. It is a mistake to read this court's cautionary words about the "but for" test as an expulsion of that notion from consideration where the question of causation is in contest. * * * The court has simply added the warning that it is necessary to temper the results thereby produced with "value judgments" and "policy considerations". This qualification has been expressed lest a party, shown to have been in breach of duty, is forever thereafter to be liable for every misfortune that follows in time whatever the breach demonstrated and however irrelevant it may appear to the damage which ensued. * * *

The plaintiff's legal onus: It is elementary to say that it is a pre-condition to recovery of damages for an established breach of a legal duty that the onus is upon the plaintiff to prove that the breach alleged was the cause of the damage shown. It is important to keep separate the questions of liability and the calculation of damages. Where, as in this case, a plaintiff relies on a claim in contract, proof of breach of that contract will entitle the plaintiff to nominal damages at least. For recovery of compensation beyond nominal damages in contract, the plaintiff must prove that the breach was the cause of the damage. This is as true of a claim based on the tort of negligence as of one framed in contract. In this sense, the legal burden of proving causation is, and remains throughout the proceedings, upon the plaintiff. It is not an insubstantial burden. In some medical contexts it has even been described as Herculean. * * * The reasons include the imprecision of, and uncertainty about, some medical conditions; the progressive nature of others; the complexity of modern medical practice and technology; and the fact that some mistakes, serious enough in themselves, have no untoward results which can properly be attributed to them. In the present case, Dr Chappel argued that he fell into the last stated class of exemption. The recognised difficulties of causation for plaintiffs in medical negligence cases have occasionally given rise to legal devices designed to lighten their burdens. * * *

Displacing apparent causation: In certain circumstances, the appearance that there is a causal connection between the breach and the damage, arising from the application of the "but for" test and the proximity of the happening of the damage, has been displaced by a demonstration that:

(a) the happening of the damage was purely coincidental and had no more than a time connection with the breach;

(b) the damage was inevitable and would probably have occurred even without the breach, for example, by the natural progression of an undetected, undiagnosed or unrevealed condition, or because the condition presented a life threatening emergency which demanded instant responses without time for the usual warnings and consents;

(c) the event was logically irrelevant to the actual damage which occurred;

(d) the event was the immediate result of unreasonable action on the part of the plaintiff; or

(e) the event was ineffective as a cause of the damage, given that the event which occurred would probably have occurred in the same way even had the breach not happened.

Reinforcing the duty to warn: In judging the performance of a health care or other professional, the law does not require perfection. It recognises the variability of professional skills. * * * However, the requirement to warn patients about the risks of medical procedures is an important one conducive to respect for the integrity of the patient and better health care. In Australia, it is a rigorous legal obligation. Its rigour was not challenged in this appeal. It must be accepted that, by establishing the requirement to warn patients of a risk to which they would be likely to attach significance, or of which they should reasonably be aware, the law intends that its obligations be carefully observed. Breaches must be treated seriously. Because in some cases the failure to warn would have no, or no relevant, consequences, proof of a breach will not of itself be sufficient to establish an entitlement to damages for every harm that thereafter occurs to the patient. To reason in such a way would involve the logical fallacy of *post hoc ergo propter hoc*. The plaintiff's legal obligation to show the causal connection remains throughout the proceedings.

Accepting subjective intentions: In considering the suggested consequences of a failure on the part of a medical practitioner to advise a patient about the risks of a particular procedure, courts in Australia have adopted a "subjective" approach which has regard to what the particular patient's response would have been had proper information been given. A contrary (objective) approach, having regard to the response of a reasonable person in the patient's situation, was not urged in this case, although it has found favour in Canada and the United States of America. The subjective criterion involves the danger of the "malleability of the recollection" even of an upright witness. Once a disaster has occurred, it would be rare, at least where litigation has commenced, that a patient would not be persuaded, in his or her own mind, that a failure to warn had significant consequences for undertaking the medical procedure at all (where it was elective) or for postponing it and getting a more experienced surgeon (as in this case). Yet, these dangers should not be overstated. Tribunals of fact can be trusted to reject absurd, self-interested assertions. Where such a conclusion is reached the case will rarely come before an appellate court. The present appeal must be approached on the footing accepted by the primary judge. This was that, if she had been warned, Mrs Hart would not have had the operation, not have suffered the physical injuries which then ensued and would have sought a more experienced surgeon when the time for operation eventually came.

Shifting the evidentiary onus: One means of alleviating the burden cast by law on a plaintiff to establish a causal relationship between the breach and the damage concerns the evidentiary onus. * * * Once a plaintiff demonstrates that a breach of duty has occurred which is closely followed by damage, a prima facie causal connection will have been established. It is then for the defendant to show, by evidence and argument, that the patient should not recover damages.

* * *

Valuing a lost chance: A further way in which, in some circumstances, the difficulties of causation for a plaintiff are alleviated is by treating the plaintiff's loss as a "loss of a chance". In cases in which this approach is permissible, it may allow evaluation of the plaintiff's loss in terms of comparing the chances of suffering harm (given the breach which has occurred) against those that would have existed (if the breach is hypothesised away). * * * It is clearly laid down by the authority of this court that, in some circumstances, a plaintiff may recover the value of a loss of a chance caused by a wrongdoer's act or omission. The approach also has some judicial support in the context of medical negligence in England, Canada and the United States. A number of commentators favour this approach because of the failure of orthodox reasoning to do justice to some patients' losses and because it invites a more empirical calculation of loss, with the use of statistics which might offer outcomes that are more accurate and fair to all concerned. On the other hand, the weight of judicial opinion in England and Canada and some academic writing appears to be critical of the application of the loss of a chance theory to cases of medical negligence. In part this is because, where medical negligence is alleged, "destiny … [has] taken its course", arguably making an analysis by reference to chance inappropriate or unnecessary in the view of the critics of this approach. Alternatively, the loss of a chance calculation has been criticised on the ground that it would discard common sense, undermine the plaintiff's onus of proving the case and submit the law to the "paralysis" of statistical abstractions.

Discounting damages: If it is established that damage was caused by the breach alleged, it remains to calculate the amount of compensation recoverable. It is then proper to reduce any damages which a defendant should pay for the harm it has caused to a proper proportion actually attributable to its breach. If, independently of the breach on the part of a defendant, the evidence shows that the plaintiff would have suffered loss, the damages may be reduced by reference to the estimate of the chances that this would have occurred. * * * Dr Chappel argued that, even if he had given the requisite warning to Mrs Hart, and she had postponed the procedure and later undergone an operation by a more experienced surgeon, there was still the same random chance that she would have suffered the complications that occurred; neither more nor less. Mrs Hart argued that the true comparison was between the loss that had in fact occurred to her and the concededly small risk that such loss would have happened at the postulated postponed operation. She resisted any reduction in her damages, submitting that a chance of injury in a postponed operation was minuscule, i.e. "speculative" in the sense described by this court.

The application of the foregoing principles to the facts of this case, as now established, presents difficult puzzles upon which reasonable minds may differ; as indeed they have. The strongest arguments for Dr Chappel, as it seems to me, are those which lay emphasis upon a logical examination of the consequences which would have flowed had he not breached his duty to warn his patient. Dissecting the facts in that way affords a powerful argument which would banish from consideration the events which in fact occurred in the operation which he carried out. All that would have happened, had he given the requisite warning, would have been a change in the timing of the operation and of the identity of the surgeon. For Dr Chappel, these were irrelevant changes as the evidence showed that, whenever the operation was performed and whoever did it, the tripartite chances which had to combine to produce the misfortune which Mrs Hart suffered were extremely rare. There was thus an equivalence of unlikelihood. They were risks inherent in the procedure, not wholly avoidable even by the most skilful and experienced of surgeons. In the view which Dr Chappel urged of the case, Mrs Hart was left with nothing more than the time sequence. To burden a surgeon, in whose actual performance no fault could be found, with civil liability for randomised chance events that followed the surgery would not be reasonable. It would penalise him for chance alone. It would do nothing to establish a superior standard in the performance of the work of surgeons generally.

For a time I was attracted to Dr Chappel's arguments. Ultimately, I have concluded against them. The "common sense" which guides courts in this area of discourse supports Mrs Hart's recovery. So does the setting of standards which uphold the importance of the legal duty that was breached here. This is the duty which all health care professionals in the position of Dr Chappel must observe: the duty of informing patients about risks, answering their questions candidly and respecting their rights, including (where they so choose) to postpone medical procedures and to go elsewhere for treatment.

* * *

* * * This was an unusual case where the patient was found to have made very clear her concerns. The practicalities are that, had those concerns been met as the law required, the overwhelming likelihood is that the patient would not, in fact, have been injured. So much was eventually conceded. In such circumstances, common sense reinforces the attribution of legal liability. It is true to say that the inherent risks of injury from rare and random causes arise in every surgical procedure. A patient, duly warned about such risks, must accept them and their consequences. Mrs Hart was ready to accept any general risks of the operation of which she was warned. However, she declined to bear the risks about which she questioned the surgeon and received no adequate response. When those risks so quickly eventuated, common sense suggests that something more than a mere coincidence or irrelevant cause has intervened. This impression is reinforced once it is accepted that Mrs Hart, if warned, would not have undergone the operation when she did.

Although no statistical or other evidence was called to demonstrate that recourse to a more experienced surgeon would necessarily have reduced the risk of the kind of injury that occurred (and while some risk was unavoidable), intuition and common sense suggest that the higher the skill of the surgeon, the less is the risk of any perforation of the oesophagus into the mediastinum. * * * And without perforation (already a rare occurrence) the second and third events necessary to produce paralysis of the vocal cords in a patient like Mrs Hart (occurrences even more rare) would not occur.

Once Mrs Hart showed the breach and the damage which had immediately eventuated, an evidentiary onus lay upon Dr Chappel to displace the inference of causation which thereupon arose. He failed to do so. Nor, in my view, causation being established, did he prove that Mrs Hart would have been exposed to the same, or substantially the same, possibilities of like injury if she had postponed the procedure and had it done by someone more experienced, as was her right. On the contrary, the evidence demonstrated that the chances of her receiving such injury in any other operation were minuscule. * * *

To the complaint that Professor Benjamin [an expert witness in the case] (or his equivalent) could not possibly undertake every Dohlman's operation (any more than the most skilful barrister can appear for every client) the answer comes back. This was not an ordinary patient. It was an inquisitive, persistent and anxious one who was found to have asked a particular question to which she received no proper answer. Had a proper answer been given, as the law required, it was found that she would not have undergone the operation at the hands of Dr Chappel when she did. It is virtually certain, then, that she would not have suffered mediastinitis at all. She therefore adequately proved causation. Dr Chappel did not displace the inferences to which her evidence gave rise. Nor was it shown that the damages to which she was entitled should be reduced on the footing that they would have occurred in any event.

As to the question of loss of a chance, Dr Chappel, by leave, added a ground of appeal to assert that Mrs Hart's damages should have been assessed in those terms. * * * At trial, the only claim for damages, which she had asserted, was in respect of the physical injury done to her vocal cords and its sequelae. She neither pleaded, nor sought to prove, a case expressed in terms of a loss of a chance. * * * The case is therefore not one in which an entirely new perspective should be adopted at such a late stage. * * * [T]his case must be approached on the footing that the loss suffered by Mrs Hart was that claimed: physical injury and its consequence—nothing more.

The appeal should be dismissed with costs.

Hayne J.

* * *

In my view, the only connection between the failure to warn and the harm the respondent has suffered is that but for the failure to warn she would not have been in harm's way. The appellant's conduct did not affect whether there would be pathogens present in the respondent's oesophagus when the procedure was carried out; his conduct did not affect whether the pathogens that were present would, in all the circumstances, produce the infection which they did; his conduct did not affect whether that infection would damage the laryngeal nerve as it did. Of course, he manipulated the instrument which perforated the oesophagus but he did so without negligence.

* * *

The law of negligence is intended to compensate those who are injured as a result of departures from standards of reasonable care. It is not intended to compensate those who have received reasonable care but who may not have had the best available care. To hold that the appellant's failure to warn the respondent of the risks of the operation caused her to lose the chance of the best available care would depart from that fundamental premise of the law of negligence.

* * *

The respondent did not establish that she had suffered damage as a result of the appellant's negligence. The claim having been framed in breach of contract and breach having been established, she is, of course, entitled to nominal damages but, in my view, to no more. I would allow the appeal.

Appeal dismissed with costs.

Notes

1. While *Chappel v. Hart* disavows the loss of a chance doctrine, is it not in fact applying it? Was not the patient's injury in fact the loss of an opportunity to have the surgery done by a more expert surgeon and thus to avoid the risk that eventuated? Does the court not hint at this in its consideration of damages?

2. A British case, *Chester v. Afshar* [2004] 4 All. E.R. 587, similarly involved a patient who, not having been warned of the small possibility of significant motor and sensory disturbance resulting from a spinal operation, had the operation and suffered the disability. The House of Lords, in a 3 to 2 decision, held for the patient, with the majority reasoning that had Miss Chester been warned she would have had surgery on a different day and would have faced only a very small chance of being injured. Subsequently in a later missed diagnosis case (*Gregg v. Scott* [2004] 1 A.C. 134) a majority of the House of Lords panel rejected the application of the loss of a chance doctrine to find causation. Can the two cases be reconciled? See Sarah Green, Coherence of Medical Negligence Cases: A Game of Doctors and Purses, 14 *Med. L. Rev.* 1 (2006).

3. An American case suggests a different approach to the problem presented by *Chappel v. Hart*. In *Johnson v. Kokemore*, 545 N.W.2d 409 (1996), a plaintiff who was severely injured by a surgery was permitted to recover damages under an informed consent claim against a surgeon who had failed to disclose that he had little experience with the particular surgery and that the mortality and morbidity rates for the particular surgery would be much worse if the surgery was performed by him than they would be if the surgery were performed by a more experienced surgeon. The court dealt with the problem of physician-specific risks, therefore, as a standard of care rather than as a causation issue.

D. Rights to Control over Patient Information

1. Confidentiality and Secrecy

Providing and paying for health care requires vast amounts of private information. Indeed, a fundamental first step in providing health care—the diagnosis—is itself information, and its accuracy depends on the ability of medical professionals to collect personal information. Much of the information used to deliver health care can be highly sensitive, such as mental health status, sensitive diseases, or sexual activity. Revealing or publishing such data can be extremely harmful to patients, so protecting the confidentiality and security of health data is extremely important. Moreover, today health privacy has become even more important and more challenging, with the creation of vast electronic databanks and "big data" algorithms that can predict one's health status using countless data points that would not qualify traditionally as "health" data, such as shopping and travel patterns, Internet searches, social networks, and financial data.

Most medical traditions call for physicians to honor their ethical obligation to keep patient confidences. This ethic is reflected in the statutes, regulations, judicial opinions, and ethical codes that require professionals to maintain patient confidentiality and secrecy. But medical traditions alone have not been able to protect patient privacy today, particularly as health-inflected data are collected, used, and disseminated by parties outside the sphere of health providers bound by ethical codes. Thus, statutory instruments have become particularly important. The first excerpt below explains why EU legislation has been influential around the world. The second excerpt includes key provisions from the EU's new General Data Protection Regulation (GDPR), followed by a comparison between U.S. and EU data protection laws. This section concludes with two cases in Italy and Taiwan regarding the legal implications of genetic databases.

Colin J. Bennett, *The European General Data Protection Regulation: An Instrument for the Globalization of Policy Standards?*

23 *Information Polity* 239–40, 243–45 (2018)

The recent revelations about Cambridge Analytica and the breach that allowed the harvesting of the personal information of some 87 million Facebook users (at latest count) has pushed privacy protection to the front pages, and focused attention on "surveillance capitalism" (Zuboff, 2017) and on the capture of personal data as the central resource for the "platform economy". * * * At no time in the past 40 years, has the protection of privacy been so prominently, globally and intensively debated. How did it get to this point?

* * *

In the 1990s, harmonization was extended through the 1995 EU Data Protection Directive (EU, 1995), Articles 25 and 26 of which stipulated that personal data on Europeans should only flow outside the boundaries of the Union to countries that can guarantee an "adequate level of protection." Through the Data Protection Directive, the harmonization of data protection then extended geographically and deepened in meaning and content (Bennett, 1997). Progressively, these harmonization efforts standardized what it meant for a country to pursue adequate data protection, and for organizations to process personal data responsibly. As more countries joined the data protection "club" so there was increasing pressure on those outside the club to pass equivalent laws.

* * *

Thus, the General Data Protection Regulation (GDPR) was born. It was first proposed in 2012 to establish a uniform set of rules that would provide enhanced protection for citizens, foster innovation in the European Single Market and make the EU, according to Commissioner Jourova, "fit for the digital age" (European Commission, 2015). After a lengthy and tortuous journey through the EU-policy-making system, involving intensive lobbying mainly from multinational business interests, the GDPR was approved by the European Parliament in April 2016, and came into force across the entire EU on May 25th, 2018. It is the most ambitious and comprehensive data protection regulation in the world. What does it require, in brief? And can we then expect it to continue the global process of policy convergence?

* * *

The mechanisms to control the transfers of personal data to "third countries" outside the EU are broadly similar to those established under the Data Protection Directive (Arts. 44–50). The Commission has the power to determine whether certain countries, territories, sectors or even international organizations offer an "adequate level of protection" for the data transferred. Those few countries that had been approved as adequate by the Commission will continue to enjoy that status, at least for four years when their status will be reviewed.

* * *

Transnational instruments for data protection have played three overlapping functions over time. They have acted as *instruments of harmonization*, as templates that any state, or organization, might use in order to fashion its own data protection policy. They have acted as *exemplars*, producing a progressive and inexorable desire to be within the community of nations that has adopted data protection legislation; the more states that adopt, the higher the pressure on the non-adopters. More recently, they have acted as *a coercive force*, with significant economic consequences for those businesses that rely upon the unimpeded international flow of personal information, and on those governments that wish to protect their domestic industries from the possible consequences of non-compliance. These instruments have built upon each other. They represent a logical progression reflecting the increasing policy interdependence of different countries.

* * *

The GDPR, like the Data Protection Directive, will continue to offer an important template of principles and provisions for other jurisdictions to emulate if they wish. Whether or not, however, it will establish the enforceable rules of the road for the processing of personal data in the global networked economy remains to be seen.

Regulation (EU) 2016/679 of the European Parliament and of the Council of 27 April 2016

on the protection of natural persons with regard to the processing of personal data and on the free movement of such data, and repealing Directive 95/46/EC (General Data Protection Regulation) OJ L 119

Whereas:

(1) The protection of natural persons in relation to the processing of personal data is a fundamental right. Article 8(1) of the Charter of Fundamental Rights of the European Union (the "Charter") and Article 16(1) of the Treaty

on the Functioning of the European Union (TFEU) provide that everyone has the right to the protection of personal data concerning him or her.

* * *

(9) The objectives and principles of Directive 95/46/EC remain sound, but it has not prevented fragmentation in the implementation of data protection across the Union, legal uncertainty or a widespread public perception that there are significant risks to the protection of natural persons, in particular with regard to online activity. Differences in the level of protection of the rights and freedoms of natural persons, in particular the right to the protection of personal data, with regard to the processing of personal data in the Member States may prevent the free flow of personal data throughout the Union. Those differences may therefore constitute an obstacle to the pursuit of economic activities at the level of the Union, distort competition and impede authorities in the discharge of their responsibilities under Union law. Such a difference in levels of protection is due to the existence of differences in the implementation and application of Directive 95/46/EC.

* * *

(35) Personal data concerning health should include all data pertaining to the health status of a data subject which reveal information relating to the past, current or future physical or mental health status of the data subject. This includes information about the natural person collected in the course of the registration for, or the provision of, health care services * * *; a number, symbol or particular assigned to a natural person to uniquely identify the natural person for health purposes; information derived from the testing or examination of a body part or bodily substance, including from genetic data and biological samples; and any information on, for example, a disease, disability, disease risk, medical history, clinical treatment or the physiological or biomedical state of the data subject independent of its source, for example from a physician or other health professional, a hospital, a medical device or an in vitro diagnostic test.

* * *

Article 1

Subject-matter and objectives

1. This Regulation lays down rules relating to the protection of natural persons with regard to the processing of personal data and rules relating to the free movement of personal data.

2. This Regulation protects fundamental rights and freedoms of natural persons and in particular their right to the protection of personal data.

* * *

Article 2

Material scope

1. This Regulation applies to the processing of personal data wholly or partly by automated means and to the processing other than by automated means of personal data which form part of a filing system or are intended to form part of a filing system.

* * *

Article 4

Definitions

For the purposes of this Regulation:

(1) 'personal data' means any information relating to an identified or identifiable natural person ('data subject'); an identifiable natural person is one who can be identified, directly or indirectly, in particular by reference to an identifier such as a name, an identification number, location data, an online identifier or to one or more factors specific to the physical, physiological, genetic, mental, economic, cultural or social identity of that natural person;

(2) 'processing' means any operation or set of operations which is performed on personal data or on sets of personal data, whether or not by automated means, such as collection, recording, organisation, structuring, storage, adaptation or alteration, retrieval, consultation, use, disclosure by transmission, dissemination or otherwise making available, alignment or combination, restriction, erasure or destruction;

* * *

(4) 'profiling' means any form of automated processing of personal data consisting of the use of personal data to evaluate certain personal aspects relating to a natural person, in particular to analyse or predict aspects concerning that natural person's performance at work, economic situation, health, personal preferences, interests, reliability, behaviour, location or movements;

* * *

(7) 'controller' means the natural or legal person, public authority, agency or other body which, alone or jointly with others, determines the purposes and means of the processing of personal data; * * *

* * *

(11) 'consent' of the data subject means any freely given, specific, informed and unambiguous indication of the data subject's wishes by which he or she, by a statement or by a clear affirmative action, signifies agreement to the processing of personal data relating to him or her;

* * *

(13) 'genetic data' means personal data relating to the inherited or acquired genetic characteristics of a natural person which give unique information

about the physiology or the health of that natural person and which result, in particular, from an analysis of a biological sample from the natural person in question;

(14) 'biometric data' means personal data resulting from specific technical processing relating to the physical, physiological or behavioural characteristics of a natural person, which allow or confirm the unique identification of that natural person, such as facial images or dactyloscopic data;

(15) 'data concerning health' means personal data related to the physical or mental health of a natural person, including the provision of health care services, which reveal information about his or her health status;

* * *

Article 5

Principles relating to processing of personal data

1. Personal data shall be:

(a) processed lawfully, fairly and in a transparent manner in relation to the data subject ('lawfulness, fairness and transparency');

(b) collected for specified, explicit and legitimate purposes and not further processed in a manner that is incompatible with those purposes * * *;

(c) adequate, relevant and limited to what is necessary in relation to the purposes for which they are processed ('data minimisation');

(d) accurate and, where necessary, kept up to date; every reasonable step must be taken to ensure that personal data that are inaccurate, having regard to the purposes for which they are processed, are erased or rectified without delay ('accuracy');

(e) kept in a form which permits identification of data subjects for no longer than is necessary for the purposes for which the personal data are processed * * * ('storage limitation');

(f) processed in a manner that ensures appropriate security of the personal data, including protection against unauthorised or unlawful processing and against accidental loss, destruction or damage, using appropriate technical or organisational measures ('integrity and confidentiality').

2. The controller shall be responsible for, and be able to demonstrate compliance with, paragraph 1 ('accountability').

* * *

Article 7

Conditions for consent

* * *

3. The data subject shall have the right to withdraw his or her consent at any time. * * * It shall be as easy to withdraw as to give consent.

4. When assessing whether consent is freely given, utmost account shall be taken of whether, inter alia, the performance of a contract, including the provision of a service, is conditional on consent to the processing of personal data that is not necessary for the performance of that contract.

* * *

Article 9

Processing of special categories of personal data

1. Processing of personal data revealing racial or ethnic origin, political opinions, religious or philosophical beliefs, or trade union membership, and the processing of genetic data, biometric data for the purpose of uniquely identifying a natural person, data concerning health or data concerning a natural person's sex life or sexual orientation shall be prohibited.

2. Paragraph 1 shall not apply if one of the following applies:

(a) the data subject has given explicit consent to the processing of those personal data for one or more specified purposes, * * *;

* * *

(h) processing is necessary for the purposes of preventive or occupational medicine, for the assessment of the working capacity of the employee, medical diagnosis, the provision of health or social care or treatment or the management of health or social care systems and services on the basis of Union or Member State law or pursuant to contract with a health professional and subject to the conditions and safeguards referred to in paragraph 3;

(i) processing is necessary for reasons of public interest in the area of public health, such as protecting against serious cross-border threats to health or ensuring high standards of quality and safety of health care and of medicinal products or medical devices, on the basis of Union or Member State law which provides for suitable and specific measures to safeguard the rights and freedoms of the data subject, in particular professional secrecy;

3. Personal data referred to in paragraph 1 may be processed for the purposes referred to in point (h) of paragraph 2 when those data are processed by or under the responsibility of a professional subject to the obligation of professional secrecy under Union or Member State law or rules established by national competent bodies or by another person also subject to an obligation of secrecy under Union or Member State law or rules established by national competent bodies.

* * *

Article 77

Right to lodge a complaint with a supervisory authority

1. Without prejudice to any other administrative or judicial remedy, every data subject shall have the right to lodge a complaint with a supervisory authority, in particular in the Member State of his or her habitual residence, place of work or place

of the alleged infringement if the data subject considers that the processing of personal data relating to him or her infringes this Regulation.

2. The supervisory authority with which the complaint has been lodged shall inform the complainant on the progress and the outcome of the complaint including the possibility of a judicial remedy pursuant to Article 78.

* * *

Article 79

Right to an effective judicial remedy against a controller or processor

1. Without prejudice to any available administrative or non-judicial remedy, including the right to lodge a complaint with a supervisory authority pursuant to Article 77, each data subject shall have the right to an effective judicial remedy where he or she considers that his or her rights under this Regulation have been infringed as a result of the processing of his or her personal data in noncompliance with this Regulation.

2. Proceedings against a controller or a processor shall be brought before the courts of the Member State where the controller or processor has an establishment. Alternatively, such proceedings may be brought before the courts of the Member State where the data subject has his or her habitual residence, unless the controller or processor is a public authority of a Member State acting in the exercise of its public powers.

* * *

Article 82

Right to compensation and liability

1. Any person who has suffered material or non-material damage as a result of an infringement of this Regulation shall have the right to receive compensation from the controller or processor for the damage suffered.

2. Any controller involved in processing shall be liable for the damage caused by processing which infringes this Regulation. A processor shall be liable for the damage caused by processing only where it has not complied with obligations of this Regulation specifically directed to processors or where it has acted outside or contrary to lawful instructions of the controller.

3. A controller or processor shall be exempt from liability under paragraph 2 if it proves that it is not in any way responsible for the event giving rise to the damage.

4. Where more than one controller or processor, or both a controller and a processor, are involved in the same processing and where they are, under paragraphs 2 and 3, responsible for any damage caused by processing, each controller or processor shall be held liable for the entire damage in order to ensure effective compensation of the data subject.

5. Where a controller or processor has, in accordance with paragraph 4, paid full compensation for the damage suffered, that controller or processor shall be entitled

to claim back from the other controllers or processors involved in the same processing that part of the compensation corresponding to their part of responsibility for the damage, in accordance with the conditions set out in paragraph 2.

6. Court proceedings for exercising the right to receive compensation shall be brought before them courts competent under the law of the Member State referred to in Article 79(2).

* * *

Note

The EU's General Data Protection Regulation (GDPR) provides other notable protections, such as the right to access one's own data (Article 15), the right to rectify inaccurate data held by controllers (Article 16), the right to be "forgotten," or to ask controllers to erase one's personal data (Article 17), the right to restrict processing in certain circumstances (Article 18), and the right to object to automated decisionmaking (Articles 21–22). This latter right allows data subjects to assert "the right not to be subject to a decision based solely on automated processing, including profiling, which produces legal effects concerning him or her or similarly significantly affects him or her." Such automated profiling could affect, for example, decisions about creditworthiness, insurability, and the like. For an early evaluation of the risks of automated decisionmaking, see Frank Pasquale, *The Black Box Society: The Secret Algorithms that Control Money and Information* (2015).

Peter Carey, *Data Protection: A Practical Guide to UK and EU Law*

xxxiii–xxxv (5th ed. 2018)

Considerable excitement and trepidation has surrounded the advent of the European Union's new Regulation on the protection of natural persons with regard to the processing of personal data and on the free movement of such data (the 'General Data Protection Regulation' or 'GDPR').

So much so, that one could be forgiven for thinking that the GDPR beholds the dawn of a new era in data protection law. However, the reality is that the Regulation mostly represents an updating measure which tweaks the pre-GDPR legal requirements that organizations were already required to undertake when processing personal data.

The real revolution was the beginning of data protection law itself, back in the 1970s. Since then, the content of the law has not altered to any Earth-shattering extent. The majority of the obligations on organizations that previously existed under Directive 95/46/EC (the former EU data protection law that was abolished by the GDPR, and upon which the UK's Data Protection Act 1998 was based) remain substantially the same under the new law. Examples include the obligation to ensure that only a minimum quantity of data are used for any particular purpose (data minimization), the obligation to process only such information on people as is relevant to the purpose/s of the processing (purpose limitation), the obligation to supply a copy of their personal data to anyone making a request (data subject access), the obligation to apply appropriate security provisions to personal data processing, and the obligation to destroy or delete data held after they have become obsolete.

* * *

But for organizations to sit back and breathe a collective sigh of relief would be mistaken for two reasons. The first is that, whilst much of the previously applicable law is reproduced in the GDPR, several new obligations present a significant challenge in both time and money—in particular, the requirements to publish certain documentation, to appoint a Data Protection Officer, and to notify breaches to both national regulators and potentially affected individuals.

The second is that many organizations are somewhat unprepared for the new law—not because they haven't taken steps to comply with the GDPR (although they may not have done), but because they didn't properly implement the *pre*-GDPR data protection legal requirements. They therefore have some catching up to do.

One possible explanation for the explosion of interest in, and awareness of, data protection legal requirements under the GDPR is the significant increase in levels of penalties that can be imposed. In particular, monetary penalties (fines, in effect) of up to 20 million euros or 4 per cent of global annual turnover are available to the national data protection regulators. Another is the global awareness that has been sparked by the apparent extra-territorial applicability of the GDPR—the law attempts to regulate organizations based outside of the EU which supply products or services to EU citizens, even where such organizations have no EU presence or establishment.

Yet a third might be that the EU chose a Regulation rather than a Directive to create the new law. To understand why this is significant, it is useful to understand the differences between a Directive and a Regulation. A Directive, which is the most common method of EU law formation, is a somewhat cumbersome legal instrument that requires implementation in each individual Member State—it sets out the goals to be achieved, and then requires Member States to implement appropriate measures in their own territories. As an example, the Data Protection Directive was implemented by the UK by the Data Protection Act 1998. France also created a Data Protection Act. As did Ireland. And as did all the remaining members of the EU. The problem with this method of law creation, especially when dealing with compliance issues across national boundaries within the EU, is that it produces twenty-eight somewhat different national laws. Even though the decisions of the Court of Justice of the European Union (which are binding in all Member States) are designed to harmonize the legal landscape across the entire region, the reality is that differences remain.

A Regulation, on the other hand, is a legal instrument that has immediate binding effect in all Member States, without any further action being required by those

States. Although Regulations can (and the GDPR does) include provisions that allow Member States to create additional rules, such as exceptions to certain requirements, the main cut and thrust of the provisions of the legal instrument is identical across the EU. This is intended to provide greater certainty for organizations that operate in multiple jurisdictions. * * * It also means that Member States' parliaments have no opportunity to 'water down' the law's requirements (as they do with a Directive) except to the extent specifically permitted under the terms of the Regulation.

In terms of guidance on what the law means, a Regulation (just like a Directive) contains both Recitals and Articles. The Articles are the important operative bits, whereas Recitals are statements that are produced by the legislators which explain the rationale behind the law. The latter are often used as 'persuasive' guides to interpretation, but they are not legally binding. * * *

But the fact that the new law has been created by a Regulation does not mean that national parliaments have no role. At the time of going to print, several Member States had introduced national legislation which provides clarification on the GDPR's applicability, including (where permitted by the GDPR) defining the scope of exceptions to some of the GDPR's provisions. The UK's own draft legislation, the Data Protection Bill 2017, is somewhat unusual in this regard since it additionally attempts to deal with the UK's legal position as regards data protection matters after Brexit. * * *

* * * [T]he Regulation has direct effect in the UK from 25 May 2018, which is at least several months prior to the earliest data that Brexit can take effect. * * *

* * *

Notes

1. In the United States, confidentiality of medical records has historically been addressed through a patchwork of state statutes, which often are limited to particular professions or institutions. Regulations issued under the Health Insurance Portability and Accountability Act of 1996 (HIPAA) and found at 45 C.F.R. Parts 160 and 164 attempt to address the issue comprehensively, at least for health plans and providers. The regulations establish a principle of confidentiality of individually identifiable health information, but include many complicated exceptions. A timely comparison of HIPAA to the new GDPR is provided by Jeremy Shapiro-Barr, *The GDPR's Impact in the U.S.: Considerations for the U.S. Health Lawyer*, 12 Journal of Health and Life Sciences Law 39 (2018). He notes, for example, how much broader the GDPR is than HIPAA. HIPAA protects only personal health data, while the GDPR applies to all kinds of personal data. The GDPR also provides data subjects with much more extensive rights, including the right to correct inaccuracies and the right to be "forgotten."

2. International transfers involving the personal data of EU residents are regulated by the GDPR. Such transfers are made significantly easier if the other country has "adequate" levels of data protection, as determined by the European Commission.

As of December 2018, the Commission designated 12 countries as meeting the minimum standards: Andorra, Argentina, Canada, the Faroe Islands, Guernsey, Israel, the Isle of Man, Jersey, New Zealand, Switzerland, Uruguay, and organizations in the United States that have been certified as meeting the "Privacy Shield" framework established by the EU and the U.S. Department of Commerce. Certification signals that the U.S. entity complies with the GDPR's privacy principles, breaches of which are enforceable in the U.S. via the Federal Trade Commission (FTC) and the U.S. Department of Transportation. *See* Commission Implementing Decision (EU) 2016/1250, OJ L 207 (Jan. 8, 2016), *at* https://ec.europa.eu/info/law/law-topic/data-protection/data-transfers-outside-eu/adequacy-protection-personal-data-non-eu-countries_en. By the end of 2018, Japan and South Korea were in various stages of seeking adequacy determinations.

Chen-Hung Chang, *Controversy over Information Privacy Arising from the Taiwan National Health Insurance Database Examining the Taiwan Taipei High Administrative Court Judgment No. 102-SU-36* (*Tsai v. NHIA*)

28 *Pace International Law Review* 27, (2016)

I. Introduction

* * *

Modern technology has increased the difficulty of protecting privacy with respect of health data due to the rapid and broad information flow. However, it is also true that the collective use of individuals' health data may aid medical research and improve medical science to benefit people. The new big data technology facilitates medical research; however, sufficient data must be supplied to make the big data technology functional. No medical research can be successful without a sizable database that accumulates sufficient data for a certain length of time.

Tsai v. NHIA, a recent and high profile lawsuit in Taiwan, illustrates the conflict between the benefits for medical research of using all citizens' medical data and the privacy threats to individuals when their medical records are exposed to others, and their most sensitive personal data are disclosed without their knowledge. * * *

The debate in *Tsai* is whether health authorities may use personal health information that they have collected in the course of performing national healthcare services for other purposes, such as allegedly promoting public welfare, without obtaining consent from the data subjects. What makes this case more complicated is that the plaintiffs whose health data were disclosed by the health agency were not unaware that the health agency had used their personal data. The data subjects strongly expressed their objections to the health agency's use of their personal data for purposes that were not communicated to them when they gave their consent. Before filing the lawsuit, the plaintiffs expressly requested that the health authority should refrain from using their health data.

Tsai involves a dilemma of two conflicting rights. The data subject plaintiffs alleged that they were exercising their privacy rights granted in the Taiwan Constitution and the privacy laws against intrusion of privacy. They added that this case did not involve just any data; their health data were at stake, and such highly sensitive information deserves greater privacy and protection. The defendant, the Taiwan National Health Insurance Administration, contested that it was reusing all citizens' health data that it previously collected with the goal of improving public healthcare services and devising healthcare policies that could benefit all citizens. * * *

II. Privacy Controversy over the Taiwan National Health Database—Examining the Taiwan Taipei High Administrative Court Judgment No. 102-SU-36

A. Background

Taiwan launched a national health insurance ("NHI") program in 1995 to provide health insurance coverage and medical care benefits to Taiwanese nationals and foreigners working in Taiwan. As of 2015, following two decades of its implementation, 99.9% of Taiwan's population is enrolled in the program. The NHI program is administered by the Taiwan National Health Insurance Administration (NHIA), the Ministry of Health and Welfare (MHW) of the Executive Yuan (formerly the Department of Health, "DOH"). The NHIA, as the government agency in charge of the national insurance program, has collected, processed and retained all insurance and medical information on the insured persons and service providers (hereinafter, "Health Insurance Data") in the course of handling the health insurance affairs.

The Health Insurance Data were not only utilized by the NHIA in providing healthcare services but were also applied by third parties entrusted by the NHIA to conduct academic research. Since 1998, the NHIA has annually sent the Health Insurance Data to the National Health Research Institutes ("NHRI"), a state-sponsored private research institution. As part of the NHRI's research work, a centralized health data center, the National Health Insurance Research Database ("NHIRD"), was created. The information stored in the NHIRD has been opened since 2000 to allow access on a per-application basis by researchers and scientists who need to conduct medical-related research.

In a continued effort to improve healthcare services and to aid the reform of public health policies, the Executive Yuan initiated a National Health Informatics Project ("NHIP") and established within the MHW the Collaboration Center of Health Information Application ("CCHIA") on May 3, 2009. Since its operation on February 1, 2011, the CCHIA has served as a national database wherein other government agencies may access the Health Insurance Data through the CCHIA. The CCHIA data may be combined with other personal data, such as household registration and tax returns, to enable the government's collaborative use of personal data, as the MHW expected when creating the CCHIA.

It was the goal of the CCHIA that the open and free flow of Health Insurance Data accessible to the government agencies and academic researchers would provide analysis and research results based on these personal data, and that would be helpful for the government to provide improved health care services to citizens. In sending the Health

Insurance Data to the CCHIA database, the NHIA has vowed to protect individuals' data privacy. Among the data privacy and security measures that the NHIA has undertaken, the NHIA has declared that all Health Insurance Data are scrambled and de-identified before being released to the CCHIA to ensure that individual identification is not traceable.

Eight individuals filed separate petitions to the NHIA in May and June of 2012 claiming that the NHIA should not transfer their personal data to any third parties for purposes not related to health insurance affairs. The petitioners were denied by the NHIA and initiated a joint administrative lawsuit with the Taiwan High Administrative Court against the NHIA, requesting that a restraining order be issued to prohibit the NHIA from disclosing their personal health data without their consent.

B. Plaintiffs' Allegation

The subjects of the data alleged that the NHIA's unauthorized transfer or disclosure of their personal data to third parties exceeded the scope of consent they originally gave when agreeing that the NHIA could collect their personal data. The plaintiffs alleged that the NHIA failed to obtain their consent when reusing the data for other purposes not indicated or agreed upon by the data subjects. According to the then-effective privacy protection law in Taiwan (i.e., the Computer-Processed Personal Data Protection Act, "CPDPA"), if the data controller wishes to use personal data in a manner inconsistent with the purposes stated when the data were collected, this manner of secondary use is not permissible unless it is necessary for the government agency to perform its duties or the situation qualifies for any statutory exemptions. The provision of personal data by NHIA to others, as the plaintiffs alleged, does not fall under the statutory functions of the NHIA, which are limited to policy making, administration and supervision of public health affairs. In other words, the data were not properly used within the necessary scope of the specific purposes of data collection.

The plaintiffs added that even if the NHIA's duty is broadly defined to justify the provision of personal health data to others for research purposes, the personal data submitted by the NHIA to NHIRD and CCHIA were not properly encrypted, leading to a possible breach of privacy by disclosing the subjects' personal identities. The data the NHIA submitted were allegedly loosely protected and may have been traceable to individuals' personal identity, and the disclosure of their personal information created significant concerns about privacy invasion. It was further argued by the plaintiffs that even if the NHIA had the authority to transfer the Health Insurance Data to the NHIRD and CCHIA without the individuals' consent, the subjects of the data should be entitled to demand that the NHIA stop using their personal data, which is part of their privacy rights as granted in the Taiwan Personal Data Protection Act.

C. The NHIA's Defenses

The NHIA argued that its use of the plaintiffs' personal data was within its statutory duty and was in compliance with the specific purposes. The NHIA argued that it has met one of the exemption[s] to reuse personal data for purposes outside the scope of the purposes of data collection as stipulated in the CPDPA, which permits data reuse when "it is necessary for the purpose of academic research and would not cause significant harm to data subjects."

In response to the plaintiffs' claim that individuals own the right to full control over their personal information both "before" and "after" the data misuse, and therefore are entitled to stop the NHIA from reusing the data, the NHIA argued that the privacy laws do not support the plaintiffs' positions. The NHIA explained that since the law has permitted the NHIA to reuse personal data for specified purposes outside the scope of the purpose of data collection, this means that the law has restricted the data subjects' right to control their personal data both before and after the NHIA's reuse of their personal data. The plaintiffs' allegation that they have the right to raise objections to stop the NHIA from using their personal information runs afoul to the purpose of allowing the NHIA to use personal data in the public interest. The NHIA alleged that if the law permits the NHIA's use of personal data without obtaining consent from the data subjects, then it is equal to permission for the NHIA to use such data without intervention from the data subjects, meaning that that the data controller's right to use personal data prevails over the interest of the individuals in refusing such use of data.

Additionally, the NHRI, which assisted the NHIA in the lawsuit, claimed that all the data provided by the NHIA was encrypted, so that the NHRI could not identify specific individuals; therefore, the data transfer by the NHIA to the NHRI is not subject to the PDPA.

D. Court Judgment

The Taipei High Administrative Court ("High Court") dismissed the plaintiffs' lawsuit on May 14, 2014. The plaintiffs filed an appeal, and the Supreme Administrative Court ("Supreme Court") remanded the case to the High Court for re-trial on November 13, 2014. The Supreme Administrative Court vacated the High Court's judgment on the grounds that the pertinent case should be governed by the "PDPA" rather than its precedent, the CPDPA (which was renamed and amended the Taiwan PDPA on May 26, 2000). The Supreme Court ruled that the High Court should re-examine the issues by applying the correct law. Because the Supreme Court vacated the High Court's judgment on the grounds of incorrect application of the law without addressing the merits of the dispute over privacy invasion, this article will focus on the reasoning of the High Court's judgment in examining the relevant privacy issues.

The High Court's judgment can be summarized as follows.

* * *

2. The NHIA's Forwarding of the Health Insurance Data to the NHRI and CCHIA is Necessary for the NHIA to Exercise Its Statutory Duty

When reviewing the issues regarding whether the NHIA may resort to its statutory duty to justify its provision of the Health Insurance Data to third parties for research purposes, the High Court gave a positive answer. In the court's findings, the Organization Act of the National Health Insurance Administration, Ministry of Health and Welfare (Organization Act of NHIA) stipulated in Article 1, and in Paragraphs 5 and 8 of Article 2, that the NHIA is in charge of the planning and implementation of policies relating to the national health insurance program and the enhancement of the quality of the nation's healthcare services and all related matters. The High Court ruled that because the NHIA is responsible for all matters relating to the national health insurance program, which should reasonably include regular review and evaluation of the implementation results through academic research to facilitate improvement of the healthcare services offered in the national health insurance program, it should be within the scope of the NHIA's duty to provide the Health Insurance Data to the NHRI and CCHIA for research purposes.

3. The NHIA's Disclosure of Health Insurance Data Qualifies for the Exemptions in the Use of Personal Data for Specific Purposes Other than Notified Purposes of Collection

The High Court ruled that the pertinent dispute should be determined pursuant to the Old Privacy Law because the New Privacy Law is silent with regard to the collection and processing of sensitive personal data. However, it also considered the relevant provisions in the New Privacy Law in rendering the judgment because the latter has offered stronger privacy protection to individuals. The Court explained that Article 8 of the Old Privacy Law provides that government agencies may only use personal data for purposes within their exercise of duties and should comply with the purposes of data collection except for the numerated exemptions. One of the exemptions is that data controllers may use collected data for other purposes if it is necessary for the purpose of academic research and that the use of personal data will not cause significant harm to the data subject. A similar but more stringent requirement for data use is set forth in the New Privacy Law. Item 5 of Article 16 of the New Privacy Law provides that government agencies shall not use personal data collected for other purposes unless "it is necessary for government agency or research institution to use data for public interest on statistics or the purpose of academic research, and such use of data will not lead to the identification of a certain person after the treatment of the provider or by the disclosure of the collector." When comparing the relevant data processing requirements in the Old Privacy Law and New Privacy Law, the Court first concluded that the latter has offered stronger protection and should apply to this dispute to fulfill the data protection requirement as declared by the Constitutional Court in its Decision No. 603, wherein the right to information privacy is officially recognized.

In reviewing whether the NHIA's disclosure of Health Insurance Data to the NHRI and CCHIA to establish the national health data center satisfied the data use requirements in both the Old and New Privacy Laws, the Court determined that this data transfer was permissible because it was conducted for academic research in the public interest. Moreover, the data involved was properly de-identified and should not harm the interests of the data subjects. Although it is true that the Health Insurance Data were not used by the NHIA for purposes directly related to the provision of national health care services, the Court took into account the academic research purpose behind the data use with the aim of improving medical services. The Court also noted that the data transferred to the NHRI and CCHIA were de-identified to avoid identification of specific individuals to protect the privacy of the data subjects. Therefore, the Court concluded that the NHIA should have satisfied the requirement of Item 7 of Article 8 of the Old Privacy Law that it is necessary for the purpose of academic research and that the use of personal data will not cause significant harm to the data subject and does not run afoul of Item 5 of Article 6 of the New Privacy Law.

4. The Right to Consent Prior to Data Use and the Right to Object after Data Use

With regard to the plaintiffs' claim that the right to information privacy encompasses the right to consent prior to use and the right to object after use, the High Court ruled that the two alleged rights bear the same nature and should be interpreted using the same rationale. The High Court found that since both the Old and New Privacy Laws permitted data use by controllers for specified purposes other than those for which the data subjects expressed consent when allowing controllers to collect their data, it is tantamount to a statutory restriction upon the rights of the data subjects in preventing their personal data from unauthorized use. The same rule also applies when the data subject wishes to exercise his right to ask the data controller to delete or remove any unwanted disclosure of personal data. If the NHIA has a legal ground in sending Health Insurance Data to the NHRI and CCHIA for research purposes, there is no reason to allow the data subjects to exercise their right to demand that the NHIA stop using their personal data. Otherwise, the statutory exemptions to allow government agencies to use personal data to serve the public interest would be in vain and would lead to the incorrect interpretation that the right to information privacy is an absolute right, which is not the intended goal of privacy laws. Given this context, if the NHIA is permitted to use the data for purposes not identified at the time of collection when the public interest is involved, the plaintiffs shall have no legal standing to stop the NHIA from using the data.

* * *

Luca Marelli & Giuseppe Testa, *Scrutinizing the EU General Data Protection Regulation*

360 *Science* 496–98 (May 2018)

On 25 May 2018, the European Union (EU) regulation 2016/679 on data protection, also known as the General Data Protection Regulation (GDPR), will take effect. The GDPR, which repeals previous European legislation on data protection (Directive 95/46/EC), is bound to have major effects on biomedical research and digital health technologies, in Europe and beyond, given the global reach of EU-based research and the prominence of international research networks requiring interoperability of standards. * * * As a timely forecast for its potential impact, we analyze the implications of the GDPR in an ongoing paradigmatic legal controversy involving the database originally assembled by one of the world's first genomic biobanks, Shardna.

* * *

Governing "Big Data" Biomedicine

Regulatory challenges of big-data biomedicine pivot around (i) the inherently open-ended potential of data, whose digital compatibility makes them valuable for research pursuits that may be wholly disjoined from the original project within which samples or data were gathered, thus undermining the classical rationale for "informed consent"; and (ii) the increasing resolution and scope of data across the full range of digitized human features (from genomes to social networks' logs), with the ensuing and often self-proclaimed erosion of privacy. Responses have come broadly in two flavors, both aiming for technical fixes, though at different levels of technological engagement.

The first includes attempts to solve the conundrums of the digital age by resorting to yet more complex digitization, as in the recent example of secure multiparty computation that enabled genomic diagnosis while preserving participants' privacy. The second resorts instead to one of the defining human technologies of our time, that is, governance, meant as the reconfiguration of power structures through procedural architectures and distributed agency, as in the proposal of trust-building techniques to skirt the zero-sum game of data privacy versus data utility by shifting emphasis from the issue of privacy, per se, to the acquisition of control over data and trust in their holders.

As one of us has empirically shown, governance mechanisms have been central to the rise of contemporary biomedicine, as well as to the shaping of European science policy, by virtue of their mutually reinforcing constitutive tenets: (i) a partial retreat of state powers and governing bodies vis-à-vis the advance of market forces and a plurality of heterogeneous "stakeholders," ushering in a substantial reshaping of decision-making ("decentralization"); and (ii) the increased reliance on soft-rule instruments—such as standards, codes of conduct, and ethical thresholds—in place of more rigid forms of legislative interventions ("standardization"). Both of these features, in turn, have been integral to the structuring of the GDPR.

* * *

Standardization

Such flexibility in data processing extends to the foundational tenet of human biomedical research—informed consent. Although the GDPR requires "specific [and] informed" consent of the data subject [Art. 6(1)(a) and Recital 32], it recognizes that researchers may face the impossibility of fully identifying all potential future research purposes at the time of data collection. Accordingly, Recital 33 states that, if too specific a consent would impinge on the purpose of research, "data subjects should be allowed to give their consent to certain areas of scientific research when in keeping with recognized ethical standards for scientific research."

This key provision, which intersects still unsettled bioethical debates on the appropriate modes of informed consent, has two major implications. First, dispelling concerns voiced in relation to previous drafts of the GDPR suggesting otherwise, it lends the full legislative weight of the GDPR in support of broad consent whenever the criterion of specific consent for specific research use at the moment of data collection proves impossible to satisfy, as in the case of biobanking.

* * *

Second, the provision contained in Recital 33 bestows on institutionalized ethics (that is, ethics committees' guidelines, along with other soft-law instruments such as professional codes of conduct, compare also Art. 40) an enhanced role in defining the scope of data processing for scientific research. More broadly, this role is enhanced in establishing general standards of practice that research with human biospecimens has been (as of yet) largely eschewing, given the absence of binding legislative requirements comparable to those regulating clinical research.

This is likely to heighten the relevance of the crucial, though still scholarly undertheorized, policy-making role of review boards and ethics committees. It also places increased emphasis on the ongoing effort lead by BBMRI-ERIC (the EU Biobanking and BioMolecular resources Research Infrastructure—European Research Infrastructure Consortium), involving major research organizations, patient advocacy groups, and industrial representatives, to develop a comprehensive code of conduct for the processing of personal data in health research (http://code-of-conduct-for-health-research.eu/). This code is envisioned as the reference standard in the field, enabling international harmonization in the EU and possibly beyond. However, it remains to be seen whether the concrete implementation of the GDPR will allow such sweeping reach by a single code of conduct. Or whether, on the contrary, the GDPR's enhanced investment in institutionalized ethics will end up promoting regulatory fragmentation through a proliferation of approaches by local ethics committees.

Testing the GDPR

For the data protection-versus-data utility conundrum, the implementation of a flexible regime of governance for European data protection, in place of rigid homogenizing provisions (and notwithstanding the possibility that Member States introduce further provisions for the processing of genetic and health-related data [Art. 9(4)], has ambivalent implications.

On one hand, in addition to controllers' discretionary prerogatives, the GDPR upholds a far-reaching "research exemption" to the strict limitations otherwise imposed on the processing of sensitive data, relaxing requirements for consent [Art. 9(2)(j)], further processing [Art. 5(1)(b)], and data storage [Art. 5(1)(e)]. The reach of this research exemption is magnified by the adoption, as per Recital 159, of an exceedingly broad definition of activities falling under the rubric of "scientific research," including "technological development and demonstration," "applied research," and "privately funded research." Through the combination of these provisions, controllers such as pharmaceutical, direct-to-consumer genetic testing, and digital technologies companies, claiming to process (sensitive) personal data within the scope of scientific research activities, stand to benefit directly from a major regulatory leeway in favor of data controllers over data subjects.

On the other hand, the context-sensitive approach entailed by mechanisms such as the compatibility test, as well as the enhanced role assigned to institutionalized ethics, could be seen—and harnessed accordingly—as laying down the conditions for increased protection of data subjects and the promotion of their substantive, rather than merely tokenistic, engagement in research.

This can be exemplified in reference to the landmark first-instance ruling of the Tribunal of Cagliari (Italy) that overturned a decision by the Italian Data Protection Authority (DPA)—the first time ever by an Italian court—that had halted the activities of the United Kingdom-based Tiziana Life Sciences Plc. with the Shardna SpA database. Shardna was an Italian genomic biobank that stored genetic, health, and genealogical data (the latter collected from municipal and parish records archived over 4 centuries) of around 12,000 genetically interrelated residents from Ogliastra, an isolated region in Sardinia, Italy, known for being one of the world's few "blue zones," areas with a high prevalence of centenarians. Shardna was purchased by Tiziana in 2016 amid arguments in local communities, including research participants seeking to halt the foreign and for-profit acquisition of Shardna's database.

The decision of the Italian DPA to impose an interim block to Tiziana's processing was made on the basis that Tiziana, as the new data controller, had to (i) inform data subjects "of the change of data controller, and the further data processing for scientific research purposes in the field of medical genetics that the new controller may intend to carry out" and (ii) recollect consent from all data subjects whose information was stored in the Shardna database. The Tribunal of Cagliari instead ruled such a provision "exorbitant" given that the new data controller "pursues the same purposes of Shardna," namely, "scientific research purposes for which consent had been given."

Although both the decision of the DPA and the ruling that overturned it unfolded with Italian data protection legislation still in place, the appeal judgment is expected to occur under the GDPR regime. Though full disentanglement of its legal complexity is beyond the scope of this paper, we argue that adjudication of this case is poised to revolve around the assessment of whether the change in data controller entails (i) a further processing of personal data, (ii) whose scope is not compatible with the original purpose for which consent had been obtained. Such assessment will arguably lead to the conclusion that it is highly implausible that Tiziana will not conduct further processing on the data set originally assembled by Shardna to advance its own research programs in oncology and immunology, irrespective of whether it (dis)continues the lines of research originally initiated by Shardna.

Assessing the compatibility of such further processing will require unpacking the abstract notion of scientific research (the stated purpose of the processing carried out by both Shardna and Tiziana). This will involve scrutinizing the research endeavors pursued by the two organizations, recognizing the substantial differences not only in their research programs and goals but also in terms of their respective governance arrangements, values, and aspirations. Shardna was established as a locally owned and governed biobank, strongly rooted in Ogliastra's communities (the name itself recalls the Shardana population inhabiting Sardinia in the Bronze Age). As such, it was able to achieve high recruitment rates in the local population for its research programs focused on the genetics of multifactorial diseases typical of Ogliastra, and thus of primarily, albeit not exclusively, local relevance. By contrast, Tiziana is an international, profit-oriented biotech company with a distinct research focus, with feeble ties to the local communities engaged in research. Consequently, irrespective of how "broad" the original consent given to Shardna was, a cogent case could be made that the relationship between data subjects and the controller—a key criterion identified by the GDPR to determine compatibility of further processing—has been considerably altered upon the change in data controller. This could be argued to make further processing incompatible with the original purpose, thus requiring re-consenting of research participants.

Whatever its outcome, this case is an exemplary testing ground because its adjudication is bound to set jurisprudence for two central issues in contemporary biomedicine that the GDPR, in its bottom-up valorization of context, leaves open to interpretive ingenuity: the reuse of personal data upon a change in the property of biobanks and data repositories and what the relevant demarcations to be traced are, in the age of big data, within the category of scientific research in its ever increasing interdependence with other socioeconomic domains. Collective engagement with the versatility of this legislative tool by European scientists and citizens will thus be key to ensure its impact is scientifically and socially robust.

In conclusion, translating into practice the tensions between greater freedom and greater accountability of research defines the very scope of the GDPR and, more broadly, of the EU's experimenting with the governance of technoscience.

Note

Massive databases like the ones at issue in Taiwan (the *Tsai* case) and Italy (the Shardna/Tiziana case) can greatly aid medical care and research, but also can easily compromise patient privacy and data security. Some of these problems were foreshadowed by earlier consideration of the privacy of genetic data, such as the Council of Europe's *Recommendation No. R (97) 5 of the Committee of Ministers to Member States on the Protection of Medical Data*, which took the bold move of including genetic data in its protections for medical data, and UNESCO's *International Declaration on Human Genetic Data* (2003), which also articulates some aspirational standards for protecting genetic data. Moreover, an early effort to create a comprehensive database of clinical information for the population of Iceland (the Health Sector Database Act No. 139/1998) was massively controversial, spurring a decision by the Icelandic Supreme Court that upheld a daughter's claim that including genetic information about her deceased father in the Health Sector Database violated her own privacy interests. *See Ragnhildur Guthmundsdóttir v. State of Iceland*, Icelandic Supreme Court, 27 Nov. 2003; Henry T. Greely, Iceland's Plan for Genomics Research: Facts and Implications, 40 *Jurimetrics J.* 153 (2000).

2. Access to Medical Records

If a patient has a right to control who can access their medical information, it would seem obvious that the patient should have access to their own information. However, traditional notions of medical paternalism, concerns about the sensitivity of medical data, and proprietary attitudes towards medical records have long limited patient access to their records. This is changing in many parts of the world (and has, by and large, changed in the United States). In common law countries, however, the change has often come by statute rather than by court decision. Though the Canadian Supreme Court decision below recognizes a far-ranging right of access to medical information, the Australian High Court decision that follows it rejects general access to records. These cases are important, not only because of their conclusion with respect to medical records, but also because of their characterizations of the physician-patient relationship. The final excerpt demonstrates how far some countries, such as Iran, have to go.

McInerney v. MacDonald

[1992] 2 Can. S.C.R. 138, 93 D.L.R. (4th) 415
(Canadian Supreme Court)

Panel: La Forest, L'Heureux-Dube, Gonthier, Stevenson* and Iacobucci JJ.

* Stevenson J. took no part in the judgment.

La Forest, J.—The central issue in this case is whether in the absence of legislation a patient is entitled to inspect and obtain copies of his or her medical records upon request.

Facts

The facts are simple. The appellant, Dr. Elizabeth McInerney, is a medical doctor who is licensed to practise in New Brunswick. The respondent, Mrs. Margaret MacDonald, was her patient. Before her consultations with Dr. McInerney, Mrs. MacDonald was treated by various physicians over a period of years. On Dr. McInerney's advice, Mrs. MacDonald ceased taking thyroid pills previously prescribed by other physicians. She then became concerned about her medical care before consulting Dr. McInerney, and wrote the latter requesting copies of the contents of her complete medical file. The doctor delivered copies of all notes, memoranda and reports she had prepared herself but refused to produce copies of consultants' reports and records she had received from other physicians, stating that they were the property of those physicians and that it would be unethical for her to release them. She suggested that Mrs. MacDonald contact the other physicians for release of their records.

An application was then made on behalf of Mrs. MacDonald to the New Brunswick Court of Queen's Bench for an order directing Dr. McInerney to provide a copy of her entire medical file relating to Mrs. MacDonald. Turnbull J. granted the application. The appeal to the Court of Appeal of New Brunswick was dismissed, * * *.

* * *

The appellant raises two issues in this appeal:

1. Are a patient's medical records prepared by a physician the property of that physician or are they the property of the patient?

2. If a patient's medical records are the property of the physician who prepares them, does a patient nevertheless have the right to examine and obtain copies of all documents in the physician's medical record, including records that the physician may have received which were prepared by other physicians?

The current position of the medical profession with respect to the right of patients to information in their medical records is reflected in the policy statement of the Canadian Medical Association published in 1985:

> The Canadian Medical Association (CMA) regards medical records as confidential documents, owned by the physician/institution/clinic that compiled them or had them compiled. Patients have a right to medical information contained in their records but not to the documents themselves. The first consideration of the physician is the well-being of the patient, and discretion must be used when conveying information contained in a medical record to a patient. This medical information often requires interpretation by a physician or other health care professional. Other disclosures of information contained in medical records to third parties (eg. physician-to-physician transfer for administrative purposes, lawyer, insurance adjuster) require written patient consent or a court order. * * *

I am prepared to accept that the physician, institution or clinic compiling the medical records owns the physical records. This leaves the remaining issue of whether the patient nevertheless has a right to examine and obtain copies of all documents in the physician's medical records. The majority of the Court of Appeal based the patient's right of access on an implied contractual term. While it may be possible to pursue the contractual route in the civil law system, I do not find it particularly helpful in the common law context. Accordingly, I am not entirely comfortable with the approach taken by the Court of Appeal. However, I do agree that a patient has a vital interest in the information contained in his or her medical records.

Medical records continue to grow in importance as the health care field becomes more and more specialized. As L. E. Rozovsky and F. A. Rozovsky put it in *The Canadian Law of Patient Records* (1984), * * *

> The twentieth century has seen a vast expansion of the health care services. Rather than relying on one individual, a physician, the patient now looks directly and indirectly to dozens and sometimes hundreds of individuals to provide him with the services he requires. He is cared for not simply by his own physician but by a veritable army of nurses, numerous consulting physicians, technologists and technicians, other allied health personnel and administrative personnel.

While a patient may, in the past, have relied primarily upon one personal physician, the trend now tends to favour referrals to a number of professionals. Each of the pieces of information provided by this "army" of health care workers joins with the other pieces to form the complete picture. As the number and use of specialists increase, the more difficult it is for the patient to gain access to that picture. If the patient is only entitled to obtain particular information from each health care provider, the number of contacts he or she may be required to make may become enormous. The problem is intensified when one considers the mobility of patients in modern society.

Medical records are also used for an increasing number of purposes. This point is well made by A. F. Westin, *Computers, Health Records, and Citizen Rights* (1976).

> As to medical records, when these were in fact used only by the physician or the hospital, it may have been only curiosity when patients asked to know their contents. But now that medical records are widely shared with health insurance companies, government payers, law enforcement agencies, welfare departments, schools, researchers, credit grantors, and employers, it is often crucial for the patient to know what is being recorded, and to correct inaccuracies that may affect education, career advancement or government benefits.

* * *

When a patient approaches a physician for health care, he or she discloses sensitive information concerning personal aspects of his or her life. The patient may also bring into the relationship information relating to work done by other medical professionals. The policy statement of the Canadian Medical Association cited earlier indicates that a physician cannot obtain access to this information without the patient's consent or a court order. Thus, at least in part, medical records contain information about the patient revealed by the patient, and information that is acquired and recorded on behalf of the patient. Of primary significance is the fact that the records consist of information that is highly private and personal to the individual. It is information that goes to the personal integrity and autonomy of the patient. * * * [S]uch information remains in a fundamental sense one's own, for the individual to communicate or retain as he or she sees fit. * * * In sum, an individual may decide to make personal information available to others to obtain certain benefits such as medical advice and treatment. Nevertheless, * * * he or she has a "basic and continuing interest in what happens to this information, and in controlling access to it".

A physician begins compiling a medical file when a patient chooses to share intimate details about his or her life in the course of medical consultation. The patient "entrusts" this personal information to the physician for medical purposes. * * * [T]he relationship between physician and patient is one in which "trust and confidence" must be placed in the physician. This statement was referred to with approval by LeBel J. * * * who himself characterized the physician-patient relationship as "fiduciary and confidential," * * *

In characterizing the physician-patient relationship as "fiduciary," I would not wish it to be thought that a fixed set of rules and principles apply in all circumstances or to all obligations arising out of the doctor-patient relationship. * * * [N]ot all fiduciary relationships and not all fiduciary obligations are the same; these are shaped by the demands of the situation. A relationship may properly be described as "fiduciary" for some purposes, but not for others. That being said, certain duties do arise from the special relationship of trust and confidence between doctor and patient. Among these are the duty of the doctor to act with utmost good faith and loyalty, and to hold information received from or about a patient in confidence. When a patient releases personal information in the context of the doctor-patient relationship, he or she does so with the legitimate expectation that these duties will be respected.

The physician-patient relationship also gives rise to the physician's duty to make proper disclosure of information to the patient. The appellant concedes that a patient has a right to be advised about the information concerning his or her health in the physician's medical record. In my view, however, the fiducial qualities of the relationship extend the physician's duty beyond this to include the obligation to grant access to the information the doctor uses in administering treatment. * * *

Certain textbooks and case law go further and assert that the patient has a "proprietary" or "property" interest in the medical records. For example, Meagher et al., supra, write:

> In the absence of an agreement, a doctor or hospital owns the records of the patient, but the patient is considered to have a property interest in the medical information contained in the record, with a right of access to it, but not to its possession.

* * *

A similar sentiment is expressed in the American text by R. D. Miller, *Problems in Hospital Law.* The author has this to say,

> The medical record is an unusual type of property because physically it belongs to the hospital and the hospital must exercise considerable control over access, but the patient and others have an interest in the information in the record. One way of viewing this is that the hospital owns the paper or other material on which the information is recorded, but it is just a custodian of the information. * * *

I find it unnecessary to reify the patient's interest in his or her medical records and, in particular, I am not inclined to go so far as to say that a doctor is merely a "custodian" of medical information. The fiduciary duty I have described is sufficient to protect the interest of the patient. The trust-like "beneficial interest" of the patient in the information indicates that, as a general rule, he or she should have a right of access to the information and that the physician should have a corresponding obligation to provide it. The patient's interest being in the information, it follows that the interest continues when that information is conveyed to another doctor who then becomes subject to the duty to afford the patient access to that information.

There is a further matter that militates in favour of disclosure of patient records. As mentioned earlier, one of the duties arising from the doctor-patient relationship is the duty of the doctor to act with utmost good faith and loyalty. If the patient is denied access to his or her records, it may not be possible for the patient to establish that this duty has been fulfilled. As I see it, it is important that the patient have access to the records for the very purposes for which it is sought to withhold the documents, namely, to ensure the proper functioning of the doctor-patient relationship and to protect the well-being of the patient. * * *

Disclosure is all the more important in our day when individuals are seeking more information about themselves. It serves to reinforce the faith of the individual in his or her treatment. The ability of a doctor to provide effective treatment is closely related to the level of trust in the relationship. A doctor is in a better position to diagnose a medical problem if the patient freely imparts personal information. The duty of confidentiality that arises from the doctor-patient relationship is meant to encourage disclosure of information and communication between doctor and patient. In my view, the trust reposed in the physician by the patient mandates that the flow of information operate both ways. * * *

* * * Indeed, H. E. Emson observes that the practice of giving patients their own records "has been said to improve patient understanding, cooperation and compliance." In this sense, reciprocity of information between the patient and physician is prima facie in the patient's best interests. It strengthens the bond of trust between physician and patient which, in turn, promotes the well-being of the patient.

While patients should as a general rule, have access to their medical records, this policy need not and, in my mind, should not be pursued blindly. The related duty of confidentiality * * * is absolute unless there is some paramount reason that overrides it. For example, "there may be cases in which reasons connected with the safety of individuals or of the public, physical or moral, would be sufficiently cogent to supersede or qualify the obligations prima facie imposed by the confidential relation." Similarly, the patient's general right of access to his or her records is not absolute. The patient's interest in his or her records is an equitable interest arising from the physician's fiduciary obligation to disclose the records upon request. * * * If the physician reasonably believes it is not in the patient's best interests to inspect his or her medical records, the physician may consider it necessary to deny access to the information. But the patient is not left at the mercy of this discretion. When called upon, equity will intervene to protect the patient from an improper exercise of the physician's discretion. In other words, the physician has a discretion to deny access, but it is circumscribed. It must be exercised on proper principles and not in an arbitrary fashion. * * *

I hasten to add that, just as a relationship may be fiduciary for some purposes and not for others, this characterization of the doctor's obligation as "fiduciary" and the patient's interest in the records as an "equitable interest" does not imply a particular remedy. Equity works in the circumstances to enforce the duty. This foundation in equity gives the court considerable discretion to refuse access to the records where non-disclosure is appropriate.

In my view, the onus properly lies on the doctor to justify an exception to the general rule of access. Not only is the information in some fundamental sense that of the patient; the doctor has primary access to it. * * * To some extent, what the documents contain is a matter of speculation for the patient. Consequently, there is a marked disparity in the ability of each party to prove its case. The burden of proof should fall on the party who is in the best position to obtain the facts.

If a physician objects to the patient's general right of access, he or she must have reasonable grounds for doing so. Although I do not intend to provide an exhaustive analysis of the circumstances in which access to medical records may be denied, some general observations may be useful. I shall make these in a response to a number of arguments that have been advanced by the appellant and in the literature for denying a patient access to medical records. These include: (1) disclosure may facilitate the initiation of unfounded law suits; (2) the medical records may be meaningless; (3) the medical records may be misinterpreted; (4) doctors may respond by keeping less thorough notes; and (5) disclosure of the contents of the records may be harmful to the patient or a third party.

* * *

Denial of access may actually encourage unfounded law suits. If a law suit is started, a patient can generally obtain access to his or her records under rules of civil procedure relating to discovery of documents. Thus, if a patient strongly wishes to see his or her records, one way of achieving this result is to commence an action before ascertaining whether or not there is a valid basis for the action.

The arguments that the records may be meaningless or that they may be misinterpreted do not justify non-disclosure in the ordinary case. If the records are, in fact, meaningless, they will not help the patient but neither will they cause harm. It is always open to the patient to obtain assistance in understanding the file. * * *

The concern that disclosure will lead to a decrease in the completeness, candour and frankness of medical records, can be answered by reference to the obligation of a physician to keep accurate records. A failure to do so may expose the physician to liability for professional misconduct or negligence. It is also easy to exaggerate the importance of this argument. Certainly physicians may become more cautious in what they record, but it cannot be assumed as a natural consequence that this will detrimentally affect the standard of care given to the patient. Generally I doubt that the quality of medical records will be measurably affected by a general rule allowing access to the patient. * * *

Non-disclosure may be warranted if there is a real potential for harm either to the patient or to a third party. This is the most persuasive ground for refusing access to medical records. However, even here, the discretion to withhold information should not be exercised readily. Particularly in situations that do not involve the interests of third parties, the court should demand compelling grounds before confirming a decision to deny access. * * * Non-disclosure can itself affect the patient's well-being. If access is denied, the patient may speculate as to what is in the records and imagine difficulties greater than those that actually exist. In addition, the physical well-being of the patient must be balanced with the patient's right to self-determination. Both are worthy of protection. In short, patients should have access to their medical records in all but a small number of circumstances. In the ordinary case, these records should be disclosed upon the request of the patient unless there is a significant likelihood of a substantial adverse effect on the physical, mental or emotional health of the patient or harm to a third party.

* * *

Since I have held that the tangible records belong to the physician, the patient is not entitled to the records themselves. Medical records play an important role in helping the physician to remember details about the patient's medical history. The physician must have continued access to the records to provide proper diagnosis and treatment. Such access will be disrupted if the patient is able to remove the records from the premises. Accordingly, the patient is entitled to reasonable access to examine and copy the records, provided the patient pays a legitimate fee for the preparation and reproduction of the information. Access is limited to the information the physician obtained in providing treatment. It does not extend to information arising outside the doctor-patient relationship.

Appeal dismissed.

Breen v. Williams

4 A.L.D. 481, 186 C.L.R. 71
(High Court of Australia, 6 Sept. 1996)

Judges: Brennan, CJ, Dawson, Toohey, Gaudron, McHugh, and Gummow, JJ.

Dawson and Toohey JJ. [The opinion of Dawson and Toohey appears after the opinion of Brennan, C.J., in the original, but is moved in front of it here because it contains the statement of facts.]

In 1977 the appellant had a bilateral augmentation mammoplasty which involved the insertion of a silicone implant in each of her breasts. Thereafter she developed bilateral breast capsules. In 1978 she consulted the respondent, who is a plastic surgeon, but not the plastic surgeon who performed the implant. The respondent advised the appellant that the capsules should be compressed and he performed that operation. The appellant experienced severe pain and, after two further consultations with her, the respondent operated and performed a bilateral capsulotomy. The appellant has not consulted the respondent since that operation, although she corresponded with him in 1983 over matters unrelated to this appeal.

In 1984 another doctor, Dr McDougall, diagnosed a lump in the appellant's left breast as silicone gel which had leaked from the breast implant. As a result, he performed a partial mastectomy upon the appellant. Since then she has had further corrective surgery on her left breast and has had the right silicone breast implant replaced. These operations were not performed by the respondent.

The appellant became interested in litigation in the United States by way of a class action against the manufacturer of the breast implants claiming that they were defective. In that litigation she was given the opportunity to "opt in" to a settlement which had been given conditional approval by a United States court. It appears that it was a condition of opting in that the appellant do so before 1 December 1994 and that she file with the United States court copies of medical records in support of any claim which she wished to make. The appellant sought to have access to the medical records kept by the respondent in her case and maintains that she did so both to secure advice whether she should opt in to the United States settlement and to comply with the condition imposed should she decide to do so. She also maintains that she has a right of access to the medical records to ensure that she has all information relating to her health at her disposal which will, in turn, ensure that she is able to make decisions regarding her future treatment.

The appellant could have secured access to the medical records by compulsory court process. It would appear that an order for discovery of the records was within the equitable jurisdiction of the Supreme Court of New South Wales. Another procedure was by way of letters rogatory. These were obtained from the United States court by several litigants in her position and orders were made by the Supreme Court of New South Wales compelling the production of medical records to the court in aid of the United States proceedings. The appellant did not avail herself of this procedure because, she said, the time available was too short. Instead, she commenced this action in the Supreme Court of New South Wales claiming a declaration that she is entitled to access to the medical records kept by the respondent in relation to herself. * * * The appellant also sought an order that the respondent allow her access to her medical records to examine them and obtain copies of the information contained in them.

Those records were not in evidence but the trial judge, Bryson J, found by inference that they comprised * * * [the defendant's handwritten notes, as well as other records].

* * * For practical purposes, the relief sought by the appellant related in the end to the respondent's handwritten notes and it was upon these that argument centred.

Of these the respondent said:

> The handwritten notes ... are prepared and maintained by me, along with the other documents described above in the belief that such records belong to me and are private to me ... [S]ome of these records will contain information supplied to me in confidence by family and friends of the patient in circumstances where I have been told by such persons that they do no[t] wish the patient to be aware of their communications with me. Often the information I receive from such sources is what I would regard as sensitive and confidential, and I would not wish to divulge my knowledge of it or source unless I judged it necessary to do so in the interest of the patient. In some cases because of the state of mind or health of the patient these records will contain information the disclosure of which in my judgment might be detrimental to the patient's well being if disclosed at all or if disclosed without full explanation. Because these notes are prepared by me in the belief that they will remain private to me, they often contain conclusions, commentary and musing which might well be different in form and substance if the notes

> were prepared by me in the knowledge that the patient was entitled to a copy of my records. I would be concerned that these notes and some of the other records maintained by me might, at least in some cases, cause confusion and unnecessary worry and stress to patients if they were made available to them without adequate explanation. Finally, in part, these notes contain information which relates solely to the business and administration of my practice and not to aspects of the treatment and management of my patients.

On 4 August 1993 the appellant's solicitors wrote to the respondent requesting copies of the appellant's medical records, not a medical report. By a letter dated 10 August 1993 the respondent replied to the appellant herself, saying:

> As [your solicitors] well know, it is a longstanding legal tradition in this country that such records are the doctor's property, an aide memoire to his treatment of the patient, and may only be released on production of a court subpoena.
>
> Accordingly the advice which I have received from my medical defence legal advis[e]rs is that this situation still holds, but that they would be very happy for me to release your records, were you to supply me with a document which would release me from any claim that might arise in relation to my treatment of you.

Despite the reference in that letter to a claim against the respondent, the appellant has not sought, nor does she seek, to make any claim against the respondent based upon his default. Had she commenced proceedings upon that basis she would have been entitled to discovery of her medical records in the ordinary course. Nevertheless, the appellant was not prepared to give the undertaking sought by the respondent's insurers and sought access to her medical records as of right.

During the trial of the appellant's action, the respondent made an open offer to provide a report in writing to the appellant about the contents of her medical records, excluding his correspondence with the New South Wales Medical Defence Union and with the appellant's solicitors. * * *. The trial judge found that the appellant did not wish to have a report such as that offered by the respondent and thus regarded himself as not called upon to consider whether the respondent's readiness to provide a report was reasonable or extended sufficiently far to satisfy any contractual duty which the respondent might have to provide a report.

Notwithstanding the purposes which the appellant asserted for wanting access to her medical records, her claim was that, in general, any patient is entitled to require from a treating doctor copies of all records relating to that patient for whatever purpose the patient has in mind. * * *

* * *

However, the appellant conceded that the right which she asserted must be subject to qualification. She accepted that "a doctor may withhold information where disclosure would be adverse to the patient's interests" and referred to this as the "therapeutic privilege".

The trial judge refused the appellant the relief which she sought. She appealed to the New South Wales Court of Appeal which, by a majority (Mahoney and Meagher JJA; Kirby P dissenting), dismissed the appeal. It is from the order of the Court of Appeal that the appellant now appeals to this court.

* * *

Proprietary right of interest

The appellant's contention is * * * that the information contained in the records can be separated from the records themselves and it is in the information that the appellant has a proprietary right or interest entitling her to access to the records. But there can be no proprietorship in information as information, because once imparted by one person to another, it belongs equally to them both. It is true, that equity acts to protect confidential information and the degree of protection afforded makes it appropriate to describe it as having a proprietary character, but that is not because property is the basis upon which protection is given. It is because of the effect of that protection. In this case, while the information provided by the appellant to the respondent was no doubt confidential, there is no question of any abuse by the respondent of that confidence and there is no property in that information in any sense upon which the appellant might base the right which she asserts.

* * *

Fiduciary duty

Whilst duties of a fiduciary nature may be imposed upon a doctor, they are confined and do not cover the entire doctor-patient relationship. Thus a doctor is under a duty to protect the confidentiality of information given by a patient. And the doctor-patient relationship is such that any substantial benefit received by the doctor from a patient (other than proper remuneration) is presumed to be the result of undue influence with the doctor bearing the onus of rebutting the presumption. Whether these aspects of the doctor-patient relationship are properly to be described as fiduciary may be a matter of debate. For example, in *Moorgate Tobacco Co Ltd v Philip Morris Ltd (No 2)*, Deane J saw the protection afforded by equity to confidential information as something separate from a wider fiduciary duty arising from the general nature of a relationship. Similarly, academic writers have classified the doctrine of undue influence as standing apart from a more general fiduciary doctrine. But the debate is not worth pursuing in the present context because it is plain that the appellant relies upon a wider fiduciary relationship between her and the respondent as giving rise to a duty on the part of the respondent to afford her access to her medical records.

The difficulty in dealing with the appellant's contention is that the law has not, as yet, been able to formulate any precise or comprehensive definition of the circumstances in which a person is constituted a fiduciary in his or her relations with another. There are accepted fiduciary relationships, such as trustee and beneficiary, agent and principal, solicitor and client, employee and employer, director and company, and partners, which may be characterised as relations of trust and confidence. In *Hospital Products Ltd v United States Surgical Corp* Mason J said:

> The critical feature of these relationships is that the fiduciary undertakes or agrees to act for or on behalf of or in the interests of another person in the exercise of a power or discretion which will affect the interests of that other person in a legal or practical sense. The relationship between the parties is therefore one which gives the fiduciary a special opportunity to exercise the power or discretion to the detriment of that other person who is accordingly vulnerable to abuse by the fiduciary of his position. The expressions "for," "on behalf of," and "in the interests of" signify that the fiduciary acts in a "representative" character in the exercise of his responsibility."

* * * It is not the case that whenever there is "a job to be performed," and entrusting the job to someone involves reposing substantial trust and confidence in that person, a fiduciary relationship arises. But it is of significance that a fiduciary acts in a representative character in the exercise of his responsibility.

A doctor is bound to exercise reasonable skill and care in treating and advising a patient, but in doing so is acting, not as a representative of the patient, but simply in the exercise of his or her professional responsibilities. No doubt the patient places trust and confidence in the doctor, but it is not because the doctor acts on behalf of the patient; it is because the patient is entitled to expect the observance of professional standards by the doctor in matters of treatment and advice and is afforded remedies in contract and tort if those standards are not observed and the patient suffers damage.

Equity requires that a person under a fiduciary obligation should not put himself or herself in a position where interest and duty conflict or, if conflict is unavoidable, should resolve it in favour of duty and, except by special arrangement, should not make a profit out of the position. The application of that requirement is quite inappropriate in the treatment of a patient by a doctor or in the giving of associated advice. There the duty of the doctor is established both in contract and in tort and it is appropriately described in terms of the observance of a standard of care and skill rather than, inappropriately, in terms of the avoidance of a conflict of interest. It has been observed that what the law exacts in a fiduciary relationship is loyalty, often of an uncompromising kind, but no more than that. The concern of the law in a fiduciary relationship is not negligence or breach of contract. Yet it is the law of negligence and contract which governs the duty of a doctor towards a patient. This leaves no need, or even room, for the imposition of fiduciary obligations. Of course, fiduciary duties may be superimposed upon contractual obligations and it is conceivable that a doctor may place himself in a position with potential for a conflict of interest—if, for example, the doctor has a financial interest in a hospital or a pathology laboratory—so as to give rise to fiduciary obligations. But that is not this case.

* * *

The appellant relied upon the decision of the Canadian Supreme Court in *McInerney v MacDonald*, in which La Forest J, delivering the judgment of the court, held that a patient is entitled to reasonable access to examine and copy the doctor's records. * * * In basing the duty upon a fiduciary relationship, La Forest J was giving expression to the view that it is the duty of the doctor to act with "utmost good faith and loyalty." Such a duty hardly fits with the undoubted duty of a doctor in this country to exercise reasonable skill and care in the giving of treatment and advice. It is, perhaps, reflective of a tendency, not found in this country, but to be seen in the United States and to a lesser extent Canada, to view a fiduciary relationship as imposing obligations which go beyond the exaction of loyalty and as displacing the role hitherto played by the law of contract and tort by becoming an independent source of positive obligations and creating new forms of civil wrong. But, with respect, that is achieved by assertion rather than analysis and, while it may effectuate a preference for a particular result, it does not involve the development or elucidation of any accepted doctrine. There is no foundation in either principle or authority in this country, however different the position may be in Canada, for the conclusion reached by La Forest J that:

> information about oneself revealed to a doctor acting in a professional capacity remains, in a fundamental sense, one's own. The doctor's position is one of trust and confidence. The information conveyed is held in a fashion somewhat akin to a trust. While the doctor is the owner of the actual record, the information is to be used by the physician for the benefit of the patient. The confiding of the information to the physician for medical purposes gives rise to an expectation that the patient's interest in and control of the information will continue.

It should be observed in relation to that passage that the court was not concerned in that case, as we are not in this, with a patient's right to information. It was concerned with access to the actual records containing the information, notwithstanding that in places the passage appears to regard "information" as interchangeable with "the actual record."

In England, § 3 of the Access to Health Records Act 1990 (UK) gives a prima facie right of access to health records by the individuals to whom they relate and other persons, but § 5(1) provides:

> Access shall not be given under section 3(2) above to any part of a health record:
>
> (a) which, in the opinion of the holder of the record, would disclose:
>
> (i) information likely to cause serious harm to the physical or mental health of the patient or of any other individual; or
>
> (ii) information relating to or provided by an individual, other than the patient, who could be identified from that information; or
>
> (b) which was made before the commencement of this Act.

That Act was passed as a result of the decision of the European Court of Human Rights in *Gaskin v United Kingdom* which held that the refusal to allow access by the applicant to certain health records was in breach of his right to respect for his private and family life under Art. 8 of the European Convention for the Protection of Human Rights and Fundamental Freedoms 1950.

In *R v Mid Glamorgan Family Health Services* the Court of Appeal upheld a decision by Popplewell J dismissing an application by a patient for access to his medical records. Popplewell J was of the view that there had been no breach of Art. 8 because the respondent had offered to make available the records (which predated the 1990 Act) to an independent medical adviser who might judge whether the information was likely to cause harm to the applicant or anyone else. However, he reached "the clearest possible conclusion" that at common law there was no right of access by the applicant to records pre-existing the Access to Health Records Act. In the Court of Appeal Nourse LJ (with whom the other members of the Court agreed) referred in his judgment to the well-known passage in the speech of Lord Templeman in *Sidaway v Governors of Bethlem Royal Hospital* in which he said:

> I do not subscribe to the theory that the patient is entitled to know everything nor to the theory that the doctor is entitled to decide everything. The relationship between doctor and patient is contractual in origin, the doctor performing services in consideration for fees payable by the patient. The doctor, obedient to the high standards set by the medical profession impliedly contracts to act at all times in the best interests of the patient. No doctor in his senses would impliedly contract at the same time to give to the patient all the information available to the doctor as a result of the doctor's training and experience and as a result of the doctor's diagnosis of the patient. An obligation to give a patient all the information available to the doctor would often be inconsistent with the doctor's contractual obligation to have regard to the patient's best interests. Some information might confuse, other information might alarm a particular patient. Whenever the occasion arises for the doctor to tell the patient the results of the doctor's diagnosis, the possible methods of treatment and the advantages and disadvantages of the recommended treatment, the doctor must decide in the light of his training and experience and in the light of his knowledge of the patient what should be said and how it should be said.

* * *

For these reasons, we would dismiss the appeal.

Brennan CJ.

The circumstances which give rise to the issues in this appeal are set out in other judgments. The appellant, who has been a patient of the respondent medical practitioner, claims a legal right to reasonable access to the records kept by the respondent with respect to the appellant and a right to inspect and/or copy those records. Subject to certain admitted exceptions, the appellant submits that that right is enforceable by declaration and injunction. The right is submitted to be based variously on contract, property and fiduciary duty. In my view, none of these bases gives any support to the appellant's claim. * * *

* * *

Contract

In the absence of special contract between a doctor and a patient, the doctor undertakes by the contract between them to advise and treat the patient with reasonable skill and care. The consideration for the undertaking may be either a payment, or promise of payment, of reward or submission by the patient, or an undertaking by the patient to submit, to the treatment proposed. A duty, similar to the duty binding on the doctor by contract, is imposed on the doctor by the law of torts. The advice and treatment required to fulfil either duty depends on the history and condition of the patient, the facilities available and all the other circumstances of the case.

The provision of advice and treatment with reasonable skill and care may not exhaust the duty of the doctor. Unless the contract between doctor and patient is especially restricted, the doctor's obligation is to maintain or improve the health of the patient generally and to use reasonable skill and care in doing so, even though the advice or treatment required on a particular occasion is in a specialist field or is to be provided only on that occasion or for a limited time. * * *

In some situations, there may be a duty to provide to the patient, or to the patient's nominee, information which the doctor has acquired in the course or for the purpose of advising or treating the patient. That is information received or otherwise acquired by the doctor pursuant to an authority given—expressly or impliedly—by the patient for the purpose of enabling the doctor to perform the doctor's contractual duty to maintain or improve the health of the patient generally. Absent the patient's permission, the doctor must not use that information for any other purpose. When the future medical treatment or physical or mental well-being of a patient might be prejudiced by an absence of information about the history or condition or treatment of the patient on an earlier occasion, the doctor who has acquired that information for the benefit of the patient's health must make it available to avoid or diminish that prejudice. Such an obligation is implied by the doctor's acceptance of the patient's authority under the contract to obtain that information. The authority is given in order to benefit the patient's health generally; the authority must be accepted and acted upon for the same purpose. As the obligation is implied, it can be excluded by express provision.

The obligation is not unqualified. As it arises from and is conditioned by the doctor's duty to benefit the patient's health generally, the obligation falls to be discharged only when the patient's health would or might be prejudiced by refusing to make the information available. And, as the service of making the information available is not ordinarily covered by the fee paid for advice or treatment, the doctor is entitled to a reasonable reward for the service.

For these reasons, I would hold that information with respect to a patient's history, condition or treatment obtained by a doctor in the course or for the purpose of giving advice or treatment to the patient must be disclosed by the doctor to the patient or the patient's nominee on request when (1) refusal to make the disclosure requested might prejudice the general health of the patient, (2) the request for disclosure is reasonable having regard to all the circumstances, and (3) reasonable reward for the service of disclosure is tendered or assured. A similar duty may be imposed on the doctor by the law of torts * * *.

An undertaking to provide information is one thing; a duty to give the patient access to, and to permit the patient to copy, the doctor's records is another. The doctor's duty to provide information not only can be discharged, but in some circumstances ought to be discharged, without allowing the patient to see the doctor's records. Where that duty can be performed without giving the patient access to the doctor's records, there is no foundation for implying any obligation to give that access. * * *

The appellant argued for an implied term in the contract between the appellant and respondent that the respondent would act in the appellant's "best interests", even to the extent of testifying for her in litigation. The propounded "best interests" obligation was said to encompass an obligation to give a patient access to the doctor's records. The term implied in the ordinary contract does not go so far. It is limited by the subject matter to which the contract relates, namely, benefiting the health of the patient.

* * * In the present case, it is not suggested that access to the respondent's records is needed for any therapeutic reason. Nor could such a suggestion be made. The respondent made an open offer to provide a report in writing relating to the history, physical examination findings, investigation results, diagnosis, proposed management plan, treatment or advice furnished to the appellant. That offer, if accepted and if fulfilled, would have discharged any obligation that might have arisen by implication from the contract between the parties. The offer was not accepted, the appellant contending not for a right to be informed but for a right of access to the doctor's records. As the contract between the appellant and respondent was wholly effective without any term entitling the appellant to access to the respondent's records and requiring the respondent to give that access, there is no foundation for implying such a term. Accordingly, the first basis of the appellant's claim fails.

Property

The appellant concedes that the property in the records as chattels is in the respondent. The concession is rightly made. Documents prepared by a professional person to assist the professional to perform his or her professional duties are not the property of the lay client; they remain the property of the professional. In the light of that principle, it is not easy to see what relevance the law of property has to the supposed right of the appellant to access to the respondent's records. If (as it was put during argument) the respondent is said to have no proprietary right that would entitle him to refuse access, the question whether the appellant has a right to be given access still remains. On that approach, the supposed right (if any) must find some basis other than property. But even on that approach, the argument is flawed. Absent some right to require, or the exercise of some power to compel, production of a document for inspection, its owner is entitled by virtue of the rights of ownership to refuse to produce it. As for copying, where the professional person is the owner of the copyright, he or she has the sole right to copy or to permit the copying of the document.

If the approach is that a right to access and to copy arises because the information contained in the records is proprietary in nature, the approach mistakes the sense in which information is described as property. * * *

* * *

Equity might restrain the respondent from disclosing without authority any information about the appellant and her medical condition that is contained in the respondent's records and, in that sense, it might be arguable that that information is the property of the appellant. Even if such a description were correct—and it is not necessary to consider that question—the description would provide no foundation for the existence of a right to access and to copy enforceable in equity. * * * There is no obligation in conscience requiring the respondent to open his records to inspection and copying by the appellant. Whichever approach is taken to the relevance of the law of property, it fails to provide any basis for the appellant's claim.

Fiduciary Duty

Fiduciary duties arise from either of two sources, which may be distinguished one from the other but which frequently overlap. One source is agency; the other is a relationship of ascendancy or influence by one party over another, or dependence or trust on the part of that other. Whichever be the source of the duty, it is necessary to identify "the subject matter over which the fiduciary obligations extend." It is erroneous to regard the duty owed by a fiduciary to his beneficiary as attaching to every aspect of the fiduciary's conduct, however irrelevant that conduct may be to the agency or relationship that is the source of fiduciary duty.

As Mason J said in *Hospital Products Ltd v United States Surgical Corp*: "it is now acknowledged generally that the scope of the fiduciary duty must be moulded according to the nature of the relationship and the facts of the case."

* * *

What is the nature of the doctor-patient relationship? Generally there is no relationship of agency. But the relationship of doctor and patient is one where the doctor acquires an ascendancy over the patient and the patient is in a position of reposing trust in the doctor. Such a relationship casts upon the doctor the onus of proving that any gift received from the patient was given free from the influence which the relationship produces. But in this case the doctor has received no gift; he has taken no step to procure an advantage for himself. Nor has he taken any advantage of his ascendancy over his patient or of her trust in him. His refusal to give access to his records does not deny his patient a benefit to which the patient was entitled either by reason of his position as the appellant's medical adviser and provider of medical treatment or by reason of the trust she reposed in him to provide medical treatment. In Canada, the Supreme Court has held that the relationship between doctor and patient casts on the doctor a fiduciary duty to provide the patient with access to his or her medical records: *McInerney v MacDonald*. But in this respect the notion of fiduciary duty in Canada does not accord with the notion in the United Kingdom. Nor, in my opinion, does the Canadian notion accord with the law of fiduciary duty as understood in this country. There is simply no fiduciary relationship which gives rise to a duty to give access to or to permit the copying of the respondent's records. There is no relevant subject matter over which the respondent's fiduciary duty extended.

* * *

The appeal should be dismissed.

Gaudron and McHugh JJ.

* * *

Australian courts have consciously refrained from attempting to provide a general test for determining when persons or classes of persons stand in a fiduciary relationship with one another. * * *

As the law stands, the doctor-patient relationship is not an accepted fiduciary relationship in the sense that the relationships of trustee and beneficiary, agent and principal, solicitor and client, employee and employer, director and company and partners are recognised as fiduciary relationships. In Hospital Products, Mason J pointed out that in all those relationships "the fiduciary acts in a 'representative' character in the exercise of his responsibility." But a doctor is not generally or even primarily a representative of his patient.

However, the categories of fiduciary relationship are not closed, and the courts have identified various circumstances that, if present, point towards, but do not determine, the existence of a fiduciary relationship. These circumstances, which are not exhaustive and may overlap, have included: the existence of a relation of confidence; inequality of bargaining power; an undertaking by one party to perform a task or fulfil a duty in the interests of another party; the scope for one party to unilaterally exercise a discretion or power which may affect the rights or interests of another; and a dependency or vulnerability on the part of one party that causes that party to rely on another.

Some aspects of the doctor-patient relationship exhibit characteristics that courts have used to find a fiduciary relationship. For example, from the most mundane consultation with a general practitioner through to the most complicated surgical procedure by a specialist surgeon, a patient is invariably dependent upon the advice and treatment of his or her doctor. Patients also invariably confide intimate personal details about themselves to their doctors. In some circumstances, the dependency of the patient or the provision of confidential information may make the relationship between a doctor and patient fiduciary in nature. But that does not mean that their relationship would be fiduciary for all purposes. * * *

* * * In the present case, if Dr Williams owed a fiduciary duty to Ms Breen, the duties and obligations which arose from their fiduciary relationship could only come from those aspects of the relationship which exhibited the characteristics of trust, confidence and vulnerability that typify the fiduciary relationship. They could only attach in respect of matters that relate to diagnosis, advice and treatment.

A consideration of the fundamental obligations of a fiduciary shows that Dr Williams owed no fiduciary duty to Ms Breen to give her access to the records that he had created. The law of fiduciary duty rests not so much on morality or conscience as on the acceptance of the implications of the biblical injunction that "[n]o man can serve two masters." Duty and self-interest, like God and Mammon, make inconsistent calls on the faithful. Equity solves the problem in a practical way by insisting that fiduciaries give undivided loyalty to the persons whom they serve * * *.

* * *

In the present case, there was no breach of fiduciary duty in the conditional denial of access because there was no pre-existing duty on the part of Dr Williams to give access to the records.

* * *

The right of access claimed by Ms Breen is not one given by the contract between her and Dr Williams. Nor can it arise from any undertaking, express or implied, by Dr Williams to act as the representative of Ms Breen because no such undertaking was given. Moreover, the contract between the parties gives her no right to or interest in the medical records. They remain the property of Dr Williams. Furthermore, a fiduciary duty that Dr Williams would always act in Ms Breen's best interests, which is the foundation of the claim of a fiduciary obligation to provide access to the records, would conflict with the narrower contractual and tortious duty to exercise reasonable care and skill in the provision of professional advice and treatment that Dr Williams undertook.

In addition, Dr Williams is the owner of the copyright in the records. By federal law, ownership of the copyright gives Dr Williams a number of exclusive proprietary rights including the right to reproduce the records in any material form. He is the beneficial owner of those rights. He does not hold them on trust for Ms Breen. In the absence of an undertaking, express or implied, on the part of Dr Williams to allow her to copy the records, it is difficult to see how Ms Breen could be allowed to copy the records even if she had a right of access to the records.

In our view, there is no basis upon which this court can hold that Dr Williams owed Ms Breen a fiduciary duty to give her access to the medical records. She seeks to impose fiduciary obligations on a class of relationship which has not traditionally been recognised as fiduciary in nature and which would significantly alter the already existing complex of legal doctrines governing the doctor-patient relationship, particularly in the areas of contract and tort. * * *

Fiduciary duties should not be superimposed on these common law duties simply to improve the nature or extent of the remedy.

Dr Cashman [the appellant's lawyer] relied strongly on the decision of the Supreme Court of Canada in *McInerney v MacDonald* to support his contention that Dr Williams owed Ms Breen a fiduciary duty to give her access to the medical records.

* * *

[T]he Canadian law on fiduciary duties is very different from the law of this country with respect to that subject. One commentator has recently pointed to the "vast differences between Australia and Canada in understanding of the nature of fiduciary obligations." One significant difference is the tendency of Canadian courts to apply fiduciary principles in an expansive manner so as to supplement tort law and provide a basis for the creation of new forms of civil wrongs. The Canadian cases also reveal a tendency to view fiduciary obligations as both proscriptive and prescriptive. However, Australian courts only recognise proscriptive fiduciary duties. This is not the place to explore the differences between the law of Canada and the law of Australia on this topic. With great respect to the Canadian courts, however, many cases in that jurisdiction pay insufficient regard to the effect that the imposition of fiduciary duties on particular relationships has on the law of negligence, contract, agency, trusts and companies in their application to those relationships. * * *

In this country, fiduciary obligations arise because a person has come under an obligation to act in another's interests. As a result, equity imposes on the fiduciary proscriptive obligations—not to obtain any unauthorised benefit from the relationship and not to be in a position of conflict. If these obligations are breached, the fiduciary must account for any profits and make good any losses arising from the breach. But the law of this country does not otherwise impose positive legal duties on the fiduciary to act in the interests of the person to whom the duty is owed. If there was a general fiduciary duty to act in the best interests of the patient, it would necessarily follow that a doctor has a duty to inform the patient that he or she has breached their contract or has been guilty of negligence in dealings with the patient. That is not the law of this country.

* * *

The appeal should be dismissed.

[Opinion of Gummow, J. omitted.]

Notes

1. Patients in Australia now have a general right to access and copy their medical records, subject to certain exceptions (for example, to protect the privacy of third parties) under the Privacy Act, 1988, and the Privacy Amendment (Private Sector) Act, 2000. For these and other privacy legislation, see Office of the Australian Information Commissioner, *Privacy Law*, at https://www.oaic.gov.au/privacy-law/.

2. Note the role that equity and the concepts of beneficial ownership in trust and fiduciary obligations play in these cases. For one thing, they make it possible to think about patients having an interest in their medical information, even though both courts accept that the legal ownership of the records rests in the physicians. The trust idea, of course, grows out of the medieval division between the English courts of law and Chancery, and has no exact equivalent in the civil law. In this instance, the common law has a means of flexibility not available in the civil law.

3. The notion of the fiduciary nature of the doctor/patient relationship has often played a key role in American decisions. The *Canterbury* decision, discussed in the preceding section, and American cases following it, relied in part on this relationship. The judges in *Breen* accept that a doctor has a fiduciary obligation not to take ad-

vantage of a patient financially, even if they reject the argument as a means to gain access to patient records. This obligation forms the basis of American prohibitions against bribes and kickbacks and self-referrals in American fraud and abuse law. See Barry R. Furrow et al., *Health Law Hornbook*, 637ff (2nd ed. 2000). Though fraud and abuse is an issue in other countries, it lacks elsewhere the political saliency that it enjoys in the United States. Why should this be true?

4. Note the rather different understanding of the notion of fiduciary that is found in these two cases. *McInerney* sees the doctor as being a fiduciary with respect to the patient, but describes the patient as a consumer. Does not the notion of a consumer assume an at-arms-length relationship, a relationship of reciprocity—rather than a relationship of dependence? *Breen* rejects the fiduciary analogy, because the relationship between doctor and patient, though characterized in part by ascendancy and dependency, is not one of representation. The duty owed by the doctor to the patient, therefore, is one of skill and competence (based in tort and contract), not of fiduciary loyalty. *Breen* seems to take a more paternalistic approach to the doctor/patient relationship, but in the end refuses to impose paternal obligations on the doctor.

5. The European Council Convention on Human Rights and Biomedicine embraces a principle of access to medical information, so this issue should become less contested in Europe. See Article 12(2), a principle that would be binding in the U.K. As recently as 1995, however, the British Court of Appeal rejected a claim of access to medical records. *R. v. Mid Glamorgan Family Health Services*, 1 All.E.R. 356 [1995], as noted in the Dawson and Toohey opinion.

Mohammad Hossein Yarmohammadian, Ahmad Reza Raeisi, Navid Tavakoli & Leila Ghaderi Nansa, *Medical Record Information Disclosure Laws and Policies among Selected Countries: A Comparative Study*

15(3) *Journal of Research in Medical Sciences* 140–49 (May–June 2010)

* * *

In Iran, there are no clear and comprehensive rules and regulations in hospitals on how to disclose patient medical records for various applications. Therefore medical record department staff [face] difficult situations for disclosure and transfer of medical records. Some hospitals have established and developed internal policies and procedures which could not adequately protect the confidentiality of patient information and/or satisfy needs of applicants in required circumstances. As the first step in striking a proper balance between the personal privacy rights of patients and the informational needs of hospitals and society in general, hospitals have to have a well defined policy and procedures on the use and disclosure of medical information. This policy should limit disclosure to essential purposes.

* * *

This research was done to review policies and laws related to disclosure of medical record information among selected countries and tried to identify the similarities and the differences between them in order to develop and adopt related policies and laws for Iranian hospitals.

Methods

This was a descriptive-comparative study done from February 2008 through October 2009. The research resources included written and electronic documents and records. Data were gathered regarding health information disclosure laws and policies related to disclosure of health information in five countries namely [the] United States, Australia, England, Malaysia and Iran. The reason for selection of [the] United States, Australia and England is their advancement and long history and experience of these countries in the field and establishment of medical record programs and departments. Malaysia is an Islamic country that in recent years has had rapid growth and development in the field of health information and communication technology. * * *

* * *

Discussion

Results showed that [the] legislative institutions of each country have ordained laws and policies * * * and in turn hospitals developed policies and procedures based on these laws. Meanwhile in all of the selected countries there are ordained limitations for release of health information for protecting health information in regard to patient rights. In Iran, however, there are sporadic laws and policies concerning disclosure of health information in the form of formal letters and bylaws. However there are no specific policies and procedures for disclosure of health information.

Regarding health information disclosure to patient[s] or family members, there is similarity in policy and procedure between [the] United States and United Kingdom. They have complete policies about disclosure of information to patient[s], but [in the] other three countries (Australia, Malaysia and Iran) policies related to disclosure of health information to patient[s] or family members are inadequate. * * *

* * *

In Iran, legal authorities should approve specific policies and laws in regard to using medical records information for patients or family members and other users of medical records, because there is major shortcoming in these fields, but findings showed that there are rigid and strong policies for legal users and law enforcement agencies.

Despite the fact that * * * agreement is [a] common requirement for disclosure of information for []payment purposes in all the selected countries, there isn't any clear and specific policy [or] procedure in Iran in this regard. There is just a general and brief recommendation for disclosure of medical records information to the patient or his or her legal representative. There is correlation between findings of current research and some other research[] which showed an ambiguity about disclosure of information for insurance companies in Iranian laws. In Iran disclosing information to insurance companies is subject to approved contracts. Insurance officers are required to investigate and prepare compatible medical records to support patients['] insurance. They should also compare records and health invoices to their own insurance terms and conditions. Lack of cooperation between hospitals especially the medical records departments and insurance companies has actually resulted in difficulty for refunding treatment expenses. Also lack of specific and clear policies despite responding to applicant requests causes violation of patient rights and neglecting the confidentiality of medical records.

Conclusions

In conclusion, legal authorities [in Iran] should approve specific policies and laws in regard to using medical records information for patients or family members and other users of medical records according to national and social circumstances of Iran. It is also recommended that further research should be conducted to do comparative studies about disclosure of health information in teaching hospitals and challenges concerning security and confidentiality of medical records.

Notes

1. The excerpt above evaluates how Iranian law compares to the laws in Australia, England, Malaysia, and the United States. Another paper involving some of the same authors compares patient access to electronic health records (EHRs) in Iran with patient access in Canada, Australia, and New Zealand. *See* Nahid Tavakoli et al., *Patient Access to Electronic Health Record: A Comparative Study on Laws, Policies, and Procedures in Selected Countries*, 67(1) Medical Archives 63–67 (Feb. 2013). How do the two papers push for reforms in Iran? What is the value of consulting the laws in other jurisdictions?

2. Scholars have examined how, in many developing countries, patients are unable to prove negligence claims because they do not have access to their own medical records. For example, patients in India and Thailand are often denied access to even basic information about their treatments. *See, e.g.*, Nathan Cortez, A Medical Malpractice Model for Developing Countries?, 4 *Drexel Law Review* 217, 227–28 (2011); Nathan Cortez, Recalibrating the Legal Risks of Cross-Border Health Care, 10 *Yale Journal of Health Policy, Law, and Ethics* 1, 29–31, 44–45 (2010).

Chapter 3

The Patient's Right to Self-Determination and Competing Considerations

A. Abortion

Abortion, the termination of a fetus before birth, remains controversial in many places across the globe. In the United States, abortion law remains politically and legally hotly contested—it is an issue that invokes debates about when personhood begins, women's rights over their bodies, religious freedom, and at times, has defined the very fabric of the political landscape. By contrast, in many other countries the issue has largely been settled in either the permissive or restrictive direction. Globally, abortion policy and practice are guided by three primary influences: religion, population policy, and economic policy. Sometimes major changes are the result of large popular social movements, but in other instances shifts occur through more quotidian bureaucratic decision-making.

In countries where the opposition to abortion is based on religious convictions, the debate raises questions about the relationship of a dominant religion and the state. For example, while Catholicism is the dominant religion in Ireland, the Irish Constitution does not endorse any state religion. However, the Irish Constitution specifically recognizes a right to life in the unborn, and attempts to liberalize abortion have been vigorously opposed by the Catholic Church—only recently has abortion been liberalized. In Belgium a stalemate existed for two decades between a parliament that wanted to liberalize one of the most restrictive abortion laws in Europe and a devout Catholic king who would have no part of it. The stalemate was only broken in 1990 when Parliament suspended the King's reign for one night to allow the law to go into effect. In Iran, a law that liberally permitted abortion, adopted under the Shah, was replaced after the 1979 Islamic Revolution with a law that made abortion illegal except where necessary to save the life of the pregnant woman. In Japan, in which Buddhism, Confucianism, and Shintoism are all influential, Shinto promotion of reproduction contributed in part to a legal ban on birth control pills, in place until 1999, which in turn contributed to a high rate of abortion as a birth control method. Sara L. Walsh, Liquid Lives and Liquid Laws: The Evolution of Abortion Law in Japan and the United States, 7 *Int'l Legal Persp.* 187 (1995); Evy F. McElmeel, Legalization of the Birth Control Pill in Japan will Reduce Reliance on Abortion as the Primary Method of Birth Control, 8 *Pac.Rim. L. & Pol'y J.* 681 (1999).

In some countries population policy plays a more important role than religion in determining abortion laws, although the two are often, as in Japan, interrelated. The most rigorous ban on abortion in modern history was probably found in Romania, where the Ceausescu regime in the 1960s adopted a strong pro-natal policy, declaring the fetus the property of the state, and vigorously prosecuting abortion. Women were examined monthly at their place of work to identify pregnancies, and women who had an illegal abortion were subject to two years in prison and were denied medical care if the abortion was botched and the woman refused to identify the abortionist. In other countries, such as Russia, abortion has been used as a relatively inexpensive means of birth control, though with high costs in terms of maternal life and health. Under China's one-child policy, abortion on demand was not only permitted, but encouraged, with abortion paid for by the state.

In many developing countries abortion practice, if not policy, is driven by economic considerations. Where both conventional birth control and additional children are unaffordable, abortion (or infanticide) remains the most viable alternative when other approaches to birth control fail. If legal abortions are unaffordable, illegal abortions become common. Making safe and effective contraception widely available, therefore, may be the most effective means of discouraging abortion in these countries. In some countries, however, abortion is also used as a means of sex selection, which is often in turn driven by economic reasons, as boys are more likely to be able to provide security to their parents in old age. India permits abortion, but outlaws abortion for selection of sex, though the law is apparently widely violated. *See* Azim A. Khan Sherwani and M. Minhajul Haq, Illegal Abortion and Women's Reproductive Health, 3 *Med. L. Int'l.* 223 (1998); Kristi Lemoine and John Tanagho, Gender Discrimination Fuels Sex Selective Abortion: The Impact of the Indian Supreme Court on the Implementation and Enforcement of the PNDT Act, 15 *U. Miami Int'l & Comp. L. Rev.* 203, 254 (2007).

The readings that follow further examine abortion law and policy throughout the world.

Abortion Policies: A Global Review

United Nations, 1–2, 4–7 (2003)

* * *

Although abortion is commonly practised throughout most of the world and has been practised since long before the beginning of recorded history, it is a subject that arouses passion and controversy. Abortion raises fundamental questions about human existence, such as when life begins and what it is that makes us human. Abortion is at the heart of such contentious issues as the right of women to control their own bodies, the nature of the State's duty to protect the unborn, the tension between secular and religious views of human life and the individual and society, the rights of spouses and parents to be involved in the abortion decision, and the conflicting rights of the mother and the foetus. Also central to the subject of abortion is one of the most highly controversial social issues of all, sexuality. * * *

* * *

* * * [T]he legal provisions governing abortion in many countries are not always conveniently located within one text. The most common place in which such provisions appear is a country's criminal code or criminal laws relating to offences against persons, for abortion has, at least in the last two centuries, been considered a criminal offence of a highly serious nature. However, with the movement during the last half of the twentieth century to liberalize abortion laws, this is no longer invariably the case; consequently, legal provisions on abortion can be found in a variety of places. Some countries have incorporated liberalized abortion provisions into their criminal codes. Others have enacted special abortion laws that are separate from criminal codes. Thus it is possible for a criminal code to prohibit abortions, while a law on abortion will describe the circumstances under which abortions are allowed. In still other countries, public health codes or medical ethics codes may contain special provisions that clarify how to interpret an abortion law. For example, a medical ethics code may specify the circumstances under which it is ethically acceptable for a physician to perform an abortion. In a final group of countries, mostly common-law countries (see below), abortion may not be governed by a specific law, but by a court decision. In a few cases, the existence of multiple texts, each with conflicting provisions, can make it difficult to determine the exact nature of the law and policy concerning abortion in a specific country.

* * *

* * * Most common law countries, other than the United States, have abortion laws that are based on various English laws and court decisions. Some take as their model the Offences Against the Person Act of 1861. Under this Act it was prohibited "unlawfully" to use any means to procure an abortion either for oneself or for another person or unlawfully to supply means for that end, and the prescribed punishment was imprisonment. Originally, this Act was interpreted as prohibiting all abortions, except those performed on the grounds of necessity, in order to save the life of the pregnant woman. Other countries follow the English court decision, *Rex* v. *Bourne*, in which it was held that abortions performed for serious physical or mental health reasons would not be considered "unlawful" under the 1861 Act. Still other countries have looked to the British Abortion Act of 1967, which sets forth broad health, foetal impairment, and socio-economic indications for abortions, in general until the twenty-fourth week of pregnancy.

The abortion laws of many civil law countries are based on the abortion provisions of the French Napoleonic Code of 1810, the 1939 French version of that Code or the 1979 abortion law of France. Under the 1810 Napoleonic Code, any person who by any means procured the abortion of a pregnant woman was punished with imprisonment, as was a pregnant woman who procured her own abortion, although it was understood that an abortion could be performed when necessary to save the life of the pregnant woman. To the provisions of the 1810 Code, the 1939 French Penal Code added language specifically allowing an abortion to be performed to save the life of the pregnant woman. The 1979 Law allows a woman who is in a state of distress to have an abortion performed on request during the first ten weeks of pregnancy after she undergoes counselling and waits a week, and later in pregnancy on other serious grounds. In contrast to the common law system, court interpretations of these laws play a minor role.

Unlike the situation in either the common law or civil law countries, no single abortion text or court case can be identified as the model for most modern Islamic abortion laws. The Quran and the *sunnah*, the two primary sources of Islamic law, do not deal specifically with abortion. Moreover, until recently, Islamic criminal laws were not always codified. Consequently, Islamic law adopts a number of approaches towards abortion, depending upon which of the five major schools of Islamic law is followed. In general, the attitude of Islamic law towards abortion is dependent upon whether the abortion is performed before ensoulment, the time at which a foetus gains a soul. This is most often viewed as occurring 120 days into a pregnancy, but is also interpreted as occurring at 40 days. Some schools permit abortion for justifiable reasons before ensoulment, while others generally prohibit it at all points of pregnancy. All schools, however, allow abortion at any time during pregnancy in order to save the life of the pregnant woman. In contrast to the situation under both common law and civil law, the punishment for abortion under classic Islamic law is payment of a sum of money to the relatives of the foetus. The amount of payment depends upon the stage of pregnancy reached at the time of the abortion. * * *

Owing to the different treatments of abortion in these three legal systems, a number of ambiguities arise in interpreting specific indications for abortion, making any comparison challenging. The most widely accepted indication for abortion—to save the life of the pregnant woman—provides a good example. Broadly speaking, this indication is valid in two categories of countries: those with abortion laws that specifically mention it and those with laws in which it is not mentioned but is inferred from the general criminal-law principles of necessity. In the latter, an abortion, although considered illegal, can be performed on the rationale that it is necessary to preserve a greater good, the life of the pregnant woman.

In practical terms, these two situations differ substantially. In the first, a physician contemplating the performance of an abortion is able to point to a specific legal provision authorizing such an act and be reasonably certain that he or she was acting within the law. In the second, no such certainty exists, only a general principle that could be raised as a defence if the physician were prosecuted for performing an illegal abortion. It would then be a matter for a court to determine after a trial. The result is that in the latter case, a physician would in general exercise much more caution in determining whether to perform an abortion to save the life of the pregnant woman.

A similar situation arises with respect to laws that permit an abortion to be performed to preserve the health of a pregnant woman. An important distinction holds between countries with laws that specifically state that an abortion is allowed to preserve the health of a pregnant woman and countries in which a court or courts have, through their interpretation of a law that lacks specific provisions, allowed such an abortion to take place. In the former, a physician can be reasonably certain of acting within the law; again, in the latter, he or she might have to rely on a court decision as a defence in criminal proceedings. * * *

Additional ambiguities are connected with the health indication for abortion. One is that a number of countries use the term "health" in their abortion laws without specifying what it encompasses. Thus it is unclear whether they intend abortions to be allowed in cases of threat to mental and physical health or only physical health. * * * The question arises as to whether health should be interpreted as historically understood or in the light of current thinking. Similarly, unless a country specifies that the threat must be serious or grave or permanently disabling, it is unclear what degree of threat to health is intended.

Other terms referring to health are even more ambiguous. Some countries allow abortions for "therapeutic" purposes or permit abortions for the purpose of "medical or surgical treatment." Others provide that the threat to health by continuation of the pregnancy must be greater than the threat posed by its termination. Statistically, during the first trimester, a pregnancy is always a greater threat to health than its termination; it is therefore difficult to determine how to interpret this phrase. A literal interpretation would allow abortion under most circumstances. Given such a lack of clarity in the laws, the designation of a country as allowing abortions for health purposes can cover a wide variety of situations. These range from allowing abortion only in cases that threaten permanent and serious damage to physical health, to cases that threaten mental health owing to socio-economic distress, to the case of "medical or surgical treatment", which is essentially abortion on request. Unless the issue has been the subject of litigation in the courts, or a target of significant legal analysis of the nature of the threat in legal commentaries, it is difficult to ascertain exactly what the circumstances must be to justify an abortion.

Procedural requirements to establish the presence of an indication for abortion are also a factor in determining the exact nature of an indication for abortion. In the context of the indication of health, it may be necessary for two or three physicians to attest to the threat to health. A great deal of difference exists between this and the situation in which the physician who is willing to perform the abortion is the only judge of whether the indication is present. In the context of abortions performed in cases of pregnancy due to rape or incest, a variety of mandated procedures also prevail. In some countries, the incident of rape or incest must be reported to police or judicial authorities, while in others the pregnant woman must only reasonably believe that the pregnancy was the result of rape or incest. Some specify no procedural requirements or, conversely, require a judicial determination that the pregnancy was the result of rape or incest. Such differences again produce a significant variation on the nature of the indication of pregnancy due to rape or incest in various countries.

The terminology employed under Islamic law presents another formidable challenge in comparing abortion laws. The principles underlying Islamic law differ fundamentally from those of common and civil law, which have at the most basic level a Western orientation; it is therefore difficult to compare laws under the two systems. An example of this problem involves the notion under Islamic law that the crime of abortion is punished not by imprisonment and government-imposed fines, but by the payment of compensation by the perpetrator of the crime to the relatives of the victim of the crime. In the context of abortion, this is entirely foreign to Western law. The problem is also illustrated in the definition of the stages of pregnancy. While Western law does recognize different stages of pregnancy, in present-day law they are almost exclusively defined by weeks of gestation; under Islamic law they can be defined in more descriptive terms such as "the lump," "something that clings," "ensoulment," or "the forming of organs and limbs".

Beyond these conceptual challenges, determining whether the written law or policy of a country conforms to the practice observed or inferred remains a major problem. In many countries where the performance of abortions is generally illegal, statistics indicate that large numbers are being carried out, most of them illegally, with few prosecutions. Of the approximately 50 million abortions carried out every year in the world, estimates place the number performed illegally at 40 percent. In these countries, law enforcement authorities ignore or tolerate the performance of illegal abortions or even unofficially license clinics for that purpose. A number of factors are responsible for this situation. Among these are the ease with which abortions can be performed, the lack of will or resources to prosecute, particularly in the light of more pressing social needs, and the clandestine nature of the procedure. In some countries where abortion is technically legal, access to authorized facilities and personnel may be limited, or resources to pay for the abortion may be lacking, resulting in more illegal abortions. In a few cases, although abortion is authorized, the Government may not have issued regulations allowing the law to be effectively implemented. In all of these situations, legal action is rarely taken except in the most egregious cases, usually involving the death of a pregnant woman. In some countries, the indifference to abortion is so great that most of those performing abortions or enforcing laws do not know what the provisions of the law actually are. The advent of new scientific developments such as RU 486, the so called "abortion pill", which makes abortion even easier to perform without the need for special facilities, will in all probability only increase the gap between law and practice.

Notes

1. Although religion can be a key factor in determining a country's abortion policy, the entrenchment of a national religion in the legal system is not always directly related to the role played by religion in that country. The United States, for example, prohibits the establishment of religion in its Constitution, but religious conviction has been highly influential in shaping the national political landscape. Great Britain, in contrast, has an established church, but its politics are largely unaffected by religiosity. Even within a country we see significant variation: For example, in Germany, every state has an established church. However, religion has played a major role in abortion politics only in Bavaria and Baden-Württemburg, the Catholic states of the south.

2. Economic factors create some of the most serious barriers to abortion in the world. Many women simply cannot access safe and legal abortions because they cannot afford the procedure itself or because they cannot access the procedure locally and the cost of travel to a region or country where abortions are available is prohibitive. Some countries, including the United States, have severely restricted the use of public funds to support abortion. For further reading on this topic *see* Martha F. Davis, Abortion Access in the Global Marketplace, 88 *N.C. L. Rev.* 1657, 1685 (2010).

3. Beyond banning or permitting abortion, there is a third model, the "counseling model" or "conflict (emergency)-oriented discourse model." *See* Albin Eser and Hans-Georg Koch, *Abortion and the Law: From International Comparison to Legal Policy*, (The Hague: T.M.C. Asser Press, 2005) 298; Sjef Gevers, Abortion Legislation and the Future of the "Counseling Model," 13 *Eur. J. Health L.* 27 (2006). Under this model, the law establishes grounds (such as an emergency) under which an abortion is legal, but leaves the decision as to whether such grounds exist to the woman. The following excerpt explains these different regulatory regimes further and details the ways they have been constitutionalized around the world:

Reva Siegal, *The Constitutionalization of Abortion*

1071–1075, in Abortion Law in Transnational Perspective: Cases and Controversies (ed. Rebecca Cook, Joanna Erdman & Bernard Dickens 2014)

III. Contemporary Constitutional Frameworks

* * *

* * * Today, we can see constitutionalization of abortion taking several forms. Some jurisdictions require government to respect women's dignity in making decisions about abortion, and consequently require legislators to provide women control, for all or some period of pregnancy, over the decision whether to become a mother. Many jurisdictions require constitutional protection for unborn life, criminalizing abortion while permitting exceptions on an indications basis to protect women's physical or emotional welfare, but not their autonomy. Yet other jurisdictions protect unborn life through counseling regimes that are result-open; these jurisdictions begin by recognizing women's autonomy for the putatively instrumental reason that it is the best method of managing the modern female citizen, and then come to embrace protecting women's dignity as a concurrent constitutional aim of depenalizing abortion.

In what follows, I explore these three forms of constitutionalization, in order of their historical emergence, and briefly illustrate with contemporary examples. The forms are distinguishable along several dimensions. As will become apparent, the frameworks of review that jurisdictions have adopted vary in the constitutional values that courts expect abortion legislation to vindicate (e.g. respecting women's dignity, protecting unborn life, protecting women's welfare), and the legislative regimes associated historically and symbolically with the vindication of these constitutional values (e.g. 'periodic' regimes which allow abortion at a woman's request for a period of pregnancy; 'indications' regimes which prohibit abortion except on indications determined by a third party; and 'result-open' dissuasive counseling regimes which allow a woman to make the ultimate decision after she is counseled against abortion). Historical and symbolic ties between constitutional values and particular legislative abortion regimes have endowed those regimes with powerful social meaning, even as enforcement of abortion legislation may provide women access in striking variance. Finally, there is variance within these forms in the judicial constraints courts impose on representative government (do courts allow, require, or prohibit legislation vindicating particular constitutional values?). In some cases, these differences in judicial constraint seem connected to the values the case law vindicates; but in others they suggest an interesting story about the interaction of courts and representative government in the articulation of constitutional law.

There are other expressions of this evolving relationship between courts and legislatures. Over the decades, constitutions have been amended to address abortion more or less directly, and statutes have been enacted that include constitutionalized preambles, either in response to antecedent constitutional law or in an effort to call into being new bodies of constitutional law. With the growth of legislative constitutionalism in abortion regulation, the boundaries between constitutional law and politics grow ever blurrier.

1. Respecting Women's Dignity: Periodic Legislation

This approach, originating in the United States, constitutionalizes the regulation of abortion with attention to women's autonomy and welfare. It is associated with periodic legislation which coordinates values of decisional autonomy and protecting life by giving women control over the abortion decision, often for an initial period of the pregnancy, thereafter allowing restrictions on abortion except on limited indications (e.g. for life or health).

This approach begins in court decisions but now also finds expression in constitutionalized preambles. In South Africa, for example, the preamble to a statute allowing abortion on request in the first 12 weeks of pregnancy announces that it vindicates 'the values of human dignity, the achievement of equality, security of the person, non-racialism and non-sexism, and the advancement of human rights and freedoms which underlie a democratic South Africa.' The High Court upheld the legislation's constitutionality in a 2004 decision: 'the Constitution not only permits the Choice on Termination of Pregnancy Act to make a pregnant woman's informed consent the cornerstone of its regulation of the termination of her pregnancy, but indeed requires the Choice Act to do so.

Legislation recently enacted in Mexico City providing for abortion on request during the First 12 weeks of pregnancy appeals to a constitutional provision that guarantees Mexican citizens the freedom to decide the number and spacing of children; the preamble to the Mexico City statute provides: 'Sexual and reproductive health care is a priority. Services provided in this matter constitute a means for the exercise of the right of all persons to decide freely, responsibly and in an informed manner on the number and spacing of children.' The Supreme Court of Mexico recently confirmed the constitutionality of the legislation. The state was constitutionally permitted to decriminalize abortion.

2. Protecting Life/Protecting Women: Indications Legislation

Other jurisdictions follow the German tradition in constitutionalizing a duty to protect life; these jurisdictions require action in furtherance of the duty to protect, and typically require or authorize legislatures to criminalize abortion with certain exceptions or indications determined by a committee of doctors or some decision-maker other than the pregnant woman. As we have seen, constitutional judgments about women are inevitably nested within the constitutional duty to protect life, and emerge in any effort to specify the terms on which abortion is to be banned (and thus also permitted). Constitutionalization in this form has tended to incorporate gender-conventional, role-based views of women's citizenship—for example that the burdens of pregnancy are naturally assumed by women, or by women who have consented to sex, except when such burdens exceed what is normally to be expected of women, at which point women may be exempt from penal sanction for aborting a pregnancy.

Constitutionalization in this form is paternalist, in its conception of women as well as the unborn, reasoning about women as dependants who may deserve protection, and protecting them against injuries to their physical and emotional welfare, rather than to their autonomy. (Jurisdictions that protect unborn life by banning abortion except on third party indication typically excuse women from the duty to bear a child to protect women's physical survival and to protect women's physical and emotional welfare; only recently have some considered protecting women's dignity.) Courts' reasoning in this tradition typically permit, but do not require, abortion legislation to protect the welfare and autonomy of women citizens who are pregnant; courts may, however, hold that a constitution requires the state to allow abortion to save a woman's life.

The Republic of Ireland, which first amended its Constitution to address abortion, expressly relates the protections it accords the life of the unborn and the life of the mother: "The State acknowledges the right to life of the unborn and, with due regard to the equal right to life of the mother, guarantees in its laws to respect, and, as far as practicable, by its laws to defend and vindicate that right.' Ireland seems to construe a woman's 'equal right to life' as including protection for a woman's physical survival but not her dignity. When an adolescent woman who was pregnant by rape was enjoined from traveling abroad for an abortion, the Irish Supreme Court overturned the injunction, reasoning that the young woman's risk of suicide satisfied the standard of a 'real and substantial risk' to the pregnant woman's life. In other words, in order to fit the case within the right to life that Ireland guarantees equally to women and the unborn, the Court had to efface the young women's agency—her refusal to have sex with her rapist and the consequent risk she might harm herself if compelled to bear her rapist's child; instead the Court approached the young woman's case as if it concerned a physiological risk from pregnancy. The Court explained that its Constitution's abortion clause should be interpreted in terms informed by the virtue of charity: 'not the charity which consists of giving to the deserving, for that is justice, but the charity which is also called mercy.

In 1985 the Spanish Constitutional Court declared that its Constitution protected the life of the unborn, in the tradition of the first West German judgment, yet declared that it was constitutional for the legislature to allow abortion on several indications, including rape. In discussing the justification for the indication for rape, the Spanish Court emphasized that in such a case 'gestation was caused by an act ... harming to a maximum degree her [a woman's] personal dignity and the free development of her personality', emphasizing that 'the woman's dignity requires that she cannot be considered as a mere instrument.' Even so, the Court reasoned that the exceptions to Spain's abortion law were constitutionally permitted, not required, and emphasized that the legislation was enacted for the purpose of protecting unborn life.

A more recent decision of the Colombian Supreme Court interpreting a constitution understood to protect unborn life offers a striking contrast. The Colombian Court held that a statute banning abortion was constitutionally required to contain exceptions for certain indications in light of 'the constitutional importance of the bearer of the rights ... the pregnant woman'. '[W]hen the legislature enacts criminal laws, it cannot ignore that a woman is a human being entitled to dignity and that she must be treated as such, as opposed to being treated as a reproductive instrument for the human race.' '[A] criminal law that prohibits abortion in all circumstances extinguishes the woman's fundamental rights, and thereby violates her dignity by reducing her to a mere receptacle for the fetus, without rights or interests of constitutional relevance worthy of protection.'

Thus, the Colombian Court held that the legislature was constitutionally obliged, and not merely permitted, to include indications in its abortion law. The Court explained that failure to allow for abortion in cases of rape would be in 'complete disregard for human dignity and the right to the free development of the pregnant woman whose pregnancy is not the result of a free and conscious decision, but the result of arbitrary, criminal acts against her in violation of her autonomy.' 'A woman's right to dignity prohibits her treatment as a mere instrument for reproduction, and her consent is therefore essential to the fundamental, life-changing decision to give birth to another person.' By this same reasoning, however, the legislature was allowed to criminalize abortion in cases of consensual sex, aso long as the legislature provided exceptions for women's life, health, and cases of fetal anomaly. This approach presumes that, for women, consent to sex is consent to procreation.

3. Protecting Life/Respecting Women: Result-Open Counseling

Yet other jurisdictions begin from a constitutional duty to protect life, and, like Germany, have begun to explore approaches for vindicating the duty to protect life that do not involve the threat of criminal prosecution. These jurisdictions constitutionally justify depenalization of abortion, coupled with abortion-dissuasive, result-open counseling, as more effective in protecting the unborn than the threat of criminal punishment. The justifications for life-protective counseling, as well as its form, are evolving over time, in ways that progressively incorporate values of women's autonomy. At a minimum, these jurisdictions recognize women as the type of modern citizens who possess autonomy of a kind that law must take into consideration if it hopes to affect their conduct; some go further and are beginning to embrace protecting women's dignity as a concurrent constitutional aim.

Constitutional review of counseling regimes originates in the German cases. In 1975, the German Court endorsed abortion-dissuasive counseling as a mode of protecting life in cases where the legislature deemed abortion non-exactable; in 1993, the German Court expanded that approach, reasoning that a legislature might find counseling coupled with depenalization of abortion generally more effective than the threat of criminal punishment in meeting its duty to protect life, observing that depenalization was also consistent with women's autonomy.

The Hungarian Court has amplified the woman-respecting aspects of this approach. In 1998, the Hungarian Court held that it was unconstitutional for the state to make verification of a 'situation of serious crisis' indication depend solely on woman's signature: 'Such provisions themselves cannot secure for the foetus the level of minimum protection required by the [Constitution] ... and in fact, they do not secure any protection, as the regulation is concerned with the mother's right to self-determination, only.' The Court explicitly rejected this legislative scheme as a concealed version of periodic regulation, while holding that the state could remedy the legislation through directed counseling measures or third party verification. The Court then discussed abortion-dissuasive counseling as a method of protecting unborn life that was also respectful of women's rights. 'In principle, such a consulting service would not ... violate her freedom of conscience'. While 'the state may not compel anyone to accept a situation which sows discord within, or is irreconcilable with the fundamental convictions which mould that person's identity' obligatory participation in counseling violates neither principle 'having particular regard to the fact that she [the pregnant woman] is only obligated to participate without any [further] obligation ... [A]s far as its outcome is concerned, the consultation—while clearly focusing on the protection of the fetus—must be open.'

Portugal has taken further steps in this direction. In upholding legislation that allowed abortion during the first ten weeks of pregnancy after a waiting period and result-open counseling, the Portuguese Constitutional Court emphasized that the new law was an elective means of protecting life. However, a counseling regime the Court upheld was not expressly dissuasive. Strikingly, the recent Portuguese decision employed the reasoning of the 1993 German decision to dispense with the need for expressly dissuasive counseling of the kind mandated by the 1993 German decision. As it did so, the Portuguese decision invoked women's dignity as a justification for result-open counseling. The Portuguese case thus features emergent elements of women's rights, both as to justification and as to legislative form. But the constitutional framework yet remains at some distance from the women's dignity-periodic access cases of jurisdictions such as the United States and South Africa. The Portuguese Court ruled that a result-open counseling framework in the early period of pregnancy is constitutionally permitted, not required, as it would be in a traditional woman's rights framework.

The abortion legislation Spain enacted in 2010 presses result-open counseling in ways that even more robustly associate it with protecting women's rights. The legislation allows abortion on request in the First 14 weeks, subject to counseling. Its preamble reasons in constitutionalized terms about the values the legislation is designed to vindicate, including both 'the rights and interests of women and prenatal life'. The preamble asserts that 'protecting prenatal life is more effective through active policies to support pregnant women and maternity', and therefore that 'protection of the legal right at the very beginning of pregnancy is articulated through the will of the woman, and not against it', and directing public officials to 'establish the conditions for adopting a free and responsible decision'.

In the decades since the German Court's 1993 decision, this hybrid framework has spread, legitimating result-open counseling early in pregnancy as a method of protecting unborn life, while increasingly acknowledging, accommodating, and sometimes even explicitly respecting women's autonomy in making decisions about motherhood. Whether or not the fetal-protective justification for results-open counseling is accompanied by a women's dignity-respecting justification, women are accorded the final word in decisions about whether they become mothers. Drawing elements from two disparate forms of constitutionalization, this hybrid form has transformative potential: one day it might combine community obligation to support those who nurture life with community obligation to respect their judgments. Realization of this potential depends on both expressive and practical aspects of implementation.

The emergence in the last two decades of fetal-protective justifications for providing women control over decisions concerning abortion is especially striking in light of the concurrent spread of woman-protective justifications for denying women access to abortion (e.g. banning or restricting abortion for the asserted purpose of protecting women from harm or coercion). In both cases, a particular legislative regime is justified by appeal to constitutional values historically associated with an opposing form of abortion regulation: legislation that allows abortion is associated with the constitutional protection of unborn life, and legislation that restricts abortion is associated with the constitutional protection of women. Rhetorical inversions of this kind may be produced through social movement struggle, or they may emerge as movements employ the discourse of a reigning constitutional order in order to challenge it.

After decades of conflict, a constitutional framework is emerging in Europe that allows legislators to vindicate the duty to protect unborn life by providing women dissuasive counseling and the ability to make their own decisions about abortion. Constitutionalization in this form values women as mothers first, yet addresses women as the kind of citizens who are autonomous in making decisions about motherhood, and may even warrant respect as such. The spread of constitutionalization in this form attests to passionate conflict over abortion and women's family roles; it also suggests increasing acceptance of claims the women's movement has advanced in the last 40 years, however controverted they remain. Jurisdictions that permit result-open counseling in satisfaction of the duty to protect unborn life express evolving understandings of women as citizens, in terms that reflect community ambivalence and assuage community division, while continuing to engender change.

* * *

Note

1. The law of abortion has been constitutionalized to a greater extent in the U.S. than any other health law issue. In the United States Supreme Court's 1973 landmark decision *Roe v. Wade*, the Court held that a woman's right of privacy under the Fourteenth Amendment of the United State's Constitution encompasses a woman's decision to terminate her pregnancy. However, the Court also found that a state can infringe on that right if it has "assert[ed] important interests in safeguarding health, in maintaining medical standards, and in protecting potential life." *Roe v. Wade*, 410 U.S. 113, 154 (1973). In so holding, *Roe* pioneered the "Periodic Legislation" paradigm of abortion regulation discussed above by establishing a term, or in this case trimester, framework in which the state's interest, and therefore its ability to regulate, grows as the fetus approaches viability.

Although this trimester framework was eventually modified in *Planned Parenthood of Southeastern Pennsylvania v. Casey*, excerpted immediately below, to this day the U.S. courts continue to balance the rights of women with the interests of the state. For a summary of some of the important cases between *Roe* and *Casey*, *see* Rachael K. Pirner & Laurie B. Williams, *Roe* to *Casey*: A Survey of Abortion Law, 32 Washburn L.J. 166 (1993).

* * *

Planned Parenthood of Southeastern Pennsylvania v. Casey

505 U.S. 833 (1992)
U.S. Supreme Court

O'Connor, Kennedy, and Souter, Justices.

Liberty finds no refuge in a jurisprudence of doubt. Yet 19 years after our holding that the Constitution protects a woman's right to terminate her pregnancy in its early stages, Roe v. Wade, 410 U.S. 113 (1973), that definition of liberty is still questioned. Joining the respondents as amicus curiae, the United States, as it has done in five other cases in the last decade, again asks us to overrule *Roe*.

At issue in these cases are five provisions of the Pennsylvania Abortion Control Act of 1982 as amended in 1988 and 1989. 18 Pa. Cons. Stat. §§ 3203–3220 (1990). The Act requires that a woman seeking an abortion give her informed consent prior to the abortion procedure, and specifies that she be provided with certain information at least 24 hours before the abortion is performed. For a minor to obtain an abortion, the Act requires the informed consent of one of her parents, but provides for a judicial bypass option if the minor does not wish to or cannot obtain a parent's consent. Another provision of the Act requires that, unless certain exceptions apply, a married woman seeking an abortion must sign a statement indicating that she has notified her husband of her intended abortion. The Act exempts compliance with these three requirements in the event of a "medical emergency." In addition to the above provisions regulating the performance of abortions, the Act imposes certain reporting requirements on facilities that provide abortion services. * * *

After considering the fundamental constitutional questions resolved by *Roe*, principles of institutional integrity, and the rule of stare decisis, we are led to conclude this: The essential holding of *Roe v. Wade* should be retained and once again reaffirmed. * * *

Constitutional protection of the woman's decision to terminate her pregnancy derives from the due process clause of the Fourteenth Amendment. * * *

Our law affords constitutional protection to [certain] personal decisions relating to marriage, procreation, contraception, family relationships, child rearing, and education. * * * These matters, involving the most intimate and personal choices a person may make in a lifetime, choices central to personal dignity and autonomy, are central to the liberty protected by the Fourteenth Amendment. At the heart of liberty is the right to define one's own concept of existence, of meaning, of the universe, and of the mystery of human life. Beliefs about these matters could not define the attributes of personhood were they formed under compulsion of the state.

These considerations begin our analysis of the woman's interest in terminating her pregnancy but cannot end it, for this reason: Though the abortion decision may originate within the zone of conscience and belief, it is more than a philosophic exercise. Abortion is a unique act. It is an act fraught with consequences for others: for the woman who must live with the implications of her decision; for the persons who perform and assist in the procedure; for the spouse, family, and society which must confront the knowledge that these procedures exist, procedures some deem nothing short of an act of violence against innocent human life; and, depending on one's beliefs, for the life or potential life that is aborted. Though abortion is conduct, it does not follow that the state is entitled to proscribe it in all instances. That is because the liberty of the woman is at stake in a sense unique to the human condition and so unique to the law. The mother who carries a child to full term is subject to anxieties, to physical constraints, to pain that only she must bear. That these sacrifices have from the beginning of the human race been endured by woman with a pride that ennobles her in the eyes of others and gives to the infant a bond of love cannot alone be grounds for the state to insist she make the sacrifice. Her suffering is too intimate and personal for the state to insist, without more, upon its own vision of the woman's role, however dominant that vision has been in the course of our history and our culture. The destiny of the woman must be shaped to a large extent on her own conception of her spiritual imperatives and her place in society.

It should be recognized, moreover, that in some critical respects the abortion decision is of the same character as the decision to use contraception, to which *Griswold v. Connecticut*, *Eisenstadt v. Baird*, and *Carey v. Population Services International*, afford constitutional protection. We have no doubt as to the correctness of those decisions. * * *

While we appreciate the weight of the arguments made on behalf of the state in the case before us, arguments which in their ultimate formulation conclude that *Roe* should be overruled, the reservations any of us may have in reaffirming the central holding of *Roe* are outweighed by the explication of individual liberty we have given combined with the force of stare decisis. We turn now to that doctrine.

[The Justices then reviewed the importance of *stare decisis* in constitutional cases, and concluded that Roe v. Wade should not be overruled.]

From what we have said so far it follows that it is a constitutional liberty of the woman to have some freedom to terminate her pregnancy. We conclude that the basic decision in *Roe* was based on a constitutional analysis which we cannot now repudiate. The woman's liberty is not so unlimited, however, that from the outset the state cannot show its concern for the life of the unborn, and at a later point in fetal development the state's interest in life has sufficient force so that the right of the woman to terminate the pregnancy can be restricted. * * *

We conclude the line should be drawn at *viability*, so that before that time the woman has a right to choose to terminate her pregnancy. We adhere to this principle for two reasons. First, as we have said, is the doctrine of *stare decisis*. Any judicial act of line-drawing may seem somewhat arbitrary, but *Roe* was a reasoned statement, elaborated with great care. We have twice reaffirmed it in the face of great opposition. * * *

The second reason is that the concept of viability, as we noted in *Roe*, is the time at which there is a realistic possibility of maintaining and nourishing a life outside the womb, so that the independent existence of the second life can in reason and all fairness be the object of state protection that now overrides the rights of the woman. See Roe v. Wade, 410 U.S., at 163. * * * [T]here may be some medical developments that affect the precise point of viability, but this is an imprecision within tolerable limits. * * * The viability line also has, as a practical matter, an element of fairness. In some broad sense it might be said that a woman who fails to act before viability has consented to the state's intervention on behalf of the developing child.

The woman's right to terminate her pregnancy before viability is the most central principle of Roe v. Wade. It is a rule of law and a component of liberty we cannot renounce. * * * On the other side of the equation is the interest of the state in the protection of potential life. The *Roe* Court recognized the state's "important and legitimate interest in protecting the potentiality of human life." The weight to be given this state interest, not the strength of the woman's interest, was the difficult question faced in *Roe*. * * * [W]e have concluded that the essential holding of *Roe* should be reaffirmed.

Yet it must be remembered that Roe v. Wade speaks with clarity in establishing not only the woman's liberty but also the state's "important and legitimate interest in potential life." That portion of the decision in *Roe* has been given too little acknowledgment and implementation by the Court in its subsequent cases. Those cases decided that any regulation touching upon the abortion decision must survive strict scrutiny, to be sustained only if drawn in narrow terms to further a compelling state interest. Not all of the cases decided under that formulation can be reconciled with the holding in *Roe* itself that the state has legitimate interests in the health of the woman and in protecting the potential life within her. In resolving this tension, we choose to rely upon *Roe*, as against the later cases. * * * Most of our cases since *Roe* have involved the application of rules derived from the trimester framework. * * *

We reject the trimester framework, which we do not consider to be part of the essential holding of *Roe*. Measures aimed at ensuring that a woman's choice contemplates the consequences for the fetus do not necessarily interfere with the right recognized in *Roe*, although those measures have been found to be inconsistent with the rigid trimester framework announced in that case. A logical reading of the central holding in *Roe* itself, and a necessary reconciliation of the liberty of the woman and the interest of the state in promoting prenatal life, require, in our view, that we abandon the trimester framework as a rigid prohibition on all provability regulation aimed at the protection of fetal life. The trimester framework suffers from these basic flaws: In its formulation it misconceives the nature of the pregnant woman's interest; and in practice it undervalues the state's interest in potential life, as recognized in *Roe*. * * *

The very notion that the state has a substantial interest in potential life leads to the conclusion that not all regulations must be deemed unwarranted. Not all burdens on the right to decide whether to terminate a pregnancy will be undue. In our view, the undue burden standard is the appropriate means of reconciling the state's interest with the woman's constitutionally protected liberty. * * * Because we set forth a standard of general application to which we intend to adhere, it is important to clarify what is meant by an undue burden.

A finding of an undue burden is a shorthand for the conclusion that a state regulation has the purpose or effect of placing a substantial obstacle in the path of a woman seeking an abortion of a nonviable fetus. A statute with this purpose is invalid because the means chosen by the state to further the interest in potential life must be calculated to inform the woman's free choice, not hinder it. And a statute which, while furthering the interest in potential life or some other valid state interest, has the effect of placing a substantial obstacle in the path of a woman's choice cannot be considered a permissible means of serving its legitimate ends. * * * Understood another way, we answer the question, left open in previous opinions discussing the undue burden formulation, whether a law designed to further the state's interest in fetal life which imposes an undue burden on the woman's decision before fetal viability could be constitutional. The answer is no.

Some guiding principles should emerge. What is at stake is the woman's right to make the ultimate decision, not a right to be insulated from all others in doing so. Regulations which do no more than create a structural mechanism by which the state, or the parent or guardian of a minor, may express profound respect for the life of the unborn are permitted, if they are not a substantial obstacle to the woman's exercise of the right to choose. Unless it has that effect on her right of choice, a state measure designed to persuade her to choose childbirth over abortion will be upheld if reasonably related to that goal. Regulations designed to foster the health of a woman seeking an abortion are valid if they do not constitute an undue burden. * * *

We give this summary:

(a) To protect the central right recognized by Roe v. Wade while at the same time accommodating the state's profound interest in potential life, we will employ the undue burden analysis as explained in this opinion. An undue burden exists, and therefore a provision of law is invalid, if its purpose or effect is to place a substantial obstacle in the path of a woman seeking an abortion before the fetus attains viability.

(b) We reject the rigid trimester framework of Roe v. Wade. To promote the state's profound interest in potential life, throughout pregnancy the state may take measures to ensure that the woman's choice is informed, and measures designed to advance this interest will not be invalidated as long as their purpose is to persuade the woman to choose childbirth over abortion. These measures must not be an undue burden on the right.

(c) As with any medical procedure, the state may enact regulations to further the health or safety of a woman seeking an abortion. Unnecessary health regulations that have the purpose or effect of presenting a substantial obstacle to a woman seeking an abortion impose an undue burden on the right.

(d) Our adoption of the undue burden analysis does not disturb the central holding of Roe v. Wade, and we reaffirm that holding. Regardless of whether exceptions are made for particular circumstances, a state may not prohibit any woman from making the ultimate decision to terminate her pregnancy before viability.

(e) We also reaffirm *Roe*'s holding that "subsequent to viability, the state in promoting its interest in the potentiality of human life may, if it chooses, regulate, and even proscribe, abortion except where it is necessary, in appropriate medical judgment, for the preservation of the life or health of the mother." Roe v. Wade, 410 U.S., at 164–165.

These principles control our assessment of the Pennsylvania statute, and we now turn to the issue of the validity of its challenged provisions.

Because it is central to the operation of various other requirements, we begin with the statute's definition of medical emergency. * * * [T]he court of appeals construed the phrase "serious risk" to include those circumstances. It stated: "we read the medical emergency exception as intended by the Pennsylvania legislature to assure that compliance with its abortion regulations would not in any way pose a significant threat to the life or health of a woman." ... We adhere to that course today, and conclude that, as construed by the court of appeals, the medical emergency definition imposes no undue burden on a woman's abortion right.

We next consider the informed consent requirement. Except in a medical emergency, the statute requires that at least 24 hours before performing an abortion a physician inform the woman of the nature of the procedure, the health risks of the abortion and of childbirth, and the "probable gestational age of the unborn child." The physician or a qualified nonphysician must inform the woman of the availability of printed materials published by the state describing the fetus and providing information about medical assistance for childbirth, information about child support from the father, and a list of agencies which provide adoption and other services as alternatives to abortion. An abortion may not be performed unless the woman certifies in writing that she has been informed of the availability of these printed materials and has been provided them if she chooses to view them.

Our prior decisions establish that as with any medical procedure, the state may require a woman to give her written informed consent to an abortion. In this respect, the statute is unexceptional. Petitioners challenge the statute's definition of informed consent because it includes the provision of specific information by the doctor and the mandatory 24-hour waiting period. The conclusions reached by a majority of the Justices in the separate opinions filed today and the undue burden standard adopted in this opinion require us to overrule in part some of the Court's past decisions, decisions driven by the trimester framework's prohibition of all previability regulations designed to further the state's interest in fetal life. * * *

To the extent [that our prior decisions] find a constitutional violation when the government requires, as it does here, the giving of truthful, nonmisleading information about the nature of the procedure, the attendant health risks and those of childbirth, and the "probable gestational age" of the fetus, those cases go too far, are inconsistent with *Roe*'s acknowledgment of an important interest in potential life, and are overruled. * * *

Whether the mandatory 24-hour waiting period is ... invalid because in practice it is a substantial obstacle to a woman's choice to terminate her pregnancy is a close question. The findings of fact by the district court indicate that because of the distances many women must travel to reach an abortion provider, the practical effect will often be a delay of much more than a day because the waiting period requires that a woman seeking an abortion make at least two visits to the doctor. The district court also found that in many instances this will increase the exposure of women seeking abortions to "the harassment and hostility of anti-abortion protestors demonstrating outside a clinic." As a result, the district court found that for those women who have the fewest financial resources, those who must travel long distances, and those who have difficulty explaining their whereabouts to husbands, employers, or others, the 24-hour waiting period will be "particularly burdensome."

These findings are troubling in some respects, but they do not demonstrate that the waiting period constitutes an undue burden. We do not doubt that, as the district court held, the waiting period has the effect of "increasing the cost and risk of delay of abortions," but the district court did not conclude that the increased costs and potential delays amount to substantial obstacles. * * *

We also disagree with the district court's conclusion that the "particularly burdensome" effects of the waiting period on some women require its invalidation. A particular burden is not of necessity a substantial obstacle. Whether a burden falls on a particular group is a distinct inquiry from whether it is a substantial obstacle even as to the women in that group. And the district court did not conclude that the waiting period is such an obstacle even for the women who are most burdened by it. Hence, on the record before us, and in the context of this facial challenge, we are not convinced that the 24-hour waiting period constitutes an undue burden. * * *

[The court also strikes down provisions of Pennsylvania law related to spousal notification but upholds provisions related to parental consent]

Our Constitution is a covenant running from the first generation of Americans to us and then to future generations. It is a coherent succession. Each generation must learn anew that the Constitution's written terms embody ideas and aspirations that must survive more ages than one. We accept our responsibility not to retreat from interpreting the full meaning of the covenant in light of all of our precedents. We invoke it once again to define the freedom guaranteed by the Constitution's own promise, the promise of liberty. * * *

[An opinion by Justice Blackmun, concurring in part, concurring in the judgment in part, and dissenting in part is omitted].

Rehnquist, Chief Justice, with whom White, Scalia, and Thomas, Justices, join, concurring in the judgment in part and dissenting in part:

The joint opinion, following its newly-minted variation on *stare decisis*, retains the outer shell of Roe v. Wade, but beats a wholesale retreat from the substance of that case. We believe that *Roe* was wrongly decided, and that it can and should be overruled consistently with our traditional approach to *stare decisis* in constitutional cases. We would adopt the approach of the plurality in Webster v. Reproductive Health Services, 492 U.S. 490 (1989), and uphold the challenged provisions of the Pennsylvania statute in their entirety. * * *

In construing the phrase *liberty* incorporated in the due process clause of the Fourteenth Amendment, we have recognized that its meaning extends beyond freedom from physical restraint. In Pierce v. Society of Sisters, 268 U.S. 510 (1925), we held that it included a parent's right to send a child to private school; in Meyer v. Nebraska, 262 U.S. 390 (1923), we held that it included a right to teach a foreign language in a parochial school. Building on these cases, we have held that the term *liberty* includes a right to marry, Loving v. Virginia, 388 U.S. 1 (1967); a right to procreate, Skinner v. Oklahoma ex rel. Williamson, 316 U.S. 535 (1942); and a right to use contraceptives. Griswold v. Connecticut, 381 U.S. 479 (1965); Eisenstadt v. Baird, 405 U.S. 438 (1972). But a reading of these opinions makes clear that they do not endorse any all-encompassing "right of privacy." ...

Nor do the historical traditions of the American people support the view that the right to terminate one's pregnancy is "fundamental." ...

We think, therefore, both in view of this history and of our decided cases dealing with substantive liberty under the due process clause, that the Court was mistaken in *Roe* when it classified a woman's decision to terminate her pregnancy as a "fundamental right" that could be abridged only in a manner which withstood "strict scrutiny." ...

The joint opinion of Justices O'Connor, Kennedy, and Souter cannot bring itself to say that *Roe* was correct as an original matter, but the authors are of the view that "the immediate question is not the soundness of *Roe*'s resolution of the issue, but the precedential force that must be accorded to its holding." Instead of claiming that *Roe* was correct as a matter of original constitutional interpretation, the opinion therefore contains an elaborate discussion of *stare decisis*. This discussion of the principle of *stare decisis* appears to be almost entirely dicta, because the joint opinion does not apply that principle in dealing with *Roe*. *Roe* decided that a woman had a fundamental right to an abortion. The joint opinion rejects that view. *Roe* decided that abortion regulations were to be subjected to "strict scrutiny" and could be justified only in the light of "compelling state interests." The joint opinion rejects that view. *Roe* analyzed abortion regulation under a rigid trimester framework, a framework which has guided this Court's decisionmaking for 19 years. The joint opinion rejects that framework.

The sum of the joint opinion's labors in the name of *stare decisis* and "legitimacy" is this: Roe v. Wade stands as a sort of judicial Potemkin Village, which may be pointed out to passers by as a monument to the importance of adhering to precedent. But behind the facade, an entirely new method of analysis, without any roots in constitutional law, is imported to decide the constitutionality of state laws regulating abortion. Neither *stare decisis* nor "legitimacy" are truly served by such an effort.

We have stated above our belief that the Constitution does not subject state abortion regulations to heightened scrutiny. Accordingly, we think that the correct analysis is that set forth by the plurality opinion in *Webster*. A woman's interest in having an abortion is a form of liberty protected by the due process clause, but states may regulate abortion procedures in ways rationally related to a legitimate state interest. * * *

We therefore would hold that each of the challenged provisions of the Pennsylvania statute is consistent with the Constitution. It bears emphasis that our conclusion in this regard does not carry with it any necessary approval of these regulations. Our task is, as always, to decide only whether the challenged provisions of a law comport with the United States Constitution. If, as we believe, these do, their wisdom as a matter of public policy is for the people of Pennsylvania to decide.

* * *

Note

The constitutional rights surrounding reproduction in the United States are not positive liberty rights. As the late John Robertson put it: "[P]rocreative liberty is a negative right against state interference with choices to procreate or to avoid procreation." It is not "a positive right to have the state or particular persons provide the means or resources necessary to have or avoid having children." John Robertson, Children of Choice (1994). Do you see the difference that comes from viewing procreative liberty as essentially the right to be left alone (by the state) in one's quest to achieve or avoid parenthood, as opposed to a claim for assistance?

As you read the following 1988 case, *R. v. Morgentaler*, consider how the Canadian Supreme Court struggles with a similar question: should it define a woman's right to abortion, as a positive right of access or merely a promise of non-interference?

Morgentaler was one of the earliest cases that interpreted the Canadian Charter of Rights and Freedoms, Canada's constitution, which only became effective in 1982. In this decision, the Canadian Supreme Court held that the Canadian Criminal Code provisions on abortion violated pregnant women's rights under the Charter and the Canadian Bill of Rights, a federal statute that antedated the Charter. Throughout the opinion, the Canadian Supreme Court engages with the United States Supreme Court's abortion jurisprudence as it then stood (after *Roe v. Wade* but before *Planned Parenthood v. Casey*). As you read, take note of the several places where the two courts employ similar step-by-step, balancing of the interests rationales, as well as where there are stark deviations.

R. v. Morgentaler

(1988) 1 Can. S.C.R. 30, 44 D.L.R. (4th) 385,
Supreme Court of Canada

Dickson C.J. and Beetz, Estey, McIntyre, Lamer, Wilson and La Forest JJ.

Dickson C.J. [Lamer J. concurring—] The principal issue raised by this appeal is whether the abortion provisions of the Criminal Code infringe the "right to life, liberty and security of the person and the right not to be deprived thereof except in accordance with the principles of fundamental justice" as formulated in s. 7 of the Canadian Charter of Rights and Freedoms. * * *

* * *

The Canadian Charter of Rights and Freedoms:

> [Sec.] 1. The Canadian Charter of Rights and Freedoms guarantees the rights and freedoms set out in it subject only to such reasonable limits prescribed by law as can be demonstrably justified in a free and democratic society.
>
> [Sec.] 7. Everyone has the right to life, liberty and security of the person and the right not to be deprived thereof except in accordance with the principles of fundamental justice.

* * *

The three appellants are all duly qualified medical practitioners who together set up a clinic in Toronto to perform abortions upon women who had not obtained a certificate from a therapeutic abortion committee of an accredited or approved hospital as required by s. 251(4). The doctors had made public statements questioning the wisdom of the abortion laws in Canada and asserting that a woman has an unfettered right to choose whether or not an abortion is appropriate in her individual circumstances.

Indictments were preferred against the appellants charging that they conspired with each other between November 1982 and July 1983 with intent to procure the miscarriage of female persons, using an induced suction technique to carry out that intent, contrary to s. 423(1)(d) and s. 251(1) of the Criminal Code.

Counsel for the appellants moved to quash the indictment or to stay the proceedings before pleas were entered on the grounds that s. 251 of the Criminal Code * * * infringed ss. 2(a), 7 and 12 of the Charter, and was inconsistent with s. 1(b) of the Canadian Bill of Rights. The trial judge, Parker A.C.J.H.C., dismissed the motion, and an appeal to the Ontario Court of Appeal was dismissed. The trial proceeded before Parker A.C.J.H.C. and a jury, and the three accused were acquitted. The Crown appealed the acquittal to the Court of Appeal and the appellants filed a cross-appeal. The Court of Appeal allowed the appeal, set aside the verdict of acquittal and ordered a new trial. The Court held that the cross-appeal related to issues already raised in the appeal, and the issues were therefore examined as part of the appeal.

* * *

Section 7 of the Charter

In his submissions, counsel for the appellants argued that the Court should recognize a very wide ambit for the rights protected under s. 7 of the Charter. Basing his argument largely on American constitutional theories and authorities, Mr. Manning submitted that the right to "life, liberty and security of the person" is a wide-ranging right to control one's own life and to promote one's individual autonomy. The right would therefore include a right to privacy and a right to make unfettered decisions about one's own life.

In my opinion, it is neither necessary nor wise in this appeal to explore the broadest implications of s. 7 as counsel would wish us to do. I prefer to rest my conclusions on a narrower analysis than that put forward on behalf of the appellants. I do not think it would be appropriate to attempt an all encompassing explication of so important a provision as s. 7 so early in the history of Charter interpretation. The Court should be presented with a wide variety of claims and factual situations before articulating the full range of s. 7 rights. I will therefore limit my comments to some interpretive principles already set down by the Court and to an analysis of only two aspects of s. 7, the right to "security of the person" and "the principles of fundamental justice."

A. Interpreting Section 7

The goal of Charter interpretation is to secure for all people "the full benefit of the Charter's protection". To attain that goal, this Court has held consistently that the proper technique for the interpretation of Charter provisions is to pursue a "purposive" analysis of the right guaranteed. A right recognized in the Charter is "to be understood, in other words, in the light of the interests it was meant to protect".

* * *

With respect to the second part of s. 7, in early academic commentary one of the principal concerns was whether the reference to "principles of fundamental justice" enables the courts to review the substance of legislation. In *Re B.C. Motor Vehicle Act*,

Lamer J. noted that any attempt to draw a sharp line between procedure and substance would be ill-conceived. He suggested further that it would not be beneficial in Canada to allow a debate which is rooted in United States constitutional dilemmas to shape our interpretation of s. 7:

> We would, in my view, do our own Constitution a disservice to simply allow the American debate to define the issue for us, all the while ignoring the truly fundamental structural differences between the two constitutions.

* * *

I have no doubt that s. 7 does impose upon courts the duty to review the substance of legislation once it has been determined that the legislation infringes an individual's right to "life, liberty and security of the person". The section states clearly that those interests may only be impaired if the principles of fundamental justice are respected. Lamer J. emphasized, however, that the courts should avoid "adjudication of the merits of public policy". In the present case, I do not believe that it is necessary for the Court to tread the fine line between substantive review and the adjudication of public policy. * * * [I]t will be sufficient to investigate whether or not the impugned legislative provisions meet the procedural standards of fundamental justice. First, it is necessary to determine whether s. 251 of the Criminal Code impairs the security of the person.

B. Security of the Person

The law has long recognized that the human body ought to be protected from interference by others. At common law, for example, any medical procedure carried out on a person without that person's consent is an assault. Only in emergency circumstances does the law allow others to make decisions of this nature. * * * "Security of the person", in other words, is not a value alien to our legal landscape. With the advent of the Charter, security of the person has been elevated to the status of a constitutional norm. This is not to say that the various forms of protection accorded to the human body by the common and civil law occupy a similar status. "Security of the person" must be given content in a manner sensitive to its constitutional position. The above examples are simply illustrative of our respect for individual physical integrity. Nor is it to say that the state can never impair personal security interests. There may well be valid reasons for interfering with security of the person. It is to say, however, that if the state does interfere with security of the person, the Charter requires such interference to conform with the principles of fundamental justice.

The appellants submitted that the "security of the person" protected by the Charter is an explicit right to control one's body and to make fundamental decisions about one's life. The Crown contended that "security of the person" is a more circumscribed interest and that, like all of the elements of s. 7, it at most relates to the concept of physical control, simply protecting the individual's interest in his or her bodily integrity.

Canadian courts have already had occasion to address the scope of the interest protected under the rubric of "security of the person". * * * The Ontario Court of Appeal has held that the right to life, liberty and security of the person "would appear to relate to one's physical or mental integrity and one's control over these …"

* * * In *Mills*, Lamer J. * * * stressed the close connection between the specific rights in ss. 8 to 14 and the more generally applicable rights expressed in s. 7 * * *:

> ... security of the person is not restricted to physical integrity; rather, it encompasses protection against "overlong subjection to the vexations and vicissitudes of a pending criminal accusation" ... These include stigmatization of the accused, loss of privacy, stress and anxiety resulting from a multitude of factors, including possible disruption of family, social life and work, legal costs, uncertainty as to the outcome and sanction.

* * *

The case law leads me to the conclusion that state interference with bodily integrity and serious state-imposed psychological stress, at least in the criminal law context, constitute a breach of security of the person. It is not necessary in this case to determine whether the right extends further, to protect either interests central to personal autonomy, such as a right to privacy, or interests unrelated to criminal justice.

I wish to reiterate that finding a violation of security of the person does not end the s. 7 inquiry. Parliament could choose to infringe security of the person if it did so in a manner consistent with the principles of fundamental justice. The present discussion should therefore be seen as a threshold inquiry and the conclusions do not dispose definitively of all the issues relevant to s. 7. With that caution, I have no difficulty in concluding that the encyclopedic factual submissions addressed to us by counsel in the present appeal establish beyond any doubt that s. 251 of the Criminal Code is prima facie a violation of the security of the person of thousands of Canadian women who have made the difficult decision that they do not wish to continue with a pregnancy.

At the most basic, physical and emotional level, every pregnant woman is told by the section that she cannot submit to a generally safe medical procedure that might be of clear benefit to her unless she meets criteria entirely unrelated to her own priorities and aspirations. Not only does the removal of decision-making power threaten women in a physical sense; the indecision of knowing whether an abortion will be granted inflicts emotional stress. Section 251 clearly interferes with a woman's bodily integrity in both a physical and emotional sense. Forcing a woman, by threat of criminal sanction, to carry a foetus to term unless she meets certain criteria unrelated to her own priorities and aspirations, is a profound interference with a woman's body and thus a violation of security of the person. Section 251, therefore, is required by the Charter to comport with the principles of fundamental justice.

Although this interference with physical and emotional integrity is sufficient in itself to trigger a review of s. 251 against the principles of fundamental justice, the operation of the decision-making mechanism set out in s. 251 creates additional glaring breaches of security of the person. The evidence indicates that s. 251 causes a certain amount of delay for women who are successful in meeting its criteria. In the context of abortion, any unnecessary delay can have profound consequences on the woman's physical and emotional well-being.

More specifically, in 1977, the Report of the Committee on the Operation of the Abortion Law (the Badgley Report) revealed that the average delay between a pregnant woman's first contact with a physician and a subsequent therapeutic abortion was eight weeks. Although the situation appears to have improved since 1977, the extent of the improvement is not clear. * * *

* * *

These periods of delay may not seem unduly long, but in the case of abortion, the implications of any delay, according to the evidence, are potentially devastating. The first factor to consider is that different medical techniques are employed to perform abortions at different stages of pregnancy. The testimony of expert doctors at trial indicated that in the first twelve weeks of pregnancy, the relatively safe and simple suction dilation and curettage method of abortion is typically used in North America. From the thirteenth to the sixteenth week, the more dangerous dilation and evacuation procedure is performed, although much less often in Canada than in the United States. From the sixteenth week of pregnancy, the instillation method is commonly employed in Canada. This method requires the intra-amniotic introduction of prostaglandin, urea, or a saline solution, which causes a woman to go into labour, giving birth to a foetus which is usually dead, but not invariably so. The uncontroverted evidence showed that each method of abortion progressively increases risks to the woman.

The second consideration is that even within the periods appropriate to each method of abortion, the evidence indicated that the earlier the abortion was performed, the fewer the complications and the lower the risk of mortality. * * * Even more revealing were the overall mortality statistics evaluated by Drs. Cates and Grimes. They concluded from their study of the relevant data that:

> Anything that contributes to delay in performing abortions increases the complication rates by 15 to 30%, and the chance of dying by 50% for each week of delay.

* * *

It is no doubt true that the overall complication and mortality rates for women who undergo abortions are very low, but the increasing risks caused by delay are so clearly established that I have no difficulty in concluding that the delay in obtaining therapeutic abortions caused by the mandatory procedures of s. 251 is an infringement of the purely physical aspect of the individual's right to security of the person. * * *

The above physical interference caused by the delays created by s. 251, involving a clear risk of damage to the physical well-being of a woman, is sufficient, in my view, to warrant inquiring whether s. 251 comports with the principles of fundamental justice. However, there is yet another infringement of security of the person. It is clear from the evidence that s. 251 harms the psychological integrity of women seeking abortions. A 1985 report of the Canadian Medical Association, * * * emphasized that the procedure involved in s. 251, with the concomitant delays, greatly increases the stress levels of patients and that this can lead to more physical complications associated with abortion. * * *

* * *

In summary, s. 251 is a law which forces women to carry a foetus to term contrary to their own priorities and aspirations and which imposes serious delay causing increased physical and psychological trauma to those women who meet its criteria. It must, therefore, be determined whether that infringement is accomplished in accordance with the principles of fundamental justice, thereby saving s. 251 under the second part of s. 7.

* * *

In outline, s. 251 operates in the following manner. Subsection (1) creates an indictable offence for any person to use any means with the intent "to procure the miscarriage of a female person". Subsection (2) establishes a parallel indictable offence for any pregnant woman to use or to permit any means to be used with the intent "to procure her own miscarriage". The "means" referred to in subs. (1) and (2) are defined in subs. (3) as the administration of a drug or "other noxious thing", the use of an instrument, and "manipulation of any kind". The crucial provision for the purposes of the present appeal is subs. (4) which states that the offences created in subss. (1) and (2) "do not apply" in certain circumstances. * * *

The procedure surrounding the defence is rather complex. A pregnant woman who desires to have an abortion must apply to the "therapeutic abortion committee" of an "accredited or approved hospital". Such a committee is empowered to issue a certificate in writing stating that in the opinion of a majority of the committee, the continuation of the pregnancy would be likely to endanger the pregnant woman's life or health. Once a copy of the certificate is given to a qualified medical practitioner who is not a member of the therapeutic abortion committee, he or she is permitted to perform an abortion on the pregnant woman and both the doctor and the woman are freed from any criminal liability.

* * *

* * * In order to understand the true nature and scope of s. 251, it is necessary to investigate the practical operation of the provisions. The Court has been provided with a myriad of factual submissions in this area. One of the most useful sources of information is the Badgley Report. The Badgley Report contains a wealth of detailed information which demonstrates[] that many of the most serious problems with the functioning of s. 251 are created by procedural and administrative requirements established in the law. For example, the Badgley Committee noted, that:

> … the Abortion Law implicitly establishes a minimum requirement of three qualified physicians to serve on a therapeutic abortion committee, plus a qualified medical practitioner who is not a member of the therapeutic abortion committee, to perform the procedure. * * *
>
> Of the 1,348 civilian hospitals in operation in 1976, at least 331 hospitals had less than four physicians on their medical staff. In terms of the distribution of physicians, 24.6 percent of hospitals in Canada did not have a med-

ical staff which was large enough to establish a therapeutic abortion committee and to perform the abortion procedure.

* * *

The Powell Report reveals another serious difficulty with s. 251 procedures. The requirement that therapeutic abortions be performed only in "accredited" or "approved" hospitals effectively means that the practical availability of the exculpatory provisions of subs. (4) may be heavily restricted, even denied, through provincial regulation. In Ontario, for example, the provincial government promulgated O. Reg. 248/70 under The Public Hospitals Act. This regulation provides that therapeutic abortion committees can only be established where there are ten or more members on the active medical staff. A minister of health is not prevented from imposing harsher restrictions. * * *

A further flaw with the administrative system established in s. 251(4) is the failure to provide an adequate standard for therapeutic abortion committees which must determine when a therapeutic abortion should, as a matter of law, be granted. Subsection (4) states simply that a therapeutic abortion committee may grant a certificate when it determines that a continuation of a pregnancy would be likely to endanger the "life or health" of the pregnant woman. It was noted above that "health" is not defined for the purposes of the section. * * *

* * *

Various expert doctors testified at trial that therapeutic abortion committees apply widely differing definitions of health. For some committees, psychological health is a justification for therapeutic abortion; for others it is not. Some committees routinely refuse abortions to married women unless they are in physical danger, while for other committees it is possible for a married woman to show that she would suffer psychological harm if she continued with a pregnancy, thereby justifying an abortion.

* * *

The combined effect of all of these problems with the procedure stipulated in s. 251 for access to therapeutic abortions is a failure to comply with the principles of fundamental justice. * * * One of the basic tenets of our system of criminal justice is that when Parliament creates a defence to a criminal charge, the defence should not be illusory or so difficult to attain as to be practically illusory.

* * *

I conclude that the procedures created in s. 251 of the Criminal Code for obtaining a therapeutic abortion do not comport with the principles of fundamental justice. It is not necessary to determine whether s. 7 also contains a substantive content leading to the conclusion that, in some circumstances at least, the deprivation of a pregnant woman's right to security of the person can never comport with fundamental justice. Simply put, assuming Parliament can act, it must do so properly. For the reasons given earlier, the deprivation of security of the person caused by s. 251 as a whole is not in accordance with the second clause of s. 7. It remains to be seen whether s. 251 can be justified for the purposes of s. 1 of the Charter.

Section 1 Analysis

Section 1 of the Charter can potentially be used to "salvage" a legislative provision which breaches s. 7. * * * A statutory provision which infringes any section of the Charter can only be saved under s. 1 if the party seeking to uphold the provision can demonstrate first, that the objective of the provision is "of sufficient importance to warrant overriding a constitutionally protected right or freedom", and second, that the means chosen in overriding the right or freedom are reasonable and demonstrably justified in a free and democratic society. This second aspect ensures that the legislative means are proportional to the legislative ends. In *Oakes*, the Court referred to three considerations which are typically useful in assessing the proportionality of means to ends. First, the means chosen to achieve an important objective should be rational, fair and not arbitrary. Second, the legislative means should impair as little as possible the right or freedom under consideration. Third, the effects of the limitation upon the relevant right or freedom should not be out of proportion to the objective sought to be achieved.

The appellants contended that the sole purpose of s. 251 of the Criminal Code is to protect the life and health of pregnant women. The respondent Crown submitted that s. 251 seeks to protect not only the life and health of pregnant women, but also the interests of the foetus. On the other hand, the Crown conceded that the Court is not called upon in this appeal to evaluate any claim to "foetal rights" or to assess the meaning of "the right to life". I expressly refrain from so doing. In my view, it is unnecessary for the purpose of deciding this appeal to evaluate or assess "foetal rights" as an independent constitutional value. Nor are we required to measure the full extent of the state's interest in establishing criteria unrelated to the pregnant woman's own priorities and aspirations. What we must do is evaluate the particular balance struck by Parliament in s. 251, as it relates to the priorities and aspirations of pregnant women and the government's interests in the protection of the foetus.

Section 251 provides that foetal interests are not to be protected where the "life or health" of the woman is threatened. Thus, Parliament itself has expressly stated in s. 251 that the "life or health" of pregnant women is paramount. The procedures of s. 251(4) are clearly related to the pregnant woman's "life or health" for that is the very phrase used by the subsection. [T]he aim of s. 251(4) is "to restrict abortion to cases where the continuation of the pregnancy would, or would likely, be injurious to the life or health of the woman concerned, not to provide unrestricted access to abortion." I have no difficulty in concluding that the objective of s. 251 as a whole, namely, to balance the competing interests identified by Parliament, is sufficiently important to meet the requirements of the first step in the *Oakes* inquiry under s. 1. I think the protection of the interests of pregnant women is a valid governmental objective, where life and health can be jeopardized by criminal sanctions. Like Beetz and Wilson JJ., I agree that protection of foetal interests by Parliament is also a valid governmental objective. It follows that balancing these interests, with the lives and health of women a major factor, is clearly an important governmental objective. * * *

I am equally convinced, however, that the means chosen to advance the legislative objectives of s. 251 do not satisfy any of the three elements of the proportionality component of *R. v. Oakes*. The evidence has led me to conclude that the infringement of the security of the person of pregnant women caused by s. 251 is not accomplished in accordance with the principles of fundamental justice. It has been demonstrated that the procedures and administrative structures created by s. 251 are often arbitrary and unfair. The procedures established to implement the policy of s. 251 impair s. 7 rights far more than is necessary because they hold out an illusory defence to many women who would prima facie qualify under the exculpatory provisions of s. 251(4). In other words, many women whom Parliament professes not to wish to subject to criminal liability will nevertheless be forced by the practical unavailability of the supposed defence to risk liability or to suffer other harm such as a traumatic late abortion caused by the delay inherent in the s. 251 system. Finally, the effects of the limitation upon the s. 7 rights of many pregnant women are out of proportion to the objective sought to be achieved. Indeed, to the extent that s. 251(4) is designed to protect the life and health of women, the procedures it establishes may actually defeat that objective. * * *

I conclude, therefore, that the cumbersome structure of subs. (4) not only unduly subordinates the s. 7 rights of pregnant women but may also defeat the value Parliament itself has established as paramount, namely, the life and health of the mother. * * * State protection of foetal interests may well be deserving of constitutional recognition under s. 1. Still, there can be no escape from the fact that Parliament has failed to establish either a standard or a procedure whereby any such interests might prevail over those of the woman in a fair and non-arbitrary fashion.

Section 251 of the Criminal Code cannot be saved, therefore, under s. 1 of the Charter.

* * *

[The concurring opinion of Beetz and Estey, JJ. is ommitted.]

McIntyre, J. (dissenting) [with Le Forest J. concurring]

* * *

The judgment of my colleague, Wilson J., is based upon the proposition that a pregnant woman has a right, under s. 7 of the Charter, to have an abortion.

* * *

The proposition that women enjoy a constitutional right to have an abortion is devoid of support in the language of s. 7 of the Charter or any other section. While some human rights documents, such as the American Convention on Human Rights, 1969 (Article 4(1)), expressly address the question of abortion, the Charter is entirely silent on the point. It may be of some significance that the Charter uses specific language in dealing with other topics, such as voting rights, religion, expression and such controversial matters as mobility rights, language rights and minority rights, but remains silent on the question of abortion which, at the time the Charter was under consideration, was as much a subject of public controversy as it is today. Furthermore, it would appear that the history of the constitutional text of the Charter affords no support for the appellants' proposition. * * *

* * *

* * * It follows then, in my view, that the interpretive approach to the Charter, which has been accepted in this Court, affords no support for the entrenchment of a constitutional right of abortion.

As to an asserted right to be free from any state interference with bodily integrity and serious state-imposed psychological stress, I would say that to be accepted, as a constitutional right, it would have to be based on something more than the mere imposition, by the State, of such stress and anxiety. It must, surely, be evident that many forms of government action deemed to be reasonable, and even necessary in our society, will cause stress and anxiety to many, while at the same time being acceptable exercises of government power in pursuit of socially desirable goals. The very facts of life in a modern society would preclude the entrenchment of such a constitutional right. * * * In the interests of public health and welfare, governments must have and exercise the power to regulate, control—and even suppress—aspects of the manufacture, sale and distribution of alcohol and drugs and other dangerous substances. Stress and anxiety resulting from the exercise of such powers cannot be a basis for denying them to the authorities. At the present time there is great pressure on governments to restrict—and even forbid—the use of tobacco. Government action in this field will produce much stress and anxiety among smokers and growers of tobacco, but it cannot be said that this will render unconstitutional control and regulatory measures adopted by governments. Other illustrations abound to make the point.

To invade the s. 7 right of security of the person, there would have to be more than state-imposed stress or strain. A breach of the right would have to be based upon an infringement of some interest which would be of such nature and such importance as to warrant constitutional protection. This, it would seem to me, would be limited to cases where the state-action complained of, in addition to imposing stress and strain, also infringed another right, freedom or interest which was deserving of protection under the concept of security of the person. For the reasons outlined above, the right to have an abortion—given the language, structure and history of the Charter and given the history, traditions and underlying philosophies of our society—is not such an interest. * * *

* * *

It is for these reasons I would conclude, that save for the provisions of the Criminal Code, which permit abortion where the life or health of the woman is at risk, no right of abortion can be found in Canadian law, custom or tradition, and that the Charter, including s. 7, creates no further right. * * *

* * *

Wilson, J.

* * *

With all due respect, I think that the Court must tackle the primary issue first. If a pregnant woman cannot, as a constitutional matter, be compelled by law to carry the foetus to term against her will, a review of the procedural requirements by which she may be compelled to do so seems pointless.

* * *

The idea of human dignity finds expression in almost every right and freedom guaranteed in the Charter. Individuals are afforded the right to choose their own religion and their own philosophy of life, the right to choose with whom they will associate and how they will express themselves, the right to choose where they will live and what occupation they will pursue. These are all examples of the basic theory underlying the Charter, namely that the state will respect choices made by individuals and, to the greatest extent possible, will avoid subordinating these choices to any one conception of the good life.

Thus, an aspect of the respect for human dignity on which the Charter is founded is the right to make fundamental personal decisions without interference from the state. This right is a critical component of the right to liberty. * * *

* * *

The question then becomes whether the decision of a woman to terminate her pregnancy falls within this class of protected decisions. I have no doubt that it does. This decision is one that will have profound psychological, economic and social consequences for the pregnant woman. The circumstances giving rise to it can be complex and varied and there may be, and usually are, powerful considerations militating in opposite directions. It is a decision that deeply reflects the way the woman thinks about herself and her relationship to others and to society at large. It is not just a medical decision; it is a profound social and ethical one as well. Her response to it will be the response of the whole person.

* * *

It seems to me, therefore, that in a free and democratic society "freedom of conscience and religion" should be broadly construed to extend to conscientiously-held beliefs, whether grounded in religion or in a secular morality. Indeed, as a matter of statutory interpretation, "conscience" and "religion" should not be treated as tautologous if capable of independent, although related, meaning. Accordingly, for the state to take sides on the issue of abortion, as it does in the impugned legislation by making it a criminal offence for the pregnant woman to exercise one of her options, is not only to endorse but also to enforce, on pain of a further loss of liberty through actual imprisonment, one conscientiously-held view at the expense of another. It is to deny freedom of conscience to some, to treat them as means to an end, to deprive them, as Professor MacCormick puts it, of their "essential humanity". * * *

* * *

Notes

1. Judges who lack relevant subject matter expertise are often confronted with highly technical medical or public health evidence when considering cases on abortion.

In *Morgentaler*, the Canadian Supreme Court's decision took the power to regulate abortion out of the hands of medical professionals on "abortion committees" because, in their non-expert judgment, that system of professional regulation imposed burdens that threatened the health and therefore the right to security of women seeking abortion. Consider what role courts should have in evaluating medical and other scientific evidence. How much should the answer vary between jurisdictions?

2. Until 2006, Colombia's abortion policy was one of the most restrictive in the world and criminalized abortion in all contexts. The Colombian Penal Code did allow for mitigation under some circumstances, like rape and incest, but the procedure was still criminal even in those circumstances. As a result, almost 35,000 illegal abortions were performed annually. The following translated excerpts come from the 600-page decision that overturned this policy courtesy of Rebecca Cook & Women's Link Worldwide, Excerpts of the Constitutional Court's Ruling That Liberalized Abortion in Colombia, 15 *Reproductive Health Matters* 160–62 (2007).

Excerpts of the Constitutional Court's Ruling That Liberalized Abortion in Colombia

C-355/2006

Writing for the majority of the Court:

Honorable Justice JAIME ARAÚJO RENTERÍA

Honorable Justice CLARA INÉS VARGAS HERNÁNDEZ

... Colombian citizens Mónica del Pilar Roa López, Pablo Jaramillo Valencia, Marcela Abadía Cubillos, Juana Dávila Sáenz and Laura Porras Santillana ("the Plaintiffs") request in separate complaints that this Court declare unconstitutional paragraph 7 of article 32, articles 122 and 124, as well as the expression "or on a woman of less than 14 years of age" contained in article 123 of Law 599, 2000 "by which the Penal Code is enacted." [These sections of the Penal Code criminalized abortion, allowed for mitigation of punishment under some circumstances, and issued a full ban of abortion in all circumstances when it was performed without the consent of the woman or when it was performed on a woman of less than 14 years of age.]

The Plaintiffs assert that the articles and paragraphs in question violate the following constitutional rights: the right to dignity (Constitutional Preamble and article 1 of the Constitution); the right to life (article 11 of the Constitution); the right to bodily integrity (article 12 of the Constitution); the right to equality and the general right to liberty (article 13 of the Constitution); the right to the free development of the individual (article 16 of the Constitution); the right to reproductive autonomy (article 42 of the Constitution); the right to health (article 49 of the Constitution); and obligations under international human rights law (article 93 of the Constitution).

* * *

5. "Life" as a relevant constitutional value that must be protected by the Colombian state and as distinguished from the "right to life"

* * *

... Although it is Congress' role to determine and adopt ideal measures for complying with the duty to protect life, this does not mean that all norms aimed at that goal are justified, for, although "life" has constitutional relevance, it does not have an absolute value nor is it an absolute right; it must be weighed against other values and constitutional rights....

Within the legal system, life receives different normative treatments. For instance, there is a distinction between the right to life in article 11 of the Constitution and life as a value protected by the Constitution. The right to life requires that an individual be entitled to it and claim the right. As with all other rights, the right to life is restricted to human persons, while the protection of life can be afforded to those who have not yet reached the human condition....

Following this reasoning, "life" and "the right to life" are different phenomena. Human life passes through various stages and manifests in various forms, which are entitled to different forms of legal protection. Even though the legal system protects the fetus, it does not grant it the same level or degree of protection it grants a human person. These differences are notable in most legal systems where, for example, the criminal punishment for infanticide or for homicide is greater than the punishment for abortion. That is, the protected life is not identical in all cases and therefore the legal implications of the offence carry different degrees of reprisal and thus a proportional punishment.

These considerations must be taken into account by the legislature if it finds it appropriate to enact public policies regarding abortion, including imposing criminal penalties where the Constitution permits, while respecting the rights of women.

* * *

7. Fundamental rights of women under the Colombian National Constitution and international law

The Colombian National Constitution of 1991 brought important changes regarding the rights of women in Colombian society and in relation to the state....

The 1991 Constitution expressly sets out the goal of recognizing and enhancing the rights of women, as well as of reinforcing these rights by protecting them in an effective and decisive manner. Thus, women are now entitled to special constitutional protection and their rights must be recognized and protected by government authorities, including those within the legal system, without exception....

It is worth noting that there are situations that affect women differently and to a greater extent, like those that affect their lives and particularly those concerning their bodies, their sexuality and their reproduction.

Women's rights have achieved an important place in United Nations world conferences and the treaties that come out of these conferences. These conference documents provide an essential framework for interpreting the rights contained in the international treaties themselves.

* * *

[The court lists the various United Nations initiatives and conferences that affirmed the importance of women's reproductive rights in international law, including the World Conference on Human Rights in Vienna in 1993, the Programme of Action of the 1994 United Nations International Conference on Population and Development in Cairo, and the Fourth World Conference on Women.]

In effect, various international treaties form the basis for the recognition and protection of women's reproductive rights, which derive from the protection of other fundamental rights such as the right to life, health, equality, the right to be free from discrimination, the right to liberty, bodily integrity and the right to be free from violence—all of which constitute the essential core of reproductive rights. Other fundamental rights, such as the right to work and the right to education—which are also affected when women's reproductive rights are violated—serve as parameters to protect and guarantee sexual and reproductive rights.

It must be noted that in addition to the protections for women's rights in the Universal Declaration of Human Rights; the International Covenant on Civil and Political Rights; the International Covenant on Economic, Social and Cultural Rights; and the American Convention on Human Rights, special protection for the rights of Latin American women are found in the Convention on the Elimination of All Forms of Discrimination against Women (CEDAW), which entered into force in Colombia on February 19, 1982, with the passage of Law 51, 1981, and the Inter-American Convention on the Prevention, Punishment and Eradication of Violence Against Women (Convention of Belém do Pará), which entered into force in Colombia on December 15, 1996, by means of Law 248, 1995. These documents, together with those signed by the governments of the signatory countries in the World Conferences, are fundamental to the protection and guarantee of the rights of women as they form the point of reference for establishing concepts which contribute to their interpretation both in the national and international spheres.

The right to health, which includes the right to reproductive health and family planning, has been interpreted by international bodies on the basis of international treaties, including CEDAW, to include the duty of all states to offer a wide range of high quality and accessible health services, which must include sexual and reproductive health services. Furthermore, these international bodies also recommend that a gender perspective be included in the design of public health policies and programs. These same international bodies have also expressed concern for the health of women living in poverty, women living in rural areas, indigenous women and adolescents, as well as with obstacles to access to contraceptive methods.

In the area of health, all states should also eliminate all obstacles that impede women's access to services, education and information on sexual and reproductive health. CEDAW has emphasized that laws criminalizing medical interventions that specially affect women constitute a barrier to women's access to needed medical care, compromising women's right to gender equality in the area of health, and amounting to a violation of states' international obligations to respect those internationally recognized rights.

The international community has also recognized that violence against women infringes on human rights and fundamental freedoms, and has established, specifically, the right of women to live free from violence based on sex or gender.

The diverse forms of gender violence constitute a violation of women's reproductive rights, due to the fact that violence affects women's health as well as their reproductive and sexual autonomy. Sexual violence infringes on women's reproductive rights, particularly the right to bodily integrity and the right to control their sexuality and reproductive capacity. Sexual violence also threatens women's right to health, not only physical health but also psychological, reproductive and sexual health.

CEDAW declared that "Gender-based violence is a form of discrimination that seriously inhibits women's ability to enjoy rights and freedoms on a basis of equality with men." The Convention of Belém do Pará, in force since March 5, 1995, and in force in Colombia since December 15, 1996—Law 248, 1995—is one of the most important instruments for protecting women's rights against the various forms of violence faced by women in diverse spheres of their lives. The Convention establishes two elements that make it particularly effective.

First, it defines violence against women both in the public and private spheres as a violation of women's human rights and fundamental freedoms. Second, the Convention establishes the state's responsibility for perpetrating or tolerating any such violence, regardless of where it occurs.

It is also important to highlight that the Rome Statute establishes, among other things, that violence and other reproductive and sexual crimes are at the same level as the other most atrocious international crimes, and may amount to torture and genocide. The Rome Statute also recognizes for the first time that violations of women's right to reproductive autonomy, both by means of forced pregnancy and forced sterilization, are amongst the most serious crimes under international human rights law.

One of the essential components of reproductive and sexual rights is women's right to choose freely the number and spacing of children. This is based on the principles of human dignity and the right to autonomy and intimacy, as has been recognized by various international conventions. CEDAW has established that a woman's right to reproductive autonomy is infringed upon by obstacles to her access to the means of controlling her fertility. Thus, non-consensual sterilization and imposed birth control methods constitute serious violations of this right. Similarly, various committees have stated that the right to freely decide the number of children is directly linked to women's right to life when there are highly restrictive or prohibitive abortion laws that result in high maternal mortality rates.

Other sexual and reproductive rights are based on the right of freedom to marry and start a family. The right to privacy is also connected to reproductive rights and is infringed upon when the state or private citizens interfere with a woman's right to make decisions about her body and her reproductive capacity. The right to privacy includes the right of a patient to have her confidentiality respected by her doctor. Therefore, the right to intimacy is infringed upon when the doctor is legally obliged to report a woman who has undergone an abortion.

With regard to the right to equality and to be free from discrimination, the Women's Convention (CEDAW) establishes women's right to enjoy human rights in conditions of equality with men. It also prescribes the elimination of barriers impeding women's effective enjoyment of their internationally recognized rights, as well as of those found in national legislation. It also establishes measures to prevent and sanction acts of discrimination.

Finally, the right to education is closely linked to reproductive rights at various levels. Having access to basic education empowers women within their families and their communities, and it raises their consciousness regarding their rights. Furthermore, the right to an education includes education on reproductive health and on the right to choose freely and responsibly the number of children and the spacing between them.

To conclude, women's sexual and reproductive rights have finally been recognized as human rights, and, as such, they have become part of constitutional rights, which are the fundamental basis of all democratic states.

Sexual and reproductive rights also emerge from the recognition that equality in general, gender equality in particular, and the emancipation of women and girls are essential to society. Protecting sexual and reproductive rights is a direct path to promoting the dignity of all human beings and a step forward in humanity's advancement towards social justice.

Nonetheless, neither a mandate to decriminalize abortion nor a prohibition on the legislature's adoption of criminal abortion laws derives from international treaties or constitutional articles on the topic. Congress has a wide range of discretion to adopt public policies on abortion. However, this discretion is not unlimited. As this Court has held, even in criminal matters, the legislature must respect two constitutional limits. First, the legislature cannot disproportionately encroach upon constitutional rights. Second, the legislature must not leave certain constitutional values unprotected. At the same time, the legislature must recognize the principle that criminal law, due to its potential to restrict liberties, must always be a measure of last resort.

* * *

8.1. The fundamental right to dignity as a limit on the legislature's discretion over criminal matters

As with "life," the concept of "dignity" has various functions in Colombian constitutional law, as has been recognized by constitutional jurisprudence. This Court has stated that "human dignity" has three different roles: (i) it is a foundational principle of the legal system and as such, it has an axiological dimension as a constitutional value; (ii) it is a constitutional principle; and (iii) it is a fundamental right....

[T]he rules which flow from the concept of human dignity—both the constitutional principle and the fundamental right to dignity—coincide in protecting the same type of conduct. This Court has held that in those cases where dignity is used as a criterion in a judicial decision, it must be understood that dignity protects the following: (i) autonomy, or the possibility of designing one's life plan and living in accordance with it (to live life as one wishes); (ii) certain material conditions of existence (to live well); and (iii) intangible goods such as physical integrity and moral integrity (to live free of humiliation)....

Human dignity warrants a sphere of autonomy and moral integrity that must be respected by public authorities and by private citizens. The sphere of protection for women's human dignity includes decisions related to their choice of life plan, among them decisions regarding reproductive autonomy. This protection also includes a guarantee of their moral integrity, which manifests itself in prohibitions against assigning women stigmatizing gender roles or imposing deliberate moral suffering....

In this way, the need to respect human dignity places a limit on the legislature's discretion with regard to criminal matters, even in circumstances where the legislature aims to protect other relevant constitutional values such as life.

Therefore, when the legislature enacts criminal laws, it cannot ignore that a woman is a human being entitled to dignity and that she must be treated as such, as opposed to being treated as a reproductive instrument for the human race. The legislature must not impose the role of procreator on a woman against her will.

* * *

8.3. Health, life and bodily integrity as limits on the discretion of the legislature over criminal matters

... The Constitutional Court has said on various occasions that the right to health, even though it is not expressly found in the Constitution as a fundamental right, has a fundamental character when it is in close relation to the right to life....

The right to health encompasses not only physical, but also mental health. As the Court has said, "The Constitution proclaims the fundamental right to personal integrity, and by doing so, refers not only to the physical aspects of the person, but also to the broad range of elements that affect one's mental health and psychological well-being. Accordingly, both the physical and psychological aspects of integrity most be preserved. A threat to one or the other, by action or omission, infringes upon this fundamental right and endangers the right to life with a minimum degree of dignity."

The right to health is an integral right that includes mental and physical wellbeing. Furthermore, for women, it includes reproductive health, which is closely linked to both induced and spontaneous abortion. Induced abortions and miscarriages may in numerous circumstances put a woman's health or life at risk, or require medical intervention to preserve her reproductive capacity....

The constitutional right to health has a service provision dimension as well as an element of protection against government and third party intrusion or interference with this right. This latter dimension of protection from violation, or obligation on the state to not interfere, is closely related to the duty of every individual to be responsible for his or her own health. From this perspective, certain measures adopted by the legislature that disproportionately restrict the right to health are unconstitutional. This is so even when those measures are adopted in order to protect the constitutional rights of others.

Prima facie, it is not proportionate or reasonable for the Colombian state to obligate a person to sacrifice her or his health in the interest of protecting third parties, even when those interests are also constitutionally relevant.

* * *

10. The case before the Court

10.1. The unconstitutionality of a total prohibition of abortion

... In the case at hand, as has been held numerous times, the life of the fetus is entitled to protection under constitutional law and therefore the decisions of the pregnant woman regarding the termination of her pregnancy go beyond the sphere of her private autonomy and implicate the interests of both the state and the legislature.... ***

Even though the protection of the fetus through criminal law is not in itself disproportionate and penalizing abortion may be constitutional, the criminalization of abortion in all circumstances entails the complete pre-eminence of the life of the fetus and the absolute sacrifice of the pregnant woman's fundamental rights. This result is, without a doubt, unconstitutional. ***

Thus, a criminal law that prohibits abortion in all circumstances extinguishes the woman's fundamental rights, and thereby violates her dignity by reducing her to a mere receptacle for the fetus, without rights or interests of constitutional relevance worthy of protection.

Determining under which circumstances it is excessive to require a woman to continue a pregnancy because it results in an infringement of a woman's fundamental rights is an exercise within the legislature's sphere. Once the legislature has decided that criminal law is the most appropriate way to protect the life of the fetus, then the legislature must set out the circumstances under which it is not excessive to sacrifice the rights of the pregnant woman. Nonetheless, if the legislature does not establish those circumstances, it is then up to the constitutional judge to prevent a disproportionate infringement of the fundamental rights of the pregnant woman. This does not mean, however, that the legislature lacks discretion to deal with this matter within constitutional limits.

Even though the Penal Code contains a general prohibition of abortion, the articles in question demonstrate that under certain circumstances the legislature did establish mitigating factors and even provided the judiciary with the discretion to not impose a penalty in a particular case. This exclusion relates to pregnancies resulting from rape, sexual abuse, non-consensual artificial insemination or implantation of a fertilized ovule (article 124 of the Penal Code).

In these circumstances, the legislature decided that the penalty for abortion should be mitigated in light of the fundamental rights of the woman involved, such as her dignity and her right to the free development of the individual. However, the legislature decided that even in those circumstances, where the woman's dignity and free development were imperiled, she should be tried and sentenced as a criminal. A measure such as this is disproportionate because the conduct continues to be criminal, which seriously infringes on the constitutional rights of the pregnant woman.

This Court is of the view that under the enumerated circumstances, abortion does not constitute a crime. This is not only because that result was originally contemplated by the legislature, but also because the absolute prevalence of the fetus' rights in these circumstances implies a complete disregard for human dignity and the right to the free development of the pregnant woman whose pregnancy is not the result of a free and conscious decision, but the result of arbitrary, criminal acts against her in violation of her autonomy; acts that are penalized in the Penal Code. ***

Taking the duty to protect the life of the fetus in these exceptional circumstances to the extreme of criminalizing the termination of pregnancy is to give an absolute privilege to the life of the fetus over the fundamental rights of the pregnant woman, in particular, her right to choose whether or not to carry to term an unwanted pregnancy. Such an intrusion by the state on her right to the free development of the individual and her human dignity is disproportionate and arbitrary. A woman's right to dignity prohibits her treatment as a mere instrument for reproduction, and her consent is therefore essential to the fundamental, life-changing decision to give birth to another person.

Pregnancy resulting from incest should also be included within these exceptional circumstances because it represents another example of a pregnancy resulting from a punishable act, where, in most cases, the woman does not consent. Even when there is no physical violence involved, incest generally infringes on a woman's autonomy. It also affects the stability of the family (an institution protected by the Constitution) and results in a violation of the constitutional principle of solidarity, which is, as has been held previously by this Court, a fundamental guiding principle of the Constitution. The criminalization of abortion in this circumstance amounts to a disproportionate and unreasonable infringement on the liberty and dignity of women.

When the pregnancy is the result of rape, sexual abuse, non-consensual artificial insemination or implantation of a fertilized ovule, or incest, it is necessary that such criminal acts be reported accordingly to the competent authorities.

To this end, the legislature may enact regulations as long as the regulations do not preclude access to abortion and do not impose a disproportionate burden on the rights of women. For instance, the regulations cannot require forensic evidence of actual penetration after a report of rape or require evidence to establish lack of consent to the sexual relationship. Nor can they require that a judge or a police officer find that the rape actually occurred; or require that the woman obtain permission from, or be required to notify, her husband or her parents.

The circumstances above are not the only ones in which it is disproportionate to criminalize abortion.

Also, when there is a risk to the health and life of the pregnant woman, it is clearly excessive to criminalize abortion since it would require the sacrifice of the fully formed life of the woman in favor of the developing life of the fetus. If the criminal penalty for abortion rests on valuing the life of the developing fetus over other constitutional interests involved, then criminalization of abortion in these circumstances would mean that there is no equivalent recognition of the right to life and health of the mother.

This Court has held on several occasions that the state cannot oblige a person, in this case a pregnant woman, to perform heroic sacrifices and give up her own rights for the benefit of others or for the benefit of society in general. Such an obligation is unenforceable, even if the pregnancy is the result of a consensual act, in light of article 49 of the Constitution, which mandates that all persons take care of their own health. ***

For the present analysis, it is relevant to consider various international human rights bodies' interpretation of international treaties that guarantee women's right to life and health. [After reviewing several treaties, the Court posits that] the prohibition of abortion where the life and health of the mother are at risk may therefore violate Colombia's obligations under international law.

These obligations do not pertain only where the woman's physical health is at risk, but also where her mental health is at risk. It must be noted that the right to health, under article 12 of the International Covenant on Economic, Social and Cultural Rights, includes the right to the highest achievable level of both physical and mental well-being. Pregnancy may at times cause severe anguish or even mental disorders, which may justify its termination if so certified by a doctor.

Some of the interveners argue that when the life or the health of the pregnant woman are at risk due to the pregnancy, article 32-7 of the Penal Code allows for the invocation of the necessity defense to avoid criminal liability. On this point, this Court must warn that the necessity defense does not resolve the constitutional tension at issue here for two reasons. First, application of the necessity defense presupposes that the legislature can completely criminalize abortion, which, as has been discussed here, is unconstitutional because it disregards the right to life and health of the mother in favor of protecting the fetus, regardless of the woman's particular circumstances. Second, for the necessity defense to apply under article 32-7, there must be actual and imminent danger which is not preventable in any other way, which was not willfully caused, and which the person does not have the legal duty to bear. These requirements do not clearly address the risks to the life or health of a pregnant woman and they impose an unreasonable burden on her.

A final circumstance that must be addressed involves medically-certified malformations of the fetus. Although there are different types of malformations, those extreme malformations incompatible with life outside the womb pose a constitutional issue that must be resolved. Those circumstances are different from having identified an illness of the fetus that may be cured during pregnancy or after birth. Rather, those circumstances involve a fetus that is unlikely to survive due to a severe malformation, as certified by a doctor. In these cases, the duty of the state to protect the fetus loses weight, since this life is in fact not viable. Thus, the rights of the woman prevail and the legislature cannot require her, under the threat of a criminal penalty, to carry a pregnancy to term.

An additional reason for the decriminalization of abortion in these extreme circumstances is that imposing a criminal penalty in order to protect the fetus results in the imposition of an unreasonable burden on the pregnant woman, who is forced to go through a pregnancy only to lose the growing life due to the malformation.

Furthermore, in a situation where the fetus is not viable, forcing the mother, under the threat of criminal charges, to carry the pregnancy to term amounts to cruel, inhumane and degrading treatment, which affects her moral well-being and her right to dignity.

In both cases described above, where the continuation of the pregnancy puts the life or health of the pregnant woman at risk or when there are serious malformations of the fetus incompatible with life outside the womb, there should be a medical certificate to validate the circumstances under which the abortion cannot be penalized.

It is not in the realm of the Court's knowledge to stipulate when the continuation of a pregnancy puts the life or health of the mother at risk or when there are serious malformations of the fetus. Such determinations are to be made by medical practitioners acting within the ethical standards of their profession.

From a constitutional standpoint, if these requirements are met—a medical certificate or a report to the authorities, depending on the circumstances—neither the pregnant woman nor the doctor who performs the abortion can be the subject of criminal charges under the three circumstances in which article 122 has been found unconstitutional. Each of these three circumstances is independent from one another. Therefore, it cannot be required, for example, to establish after a rape that the life or health of the mother is at risk or that the fetus is not viable. In the case of rape or incest, the good faith of the woman who reports the incident to the authorities shall be presumed and it is enough for her to show a copy of the report to the doctor.

It must be noted that conscientious objection is not a right that legal entities or the state can exercise. It is only possible for natural persons to exercise this right. Hospitals, clinics or other health centers cannot raise a conscientious objection to performing an abortion when all the requirements established by this decision are met. When it comes to natural persons, it must be underscored that a conscientious objection relates to a religious belief and the opinion of the doctor with regard to abortion should not be questioned. However, women's fundamental rights cannot be disregarded, thus, if the doctor raises a conscientious objection, the doctor must immediately refer the pregnant woman to another medical practitioner who can perform the abortion. That referral is without prejudice to a determination that may be made afterwards, through mechanisms established by the medical profession, regarding whether the objection was legitimate.

Even though regulations are not necessary for the immediate decriminalization of abortion in the three circumstances presented in this decision, the legislature or the authorities regulating social and health services are not prevented from adopting decisions within their discretion and in order to fulfill their duties with respect to the constitutional rights of women; for example, taking measures that will effectively ensure women access in conditions of equality and safety in the area of health and social services.

In these three circumstances, the legislature is proscribed from establishing requirements that limit access to abortion services or that amount to a disproportionate burden on the rights of women.

The above analysis demonstrates that even though the decision to criminalize abortion as a measure to protect the life of the fetus is constitutionally [permissible] ... the total prohibition of abortion in all cases is a blatantly disproportionate measure as it infringes upon the rights of the pregnant woman, protected by the Constitution of 1991 as well as by the international human rights treaties that are part of the Constitutional Bundle.

The protection of women's rights does not call for the complete invalidation of article 122, because this would leave life unprotected. Furthermore, it would prevent the legal system from regulating abortion in circumstances where the Constitution allows for it.

To conclude, under the principle that calls for the preservation of laws, it is necessary to declare the conditional constitutionality of the challenged article. In accordance with this decision, abortion will not be considered a crime in the circumstances described herein. In this manner, protection for the life of the fetus will not disproportionately override the rights of the pregnant woman.

The Court declares that article 122 of the Penal Code is constitutional with the understanding that abortion is not criminal in the following circumstances: a) when the continuation of the pregnancy presents risks to the life or the health of the woman, as certified by a medical doctor; b) when there are serious malformations of the fetus that make the fetus not viable, as certified by a medical doctor; and c) when the pregnancy is the result of any of the following criminal acts, duly reported to the authorities: incest, rape, sexual abuse, or artificial insemination or implantation of a fertilized ovule without the consent of the woman.

[The Court also struck down the Penal Code's strict criminalization of abortion "on a woman of less than 14 years of age" because it "annuls the pregnant minor's fundamental rights to the free development of the individual, autonomy and dignity, and is inadequate to achieve its stated goals" and "therefore clearly disproportionate and unconstitutional." Hence, the expression "or on a woman of less than 14 years of age" is hereby declared unconstitutional.]

10.3. On the constitutionality of article 124 of the Penal Code

All of the circumstances cited as mitigating factors in the challenged article are included, by virtue of this decision, together with those not expressly mentioned in the article, as circumstances under which abortion is not a crime.

As a consequence of this decision, the article in question and the paragraph in question are superfluous because the Court declares that, instead of constituting mitigating factors, the circumstances no longer constitute a crime. The article shall be deleted from the Code....

* * *

Notes

1. The Columbian Constitution incorporates international law and treaties directly into its national legal system in what is termed a "constitutional bundle." While both the Canadian and United States' abortion jurisprudence is concerned with applying certain universal constitutional rights to women, like the right to dignity and privacy, the Colombian Constitutional Court is able to consider rights and freedoms guaranteed specifically to women under international law. In your opinion, does this facet of the Colombian Court's approach—which considers not only the physical and mental implications of barring women's access to abortion but the broader impacts on women's ability to work and access education—make the opinion more persuasive than the less gendered approaches of the other courts discussed?

2. When discussing abortion, courts often weigh a woman's right to terminate her pregnancy against a fetus' right to life. Very rarely (Irish law serves as an exception) is the fetus afforded full status as a human being and full protection of human rights law. What are the legal consequences of recognizing the fetus as a person? How does the Hungarian Constitutional Court case, reproduced below, address the question of the personhood of the fetus?

Decision 48/1998 (XI. 23.) AB

Hungarian Constitutional Court,
pages 1–21, 23, 26–28 (1998)

The Constitutional Court establishes that it is not unconstitutional to enact an Act of the Parliament permitting abortion in case the pregnant woman is in a situation of serious crisis. However, the legislature may only dispense, in a constitutional way, with the examination of the existence of a serious crisis situation if, at the same time, it establishes provisions creating adequate counterbalance with a view to protecting foetal life.

The Constitutional Court establishes that the concept and the application criteria for a situation of serious crisis may only be defined in an Act of the Parliament; the lack of such a definition may not be substituted for either in statute of a lower level, or by way of judicial interpretation.

* * *

The Constitutional Court rejects the petition proposing that the Constitutional Court decide whether or not the foetus is a human.

* * *

According to Section 6 para. (1) item d) of the Act on the Protection of the Foetus, abortion may be procured until the 12th week of pregnancy if the pregnant woman is in a situation of serious crisis. Almost all the petitioners challenged the above provision, arguing that—taking into account Section 12 para. (6) defining the concept of a situation of serious crisis—it practically allows unrestricted abortion. In this context, one of the petitioners claimed the unconstitutionality of Section 9 para. (3) of the Implementing Decree, by which the existence of a situation of serious crisis is verified by the statement of the pregnant woman seeking abortion, and the staff member of the Family Protection Service has no discretionary powers concerning the contents and the validity of her representation.

One of the petitioners claimed the unconstitutionality of Section 6 para. (2) item b) of the Act on the Protection of the Foetus allowed the time limit for procuring abortion to the 18th week of pregnancy to be extended if the pregnant woman did not realise her pregnancy earlier due to a medical error or a health-related cause beyond her scope of responsibility, or if exceeding the 12th week of pregnancy was caused by the default of a healthcare institution or an authority.

Some of the petitioners challenged the entire Act on the Protection of the Foetus as unconstitutional, claiming that—contrary to its title—it does not contain any concrete provision on the protection and the rights of the foetus, and it does not declare the legal subjectivity of the foetus. Therefore, one of the petitioners asked the Constitutional Court to decide whether or not the foetus is a human.

The petitioners referred to several provisions of the Constitution, including: Article 54 para. (1) (the right to life and human dignity), Article 8 para. (1) (the obligation of the State to protect fundamental human rights), Article 66 para. (2) (mothers shall receive State support and protection before and after the birth of the child), Article 70/D (the right to physical and mental health), and Article 70/E (the right to social security). Similarly, all of the petitioners referred to Decision 64/1991 (XII. 17.) AB of the Constitutional Court (ABH 1991, 297; hereinafter: the "Decision of the Constitutional Court") concerning the former regulations on abortion. The petitioners claimed that when adopting the regulations in force, the legislature had not complied with the constitutional requirements specified in the Decision of the Constitutional Court.

* * *

The following provisions of the Act on the Protection of the Foetus and of the Implementing Decree are examined in the present decision:

* * *

Act on the Protection of the Foetus:

SECTION 6 para. (1) Abortion may be procured until the 12th week of pregnancy if

a) it is justified by a cause seriously endangering the pregnant woman's health;

b) it is medically probable that the foetus suffers from a serious deficiency or any other damage;

c) the pregnancy is the result of a criminal act, and

d) the pregnant woman is in a situation of serious crisis.

* * *

SECTION 12 para. (6) A situation of serious crisis is one which causes physical or mental breakdown or a subsequent impossible situation in social terms, thus endangering the healthy development of the foetus. The pregnant woman verifies the existence of the situation of serious crisis by signing the application form.

* * *

According to Article 2 paragraph (1) of the [European] Convention [on the Protection of Human Rights and Fundamental Freedoms], "Everyone's right to life shall be protected by law. No one shall be deprived of his life intentionally (…)". When interpreting the words of the Convention, one may face the same problem as in the case of Article 54 para. (1) of the Constitution, namely, whether it can be stated beyond any doubt that the term "everyone" * * * obligatorily covers the foetus as well; in other words, does the Convention protect the foetus' right to life the same way as in the case of a man born? The practice of the European Human Rights Commission has been consistent in addressing this issue in several concrete cases: it has, namely, not taken a stand. In the Case *X v United Kingdom* it stated concerning Article 2 paragraph (1) of the Convention the following: "It seems that the term 'everyone' cannot be applied to an unborn child". It was added in the decision that even if supposing that the provision concerned secured for the foetus the right to life from the moment of conception, this right may be restricted—including by abortion—in order to protect the mother's life and health. * * * Therefore, in the opinion of the Commission, the Member States have certain discretion on the basis of the Convention in regulating abortion.

* * *

The Constitutional Court establishes that—although the Act on the Protection of the Foetus does not contain an explicit provision on the legal subjectivity of the foetus—the Act in question regarding abortion expresses the implicit opinion of the Parliament on the foetus not being a human in legal terms. * * *

However, the lack of granting legal subjectivity for the foetus does not mean that foetal life is not protected by the Constitution. As explained in the Decision of the Constitutional Court, the foetus must enjoy protection—which is not absolute—resulting from the right to life (Article 54 para. (1) of the Constitution), to be secured by the State for conceived human life during its formation. This protection is not questioned by the Act on the Protection of the Foetus and, in line with the above concept, the legislator stated in the Preamble of the Act that "foetal life which starts in the moment of conception must be respected and protected" and repeated it in the text of the legal norm in the following form: "the foetus formed by the unification of an ovum and a spermatozoon, and developing in the womb, as well as the pregnant woman must be supported and protected." * * *

* * *

As stated in the Decision of the Constitutional Court, if the legislature or the body adopting the Constitution decides that the foetus is not a human from a legal point of view, i.e. a subject of law under Article 56 of the Constitution, and therefore, does not have the right to life and dignity, then—in accordance with the Constitution—it is not only possible but inevitable for the State to protect foetal life together with determining and considering other values defined in, and protected by, the Constitution against the mother's right to self-determination, and her other fundamental rights.

It is reinforced by the Constitutional Court that according to Article 54 para. (1) and Article 8 para. (1) of the Constitution, the protection of human life is "the primary obligation of the State". The State's duty to "respect and protect" these fundamental rights is not exhausted by the duty not to encroach on them, but incorporates the obligation to ensure the conditions necessary for their realisation. * * *

* * *

For the individual, the subjective right to life serves to ensure his/her own life. However, the duty of the State based on the right to life goes beyond its obligation not to violate the individual's subjective right to life and to employ its legislative and administrative measures to protect this right, but it must protect human life in general and the conditions thereof. The protection of human life cannot be limited to the protection of the life of men born and having legal subjectivity. Human life is a continuous process starting in the moment of conception. Primarily as legal subjectivity is regarded, certain sections of the life of the same individual human being are, however, qualified by the legislation in force in a different manner as permitted rather than made obligatory by the Constitution. The State's duty of protecting life is qualitatively different from aggregating the right to life of individuals; it is "human life" in general, and consequently, human life as a value that is the subject of protection. Hence, the State's objective and institutionalised duty to protect human life extends to lives which are in their formation. This duty, in contrast with the right to life, is not absolute. This is why the legislature may consider other rights—such as the mother's right to health or self-determination—against it.

* * *

For the above balancing act, the Constitutional Court may only designate the constitutional boundaries of the freedom of the legislature wherein the law must lie; and alternatively, it can establish an unconstitutional omission of legislative duty if the legislature has failed to extend the constitutionally required minimum protection either to the mother's right or to the foetus' life. Accordingly, if the foetus' legal capacity is not recognised, the legislature—when called upon to designate conditions authorising abortion—may not ignore the sometimes conflicting rights and obligations determining the contents of regulation: this way, it must weigh both the woman's right to self-determination, to life and to physical integrity as well as the State's duty to protect life—including foetal life—that follows from the right to life.

A complete ban on abortion would, therefore, be unconstitutional. It would likewise not be constitutional if regulations would favour exclusively the mother's right to self-determination. The State has a duty to protect human life from the moment of conception, and hence, the mother's right to self-determination cannot prevail alone even in the earliest stages of pregnancy. This objective duty to protect life means that the State may not constitutionally permit unjustified abortion. Justification is especially necessary in the case of abortion as the State's duty to safeguard human life does not serve the purpose of averting or minimising anonymous statistical risks but concerns the wilful termination of individual human lives being formed. * * *

* * * The State's objective duty to protect life has the same status when applied to the protection of conceived individual human life. As explained in the Decision of the Constitutional Court, the above circumstances do not require that the foetus be declared a special subject of law. * * * Nevertheless, it is pointed out by the Constitutional Court that the special significance of foetal life to be protected under the State's duty to protect life may, in other legal systems, be reflected in the establishment of individual fundamental rights as "the human dignity of unborn human life" and "the unborn man's own right to life". For example, the German Federal Constitutional Court established that the foetus has its own individual right to life.

According to the petitions, the Parliament did not act in compliance with the Constitution when * * * the legislature allowed abortion to be procured if the pregnant woman is in a situation of serious crisis, and * * * the existence of a situation of serious crisis may be justified exclusively by the pregnant woman's declaration, without any control by another person. * * *

* * *

The pregnant woman's "situation of serious crisis" is a criterion used in the legal systems of several countries when regulating abortion, although it may have different meanings and functions. It can be established in general that the situation of serious crisis is practically a concrete application of the condition of proportionality to the particular statutory definition of abortion. If a legal system—as most of the European legal systems—applies the State's obligation to protect foetal life or—exceptionally—the foetus' own right to life, which can nevertheless be restricted by the mother's right to self-determination, restricting the protection of foetal life by the mother's right becomes proportionate on the ground of assuming that bearing the child, i.e. enforcing the protection (in other legal systems: the right) of the foetus, would put a burden on the pregnant woman which is far bigger than the usual burden of pregnancy, and this way, the continuation of pregnancy cannot be expected from the woman. In a broad sense, all classically accepted indications are "situations of serious crisis": medical and ethical indications as far as the mother and genetic-teratological ones as far as the foetus are concerned. However, in a narrow sense, the term "situation of crisis" is a social indication, which is a more recent concept subject to many debates. * * * [T]he *state of the pregnant woman* is the focus and the enforcement of *her right* is justified by the "situation of serious crisis" *in conflict* with the "right" or the constitutionally protected legal status of the foetus. * * *

The American law approaches in a different way the conflict between the pregnant woman and the foetus. There, for the last two decades, the mother's right to decide on abortion in the first trimester of pregnancy has been accepted as a constitutional right [(Roe v. Wade, 410 U.S. 113 (1973)]. However, it became clear by 1992 that due to changes first occurring a decade ago, the State's right to intervene into the mother's right to privacy in the foetus' interest should be accepted even in the first trimester. Although no majority opinion has been accepted concerning the constitutional standard of intervention, a concept that seems to correspond to the "situation of serious crisis" is presented in the opinions of three judges: restrictions by the State cannot unduly burden the woman's freedom of decision. Thus, the function of undue burden is exactly the opposite as in Europe: it is not the exceptional burden of pregnancy why a woman cannot be expected to perform the obligation—that would normally result from the "foetus' right to life" or the State's duty to protect foetal life—of bearing the foetus and giving birth to the child, but her constitutionally protected freedom of decision is protected from being "unduly" restricted by the State. It is the concept of "undue burden" that limits (constitutionally allowed) intervention by the State, including consultations aimed at preventing abortion, useless medical examinations etc. * * *

In the Hungarian law—similarly to other European legal systems using the concept of a situation of serious crisis, the theoretical basis of which is different from the American approach to abortion—the seriously critical state of the pregnant woman, as an independent indication, must qualify the state of the pregnant woman whose situation may justify derogation from the protection of the foetus. * * *

* * *

According to Section 12 para. (6) of the Act on the Protection of the Foetus, in case of a pregnant woman, a situation of serious crisis is one which causes physical or mental breakdown or a subsequent impossible situation in social terms, *thus* endangering the healthy development of the foetus. * * *

To the alternative criteria of physical or mental breakdown or a subsequent impossible situation in social terms, the Parliament must have added as a conjunctive condition the resulting endangerment of the healthy development of the foetus in order to render more stringent the criteria for a situation of serious crisis and—supposedly—to harmonise it with the principle contained in the Act at the beginning of the chapter on abortion, specifying that abortion may only be procured in case of endangerment, under the conditions laid down in the Act (Section 5). The conditions (Section 6) then take into account the endangerment of both the mother and the foetus. When defining the situation of serious crisis, the Act represents the endangerment of both of them.

However, as the definition of a situation of serious crisis puts the conditions into not only a conjunctive relation, but a relation of cause and effect as well, the endangerment of the healthy development of the foetus becomes the decisive feature in an indication the essence and the aim of which as well as its constitutional acknowledgement may only be justified by circumstances in the mother's life demanding disproportionate sacrifice.* * * This construction of cause and effect results in further logical contradictions. As already pointed out by the Constitutional Court, the mother being in a situation of serious crisis is the reason for restricting the State's duty to protect foetal life; therefore, these two aspects must be weighed against each other: the mother's rights and the State's duty to protect foetal life restrict each other.

The protection of foetal life may only exceptionally be restricted with reference to the endangerment of the foetus' health—a cause not related to the mother. This, of course, requires the verification of a serious foetal damage under strictly controlled medical circumstances. * * * Serious foetal disability is accepted by the law as a legitimate indication of abortion because, on the one hand, the law is aimed at protecting the foetus from the burdens of disabled life in the future * * * and, on the other hand, it is not expected from the mother to bear the mental and physical burdens caused by the disability of her child. Therefore, in case of a genetic indication, the mother's situation of serious crisis is not the cause, but a result of the foetus' genetic disorder. Nevertheless, the statutory definition of the situation of serious crisis turns this relationship upside down.

* * *

Based on the above, the Constitutional Court establishes that the first sentence of Section 12 para. (6) of the Act on the Protection of the Foetus is contrary to the principle of legal certainty, thus violating Article 2 para. (1) of the Constitution. Due to its further deficiencies, it does not meet the State's obligation to protect foetal life either, and therefore, it violates Article 54 para. (1) of the Constitution as well.

However, it is necessary to examine the statutory definition of a situation of serious crisis, as a legitimate indication, in the context of all the legal criteria of abortion, as it is not applied in itself and the criteria of its enforcement together with its wider legal environment gives rise to further important constitutional concerns. According to Section 12 para. (6) of the Act on the Protection of the Foetus, the pregnant woman verifies the existence of a situation of serious crisis by signing the application form. According to Section 9 para. (3) of the Implementing Decree, the staff member of the Family Protection Service—who is in charge of verifying the statutory indication of abortion—has no discretionary powers concerning the contents and the validity of her representation.

* * *

It is a fact that in the law of many European countries, there has been a shift from the objective and professionally controlled social indication to a subjective and uncontrollable "general situation of crisis" based on a statement by the pregnant woman. The most significant shift may be seen in the German Federal Constitutional Court's decisions on abortion adopted between 1975 and 1993 and the resulting changes in legislation. The first decision allowed the legislature to declare that the pregnant woman may not be expected to continue pregnancy in case it represents an extreme burden similar to the weight of a state seriously endangering the pregnant woman's life or health, which is another legitimate indication of abortion. The existence of this indication of abortion, called a general state of emergency or social indication, had to be verified. However, the decision of 1993 and the amendments of the Act that followed it in 1995 expressly renounce verification of the indication by a third party, and what is more, it is not necessary to reveal the mother's identity during the obligatory consulting session.* * *

A similar indication has been introduced by the Belgian Act on Abortion in 3 April, 1990. Accordingly, abortion is legitimate in the first 12 weeks of pregnancy if there is a state of emergency and it is the firm will of the pregnant woman to have an abortion. However, as stated in the reasoning of the draft of the Act, there is practically no difference between these two conditions: the woman's determined and constant reluctance to have a child is, in fact, the state of emergency. * * *

* * *

It is only a decision made by the Polish Constitutional Court in 1997 that follows a contrary approach. Accordingly, allowing abortion on the basis of the pregnant woman's financial or social difficulties violates the principle of proportionality of constitutional values. As stated in the reasoning of the decision, in the conflict of protecting the woman's interests on the basis of her subjective evaluation of the situation and the right to life, the latter has primacy.

* * *

It has been constantly stated by the Constitutional Court that among the rights to be weighed against the State's duty to give increased protection to foetal life, the mother's right to self-determination—as part of the right to human dignity—is the most important one. Undoubtedly, revealing details of the situation of crisis and having it assessed by a third party violate the woman's privacy and may in some cases violate her right to human dignity as well. Any violation of the above fundamental rights may only be evaluated in the context of abortion, where it collides with the State's duty to protect foetal life. * * * [I]ndeed, it is constitutionally required to have a balance in the mutually restrictive relationship between the woman's right to self-determination and the State's duty to protect life. * *

Contrary to the interpretation of the American Constitution, according to the Constitutional Court it follows ab ovo from the Constitution of Hungary that—if the legal subjectivity of the foetus is not acknowledged by the law—the woman's right to dignity and privacy must be weighed against the State's duty to protect foetal life. It is always the State's life protecting duty—in the present case, protection from the wilful termination of an individual foetal life—which must be weighed against the woman's rights. In the conflict of the above rights and duties, obliging the woman by the law to give details on her situation of serious crisis does not qualify as a disproportionate restriction of the woman's right to privacy and dignity. * * *

* * *

Instituting a general indication of crisis and waiving the assessment of the case practically result in applying the deadline method, i.e. allowing abortion in the first 12 weeks at the pregnant woman's request without any further condition or discretion. * * * Maintaining the statutory requirement of a serious, disproportionate, extraordinary, unbearable etc. situation of crisis in the field of legitimate causes of abortion—as the most important and in constitutional terms most sensitive point of the former legal regulation of abortion—is aimed at demonstrating that the State, at least in principle and on constitutional grounds, does not give a free way to abortion, an act acknowledged by the law only in exceptional cases: abortion may only be legally implemented in case there is a serious conflict related to conscience or to a personal situation of life, and if the woman's rights to life, health and self-determination are violated to a great extent.

* * *

If the right to verify the situation of crisis is waived by the law, other means are to be found to remedy the protection lost. In the international practice, the State's acknowledging a situation of serious crisis means a shift in the focus of protection from expressly banning and punishing abortion to regulating the circumstances thereof.

* * *

Section 12 para. (6) of the Act on the Protection of the Foetus and Section 9 para. (3) of the Implementing Decree—examining the norms themselves—are unconstitutional on the basis of the foregoing.

* * * [I]t is incompatible with the State's duty to protect foetal life to have the situation of serious crisis verified simply by the pregnant woman's signing the application form. * * * The staff member of the Family Protection Service—who is in charge of verifying the statutory indication of abortion—has no discretionary powers concerning the contents and the validity of her representation. Such provisions themselves cannot secure for the foetus the level of minimum protection required by the constitutional interpretation of the Constitutional Court, and in fact, they do not secure any protection, as the regulation is concerned with the mother's right to self-determination only. * * * Consequently, the legislature has failed to comply with the constitutional criteria specified in the Decision of the Constitutional Court for the case of the Parliament not acknowledging the legal subjectivity of the foetus.

* * *

* * * [L]egal certainty (Article 2 para. (1) of the Constitution) requires that one could prove the existence of a particular circumstance exceptionally excluding the unlawful nature of an act which is dangerous to the society, and therefore, punishable in principle, and such an exception must be verified by the court or another competent

institution. If abortion is allowed on the basis of a situation of serious crisis, the staff member of the institution concerned, i.e. the Family Protection Service, may only complete the form authorising abortion, but his or her right to verify the existence of the cause regarding the contents or truthfulness of the representation specifying the cause is expressly withdrawn by the law: in essence, the right to establish the cause excluding unlawfulness is allocated by the Act on the Protection of the Foetus and the Implementing Decree solely to the pregnant woman requesting abortion. As a consequence, Section 12 para. (6) of the Act on the Protection of the Foetus and Section 9 para. (3) of the Implementing Decree violate the principle of legal certainty in the context of Section 169 of the CC.

All this shall not mean that the State may not take certain cases of abortion out of the scope of criminal punishment, with reference either to the lack of actual endangerment of the society and the lack of unlawfulness (e.g. abortion based on medical or ethical indication), or to the supposed inefficiency of criminal punishment, where the State wishes to use other means to perform its constitutional duty of protecting life.* * *

The Constitutional Court establishes that Section 9 of the Act on the Protection of the Foetus assigns a merely informative task to the staff member of the Family Protection Service. After receiving the application for abortion, the staff member shall inform the pregnant woman of the statutory conditions of abortion [paragraph 1(a)], then of the financial allowances and benefits in kind available in case the child is born, as well as of the institutions offering support, the conditions of adoption, the circumstances, the method and the dangers of abortion, the medical institutions that perform abortion, and finally, the methods of contraception proposed personally to the woman concerned. According to paragraph 2, after giving the above information, the staff member shall complete the appropriate application form to be signed by the applicant [as a verification of the situation of serious crisis in line with Section 12 para. (6)], and at the same time, he or she designates the institution chosen to perform the abortion. According to the Implementing Decree, in addition to the above information service, the Family Protection Service shall have administrative tasks only (Sections 9 and 10). * * * Finally, according to Section 15 of the Act on the Protection of the Foetus, it is banned to advertise or propagate abortion, institutions performing abortion, and tools or substances that may be used for abortion. In contrast, according to Section 2 of the Act on the Protection of the Foetus, elementary and secondary-level educational institutions have the duty of instruction on the value of health and human life, a healthy way of life, a responsible relationship between man and woman, family life meeting human standards, and contraceptive methods that are not detrimental to health; at the same time, the State supports the publication and the presentation in the mass media of brochures that serve the purpose of protecting foetal life.

The Constitutional Court establishes that the provisions of the Act on the Protection of the Foetus and of the Implementing Decree referred to before are not suitable for remedying the unconstitutional situation caused by the provisions of the Act. The pregnant woman's personality rights, and in particular, her right to self-determination may have primacy over the right to life and the State's obligation to protect foetal life only in exceptional cases when there is a conflict arising from the mother's rights being seriously endangered. In case the enforcement of such rights is allowed by the law to as great an extent as provided by the Act on the Protection of the Foetus when regulating the situation of serious crisis, foetal life, too, must be protected by firm and effective provisions in order to re-establish the constitutional balance. * * *

* * *

After the nullification of Section 12 para. (6), with Section 6 para. (1) item d) remaining in force, the Act on the Protection of the Foetus may only comply with the requirements—already established in the Decision of the Constitutional Court—resulting from Article 8 para. (2) of the Constitution as far as the level of regulating the indication of a situation of serious crisis is concerned if the contents of the concept of a situation of serious crisis and the respective application criteria are regulated on the level of an Act of the Parliament.

* * *

Dissenting opinion by Dr. Tamás Lábady, Judge of the Constitutional Court

* * *

All abortions violate the right to life. The State must use the tools of legislation, information, training and education in acting against abortion. The legal norms and the constitutional concept of the State should not suggest that such a tolerated phenomenon is in line with the values and the human image of the Constitution. * * *

In my opinion, a more severe constitutional requirement should have been specified in the decision of the Constitutional Court—even on the grounds of its concept—for the objective protection of the right to life, taking into account the individuality of foetal life, i.e. the fact that each and every foetal life is the origin of an individual and irreproducible human life. Therefore, the State must—in addition to cutting the "statistical risk" of abortion—work on letting all foetuses be born without any discrimination.

Notes

1. The Hungarian Constitutional Court relies explicitly on comparative law in its analysis. Consider the comparison it makes to the U.S. Constitutional treatment: "the function of undue burden is exactly the opposite as in Europe: it is not the exceptional burden of pregnancy why a woman cannot be expected to perform the obligation—that would normally result from the 'foetus' right to life' or the State's duty to protect foetal life—of bearing the foetus and giving birth to the child, but her constitutionally protected freedom of decision is protected from being 'unduly' restricted by the State." Is the difference in approach inherent to higher order constitutional or political differences between the two countries? For example, the tendency of Americans to view the Constitution as a bulwark against threats *from* their government?

2. Another country that has struggled with the constitutionality of abortion is Ireland. The Eighth Amendment to the Irish Constitution, adopted in 1983, recognizes a right to life in the unborn. This provision was adopted in part, apparently, to forestall the application of European human rights and community law to preempt Irish statutes prohibiting abortion. After a widely publicized 1992 case in which a fourteen year old girl who had been raped by her friend's father was enjoined from leaving Ireland to get an abortion (a decision eventually reversed by the Irish Supreme Court, though on grounds that left the right to travel very unclear), Ireland adopted by referendum two new constitutional amendments. Amendments 13 and 14 to the Irish Constitution recognized the right of women to travel abroad to have an abortion, and to receive within Ireland information about the availability of abortions abroad. In 1995, the Irish parliament adopted a statute that permitted the dissemination of information respecting abortion, but prohibited the distribution of information that would counsel or advocate abortion, and forbade professionals within Ireland from arranging abortions elsewhere. The Irish Supreme Court subsequently upheld this statute against attacks from both those who opposed and those who supported abortion rights. See Patrick Hanafin, Reproductive Rights and the Irish Constitution: From Sanctity of Life to Sanctity of Autonomy? 3 *European J. Health L.* 179 (1996); Keith S. Koegler, Ireland's Abortion Information Act of 1995, 29 *Vand.J.Transnat'l L.* 117 (1996); Bryan Mercurio, Abortion in Ireland: An Analysis of the Legal Transformation Resulting from Membership in the European Union, 11 *Tul. J. Int'l & Comp. L.* 141 (2003). An attempt in 2002 to amend the Irish Constitution to outlaw abortion except when necessary to save the life of the mother (other than by threat of suicide) was narrowly defeated. Under Irish law, however, human life begins at implantation, thus the "morning after" pill or the use of coils is not specifically illegal. See Simon Mills and R.A.J. Spence, *Clinical Practice and the Law,* 287–89 (2002). The Irish situation changed only in 2018 when the Republic of Ireland voted overwhelmingly to overturn the abortion ban by 66.4% to 33.6%.

3. A number of countries have also adopted laws prohibiting or severely restricting research involving human embryos, recognizing that embryos are potential human life. The Council of Europe, Convention on Human Rights and Biomedicine provides:

> Article 18—Research on embryos *in vitro*
>
> 1 Where the law allows research on embryos *in vitro*, it shall ensure adequate protection of the embryo.
>
> 2 The creation of human embryos for research purposes is prohibited.

See, discussing the impact of this provision, Jennifer Gunning, Article 18 of the European Biomedicine Convention: What Impact on Assisted Reproduction, 6 *European J. Health L.* 165 (1999). For a multination study, see Albin Eser, Hans-George Koch, Carola Seith, editors, *International Perspectives on the Status and Protection of the Extracorporeal Embryo* (2007).

B. Assisted Reproduction

Since in vitro fertilization first became possible in the late 1970s, developed nations have had to confront the question of whether and to what extent to regulate the availability and terms and conditions of assisted reproduction. In fact, many nations even before this time regulated artificial insemination, which has been available at least since the 18th century. Not surprisingly, national responses to assisted reproduction have varied considerably. As reproductive technology has continued to develop, its legal status has continued to evolve, although legal developments have not always kept pace with technological change.

As the following excerpts illustrate, most countries permit some forms of assisted reproduction. Other forms, most notably commercial surrogacy and cloning are generally prohibited where addressed. Assisted reproduction is normally regulated, however, rather than prohibited. Topics addressed by law or regulation include licensing of facilities that offer this service, requirements for fully informed consent of recipients, provisions of rules for determining parentage, restrictions on commercialization, and protection of the confidentiality of donors. A separate question in many countries is whether public health insurance will pay for assisted reproduction technology. A number of countries that permit assisted reproduction do not finance it because of its cost.

The primary consideration driving assisted reproduction policy is a concern for assisting families with fertility problems. A common concern, however, is whether assisted reproduction should be limited to situations involving infertility, or whether it should also be available to single women or gays and lesbians who are not otherwise infertile, but prefer not to procreate naturally. Most countries limit the availability of assisted reproduction to infertile women or couples (or to situations where natural reproduction would risk passing on genetic disorders), but in a few countries, a broader policy favoring reproductive autonomy would permit assisted reproduction in other situations. One policy consideration that counsels restrictions on assisted reproduction is a concern for avoiding increased risks of genetic abnormalities, present in some forms of assisted reproduction. Screening of sperm is also common to avoid transmission of HIV or other diseases. Concern for protection of human life, or potential human life, present in gametes and embryos, also affects policy. Some states, for example, limit the storage of embryos. Concern for potential children also grounds recipient screening policies that consider the age, mental health, and character of potential parents. Another issue is the potential problems posed by multiple births, which are common with some forms of artificial reproduction. The relative weight given to these various concerns in different countries, and the varying ways in which these concerns affect different reproductive technologies, results in a range of regulatory approaches.

To see this variety of attitudes at work consider the following excerpts from academic articles describing the approach to reproductive technologies of several different countries.

Dov Fox, *Reproductive Negligence*

117 Colum. L. Rev. 149, 163–65 (2017)

* * *

[In the United States,] elected officials decline to regulate procreative conduct outside abortion and surrogacy. The single federal statute that deals with reproductive technology asks practitioners to do no more than report the rates at which patients get pregnant, and even then imposes no penalty for refusal. Few states regulate assisted reproduction either. One reason for this regulatory vacuum is that interventions in the processes of procreation invoke values about sex, family, and parenting that are often charged, complex, and even contradictory. These interventions implicate the blessings of parenthood as much as freedom from it, for example, and dreams of having children with particular traits as much as wishes for offspring without those very same features. Such questions tend to divide voters not only across traditional political constituencies but also within them. The "historical stigma of infertility" might also relieve what political pressure might otherwise be applied by keeping reproductive negligence "a secret between an individual and her physician." Another explanation is that the multibillion-dollar fertility industry in America mounts powerful lobbying forces against occasional calls for regulation. Private organizations that oversee the field do not meaningfully enforce their guidelines except by revocation of membership. The absence of external surveillance or effective self-policing leaves little by way of deterrence against reproductive negligence. This leaves potential victims to rely instead on nonpolitical, after-the-fact forms of protection.

* * *

Marsha Garrison, *Regulating Reproduction*

76 Geo. Wash. L. Rev. 1623, 1623–24 (2008)

* * *

The United Kingdom has the most comprehensive regulatory scheme [for reproductive technology]; the pioneering Human Fertilisation and Embryology Act of 19908 ("Act") was drafted to ensure that ... sensitive issues of moral and legal complexity are dealt with in a clear framework.... to balance what are the sometimes conflicting interests of the involuntarily childless and the children of the reproduction resolution.... [and] to mediate between the families who may benefit from research into the causes of genetically inherited disease ... and the human embryo or foetus. The Act sets out a comprehensive regulatory framework that governs artificial insemination, in vitro fertilization ("IVF"), surrogacy, and research involving pre-embryos; it also establishes a governmental agency to license ART providers and to resolve issues not dealt with in the statute. As a result of this comprehensive regulatory scheme, in the U.K., it is public policy, not market forces, that determines whether sex selection is offered to would-be parents and how a host of other reproductive technology questions should be resolved.

* * *

Doron Dorfman, *The Inaccessible Road to Motherhood—The Tragic Consequence of Not Having Reproductive Policies for Israelis with Disabilities*

30 Colum. J. Gender & L. 49, 55–59 (2015)

* * *

ART policy in Israel is regarded as exceptional in international terms: fertility treatments are funded by the state (for the first two live births per family) and are offered to women of all family statuses and sexual orientations up to the age of forty-five to fifty-one depending on whether or not a donor egg is needed. Israel was found to have the world's highest number of In Vitro Fertilization ("IVF") treatment cycles per capita. Israel also protects the right of a woman or a man to be absent from work for fertility treatments and prohibits employers from firing any employee who undergoes such procedures. However, when it comes to methods of having children without the woman carrying them in her womb, i.e., through adoption or surrogacy (whether with a gestational carrier or a "classic surrogate"), the policies are much more restricted. The cross-cultural rationale for the stricter rules regarding those methods of third-party reproduction is that they are considered to be more susceptive to misuse and ethical concerns regarding the third-party. A second, more local rationale for the sharp distinction between the ART and the third-party reproduction policies in Israel has to do with ensuring the religious-ideological-political idea of the natural Jewish family. Making sure that offspring are of common origin as the other Jewish collective is a disclosed interest of the Jewish state, which can only be guaranteed through ART and not third-party reproduction.

Adoption in Israel is an excruciating process that entails much bureaucratic hassle and extensive waiting periods. Domestic adoption is only available to those who fulfill strict conditions. Only heterosexual couples who are legally married (meaning married through the rabbinical courts) for three years, who are not more than forty-three years older than the adopted child, and have no other children are eligible to adopt. The couple should also have at least twelve years of schooling, have shown that they have a regular source of income at least within the national average income, and that they have a home where the child could have her own room. The prospective adopting couple also needs to be of the same religion as the child's birth family, and the couple is assessed for their spousal, familial, and social functioning. Single individuals are only allowed to adopt children who could not be placed with an adoptive couple. The waiting period for a domestic adoption is five to six years on average.

Inter-country adoption is also quite cumbersome. Foreign adoption is much less restrictive from the prospective parents' side in comparison with domestic adoption (applicants must only undergo a psychologist's assessment of their parenthood abilities and comply with the adoptee's country requirements). However, Israel is very suspicious of foreign adoption agencies, and those agencies are subject to strict investigation before approving the adoption. It needs to be mentioned that inter-country adoption is quite expensive and is usually equated to a person's entire annual income, meaning it is thus beyond the reach of most couples or single persons.

Surrogacy in Israel is likewise a strictly regulated process. It is only available to heterosexual couples who can prove their infertility. The prospective parents and the surrogate must all share the same religion. The surrogate must be an unmarried woman (i.e., single, widowed, or divorced) who has a child of her own and cannot be biologically related to either of the prospective parents. Surrogacy in Israel is also illegal as a career. Despite being a highly contentious issue, "reproductive tourism" involving surrogacy abroad (especially in third world countries), is quite popular in Israel due to the high demand. Many gay and straight couples turn to that option; they find a surrogate outside the country to be inseminated with a fertilized egg (containing the genetic materials of one or both prospective parents) and carry the baby. Once the baby is born, the parents bring her back to their home country. This option requires not only a tremendous investment of time, money, and other resources, but it is also dependent on fast-changing policies of the foreign country, and on a highly bureaucratic process of bringing the child back and determining her religion and citizenship status by proving the genetic connection to at least one of the parents.

While the disparity between ART and the third-party reproduction methods of adoption and surrogacy in Israel might be justified, it obviously excludes or even discriminates against individuals and populations who cannot bear children like infertile women, single straight or gay men, gay couples, or people with disabilities. Specifically with regard to people with disabilities, although the Israeli legal treatment of this population was highly influenced by the American disability rights advocacy, academia, and legislation, the Israeli counterpart for the ADA, the Equal Rights for People with Disabilities Law, was never interpreted by the Israeli courts to include procreation as a "major life activity" like the American Supreme Court had in *Bragdon v. Abbott*. There is currently no Israeli legislation or significant body of case law that discusses reproductive and family policy for people with disabilities.

* * *

Martin Hevia & Carlos Herrera Vacaflor, *The Legal Status of In Vitro Fertilization in Latin America and the American Convention on Human Rights*

36 Suffolk Transnat'l L. Rev. 51, 58–62 (2013)

* * *

Let us begin by examining the legal status of IVF. First, there are states that explicitly regulate access to IVF. Peru allows infertile women access to IVF as a treatment. Similarly, in Mexico, married women have access to insemination, given the consent of their husbands. Colombia, in turn, tentatively allows procreation by means of IVF; article 42(6) of its Constitution dictates that children can be conceived with scientific assistance. Colombia's Health Ministry regulates the donation of gametes for assisted reproduction technology, including IVF.

Second, there are states that only informally regulate access to IVF. Brazil regulates only through resolutions enacted by the Federal Council of Medicine, and subsidiary laws about scientific research on embryos or emergency contraceptives. The Federal Council of Medicine permits IVF not only for couples, but also for single women. It also prohibits the destruction of embryos, though it does allow their cryopreservation and selection. In early 2011, it issued a resolution allowing access to IVF for "all competent persons," a phrase that came to include unwed individuals and same-sex couples. Additionally, a 2005 law, known as the "Law of Biosecurity," permits and regulates medically or therapeutically motivated research on cells and embryos obtained through IVF, including mother cells, embryonic cells, non-viable embryos, and embryos that had been cryopreserved for more than 3 years. All of this offers a positive outlook for access to IVF, and the limits present when it is balanced against protecting other interests like the right to life.

The situation in Chile is similar. The Chilean Ministry of Health published a report, devoid of legal force, establishing general steps for IVF. The report required transferring all created embryos to the mother, and prohibiting their cryopreservation. In 1998, Chile enacted law 19.585 regulating kinship, and established that "the father and the mother of a child conceived through the application of assisted human reproductive technology are the man and woman who committed to it." In 2006, it enacted law 20.120 "on scientific research on the human being, its genome, and prohibiting human cloning." This law protects human life from the moment of conception, and therefore, forbids human cloning and destroying human embryos for the acquisition of embryonic stem cells.

Finally, there are states that do not expressly regulate IVF, though ethical regulations specific to health care providers may be present. In Argentina, there is no national law that regulates IVF, despite many attempts to formulate one. Provinces independently are trying to regulate the practice. Currently, the only province that specifically regulates assisted reproduction is the province of Buenos Aires. Ecuador also does not regulate IVF. The practice is completely "de facto," leaving the ethical and practical challenges of IVF directly in the hands of doctors.

* * *

Rosario M. Isasi, Bartha M. Knoppers, Peter A. Singer & Abdallah S. Daar, *Legal and Ethical Approaches to Stem Cell and Cloning Research: A Comparative Analysis of Policies in Latin America, Asia, and Africa*

32 J.L. Med. & Ethics 626, 629 (2004)

* * *

In the African continent, there is little regulation on genetic research and human reproductive technologies. Like Brazil, South Africa is undergoing a process of policy redesign, moving from a restrictive to a moderate approach in regulating cloning and embryo research. Currently, the Parliament of South Africa is discussing a draft of the National Health Bill, which would repeal the Human Tissue Act. The draft bill prohibits the reproductive cloning of human beings but would allow research or therapeutic cloning and stem cell research with the prior authorization of the Minister of Health. It also would prohibit the importation or exportation of human embryos and zygotes (unless expressly authorized by the Minister).

* * *

Moving from the general to the specific, the materials that follow examine how specific legal controversies involving reproductive technology play out in several jurisdictions. As discussed above, the U.K. has one of the more intensive forms of regulation of assisted reproduction. The following materials compare the way it and the U.S. have regulated the difficult question of so-called "savior siblings"—children born through assisted reproduction to be potential bone marrow donors or otherwise help existing sick siblings.

Regina (Quintavalle) v. Human Fertilisation and Embryology Authority

House of Lords, [2005] UKHL 28, [2005] 2 A.C. 561 (2005)

* * *

This was an appeal, by leave of the House of Lords, by the claimant, Josephine Quintavalle, on behalf of Comment on Reproductive Ethics, against the judgment of the Court of Appeal allowing an appeal by the defendant, the Human Fertilisation and Embryology Authority ("the authority") from the order of Maurice Kay J quashing, by way of judicial review, the decision in principle made by the authority, dated 13 December 2001, to allow HLA typing in order to test an embryo for tissue compatibility with an affected sibling, pursuant to section 11 of the Human Fertilisation and Embryology Act 1990.

* * *

Lord Hoffmann

My Lords, Zain Hashmi is a little boy, now aged six, who suffers from a serious genetic disorder called beta thalassaemia major. His bone marrow does not produce enough red blood cells and in consequence he is often very poorly and needs daily drugs and regular blood transfusions to keep him alive. But he could be restored to normal life by a transplant of stem cells from a tissue compatible donor.

The problem is to find compatible tissue which Zain's immune system will not reject. The chances of finding a compatible donor who is not a sibling are extremely low. Even in the case of siblings, the chances are only one in four. None of Zain's three elder siblings is compatible. In addition, the donor must be free of the same disorder. That lengthens the odds even more. Zain's mother, Mrs Hashmi, has twice conceived in the hope of giving birth to a child whose umbilical blood could provide stem cells for Zain. Once the foetus was found to have beta thalassaemia major and she had an abortion. On the second occasion, she gave birth to a child whose tissue turned out not to be compatible.

There is a way to save the Hashmi family from having to play dice with conception. * * * In vitro fertilisation ("IVF") has enabled many couples who could not achieve natural fertilisation to have children. More recently, it has become possible to perform a biopsy upon the newly fertilised IVF embryo and remove a single cell to test it for genetic disorders. This is called pre-implantation genetic diagnosis ("PGD"). It provides a woman with information about the embryo proposed to be implanted in her body so that she may decide whether or not to proceed. Mrs Hashmi, for example, would have been spared having to have her foetus carrying beta thalassaemia major aborted if the embryo had been created by IVF and the disorder diagnosed by PGD.

Still more recently, and so far only in the United States, it has become possible to use the same single cell biopsy technique to test for tissue compatibility. This involves examination of the human leukocyte antigens ("HLA") and is known as HLA typing. That means that if Mr and Mrs Hashmi's sperm and eggs are used to create IVF embryos which are then tested for beta thalassaemia major by PGD and for tissue compatibility with Zain by HLA typing, they can know that the child Mrs Hashmi conceives will have stem cells which could cure Zain. The question in this appeal is whether this can lawfully be done in the United Kingdom.

After the birth of the first IVF child or "test tube baby" in 1978, it became clear that the new technique, together with other potential developments in embryology and genetics, could raise serious medical and ethical issues. The government appointed a committee under the chairmanship of Dame Mary Warnock DBE to advise. * * * The centrepiece of the committee's recommendations was the creation of a statutory licensing authority to regulate all research and treatment which involved the use of IVF embryos.

This recommendation was given effect by the Human Fertilisation and Embryology Act 1990, which set up the Human Fertilisation and Embryology Authority ("the authority"). Members are appointed by the Secretary of State and it has to have a lay (i.e. not medically qualified or engaged in IVF treatment or research) chairman and deputy chairman and a majority of lay members.* * *

The source of the authority's power is section 3(1), which makes it a criminal offence to bring about the creation of an embryo or keep or use an embryo except pursuant to a licence from the authority. The proposed treatment of Mrs Hashmi to assist her in bearing a tissue-compatible child involves the creation and use of embryos and therefore requires a licence. In this case, the authority has granted a licence which permits both PGD and HLA typing. But Ms Quintavalle, the claimant in these proceedings, who is director and founder of a group which believes in absolute respect for the human embryo, says that the authority has no power to authorise HLA typing. She brought judicial review proceedings for a declaration to that effect. It was granted * * * but an appeal was allowed and the application dismissed by the Court of Appeal.

* * *

In this case, we are particularly concerned with the activities which may be authorised to be done in the course of providing treatment services. "Treatment services" are defined by section 2(1) to mean, among other things, medical services provided to the public for the purpose of assisting women to carry children. IVF is of course such a service; the proposal is to assist Mrs Hashmi to carry a child conceived by the implantation of an IVF embryo. So the question is whether PGD and HLA typing are activities which the authority can authorise to be done "in the course" of providing her with IVF treatment.

To find the answer, one must look at the list of activities in para 1 of Schedule 2. Para 1(3) provides that the authority may licence an activity on the list only if it appears to the authority to be "necessary or desirable for the purpose of providing treatment services". The activities include: "1(1) ... (d) practices designed to secure that embryos are in a suitable condition to be placed in a woman or to determine whether embryos are suitable for that purpose."

The authority's case is that both PGD and HLA typing are to determine whether an embryo would be suitable for the purpose of being placed in Mrs Hashmi. The definition of treatment services focuses upon the woman as the person to whom the services are provided. The authority says that Mrs Hashmi is entitled to regard an embryo as unsuitable unless it is both free of abnormality and tissue compatible with Zain. Without such testing, she cannot make an informed choice as to whether she wants the embryo placed in her body or not. The authority considers it desirable for the purpose of providing her with treatment services, i.e., IVF treatment, that she should be able to make such a choice. Mr Pannick, who appeared for the authority, pointed out that the Act does not require that PGD or HLA typing should *constitute* treatment services. They must be activities *in the course* of such services, i.e. in the course of providing IVF treatment.

The claimant, on the other hand, says that this gives far too wide a meaning to the notion of being suitable. It would enable the authority to authorise a single cell biopsy to test the embryo for whatever characteristics the mother might wish to know: whether the child would be male or female, dark or blonde, perhaps even, in time to come, intelligent or stupid. Suitable must therefore have a narrower meaning than suitable for that particular mother. Maurice Kay J thought that suitable meant only that the embryo would be viable. That would rule out a good deal of PGD, because many genetic abnormalities do not affect the viability of the foetus. * * * The narrower meaning is particularly difficult to support when paragraph 3(2)(e) lists, among the research projects which may be licensed, "developing methods for detecting the presence of gene or chromosome abnormalities in embryos before implantation". It would be very odd if Parliament contemplated research to develop techniques which could not lawfully be used. So Lord Brennan [representing the claimant] accepts that suitable means more than viable. Building on paragraph 3(2)(e), he says that an embryo is suitable if it is capable of becoming a healthy child, free of abnormalities. PGD to establish that the embryo is free from genetic abnormalities is therefore acceptable. But not HLA typing. A baby which is not tissue compatible with Zain would not be in any way abnormal. It just would not answer the particular needs of the Hashmi family.

"Suitable" is one of those adjectives which leaves its content to be determined entirely by context. As my noble and learned friend, Lord Scott of Foscote, put it in argument, a suitable hat for Royal Ascot is very different from a suitable hat for the Banbury cattle market. The context must be found in the scheme of the 1990 Act and the background against which it was enacted.* * *

The Warnock Report discussed possible future developments in embryology. Some of these, such as creating children in vitro or the gestation of human embryos in other species, it recommended should be unequivocally banned. On others, it made no such recommendations. One of these was embryonic biopsy, such as can now be used for PGD and HLA typing. It described, in para 12.13, the advantages of PGD in detecting abnormalities before implantation * * * and its disadvantages, namely the need to use IVF. It concluded that it was unlikely that embryonic biopsy would become a feasible method of detecting abnormal embryos for some considerable time.

For present purposes, the most relevant discussion in the Warnock Report concerned gender identification. * * * Such information could be used to select embryos to "prevent the birth of a child with a sex-linked hereditary disease". The committee saw no reason why this should not be done: para 9.11. It then went on to consider the use of gender identification to select the sex of a child "for purely social reasons". After some discussion of the social issues (population distribution, the role of women in society), the committee said that it was unable to make any positive recommendations.* * *

* * *

The conclusion which I draw is that the committee contemplated that the authority would decide the circumstances, if any, in which sex selection on social grounds should be authorised. As sex selection on social grounds is the most obvious case of selecting an embryo on grounds other than its health, I would infer that the Warnock committee did not intend that selection of IVF embryos on grounds which went beyond genetic abnormality should be altogether banned.

* * * The intention [or Parliament as evidenced by the White Paper that preceded the legislation] was therefore to define the functions of the authority in very broad terms. To ensure that the legislation was flexible enough to deal with "as yet unforeseen treatment developments which may raise new ethical issues", the Bill would "contain powers to make regulations (subject to the affirmative resolution procedure) to add to or subtract from the range of matters coming within the regulatory scope of the [authority]".

* * *

Included in the matters which were to be prohibited were what journalists commonly call "designer babies" or, as the White Paper put it, in para 37: "the artificial creation of human beings with certain predetermined characteristics through modification of an early embryo's genetic structure." Another was the cloning of individuals by nuclear substitution. But, relevantly for present purposes, there was no proposal to include in the "clearly prohibited" list the testing of embryos to enable the mother to choose to carry a child with characteristics of her choice. One infers that the White Paper intended the fundamental ethical issues which such activities might raise to be determined by the statutory authority, subject to the regulation-making power by which Parliament could impose its own decision.

* * * Section 3(3)(a) prevents, as the Warnock Committee recommended, the development of the foetus in vitro by providing that a licence may not authorise the keeping or use of an embryo after the appearance of the primitive streak. Nor may the authority authorise the placing of an embryo in an animal (subsection (3)(b)) or the cloning of an embryo (subsection (3)(d)). By para 1(4) of Schedule 2, a licence may not authorise altering the genetic structure of any cell while it forms part of an embryo.* * *

Subject to these prohibitions, the licensing power of the authority is defined in broad terms. Paragraph 1(1) of Schedule 2 enables it to authorise a variety of activities (with the possibility of others being added by regulation) provided only that they are done "in the course of" providing IVF services to the public and appear to the authority "necessary or desirable" for the purpose of providing those services. Thus, if the concept of suitability in sub-paragraph (d) of 1(1) is broad enough to include suitability for the purposes of the particular mother, it seems to me clear enough that the activity of determining the genetic characteristics of the embryo by way of PGD or HLA typing would be "in the course of" providing the mother with IVF services and that the authority would be entitled to take the view that it was necessary or desirable for the purpose of providing such services.

The chief argument of Lord Brennan [counsel for the claimant] against interpreting suitability in this sense was that, once one allowed the mother's choice to be a legitimate ground for selection, one could not stop short of allowing it to be based upon such frivolous reasons as eye or hair colour as well as more sinister eugenic practices. It was, he said, inconceivable that Parliament could have contemplated the possibility of this happening.

Let it be accepted that a broad interpretation of the concept of suitability would include activities highly unlikely to be acceptable to majority public opinion. It could nevertheless be more sensible for Parliament to confine itself to a few prohibitions which could be clearly defined but otherwise to leave the authority to decide what should be acceptable. The fact that these decisions might raise difficult ethical questions is no objection. The membership of the authority and the proposals of the Warnock committee and the White Paper make it clear that it was intended to grapple with such issues.

In this case, as I have said, Maurice Kay J thought that suitable meant no more than suitable to produce a viable foetus but Lord Brennan, understandably unwilling to argue that Parliament might have outlawed PGD, said that it meant suitable to produce a healthy foetus, free of genetic defects. But this definition is itself not free from difficulty. What amounts to a genetic defect? Marie Stopes, an enthusiastic believer in eugenics, cut off relations with her son because she considered that the woman he chose to marry suffered from a genetic defect: she was short-sighted and had to wear spectacles. Surely it would be more sensible to concentrate on whether choice on such grounds was ethically acceptable rather than to argue over whether it counted as a genetic defect. The great advantage which Parliament would have seen in using broad concepts to define the remit of the authority is that it would avoid sterile arguments over questions of definition and focus attention upon the ethical issues.

Even in cases in which one could clearly say that the ground for selection was not a genetic defect, a total prohibition might exclude cases which many people would think ethically acceptable. Mr Pannick drew attention to the facts of Leeds Teaching Hospitals NHS Trust v A [2003] 1 FLR 1091. In the course of providing IVF treatment to a husband and wife, the hospital mixed up the sperm provided by the husband with that of another man. As a result, a woman gave birth to twins, the father of whom was a stranger. But they suffered from no genetic defects and Mr Pannick points out that if the muddle had been suspected before implantation of the embryo, Lord Brennan's construction of suitability would have prevented any tests to check the embryo's DNA. * * *

* * *

I would * * * accept Mr Pannick's argument and hold that both PGD and HLA typing could lawfully be authorised by the authority as activities to determine the suitability of the embryo for implantation within the meaning of paragraph 1(1)(d).

* * *

Another point on which the authority has shifted its position is the use of bone marrow rather than umbilical cord blood as a source of stem cells. Bone marrow may in some cases be more suitable but involves a far more intrusive operation upon the donor child than taking cord blood. The policy formulated by the authority in 2001 (under which the licence which authorised the treatment of Mrs Hashmi was granted) required a condition that "the intention" should be only to take cord blood. After a review in 2004, the authority decided to delete this condition. It was in practice unenforceable because once the embryo had been implanted and the child conceived, the case passed out of the jurisdiction of the authority. * * *

* * *

In my opinion, however, it is unnecessary to express any view about Lord Brennan's criticisms of the way the authority has exercised its jurisdiction. There has never been any suggestion that the authority acted unreasonably in granting a licence. The case has always been that it had no power to do so. In my opinion it did, and I would therefore dismiss the appeal. *Appeal dismissed.*

* * *

Notes

1. Lisa and Jack Nash's first child, Molly, was born with *Franconi Anemia*, a rare and life-threatening genetic bone marrow disorder. In an effort to save Molly's life, the Nash's used PGD to select an embryo that fit two criteria. First, the embryo could not carry *Franconi Anemia*. Second, the embryo needed to be an exact tissue match with Molly to facilitate a blood donation. Adam Nash was born on August 29, 2000 by Caesarean section. In October, blood from Adam's umbilical cord was successfully transplanted to his sister. Afterward, Adam was heralded "the world's first savior sibling." Horsey, "U.S. 'saviour siblings' spark debate", *BioNews London*, May 5, 2004. Given the ethical questions involved in birthing a child to save another child's life, the event was saturated with controversy, and even led to a novel by Jodi Picoult, *My Sister's Keeper*.

2. Susan Wolf et al. tackle the question of how to regulate savior siblings in their article *Using Preimplantation Genetic Diagnosis to Create Stem Cell Donor: Issues, Guidelines & Limits*, 31 Journal of Law, Medicine & Ethics 327 (2003). The authors propose a concrete set of requirements for families to meet prior to using PGD to select and birth a donor baby. The requirements function as protections for the donor-to-be from potentially exploitative parents. Some of the requirements include mandatory psychological evaluations of parents both before donor conception and before any tissue donation from the donor baby, independent physician requirements for the donor-to-be and the donor children, and a requirement that the donor baby not be placed at greater risk because of a donation.

However, much of the mooring for these requirements are attached to the future interests of the donor-to-be. The law does not typically favor interests of potential humans over those that are currently living. Given that at least some of these requirements are justified by placing a premium on a potential future being's interests, are these requirements untenable? Would requirements like these delay the process of birthing a donor baby such that many potential donee's would die? If so, do these regulations result in a net gain or a net loss to society? Can a donor-to-be baby actually be harmed by even the most exploitative donor practices if the counterfactual to such exploitation is non-existence?

* * *

As ART evolves, it breaks into distinct categories of usage that give rise to different kinds of conflicts and regulatory challenges for nations. The remainder of this section of the chapter is broken into five subsections, meant to cover the most important of these categories.

1. Anonymous Sperm (and Egg) Donation

Should sperm (and egg) donors be allowed to be anonymous or do donor-conceived children have a right to access the names and identifying information of their sperm (and egg) donor? The materials that follow compare and contrast the approach of different jurisdictions. One point of nomenclature is worth raising at the outset—

while the term "donor" is often used, perhaps "vendor" might be more appropriate, as in many cases those who provide sperm and egg are compensated for doing so.

Pratten v. British Columbia (Attorney General)

2011 BCSC 656 (2011)
Supreme Court of British Columbia

Olivia Pratten is a successful journalist in her late twenties. In 1981, she was conceived using sperm from an anonymous donor. Like many donor offspring, Ms. Pratten knows almost nothing about the man who provided one-half of her genetic makeup. She has long felt that a part of her identity is missing. She risks inadvertently forming a romantic relationship with a half-sibling. She worries her health, and the health of her future children, could be comprised by the lack of information. Ms. Pratten went to Dr. Gerald Korn, the Vancouver doctor who performed the insemination, seeking information about her donor. As of November 2002, when he retired, Dr. Korn was not obliged to keep records for a patient for more than six years from the last entry recorded, according to the rules of the College of Physicians and Surgeons of British Columbia (the "College") then in place. Dr. Korn says he no longer has any records relating to Ms. Pratten's donor, and that all records have been destroyed. Ms. Pratten says that the government of British Columbia (the "Province") permitted the destruction, thereby depriving her of basic personal information that is necessary for her physical and psychological health ... Ms. Pratten asserts that this situation is profoundly unfair and discriminatory, and contrary to the Canadian Charter of Rights and Freedoms. She has therefore brought a constitutional challenge to the absence of legislation that would ensure information about gamete donors is recorded and preserved for donor offspring, and could be made available to them. Ms. Pratten's challenge has two parts. The first part is a claim under s. 15 of the Charter alleging discrimination as between adoptees and donor offspring. Ms. Pratten says that the Province has discriminated against donor offspring by enacting underinclusive legislation—namely, the Adoption Act and Adoption Regulation—and by failing to enact any legislation to provide her and other donor offspring with the rights and opportunities to know their origins that most Canadians take for granted. The second part is a claim under s. 7 of the Charter that the liberty and security rights of donor offspring are violated by the Province's failure to enact legislation to protect fundamental aspects of their personal autonomy and health. Here, Ms. Pratten argues that s. 7 of the Charter guarantees a positive right to liberty and security of the person, and therefore guarantees a free-standing constitutional right to know one's origins and genetic heritage. Ms. Pratten seeks, on her own behalf and on behalf of all donor offspring, the right to the identity of the donor, irrespective of when donor offspring were conceived, and irrespective of whether the donor believed that he would remain anonymous.

* * *

Section 15(1) of the Charter provides:

> 15 (1) Every individual is equal before and under the law and has the right to the equal protection and equal benefit of the law without discrimination and, in particular, without discrimination based on race, national or ethnic origin, colour, religion, sex, age or mental or physical disability.

Section 15 is a constitutional guarantee against discrimination and a guarantee of substantively equal protection and benefit of the law. In other words, it is a guarantee of substantive—and not just formal—equality[.] ... The purpose of s. 15 is to ensure equality in the formulation and application of the law, and to promote a society in which all are secure in the knowledge that they are recognized at law as human beings equally deserving of concern, respect and consideration[.] The s. 15(1) guarantee is the broadest of all guarantees, and it applies to and supports all other rights guaranteed by the Charter[.]

The test for showing discrimination under s. 15(1) has two parts: (1) Does the law create a distinction based on an enumerated or analogous ground? (2) Does the distinction create a disadvantage by perpetuating prejudice or stereotyping?

* * *

I conclude that the appropriate comparison at step one of the analysis under s. 15(1) is between adoptees and donor offspring. I conclude further that excluding donor offspring from the benefits and protections of the Adoption Act and Adoption Regulation creates a distinction between adoptees and donor offspring, and that distinction is based on an analogous ground, namely manner of conception. Except for s. 4(1)(e) to (h) of the Regulation, the omission of donor offspring from the provisions of the Adoption Act and Adoption Regulation set out in Schedule "A" is discriminatory. I conclude that the omission of donor offspring from s. 4(1)(e) to (h) of the Regulation, which concern information about a child already born, is not discriminatory ... In context, the distinction made between adoptees and donor offspring creates a disadvantage to donor offspring by perpetuating stereotypes about donor offspring.

As a result, there is a violation of the rights of Ms. Pratten and donor offspring under s. 15(1) of the Charter.

* * *

Section 7 of the Charter provides that:

Everyone has the right to life, liberty and security of the person and the right not to be deprived thereof except in accordance with the principles of fundamental justice....

Ms. Pratten argues that s. 7 of the Charter should be interpreted as comprising two rights, one positive and one negative. She says that s. 7 guarantees a positive right to liberty and security of the person, and as such, she need not show that a breach of her rights violates any principles of fundamental justice. In the alternative, Ms. Pratten argues that she and other donor offspring are deprived of liberty and security of the person because the state (i.e., the Province), by virtue of its oversight of the bylaws of the College, continues to permit the destruction of records containing identity and health information about donors, and this breach of s. 7 violates the principles of fundamental justice.

The [Attorney General of British Columbia (AGBC)] submits that s. 7 does not impose upon the Province an obligation to legislate and that the issues raised by Ms. Pratten in her "positive rights" argument are not justiciable. Further, the AGBC argues that there is no constitutional right to know one's genetic heritage, and that, based on the evidence, there has been no deprivation of the right to liberty or security of the person in this case. The AGBC says that, even it could be argued that s. 7 creates positive rights to legislate, the unprecedented, novel approach advanced by Mr. Arvay on behalf of Ms. Pratten should not be adopted here. Finally, the AGBC submits that the legislation establishing the College and providing a mechanism for the College to make rules cannot constitute the requisite state action.

The potential implications of a free-standing constitutional right to know one's biological origins are uncertain and may be enormous. In my view, they go far beyond anything that might be required to address Ms. Pratten's complaints in this case, particularly given my conclusion that her rights under s. 15 have been breached. Courts in Ontario, [Canada] in the context of adoption legislation, have rejected the proposition that there is a constitutionally-protected right to "know one's past." In that light, I have concluded that this case will not be the "one day" when s. 7 is interpreted to impose on the state a positive duty to act and legislate where it has not done so.

* * *

I turn then to consider Ms. Pratten's "negative rights" argument: her assertion that she has been deprived of the right to liberty and security of the person, contrary to s. 7.

Ms. Pratten claims she and other donor offspring have been deprived of both liberty and security of the person. [The court reviews the College of Physicians rules and considers whether they establish state action].

... At best, the state action in this case amounts to no more than the tacit permission given through the approval given to the College's rules by the Lieutenant Governor in Council, and the theoretical failure of the minister to require the College's rules and bylaws to contain particular provisions concerning records relating to donors and donor offspring. However, the argument assumes a positive obligation on the Province to act in a particular way. In my view, this amounts to simply an alternative statement of Mr. Arvay's "positive rights" interpretation of s. 7, which I have rejected ... Since, in my view, there is insufficient state action to support Ms. Pratten's s. 7 claim, I do not need to address whether there has been a deprivation contrary to the principles of fundamental justice.

* * *

I have found a violation under s. 15 of the Charter of the equality rights of Ms. Pratten and donor offspring. Accordingly, the burden falls on the AGBC to prove that such a limit on their rights is a reasonable one that is demonstrably justifiable in a free and democratic society.

[The court applies a two-step test referred to as the *Oakes* test to determine whether the limitations on Ms. Pratten and the donor offspring are reasonable and demonstrably justifiable. If such limits are justifiable, British Columbia will win the case. The court concludes that AGBC failed the first prong of the test by failing "to establish that the objective of the omission of donor offspring was or is pressing and substantial."]

* * *

When a law produces an unconstitutional effect, the usual remedy lies under s. 52(1) of the Constitution Act, 1982, which provides that the law is of no force or effect to the extent that it is inconsistent with the Charter. Depending on the circumstances, a court may simply strike down the law; it may strike down and temporarily suspend the declaration of invalidity; or it may resort to the techniques of reading down or reading in[.]

... Here, I have determined that the omission of donor offspring from the provisions of the Adoption Act and Adoption Regulation set out in Schedule "A" (except for s. 4(1)(e) to (h) of the Regulation) is discriminatory and breaches s. 15 of the Charter. That is the extent of the inconsistency between the legislation and the Charter. The appropriate remedy is to grant a declaration that those provisions are of no force or effect.

A suspension of that declaration is essential. In this case, the problem is that the legislation is underinclusive, and an immediate declaration of invalidity harms those who rightly benefit from the legislative scheme, while extending nothing to those who have been excluded from it: see Schachter, at p. 719. The only issue is the length of the suspension.

I have concluded that the declaration should be suspended for a period of fifteen months from the date of this judgment.

... I decline to make the declaration sought by Ms. Pratten concerning the content of new legislation, as I do not believe it is either appropriate or necessary in the circumstances of this case. It will be the Province's responsibility to draft and enact legislation that complies with the Charter, in the light of these reasons.

Finally, with respect to the continuation of the injunction ordered by Madam Justice Gerow concerning Gamete Donor Records ... [I] pronounce a permanent injunction prohibiting the destruction, disposal, redaction or transfer out of British Columbia of Gamete Donor Records, as those are defined in Madam Justice Gerow's order pronounced December 18, 2008.

* * *

[Following this decision, the AGBC appealed to the British Columbia Court of Appeals (BCCA). The BCCA reversed, finding that Section 15(2) was in fact constitutional. Relying on a Supreme Court of Canada decision, *R v. Kapp*, 2 SCR 483 (2008), the court concluded that the BCSC had conducted its analysis in the wrong order. Before deciding whether the Adoption Act is in fact discriminatory, the court must find that the act does not fall into the category of an "ameliorative program" laid out in Section

15(2) of the Charter. The BCCA found that it did not need to reach the question of whether the Adoption Act was discriminatory because it qualified as an "ameliorative program" under Section 15(2). The BCCA then affirmed the BCSC's finding that Section 7 did not confer a positive right on Ms. Pratten to know her biological origins.]

* * *

By statute, in the UK, donor anonymity has been prohibited:

The Human Fertilisation and Embryology Authority (Disclosure of Donor Information) Regulations (2004)

Citation, commencement and interpretation

1.—(1) These Regulations may be cited as the Human Fertilisation and Embryology Authority (Disclosure of Donor Information) Regulations 2004 and come into force on 1st July 2004.

(2) In these Regulations—

"the Act" means the Human Fertilisation and Embryology Act 1990;

"applicant" means a person who has requested information under section 31(4) of the Act;

"donor" means the person who has provided the sperm, eggs or embryos that have been used for treatment services in consequence of which the applicant was, or may have been, born.

Information that the Authority is required to give

2.—(1) Subject to paragraph (4), the information contained in the register which the Authority is required to give an applicant by virtue of section 31(4)(a) of the Act is any information to which paragraph (2) or (3) applies.

(2) This paragraph applies to information as to—

(a) the sex, height, weight, ethnic group, eye colour, hair colour, skin colour, year of birth, country of birth and marital status of the donor;

(b) whether the donor was adopted;

(c) the ethnic group or groups of the donor's parents;

(d) the screening tests carried out on the donor and information on his personal and family medical history;

(e) where the donor has a child, the sex of that child and where the donor has children, the number of those children and the sex of each of them;

(f) the donor's religion, occupation, interests and skills and why the donor provided sperm, eggs or embryos;

(g) matters contained in any description of himself as a person which the donor has provided;

(h) any additional matter which the donor has provided with the intention that it be made available to an applicant; but does not include information which may identify the donor by itself or in combination with any other information which is in, or is likely to come into, the possession of the applicant.

(3) This paragraph applies to information from which the donor may be identified which he provides after 31st March 2005 to a person to whom a licence applies, being information as to—

(a) any matter specified in sub-paragraphs (a) to (h) of paragraph (2);

(b) the surname and each forename of the donor and, if different, the surname and each forename of the donor used for the registration of his birth;

(c) the date of birth of the donor and the town or district in which he was born;

(d) the appearance of the donor;

(e) the last known postal address of the donor.

(4) The information which the Authority is required to give to the applicant does not include any information which at the time of his request the applicant indicates that he does not wish to receive.

Notes

1. Gaia Bernstein notes that a number of international jurisdictions, including Sweden, Australia, the Netherlands, and the United Kingdom, have adopted prohibitions on gamete donor anonymity. She claims that these prohibitions have led to shortages in egg and sperm supply. As some U.S. states contemplate a shift to a similar open-identity system, Bernstein warns that such a shortage could lead to the use of legally disfavored practices, such as "traditional" surrogacy, creating further legal uncertainty for these lesser-used forms of ART. See Gaia Bernstein, *Unintended Consequences: Prohibitions On Gamete Donor Anonymity And The Fragile Practice Of Surrogacy*, 10 Ind. Health L. Rev. 291 (2013). The effect of these disclosure laws and whether their effects on donor recruitment are long term or short term remains contested. It may also be possible to counteract any negative effect on sperm donation when anonymity is prohibited by increasing compensation for sperm donors, at least in jurisdictions where it is permitted. I. Glenn Cohen, Travis Coan, Michelle Ottey, Christina Boyd, *Sperm Donor Anonymity and Compensation: An Experiment with American Sperm Donors*, 3 J. L. & Biosciences 468 (2016).

2. Naomi Cahn argues that offspring successfully conceived and born via sperm donation have no say in the contracts securing the donor's anonymity. Cahn further underscores the law's focus on the parent-child relationship in resolving these anonymity disputes, rather than an acknowledgement of the rights of donor-conceived adults. The result, as the argument goes, is that donor-conceived offspring's own identity interest is discounted in favor of the donor's anonymity, even when the autonomy of the donor may not be at stake. Naomi Cahn, *Do Tell! The Rights of Donor Conceived Offspring*, 42 Hofstra L. Rev. 1077 (2014). By contrast, Glenn Cohen challenges Cahn's argument that donor conceived offspring are harmed at all by pointing to a logical problem with the reasoning: regulations prohibiting anonymous sperm donation change

with whom individuals seeking donated sperm reproduce by shifting sperm donation from opportunists to altruistic donors. Even if the supply of gametes were to remain identical pre and post prohibition, the population who is donating changes, meaning "the regulation would 'protect' these particular children [who would be conceived under an anonymous regime] out of existence." See I. Glenn Cohen, *Sperm and Egg Donor Anonymity: Legal and Ethical Issues*, The Oxford Handbook of Reproductive Ethics (Leslie Francis ed., 2016) (citing Cohen, *Rethinking Sperm-Donor Anonymity: Of Changed Selves, Nonidentity, and One-Night Stands*, 100 Geo. L.J. 431, 436–37 (2012)).

3. For further reading on the disclosure/non-disclosure debate, see *Abolishing Anonymity: A Rights-Based Approach To Evaluating Anonymous Sperm Donation*, 20 UCLA Women's L.J. 111 (2013); *A Balancing Act? The Rights Of Donor-Conceived Children To Know Their Biological Origins*, 40 Ga. J. Int'l & Comp. L. 619 (2012); *Protecting A Man's Right To Choose: Why Mandatory Identity Release For Sperm Donors Is A Bad Idea*, 16 Mich. St. U. J. Med. & L. 429 (2012); *Anonymously Provided Sperm And The Constitution*, 23 Colum. J. Gender & L. 1 (2012).

2. Embryo Disposition Disputes

Individuals in intimate relationships (most commonly husbands and wives) invest heavily financially, emotionally, and medically, in attempt to produce children through in vitro fertilization. That process often produces significant numbers of embryos. Typically, only a small number of embryos are implanted in each attempt because higher order multiple births are associated with bad outcomes for mother and child. The remaining embryos are cryopreserved for future use. What happens when circumstances change for a couple seeking to reproduce together—most notable divorce and death? How should courts resolve contentious battles between one party who wants to reproduce with the cryopreserved embryos and one who is opposed to that happening? Does it matter whether the two parties put in place a prior agreement? The cases that follow consider show how different jurisdictions have handled these issues. One piece of nomenclature—some courts and scholars refer to the embryo at the stage of development where it is frozen as a "pre-embryo" while others simply refer to it as an "embryo," but nothing in the reasoning turns on that distinction.

J.B., Plaintiff-Respondent, v. M.B., Defendant-Appellant, and C.C., Defendant

783 A.2d 707 (2001)
Supreme Court of New Jersey

The opinion of the Court was delivered by PORITZ, C.J.

In this case, a divorced couple disagree about the disposition of seven preembryos that remain in storage after the couple, during their marriage, undertook in vitro fertilization procedures. We must first decide whether the husband and wife have entered into an enforceable contract that is now determinative on the disposition issue. If not, we must consider how such conflicts should be resolved by our courts.

Although the reproductive technology to accomplish in vitro fertilization has existed since the 1970s, there is little caselaw to guide us in our inquiry.

* * *

M.B. contends that he and J.B. entered into an agreement to use or donate the preembryos, and J.B. disputes the existence of any such agreement. As an initial matter, then, we must decide whether this case involves a contract for the disposition of the cryopreserved preembryos resulting from in vitro fertilization. We begin, therefore, with the consent form provided to J.B. and M.B. by the Cooper Center. That form states, among other things:

> The control and disposition of the embryos belongs to the Patient and her Partner. You will be asked to execute the attached legal statement regarding control and disposition of cryopreserved embryos.

The attachment, executed by J.B. and M.B., provides further detail in respect of the parties' "control and disposition":

> I, J.B. (patient) and M.B. (partner) agree that all control, direction, and ownership of our tissues will be relinquished to the IVF Program under the following circumstances:
>
> 1. A dissolution of our marriage by court order, unless the court specifies who takes control and direction of the tissues, or
>
> 2. In the event of death of both of the above named individuals, or unless provisions are made in a Will, or
>
> 3. When the patient is no longer capable of sustaining a normal pregnancy, however, the couple has the right to keep embryos maintained for up to two years before making a decision [regarding a] "host womb" or
>
> 4. At any time by our/my election which shall be in writing, or
>
> 5. When a patient fails to pay periodic embryo maintenance payment.

The consent form, and more importantly, the attachment, do not manifest a clear intent by J.B. and M.B. regarding disposition of the preembryos in the event of "[a] dissolution of [their] marriage." Although the attachment indicates that the preembryos "will be relinquished" to the clinic if the parties divorce, it carves out an exception that permits the parties to obtain a court order directing disposition of the preembryos. That reading is consistent with other provisions of the attachment allowing for disposition by a last will and testament "[i]n the event of death," or "by our/my election ... in writing." Clearly, the thrust of the document signed by J.B. and M.B. is that the Cooper Center obtains control over the preembryos unless the parties choose otherwise in a writing, or unless a court specifically directs otherwise in an order of divorce.

* * *

M.B. asserts, however, that he and J.B. jointly intended another disposition. Because there are no other writings that express the parties' intentions, M.B. asks the Court either to remand for an evidentiary hearing on that issue or to consider his certified statement. In his statement, he claims that before undergoing in vitro fertilization the couple engaged in extensive discussions in which they agreed to use the preembryos themselves or donate them to others. In opposition, J.B. has certified that the parties never discussed the disposition of unused preembryos and that there was no agreement on that issue.

We find no need for a remand to determine the parties' intentions at the time of the in vitro fertilization process. Assuming that it would be possible to enter into a valid agreement at that time, irrevocably deciding the disposition of preembryos in circumstances such as we have here, a formal, unambiguous memorialization of the parties' intentions would be required to confirm their joint determination. The parties do not contest the lack of such a writing. We hold, therefore, that J.B. and M.B. never entered into a separate binding contract providing for the disposition of the cryopreserved preembryos now in the possession of the Cooper Center.

* * *

In essence, J.B. and M.B. have agreed only that on their divorce the decision in respect of control, and therefore disposition, of their cryopreserved preembryos will be directed by the court ... Without guidance from the Legislature, we must consider a means by which courts can engage in a principled review of the issues presented in such cases in order to achieve a just result. Because the claims before us derive, in part, from concepts found in the Federal Constitution and the Constitution of this State, we begin with those concepts.

Both parties and the ACLU Amici invoke the right to privacy in support of their respective positions. More specifically, they claim procreational autonomy as a fundamental attribute of the privacy rights guaranteed by both the Federal and New Jersey Constitutions. Their arguments are based on various opinions of the United States Supreme Court that discuss the right to be free from governmental interference with procreational decisions. See *Eisenstadt v. Baird,* 405 *U.S.* 438, 453 (1972); *Griswold v. Connecticut,* 381 *U.S.* 479, 485–86 (1965); *Skinner v. Oklahoma,* 316 *U.S.* 535, 541 (1942).

In *Skinner v. Oklahoma, supra,* the Court spoke of that most "basic liberty[ ]" when rejecting, on equal protection grounds, an Oklahoma statute that required sterilization of certain repeat criminal offenders. 316 U.S. at 541. "Marriage and procreation," said Justice Douglas, "are fundamental to the very existence and survival of the race." *Ibid.* Later, in *Griswold, supra,* and *Eisenstadt, supra,* the Court invalidated statutes restricting use of and access to contraceptives by both married and unmarried couples, stating in *Griswold* that prohibitions on the use of contraceptives unconstitutionally infringe on the sanctity and privacy of the marital relationship, 381 *U.S.* at 485–86, and, in *Eisenstadt,* that "[i]f the right of privacy means anything, it is the right of the individual, married or single, to be free from unwarranted governmental intrusion into matters so fundamentally affecting a person as the decision whether to bear or beget a child," 405 U.S. at 453.

This Court also has recognized the fundamental nature of procreational rights. In *In re Baby M,* we considered a custody dispute between a father and a surrogate mother. 537 *A.*2d 1227 (1988). Although the case involved the enforceability of a surrogacy contract, the father asserted that his right to procreate supported his claim for custody of Baby M. We held that the right to procreate was not implicated by the custody battle, which dealt with parental rights after birth. We observed, however, that "the rights of personal intimacy, of marriage, of sex, of family, of procreation ... are fundamental rights protected by both the federal and state Constitutions." *Id.* at 1227....

Those decisions provide a framework within which disputes over the disposition of preembryos can be resolved. In *Davis [v. Davis]*, for example, a divorced couple could not agree on the disposition of their unused, cryopreserved preembryos. 842 *S.W.*2d at 589. The Tennessee Supreme Court balanced the right to procreate of the party seeking to donate the preembryos (the wife), against the right not to procreate of the party seeking destruction of the preembryos (the husband). *Id.* at 603. The court concluded that the husband's right would be significantly affected by unwanted parenthood "with all of its possible financial and psychological consequences." *Ibid.* In his case, that burden was the greater because, as a child, he had been separated from his parents after they divorced and his mother suffered a nervous breakdown. *Id.* at 603–04. Because of his personal experiences, the husband was "vehemently opposed to fathering a child that would not live with both parents." *Id.* at 604.

Against that interest, the court weighed the wife's "burden of knowing that the lengthy IVF procedures she underwent were futile, and that the preembryos to which she contributed genetic material would never become children." *Ibid.* Although that burden was not insignificant, the court found that it did not outweigh the father's interest in avoiding procreation. *Ibid.* The court held that the scales "[o]rdinarily" would tip in favor of the right not to procreate if the opposing party could become a parent through other reasonable means. *Ibid.*

* * *

We agree with the Tennessee Supreme Court that "[o]rdinarily, the party wishing to avoid procreation should prevail." *Ibid.* Here, the Appellate Division succinctly described the "apparent" conflict between J.B. and M.B.:

> In the present case, the wife's right not to become a parent seemingly conflicts with the husband's right to procreate. The conflict, however, is more apparent than real. Recognition and enforcement of the wife's right would not seriously impair the husband's right to procreate. Though his right to procreate [717] using the wife's egg would be terminated, he retains the capacity to father children.

In other words, M.B.'s right to procreate is not lost if he is denied an opportunity to use or donate the preembryos. M.B. is already a father and is able to become a father to additional children, whether through natural procreation or further in vitro fertilization. In contrast, J.B.'s right not to procreate may be lost through attempted use or through donation of the preembryos. Implantation, if successful, would result in the birth of her biological child and could have life-long emotional and psychological repercussions. Her fundamental right not to procreate is irrevocably extinguished if a surrogate mother bears J.B.'s child. We will not force J.B. to become a biological parent against her will.

* * *

[The] laws of New Jersey also evince a policy against enforcing private contracts to enter into or terminate familial relationships. New Jersey has, by statute, abolished the cause of action for breach of contract to marry. Private placement adoptions are disfavored, and may be approved over the objection of a parent only if that parent has failed or is unable to perform "the regular and expected parental functions of care and support of the child."

That public policy also led this Court to conclude in *Baby M*, *supra*, that a surrogacy contract was unenforceable. We held that public policy prohibited a binding agreement to require a surrogate, there the biological mother, to surrender her parental rights.... In an action by the father to enforce the surrogacy contract, we held that the contract conflicted with "(1) laws prohibiting the use of money in connection with adoptions; (2) laws requiring proof of parental unfitness or abandonment before termination of parental rights is ordered or an adoption is granted; and (3) laws that make surrender of custody and consent to adoption revocable in private placement adoptions." 537 A.2d 1227. Our decision was consistent with the policy expressed earlier in [earlier cases] that consent to terminate parental rights was revocable in all but statutorily approved circumstances.

Enforcement of a contract that would allow the implantation of preembryos at some future date in a case where one party has reconsidered his or her earlier acquiescence raises similar issues. If implantation is successful, that party will have been forced to become a biological parent against his or her will. We note disagreement on the issue both among legal commentators and in the limited caselaw on the subject. *Kass*, *supra*, held that "[a]greements between progenitors, or gamete donors, regarding disposition of their prezygotes should generally be presumed valid and binding, and enforced in a dispute between them...." 696 N.E.2d at 180. The New York court emphasized that such agreements would "avoid costly litigation," "minimize misunderstandings and maximize procreative liberty by reserving to the progenitors the authority to make what is in the first instance a quintessentially personal private decision." *Ibid.*

We recognize that persuasive reasons exist for enforcing preembryo disposition agreements. Both the *Kass* and *Davis* decisions pointed out the benefits of enforcing agreements between the parties. See *Kass*, *supra*, 696 N.E.2d at 179 (noting "need for clear, consistent principles to guide parties in protecting their interests and resolving their disputes"); *Davis*, *supra*, 842 S.W.2d at 597 (discussing benefit of guidance to parties undertaking in vitro fertilization procedures). We also recognize that in vitro fertilization is in widespread use, and that there is a need for agreements between the participants and the clinics that perform the procedure. We believe that the better rule, and the one we adopt, is to enforce agreements entered into at the time in vitro fertilization is begun, subject to the right of either party to change his or her mind about disposition up to the point of use or destruction of any stored preembryos.

The public policy concerns that underlie limitations on contracts involving family relationships are protected by permitting either party to object at a later date to provisions specifying a disposition of preembryos that that party no longer accepts. Moreover, despite the conditional nature of the disposition provisions, in the large majority of cases the agreements will control, permitting fertility clinics and other like facilities to rely on their terms. Only when a party affirmatively notifies a clinic in writing of a change in intention should the disposition issue be reopened. Principles of fairness dictate that agreements provided by a clinic should be written in plain language, and that a qualified clinic representative should review the terms with the parties prior to execution. Agreements should not be signed in blank ... or in a manner suggesting that the parties have not given due consideration to the disposition question. Those and other reasonable safeguards should serve to limit later disputes.

Finally, if there is disagreement as to disposition because one party has reconsidered his or her earlier decision, the interests of both parties must be evaluated. Because ordinarily the party choosing not to become a biological parent will prevail, we do not anticipate increased litigation as a result of our decision. In this case, after having considered that M.B. is a father and is capable of fathering additional children, we have affirmed J.B.'s right to prevent implantation of the preembryos. We express no opinion in respect of a case in which a party who has become infertile seeks use of stored preembryos against the wishes of his or her partner, noting only that the possibility of adoption also may be a consideration, among others, in the court's assessment.

Under the judgment of the Appellate Division, the seven remaining preembryos are to be destroyed.

VERNIERO, J., concurring.

I join in the disposition of this case and in all but one aspect of the Court's opinion. I do not agree with the Court's suggestion, in *dicta,*that the right to procreate may depend on adoption as a consideration.

I also write to express my view that the same principles that compel the outcome in this case would permit an infertile party to assert his or her right to use a preembryo against the objections of the other party, if such use were the only means of procreation. In that instance, the balance arguably would weigh in favor of the infertile party absent countervailing factors of greater weight. I do not decide that profound question today, and the Court should not decide it or suggest a result, because it is absent from this case.

* * *

Evans v. UK

Application no. 6339/05, Judgment 10 April 2007
The European Court of Human Rights

On 12 July 2000, the applicant and her partner, J. (born in November 1976), commenced treatment at the Bath Assisted Conception Clinic ("the clinic"). The applicant had been referred for treatment at the clinic five years earlier, when she was married, but had not pursued it because of the breakdown of her marriage.

On 10 October 2001, the applicant and J. were informed, during an appointment at the clinic, that preliminary tests had revealed that the applicant had serious pre-cancerous tumours in both ovaries, and that her ovaries would have to be removed. They were told that because the tumours were growing slowly it would be possible first to extract some eggs for in vitro fertilisation ("IVF"), but that this would have to be done quickly.

The consultation of 10 October 2001 lasted approximately an hour in total. A nurse explained that the applicant and J. would each have to sign a form consenting to the IVF treatment and that, in accordance with the provisions of the Human Fertilisation and Embryology Act 1990 ("the 1990 Act"), it would be possible for either to withdraw his or her consent at any time before the embryos were implanted in the applicant's uterus (see paragraph 37 below). The applicant asked the nurse whether it would be possible to freeze her unfertilised eggs, but was informed that this procedure, which had a much lower chance of success, was not performed at the clinic. At that point, J. reassured the applicant that they were not going to split up, that she did not need to consider the freezing of her eggs, that she should not be negative and that he wanted to be the father of her child.

Thereafter, the couple entered into the necessary consents, by signing the forms required by the 1990 Act (see paragraph 37 below). Immediately beneath the title to the form appeared the following words:

> "NB—do not sign this form unless you have received information about these matters and have been offered counselling. You may vary the terms of this consent at any time except in relation to sperm or embryos which have already been used. Please insert numbers or tick boxes as appropriate."

J. ticked the boxes which recorded his consent to use his sperm to fertilise the applicant's eggs in vitro and the use of the embryos thus created for the treatment of himself and the applicant together. He further ticked the box headed "Storage", opting for the storage of embryos developed in vitro from his sperm for the maximum period of ten years and also opted for sperm and embryos to continue in storage should he die or become mentally incapacitated within that period. The applicant signed a form which, while referring to eggs rather than sperm, essentially replicated that signed by J. Like J., she ticked the boxes providing for the treatment of herself and for the treatment "of myself with a named partner."

On 12 November 2001, the couple attended the clinic and eleven eggs were harvested and fertilised. Six embryos were created and consigned to storage. On 26 November, the applicant underwent an operation to remove her ovaries. She was told that she should wait two years before attempting to implant any of the embryos in her uterus.

In May 2002 the relationship broke down. The future of the embryos was discussed between the parties. On 4 July 2002, J. wrote to the clinic to notify it of the separation and to state that the embryos should be destroyed.

The clinic notified the applicant of J.'s withdrawal of consent to further use of the embryos and informed her that it was now under a legal obligation to destroy them, pursuant to paragraph 8(2) of Schedule 3 to the 1990 Act (see paragraph 37 below). The applicant commenced proceedings in the High Court, seeking an injunction requiring J. to restore his consent to the use and storage of the embryos and a declaration, inter alia, that he had not varied and could not vary his consent of 10 October 2001. Additionally she sought a declaration of incompatibility under the Human Rights Act 1998 to the effect that section 12 of, and Schedule 3 to, the 1990 Act breached her rights under Articles 8, 12 and 14 of the Convention. She also pleaded that the embryos were entitled to protection under Articles 2 and 8. Interim orders were made requiring the clinic to preserve the embryos until the end of the proceedings. [The proceedings then wound their way up the chain to the European Court of Human Rights].

* * *

In her original application and in her observations before the Chamber, the applicant complained that the provisions of English law requiring the embryos to be destroyed once J. withdrew his consent to their continued storage violated the embryos' right to life, contrary to Article 2 of the Convention, which reads as follows:

> "1. Everyone's right to life shall be protected by law...."

In its judgment of 7 March 2006, the Chamber observed that in Vo v. France [GC], no. 53924/00, § 82, ECHR 2004-VIII, the Grand Chamber had held that, in the absence of any European consensus on the scientific and legal definition of the beginning of life, the issue of when the right to life begins comes within the margin of appreciation which the Court generally considers that States should enjoy in this sphere. Under English law, as was made clear by the domestic courts in the present applicant's case, an embryo does not have independent rights or interests and cannot claim—or have claimed on its behalf—a right to life under Article 2. There had not, accordingly, been a violation of that provision....

The Grand Chamber, for the reasons given by the Chamber, finds that the embryos created by the applicant and J. do not have a right to life within the meaning of Article 2 of the Convention, and that there has not, therefore, been a violation of that provision.

* * *

Article 8 of the Convention, which states:

"1. Everyone has the right to respect for his private and family life ...

2. There shall be no interference by a public authority with the exercise of this right except such as is in accordance with the law and is necessary in a democratic society in the interests of national security, public safety or the economic well-being of the country, for the prevention of disorder or crime, for the protection of health or morals, or for the protection of the rights and freedoms of others." ...

It is not disputed between the parties that Article 8 is applicable and that the case concerns the applicant's right to respect for her private life. The Grand Chamber agrees with the Chamber that "private life", which is a broad term encompassing, *inter alia*, aspects of an individual's physical and social identity including the right to personal autonomy, personal development and to establish and develop relationships with other human beings and the outside world (see *Pretty* [found at page 376 of this book]), incorporates the right to respect for both the decisions to become and not to become a parent.

It must be noted, however, that the applicant does not complain that she is in any way prevented from becoming a mother in a social, legal, or even physical sense, since there is no rule of domestic law or practice to stop her from adopting a child or even giving birth to a child originally created *in vitro* from donated gametes. The applicant's complaint is, more precisely, that the consent provisions of the 1990 Act prevent her from using the embryos she and J. created together, and thus, given her particular circumstances, from ever having a child to whom she is genetically related. The Grand Chamber considers that this more limited issue, concerning the right to respect for the decision to become a parent in the genetic sense, also falls within the scope of Article 8.

The dilemma central to the present case is that it involves a conflict between the Article 8 rights of two private individuals: the applicant and J. Moreover, each person's interest is entirely irreconcilable with the other's, since if the applicant is permitted to use the embryos, J. will be forced to become a father, whereas if J.'s refusal or withdrawal of consent is upheld the applicant will be denied the opportunity of becoming a genetic parent. In the difficult circumstances of this case, whatever solution the national authorities might adopt would result in the interests of one or the other parties to the IVF treatment being wholly frustrated....

A number of factors must be taken into account when determining the breadth of the margin of appreciation to be enjoyed by the State in any case under Article 8. Where a particularly important facet of an individual's existence or identity is at stake, the margin allowed to the State will be restricted. Where, however, there is no consensus within the member States of the Council of Europe, either as to the relative importance of the interest at stake or as to the best means of protecting it, particularly where the case raises sensitive moral or ethical issues, the margin will be wider. There will also usually be a wide margin if the State is required to strike a balance between competing private and public interests or Convention rights....

In addition, while the Court is mindful of the applicant's submission to treat the comparative law data with caution, it is at least clear, and the applicant does not contend otherwise, that there is no uniform European approach in this field. Certain States have enacted primary or secondary legislation to control the use of IVF treatment, whereas in others, this is a matter left to medical practice and guidelines. While the United Kingdom is not alone in permitting storage of embryos and in providing both gamete providers with the power freely and effectively to withdraw consent up until the moment of implantation, different rules and practices are applied elsewhere in Europe. It cannot be said that there is any consensus as to the stage in IVF treatment when the gamete providers' consent becomes irrevocable …

As regards to the balance struck between the conflicting Article 8 rights of the parties to the IVF treatment, the Grand Chamber, in common with every other court which has examined this case, has great sympathy for the applicant, who clearly desires a genetically related child above all else. However, given the above considerations, including the lack of any European consensus on this point [ ], it does not consider that the applicant's right to respect for the decision to become a parent in the genetic sense should be accorded greater weight than J.'s right to respect for his decision not to have a genetically related child with her.

* * *

In her application and in the proceedings before the Chamber, the applicant complained of discrimination contrary to Article 14 of the Convention taken in conjunction with Article 8, reasoning that a woman who was able to conceive without assistance was subject to no control or influence over how the embryos developed from the moment of fertilisation, whereas a woman such as herself who could conceive only with IVF was, under the 1990 Act, subject to the will of the sperm donor.

In her observations to the Grand Chamber, however, the applicant submitted that her complaints under Articles 8 and 14 were inextricably linked, and that if the Court found that the impugned provision of domestic law was proportionate under Article 8, it should also find the scheme reasonably and objectively justified under Article 14.

The Grand Chamber agrees with the Chamber and the parties that it is not required to decide in the present case whether the applicant could properly complain of a difference of treatment as compared to another woman in an analogous position, because the reasons given for finding that there was no violation of Article 8 also afford a reasonable and objective justification under Article 14 (see, mutatis mutandis, Pretty, cited above, § 89).

Consequently, there has been no violation of Article 14 of the Convention.

Notes

1. Other pre-embryo disposition dispute cases use a "contractual approach" to resolving the matter rather than looking to the contemporaneous mutual consent of the

parties, as in the two preceding cases. For instance, the majority opinion of Justice Tal in the Israeli case *Nahmani v. Nahmani* resolved a disposition dispute by relying on contract principles. Justice Tal's opinion argued that the husband was estopped from opposing the implantation of an embryo fertilized by his sperm in his ex-wife because she reasonably relied on his consent when the embryo was fertilized, creating a valid case of promissory estoppel. In the U.S. case *Kass v. Kass*, the parties agreed in a consent form prior to retrieving and freezing embryos that, if the couple could not agree on using stored, frozen embryos, then those embryos would be donated to a research program. The court ultimately upheld and enforced this consent form as a valid and binding contract expressing the will of the parties at the time of embryo storage.

2. Carl Coleman argues in his article, *Procreative Liberty and Contemporaneous Choice: An Inalienable Rights Approach to Frozen Embryo Disputes*, 84 Minn. L. Rev. 55 (1999), that the contractual approach leaves much to be desired in settling embryo disposition disputes. Instead, Coleman advocates for contemporaneous mutual consent as an inalienable right and one that should govern the pre-embryo distribution disputes from wall-to-wall. The bedrock of his principle stems from the idea that, if one party objects to the use of a frozen embryo, then the use of that embryo will always be a higher burden than prohibiting the party that wants to implant the frozen embryo from doing so. Thus, the contemporaneous mutual consent approach seeks the highest aggregate well-being of all parties by avoiding the inevitable winner/loser outcome that emerges when a court enforces a contract over the objection of a previously-consenting party.

3. Glenn Cohen confronts the question of whether the law should protect a party's interest in not being a genetic parent at all. Cohen breaks down parenthood rights into three categories: gestational, legal, and genetic. He argues that the normative mooring for the right not to be a genetic parent is attached to a type of harm called "attributional parenthood" where a genetic parent is associated with a genetic son, despite having no parent-child relationship. Given this harm, he claims that the right not to be a genetic parent should be recognized by courts taking a contractual approach, though he also asserts that the right should be waivable at the contracting stage. I. Glenn Cohen, *The Right Not to be a Genetic Parent?*, 81 S. Cal. L. Rev. 1115 (2008).

3. Surrogacy

Surrogacy comes in two forms. In "traditional" or "full," there is typically an intended father who plans to rear the child. The father often though not always has a marital or romantic partner, heterosexual or gay. The intended father provides sperm that is used to inseminate a surrogate. The surrogate is both the genetic and gestational mother of the child, but the point of the arrangement is that the genetic father (and if appropriate his partner) will rear the child. In "gestational" surrogacy, there is typically an intended mother and father. They provide sperm and egg respectively, the egg is fertilized with the sperm through in vitro fertilization, and then the embryo is placed in the gestational surrogate to carry to term. The point of the arrangement is for the intended parents to carry the child. Typically, surrogacy arrangements are "commercial," in the sense that the surrogate is paid to gestate the child, though there are also instances of "altruistic" surrogacy. Most jurisdictions are much more favorable to gestational than traditional surrogacy, and gestational surrogacy is by far the most common. Countries take radically different approaches to surrogacy, which leads to significant amounts of fertility tourism.

Katherine Voskoboynik, *Clipping the Stork's Wings: Commercial Surrogacy Regulation and Its Impact on Fertility Tourism*

26 Ind. Int'l & Comp. L. Rev. 336, 341–352 (2016)

1. The United States of America

As nations that have legalized commercial surrogacy begin to impose legislative and/or cost-prohibitive restrictions, the link between surrogacy and fertility tourism becomes stronger than ever. The United States perceives surrogacy as a state law matter. Some states, such as California and Illinois, are very favorable toward commercial surrogacy. Meanwhile, states such as New York and Michigan not only ban the practice, but also effectuate civil and criminal sanctions upon those who participate in surrogacy arrangements. For example, the District of Columbia and New York hold parties who enter into a commercial surrogacy contract civilly liable. Michigan imposes penalties such as a fine of up to $10,000 and/or one year in prison for surrogates in a commercial surrogacy arrangement. Other states, such as Arizona, Indiana, North Dakota, and Louisiana prohibit both commercial and altruistic surrogacy. Rather than impose sanctions, they simply consider surrogacy contracts unenforceable.

Meanwhile, certain states "implicitly permit altruistic surrogacy" because their legislation explicitly prohibits only commercial surrogacy. For example, Washington and Louisiana consider commercial surrogacy arrangements as void against public policy, while Kentucky and Nebraska explicitly prohibit commercial surrogacy. Arkansas, Florida, Nevada, New Hampshire, New Mexico, and Virginia permit altruistic surrogacy arrangements that are heavily regulated. For example, both the New Hampshire and Florida statutes dictate that the intended parents must demonstrate a medical need for surrogacy. Regulations in other states vary in strictness. New Hampshire requires the intended parents, the surrogate, and her husband to attend counseling prior to entering into a surrogacy arrangement. Florida does not have such a requirement, but the statute mandates specific qualifications such as the marital status of the parties (the intended parents must be married).

Illinois, Texas, and Utah explicitly permit commercial surrogacy, and California implicitly allows commercial surrogacy. Texas and Utah's statutes recognize "reasonable remuneration paid to the surrogate." However, these statutes impose heavy restrictions on commercial surrogacy. For example, the Illinois Gestational Surrogacy Act of 1995 limits recognition of commercial surrogacy arrangements to gestational surrogacy. The statute also necessitates a demonstration of medical need, typically procured through a doctor's affidavit, and requires that intended parents and the gestational surrogate submit to a psychological evaluation. While California is legislatively silent on surrogacy, its case law indicates that California courts will enforce surrogacy agreements and establish legal parentage in the intended parents rather than the surrogate. States that expressly and implicitly permit commercial surrogacy are more popular destinations.

Surrogacy legislation has recently become a heavily debated issue in state legislatures. New Hampshire followed the example of pro-surrogacy states such as Illinois and California and, in 2014, enacted a law allowing commercial surrogacy. As states move towards legalizing surrogacy, more avenues become open to potential intended parents who can afford the cost of surrogacy in the United States. The number of babies born through surrogacy in the United States has tripled over the last ten years. In 2014, over two thousand babies were born through gestational surrogacy in the United States.

2. India

Individuals unable to pursue surrogacy in the United States have often utilized India as a cheaper alternative. Surrogacy became legal in India in 2002, and the industry has grown to be the "world's top destination for commercial surrogacy." The approximately three thousand clinics that provide surrogacy services to international clients in India generate more than $400 million per year, and the number of clinics is increasing yearly by twenty-five percent. Indian surrogates give birth to approximately two thousand "foreign babies each year." India's dominance is attributed to its affordability, high-quality private healthcare, English-speaking clinics, extensive number of women willing to participate in surrogacy, a "business climate that encourages the outsourcing of Indian labor," and the legality of commercial surrogacy. However, in 2013, India enacted a law restricting surrogacy only to heterosexual couples who have been married for a minimum of two years, and who come from countries where surrogacy is legal. This legislation bans single, same-sex, and unmarried individuals from pursuing surrogacy in India, as well as those "circumventing their home laws to have children."

3. Ukraine

Ukraine is "quickly gaining traction" as an international surrogacy destination due to its liberal surrogacy laws. In Ukraine, only infertile, legally married heterosexual couples are permitted to pursue surrogacy, but the laws are otherwise surrogacy-friendly. Ukraine legally recognizes commercial surrogacy and is protective of intended parents' rights by granting them legal parentage upon the notarized written consent of the surrogate. Ukraine is home to numerous surrogacy clinics that "advertise the ... favorable policies toward intended parents as selling points." Statistics for the annual number of surrogacy arrangements are difficult to obtain, as no regulatory bodies exist to monitor surrogacy in Ukraine. A news source recently stated that in 2011, one hundred and twenty successful surrogacy pregnancies occurred in Ukraine. However, that number is believed to be much higher because surrogacy agencies are not required to report statistics to a governing body. Roughly half of the surrogacy arrangements in Ukraine involve international intended parents. In Ukraine, foreign intended parents spend approximately $30,000 to $45,000, with the surrogate receiving $10,000 to $15,000. Ukraine is currently experiencing a "surplus of women who desire to be surrogates" and the costs of surrogates are expected to decrease as a result.

4. Russia

India's strict restrictions and Ukraine's unfavorable treatment of unmarried persons and same-sex couples are popularizing other surrogacy destinations, such as Russia, Mexico, and Thailand. In Russia, gestational surrogacy is officially only legal for married heterosexual couples and single women. However, the law's position on same-sex couples, unmarried couples, and single persons "is not clearly spelled out," and as a result, "surrogacy is largely unrestricted." Therefore, unlike India and Ukraine, Russia does not expressly ban same-sex couples and single persons from pursuing surrogacy. Russian law does not acknowledge samesex marriage, and lesbian couples are treated as single women for purposes of surrogacy. Similar to Ukraine, Russia also protects intended parents' rights by granting legal parentage upon notarized written consent of the surrogate. With the ongoing restrictions in India and Ukraine, "Russia is one such country that commentators have suggested foreign intended parents may travel to now because it is one of the countries where commercial surrogacy is legal and the cost appears to be relatively low."

5. Mexico

Mexico is another destination where international clients are "[flock]ing" to evade other countries' restrictive laws. Mexico does not address surrogacy, except in the state of Tabasco. Tabasco's civil code legalized gestational surrogacy in 1998. However, international surrogacy arrangements are considered relatively new in Tabasco, as foreign intended parents have only recently begun favoring countries such as Russia, Mexico, and Thailand over the United States, Ukraine, and India. Agencies were first based in Cancun, which is "already an established cent[er] of medical tourism." Many surrogacy programs, agencies, and clinics now exist throughout Mexico, where IVF treatment is permitted anywhere as long as the babies are born in Tabasco. The law allows payment for surrogates' medical and living expenses, but contains an "altruism requirement." Nevertheless, commercial surrogacy persists, as this requirement is "an easily circumvented legal nuance." Agencies do not mention surrogate compensation on their websites or marketing materials, but calling the earnings "economic assistance" renders the payments permissible.

6. Thailand

Until recently, Thailand was another desirable destination for foreign clients because no laws against surrogacy existed. Therefore, surrogacy was de facto legal. Thailand's Medical Council banned commercial surrogacy in 1997, imposing restrictions such as "no compensation may be made" to the woman carrying the baby and that the surrogate must be "relative by blood of either party of the couple." Nonetheless, Thailand experienced a boom of surrogacy-related tourism due to its large IVF market and restrictive legislation in other countries where commercial surrogacy is legal. Over the past few years, the use of surrogacy in Thailand has increased by fifty-four percent. Compared to the United States, surrogacy is also considerably more affordable, costing between $38,000 and $50,000.

However, a series of surrogacy-related scandals erupted in the summer of 2014, such as an Australian couple's alleged abandonment of a baby with Down syndrome while taking home his healthy twin sister. As a result of the industry's rapid growth and the outrage created by the scandals, a draft bill banning and criminalizing commercial surrogacy passed its first reading with overwhelming support in November 2014. Thailand's Parliament passed the bill in February 2015, which prevents foreigners from pursuing surrogacy in Thailand, forbids the "recei[pt] of any assets or benefits" stemming from a surrogacy arrangement[,] and seeks to punish violators with up to ten years in prison. The future of ongoing commercial surrogacy arrangements in Thailand is presently unclear, as the government seeking to pass the bill is composed of military junta members that took power through a coup d'état in May 2014. Additionally, Dr. Somsak Lolekha, a member of the Thai Medical Council, stated in a recent interview with the British Broadcasting Corporation that "[w]e have no law enforcement ... [j]ust like drinking and driving. We have the law. But they never enforce it ... [t]hat is a weak point of Thailand." According to a representative of Families Through Surrogacy in Australia, "[h]undreds of intended parents from Australia, or the US and European countries currently have pregnancies underway with Thai surrogates." Foreign intended parents with present surrogacy arrangements in Thailand may now be caught in limbo.

* * *

In re Baby M

109 N.J. 396 (1988)

The Supreme Court of New Jersey

The opinion of the Court was delivered by WILENTZ, C.J.

In this matter, the Court is asked to determine the validity of a contract that purports to provide a new way of bringing children into a family. For a fee of $10,000, a woman agrees to be artificially inseminated with the semen of another woman's husband; she is to conceive a child, carry it to term, and after its birth surrender it to the natural father and his wife. The intent of the contract is that the child's natural mother will thereafter be forever separated from her child. The wife is to adopt the child, and she and the natural father are to be regarded as its parents for all purposes. The contract providing for this is called a "surrogacy contract," the natural mother inappropriately called the "surrogate mother."

We invalidate the surrogacy contract because it conflicts with the law and public policy of this State. While we recognize the depth of the yearning of infertile couples to have their own children, we find the payment of money to a "surrogate" mother illegal, perhaps criminal, and potentially degrading to women. Although in this case we grant custody to the natural father, the evidence having clearly proved such custody to be in the best interests of the infant, we void both the termination of the surrogate mother's parental rights and the adoption of the child by the wife/stepparent. We thus restore the "surrogate" as the mother of the child.

We find no offense to our present laws where a woman voluntarily and without payment agrees to act as a "surrogate" mother, provided that she is not subject to a binding agreement to surrender her child. Moreover, our holding today does not preclude the Legislature from altering the current statutory scheme, within constitutional limits, so as to permit surrogacy contracts. Under current law, however, the surrogacy agreement before us is illegal and invalid.

* * *

Notes

1. *Baby M*, perhaps the most famous U.S. surrogacy case, concerned traditional surrogacy. Some U.S. states are more permissive in enforcing surrogacy agreements when they are gestational not traditional surrogacy arrangements. In California, for example, the lead case is *Johnson v. Calvert*, 851 P.2d 776 (Cal. 1993) which addressed the question: [i]f a gestational surrogate, pursuant to a surrogacy agreement, gives birth to the genetic child of a couple and wants to retain the child contrary to the terms of the agreement, who is the child's natural mother? The California court ultimately determined that the husband and wife who provided the fertilized embryo were the child's natural parents, not the gestational surrogate. The court reasoned that the interest of the genetic mother "tied" with the interest of the gestational mother, and the intent of the parties, expressed through the surrogacy agreement, broke the tie.

2. Thailand has recently implemented a complete ban on commercial surrogacy, marking a dramatic shift from a no-regulation policy. The shift came, in part, thanks to a few scandals where foreign nationals exploited Thai surrogates. However, one author argues that this ban will only drive commercial surrogacy underground, marginalizing Thai surrogates even further. Instead, the author argues that Thailand should adopt Israel's approach to regulating surrogacy, striking a balance between a laissez-faire environment and a complete ban. See Zimmerman, *Thailand's Ban on Commercial Surrogacy: Why Thailand Should Regulate, Not Attempt to Eradicate*, 41 Brook. J. Int'l L. 917 (2016).

3. In 1991, the Cour de Cassation, France's highest civil court, ruled than an *altruistic* surrogacy agreement was contrary to the nation's public policy, effectively banning any surrogacy arrangement. Cour de cassation 6 April 2011 n° 09-66.486 and 10-19.053 and 09-17.73. The court's decision was codified by the Bioethics Act of 1994. Specifically, the law prohibits granting French citizenship to children born abroad via surrogacy arrangements involving French citizens as the intended parents, and also prohibited either intended parent from obtaining parental rights. In subsequent years, pushed in part by the decisions of the European Court of Human Rights, the French approach has become more permissive. As Richard Storrow recently summarized the current state of play:

> As of July of 2017, the Cour de Cassation has issued a series of decisions allowing the recording of birth certificates, at least insofar as the genetic parent

> is concerned. New questions of law are emerging. In the cases of the heterosexual married couples, the high court ordered the registration of the certificates insofar as paternity is concerned but not maternity. In the case of the gay male married couple that requested that the non-biological parent be allowed to adopt the child, the question of the gestational mother's consent to the adoption was raised. Both decisions seem far afield from the high court's rigid stance before the involvement of the ECHR.
>
> In response to the decisions of the ECHR, which sent the strong message that protecting children takes priority over a law that attempts to stamp out the means by which they were conceived, French courts have developed the technical solution of separating the policy position that surrogacy contracts are illicit from the reality that the children in these cases have biological fathers who are French. It is fair to conclude, then, that the ECHR has had a fairly radical influence on the position of the French high court, which in 2013, declared that "requests for recognition were the result of a fraudulent process that can be given no effect." The French courts' new stance on the rights of children born via surrogacy has re-stoked the debate over surrogacy in France, with supporters applauding the outcomes and opponents sensing a destabilization of the French prohibition on surrogacy. Nonetheless, both the Valls and Philippe governments have assured worried citizens that the government has no intention of supporting a repeal of the ban on surrogacy.

Richard F. Storrow, International Surrogacy in the European Court of Human Rights, 43 *N.C.J. Int'l L.* 38, 53–54 (2018)

4. The Australian case *Re EMC*, [2012] NSWSC 1626 (2012) addresses the question of what constitutes a commercial surrogacy agreement based on laws in the state of New South Wales banning the practice. A gay couple donated sperm to a surrogate mother and paid her reimbursement expenses for lost wages during the surrogacy. After the baby was born, the couple attempted to get a parentage order declaring them the legal parents of the child. They were refused and had to litigate. The question was whether paying those reimbursement expenses created a prohibited commercial surrogacy arrangement, which would bar transfer of parentage to the couple. The Supreme Court of New South Wales concluded the payments did not constitute commercial surrogacy since they were only for the birth mother's "reasonable expenses."

The Australian state of Victoria allows heterosexual or same sex couples who are unable to conceive or give birth to their own children (or who will pass on a severe genetic defect) to be considered for surrogacy under the Assisted Reproductive Treatment Act of 2008. The Act only allows for altruistic surrogacy, though couples may pay for the medical expenses of the birth mother related to the surrogacy. The birth mother must be over twenty-five and cannot have any genetic link to the child (i.e. traditional surrogacy is prohibited). Couples must pass criminal background checks and must undergo independent counseling. Every surrogacy arrangement must also be approved by the "Patient Review Panel." Do these strict requirements help eliminate the problems that lead to litigation in other regimes? Or are these requirements so burdensome that couples will travel abroad to seek jurisdictions where commercial surrogacy is legal and inexpensive? In the following section, we discuss the practice of "fertility tourism," where couples travel abroad to find surrogacy (and other reproductive) services. Many such cases arise because a person or couple's home country either bans or heavily restricts surrogacy. But as we will see in the next section, fertility tourism can often be fraught with legal peril for both the children and the intended parents.

4. Fertility Tourism

"Fertility Tourism" refers to the practice of traveling from one's home country to a destination country in order to get reproductive technology services that are not available at home. It typically is a form of "circumvention tourism," in that it takes advantage of the opportunity offered by travel to enable the circumvention of a domestic regulatory regime. See I. Glenn Cohen, *Circumvention Tourism*, 97 Cornell L. Rev. 1309 (2012). Fertility tourism raises a series of difficult ethical and legal questions. Among those: should a home country that prohibits commercial surrogacy out of fears of exploitation of its citizens defer to another country's contrary perception when it comes to that country's citizens? Should criminal prohibitions on commercial surrogacy be extended extraterritorially? How should the home country handle bestowing citizenship on children born abroad through surrogacy? What about recognizing parental status for the intended parents in cases of circumvention tourism for surrogacy? Consider these complicated questions as you read more about this practice in what follows.

Lisa C. Ikemoto, *Reproductive Tourism: Equality Concerns in the Global Market for Fertility Services*

27 Law & Ineq. 277, 281–282, 285–287, 296–301 (2009)

Both the media and scholars use the term "reproductive tourism" to refer to an interrelated set of practices. "Reproductive tourism" often refers most explicitly to the demand side of the industry—to those who travel outside of their jurisdiction of residence to access reproductive technologies. In this Article, I use "reproductive tourism" narrowly to refer to those seeking ART access for the purpose of becoming parents. Some fertility travelers seek services within their home country, while some travel across country borders. Some fertility travelers use ART in hopes of having a genetically related child. Others use technology to have a child, regardless of genetic ties. A long list of market participants forms the supply side of the global market in fertility services. This list includes health care providers, health care facilities such as clinics and hospitals, brokers, and those who provide the raw materials: the men and women who provide gametes, and the women who carry and give birth to children according to surrogacy arrangements.

* * *

Reproductive tourism spans the globe. The destination spots and points of departure in the global fertility market include both developed and developing countries.

Australia, Canada, Germany, India, Israel, and South Africa are among the many destination spots. Fertility travelers hail from a range of countries such as Costa Rica, Japan, Mexico, and the United Kingdom.

Many jurisdictions, such as Australia, Italy, and Germany, are both destination spots and points of departure. The United States is also a major presence on both the supply and the demand side of the market. United States residents travel within the United States to access ART that is not readily available in their home states or regions. United States suppliers also serve many who enter the United States in order to access ART. At the same time, many United States residents cross borders to seek fertility services outside the United States.

Often, fertility travelers have racial or gender preferences that inform their choice of fertility destination. Many seeking third-party gametes want gametes from individuals whose race matches their own. As a result, Romania and the Ukraine are among the popular destination spots for egg donation among Whites. Because of its racial diversity, the United States is popular among travelers from Asia and Latin America, as well as countries with predominantly White populations. Jurisdictions that permit PGD use for sex selection attract those who wish to choose the sex of their child.

Some destinations are attractive because of their religious or social norms. Fertility clinics in Israel provide ART for Jewish women and couples from other countries who seek assurance that procedures comply with Jewish law. In some jurisdictions, either legal regulation or clinic-imposed rules restrict ART access based on marital status and/or sexual orientation. On the other hand, some clinics have formed for the express purpose of providing access to single people and lesbian and gay couples. Some regions or clinics offer services on an inclusive basis because it is good for business. Other jurisdictions have civil rights laws that apply to providers, thus prohibiting them from refusing patients based on marital status and/or sexual orientation. As a result, there are destination spots for single women and men, and lesbian and gay couples who want access to ART, such as Belgium, Finland, Greece, India, and the United States.

* * *

Legal restrictions on the use of ART in one jurisdiction create an incentive to travel to a jurisdiction where the technology is subject to fewer or no restrictions and therefore available for use. A few examples follow.

It is not a coincidence that Swedes, Norwegians, and the Dutch travel to Denmark for sperm. These points of departure permit only known donors. That is, these countries prohibit anonymous donation. As a result, sperm supply is low in Sweden, Norway, and the Netherlands. Denmark, on the other hand, permits anonymous donation. Supply is high there. In fact, Cryos International (Cryos), one of the world's largest sperm banks, is located in Denmark. Cryos estimates its banked sperm has led to 10,000 pregnancies throughout the world since 1987. There are many types of regulations that restrict availability of third-party sperm, and thus prompt fertility travel. The disclosure requirements nicely illustrate the role of law in promoting reproductive tourism, because distinct travel patterns emerged in response to the restrictions. The adoption of disclosure requirements for sperm donors dramatically changed the flow of sperm commerce.

Spain and Romania are two of the most popular destination spots for IVF and donor eggs in Western Europe. Both countries permit payment to egg donors and donor anonymity. Previously, Italy was such a spot. ART use in Italy was substantially unregulated, and at least a few providers were willing to use ART in ways that challenged social norms. For example, Italy had one of the highest number of pregnancies among postmenopausal women due to ART use. In 2004, however, Italy enacted some of most restrictive regulations of ART use. Among the restrictions is a ban on egg and sperm donation, and a ban on the cryopreservation of embryos in most cases. Italy switched positions from a destination spot to point of departure. In 2005, the United Kingdom prohibited payment for eggs. A long waiting list for donor eggs and reproductive tourism to Spain and Romania resulted. Even more recently, Taiwan enacted a law that enables payment, in the form of reimbursement, for 'nutritional supplements' to egg donors. Given bans on payment to egg donors in mainland China and Japan, Taiwan's new law may make that country the premier ART destination spot of East Asia.

India and the United States are two additional major destination spots for surrogacy. India permits commercial surrogacy, although restrictive laws have recently been proposed. In the United States, surrogacy is a matter of state law. Some states permit commercial surrogacy. Not surprisingly, states with laws that enable commercial surrogacy have become more popular destination spots. In California, a 1994 state supreme court decision addressed a parentage dispute arising from a gestational surrogacy agreement in which the intended parents were also the gamete donors. The court determined that Crispina Calvert, who provided the eggs and entered the contract for the purpose of having a child to raise, was the legal mother. The outcome of the case, which effectively enforced the contract with respect to parentage, has made California a surrogacy destination spot within the United States and in the global market. In addition, neither India nor the United States has laws denying the use of ART based on marital status or sexual orientation. Thus, the two countries are both major destinations and niche markets in reproductive tourism.

* * *

Reproductive tourism often makes ART use affordable, or at least less expensive. The lack of substantial regulation makes the full range of ART available in the United States, but many United States residents travel abroad for ART use. In some jurisdictions, health insurance makes ART use affordable at home for those who could not otherwise pay for it. As of 2007, six countries with national health plans—Belgium, France, Greece, Israel, Slovenia, and Sweden—provided substantial coverage for ART. Of the countries for which there is data, approximately half have no insurance coverage for ART use. In the United States, less than one-third of the states have benefit mandates for ART, and those that do tend to limit coverage to married couples, for a limited range of services. Health insurance, especially coverage under national health insurance, is not usually portable. As a result, many, if not most, people who use ART pay out of pocket. Travelling abroad to a jurisdiction where IVF, donor gametes, surrogacy, or other services cost significantly less saves money for some. For others, it makes ART financially accessible.

* * *

Exclusionary social or religious rules often translate into clinic restrictions. Clinic rules are not enforceable at law, but when widely used, effectively limit access within a jurisdiction. As discussed above, marital status and sexual orientation are commonly used to restrict ART access. In some jurisdictions, those rules are law. In others, they have resulted in restrictive clinic policy. For example, in the United Kingdom, clinic refusals to provide services to single women and lesbians have given many reason to travel to other countries where ART is available to them.

In some jurisdictions, religion influences the availability of ART. In many South American countries, where the Catholic Church is powerful, only a handful of clinics exist. Catholic doctrine prohibits use of most ART, including IVF and any technology using third-party gametes. Of those countries in which insurance is not available to cover infertility treatment, many are Catholic. So, for residents of these countries who want ART access, travel may be the best means of obtaining it.

In some jurisdictions, and for some individuals in any region, infertility is stigmatized. ART use is sought in secrecy. Travel is a way of avoiding detection. The trip abroad is described to friends, neighbors, and co-workers as a vacation. The trip may also be described as a "fertility holiday," but its primary purpose is to seek ART use while avoiding the stigma of infertility.

Notes

1. The European Court of Human Rights (ECHR) has confronted difficult legal issues arising out of fertility tourism in two recent cases. The first, *Mennesson v. France*, HUDOC 65192/11 (Eur. Ct. H.R. June 26, 2014), involved two French citizens intending to be parents to a child born of California gestational surrogate using the intended father's sperm and a donor egg. The citizens sought French recognition of the California birth certificate. France's public policy is hostile to surrogacy, and thus the French government argued the birth certificate should not be recognized by France. The lower court agreed with the French government.

However, the Fifth Section of the ECHR reversed, concluding that while France had the ability to enforce its surrogacy public policy, the interest of the child in establishing its identity through the legal parent-child relationship was sufficient to give rise to a violation of Article 8 of the Convention for the Protection of Human Rights and Fundamental Freedoms.

The second case, *Paradiso and Campanelli v. Italy*, HUDOC 25358/12 5 37 (Eur. Ct. H.R. Jan. 24, 2017), was decided by the Grand Chamber of the ECHR in early 2017, and reached the opposite conclusion of the Fifth Section. In *Campanelli*, a couple used a Russian gestational surrogate but without providing either sperm or egg. Given the lack of a genetic tie, the court found that Italy could deny parentage to the intended parents and simultaneously prohibit the parents from adopting the child.

Is the court's justification regarding genetic ties in *Campanelli* enough to sustain its conclusion? What other factors might the court have relied upon in reaching its decision?

2. Consider the following critiques of the ECHR's argument. First, in *Mennesson* the parental act of using a commercial surrogate is criminalized. Denying the child citizenship may seem harsh in a vacuum, but compared with the potential of granting a child citizenship only to be placed in the custody of incarcerated parents, such a denial of citizenship seems less cruel. Second, arguing that a denial of citizenship constitutes a deprivation to the child necessarily requires that the child was entitled to citizenship, which is far from clear. Third, if a combination of denial of citizenship and a criminal penalty imposed on the parents results in zero attempted fertility tourism surrogacies no children will suffer the harm of these cases, and thus such rules are justified. On the other hand, if the rules have no deterrent value, every child in these countries born through fertility tourism will be harmed by the policy, making it unjustifiable. The goal, then, should be to determine the deterrent effect of these policies before deciding whether denial of citizenship is or is not proper. Do you agree with parts, or all, of this reasoning? Why or why not?

3. Some of the quandaries associated with fertility tourism could be solved with a comprehensive international regime, adopted by treaty. However, in the short term, such a regime seems unrealistic. One of the most significant barriers standing in the way is the large variance in regulatory schemes controlling fertility tourism. Even two fairly similar countries (such as two nations in the European Union) may have completely divergent approaches to regulating fertility tourism. For an in-depth discussion of potential methods for fertility tourism regulation, current problems with fertility tourism, and potential future conflicts, see I. Glenn Cohen, *Patients with Passports*, Oxford University Press (2014).

5. Wrongful Birth/Life Actions

What happens when something goes wrong in reproductive technology use or genetic diagnosis? How does the tort system handle lawsuits alleging negligence? This section discusses the variation in approaches across jurisdictions.

Ivo Giesen, *Of Wrongful Birth, Wrongful Life, Comparative Law, and the Politics of Tort Law Systems*

Tydskrif vir Heedendaagse Romeins-Hollandse Reg (THRHR), Vol. 72, pp. 257, 259–265 (2009)

The topic of this article encompasses two types of causes of action for damages against medical practitioners. First, a so called wrongful birth claim involves a claim for damages by the parents of a child for, most importantly, the costs of bringing up the child. The claim is filed because the parents did not want any (more) children, for whatever reason, or did not want the child in question to be born (because of a genetic disability detected during pregnancy), but became parents (again) anyway because of the fault of a third person, that is, the doctor, by not preventing the conception from occurring (also known as wrongful conception: failing to implant a contraceptive in the right manner, not warning about risks of getting pregnant anyway, etcetera), by not terminating the pregnancy correctly after it has come about (failed abortion) or by not correctly performing the necessary genetic tests. An example is of course the situation in which a birth control operation was performed but turned out to be unsuccessful because of a fault of the doctor. In the cases we are dealing with here, the child being born can thus either be a healthy or a disabled child. This is in principle of no consequence to the possibilities of a wrongful birth action. Although in some legal systems, this fact is considered relevant (see below). The most important heads of damages are the cost of raising the child (which is considered to be pure economic loss) and non-pecuniary losses (in principle for both the mother and the father for interference with family life).

A wrongful life claim on the other hand is a claim by a child, and this will always be a disabled child, issued by its representatives, that is, most notably the parents, against a doctor or obstetrician for having to live a life full of suffering because of a handicap while the child was not supposed to have been born at all but is born anyway because of a negligent act by the doctor or assistant. For instance, if one fails to order or correctly perform prenatal research (for example, a chromosome test) as to the state of health of the foetus (wrongful genetic counselling), a handicapped child might be born where otherwise, had the testing been done correctly, the pregnancy would have been terminated by the parents. Had the testing indeed been performed correctly, they would have known the child would be born severely disabled and then they would have chosen an abortion to end the pregnancy. Due to the doctor's fault, however, they never got round to making or being able to make that decision. Damages in these cases consist of the cost of living for the child (which, arguably, seem to be purely economical in nature), that is, the cost of rearing the child for the person taking that task upon himself, including the extra costs related to the disability, and possibly also nonpecuniary loss for the child.

* * *

What is the current state of the law in this regard? Focusing first on wrongful birth claims and paying attention only to the cost of maintaining the child and non-pecuniary damages as the most important heads of damages for the parents suing the doctor or hospital, the following picture emerges.

In the Netherlands, wrongful birth claims have been allowed since the 1997 case of the so-called Missing IUD in which the Dutch Supreme Court (the Hoge Raad) awarded the maintenance costs for raising the child as well as nonpecuniary losses to the mother. The case concerned a family that had specifically decided not to have any more children because of their troublesome financial state of affairs. The sterilisation operation failed, by negligence on the doctor's part, and a fourth (healthy) child was born. The Supreme Court approached the case as a matter of applying Dutch law of damages to a certain pattern of facts in a technical manner. In doing so, they avoided the moral and political issues.

In England, claims for wrongful birth have been rejected to a large extent in the case of *MacFarlane v Tayside Health Board*. The House of Lords decided—in essence—that there was no duty of care for a doctor towards the parents, since we are dealing here with an instance of pure economic loss and accepting a duty in this case would not be fair, just and reasonable. Since these are in fact pure economic loss cases, the well-known Common Law reluctance in that regard comes into play as well. But non-pecuniary losses are being awarded to the mother for pain and suffering related to having to give birth to the child. In *Rees v Darlington Memorial Hospital*, however, a conventional award (and not a compensatory one) was granted to the mother in question who had sought to prevent having any children because she felt she could not take care properly of a child due to her own blindness. Her sterilisation failed and a healthy son was born. The reason for granting the sum of £15,000 was to recognise the fact that she had suffered a legal wrong. According to Van Dam, this award indicates that the outcome reached previously in the MacFarlane was not considered completely satisfactory. I agree. The *Rees* case might actually be a first step towards granting some form of relief with regard to maintenance costs (again, because English law had awarded damages before *MacFarlane*).

The situation in Germany is rather difficult when it comes to maintenance loss (non-pecuniary losses are awarded for the mother). There is a strong divide of opinion: The German Bundesgerichtshof is in favour of allowing a wrongful birth claim, awarding the costs of raising the child under certain conditions, but the Second Chamber of the constitutional court, the Bundesverfassungsgericht, is against this, considering these damages to be contrary to the dignity of the child. The Bundesgerichtshof has remained true to its opinion, however, so these costs are generally compensated.

In France, a wrongful birth claim is only possible to some extent, that is only in so far as there is a special loss that exceeds the normal burdens of motherhood. So, when a healthy child is born there is in principal no valid claim to be launched. A claim for maintenance costs is possible, however, if the child is born handicapped (in that case non-pecuniary loss is granted as well), if the mother is in bad financial condition or if she suffers mental problems as a result of the birth.

So, at the European front, the claim for compensation for wrongful birth has been acknowledged by most jurisdictions, at least to some extent. The same is true for (most of) the United States of America. The Australian highest court has done the same in *Cattanach v Melchior* but some Australian federal legislators have reversed that decision. Under South African law, filing suit in a wrongful birth action will stand up in court with regard to the costs of maintenance of the child, but not for non-pecuniary losses, as was decided in *Administrator, Natal v Edouard* and in *Mukheiber v Raath*.

* * *

How are wrongful life claims resolved? In the Netherlands, not only a wrongful birth claim is possible, but the same goes for wrongful life claims. This was decided in 2005 by the Dutch Supreme Court in the *Kelly* case. The court granted her the cost of living (that is, her upbringing), as well as the extra costs related to her handicaps and non-pecuniary losses for her suffering. The Dutch legislator did not intervene afterwards, not even when asked specifically to think about doing so, basically stating that this Supreme Court decision seemed to be handed down in accordance with the rules of private law in the Netherlands and that there was no apparent reason for the legislator to decide otherwise.

The German legal system denied the possibility of issuing a wrongful life claim in a Bundesgerichtshof case of a foetus being exposed to the Rubella disease contracted by the mother. The reason is that there is no direct duty to prevent the birth of a foreseeable handicapped child because human life might appear valueless if such a duty would be accepted.

In England, section 1 of the Congenital Disabilities (Civil Liability) Act 1976 does allow a prenatal harm claim for a child if it is born alive and disabled if the defendant was liable to either parent for the act which led to the disability. This wording however excludes cases of naturally caused handicaps, such as a genetic defect not detected because it was not properly tested for. The legislator thus stepped in to prohibit (future) wrongful life claims. The courts agree with this position. In *McKay v Essex Area Health Authority*, a case of an undetected Rubella disease again, the wrongful life claim was rejected on public policy grounds: There is no duty to abort a disabled child, accepting such a duty would be a violation of the sanctity of human life, and the assessment of damages (comparing the situation of a disabled child with that of a "not born foetus") is impossible.

The French Cour de cassation made room for a wrongful life claim for the costs of the handicap in the famous Perruche case. Nicolas Perruche was born severely handicapped because his mother contracted the rubella disease thinking—because her physician told her so—that she was immunised against the disease. After the decision was handed down, the French legislator stepped in by enacting that nobody can be indemnified for his birth, even if handicapped. This so-called "Loi Anti Perruche" from 2002 thus overruled the Cour de cassation.

The French legislators' decision is in line with what is commonly decided across continental Europe. Canadian and (most) American courts also turned down this cause of action. In Australia, the case of *Harriton v Stephens* was (again) about a doctor who failed to diagnose the mother's rubella infection during pregnancy and who failed to warn the mother of the risk of serious disability as a consequence of that infection. The High Court of Australia decided by a majority that the wrongful life claim should be denied.

In *Friedman v Glicksman*, Goldblatt J in the Witwatersrand Local Division upheld the wrongful birth claim for South African law, in line with the state of South African law mentioned earlier, but he denied the admissibility of the wrongful life claim initiated by the mother in that case on behalf of her child. The same solution, a denial of the wrongful life claim—on public policy grounds—was handed down by the Supreme Court of Appeal in *Stewart v Botha.*

Notes

1. The Non-Identity Problem. Glenn Cohen highlights a major problem with wrongful life tort cases in his article *Regulating Reproduction: The Problem with Best Interests*, 96 Minn. L. Rev. 423, 443 (2011) called "the non-identity problem," introduced by the philosopher Derek Partift in the philosophical literature: "[T]ort liability in wrongful life cases would run afoul of the Non-Identity Problem because (assuming they are given a life worth living) the children born cannot be said to be harmed by their conception, for had their parents been properly informed of the risk of their health difficulties and delayed conception or chosen a different reproductive partner, they would not have come into existence; instead a different child would have."

2. The Supreme Court of Illinois in *Siemieniec v. Lutheran*, 512 N.E.2d 691 (Ill. 1987), in a contentious decision with multiple concurrences, implicitly engaged with the Non-Identity Problem for a wrongful life claim and barred a child from bringing such an action, citing its own public policy respecting human life as evidence that the child did not have a life not worth living. However, the court allowed the parents to sustain a wrongful birth action against the doctor for failing to foresee problems with their child that would have led to the parents aborting him/her. Importantly, the court only allowed recovery for "extraordinary expenses"—those beyond what it would cost to raise a average, healthy child—until the child reached the age of majority.

3. The California Supreme Court in *Turpin v. Sortini*, 643 P.2d 954 (Cal. 1982) also denied a child's ability to bring a wrongful birth action. However, Justice Mosk, in a dissenting opinion, reasoned that a child should be able to sustain the action, relying on the pain and suffering experienced via the often debilitating medical conditions that children who bring these sorts of actions experience. Is this intuitive appeal to compensate an infant for its pain and suffering a simpler way to view this problem? Or is it simply relying on emotional appeal to skirt a logical problem?

4. The High Court of Australia has also grappled with wrongful life tort cases. In *Harriton v. Stephens*, 226 CLR 52, 72, 84 (High Court of Australia 2006), the majority of the court ruled against the plaintiff seeking to bring a wrongful life action, with the plurality opinion drawing upon the non-identity problem for its main support. Justice Kirby, however, dissented, arguing that precluding the wrongful life action gave "exceptional immunity to health care providers." In an attempt to address the non-identity problem, Justice Kirby opined:

> "[T]he courts have been willing to assign monetary values to many intangible injuries and nebulous losses", and that, "it has long been established that dif-

ficulties of quantification do not preclude relief where it is accepted that the plaintiff has suffered actionable damage."

Does this argument answer the issue?

C. End of Life: Withdrawal

Decisions at and about the end of life remain controversial around the world. The United States has recognized for several decades a constitutional right to refuse life-prolonging medical treatment, but the Supreme Court has declined to extend that constitutional right to encompass access to life-ending medical care, essentially deferring to states' individual laws. See Cruzan v. Director, Missouri Dept. of Health, 497 U.S. 261 (1990); see also Vacco v. Quill, 521 U.S. 793 (1997); see also Washington v. Glucksberg, 521 U.S. 702 (1997). In recent years, a handful of states, beginning with Oregon, have begun allowing for life-ending medical care—that is, prescriptions or injections that result directly in the end of life. This brings the U.S. more in line with the positions of several European countries, such as Belgium and the Netherlands, and Canada, where some version of the right to seek affirmative life-ending treatment is recognized. At the same time, some jurisdictions maintain strong prohibitions—for example, Russia, where aiding another person in ending his or her own life is statutorily criminalized. See Federal Law No.323-FZ *On the Basics of Healthcare Protection of Citizens in Russian Federation* (enacted on Nov. 21, 2011, amended on April 3, 2017).

This chapter begins by examining the refusal of life-sustaining or life-prolonging treatment ("refusal of treatment"). In what we will call refusal of treatment, a medical professional follows a patient's (or their legally designated surrogate's) request to withhold, or withdraw then withhold, life-sustaining or life-prolonging medical treatment, resulting in the patient's death. The chapter then looks at cases where an affirmative act is undertaken in order to end a life, either a prescription for a lethal dose of medication, which the patient themselves administers ("prescription"), or a physician-administered drug that results in the patient's death ("injection").

While the nomenclature of these various approaches is controversial, politicized, and slippery, we endeavor to use a uniform terminology that is as neutral as possible. We do not contend that our terminology is undisputed. Indeed, other terminology is also in wide usage—for example, the term "euthanasia," where refusal is passive euthanasia, and prescription and injection are active euthanasia. However, we believe our chosen vocabulary is well-established enough to be the most useful here.

1. Refusal of Treatment

Although a patient's right to decide whether to discontinue life-sustaining treatment has been recognized in the United States since the *Quinlan* case in 1976, and every state subsequently passed legislation governing advance directives, the right to die has developed more slowly, and along different lines, in most other nations. A few, primarily Western, countries have statutes recognizing the right to refuse or discontinue life-sustaining treatment. The legal situation in Canada, where most provinces have adopted laws recognizing advance directives, and several have appellate court decisions recognizing a right to die, arguably resembles that of the United States most closely. See Decision-Making at the End of Life, in *Canadian Health Law and Policy* 501–532 (Jocelyn Downie, Timothy Caulfield, and Colleen Flood, eds., 2d. ed. (2002)). Advance directives are also recognized under Singaporean law, see, Ter Kah Leng and Susanna Leong Huey Sy, Advance Medical Directives in Singapore, 5 *Med. L. Rev.* 63 (1997), and in a number of the Australian states and territories, see Michael Eburn, Withdrawing, Withholding, and Refusing Emergency Resuscitation, 2 *J. L. & Med.* 131 (1994). Denmark has a statute governing advance directives, and Finland and the Netherlands recognize them as well—though they do not regulate them in detail. See Herman Nys, Emerging Legislation in Europe on the Legal Status of Advance Directives and Medical Decision-Making with Respect to an Incompetent Patient ("Living-Wills"), 4 *Eur. J. Health L.* 179 (1997); see also David Jessop, Patients' Rights and Doctors' Responsibilities: Confluence and Conflict, 3 *Med. L. Int.* 197 (1997) (discussing the English situation, where advance directives have common law, though not statutory, authority); see also Kristina Stern, Advance Directives, 2 *Med. L. Rev.* 57 (1994).

In much of the world, however, death and dying issues are instead governed by court decisions interpreting code provisions prohibiting homicide and assisted suicide, and by the ethical codes, opinions, and disciplinary decisions of medical associations and licensure boards. These decisions and opinions often vary from their United States counterparts in important respects. First, in the United States, the right to refuse life-sustaining treatment followed quite directly from the right of patients to autonomous decision making—that is, the right to informed consent. In other parts of the world, this connection has not seemed so obvious. Though the right to consent to treatment is recognized almost everywhere (in theory, if not in practice), in some countries this right is seen primarily as a right to bodily integrity—the right to not have one's body invaded without consent. It is not obvious in these countries that the right extends to patient involvement in medical decisions generally, or that it covers interventions like the provision of artificial nutrition or hydration. See Sjef Gevers, Patient Involvement in Non-Treatment Decisions, 4 *Eur. J. Health L.* 145 (1997).

Second, in some countries the right of the doctor to determine the appropriate treatment for his or her patient must be balanced with the patient's rights. One organization, responding to the 1994 British Select Committee on Medical Ethics, stated that "it would be bizarre in the extreme to require a skilled professional doctor to adhere to the stipulations of a living will which did not accord with his/her expert opinion of what would be in the best interests of the patient's health" (quoted in Anne Morris, Life and Death Decisions: "Die, My Dear Doctor? That's the Last Thing I Shall Do!" 3 *European J. Health L.* 9, 26 (1996)). Though this statement is extreme, courts in other countries do afford much more deference than do American courts to the opinions of medical professionals as to whether treatment should be continued. In fact, in some countries a doctor may be found to have violated his or her ethical obligations by withholding or withdrawing treatment and allowing a patient to die, even if the patient requested that medical interventions cease.

Third, some countries seem to afford the courts a more central role in end-of-life decisions where the patient is incompetent. Though courts and legislatures in the United States are increasingly willing to leave these decisions to patients and their families, judicial oversight remains more prominent in other countries. Consequently, the role of the family is given less weight. See Cameron Stewart, Who Decides When I Can Die? Problems Concerning Proxy Decisions to Forego Medical Treatment, 4 *J. L. & Med.* 386 (1997).

Fourth and finally, the Western "substituted judgment" approach to decision-making—in which a surrogate decision-maker attempts to make the decision the patient would have made if competent—is generally elsewhere rejected in favor of a "best interests" test, under which caregivers and courts attempt to figure out what is best for the patient.

The following reading considers the contrasting laws of several European countries on the right-to-die issue. While each country has relevant codified law, they differ in their courts' interpretations of that law, and in the relative weight accorded to a patient's right to self-determination—in the Netherlands, for example, that right is paramount—versus a physician's right to practice as he or she sees prudent—for example, the United Kingdom has afforded the doctor's input more weight. *See* Great Ormund Street Hospital v. Yates, No. [2017] EWHC 972 (Fam) (Apr. 11, 2017) (affording hospital's recommendation for palliative care over experimental life-saving care, over the parent's wishes, in the Charlie Gard case).

Herman Nys, *Physician Involvement in a Patient's Death: A Continental European Perspective*

(text originally from Medical Law Review, vol. 7 (1999), updated by Herman Nys, 2007)

I. Introduction

This article contains an analysis of recent legal developments in Europe (which is the supranational and international level of the Council of Europe and the European Union) and in some continental European countries regarding physician involvement in a patient's death.

Four types of physician involvement in a patient's death have been distinguished. Firstly, a physician may become involved in a patient's death because the patient refuses a treatment that may possibly save his life. Is there a legally recognised obligation for a physician to respect the right of a patient to refuse treatment when death may be the consequence of such refusal? What is the legal value of an advance refusal of such a treatment (the so-called living will)? And what is the role played by formally appointed representatives and close relatives?

Secondly, a physician may become involved in a patient's death as the result of a non[-]treatment decision. If this decision is the consequence of a refusal of the treatment by the patient, it falls under the first category. Non-treatment or abstinence decisions however, mainly refer to the patient whose condition is agreed to be hopeless either in the sense that the treatment has no chance of success or that it would be (or has become) disproportionate to any benefit for the patient.

Thirdly, a physician may become involved in a patient's death because of the use of drugs to alleviate pain or other symptoms even though the dose used will more or less certainly hasten the moment of death. I will refer to this category as "pain relief (decisions)".

Fourthly, physician involvement in a patient's death when the physician intentionally terminates the life, at the patient's request or not. If this is done at the request of the patient I term this (mainly under the influence of Dutch jurisprudence) euthanasia. However, I am aware that this term is also used (together with adjectives as active or passive, direct or indirect) in a much broader sense in other countries. In a comparative analysis, the term euthanasia is therefore useless. I will for this reason use a more neutral term, termination of life on request. This category also covers doctor-assisted suicide although I am aware that to many people "active, voluntary euthanasia" and "doctor-assisted suicide" are distinct categories. [The author's discussion of assisted suicide and euthanasia is found in the next section of this book.]

II. Developments in European Law

A. The Right of a Patient to Refuse a Medical Treatment

1. General remarks

A treatment against the will of a competent patient may first of all be considered as a violation of Article 8 of the European Convention for the protection of Human Rights (ECHR). This article reads as follows:

> 1. Everyone has the right to respect for his private and family life, home and correspondence.
>
> 2. There shall be no interference by a public authority with the exercise of this right except such as in accordance with the law and necessary in a democratic society in the interests of national security, public safety or the economy wellbeing of the country, for the prevention of disorder or crime, for the protection of health or morals, or for the protection of the rights and freedoms of others.

The right to respect for his private life protected by Article 8 ECHR is most clearly concerned with individual choices as to bodily autonomy. The European Commission on Human Rights has decided that medical intervention against the will of the patient, even of minimal importance, violates the right to respect of privacy.

The European Court of Justice of the European Communities (established in Luxembourg and not to be confused with the European Court of Human Rights in Strasbourg) has decided that "the right for private life requires that a person's refusal (of an HIV test in the particular case) be respected in its entirety". This aspect of article 8 also includes the right not to be treated medically without consent. For this reason, the Court found a violation of article 8 in the *Glass* case (2004). In the *Pretty* case (2002), the Court held as follows: "in the sphere of medical treatment, the refusal to accept a particular treatment might, inevitably, lead to a fatal outcome, yet the imposition of medical treatment, without the consent of a mentally competent adult patient, would interfere with a person's physical integrity in a manner capable of engaging the rights protected under article 8 (1) of the Convention".

Bodily autonomy is also protected by Article 2 that protects the right to life, and Article 3 that protects the right to be free from torture or inhuman, or degrading treatment, or punishment. The case law associated with Article 3, however, indicates that it is mainly concerned with punishment. Even though the article protects an individual from "degrading treatment[,"] a term which terminally ill persons may associate with the intrusive procedures and loss of dignity accompanying their illness, it seems not applicable with respect to a medical treatment against the expressed refusal of a competent patient. With regard to refusal by an incompetent patient, in the case of *Herczegfalvy*, the Court decided that it was for the medical authorities to decide, on the basis of the recognised rules of medical science on the therapeutic methods to be used, by force if necessary, to preserve the physical and mental health of patients who are entirely incapable of deciding for themselves. In general, a medical treatment that is necessary cannot be considered as inhuman or degrading. Article 5 ECHR ("Everyone has the right to liberty and security of person") that protects personal freedom can also be of relevance although it is mainly of importance to protect a patient against illegal deprival of freedom. When the refusal of a lifesaving treatment is also inspired by religious reasons (cf. Jehovah's Witness), Article 9 ECHR that guarantees the freedom of conviction and religion is of relevance.

Nowadays, the protection of European citizens of medical treatment against their refusal cannot only be deduced from Article 8 ECHR. On 1 December 1999, the European Convention on Human Rights and Biomedicine of 4 April 1997 became effective. Article 5 of this Convention reads as follows:

> An intervention in the health field may only be carried out after the person concerned has given free and informed consent to it. This person shall before hand be given appropriate information as to the purpose and nature of the intervention as well as on its consequences and risks. The person concerned may freely withdraw consent at any time.

2. Advance refusal of a treatment (Living will)

The ECHR does not contain any direct reference to an advance refusal of a medical treatment. In this respect, Article 9 of the Convention on Human Rights and Biomedicine is of direct relevance. It reads as follows:

> The previously expressed wishes relating to a medical intervention by a patient who is not, at the time of the intervention, in a state to express his or her

> wishes shall be taken into account. "Taking into account" is only a weak recognition of the right to refuse medical treatment in advance. According to the Explanatory Report, taking previously expressed wishes into account does not mean that they should necessarily be followed. For example, when the wishes were expressed a long time before the intervention and science has since progressed, there may be grounds for not heeding the patient's opinion. The practitioner should thus, as far as possible, be satisfied that the wishes of the patient apply to the present situation and are still valid taking into account in particular of technical progress in medicine.

This cautious approach of the Convention reflects the lack of consensus in many European countries as to the validity of an advance refusal of treatment, especially life supporting treatment (infra).

3. Refusal by a representative

Article 6 of the Convention on Human Rights and Biomedicine contains a mechanism to protect persons not able to consent. Article 6(3) reads as follows:

> Where, according to law, an adult does not have the capacity to consent to an intervention because of a mental disability, a disease or for similar reasons, the intervention may only be carried out with the authorisation of his or her representative or a person or body provided for by law. The individual concerned shall as far as possible take part in the authorisation.

Article 6(5) provides that the authorisation may be withdrawn at any time in the best interests of the person concerned. Although the refusal of a treatment is not mentioned here expressly, the explanatory memorandum makes it clear that a representative may refuse a treatment: "It was not considered necessary to provide in this article for a right of appeal against the decision of the legal representative to authorise or refuse to authorise an interventions."

B. Non-treatment Decisions

The European Commission has been confronted with the question whether Article 2 ECHR (right to life) obliges a Member State to protect its citizens against non-treatment decisions. A Swiss citizen lodged a complaint before the European Commission because of what he considered as a case of "passive euthanasia" on his father who suffered from Parkinson's disease. The facts of the application do not reveal the medical treatment or under what circumstances it was withdrawn. Regardless, his complaint before the Swiss Courts was dismissed and finally the Swiss Federal Supreme Court declared his appeal inadmissible. Before the European Commission, the applicant complained that Swiss law violates the right to life (Article 2 ECHR) because it does not condemn *expressis verbis* a so-called "passive euthanasia" applied without the written and express consent of the patient. The applicant also considered this legal vacuum as a violation of Article 8 ECHR because not respecting the will of the patient constitutes a violation of his right to privacy. According to the Commission, Article 2 obliges a state not only to abstain from intentionally killing a person, but also that it takes adequate measures to protect life. The European Commission declared the complaint inadmissible because the Swiss law incriminates the fact of taking life by negligence or by guilty imprudence. By offering this protection Swiss law complies with the obligation imposed by Article 2 ECHR.

Unfortunately, the Commission has not given an answer with respect to the violation of Article 8. In the *Glass* case (2004), the Court did not consider it necessary to examine separately the applicants' complaint regarding the inclusion of a DNR notice in the first applicant's (a severely disabled child) case notes without the consent and knowledge of the second applicant (his mother). It however observed in line with its admissibility decision that the notice was only directed against the application of vigorous cardiac massage and intensive respiratory support, and did not exclude the use of other techniques, such as the provision of oxygen, to keep the first applicant alive. The participation of the patient (or his legal representative) in a non-treatment decision has also otherwise not received much attention until recently. In much of the literature, in statements by international organisations, and in many national legal documents, informed consent by the patient is not related to the concept of "medical decisions" but to the narrower concept of "intervention" or even "treatment[."] For example, Article 5 of the Convention on Human Rights and Biomedicine (supra) limits the right to give informed consent to such "intervention". Although the term "intervention" must be understood here in a broad sense—it covers all medical acts, in particular interventions performed for the purpose of preventive care diagnosis, treatment or rehabilitation, or in a research context—it nevertheless is limited to "acts." If informed consent is only required before a medical intervention is carried out, in fact only one albeit important aspect of patient participation in medical decision making (the possibility to refuse an intervention after adequate information has been provided) has the status of a legal obligation for the physician. This creates the risk that in other medical decisions involving the patient, such as non-treatment decisions, he may be left at the discretion of the health professional or that it may be considered only a matter of good practice to ask for the opinion of the patient, and not necessarily a legal duty.

This limited approach of patient participation in medical decisions may be explained because informed consent is viewed traditionally and essentially as a justification for unauthorised, intentional touching of another person. Moreover, in this opinion a medical intervention is only justified when the physician acts with a therapeutic intention. If, however, according to the physician the situation of the patient is such that his intervention cannot serve any therapeutic purpose, he not only has a right but a duty to withdraw the treatment. This reasoning leaves no room for an active patient (or his relatives) participation in a non-treatment decision.

C. Pain Relief

In the *Glass* case (2004), the European Court considered that the decision to impose pain relieving treatment on the severely handicapped child in defiance of his mother's objections gave rise to an interference with the first applicant's right to respect for his private life, and in particular his right to physical integrity.

D. Termination of life on request

According to the European Court, Article 2 ECHR cannot be said to guarantee to anyone a right to die, and, therefore, it cannot be regarded as an avenue for challenging national legislation prohibiting termination of life on request or assisted suicide (*Pretty* case, 2002). With regard to Article 3 ECHR the Court concluded that no positive obligation arises under this article to require a State to provide a lawful opportunity for any form of assisted suicide. However, the Court was not prepared to exclude the possibility that a complete ban on assisted suicide constitutes an interference with the right to respect for private life as guaranteed under Article 8 (1) ECHR.

III. Developments in National Law

A. Denmark

1. The right to refuse a medical treatment

In Denmark, the right to refuse a medical treatment has explicitly been recognised by statute []. Section 25 of the of Law No. 546 of 24 June 2005 on Health that entered into force 1 January 2007 reads as follows:

> A terminal patient may reject treatment entirely aimed at delaying the time of death.

One of the implications of this disposition is that the patient can reject treatment and can thus, for example, avoid being kept alive artificially. The Danish Parliament has attached decisive emphasis to respecting the patient's right of self-determination and to avoiding the sustenance of life at any cost. Under Danish legislation, the doctor must respect the patient's autonomy with regard to foregoing treatment alternatives. If the patient makes a non-treatment decision, the doctor must comply with the patient's wishes.

Law No. 546 of 24 June 2005 has also expressly recognized the validity of advance refusals or living wills. Section 26 (1) of this act provides as follows:

> Any person over the age of 18 and not under guardianship may establish a living will. In the living will the patient may express his wishes regarding treatment, in case he experiences a condition where he is no longer able to perform his right to self-determination.

According to subsection 2 in a living will it is possible to record conditions regarding:

> a) refusal of life prolonging treatment in situations where the patient is terminally ill, and
>
> b) refusal of life prolonging treatment in case of illness, progressed decrepitude, accident, heart failure or the like leaving the patient permanently unable to take care of himself or herself physically and mentally.

Life prolonging treatment is defined in subsection 3 as treatment with no prospect of cure, improvement or relief, but only for some life prolonging. It does not include life-supporting treatment.

According to subsection 5, the wishes expressed according to subsection 2 (a) (terminally ill patient refusing life prolonging treatment) are binding for the health care provider who in other words is obliged to respect the patient's request to omit treatment. The law requires that only the assessment of the patient's medical condition may be taken into consideration, whereas other factors may not be considered relevant, e.g. the physician's personal preferences, research interests or economic motives. A wish expressed according to subsection 2 (b) ([]permanently severely impaired patient refusing life prolonging treatment) however is a recommendation for the health care provider and must be taken into consideration as such. The law presupposes that the request in such a living will, although legally not binding, may only be overruled due to reasons of a very substantial nature. In the physician's considerations, a number of factors might be included, e.g. the nature and progression of the illness, the treatment options, the patient's age and life situation, the relative's opinions etc. The physician's discretionary power in this respect is rather wide and vague.

Section 26 (4) stipulates that in case a health care provider, when the patient is unable to perform his right to self-determination, is planning the initiation of life-extending treatment to a terminally ill patient, or plans on continuing life prolonging treatment in a situation as described in subsection 2 (b), he must contact the living will registry established according to section 27 to check for the existence of a living will. Section 27 empowers the Interior and Health Minister to establish a living wills register and determine regulations for the issue, design, registration and withdrawal of living wills. The registration procedure currently costs about 7€. The validity of an advance directive is not limited to a set period of time. A clear statement issued in a different manner may be given legal status equivalent to an advance directive filed on the official formula, if a physician becomes aware of its existence and content. A patient may always revoke the living will by issuing a written and clear notification to the Registry. In connection with a current illness, the living will may informally be revoked by a plain statement, e.g. to the responsible physician or another health care professional.

2. Non-treatment decision

Section 25 (2) of Law No 546 of 24 June 2005 reads as follows:

> In case a patient is no longer able to practice his right to self-determination, the health care person may refrain from initiating or proceeding with life-extending treatment.

3. Pain relief

Section 25 (3) of this Law provides:

> A terminal patient may receive pain-relieving, sedative or similar medication necessary to relieve the condition of the patient, even if this might accelerate the time of death.

B. France[1]

1. The right to refuse a medical treatment

Article 3 of Law No. 94-653 of 29 July 1994 regarding respect for the human body (one of the so-called Bioethics laws) has amended Article 16 of the French Civil Code. Following amendments in 1999 and 2004, Article 16(3) now reads as follows:

> The integrity of the human body may only be violated in case of medical necessity for the person concerned.... The consent of the person concerned has to be given beforehand except when his state of health requires a medical intervention to which he cannot give his consent.

The right to refuse a medical intervention is clearly recognised. As a consequence of this law, the French Court of Cassation has already changed its jurisprudence as to what party—the patient or the physician—has to prove whether the patient has given his informed consent. Until 1997, the Court laid the burden of proof upon the patient. In a decision of 25 February 1997, however, the Court revised its position: it is now to the physician to demonstrate that he has obtained the informed consent. This change follows logically from Article 16(3) of the French Civil Code: a violation of the human body is prohibited unless for medical reasons and unless the person concerned has consented to it. A physician who violates this prohibition must demonstrate that these conditions are present. It also means that a physician has to accept the refusal of a patient because without consent of the patient, he may not violate the bodily integrity of the patient to refuse a medical treatment.

Since its amendment in 1995, Article 36 of the professional ethics Code of the French Order of Physicians is also very clear with respect to the right of a patient to refuse a medical treatment. It reads as follows:

> Consent of the person concerned has to be sought before any diagnostic procedure or treatment. If a competent patient refuses a diagnostic procedure or treatment, the physician has to respect this refusal after having informed the patient of all its consequences.

Finally, in 2002 a far-reaching provision was introduced by Law No 2002-303 of 4 March 2002 on the rights of patients in the Code of Public Health (section L1111-4). After being amended by Law No 2005-370 of 22 April 2005 on the rights of patients and the end of life, section L1111-4 reads as follows:

> Each person takes his own decisions regarding his health, in conjunction with the healthcare professional and taking account of the information and recommendations furnished by him.

The physician must respect the will of the person after having informed him of the consequences of his choices. If the patient's decision to refuse or stop any treatment

1. See note 2 after this excerpt.

puts his life in danger, the physician must do all he can to convince him to accept the needed treatment. He can consult a colleague. In any case, the patient has to reiterate his decision after a reasonable period of time. This is added to his medical file. The physician preserves the dignity of the dying patient and assures the quality of the end of life.

No medical act and no treatment can be provided without the free and informed consent of the person. This consent can be withdrawn at any time.

The obligation to help a person in danger, provided for in Article 223-6, section 2 of the French New Criminal Code (Article 63, old Criminal Code) is not an absolute one and has to yield when a competent patient has knowingly expressed a refusal to receive a treatment, according to the French Court of Cassation in a famous decision of 3 January 1973. A decision of the French Council of State nullified a disciplinary sanction imposed by the French Order of Physicians on a physician who had prescribed a palliative treatment to a woman who refused an efficient treatment for cancer. Against the background of this jurisprudence and the legislative change in 1994, the decision by the Council of State in the *Granier* case surprised most commentators. In this decision, the Council of State indeed confirmed a disciplinary sanction imposed upon a physician by the French Order of Physicians. Confronted with a patient suffering from breast cancer and who had explicitly refused a [mastectomy] and radiotherapy, the physician had limited himself to offer palliative care. After a complaint by a colleague the physician was sentenced by the order of physicians to a prohibition of three, and after appeal, six months of practice of medicine. After the appeal of the physician, the Council of State confirmed this severe sanction. For Dubouis, this sanction cannot be reconciled with the right of the patient to refuse a treatment and the duty of the physician to respect this refusal, the more so because in a previous decision the Council had reached an opposite conclusion. For Dunet-Larousse, the practical consequences of the *Granier* decision should not be exaggerated because the palliative treatment offered to the patient was of a scientifically disputable nature. But having regard to the principles at stake, the decision is incompatible with civil law and the code of professional ethics.

The development introduced by the Council of State with the *Granier* decision has recently been confirmed by lower administrative court decisions. The Paris Administrative Court of Appeal had to decide whether a physician could lawfully carry out a blood transfusion against the express refusal of a Jehovah's Witness. In both cases the patient had clearly expressed his refusal to undergo a blood transfusion. The widow of the patient in the first case (notwithstanding the blood transfusion the patient had died) and the patient herself in the second case argued that the treating physician had not respected obligations imposed both by European and French law. With respect to European law, they referred to Articles 3, 5, and Article 9 ECHR. Rather surprisingly they did not mention Article 8 ECHR. The Court decided that there was no violation of Articles 3 and 5. The blood transfusion could be regarded as a violation of the freedom of religion (Article 9 ECHR) but in this particular case it was justified by the duty of the physician to save the life of the patient. With respect to French law, the Court considered that Article 36 of the Code of Professional Ethics of the Order of Physicians that had been approved by decree and thus had a binding force, and Article 16(3) of the Civil Code, obliged a physician to respect the will of the patient. However, the Court added, the obligation of the physician to respect the will of the patient is limited by another obligation of the physician to save the health and life of the patient if the following three conditions are met: Firstly, the medical intervention is urgently needed; secondly, the life of the patient is in danger; and thirdly, there is no alternative solution.

Both decisions leave many questions unanswered. First, one may wonder [w]hether the Court would have reached the same conclusion if a life-saving treatment was refused not because of religious reasons as was the case here, but because the patient did not want to live any more. A Jehovah's Witness who refuses blood does not want to be dead, but accepts death as a consequence of refusal. The fact that no referral was made to Article 8 ECHR may be understood in this context. Although both decisions are silent on this, the advice of the Commissioner of the Government to the Court made it clear that even if the refusal was based on the right of the patient to refuse a treatment and not on religious reasons, the attending physician had not to respect the will of the patient. According to the Commissioner, it is not for the Courts to recognize in a praetorian-way a right to die by refusing relatively simple and efficient medical care, whereas the legislator has not legalized euthanasia. In other words, recognizing a right to refuse life-saving treatment is considered as paving the way to a right to be killed on request and that is a matter that has to be decided by Parliament. Another important and not clearly answered question is the legal basis of the duty of a physician to save the life and health of the patient. This cannot be the obligation imposed by the Criminal Code to help a person who is in danger because it is generally accepted in French law that this obligation is limited by a refusal of the patient.

The French Council of State has confirmed both decisions. Given the *Granier* opinion, it would have been surprising if the Council had nullified them. It was not clear whether this decision would survive the recognition of the right to refuse a life saving treatment as a patient right in 2002. In August 2002, the Council of State, however, confirmed its decision. Despite the numerous legislative declarations of the patient's right to self-determination the French courts are not inclined to force physicians to respect patient's refusals of life-saving treatment. It remains to be seen whether the legislative change in 2005 will be more effective.

The forgoing relates in general to the refusal of a life saving treatment by any patient. With regard to the refusal of any treatment by a terminally ill patient, Article L.1111-10 of the Public Health Code provides that the physician has to respect his wish after having informed him of the consequences of his choice. The decision of the patient is added to his medical file.

The law No 2005-370 of 22 April 2005 on the rights of patients and the end of life has also created a legal basis for advance directives and proxy decisions. Article L1111-11 reads as follows:

> Every adult person may make up advance directives in case he is no longer capable to express his will. These advance directives indicate the wishes of the person concerning the conditions to limit or to stop treatment at the end of his life. They may be revoked at any time.

On the condition that they have been made up three years before the person became unconscious: the physician takes them into consideration before taking a decision to diagnose, intervene, or treat.

Article L.1111-12 of the Code of Public Health provides:

> If a terminally ill person who is incapable to express his will has designated a person of confidence the opinion of this person prevails, except in a case of urgency or impossibility, to any other non medical opinion, with the exclusion of advance directives, in decisions taken by a physician to diagnose, intervene or treat the incapable patient.

2. Non-treatment decisions

The Court of Appeal of Rouen on 6 March 1996 condemned an [anesthesiologist] for involuntary homicide: he had decided to extubate a patient and to withdraw reanimation of that patient. According to the Court both decisions had been taken against logic and medical ethics and against the accepted rules of good practice. The physician appealed against this decision. He argued that no causal relationship had been demonstrated between the decision to stop the reanimation and the death of the patient because the Court had itself ascertained that the patient had no chance of recovery or survival. The Court of Cassation confirmed the decision of the Court of Appeal in a judgment of 19 February 1997. According to the Court of Cassation the Court of Appeal had correctly interpreted the facts of the case.

More important than the decision of the Court of Cassation itself—after all the Court hides itself behind the sovereign appreciation of the facts by the Court of Appeal—are the comments on this decision in the literature. Both Legros and Chevallier have difficulties with the legal qualification of the decision to stop reanimating followed by the death of the patient as an involuntary homicide. They argue that the correct qualification would have been a voluntary homicide. According to Chevallier there is a deliberate policy underlying this qualification. A voluntary homicide (euthanasia) has to be judged by a jury composed of lay persons and one may fear that they would be too lenient, misled by emotions. By qualifying the withdrawal of reanimation as an involuntary homicide, it has to be judged by professional judges. This will result in a more efficient fight against euthanasia according to Chevallier who admits that the judgment of the Court of Cassation was a severe one. This severity is inspired by the desire of the Court to combat certain contemporary tendencies to deliberately end the pain and suffering of patients who are manifestly condemned to die in a short time. There is no doubt, according to Chevallier, that the decision of the Court of Cassation has to be situated within a more general approach of the jurisprudence to combat immoral practices tending towards euthanasia and instead to impose, respecting the traditional Hippocratic oath, what some call incorrectly therapeutic obstination.

In 1987 the District Court of Paris was confronted with two conflicting requests by relatives of a 61-year-old cancer patient who was at that moment terminally ill. The father of the patient asked the Court to continue giving him chemotherapy while his daughter-in-law (the spouse of the patient) asked that this therapy be discontinued and replaced by an alternative treatment. The Court appointed experts who came to the conclusion that continuation of chemotherapy did not cause unbearable suffering to the patient. But before the Court had taken a decision on the request to discontinue this treatment, the patient died.

Law No 2005-370 on the rights of patients and the end of life has also introduced some rules regarding non-treatment decisions. Article L 1111-4 (4) of the Code of Public Health provides the following:

> When the patient cannot express his will, limiting or withdrawing a treatment so that his life may be endangered may not be decided without consulting colleagues and without asking the opinion of the person of confidence appointed by the patient or his family or his relatives and taking into consideration his advance directives. The decision to limit or withdraw treatment has to be added to his medical file.

Article L 1111-13 relates to terminally ill patients who cannot express their will. If a physician wants to limit or to withdraw treatment because it is futile, disproportionate or only prolonging artificially the life of the patient he has to consult colleagues and ask the opinion of the person of confidence appointed by the patient or his family or his relatives and take into consideration his advance directives.

3. Pain relief

In 2000 the Council of State approved the decision taken by the National Council of the Order of physicians in a case where a physician had admitted injecting his terminally ill patient with potassium chloride in order to prevent her suffering atrociously during the last few hours of her life. The National Council condemned him because he had not attempted to relieve her pain by palliative care.

Law No 2002-303 on the rights of patients has stipulated that any person has a right to receive pain-relieving treatment (Article L.1110-5 Code of Public Health). Law No 2005-370 on the rights of patients and the end of life has supplemented this article by the following provision:

If a physician is convinced that he cannot relieve the pain of a terminally ill patient otherwise than by applying a treatment that may have the secondary effect to shorten the life of the patient, he must inform the patient, his person of confidence, his family or his relatives. His decision has to be added to his medical file.

C. *Germany*

1. The right to refuse a medical treatment

In Germany, the citizen's right of self-determination is explicitly protected by Article 2(1) of the *GrundGesetz*. Not surprisingly, it has long been recognized in jurisprudence that a patient capable of making a decision can refuse a medical treatment, even if the treatment is vital. In a landmark case of 13 September 1994 a Criminal Panel of the German Supreme Court (re)emphasized a patient's right of self-determination, a right to be respected even in the case of a dangerously ill patient. The decision makes clear that withdrawal of treatment or care which leads to death may be done consistently with a patient's rights: indeed may be a vindication of them even where there is a constitutionally protected "right to life." As early as 1957 the Supreme Court had recognised the right to refuse a medical treatment.

The Judgment of the Supreme Court of 13 September 1994 was also important in another respect. As a consequence, the German Medical Association decided to amend its guidelines on medical *Sterbebegleitung* (aid-in-dying). The amended guideline is unambiguous as to the right of a patient to refuse a medical treatment: if a patient is competent, the physician has to respect the contemporaneously expressed will of a well informed patient, even if this will does not correspond with medically indicated measures. This is also valid for a request to end life-supporting measures that have already been started. The physician must help a patient who refuses a life-saving treatment to consider the consequences.

In the decision of 13 September 1994, the Court also laid the basis for widespread acceptance of living wills in Germany. A 70-year-old patient who suffered serious, irreversible brain damage caused by a cardiac arrest in 1990, was unable to express her wishes. She could not swallow and had to be artificially fed through a tube. Her son had been appointed as her guardian. In March 1993, her doctor and her son ordered the nursing staff to discontinue artificial feeding. The staff however refused to do so and informed the guardian Court, which in turn, informed the prosecutor. As a result, the doctor and the son were prosecuted for attempted manslaughter. The District Court found them both guilty of attempted manslaughter. The defendants appealed to the Federal Supreme Court. The Court allowed the appeal and remanded the case for retrial. According to the Court:

> 1. The District Court erred in holding that allowing someone with cardiac activity, respiratory activity and proper circulation to die by way of terminating medical treatment, automatically gives rise to criminal liability. Provision must be made for exceptional cases such as this where regard must be given to the patient's right of self-determination which embraces the right to refuse life-sustaining medical treatment.
>
> 2. Where the wishes of an incompetent person must be presumed, the need to protect human life demands that a high evidential standard be satisfied. Account must be taken of the patient's written or oral indications, religious views, other value-systems and expectations of life. Objective criteria may be clues to individual hypothetical intention, but should not be accorded significant weight unless the patient's presumed intention is indeterminate.

Subsequently, the District Court (judgment of 17 May 1995) acquitted both defendants on the basis of the "presumed consent or will" test of the German Supreme Court. Applying what the Court termed "strict evidential requirements" to determine the patient's presumed will, the District Court set out its approach based upon the Supreme Court's decision as follows:

> Single utterances alone will not as a rule amount to a proper basis as they could have been made during a passing mood. Things do not depend solely on former, verbal or written declarations by the patient. Such declarations may not be assessed in isolation, but have to be looked at together with further indicia which go to reveal the patient's will. The Federal Supreme Court listed a number of indicia which are not exhaustive. What is decisive in ascertaining the patient's presumed consent are her religious beliefs, her other personal value beliefs, her expectations of life (bearing in mind her age), the pain she suffers and the burden to the patient of her pain, the reasonableness of medical intervention, as well as the individual views of the patient.

Hence, the physician and the son were declared not guilty. From the decisions of the District Court, and the Supreme Court, it follows that the presumed consent of a patient in withdrawing life supporting treatment is binding on the attending physician.

Although the expression "advance directive" or "living will" does not appear even once in the decision of the German Supreme Court, according to a German annotator[,] "you can almost hear the sigh of the judge who wrote the judgment: 'How much easier this case would have been had the patient made use of such an advance directive.' "

As consequence of this judgment by the Supreme Court, more and more use is made in Germany of written refusals of life-supporting treatment in the event of an irreversible state of unconsciousness. Such a will is considered to be binding on the attending physician, the guardian and the guardian Court as the writer is aware that, at the moment of drawing up, he will not be able to change his mind. However a more recent decision of a Guardianship Panel of the German Supreme Court of 7 March 2003 has cast doubt on the legal validity of living wills. Unlike the Criminal Panel which relate exclusively to the declared or presumed wish of the patient, the Guardianship Panel demands "objective medical" criteria. This means that the wishes of a patient expressed in a living will are not exclusively decisive.

In its decision of 13 September 1994, the Supreme Court did not have to deal with [the question of appointing a guardian] as a guardian had already been appointed [] (the son of the patient) before the problem of withdrawing life-supporting treatment had arisen. For the majority of German commentators it is obvious, however, that the intervention of a guardian is a necessity before a decision to withdraw a life supporting treatment is taken.

Another important question is whether the guardianship court must be involved in such a decision. According to Article 1904, German Civil Code, the guardian's consent concerning medical examination, treatment or surgical intervention has to be approved by the guardianship court if the envisioned procedure poses a danger to the patient's life, or a long and serious injury to his health. In its decision of 13 September 1994 the German Supreme Court argued for an application mutatis mutandis of this rule in cases of withdrawal of treatment, at least if the process of dying had not yet begun. This opinion has been confirmed in a decision of the Central District Court of Frankfurt-am-Main of 17 July 1998. Also, the revised (in 1998 and amended again in 2004) Guidelines of the German Medical Association state that the request of the guardian to end a life-supporting treatment has to be confirmed by a guardianship court when the process of dying has not yet begun. However there is no consensus on this and some District Courts (München I, Augsburg, Karlruhe/Freiburg) have taken the view that a decision to withdraw treatment is a very personal one which cannot be delegated to a guardian in any case.

2. Pain relief

In another landmark decision of 15 November 1996, the German Supreme Court decided that a medically indicated pain relief treatment, in accordance with the express or presumed consent of a dying patient, does not become an illegal act because of the unwanted but unavoidable consequence that the process of dying is accelerated.

This was the first decision by the German Supreme Court dealing with "indirekten Sterbehiffe" (indirect euthanasia). Together with the decision of 13 September 1994 it is an important determination regarding the limits of the duty to treat by a physician. It is also a significant decision because it may free physicians from the fear of prosecution for homicide when they apply pain relief treatment. According to Verrel the opposite is the case: a physician who withholds from his patient a medically indicated pain treatment violates the bodily integrity of that patient. A more recent decision of the German Supreme Court of 7 February 2001 has confirmed this case law and in more concrete terms stated that "indirect euthanasia" is [justified] through the emergency regulation of Article 34 of the German Criminal Code. The guidelines of the German Medical Association (as amended in 2004) reflect the unanimity on this: "in cases of mortal illness the alleviation of suffering may have priority to such an extent that the possibility of an unavoidable shortening of the patient's life will become acceptable."

D. *The Netherlands*

1. The right to refuse a medical treatment

In the not too distant past, Dutch physicians have tended to be rather authoritarian and the law accepted this, but now the patient's unqualified right to self-determination in this regard is no longer subject to doubt. It may be a right whose exercise is not always made easy for the patient, but as a matter of legal principle the doctor who imposes treatment on a patient without his consent is without question guilty of a number of medical disciplinary, civil and even criminal offences. Thus, a competent patient has the legal right, for whatever reason, to refuse (further) treatment, even if the treatment is in the opinion of the doctor indicated and necessary to continued life. It is not relevant that the patient exercises this right in order to shorten his life; nor is it relevant that the doctor (or anyone else) agree with the patient's decision.

With regard to an advance refusal of a medical treatment or living will, Article 450(3) of the Act on the Medical Contract provides for the following:

> In the case of an incompetent patient of 16 years or older, the physician has to follow the clearly expressed opinions of the patient in a written form at a moment that he was competent and containing a refusal of consent. The physician may override this refusal if he has well founded reasons for doing so.

It has taken much pressure from the Dutch Parliament to have this provision incorporated into the Act on Medical Contract. Against the wishes of the government, and at the last moment, a majority in Parliament approved an amendment. The main issue of discussion was the value that should be attached to written anticipatory decisions. For the government the amendment added little to the already accepted principle of informed consent whilst in the view of Parliament, the amendment was necessary to end the uncertainty that surrounded advance refusals in daily life.

The authority of the physician to override an advance refusal should not be used too extensively, otherwise the provision would become senseless. Preferably, health care providers should use this power only in situations in which the statement is apparently unspecific and/or outdated. The same legislation provides that appointed representatives and close relatives of the patient can exercise the right on his behalf. A physician who, at the request of the patient, abstains from treatment that is necessary for the preservation of life is not regarded as having killed the patient, in the sense of homicide. The patient's death is considered due to a "natural" cause, which means that no special legal controls exist.

2. Non-treatment decisions

Not initiating, or terminating, life-prolonging treatment when this is "medically futile[,"] either in the sense that the treatment has no chance of success or that it would be (or has become) disproportionate to any benefit for the patient, is considered to fall within the scope of the "normal medical practice" that a physician is authorised to perform.

What constitutes "medical treatment" in this connection has been the subject of considerable discussion. In June 1987 Gerard Stinissen brought a civil action in the District Court of Almelo, asking for a judgment that further treatment of his wife should be stopped. She had been in coma since March 1974 as a result of a medical mistake during a Caesarean delivery. In 1976 her husband had asked the nursing home where she was being kept alive to allow her to die. The nursing home refused, initially because they were opposed to taking an "active" decision to let a patient die, but later because they were unsure of their legal position. Stinissen requested the District Court to order that the artificial feeding of his wife be stopped, that possible complications not be treated, and that the nursing home confine itself to care aimed at the relief of suffering. Stinissen argued that medical treatment was futile and that the patient could not be considered to have given consent to it. The Court ruled that the artificial feeding of Ms Stinissen should be considered medical treatment and therefore fell within the authority of a doctor to terminate futile medical treatment.

But it considered the doctor's decision to keep her alive legitimate and refused to intervene. The Court of Appeal of Arnhem likewise rejected Stinissen's request that artificial feeding be stopped. The Court argued that doctors should make judgments concerning medical treatment. The Court also confirmed the ruling of the District Court that the artificial feeding should be considered medical treatment. After the Court of Appeal's decision, her physician decided to stop the artificial feeding.

With regard to patient participation in a non-treatment decision, a doctor is not required to accede to a patient's (or his representative) insistence on treatment the doctor considers futile. On general principles, it would seem that he must at least inform the patient, or in the case of a non-competent patient, the family or others responsible for the patient, of the fact that he proposes to abstain from treatment he considers futile, if only so that they can seek a second professional opinion.

Unless based on the patient's request, DNR instructions and other advance decisions not to administer life-prolonging treatment under specific conditions also fall in this category. It has recently been argued in connection with a hospital protocol for such decisions that the greater the role that proportionality or "quality-of-life" considerations play, the greater the role of the patient (or his representative) in the decision-making should be.

IV. Conclusion: Strengths and Weaknesses of Continental European Medical Law

Comparative studies in the area of health law are rare. It is easy to identify a number of factors which have contributed to this paucity of comparative analysis. The linguistic differences have no doubt made their contribution. Also the differences in legal culture make comparative health law a difficult undertaking. With regard to the law of physician involvement in a patient's death, these difficulties are amplified by the lack of uniformity in terminology.

I will limit myself in this concluding part to draw the attention to some remarkable differences and resemblances in the legal approach of physician involvement in a patient's death in the countries I have studied.

The most interesting and surprising conclusion to me is the role played by the jurisprudence in France and Germany, and the different directions in which both countries have evolved under the influence of that jurisprudence during the last decennium.

There is, of course, one important common feature: the prohibition of termination of life by a physician at the request of a patient is considered to be an absolute limit to legally acceptable physician involvement in a patient's death. But with the same objective in mind, namely safeguarding this limit, the jurisprudence in both countries has created a totally different system. In France, the right of a patient to refuse a life-saving treatment, and the right of the physician to take a non-treatment decision, are considered as a threat to the prohibition of termination of life upon request. Admittedly, this is not said in so many words in the judgments; there are differences in approach between the Council of State and the Court of Cassation; the actual facts of the case may influence decisively a judgment and comments on these judgments are rather rare. But we cannot close our eyes to the apparent fact that the French jurisprudence has evolved during the 1990s in a direction that makes it difficult for patient and physician alike to opt for death with dignity. That the French jurisprudence prefers therapeutic obstination over dying with dignity in order to prevent the slippery slope to termination of life request may be too strong a statement because there are also signs pointing in another direction (especially in some comments on this jurisprudence). Nonetheless, there is a French model in the law of physician involvement in a patient's death. A model that aims at preventing that termination of life on request becomes an accepted practice by refusing patient and physician alike to take decisions that may eventually lead to the death of the patient. Not surprisingly, this jurisprudence expressly refers to accepted medical professional ethics that tends to be rather conservative. In 2002 and subsequently in 2005 the French legislature has intervened to strengthen the rights of patients in general (2002) and of dying patients in particular. And although the right to refuse a treatment even in an advance directive is now legally accepted, medical and legal practice still are profoundly influenced by the habits and attitudes of the last decennium of the previous century.

On the other hand, the Criminal Panel of the German Federal Supreme Court has built up during the last decennium or so a jurisprudence that lays the decisions regarding the refusal of medical treatment, non-treatment and pain relief with the patient. In interviews in legal journals, judges of the Court with a remarkable openness have explained that the right to determination is the red thread in a strategy to make termination of life on request more or less superfluous. There is also a German model in the law of physician involvement in a patient's death. A model that aims at preventing that termination of life on request becomes an accepted practice by recognising the right of the patient to refuse treatment and to participate in non-treatment and pain relief decisions. In this jurisprudence, no referral is made to existing medical professional guidelines. Just the opposite is true: these guidelines have been adjusted to the jurisprudence.

Notes

1. Though the law pertaining to rights to refuse treatment varies from state to state in the United States, the law has become increasingly uniform over the years. The emergence of a fairly widely held consensus on what the law should be has been led by three Supreme Court decisions, *Cruzan v. Director, Missouri Dept. of Health*, 497 U.S. 261 (1990) (holding that medical professionals need not withdraw life-sustaining treatment absent clear and convincing evidence that the patient would have wanted that); *Washington v. Glucksberg*, 521 U.S. 702 (1997) (allowing state ban on assisted suicide to stand, as it did not violate any constitutionally-protected liberty interest); and *Vacco v. Quill*, 521 U.S. 793 (1997) (holding that New York's prohibition on assisting suicide did not violate Equal Protection Clause of Fourteenth Amendment), which have laid out several basic principles. These principles are, first, that the right to make decisions at the end of life is a constitutionally protected liberty interest. Second, that right does not extend to requesting assistance with suicide (prescription or injection). The Court in *Vacco* opined that refusing end of life care and requesting as-

sistance in bringing an end to life were distinguishable both in terms of causation and intent. That said, as is discussed later in this chapter, while the Supreme Court has not held decriminalization or authorization of assisted suicide constitutionally *mandated*, nor has it declared constitutionally *prohibited*. This has resulted in a few states authorizing it and many others prohibiting it. Third, the right to refuse treatment survives incompetency, and decisions affecting incompetents will normally be made on a substituted judgment basis, though best interest judgments may be permissible if there is insufficient evidence of the subject's desires to ground a substituted judgment decision. States may, according to *Cruzan*, require clear and convincing evidence to permit termination of treatment. Most states do, though the vigor with which the standard is enforced varies considerably from state to state. Artificial provision of nutrition and hydration (tube feeding) is treated as a medical procedure, and may be refused like others, though some states place more stringent requirements on terminating tube feeding than on terminating other procedures. All states provide for advanced directives, usually living wills and durable powers of attorney, and these are either decisive or are given considerable weight in decision making. For a state-by-state survey, see American Bar Association, *State Health Care Power of Attorney Statutes* (January 2018), https://www.americanbar.org/content/dam/aba/administrative/law_aging/state-health-care-power-of-attorney-statutes.authcheckdam.pdf.

2. As the above excerpt from Nys reflects, France has effectively two Supreme Courts, the Cour de Cassation, the court of last resort for reviewing judicial decisions; and the Council of State, the final court of appeal for administrative decisions. Are the decisions of these two bodies in this instance consistent? Note the powerful role which the duty to rescue in emergencies plays in the French right to die law. The "Commissioner of the Government" who played a role in the Jehovah's Witness case is a functionary who presents the position of the state in French court cases. This role is a bit like that of the solicitor general in the United States, but is more frequently exercised. See Mitchel de S.-O.-l'E Lasser, Comparative Law and Comparative Literature: A Project in Progress, 1997 *Utah L. Rev.* 471.

3. Although the Nys article is mostly up-to-date, Germany has since changed its position on living wills. See Germany: Court Clarifies Requirements for Living Wills and Durable Healthcare Powers of Attorney, Library of Congress (Sept. 30, 2016), http://www.loc.gov/law/foreign-news/article/germany-court-clarifies-requirements-for-living-wills-and-durable-healthcare-powers-of-attorney/; see also Living Will Law 'Strikes a Successful Balance', Spiegel Online, http://www.spiegel.de/international/germany/the-world-from-berlin-living-will-law-strikes-a-successful-balance-a-631447.html. Germany recognizes living wills, but they are not legally binding on the patient's authorized representative unless they are exceedingly specific. For example, a patient's living will stating that they do not wish to receive "life-prolonging treatment" is not specific enough; the German court said the patient would have had to list specific medical treatments they did not wish to receive in order to have their living will honored. See id. Germany has consistently taken a strong right-to-life position in most of the issues that we have studied. It has also, however, taken a strong position

supporting autonomous patient decisionmaking. Are these two positions in conflict here? Or has Germany found a way to reconcile them?

4. In the United States, the issue that Nys identifies as "non-treatment" decisions is usually discussed under the rubric of medical "futility". The issue is raised when further medical care serves no purpose, and involves the obligation or right the physician has at that point to terminate care. In one well-known American case, *In the Matter of Baby K*, 16 F.3d 590 (1994), the Fourth Circuit Court of Appeals held that the Emergency Medical Treatment and Active Labor Act (EMTALA) prohibits denial of treatment to an anencephalic newborn even when further care would be "futile". See also Roberts v. Galen of Virginia, Inc., 525 U.S. 249 (1999) (holding that a hospital need not act with malice in removal of treatment to have violated EMTALA). In a similar case in the United Kingdom, *In re J*, 4 All E.R. 614 (C.A. 1992), the court decided that the family could not compel the doctors to treat a baby where treatment was counter-indicated. See James Munby, Rhetoric and Reality: The Limitations of Patient Self-Determination in Contemporary English Law, 14 *J. Contemp. Health L. & Pol'y* 315 (1998). For reporting on a similar more recent British Case, see Margot Brazier, Commentary: An Intractable Dispute: When Parents and Professionals Disagree, 13 *Med. L. Rev.* 412 (2005). The parent-physician dispute played out again in the recent Charlie Gard case, where a court ultimately ceded to a hospital's recommendation to take an infant off of life support over the parents' protestations. *See* Debra Goldschmidt & Hilary Clarke, *Baby Charlie Gard Dies After Life Support Withdrawn*, CNN (July 29, 2019, 1:36 AM), http://www.cnn.com/2017/07/28/health/charlie-gard-death/index.html; *see also* Robert D. Truog, The United Kingdom Sets Limits on Experimental Treatments: The Case of Charlie Gard, 318 *JAMA* 1001 (2017).

5. Undertreatment of pain has traditionally been common throughout the world, and in particular in the United States. There has been a concerted effort in recent years to remove regulatory and law enforcement barriers to effective pain management at the end-of-life. Special symposium issues of the Journal of Law Medicine and Ethics in 1996 and 1998 highlighted this issue. The Supreme Court in *Washington v. Glucksberg*, 521 U.S. 702, 702 (1997), allowed Washington state's ban on assisted suicide to stand, but in their concurrences Justices Souter and O'Connor countenanced the possibility of "terminal sedation"—providing pain relief in high enough quantities to cause death, if the intent of the medical professional was to diminish pain, Id. at 738 and 785, n.16. Other countries seem also to be increasingly aware of this problem. On pain and end of life care, see Timothy Jost & Danuta Mendelson, A Comparative Study of the Law of Palliative Care and End of Life Treatment, 21 *J. L. Med. & Ethics* 130 (2003). A 2004 European Court of Human Rights case, however, held that an English court violated Article 8 of the European Convention of Human Rights guarantying a right to physical and moral integrity when it refused to block a hospital from administering morphine and coding as do not resuscitate a severely disabled child suffering postoperative complications at the insistence of the child's mother. ECHR 2004/9 *Case of Glass v. The United Kingdom*, 9 March 2004, no. 61827/00.

6. The Terri Schiavo controversy in the United States raised in the public consciousness the question of when nutrition and hydration should be removed when there is a dispute among close relatives as to what the person would have wanted, and even as to the nature of the patient's condition. See, discussing the *Schiavo* case in an international comparative perspective, Symposium, 12 *Eur. J. Health L.* 317ff (2005), including articles on German, U.K. and Dutch law.

7. Note that other countries seem to give far less authority to advanced directives than do American jurisdictions. Why is this? Some American commentators have also begun to question whether advanced directives should always be given decisive weight, particularly when the mental state of the person who signed the directive has changed dramatically. See Rebecca Dresser, Missing Persons: Perceptions of Incompetent Persons, 46 *Rutgers L. Rev.* 609 (1994); see also, Hans-Georg Koch, Erwin Bernat and Alan Meisel, Self-Determination, Privacy and the Right to Die. A Comparative Law Analysis (Germany, United States of America, Japan), 4 *Eur. J. Health L.* 127 (1997).

8. Why do European countries seem to prefer "best interest" to "substituted judgment" standards for making termination of treatment decisions? Might our "substituted judgment" standard be explained by our grounding "right-to-die" law heavily on the doctrine of informed consent compared to European law being arguably based more directly on therapeutic judgment?

9. A leading British decision concerning the right-to-die issue with respect to incompetent patients remains *Airedale NHS Trust v. Bland*, [1993] All ER 275. In this case the British House of Lords decided that discontinuance of the provision of artificial nutrition and hydration would be in the best interests of a patient in a persistent vegetative state, even though it would cause his death. The court concluded that the best interests test was appropriate for these cases, and that this standard should be applied by a court, placing considerable weight on medical opinion. For discussion of this case, see Ian Freckelton, Withdrawal of Life Support: The "Persistent Vegetative State" Conundrum, 1 *J.L. & Med.* 35 (1993); Andrew Grubb, The Persistent Vegetative State: A Duty (Not) to Treat and Conscientious Objection, 4 *Eur. J. Health L.* 157 (1997). The legislature extended the test in the Mental Capacity Act of 2005, which instructs medical professionals to care for individuals who lack capacity—for example, those who have suffered some forms of brain injury, or who have some forms of dementia—by acting in their best interests. See 2005 c 9.

10. For an example of the Irish approach, which takes a relatively liberal view toward end-of-life decisionmaking, see In the Matter of A Ward of Court, 2 I.L.R.M. 401 (Irish Supreme Court, 27 July 1995) (recognizing rights to autonomy, privacy, dignity, bodily integrity, life, death, and equality in ordering the removal of a feeding tube, at a family's wishes and over a hospital's objections). Is there any inconsistency between this and the relatively conservative Irish view of abortion? Note that Germany is similarly conservative on abortion but open to termination of life support at the end of life. See Dermont Feenan, A "Terrible Beauty," the Irish Supreme Court, and Dying, 3 *Eur. J. Health L.* 29 (1996).

Although most of the published literature about refusal and withdrawal focuses on the North American and Western European perspectives, there is emerging literature considering the approaches of other jurisdictions. The following excerpt, for example, explores the Chinese perspective:

Konstantin Tretyakov, *The Right to Die in the United States, Canada, and China: Legal Fictions and Their Utility in a Comparative Perspective*

21 U. Pa. J.L. & Soc. Change 79, 108–113 (2018)

Exploring the Chinese approaches to the right to die can be a difficult task, for both the doctrinal underpinnings of the right in question and the practices of its implementation are very different from those in the United States and Canada. Furthermore, the regulations of the right to die are much less certain than in many Western countries. Therefore, the Chinese experience does not so readily present available parallels to the situation in the United States as the Canadian experience does. At the same time, the Chinese views on the right to die can still be instructive for the U.S. audience, as they help both to flesh out the problem of legal fictions and to illuminate the importance of the doctrinal elements of the right to die and their careful balancing.

In what follows I shall analyze the Chinese doctrine of informed consent and a corresponding doctrine of the right to refuse life-saving medical treatment in terms of their statutory and regulatory content, central premises (including causation and intention), and application by the people's courts in China[].

As far as [w]ithdrawal [of life sustaining treatment] is concerned, in China it originates from the patient's right of informed consent and the corresponding right to refuse medical treatment. The legal pedigree of these rights in China, however, seems much less robust than in the United States, as they are mostly statutory and regulatory constructs that have been developing in the Chinese law since the early 1990s.

In China, the provisions on the right of informed consent (from which the right to refuse treatment can be deduced) can be found in statutes and regulations about the medical profession, among which are Law on Tort Liability, Law on Practicing Doctors, Rules on Handling Medical Accidents, Rules on Management of Medical Institutions, and Enforcement Rules for the Rules of Management of Medical Institutions.

In addition to these acts, there are also several laws and regulations that provide for the involuntary medical treatment of certain groups of patients, including the Law on Prevention and Treatment of Infectious Diseases and Mental Health Law. I do not address these two laws, not because their provisions are less important, but rather because they concern special categories of patients and do not give a general picture of the law of informed consent in China.

The rules in the general documents on informed consent are somewhat vague and in part contradictory. For example, while some of the documents speak of "the patient's consent" (患者同意, *huànzhě tóngyì*), other documents suggest more strongly that the patient's consent must be informed (知情同意, *zhīqíng tóngyì*). The documents also provide for the doctors' duty to obtain consent from their patients and/or their family members for certain (but not all) kinds of treatment, and the list of types of treatment for which consent is required differs between statutes and regulations. Finally, while some documents state that the doctors must rescue patients in critical condition without their consent or consent from family members, a more recent statute provides that there is no such duty.

Despite these discrepancies, there are several common characteristics of the Chinese regime of informed consent that can be discerned from these statutes and regulations. First, the patient's "right" of informed consent (and the corresponding right to refuse medical treatment) apparently exists in China, although it finds no direct stipulation in the black letter of the Chinese law. Instead, the Chinese statutes and regulations speak of the doctors' duty to obtain consent (informed or not) from their patients and/or their family members. A violation of that duty results in tort, disciplinary, or administrative liability of doctors and medical institutions. Some examples demonstrate that the hospitals and the people's courts in China construe this duty formally with little regard to the patients' best interests. A pertinent example here is the case of Xiao Zhijun (肖志军), who refused to give written consent for caesarian section surgery on behalf of his wife. The hospital did not perform the surgery, and both the woman and her fetus died. This case, which happened in 2007, provoked social debates of wide magnitude, and many blamed the hospital for its formalistic approach to patient's consent. Nevertheless, the authorities stated that the hospital's inaction was lawful.

Second, the patient's right to choose the course of her treatment or to refuse it is subject to the wider discretion of physicians and the patient's family members, who can conceal information from the patient in order not to hurt her and make decisions about the treatment behind her back. The laws and regulations also frequently mention the duty to obtain the patient's consent together with the duty not to harm the patient by disclosing relevant information. All this leads to significant abridgments of the patient's autonomy in medical decision-making. A pertinent example here comes from the province of Guangzhou, where a woman was in active labor but refused to grant consent for a caesarian section. The doctors consulted her family members who gave their consent on the surgery. The fetus died, but the woman survived, and the doctors were not held liable for the treatment they performed against the patient's wishes. Studies undertaken by several authors also demonstrate that doctors working in intensive care units do not disclose the truth about diagnosis and prognosis to their patients out of concerns about their well-being (consequentialism) and instead refer to the patient's families to make decisions about treatment.

Third, a patient's consent is required only for certain types of medical procedures. The list of medical interventions requiring the patient's (and her family's) consent drawn up by the Ministry of Health may be broad, but it is still a list—and not, for example, a blanket disposition to the effect that informed consent is required in all situations unless specified otherwise. With respect to [w]ithdrawal, it is unclear whether life-sustaining medical treatments (such as putting the patient on a ventilator or inserting a nasogastric tube into a patient's body) are within the list of medical interventions that require consent, although it seems likely that they are: life-saving treatment is costly and, if not covered by insurance, can be a significant economic burden to patients and their families.

A doctrine of [w]ithdrawal that emerges from these rules and the practice of their implementation differs significantly from its U.S. counterpart. First, the autonomy of the patient (and her corresponding right) has a much weaker presence in the doctrine. In fact, the will of the patient regarding her treatment (or refusing it) may well be overridden by the will of her family members. Furthermore, the doctor's orientation toward the patient's family in the medical decision-making process often leaves the patient unaware of her current condition and further impedes her autonomous decision-making.

Second, the thrust of the Chinese doctrine of informed consent (and a corresponding doctrine of [w]ithdrawal) seems to be more consequentialist than in the United States. This is apparent from (1) the types of treatment for which the patient's (or her family's) consent is required (the kinds of treatment that are likely to produce significant impact on the patient's and/or her family's physical, emotional, or financial well-being) and (2) the protective orientation of informed consent rules meant not to harm the patients by disclosing certain sensitive information to them. Furthermore, the very idea of informed consent in China emerges in the context of liability of the doctors and medical institutions; in other words, the basis of the need for consent is not so much the patient's right as the negative consequences the medical professionals would suffer if they don't obtain it.

Finally, the doctrine of [w]ithdrawal [of life-sustaining treatment] that can be deduced from the rules on informed consent in the context of civil, administrative, or disciplinary liability necessarily puts emphasis on the issues of intention and causation that are important in imposing that liability. At the same time, as the implementation of the doctrine suggests, if the patient's family members agree on withdrawal of life-saving treatment from their relative, a commencement of a court action to bring the doctor or the hospital to liability is unlikely. (In the situations when the family is divided on whether the patient should be removed from life support or not, the doctors are likely not to discontinue life-saving treatment, as being alive is presumably better for the patient than being dead and the doctors are highly unlikely to be held liable for a "wrongful life" of the patient.) In a very unlikely situation when such an issue is presented before the people's court, it will likely defer to medical experts on the issue of what caused the death of the patient. The doctor's intention will likely be construed broadly enough to embrace both purpose (desire) and foresight, which is in line with the consequentialist notion of intentionality.

Notes

1. Russia has also seen recent developments in its right to refuse or withdraw treatment, with the criminalization of the dissemination of information about how to seek end-of-life care, even by a medical professional on a patient's request. The law

was intended to curb online dissemination of instructions on how to commit suicide; that it criminalizes seeking medical care could be an unintended side effect. The law does allow the refusal or withdrawal of care by a patient or an authorized representative, except in for a select set of patients: for example, the mentally ill, criminals, and those suffering from an illness that could harm others. See Federal Law No.323-FZ *On the Basics of Healthcare Protection of Citizens in Russian Federation* (enacted on Nov. 21, 2011, amended on April 3, 2017).

2. The medical and legal perspectives on the right to die are often influenced by religion. For example a recent case in India considered the legality of the Jain tradition of *santhara*, fasting oneself to death, practiced by a few hundred individuals each year. A lower court initially outlawed *santhara*, citing concerns about younger Jains encouraging elders to adopt the practice in order to avoid elder care. But among concerns about religious freedom, the Supreme Court has stayed that order until it hears the case. See Jain 'Santhara' Ritual of Fast Unto Death Can Continue For Now, Says Court, NDTV, http://www.ndtv.com/india-news/jain-tradition-of-santhara-or-fasting-unto-death-allowed-by-supreme-court-1212645.

D. Physician Aid in Dying

The prior part of this Chapter reviewed withholding and withdrawal of life-sustaining treatment for the terminally ill and/or persons in persistent vegetative states. As that discussion shows, while most countries permit withdrawal and withholding, there are significant differences in the way in which the legal rules are implemented. By contrast, there is much more disagreement on the topic of directly assisting terminally ill patients to end their lives, either by providing them with life-ending medicine (prescription) or physicians or others directly administering treatment resulting in death (injection) (collectively, physician aid in dying). Comparably few jurisdictions have legalized aid in dying and it remains controversial even where it is permitted. Some advocates for legalization of physician aid in dying contend that patient autonomy and self-determination ought to be recognized as paramount values, and that there is no legitimate reason to prevent those with the competency to do so from making an informed decision to end their life. Others strongly believe that it is unethical for medical professionals to assist patients in ending their own lives. Opponents make several arguments against physician aid in dying: first, that life is sacred, doctors and patients and doctors should not play God, and physician aid in dying violates human dignity; second, that better access to palliative care would ameliorate the need for patients to seek to end their lives; third, that vulnerable, sick individuals will be coerced into ending their lives out of a concern about the burden (financial and otherwise) they impose on their families and/or society; fourth, that involving physicians and nurses in the ending of a patient's life is incompatible with the ethics of the profession; and finally, that there is no sufficient limiting principle once patient autonomy over death is the norm—in other words, a concern that once patient autonomy is recognized as the paramount value, eventually physician aid in dying will be available to all patients—not just those who are terminally ill—leading to potential for a slippery slope of abuse and exploitation of vulnerable populations. The adequacy and meaning of the empirical data is contested, and has led both sides of the debate to claim current practices support their perspective. See generally M.J. Shariff, Assisted death and the slippery slope—finding clarity amid advocacy, convergence, and complexity, 19 *Curr. Oncology* 143 (2012).

Cases on physician aid in dying tend to come before courts in one of two ways. In many instances, a patient seeks to assert a right to aid in dying and the courts have adjudicated whether such a right exists and, if so, on what basis (a right to privacy, a right to dignity, a right to life, and a right to due process and equal protection have all been considered). Less frequently, cases come before courts where a practitioner is charged with some form of culpable homicide related to the death of a patient. Both types of cases are explored below.

1. The Netherlands and Europe

The Dutch experience with aid in dying has played a major role in the development of aid in dying law around the world. The country is one of only a handful of jurisdictions to allow injection in addition to prescription. Some have argued that aid in dying enjoys widespread support in the Netherlands because the medical profession believes that its task is not simply to preserve life but also to combat pain and suffering. R.J.M. Dillmann, Euthanasia in The Netherlands: The Role of the Dutch Medical Profession, Cambridge Quarterly of Healthcare Ethics 100 (1996). When these values come in conflict, the priority of preserving life is not a foregone conclusion. Nonetheless, the circumstances under which preventing suffering can trump preserving life remain controversial—as evidenced by the *Chabot* case, excerpted below, in which a patient who was severely depressed because of her life circumstances—but not in serious physical ill health—requested and obtained assistance in suicide.

Office of Public Prosecutions v. Chabot

Supreme Court of the Netherlands, Criminal Chamber,
21 June 1994, no. 96.972, from John Griffiths, Alex Bood, and Haleen Weyers,
Euthanasia and the Law in the Netherlands 329–38 (1998)

Procedure

The appeal is from the Court of Appeals, Leeuwarden (30 September 1993), which (like the District court, Assen, 21 April 1993) found the defendant not guilty of the offence charged: "Intentionally assisting another person to commit suicide" as prohibited by article 294 of the Criminal Code. The Court of Appeals found the defense of justification due to necessity well-founded and the question on appeal is whether the Court's interpretation of the scope of the defense was legally correct and whether the facts as found support the decision.

* * *

Facts

The following facts were established by the Court of Appeals.

Defendant is a psychiatrist who on 28 September 1991 supplied to Ms. B, at her request, lethal drugs that she consumed in the presence of defendant, a GP, and her friend Ms. H. She died half an hour later. Defendant reported her death the same day to the local coroner as a suicide which he had assisted. He included what the Court of Appeals characterizes as an "extensive report" of the case, with "a very detailed account of the discussions with Ms. B (and her sister and brother-in-law), a report of the psychiatric investigation and defendant's diagnosis, his considerations concerning Ms. B's bereavement process and her refusal of treatment."

Ms. B was 50 years old. She had married at the age of 22 but the marriage was from the beginning not a happy one. She had two sons, Patrick and Rodney. In 1986 her older son, Patrick, committed suicide while in military service in Germany. From that time on her marital problems grew worse and the relationship more violent, and her wish to end her life began to manifest itself. According to her own statements, she only remained alive to care for her other son Rodney. These circumstances led to a brief admission to the psychiatric ward of a local hospital in October of 1986, followed by polyclinical psychiatric treatment, neither of which had an effect on her situation: according to the psychiatrist at the time, she was not open to any suggestion of working toward an acceptance of Patrick's death.

In December 1988, shortly after the death of her father, Ms. B left her husband, taking Rodney with her; the divorce followed in February 1990. In November 1990 Rodney was admitted to hospital in connection with a traffic accident. In the hospital he was found to be suffering from cancer, from which he died on 3 May 1991. That evening Ms. B attempted suicide with drugs that she had received from her psychiatrist in 1986 but had saved. The attempt was unsuccessful, and to her great disappointment she recovered consciousness a day and a half later. She immediately began to save drugs again with the intention of committing suicide.

Finding a way to die came to dominate her thoughts. She discussed various methods with her sister; she gave an old friend a letter that was to be opened only after her death; she arranged for cemetery plots for herself, her two sons and her former husband and had her first son reburied so that there was space for her between the graves of her two sons. She attempted to get effective drugs for committing suicide and considered other methods as well, which she discussed with various people. However, she was afraid that a second failure might lead either to an involuntary committal to a mental institution or to continued life with a serious disability. She made it known to others that she wished to die, but in a humane way that would not involuntarily confront others with her suicide.

Ms. B approached the Dutch Association for Voluntary Euthanasia and in this way came in contact with defendant, who had indicated his willingness to give psychiatric support to persons who might approach the Association for help. Between 2 August and 7 September 1991 defendant had four series of discussions with Ms. B, totalling some 24 hours. He also spoke with Ms. B's sister and brother-in-law. Beginning on 11 August, after the second series of discussions with Ms. B, defendant approached 4 consultants. He furnished them with an extensive account of his findings and requested suggestions concerning matters that he might have overlooked in the psychiatric investigation of Ms. B or that required further clarification. He also asked whether they were in agreement with his diagnosis. Later, after the third series of discussions, he approached 3 more consultants.

In considering the question "whether Ms. B was suffering from any illness" the Court of Appeals concluded that there was no indication of any somatic condition that might have been the source of Ms. B's wish to die. From the beginning of defendant's contacts with her it was clear that she was suffering from psychic traumas that in principle lent themselves to psychiatric treatment, so that defendant was justified in entering into a doctor-patient relationship with her even though that might ultimately expose him to a conflict of duties.

Defendant's professional judgment of Ms. B was that there was no question in her case of a psychiatric illness or major depressive episode, but that according to the classification system of the American Psychiatric Association (D.S.M.-III-R), she was suffering from an adjustment disorder consisting of a depressed mood, without psychotic signs, in the context of a complicated bereavement process. In his opinion, she was experiencing intense, long-term psychic suffering that, for her, was unbearable and without prospect of improvement. Her request for assistance with suicide was well-considered: in letters and discussions with him she presented the reasons for her decision clearly and consistently and showed that she understood her situation and the consequences of her decision. In his judgment, her rejection of therapy was also well-considered.

The Court of Appeals found that defendant was an experienced psychiatrist who made his diagnosis in a very careful way. The experts consulted by him were agreed that Ms. B's decision was well-considered and her suffering long-term and unbearable, and that in the circumstances there was no "concrete treatment perspective"; the majority agreed without reservation with the way he had handled the case. Several of them observed that it was highly likely that, if not given expert assistance, Ms. B would have continued her efforts to commit suicide, using increasingly violent means. Although her condition was in principle treatable, treatment would probably have been long and the chance of success was small. None of the experts consulted considered that there was in fact any realistic treatment perspective, in light of her well-established refusal of treatment. Defendant had repeatedly tried to persuade Ms. B to accept some form of therapy and the Court of Appeals accepted defendant's testimony to the effect that if there had been an available treatment with a realistic chance of success within a reasonable period, he would have continued to pressure Ms. B to accept it and, if she continued to refuse, would not have given her the requested assistance.

The experts consulted in this case, a discussion paper of the Medical Association on the subject, a discussion paper of the Inspectorate for Mental Health, and a position paper of the Dutch Association for Psychiatry all agree that from the point of view of medical ethics, there may be circumstances in which assistance with suicide is legitimate in the case of persons whose suffering does not have a somatic origin and who are not in the terminal phase of their disease.

The opinion of the Supreme Court

General Considerations

* * *

* * * [T]he circumstances of an individual case may be such that rendering assistance with suicide, like performing euthanasia, can be considered justifiable. This is the case when it is proved that the defendant acted in a situation of necessity, that is to say—speaking generally—that confronted with a choice between mutually conflicting duties, he chose to perform the one of greater weight. In particular, a doctor may be in a situation of necessity if he had to choose between the duty to preserve life and the duty as a doctor to do everything possible to relieve the unbearable and hopeless suffering [*ondraaglijk en uizichtloos lijden*] of a patient committed to his care.

When a doctor who has performed euthanasia or furnished the means for suicide claims that he acted in a situation of necessity, the trial court must investigate ... whether the doctor, especially in the light of scientifically responsible medical opinion and according to the norms recognized in medical ethics, made a choice between mutually conflicting duties that, considered objectively and in the context of the specific circumstances of the case, can be considered justifiable. In this connection it should be observed that the procedure by which the doctor responsible for treatment [*behandelende arts*] is to report cases of euthanasia and assistance with suicide, including thereby information on a number of specified items ... contains no substantive criteria which, if met by a doctor who performs euthanasia or renders assistance with suicide, entail that his behavior is justifiable. The reporting procedure offers a procedural structure within which the responsible doctor can render account of his behavior and the prosecutorial authorities or the trial court can assess it.

3.2—The Justifiability of Assistance With Suicide in the Case of Non-Somatic Suffering and a Patient Who is Not in the Terminal Phase

The first ground of appeal depends on the view that assistance with suicide by a doctor, in the case of a patient like Ms. B whose suffering is not somatic and who is not in the terminal phase, cannot [as a matter of law] be justifiable.

This view cannot be considered correct. The specific nature of the defense of necessity, which, depending upon the trial court's weighing and evaluation after the fact of the particular circumstances of the case can lead it to decide that the act was justified, does not allow for any such general limitation. A claim of necessity can therefore not be excluded simply on the ground that the patient's unbearable suffering, without prospect of improvement, does not have a somatic cause and that the patient is not in the terminal phase. The Court of Appeals found, and this is not challenged on appeal, that from the point of view of medical ethics the legitimacy of euthanasia or assistance with suicide in such circumstances is not categorically excluded. In answering the question whether in a particular case a person's suffering must be regarded as so unbearable and hopeless that an act that violates article 294 must be considered justified because performed in a situation of necessity, the suffering must be distinguished from its cause, in the sense that the cause of the suffering does not detract from the extent to which suffering is experienced. But the fact remains that when the suffering of a patient does not demonstrably follow from a somatic illness or condition, consisting simply of the experience of pain and loss of bodily functions, it is more difficult objectively to establish the fact of suffering and in particular its seriousness and lack of prospect of improvement. For this reason the trial court must in such cases approach the question whether there was a situation of necessity with exceptional care.

The Voluntariness of the Request in the Case of a Psychiatric Patient

[The second ground of appeal challenges the Court of Appeals' holding that it is possible for a psychiatric patient voluntarily to request assistance with suicide; alternatively, it is argued that the judgment of the Court of Appeals that the request was voluntary is not based on sufficient evidence. The third ground of appeal challenges the Court of Appeals' holding that the fact that a second psychiatrist had not examined Ms. B is not an obstacle to accepting the defense of necessity. The Supreme Court deals with these various contentions together.

The Court holds that the prosecution's assertion that the request for assistance with suicide of a psychiatric patient cannot be voluntary "is as a general [legal] proposition incorrect." The Court of Appeals held "that the wish to die of a person whose suffering is psychic can be based on an autonomous judgment. That holding is in itself not incorrect."

The alternative challenge—to the sufficiency of the evidence—is, however, well founded, among other things in light of the fact that Ms. B had not been examined by a second psychiatrist.]

As stated above, in a case in which the suffering of a patient is not based on a somatic disease or condition, the trial court must approach the question whether under the circumstances of the case assistance with suicide can be justified as having occurred in a situation of necessity with exceptional care.

If a doctor who affords his patient assistance with suicide has neglected before acting to check his judgment concerning the situation with which he is confronted against that of an independent colleague, whether or not the latter conducts his own examination of the patient, this need not in general preclude the possibility that the trial court, based on its own investigation of the circumstances of the case, comes to the conclusion that the doctor acted in a situation of necessity and therefore must be considered not guilty. However, the situation is different in a case like the present one.

[When the case involves] a patient whose suffering is not based on a somatic disease or condition ... the trial court, in considering whether the claim of necessity is well-founded, must—considering the exceptional care with which it is to approach this matter—base its decision among other things on the judgment of an independent medical expert who has at least seen and examined the patient himself. Since the trial court must decide whether the defense of necessity is compatible with the requirement that the course of conduct chosen be proportional to the harm to be avoided and also the least harmful choice available, the judgment of the independent colleague of the defendant, based partly on his own examination, should deal with the seriousness of the suffering and the lack of prospect for improvement, and in that connection also with other possibilities of providing help. This is because in assessing whether suffering is so unbearable and hopeless that assistance with suicide can be deemed a choice justified by a situation of necessity, there can in principle be no question of hopelessness if there is a realistic alternative to relieve the suffering which the patient has in complete freedom rejected. The independent expert must also include in his examination the question, whether the patient has made a voluntary and well-considered request, without his competence being influenced by his sickness or condition.

Absent the judgment of an expert who saw and examined Ms. B, the Court of Appeals could not properly come to the conclusion that defendant as the responsible psychiatrist was confronted with an unavoidable conflict of duties and in that situation made a justifiable choice. In such a situation, the Court of Appeals should have rejected the defense.

Judgment

[The judgment below must be reversed. In general, this would lead to referral of the case to another Court of Appeals. In the circumstances of this case such a referral—considering the absence of the essential report of an independent expert who himself examined Ms. B—could only lead to the conclusion that the defense of necessity must be rejected. In such a case it is more efficient for the Supreme Court to give final judgment itself.

The defense of necessity is rejected, and the defendant, not having made any other defense, is found guilty of the offence as charged.

However, "the person of the defendant and the circumstances in which the offence was committed ... have led the Supreme Court to apply article 9a of the Criminal Code and not to impose any punishment or other measure."]

Following the decision, further disciplinary actions were taken, described in the following excerpt from Griffiths, Bood, and Weyers, supra, at 338–39.

The medical disciplinary proceedings against Chabot

The prosecution in the criminal case had requested the responsible Medical Inspector, who was contemplating a medical disciplinary proceeding, not to go ahead with it while the criminal case was pending. When, with the decision of the Supreme Court on 21 June 1994, the criminal case was over, the disciplinary proceedings against Chabot got under way. The regional Medical Disciplinary Tribunal rendered a decision on 6 February 1995. It concluded that Chabot had "undermined confidence in the medical profession" (the basic disciplinary norm). Chabot received a relatively severe sanction: "Reprimand." On 19 April 1995 Chabot announced that he had had enough of legal proceedings and would not appeal this decision, so that the case was finally closed.

The Medical Disciplinary Tribunal held, as had the Supreme Court, that assistance with suicide can be legitimate in the case of a person whose suffering is of non-somatic origin and who is not in the terminal phase. The request must be the result of an "autonomous decision" and not of a treatable disorder. The consulted doctors must have personally examined the person concerned (the Tribunal is not entirely clear whether more than one doctor must be consulted nor whether this must be a psychiatrist).

The Tribunal considered that in the specific circumstances of the case Chabot had not adequately preserved his professional distance, particularly in light of the frequency and length of his sessions with Ms. B and the fact that these took place at Chabot's house in the countryside (where Ms. B, together with a couple who accompanied her, resided in a guest cottage on Chabot's property).

Finally, the Tribunal seems to have taken a more restrictive view than the Supreme Court on one crucial aspect of the case: the extent to which a doctor must insist on treatment as an alternative to assistance with suicide. The Supreme Court's opinion refers to a "realistic alternative," leaving room for the possibility that available treatment possibilities may not be considered "realistic." The Tribunal, on the other hand, took the position that Chabot could not properly conclude that Ms. B's condition was untreatable until after treatment had in fact been tried. "The patient's refusal of treatment should have been a reason for [Chabot] to refuse the requested assistance with suicide, at least for the time being."

This difference between the two decisions reflects the fundamental difference of opinion between the experts called by the Tribunal in the disciplinary proceeding. The Tribunal adopted the latter's view that treatment ought not to have been honored.

* * *

Notes

1. For more discussion of the Chabot case and its aftermath, see The Chabot Case: Analysis and Account of Dutch Perspectives, 5 *Med. L. Int.* 141 (2002); H.J.J. Leenan, Dutch Supreme Court about Assistance to Suicide in the Case of Severe Mental Suffering, 1 *Eur. J. Health L.* 377 (1994); Johan Legemaate & J.K.M. Gevers, Physician-Assisted Suicide in Psychiatry: Developments in the Netherlands, 6 *Cambridge Q. in Healthcare Ethics* 175 (1997); and Johanna H. Groenewoud, Physician-Assisted Death in Psychiatric Practice in the Netherlands, 336 *New Eng. J. Med.* 1795 (1997).

2. A discussion of the Dutch experience is found in John Griffiths, Alex Bood and Heleen Weyers, *Euthanasia and Law in the Netherlands* (1998). *See also*, Raphael Cohen-Almagor, Non-voluntary and Involuntary Euthanasia in the Netherlands: Dutch Perspectives, 18 *Issues in Law and Medicine* 239 (2003); Raphael Cohen-Almagor, The Guidelines for Euthanasia in the Netherlands: Reflection on Dutch Perspectives, 9 *Ethical Perspectives* 3 (2002); Margaret Pabst Battin, A Dozen Caveats

Concerning Discussion of Euthanasia in the Netherlands, in M.P. Battin, *The Least Worst Death*, 130 (1994); Sherwin B. Nuland, Physician-Assisted Suicide and Euthanasia in Practice, 342 *New Eng. J. Med.* 583 (2000); National Legal Center for the Medically Dependent and Disabled, Physician-Assisted Suicide and Euthanasia in the Netherlands: A Report to the House Judiciary Subcommittee on the Constitution, 14 *Issues L. & Med.* 301 (1998); Marcia Angell, Euthanasia in the Netherlands—Good News or Bad? 335 *New Eng. J. Med.* 1676 (1996).

3. The Dutch situation has been extensively studied independently and by the Dutch government (a series of empirical studies have been conducted on practice under the statute). See, e.g. Bregje Onwuteaka-Philipsen, et al., Taking the Final Step: Changing the Law on Euthanasia and Physician-Assisted Suicide: Dutch Experience of Monitoring Euthanasia, 331 *BMJ* 691 (2005); Jacqueline M. Cuperus-Bosma, Physician-Assisted Death: Policy-Making by the Assembly of Prosecutors General in the Netherlands, 4 *Eur. J. Health L.* 225 (1997); Johanna H. Groenewoud, et al., Clinical Problems with the Performance of Euthanasia and Physician-Assisted Suicide in the Netherlands, 342 *New Eng. J. Med.* 551 (2000); and Johanna H. Groenewoud, Physician-Assisted Death in Psychiatric Practice in the Netherlands, 336 *New Eng. J. Med.* 1795 (1997).

One concern about the empirical evidence is that Dutch aid in dying may be widely underreported (for a recent retrospective on end-of-life decisions in the Netherlands, see Agnes van der Heide et al., End-of-Life Decisions in the Netherlands over 25 Years, 377 *New Eng. J. Med.* 492 (2017)). Some commentators, however, have pointed out that these practices are probably being carried out in many other nations secretly, and are never reported. For example, a number of nations permit the practice of terminal sedation—increasing dosages of medication for persons in severe pain to the point where the medication may result in death. See J. Pereira, Legalizing Euthanasia or Assisted Suicide: the Illusion of Safeguards and Controls, 18 *Curr. Oncol.* e38–e45 (2011). Is the line between officially permitted terminal sedation or withdrawal of treatment on the one hand, and assistance in suicide on the other, meaningful?

4. The Dutch experience has critics and proponents, and is often also cited as an example of what to do (and what not to do) in setting up a regulatory regime for aid in dying. See, e.g., Trudo Lemmens, The Conflict between Open-Ended Access to Physician-Assisted Dying and the Protection of the Vulnerable: Lessons from Belgium's Euthanasia Regime for the Canadian Post-Carter Era in Catherine Régis, Lara Khoury, Robert Kouri, *Les Grands Conflits en Droit de la Santé* (Cowensville: Yvon Blais, 2016) 261–317; Jocelyn Downie, et al., Pereira's Attack on Legalizing Euthanasia or Assisted Suicide: Smoke and Mirrors, 19 *Curr. Oncology*, 133 (2012).

5. Currently the Netherlands, Belgium, Colombia, Luxembourg, and Canada are the only national jurisdictions that officially sanction and regulate physician aid in dying, though within some countries some sub-national jurisdiction do as well (e.g., the canton of Zurich in Switzerland, some U.S. states). For more on the approaches of various nations to aid in dying, see Raphael Cohen-Almagor, Euthanasia and Physician-Assisted Suicide in the Democratic World: Legal Overview, 16 *N.Y. Int. L. Rev.* 1 (2003); Hazel E. McHaffie, et al., Withholding/Withdrawing Treatment from

Neonates: Legislation and Official Guidelines Across Europe, 25 *J. Med. Ethics* 440 (1999); Michael Ashby, Of Life and Death: The Canadian and Australian Senates on Palliative Care and Euthanasia, 6 *J. L. & Med.* 40 (1997); Meredith Blake, Physician-Assisted Suicide: A Criminal Offence or a Patient's Right? 5 *Med. L. Rev.* 294 (1997). On the status of aid-in-dying under British law, see also John Keown, Euthanasia in England: Courts, Committees and Consistency, 16 *Medicine and Law* 805 (1997); and David P.T. Price, Assisted Suicide and Refusing Medical Treatment: Linguistics, Morals and Legal Contortions, 4 *Med. L. Rev.* 270 (1996); under Belgian law, Herman Nys, A Presentation of the Belgian Act on Euthanasia Against the Background of Dutch Euthanasia Law, 10 *Eur. J. Health L.* 239 (2003); Eva Strubbe, Toward a Legal Recognition for Termination of Life without Request, 7 *Eur. J. Health L.* 57 (2000); and under Canadian law, Michael Stingl, Euthanasia and Health Reform in Canada, 7 *Cambridge Q. Healthcare Ethics*, 348 (1998).

Pretty v. United Kingdom

Application no. 2346/02, Council of Europe:
European Court of Human Rights, 29 April 2002

I. THE CIRCUMSTANCES OF THE CASE

The applicant is a 43-year-old woman. She resides with her husband of twenty-five years, their daughter and granddaughter. The applicant suffers from motor neurone disease (MND). This is a progressive neuro-degenerative disease of motor cells within the central nervous system. The disease is associated with progressive muscle weakness affecting the voluntary muscles of the body. As a result of the progression of the disease, severe weakness of the arms and legs and the muscles involved in the control of breathing are affected. Death usually occurs as a result of weakness of the breathing muscles, in association with weakness of the muscles controlling speaking and swallowing, leading to respiratory failure and pneumonia. No treatment can prevent the progression of the disease.

The applicant's condition has deteriorated rapidly since MND was diagnosed in November 1999. The disease is now at an advanced stage. She is essentially paralysed from the neck down, has virtually no decipherable speech and is fed through a tube. Her life expectancy is very poor, measurable only in weeks or months. However, her intellect and capacity to make decisions are unimpaired. The final stages of the disease are exceedingly distressing and undignified. As she is frightened and distressed at the suffering and indignity that she will endure if the disease runs its course, she very strongly wishes to be able to control how and when she dies and thereby be spared that suffering and indignity.

Although it is not a crime to commit suicide under English law, the applicant is prevented by her disease from taking such a step without assistance. It is however a crime to assist another to commit suicide (section 2(1) of the Suicide Act 1961).

Intending that she might commit suicide with the assistance of her husband, the applicant's solicitor asked the Director of Public Prosecutions (DPP), in a letter dated

27 July 2001 written on her behalf, to give an undertaking not to prosecute the applicant's husband should he assist her to commit suicide in accordance with her wishes.

In a letter dated 8 August 2001, the DPP refused to give the undertaking ...

[Courts in the United Kingdom refused her request to overturn the decision. Mrs. Pretty appealed all the way to the UK House of Lords. Appeal was then sought in the European Court of Human Rights. The European court first reviewed the UK decision and relevant UK law before turning to European law.]

* * *

II. ALLEGED VIOLATION OF ARTICLE 2 OF THE CONVENTION

The relevant parts of Article 2 of the Convention provide:

"1. Everyone's right to life shall be protected by law. No one shall be deprived of his life intentionally save in the execution of a sentence of a court following his conviction of a crime for which this penalty is provided by law.

2. Deprivation of life shall not be regarded as inflicted in contravention of this Article when it results from the use of force which is no more than absolutely necessary:

(a) in defence of any person from unlawful violence;

(b) in order to effect a lawful arrest or to prevent the escape of a person lawfully detained;

(c) in action lawfully taken for the purpose of quelling a riot or insurrection."

* * *

The Court's case-law accords pre-eminence to Article 2 as one of the most fundamental provisions of the Convention (see *McCann and Others v. the United Kingdom*, judgment of 27 September 1995, Series A no. 324, pp. 45–46, §§ 146–47). It safeguards the right to life, without which enjoyment of any of the other rights and freedoms in the Convention is rendered nugatory. It sets out the limited circumstances when deprivation of life may be justified and the Court has applied a strict scrutiny when those exceptions have been relied on by the respondent States (ibid., p. 46, §§ 149–50).

The text of Article 2 expressly regulates the deliberate or intended use of lethal force by State agents. However, it has been interpreted as covering not only intentional killing but also the situations where it is permitted to "use force" which may result, as an unintended outcome, in the deprivation of life (ibid., p. 46, § 148). Furthermore, the Court has held that the first sentence of Article 2 § 1 enjoins the State not only to refrain from the intentional and unlawful taking of life, but also to take appropriate steps to safeguard the lives of those within its. This obligation extends beyond a primary duty to secure the right to life by putting in place effective criminal-law provisions to deter the commission of offences against the person backed up by law-enforcement machinery for the prevention, suppression and sanctioning of breaches of such provisions; it may also imply in certain well-defined circumstances a positive obligation on the authorities to take preventive operational measures to protect an individual whose life is at risk from the criminal acts of another individual.

More recently, in *Keenan*, Article 2 was found to apply to the situation of a mentally ill prisoner who disclosed signs of being a suicide risk (see *Keenan*, cited above, § 91).

The consistent emphasis in all the cases before the Court has been the obligation of the State to protect life. The Court is not persuaded that "the right to life" guaranteed in Article 2 can be interpreted as involving a negative aspect. While, for example in the context of Article 11 of the Convention, the freedom of association has been found to involve not only a right to join an association but a corresponding right not to be forced to join an association, the Court observes that the notion of a freedom implies some measure of choice as to its exercise ... Article 2 of the Convention is phrased in different terms. It is unconcerned with issues to do with the quality of living or what a person chooses to do with his or her life. To the extent that these aspects are recognised as so fundamental to the human condition that they require protection from State interference, they may be reflected in the rights guaranteed by other Articles of the Convention, or in other international human rights instruments. Article 2 cannot, without a distortion of language, be interpreted as conferring the diametrically opposite right, namely a right to die; nor can it create a right to self-determination in the sense of conferring on an individual the entitlement to choose death rather than life.

The Court accordingly finds that no right to die, whether at the hands of a third person or with the assistance of a public authority, can be derived from Article 2 of the Convention. It is confirmed in this view by the recent Recommendation 1418 (1999) of the Parliamentary Assembly of the Council of Europe ...

III. ALLEGED VIOLATION OF ARTICLE 3 OF THE CONVENTION

Article 3 of the Convention provides:

"No one shall be subjected to torture or to inhuman or degrading treatment or punishment."

* * *

Article 3 of the Convention, together with Article 2, must be regarded as one of the most fundamental provisions of the Convention and as enshrining core values of the democratic societies making up the Council of Europe. In contrast to the other provisions in the Convention, it is cast in absolute terms, without exception or proviso, or the possibility of derogation under Article 15 of the Convention.

An examination of the Court's case-law indicates that Article 3 has been most commonly applied in contexts in which the risk to the individual of being subjected to any of the proscribed forms of treatment emanated from intentionally inflicted acts of State agents or public authorities. It may be described in general terms as imposing a primarily negative obligation on States to refrain from inflicting serious harm on persons within their jurisdiction. However, in light of the fundamental importance of Article 3, the Court has reserved to itself sufficient flexibility to address the application of that Article in other situations that might arise.

In particular, the Court has held that the obligation on the High Contracting Parties under Article 1 of the Convention to secure to everyone within their jurisdiction the rights and freedoms defined in the Convention, taken in conjunction with Article 3, requires States to take measures designed to ensure that individuals within their jurisdiction are not subjected to torture or inhuman and degrading treatment or punishment, including such treatment administered by private individuals ... A positive obligation on the State to provide protection against inhuman or degrading treatment has been found to arise in a number of cases ... Article 3 also imposes requirements on State authorities to protect the health of persons deprived of liberty ...

As regards the types of "treatment" which fall within the scope of Article 3 of the Convention, the Court's case-law refers to "ill-treatment" that attains a minimum level of severity and involves actual bodily injury or intense physical or mental suffering ... Where treatment humiliates or debases an individual, showing a lack of respect for, or diminishing, his or her human dignity, or arouses feelings of fear, anguish or inferiority capable of breaking an individual's moral and physical resistance, it may be characterised as degrading and also fall within the prohibition of Article 3 ... The suffering which flows from naturally occurring illness, physical or mental, may be covered by Article 3, where it is, or risks being, exacerbated by treatment, whether flowing from conditions of detention, expulsion or other measures, for which the authorities can be held responsible ...

In the present case, it is beyond dispute that the respondent State has not, itself, inflicted any ill-treatment on the applicant. Nor is there any complaint that the applicant is not receiving adequate care from the State medical authorities. The situation of the applicant is therefore not comparable with that in *D. v. the United Kingdom*, in which an AIDS sufferer was threatened with removal from the United Kingdom to the island of St Kitts where no effective medical or palliative treatment for his illness was available and he would have been exposed to the risk of dying under the most distressing circumstances. The responsibility of the State would have been engaged by its act ("treatment") of removing him in those circumstances. There is no comparable act or "treatment" on the part of the United Kingdom in the present case.

The applicant has claimed rather that the refusal of the DPP to give an undertaking not to prosecute her husband if he assisted her to commit suicide and the criminal-law prohibition on assisted suicide disclose inhuman and degrading treatment for which the State is responsible as it will thereby be failing to protect her from the suffering which awaits her as her illness reaches its ultimate stages. This claim, however, places a new and extended construction on the concept of treatment, which, as found by the House of Lords, goes beyond the ordinary meaning of the word.... As found above, Article 2 of the Convention is first and foremost a prohibition on the use of lethal force or other conduct which might lead to the death of a human being and does not confer any right on an individual to require a State to permit or facilitate his or her death.

The Court cannot but be sympathetic to the applicant's apprehension that without the possibility of ending her life she faces the prospect of a distressing death. It is true that she is unable to commit suicide herself due to physical incapacity and that the state of law is such that her husband faces the risk of prosecution if he renders her assistance. Nonetheless, the positive obligation on the part of the State which is relied on in the present case would not involve the removal or mitigation of harm by, for instance, preventing any ill-treatment by public bodies or private individuals or providing improved conditions or care. It would require that the State sanction actions intended to terminate life, an obligation that cannot be derived from Article 3 of the Convention ...

IV. ALLEGED VIOLATION OF ARTICLE 8 OF THE CONVENTION

Article 8 of the Convention provides as relevant:

"1. Everyone has the right to respect for his private and family life ...

2. There shall be no interference by a public authority with the exercise of this right except such as is in accordance with the law and is necessary in a democratic society in the interests of national security, public safety or the economic well-being of the country, for the prevention of disorder or crime, for the protection of health or morals, or for the protection of the rights and freedoms of others."

* * *

1. Applicability of Article 8 § 1 of the Convention

As the Court has had previous occasion to remark, the concept of "private life" is a broad term not susceptible to exhaustive definition. It covers the physical and psychological integrity of a person. It can sometimes embrace aspects of an individual's physical and social identity. Elements such as, for example, gender identification, name and sexual orientation and sexual life fall within the personal sphere protected by Article. Article 8 also protects a right to personal development, and the right to establish and develop relationships with other human beings and the outside world. Although no previous case has established as such any right to self-determination as being contained in Article 8 of the Convention, the Court considers that the notion of personal autonomy is an important principle underlying the interpretation of its guarantees.

The Government have argued that the right to private life cannot encapsulate a right to die with assistance, such being a negation of the protection that the Convention was intended to provide. The Court would observe that the ability to conduct one's life in a manner of one's own choosing may also include the opportunity to pursue activities perceived to be of a physically or morally harmful or dangerous nature for the individual concerned. The extent to which a State can use compulsory powers or the criminal law to protect people from the consequences of their chosen lifestyle has long been a topic of moral and jurisprudential discussion, the fact that the interference is often viewed as trespassing on the private and personal sphere adding to the vigour of the debate. However, even where the conduct poses a danger to health or, arguably, where it is of a life-threatening nature, the case-law of the Convention institutions has regarded the State's imposition of compulsory or criminal measures as impinging on the private life of the applicant within the meaning of Article 8 § 1 and requiring justification in terms of the second paragraph.

While it might be pointed out that death was not the intended consequence of the applicants' conduct in the above situations, the Court does not consider that this can be a decisive factor. In the sphere of medical treatment, the refusal to accept a particular treatment might, inevitably, lead to a fatal outcome, yet the imposition of medical treatment, without the consent of a mentally competent adult patient, would interfere with a person's physical integrity in a manner capable of engaging the rights protected under Article 8 § 1 of the Convention. As recognised in domestic case-law, a person may claim to exercise a choice to die by declining to consent to treatment which might have the effect of prolonging his life.

In the present case, although medical treatment is not an issue, the applicant is suffering from the devastating effects of a degenerative disease which will cause her condition to deteriorate further and increase her physical and mental suffering. She wishes to mitigate that suffering by exercising a choice to end her life with the assistance of her husband. As stated by Lord Hope, the way she chooses to pass the closing moments of her life is part of the act of living, and she has a right to ask that this too must be respected.

The very essence of the Convention is respect for human dignity and human freedom. Without in any way negating the principle of sanctity of life protected under the Convention, the Court considers that it is under Article 8 that notions of the quality of life take on significance. In an era of growing medical sophistication combined with longer life expectancies, many people are concerned that they should not be forced to linger on in old age or in states of advanced physical or mental decrepitude which conflict with strongly held ideas of self and personal identity ...

The applicant in this case is prevented by law from exercising her choice to avoid what she considers will be an undignified and distressing end to her life. The Court is not prepared to exclude that this constitutes an interference with her right to respect for private life as guaranteed under Article 8 § 1 of the Convention. It considers below whether this interference conforms with the requirements of the second paragraph of Article 8.

2. Compliance with Article 8 § 2 of the Convention

An interference with the exercise of an Article 8 right will not be compatible with Article 8 § 2 unless it is "in accordance with the law", has an aim or aims that is or are legitimate under that paragraph and is "necessary in a democratic society" for the aforesaid aim or aims....

According to the Court's established case-law, the notion of necessity implies that the interference corresponds to a pressing social need and, in particular, that it is proportionate to the legitimate aim pursued; in determining whether an interference is "necessary in a democratic society", the Court will take into account that a margin of appreciation is left to the national authorities, whose decision remains subject to review by the Court for conformity with the requirements of the Convention. The margin of appreciation to be accorded to the competent national authorities will vary in accordance with the nature of the issues and the importance of the interests at stake.

The Court recalls that the margin of appreciation has been found to be narrow as regards interferences in the intimate area of an individual's sexual life. Although the applicant has argued that there must therefore be particularly compelling reasons for the interference in her case, the Court does not find that the matter under consideration in this case can be regarded as of the same nature, or as attracting the same reasoning.

The parties' arguments have focused on the proportionality of the interference as disclosed in the applicant's case. The applicant attacked in particular the blanket nature of the ban on assisted suicide as failing to take into account her situation as a mentally competent adult who knows her own mind, who is free from pressure and who has made a fully informed and voluntary decision, and therefore cannot be regarded as vulnerable and requiring protection. This inflexibility means, in her submission, that she will be compelled to endure the consequences of her incurable and distressing illness, at a very high personal cost.

The Court would note that although the Government argued that the applicant, as a person who is both contemplating suicide and severely disabled, must be regarded as vulnerable, this assertion is not supported by the evidence before the domestic courts or by the judgments of the House of Lords which, while emphasising that the law in the United Kingdom was there to protect the vulnerable, did not find that the applicant was in that category.

Nonetheless, the Court finds, in agreement with the House of Lords and the majority of the Canadian Supreme Court in *Rodriguez*, that States are entitled to regulate through the operation of the general criminal law activities which are detrimental to the life and safety of other individuals. The more serious the harm involved the more heavily will weigh in the balance considerations of public health and safety against the countervailing principle of personal autonomy. The law in issue in this case, section 2 of the 1961 Act, was designed to safeguard life by protecting the weak and vulnerable and especially those who are not in a condition to take informed decisions against acts intended to end life or to assist in ending life. Doubtless the condition of terminally ill individuals will vary. But many will be vulnerable and it is the vulnerability of the class which provides the rationale for the law in question. It is primarily for States to assess the risk and the likely incidence of abuse if the general prohibition on assisted suicides were relaxed or if exceptions were to be created. Clear risks of abuse do exist, notwithstanding arguments as to the possibility of safeguards and protective procedures.

The applicant's counsel attempted to persuade the Court that a finding of a violation in this case would not create a general precedent or any risk to others. It is true that it is not this Court's role under Article 34 of the Convention to issue opinions in the abstract but to apply the Convention to the concrete facts of the individual case. However, judgments issued in individual cases establish precedents albeit to a greater or lesser extent and a decision in this case could not, either in theory or practice, be framed in such a way as to prevent application in later cases.

The Court does not consider therefore that the blanket nature of the ban on assisted suicide is disproportionate. The Government have stated that flexibility is provided for in individual cases by the fact that consent is needed from the DPP to bring a prosecution and by the fact that a maximum sentence is provided, allowing lesser penalties to be imposed as appropriate. The Select Committee report indicated that between 1981 and 1992 in twenty-two cases in which "mercy killing" was an issue, there was only one conviction for murder, with a sentence of life imprisonment, while lesser offences were substituted in the others and most resulted in probation or suspended sentences (paragraph 128 of the report cited at paragraph 21 above). It does not appear to be arbitrary to the Court for the law to reflect the importance of the right to life, by prohibiting assisted suicide while providing for a system of enforcement and adjudication which allows due regard to be given in each particular case to the public interest in bringing a prosecution, as well as to the fair and proper requirements of retribution and deterrence.

Nor in the circumstances is there anything disproportionate in the refusal of the DPP to give an advance undertaking that no prosecution would be brought against the applicant's husband. Strong arguments based on the rule of law could be raised against any claim by the executive to exempt individuals or classes of individuals from the operation of the law. In any event, the seriousness of the act for which immunity was claimed was such that the decision of the DPP to refuse the undertaking sought in the present case cannot be said to be arbitrary or unreasonable.

The Court concludes that the interference in this case may be justified as "necessary in a democratic society" for the protection of the rights of others and, accordingly, that there has been no violation of Article 8 of the Convention.

* * *

VI. ALLEGED VIOLATION OF ARTICLE 14 OF THE CONVENTION

Article 14 of the Convention provides:

"The enjoyment of the rights and freedoms set forth in [the] Convention shall be secured without discrimination on any ground such as sex, race, colour, language, religion, political or other opinion, national or social origin, association with a national minority, property, birth or other status."

* * *

The Court has found above that the applicant's rights under Article 8 of the Convention were engaged. It must therefore consider the applicant's complaints that she has been discriminated against in the enjoyment of the rights guaranteed under that provision in that domestic law permits able-bodied persons to commit suicide yet prevents an incapacitated person from receiving assistance in committing suicide.

For the purposes of Article 14 a difference in treatment between persons in analogous or relevantly similar positions is discriminatory if it has no objective and reasonable justification, that is if it does not pursue a legitimate aim or if there is not a reasonable relationship of proportionality between the means employed and the aim sought to be realised. Moreover, the Contracting States enjoy a margin of appreciation in assessing whether and to what extent differences in otherwise similar situations justify a different treatment. Discrimination may also arise where States without an objective and reasonable justification fail to treat differently persons whose situations are significantly different.

Even if th[is] principle ... was applied to the applicant's situation however, there is, in the Court's view, objective and reasonable justification for not distinguishing in law between those who are and those who are not physically capable of committing suicide. Under Article 8 of the Convention, the Court has found that there are sound reasons for not introducing into the law exceptions to cater for those who are deemed not to be vulnerable ... Similar cogent reasons exist under Article 14 for not seeking to distinguish between those who are able and those who are unable to commit suicide unaided. The borderline between the two categories will often be a very fine one and to seek to build into the law an exemption for those judged to be incapable of committing suicide would seriously undermine the protection of life which the 1961 Act was intended to safeguard and greatly increase the risk of abuse ...

Notes

1. *Pretty v. UK* held the UK's policy on aid in dying was not in violation of the European Convention on Human Rights. There remain significant differences in the way E.U. Member States treat the topic. While the Netherlands is on one end of the spectrum, Ireland is an example of a European country on the other end. In *Fleming v. Ireland & Ors*, 2013 IESC 19, decided in 2013, the Irish Supreme Court refused to find a right to physician aid in dying. The high court noted, however, that the legislature was free to allow aid in dying, provided appropriate safeguards were instituted.

2. How important was the "margin of appreciation" to Court's decision in *Pretty v. UK*? As you read through the various court decisions in this chapter, consider from a comparative constitutionalism perspective whether different conceptions of deference to legislatures are doing a lot of the work in the Court decisions or whether instead courts are adjusting their deference to their preferred policy outcomes?

2. Canada

In *Rodriguez v. British Columbia*, [1993] 3 S.C.R. 519, decided in 1993, the Canadian Supreme Court held that the prohibition of prescription and injection did not violate the Canadian Charter of Rights and Freedoms. In particular, it did not violate the guarantee to security of person or the prohibition on cruel and unusual treatment. Moreover, the *Rodriguez* court held that Section 1 saved the law from violating the equality challenge. See, discussing *Rodriguez* in comparative perspective, Patrick Thompson, The Law and Active Euthanasia: Whose Life is it Anyway? 2 *J. L. & Med.* 233 (1995). It took more than 20 years for the Court to reconsider the issue, which it did in 2015. In *Carter v. Canada*, the Court came to a very different conclusion, overruling *Rodriguez* by finding a right to aid in dying inherent in the right to life, liberty, and security of person guaranteed by the Charter.

Carter v. Canada (Attorney General)

2015 SCC 5, [2015] 1 S.C.R. 331
Supreme Court of Canada

... In Canada, aiding or abetting a person to commit suicide is a criminal offence ... This means that a person cannot seek a physician-assisted death. Twenty-one years ago, this Court upheld this blanket prohibition on assisted suicide by a slim majority: *Rodriguez v. British Columbia (Attorney General)*, [1993] 3 S.C.R. 519. Sopinka J., writing for five justices, held that the prohibition did not violate s. 7 of the *Canadian Charter of Rights and Freedoms*, and that if it violated s. 15, this was justified under s. 1, as there was "no halfway measure that could be relied upon with assurance" to protect the vulnerable (p. 614). Four justices disagreed ...

Despite the Court's decision in *Rodriguez*, the debate over physician-assisted dying continued. Between 1991 and 2010, the House of Commons and its committees debated no less than six private member's bills seeking to decriminalize assisted suicide. None was passed. While opponents to legalization emphasized the inadequacy of safeguards and the potential to devalue human life, a vocal minority spoke in favour of reform, highlighting the importance of dignity and autonomy and the limits of palliative care in addressing suffering. The Senate considered the matter as well, issuing a report on assisted suicide and euthanasia in 1995. The majority expressed concerns about the risk of abuse under a permissive regime and the need for respect for life. A minority supported an exemption to the prohibition in some circumstances.

More recent reports have come down in favour of reform. In 2011, the Royal Society of Canada published a report on end-of-life decision-making and recommended that the Criminal Code be modified to permit assistance in dying in some circumstances. The Quebec National Assembly's Select Committee on Dying with Dignity issued a report in 2012, recommending amendments to legislation to recognize medical aid in dying as appropriate end-of-life care (now codified in *An Act respecting end-of-life care*, CQLR, c. S-32.0001 (not yet in force)).

The legislative landscape on the issue of physician-assisted death has changed in the two decades since *Rodriguez*. In 1993 Sopinka J. noted that no other Western democracy expressly permitted assistance in dying. By 2010, however, eight jurisdictions permitted some form of assisted dying: the Netherlands, Belgium, Luxembourg, Switzerland, Oregon, Washington, Montana, and Colombia. The process of legalization began in 1994, when Oregon, as a result of a citizens' initiative, altered its laws to permit medical aid in dying for a person suffering from a terminal disease. Colombia followed in 1997, after a decision of the constitutional court. The Dutch Parliament established a regulatory regime for assisted dying in 2002; Belgium quickly adopted a similar regime, with Luxembourg joining in 2009. Together, these regimes have produced a body of evidence about the practical and legal workings of physician-assisted death and the efficacy of safeguards for the vulnerable.

Nevertheless, physician-assisted dying remains a criminal offence in most Western countries, and a number of courts have upheld the prohibition on such assistance in the face of constitutional and human rights challenges: see, e.g., *Washington v. Glucksberg*, 521 U.S. 702 (1997); *Vacco v. Quill*, 521 U.S. 793 (1997); *Pretty v. United Kingdom*, No. 2346/02, ECHR 2002-III; and *Fleming v. Ireland*, [2013] IESC 19. In a recent decision, a majority of the Supreme Court of the United Kingdom accepted that the absolute prohibition on assisted dying breached the claimants' rights, but found the evidence on safeguards insufficient; the court concluded that Parliament should be given an opportunity to debate and amend the legislation based on the court's provisional views.

The debate in the public arena reflects the ongoing debate in the legislative sphere. Some medical practitioners see legal change as a natural extension of the principle of patient autonomy, while others fear derogation from the principles of medical ethics. Some people with disabilities oppose the legalization of assisted dying, arguing that it implicitly devalues their lives and renders them vulnerable to unwanted assistance in dying, as medical professionals assume that a disabled patient "leans towards death at a sharper angle than the acutely ill—but otherwise non-disabled—patient." Other people with disabilities take the opposite view, arguing that a regime which permits control over the manner of one's death respects, rather than threatens, their autonomy and dignity, and that the legalization of physician-assisted suicide will protect them by establishing stronger safeguards and oversight for end-of-life medical care.

The impetus for this case arose in 2009, when Gloria Taylor was diagnosed with a fatal neurodegenerative disease, amyotrophic lateral sclerosis (or ALS), which causes progressive muscle weakness. ALS patients first lose the ability to use their hands and feet, then the ability to walk, chew, swallow, speak and, eventually, breathe. Like Sue Rodriguez before her, Gloria Taylor did "not want to die slowly, piece by piece" or "wracked with pain," and brought a claim before the British Columbia Supreme Court challenging the constitutionality of Criminal Code provisions that prohibit assistance in dying, specifically ss. 14, 21, 22, 222, and 241 …

By 2010, Ms. Taylor's condition had deteriorated to the point that she required a wheelchair to go more than a short distance and was suffering pain from muscle deterioration. She required home support for assistance with the daily tasks of living, something that she described as an assault on her privacy, dignity, and self-esteem. She continued to pursue an independent life despite her illness, but found that she was steadily losing the ability to participate fully in that life. Ms. Taylor informed her family and friends of a desire to obtain a physician-assisted death. She did not want to "live in a bedridden state, stripped of dignity and independence", she said; nor did she want an "ugly death." …

Ms. Taylor, however, knew she would be unable to request a physician-assisted death when the time came, because of the Criminal Code prohibition and the fact that she lacked the financial resources to travel to Switzerland, where assisted suicide is legal and available to non-residents. This left her with what she described as the "cruel choice" between killing herself while she was still physically capable of doing so, or giving up the ability to exercise any control over the manner and timing of her death ... [R]unning through the evidence of all the witnesses is a constant theme— that they suffer from the knowledge that they lack the ability to bring a peaceful end to their lives at a time and in a manner of their own choosing.

Some describe how they had considered seeking out the traditional modes of suicide but found that choice, too, repugnant: I was going to blow my head off. I have a gun and I seriously considered doing it. I decided that I could not do that to my family. It would be horrible to put them through something like that.... I want a better choice than that ... One woman noted that the conventional methods of suicide, such as carbon monoxide asphyxiation, slitting of the wrists or overdosing on street drugs, would require that she end her life "while I am still able bodied and capable of taking my life, well ahead of when I actually need to leave this life".

* * *

In our view, two of these provisions are at the core of the constitutional challenge: s. 241(*b*), which says that everyone who aids or abets a person in committing suicide commits an indictable offence, and s. 14, which says that no person may consent to death being inflicted on them. It is these two provisions that prohibit the provision of assistance in dying. Sections 21, 22, and 222 are only engaged so long as the provision of assistance in dying is itself an "unlawful act" or offence. Section 241(*a*) does not contribute to the prohibition on assisted suicide.

The Charter states:

> **1.** The Canadian Charter of Rights and Freedoms guarantees the rights and freedoms set out in it subject only to such reasonable limits prescribed by law as can be demonstrably justified in a free and democratic society.
>
> **7.** Everyone has the right to life, liberty and security of the person and the right not to be deprived thereof except in accordance with the principles of fundamental justice.
>
> **15.** (1) Every individual is equal before and under the law and has the right to the equal protection and equal benefit of the law without discrimination and, in particular, without discrimination based on race, national or ethnic origin, colour, religion, sex, age or mental or physical disability.

* * *

The main issue in this case is whether the prohibition on physician-assisted dying found in s. 241(*b*) of the Criminal Code violates the claimants' rights under ss. 7 and 15 of the Charter. For the purposes of their claim, the appellants use "physician-assisted death" and "physician-assisted dying" to describe the situation where a physician provides or administers medication that intentionally brings about the patient's death, at the request of the patient. The appellants advance two claims: (1) that the prohibition on physician-assisted dying deprives competent adults, who suffer a grievous and irremediable medical condition that causes the person to endure physical or psychological suffering that is intolerable to that person, of their right to life, liberty and security of the person under s. 7 of the Charter; and (2) that the prohibition deprives adults who are physically disabled of their right to equal treatment under s. 15 of the Charter.

* * *

Section 7 of the Charter states that "[e]veryone has the right to life, liberty and security of the person and the right not to be deprived thereof except in accordance with the principles of fundamental justice."

In order to demonstrate a violation of s. 7, the claimants must first show that the law interferes with, or deprives them of, their life, liberty or security of the person. Once they have established that s. 7 is engaged, they must then show that the deprivation in question is not in accordance with the principles of fundamental justice.

For the reasons below, we conclude that the prohibition on physician-assisted dying infringes the right to life, liberty and security of Ms. Taylor and of persons in her position, and that it does so in a manner that is overbroad and thus is not in accordance with the principles of fundamental justice. It therefore violates s. 7.

A. *Does the Law Infringe the Right to Life, Liberty and Security of the Person?*

(1) Life

The trial judge found that the prohibition on physician-assisted dying had the effect of forcing some individuals to take their own lives prematurely, for fear that they would be incapable of doing so when they reached the point where suffering was intolerable. On that basis, she found that the right to life was engaged.

We see no basis for interfering with the trial judge's conclusion on this point. The evidence of premature death was not challenged before this Court. It is therefore established that the prohibition deprives some individuals of life.

The appellants and a number of the interveners urge us to adopt a broader, qualitative approach to the right to life. Some argue that the right to life is not restricted to the preservation of life, but protects quality of life and therefore a right to die with dignity. Others argue that the right to life protects personal autonomy and fundamental notions of self-determination and dignity, and therefore includes the right to determine whether to take one's own life.

In dissent at the Court of Appeal, Finch C.J.B.C. accepted the argument that the right to life protects more than physical existence. In his view, the life interest is "intimately connected to the way a person values his or her lived experience. The point at which the meaning of life is lost, when life's positive attributes are so diminished as to render life valueless, ... is an intensely personal decision which 'everyone' has the right to make for him or herself." Similarly, in his dissent in *Rodriguez*, Cory J. accepted that the right to life included a right to die with dignity, on the ground that "dying is an integral part of living."

The trial judge, on the other hand, rejected the "qualitative" approach to the right to life. She concluded that the right to life is only engaged when there is a threat of death as a result of government action or laws. In her words, the right to life is limited to a "right not to die."

This Court has most recently invoked the right to life in *Chaoulli*, where evidence showed that the lack of timely health care could result in death, and in *PHS*, where the clients of Insite were deprived of potentially lifesaving medical care. In each case, the right was only engaged by the threat of death. In short, the case law suggests that the right to life is engaged where the law or state action imposes death or an increased risk of death on a person, either directly or indirectly. Conversely, concerns about autonomy and quality of life have traditionally been treated as liberty and security rights. We see no reason to alter that approach in this case.

This said, we do not agree that the existential formulation of the right to life *requires* an absolute prohibition on assistance in dying, or that individuals cannot "waive" their right to life. This would create a "duty to live", rather than a "right to life", and would call into question the legality of any consent to the withdrawal or refusal of lifesaving or life-sustaining treatment. The sanctity of life is one of our most fundamental societal values. Section 7 is rooted in a profound respect for the value of human life. But s. 7 also encompasses life, liberty and security of the person during the passage to death. It is for this reason that the sanctity of life "is no longer seen to require that all human life be preserved at all costs." And it is for this reason that the law has come to recognize that, in certain circumstances, an individual's choice about the end of her life is entitled to respect. It is to this fundamental choice that we now turn.

(2) Liberty and Security of the Person

Underlying both of these rights is a concern for the protection of individual autonomy and dignity. Liberty protects "the right to make fundamental personal choices free from state interference." Security of the person encompasses "a notion of personal autonomy involving ... control over one's bodily integrity free from state interference," and it is engaged by state interference with an individual's physical or psychological integrity, including any state action that causes physical or serious psychological suffering. While liberty and security of the person are distinct interests, for the purpose of this appeal they may be considered together.

The trial judge concluded that the prohibition on assisted dying limited Ms. Taylor's s. 7 right to liberty and security of the person, by interfering with "fundamentally important and personal medical decision-making," imposing pain and psychological stress and depriving her of control over her bodily integrity. She found that the prohibition left people like Ms. Taylor to suffer physical or psychological pain and imposed stress due to the unavailability of physician-assisted dying, impinging on her security of the person. She further noted that seriously and irremediably ill persons were "denied the opportunity to make a choice that may be very important to their sense of dignity and personal integrity" and that is "consistent with their lifelong values and that reflects their life's experience."

We agree with the trial judge. An individual's response to a grievous and irremediable medical condition is a matter critical to their dignity and autonomy. The law allows people in this situation to request palliative sedation, refuse artificial nutrition and hydration, or request the removal of life-sustaining medical equipment, but denies them the right to request a physician's assistance in dying. This interferes with their ability to make decisions concerning their bodily integrity and medical care and thus trenches on liberty. And, by leaving people like Ms. Taylor to endure intolerable suffering, it impinges on their security of the person.

The law has long protected patient autonomy in medical decision-making.... This right to "decide one's own fate" entitles adults to direct the course of their own medical care it is this principle that underlies the concept of "informed consent" and is protected by s. 7's guarantee of liberty and security of the person, the right of medical self-determination is not vitiated by the fact that serious risks or consequences, including death, may flow from the patient's decision. It is this same principle that is at work in the cases dealing with the right to refuse consent to medical treatment, or to demand that treatment be withdrawn or discontinued.

[I]t is clear that anyone who seeks physician-assisted dying because they are suffering intolerably as a result of a grievous and irremediable medical condition "does so out of a deeply personal and fundamental belief about how they wish to live, or cease to live." The trial judge, too, described this as a decision that, for some people, is "very important to their sense of dignity and personal integrity, that is consistent with their lifelong values and that reflects their life's experience." This is a decision that is rooted in their control over their bodily integrity; it represents their deeply personal response to serious pain and suffering. By denying them the opportunity to make that choice, the prohibition impinges on their liberty and security of the person. As noted above, s. 7 recognizes the value of life, but it also honours the role that autonomy and dignity play at the end of that life. We therefore conclude that ss. 241 (*b*) and 14 of the *Criminal Code,* insofar as they prohibit physician-assisted dying for competent adults who seek such assistance as a result of a grievous and irremediable medical condition that causes enduring and intolerable suffering, infringe the rights to liberty and security of the person.

We note, as the trial judge did, that Lee Carter and Hollis Johnson's interest in liberty may be engaged by the threat of criminal sanction for their role in Kay Carter's death in Switzerland. However, this potential deprivation was not the focus of the arguments raised at trial, and neither Ms. Carter nor Mr. Johnson sought a personal remedy before this Court. Accordingly, we have confined ourselves to the rights of those who seek assistance in dying, rather than of those who might provide such assistance.

(3) Summary on Section 7: Life, Liberty and Security of the Person

For the foregoing reasons, we conclude that the prohibition on physician-assisted dying deprived Ms. Taylor and others suffering from grievous and irremediable medical conditions of the right to life, liberty and security of the person. The remaining question under s. 7 is whether this deprivation was in accordance with the principles of fundamental justice.

B. *The Principles of Fundamental Justice*

Section 7 does not promise that the state will never interfere with a person's life, liberty or security of the person—laws do this all the time—but rather that the state will not do so in a way that violates the principles of fundamental justice.

Section 7 does not catalogue the principles of fundamental justice to which it refers. Over the course of 32 years of *Charter* adjudication, this Court has worked to define the minimum constitutional requirements that a law that trenches on life, liberty or security of the person must meet. While the Court has recognized a number of principles of fundamental justice, three have emerged as central in the recent s. 7 jurisprudence: laws that impinge on life, liberty or security of the person must not be arbitrary, overbroad, or have consequences that are grossly disproportionate to their object.

Each of these potential vices involves comparison with the object of the law that is challenged. The first step is therefore to identify the object of the prohibition on assisted dying.

The trial judge, relying on *Rodriguez*, concluded that the object of the prohibition was to protect vulnerable persons from being induced to commit suicide at a time of weakness. All the parties except Canada accept this formulation of the object....

Before turning to the principles of fundamental justice at play, a general comment is in order. In determining whether the deprivation of life, liberty and security of the person is in accordance with the principles of fundamental justice under s. 7, courts are not concerned with competing social interests or public benefits conferred by the impugned law. These competing moral claims and broad societal benefits are more appropriately considered at the stage of justification under s. 1 of the *Charter*.

In *Bedford*, the Court noted that requiring s. 7 claimants "to establish the efficacy of the law versus its deleterious consequences on members of society as a whole, would impose the government's s. 1 burden on claimants under s. 7." A claimant under s. 7 must show that the state has deprived them of their life, liberty or security of the person and that the deprivation is not in accordance with the principles of fundamental justice. They should not be tasked with also showing that these principles are "not overridden by a valid state or communal interest in these circumstances."

It is not appropriate for the state to thwart the exercise of the accused's right by attempting to bring societal interests into the principles of fundamental justice and to thereby limit an accused's s. 7 rights. Societal interests are to be dealt with under s. 1 of the *Charter* ...

... To deprive a person of constitutional rights arbitrarily or in a way that is overbroad or grossly disproportionate diminishes that worth and dignity. If a law operates in this way, it asks the right claimant to "serve as a scapegoat." It imposes a deprivation via a process that is "fundamentally unfair" to the rights claimant.

This is not to say that such a deprivation cannot be *justified* under s. 1 of the *Charter*. In some cases the government, for practical reasons, may only be able to meet an important objective by means of a law that has some fundamental flaw. But this does not concern us when considering whether s. 7 of the *Charter* has been breached.

(1) Arbitrariness

The principle of fundamental justice that forbids arbitrariness targets the situation where there is no rational connection between the object of the law and the limit it imposes on life, liberty or security of the person. An arbitrary law is one that is not capable of fulfilling its objectives. It exacts a constitutional price in terms of rights, without furthering the public good that is said to be the object of the law.

The object of the prohibition on physician-assisted dying is to protect the vulnerable from ending their life in times of weakness. A total ban on assisted suicide clearly helps achieve this object. Therefore, individuals' rights are not limited arbitrarily.

(2) Overbreadth

The overbreadth inquiry asks whether a law that takes away rights in a way that generally supports the object of the law, goes too far by denying the rights of some individuals in a way that bears no relation to the object. Like the other principles of fundamental justice under s. 7, overbreadth is not concerned with competing social interests or ancillary benefits to the general population. A law that is drawn broadly to target conduct that bears no relation to its purpose "in order to make enforcement more practical" may therefore be overbroad. The question is not whether Parliament has chosen the least restrictive means, but whether the chosen means infringe life, liberty or security of the person in a way that has no connection with the mischief contemplated by the legislature. The focus is not on broad social impacts, but on the impact of the measure on the individuals whose life, liberty or security of the person is trammelled.

Applying this approach, we conclude that the prohibition on assisted dying is overbroad. The object of the law, as discussed, is to protect vulnerable persons from being induced to commit suicide at a moment of weakness. Canada conceded at trial that the law catches people outside this class: "It is recognised that not every person who wishes to commit suicide is vulnerable, and that there may be people with disabilities who have a considered, rational and persistent wish to end their own lives." The trial judge accepted that Ms. Taylor was such a person—competent, fully informed, and free from coercion or duress. It follows that the limitation on their rights is in at least some cases not connected to the objective of protecting *vulnerable* persons. The blanket prohibition sweeps conduct into its ambit that is unrelated to the law's objective.

Canada argues that it is difficult to conclusively identify the "vulnerable", and that therefore it cannot be said that the prohibition is overbroad. Indeed, Canada asserts, "every person is *potentially* vulnerable" from a legislative perspective.

We do not agree. The situation is analogous to that in *Bedford*, where this Court concluded that the prohibition on living on the avails of prostitution in s. 212(1) (*j*) of the *Criminal Code* was overbroad. The law in that case punished everyone who earned a living through a relationship with a prostitute, without distinguishing between those who would assist and protect them and those who would be at least potentially exploitive of them. Canada there as here argued that the line between exploitative and non-exploitative relationships was blurry, and that, as a result, the provision had to be drawn broadly to capture its targets. The Court concluded that that argument is more appropriately addressed under s. 1.

[The Court also considered but found it unnecessary to decide whether the prohibition also violates the principle against gross disproportionality.]

* * *

X. Section 1

In order to justify the infringement of the appellants' s. 7 rights under s. 1 of the *Charter*, Canada must show that the law has a pressing and substantial object and that the means chosen are proportional to that object. A law is proportionate if (1) the means adopted are rationally connected to that objective; (2) it is minimally impairing of the right in question; and (3) there is proportionality between the deleterious and salutary effects of the law.

It is difficult to justify a s. 7 violation. The rights protected by s. 7 are fundamental, and "not easily overridden by competing social interests." And it is hard to justify a law that runs afoul of the principles of fundamental justice and is thus inherently flawed. However, in some situations the state may be able to show that the public good—a matter not considered under s. 7, which looks only at the impact on the rights claimants—justifies depriving an individual of life, liberty or security of the person under s. 1 of the *Charter*. More particularly, in cases such as this where the competing societal interests are themselves protected under the *Charter*, a restriction on s. 7 rights may in the end be found to be proportionate to its objective.

Here, the limit is prescribed by law, and the appellants concede that the law has a pressing and substantial objective. The question is whether the government has demonstrated that the prohibition is proportionate.

At this stage of the analysis, the courts must accord the legislature a measure of deference. Proportionality does not require perfection. Section 1 only requires that the limits be "reasonable". This Court has emphasized that there may be a number of possible solutions to a particular social problem, and suggested that a "complex regulatory response" to a social ill will garner a high degree of deference.

On the one hand, as the trial judge noted, physician-assisted death involves complex issues of social policy and a number of competing societal values. Parliament faces a difficult task in addressing this issue; it must weigh and balance the perspective of those who might be at risk in a permissive regime against that of those who seek assistance in dying. It follows that a high degree of deference is owed to Parliament's decision to impose an absolute prohibition on assisted death. On the other hand, the trial judge also found—and we agree—that the absolute prohibition could not be described as a "complex regulatory response." The degree of deference owed to Parliament, while high, is accordingly reduced.

* * *

(2) Minimal Impairment

At this stage of the analysis, the question is whether the limit on the right is reasonably tailored to the objective. The inquiry into minimal impairment asks "whether there are less harmful means of achieving the legislative goal." The burden is on the government to show the absence of less drastic means of achieving the objective "in a real and substantial manner." The analysis at this stage is meant to ensure that the deprivation of Charter rights is confined to what is reasonably necessary to achieve the state's object.

The question in this case comes down to whether the absolute prohibition on physician-assisted dying, with its heavy impact on the claimants' s. 7 rights to life, liberty and security of the person, is the least drastic means of achieving the legislative objective. It was the task of the trial judge to determine whether a regime less restrictive of life, liberty and security of the person could address the risks associated with physician-assisted dying, or whether Canada was right to say that the risks could not adequately be addressed through the use of safeguards.

This question lies at the heart of this case and was the focus of much of the evidence at trial. In assessing minimal impairment, the trial judge heard evidence from scientists, medical practitioners, and others who were familiar with end-of-life decision-making in Canada and abroad. She also heard extensive evidence from each of the jurisdictions where physician-assisted dying is legal or regulated. In the trial judge's view, an absolute prohibition would have been necessary if the evidence showed that physicians were unable to reliably assess competence, voluntariness, and non-ambivalence in patients; that physicians fail to understand or apply the informed consent requirement for medical treatment; or if the evidence from permissive jurisdictions showed abuse of patients, carelessness, callousness, or a slippery slope, leading to the casual termination of life.

The trial judge, however, expressly rejected these possibilities. After reviewing the evidence, she concluded that a permissive regime with properly designed and administered safeguards was capable of protecting vulnerable people from abuse and error. While there are risks, to be sure, a carefully designed and managed system is capable of adequately addressing them ...

The trial judge found that it was feasible for properly qualified and experienced physicians to reliably assess patient competence and voluntariness, and that coercion, undue influence, and ambivalence could all be reliably assessed as part of that process. In reaching this conclusion, she particularly relied on the evidence on the application of the informed consent standard in other medical decision-making in Canada, including end-of-life decision-making. She concluded that it would be possible for physicians to apply the informed consent standard to patients who seek assistance in dying, adding the caution that physicians should ensure that patients are properly informed of their diagnosis and prognosis and the range of available options for medical care, including palliative care interventions aimed at reducing pain and avoiding the loss of personal dignity.

As to the risk to vulnerable populations (such as the elderly and disabled), the trial judge found that there was no evidence from permissive jurisdictions that people with disabilities are at heightened risk of accessing physician-assisted dying. She thus rejected the contention that unconscious bias by physicians would undermine the assessment process. The trial judge found there was no evidence of inordinate impact on socially vulnerable populations in the permissive jurisdictions, and that in some cases palliative care actually improved post-legalization. She also found that while the evidence suggested that the law had both negative and positive impacts on physicians, it did support the conclusion that physicians were better able to provide overall end-of-life treatment once assisted death was legalized. Finally, she found no compelling evidence that a permissive regime in Canada would result in a "practical slippery slope."

* * *

(c) *The Feasibility of Safeguards and the Possibility of a "Slippery Slope"*

At trial Canada went into some detail about the risks associated with the legalization of physician-assisted dying. In its view, there are many possible sources of error and many factors that can render a patient "decisionally vulnerable" and thereby give rise to the risk that persons without a rational and considered desire for death will in fact end up dead. It points to cognitive impairment, depression or other mental illness, coercion, undue influence, psychological or emotional manipulation, systemic prejudice (against the elderly or people with disabilities), and the possibility of ambivalence or misdiagnosis as factors that may escape detection or give rise to errors in capacity assessment. Essentially, Canada argues that, given the breadth of this list, there is no reliable way to identify those who are vulnerable and those who are not. As a result, it says, a blanket prohibition is necessary.

The evidence accepted by the trial judge does not support Canada's argument. Based on the evidence regarding assessment processes in comparable end-of-life medical decision-making in Canada, the trial judge concluded that vulnerability can be assessed on an individual basis, using the procedures that physicians apply in their assessment of informed consent and decisional capacity in the context of medical decision-making more generally. Concerns about decisional capacity and vulnerability arise in all end-of-life medical decision-making. Logically speaking, there is no reason to think that the injured, ill, and disabled who have the option to refuse or to request withdrawal of lifesaving or life-sustaining treatment, or who seek palliative sedation, are less vulnerable or less susceptible to biased decision-making than those who might seek more active assistance in dying. The risks that Canada describes are already part and parcel of our medical system.

As the trial judge noted, the individual assessment of vulnerability (whatever its source) is implicitly condoned for life-and-death decision-making in Canada. In some cases, these decisions are governed by advance directives, or made by a substitute decision-maker. Canada does not argue that the risk in those circumstances requires an absolute prohibition (indeed, there is currently no federal regulation of such practices). In *A.C.*, Abella J. adverted to the potential vulnerability of adolescents who are faced with life-and-death decisions about medical treatment. Yet, this Court implicitly accepted the viability of an individual assessment of decisional capacity in the context of that case. We accept the trial judge's conclusion that it is possible for physicians, with due care and attention to the seriousness of the decision involved, to adequately assess decisional capacity.

The trial judge, on the basis of her consideration of various regimes and how they operate, found that it is possible to establish a regime that addresses the risks associated with physician-assisted death.... We agree with the trial judge that the risks associated with physician-assisted death can be limited through a carefully designed and monitored system of safeguards.

...

The trial judge found that [the evidence] did not support [Canada's] contention that a blanket prohibition was necessary in order to substantially meet the government's objectives. We agree. A theoretical or speculative fear cannot justify an absolute prohibition. As Deschamps J. stated in *Chaoulli*, at para. 68, the claimant "d[oes] not have the burden of disproving every fear or every threat", nor can the government meet its burden simply by asserting an adverse impact on the public. Justification under s. 1 is a process of demonstration, not intuition or automatic deference to the government's assertion of risk.

Finally, it is argued that without an absolute prohibition on assisted dying, Canada will descend the slippery slope into euthanasia and condoned murder. Anecdotal examples of controversial cases abroad were cited in support of this argument, only to be countered by anecdotal examples of systems that work well. The resolution of the issue before us falls to be resolved not by competing anecdotes, but by the evidence. The trial judge, after an exhaustive review of the evidence, rejected the argument that adoption of a regulatory regime would initiate a descent down a slippery slope into homicide. We should not lightly assume that the regulatory regime will function defectively, nor should we assume that other criminal sanctions against the taking of lives will prove impotent against abuse.

We find no error in the trial judge's analysis of minimal impairment. We therefore conclude that the absolute prohibition is not minimally impairing.

* * *

We have concluded that the laws prohibiting a physician's assistance in terminating life (*Criminal Code*, s. 241 (b) and s. 14) infringe Ms. Taylor's s. 7 rights to life, liberty and security of the person in a manner that is not in accordance with the principles of fundamental justice, and that the infringement is not justified under s. 1 of the *Charter*. To the extent that the impugned laws deny the s. 7 rights of people like Ms. Taylor they are void by operation of s. 52 of the *Constitution Act, 1982*. It is for Parliament and the provincial legislatures to respond, should they so choose, by enacting legislation consistent with the constitutional parameters set out in these reasons.

The appropriate remedy is therefore a declaration that s. 241 (*b*) and s. 14 of the *Criminal Code* are void insofar as they prohibit physician-assisted death for a competent adult person who (1) clearly consents to the termination of life; and (2) has a grievous and irremediable medical condition (including an illness, disease or disability) that causes enduring suffering that is intolerable to the individual in the circumstances of his or her condition. "Irremediable", it should be added, does not require the patient to undertake treatments that are not acceptable to the individual. The scope of this declaration is intended to respond to the factual circumstances in this case. We make no pronouncement on other situations where physician-assisted dying may be sought....

In our view, nothing in the declaration of invalidity which we propose to issue would compel physicians to provide assistance in dying. The declaration simply renders the criminal prohibition invalid ...

Notes

1. When a court finds a right to aid in dying, that is often just the first step in a process of creating authorizing legislation and regulation. In June 2016, the Canadian Parliament passed legislation amending the criminal code to prevent prosecution of medical assistance in dying. Both assistance through prescribing life-ending medications and through injection of the patient with life-ending medicine are now legal, provided the patient meets the eligibility criteria set forth in the bill. For more on the regulatory challenges ahead for Canada, see generally Trudo Lemmens, The Conflict between Open-Ended Access to Physician-Assisted Dying and the Protection of the Vulnerable, in Catherine Regis, Lara Khoury, and Robert Kouri, eds., *Les Grands Conflits en Droit de la Santé* 261 (2016).

The bill restricts aid in dying to those whose "natural death" is "reasonably foreseeable." An Act to amend the Criminal Code and to make related amendments to other Acts, Statutes of Canada, 2016, c. 3 (Can.). Does this comport with *Carter*'s holding?

2. In order to prevent medical tourism to Canada for aid in dying, the Canadian government has established that only those eligible for health services funded by a government in Canada are eligible for prescription or injection. This is in contrast to other jurisdictions, like Switzerland, that do not have what is effectively a residency requirement. In Switzerland, this had led to an estimated 150–200 individuals per year traveling to the canton of Zurich to seek aid in dying. Travelers for assisted suicide came from 31 different countries but most were Europeans. Although useful, these figures are from Zurich (the primary canton for travel for assisted suicide) only, so they also might somewhat undercount the total number of individuals traveling for assisted suicide. See I. Glenn Cohen, Traveling for Assisted Suicide, 373, 378–379 in *Euthanasia and Assisted Suicide: Global Views on Choosing to End Life* (Michael J. Cholbi ed. 2016) (citing Gauthier, S., J. Mausbach, T. Reisch, and C. Bartsch, 2014). "Suicide Tourism: A Pilot Study on the Swiss Phenomenon." *J. Med. Ethics* (August 20): 1–7. doi:10.1136/medethics-2014-102091 (accessed April 24, 2015); Bosshard, G., E. Ulrich, and W. Bär. 2003. "748 Cases of Suicide Assisted by a Swiss Right-to-Die Organisation." *Swiss Medicine Weekly* 133: 310–17. doi:2003/21/smw-10212; Fischer, S., C. A. Huber, L. Imhof, R. Mahrer Imhof, M. Furter, S. J. Ziegler,

G. Bosshard. 2008. "Suicide Assisted by Two Right-to-Die Organisations." *J. Med. Ethics* 34: 310–17. doi:10.1136/jme.2007.023887.)

3. There are related bioethical legal issues that jurisdictions like Canada must address when legalizing aid in dying relating to organ donation. Should organ donors be allowed to donate to a family member? Should governments disclose to potential recipients that aid in dying was involved in the donor's end of life? Should a recipient who has moral or religious objections to aid in dying be allowed to reject an organ from a donor who died through prescription or injection? How can governments adequately protect patient autonomy of both donors and recipients?

4. Despite Canada's about-face on the issue of aid in dying, the issue does not seem likely to change anytime soon at the federal level in the United States. The U.S. Supreme Court has twice rejected arguments that the U.S. Constitution guarantees a right to aid in dying. While there is no federally recognized right to physician aid in dying, the practice is also not prohibited, and some states have legalized aid in dying. The right of states to regulate these practices is well established. See Gonzales v. Oregon, 546 U.S. 243 (2006). Oregon has been the trailblazer in the United States. The Oregon law was adopted by initiative in 1994 and upheld by a subsequent referendum. A handful of states—including Washington, Vermont, California, Washington, DC, Montana, Colorado and New Jersey—have recently legalized a right to aid in dying, modeling their laws on those of Oregon—in fact, most of the new state statutes closely track the requirements in the Oregon law. Nearly all of the states that have legalized prescription have done so through voter-backed or legislative initiatives, not through judicial decisions (Montana is the exception). See generally David Orentlicher, Thaddeus Mason Pope, and Ben A. Rich, The Changing Legal Climate for Physician Aid in Dying, 311 *JAMA* 1961 (2014).

Portions of the Oregon Death With Dignity Act are reproduced below, Or. Statutes § 127.800–897 (2015):

Form of the written request.

(1) A valid request for medication under ORS 127.800 to 127.897 shall be in substantially the form described in ORS 127.897, signed and dated by the patient and witnessed by at least two individuals who, in the presence of the patient, attest that to the best of their knowledge and belief the patient is capable, acting voluntarily, and is not being coerced to sign the request.

(2) One of the witnesses shall be a person who is not:

(a) A relative of the patient by blood, marriage or adoption;

(b) A person who at the time the request is signed would be entitled to any portion of the estate of the qualified patient upon death under any will or by operation of law; or

(c) An owner, operator or employee of a health care facility where the qualified patient is receiving medical treatment or is a resident.

(3) The patient's attending physician at the time the request is signed shall not be a witness.

(4) If the patient is a patient in a long term care facility at the time the written request is made, one of the witnesses shall be an individual designated by the facility and having the qualifications specified by the Oregon Health Authority by rule. [1995 c.3 s.2.02]

(Safeguards)

(Section 3)

Attending physician responsibilities.

(1) The attending physician shall:

(a) Make the initial determination of whether a patient has a terminal disease, is capable, and has made the request voluntarily;

(b) Request that the patient demonstrate Oregon residency pursuant to ORS 127.860;

(c) To ensure that the patient is making an informed decision, inform the patient of:

(A) His or her medical diagnosis;

(B) His or her prognosis;

(C) The potential risks associated with taking the medication to be prescribed;

(D) The probable result of taking the medication to be prescribed; and

(E) The feasible alternatives, including, but not limited to, comfort care, hospice care and pain control;

(d) Refer the patient to a consulting physician for medical confirmation of the diagnosis, and for a determination that the patient is capable and acting voluntarily;

(e) Refer the patient for counseling if appropriate pursuant to ORS 127.825;

(f) Recommend that the patient notify next of kin;

(g) Counsel the patient about the importance of having another person present when the patient takes the medication prescribed pursuant to ORS 127.800 to 127.897 and of not taking the medication in a public place;

(h) Inform the patient that he or she has an opportunity to rescind the request at any time and in any manner, and offer the patient an opportunity to rescind at the end of the 15 day waiting period pursuant to ORS 127.840;

(i) Verify, immediately prior to writing the prescription for medication under ORS 127.800 to 127.897, that the patient is making an informed decision;

(j) Fulfill the medical record documentation requirements of ORS 127.855;

(k) Ensure that all appropriate steps are carried out in accordance with ORS 127.800 to 127.897 prior to writing a prescription for medication to enable a qualified patient to end his or her life in a humane and dignified manner; and

(L)(A) Dispense medications directly, including ancillary medications intended to facilitate the desired effect to minimize the patient's discomfort, provided the attending physician is registered as a dispensing physician with the Board of Medical Examiners, has a current Drug Enforcement Administration certificate and complies with any applicable administrative rule; or

(B) With the patient's written consent:

(i) Contact a pharmacist and inform the pharmacist of the prescription; and

(ii) Deliver the written prescription personally or by mail to the pharmacist, who will dispense the medications to either the patient, the attending physician or an expressly identified agent of the patient.

(2) Notwithstanding any other provision of law, the attending physician may sign the patient's death certificate. [1995 c.3 s.3.01; 1999 c.423 s.3]

Consulting physician confirmation.

Before a patient is qualified under ORS 127.800 to 127.897, a consulting physician shall examine the patient and his or her relevant medical records and confirm, in writing, the attending physician's diagnosis that the patient is suffering from a terminal disease, and verify that the patient is capable, is acting voluntarily and has made an informed decision. [1995 c.3 s.3.02]

Counseling referral.

If in the opinion of the attending physician or the consulting physician a patient may be suffering from a psychiatric or psychological disorder or depression causing impaired judgment, either physician shall refer the patient for counseling. No medication to end a patient's life in a humane and dignified manner shall be prescribed until the person performing the counseling determines that the patient is not suffering from a psychiatric or psychological disorder or depression causing impaired judgment. [1995 c.3 s.3.03; 1999 c.423 s.4]

127.830 s.3.04. Informed decision.

No person shall receive a prescription for medication to end his or her life in a humane and dignified manner unless he or she has made an informed decision as defined in ORS 127.800 (7). Immediately prior to writing a prescription for medication under ORS 127.800 to 127.897, the attending physician shall verify that the patient is making an informed decision. [1995 c.3 s.3.04]

3. South Africa

In contrast to Canada, South Africa's Supreme Court of Appeal recently overturned a lower court's decision allowing a terminally ill patient access to a prescription for aid in dying. The court declined to find a common law or constitutional right to aid in dying.

Minister of Justice and Correctional Services v. Estate Stransham-Ford

(531/2015) 2016 ZASCA 197 (6 December 2016).
Supreme Court of South Africa

* * *

[This case concerns] Mr. Robert (commonly known and referred to as Robin) Stransham-Ford, who was dying of cancer. He approached the High Court of South Africa,

Gauteng Division, Pretoria claiming an order that a medical practitioner could either end his life by administering a lethal substance, or provide him with the lethal substance to enable him to administer it himself, and that in either event such medical practitioner would not be subject to prosecution or disciplinary steps by the relevant professional body. To that end he sought an order that the common law in relation to the crimes of murder and culpable homicide should be developed in terms of s 39(2) of the Constitution. He claimed this relief as a matter of right, sourced in the Bill of Rights under the Constitution. [This order was granted by a lower court on April 29, 2015. On April 30, 2015, Mr. Stransham-Ford died.]

Robert Stransham-Ford was an advocate. On 19 February 2013 a prostate biopsy confirmed the presence of adenocarcinoma. The cancer was aggressive and by January 2015 had spread to lymph glands elsewhere in his body. On 13 March 2015 an ultrasound biopsy confirmed the presence of lymphoma. On 15 March 2015 he was admitted to Victoria Hospital in Cape Town suffering from severe abdominal pain. On 18 March 2015 at Groote Schuur Hospital an attempt was made to insert stents in the ureters leading from his kidneys to his bladder in an endeavour to relieve the obstruction. On 25 March 2015 Dr. Cameron Bruce took over his care and was the doctor who cared for him until his death. Mr. Stransham-Ford was at this time resident in Cape Town with his former wife and daughter, where he remained until his death. His former wife and his administrative assistant from his legal practice provided his daily care. From 25 March 2015 Dr. Bruce attended upon Mr. Stransham-Ford at his former wife's home on nine occasions. In addition a palliative care nurse, Sister Yvonne Jackman from St Luke's Hospice, visited Mr. Stransham-Ford on a regular basis. As already mentioned he died on 30 May 2015 at about 8.00 am.

The application was launched on 17 April 2015 (a Friday) as an urgent application with foreshortened periods, requiring the respondents to deliver answering affidavits by Wednesday, 22 April 2015, and selecting 28 April 2015 as the date for hearing ... Mr. Stransham-Ford made it clear in his founding affidavit that he was bringing the application in his personal capacity. The prayers for relief were couched in terms personal to him and any medical practitioner who assisted him ... Mr. Stransham-Ford's death before any order could be made materially affected the application, which was concerned only with his personal situation and sought relief directed at enabling him to die. The need for the court to grant the relief he had sought was overtaken by his death. In blunt terms, no further purpose could be served by granting that relief.

[Despite ruling the case moot, the court considered the merits so that the prior decision did not have precedential effect.] *** The [lower] court assumed that our law in this delicate area is both clear and simple. It said the following in para 10 of the judgment:

> 'The current legal position is that assisted suicide or active voluntary euthanasia is unlawful.

See: *S v De Bellocq* 1975 (3) SA 538 (T) at 539 d; and *S v Marengo* 1991 (2) SACR 43 (W) 47 A–B; and *Ex parte Minister van Justisie: In re S v Grotjohn* 1970 (2) SA 355 A.'

That statement, which was assumed to be correct in the arguments addressed to us on behalf of the various parties and amici, was not only not supported by the authorities relied upon, but was a wholly inadequate analysis of the relevant law in this area. Two of the cited cases did not deal with either voluntary euthanasia or assisted suicide and the third, which dealt with encouraging and facilitating suicide, was concerned with a domestic situation far removed from the matters with which we are concerned. A brief exposition of the current state of our law in this area is called for.

* * *

Mercy killing and active voluntary euthanasia (PAE)

On the other side of the coin a 'mercy killing' undoubtedly constitutes the crime of murder. That emerges clearly from the cases of *Hartmann* and *De Bellocq*, reported alongside one another in the law reports although six years apart in point of time. In *Hartmann*, the accused, a medical practitioner, inserted a lethal dose of pentothal into an intravenous drip in his father's arm. His father was 87 years of age, bedridden, dying of cancer and in a critical state of health and great pain. The son's motive in doing this was entirely in what he conceived to be his father's best interests. He was nonetheless convicted of murder, but sentenced to a year's imprisonment of which all but the period until the rising of the court was suspended for one year.

Mrs. de Bellocq's situation was equally tragic. She and her husband were in South Africa temporarily, had been but recently married and she was expecting their first child. The baby was born prematurely and after a short period was found to have toxoplasmosis, which had left it severely disabled, unable to receive nourishment, other than through a naso-gastric tube, and grievously mentally handicapped. Its prognosis was poor. A few weeks after she took the child home, whilst herself suffering from post-natal depression, she decided on the spur of the moment to drown her child while bathing it. As was the case in *Hartmann* the contention that this was culpable homicide was rejected and she was convicted of murder. She was discharged on her own recognizance that she would come up for sentence six months later, at which time it was anticipated that she and her husband would be about to return home.

Neither of these cases, nor *Marengo*, which was also cited by Fabricius J., had anything to do with either assisted suicide (PAS) or active voluntary euthanasia (PAE). They were all cases of euthanasia of the kind usually referred to as 'mercy killing'. They did not involve suicide and in none of them had the person who died asked to have their life ended. They are only relevant in identifying the issue arising from PAE, which is whether the consent of the patient makes any difference to the legal consequences of the medical practitioner's conduct. The answer, as the law stands, is that it does not. Insofar as the crime of murder is concerned, consent is not a defence available to the person who brings about the death of the deceased. Nor does the fact of consent justify a conviction on the lesser charge of culpable homicide.

That principle is graphically illustrated by circumstances far removed from the present. They were aptly described in a judgment by Holmes J.A. as involving:

'... a grim and sombre drama of despair and mercenary death, uniquely macabre because the deceased arranged his own murder, in circumstances of dire financial stress, for the purpose of insurance gain to his widow and his avoidance of the prospects of imprisonment for fraud.'

As this characteristically pithy summary reveals, the deceased, Mr. Jackson, had arranged with others, including his wife and a friend to have himself killed. Mr. Robinson was hired for the purpose of undertaking the killing. After driving with the deceased to a suitably lonely spot, where they consumed a considerable quantity of alcohol, he shot and killed Mr. Jackson. Relying on *Peverett*, and certain of the early writers on criminal law, Holmes J.A. held that consent is no defence to criminal responsibility for intentionally killing another person.

PAE therefore constitutes the crime of murder. A medical practitioner who administers a lethal agent to a patient at the latter's request commits the crime of murder. No doubt if they did so the circumstances would materially affect the sentence imposed for that crime, but nonetheless the conviction would stand. While I have dealt with the problem as if the only person who could be in this situation would be a medical practitioner administering the lethal dose, I can see no reason for distinguishing their situation from that of a family member or friend who did the same.

The critical question posed by this aspect of the relief sought by Mr. Stransham-Ford, was therefore whether the law in regard to consent as a defence to a charge of murder should be changed. It involved a challenge to the principle laid down in *Peverett*, and repeated in *Robinson*, but neither the principle, nor these cases, was addressed by the high court. If the common law were to be developed, a topic to which I turn below, this needed to be confronted squarely and the scope and ambit of the requisite exception to, or departure from, existing principle had to be defined. Regard needed to be had to the fact that there are [editor's note: at the time the court was writing] only four countries in the world that permit PAE. All I would say at this stage is that, as there was no attempt by either the parties or the court below to identify this as an issue calling for consideration, it was not given full and proper consideration by the court below. An order making such a profound change to our law of murder, without any consideration of applicable principles, should not have been made and it must now be set aside. Furthermore, on the facts of the matter, the question did not arise. No doctors came forward to say that they were willing to administer a lethal substance to Mr. Stransham-Ford or to say that they thought that appropriate in the circumstances of his situation. The possibility of PAE was accordingly academic. The high court was not in a position to consider whether and subject to what conditions the law in regard to consent as a defence to a charge of murder needed to be altered. Even had Mr. Stransham-Ford not died when he did, the court should have refused to enter into this academic question.

Assisted suicide (PAS)

Mr. Stransham-Ford sought in the alternative an order that a medical practitioner be authorised to enable him to terminate his own life by providing him with an appropriate lethal agent that he could administer himself in order to terminate his life. Although not mentioned in the affidavits, which speak only of Mr. Stransham-Ford wishing to avoid dying in circumstances he regarded as infringing on his right to dignity, the reality is that he said that he wished to be able to commit suicide in a manner and at a time of his own choosing, no doubt because he believed that this would be simpler, less painful and distressing and more certain of being efficacious than any other means open to him. As pointed out … above his act in committing, or attempting to commit, suicide would attract no criminal consequences for him. Any criminal liability would attach to the medical practitioner who prescribed the means whereby he could commit suicide.

It is here that the case of *Grotjohn* referred to and relied on by [the lower court] is relevant to the issue of PAS. Whether it has the effect he attributed to it requires a detailed consideration of what was in issue in the case and what it decided.

Grotjohn arose from a distressing domestic situation. Mr. and Mrs. Grotjohn were unhappily married. She was partially paralysed and bipolar, and he was having an affair with another woman. On the day in question they had a heated argument in the course of which she claimed that a rifle he owned was not in working order. He produced the rifle, undertook some makeshift repairs that involved the removal of the trigger guard and, when she suggested it would not work, found a bullet and demonstrated it was in working order by firing the bullet from their flat into the ground outside. Thereafter the argument continued about his affair. Eventually Mrs. Grotjohn became furiously angry and said that she would shoot herself. The accused obtained another bullet from elsewhere in their flat, loaded the gun in her presence and handed it to her saying 'Shoot yourself then if you will because you are a burden'. Mrs. Grotjohn placed the butt of the rifle on the floor, the muzzle under her chin and fired it by pulling the trigger with her foot, thereby killing herself.

Mr. Grotjohn was acquitted of his wife's murder on the ground that her death had been occasioned by her own independent act in committing suicide and that this broke the chain of causation between any action on his part and her death. In reaching that conclusion the trial court relied on an earlier, somewhat different case, involving a failed suicide pact. There, the wife of a married man engaged in an affair confronted him over the affair. After he broke the news to his girlfriend, they discussed the impossibility of their situation and decided to commit suicide together. To that end he acquired sleeping pills in addition to some he already had in his possession and that evening they went to a secluded spot near a beach, divided the pills into two equal portions and consumed them together. Some hours later he awoke and found that his girlfriend was dead beside him in the car. He then tried to commit suicide by drowning but was rescued by fishermen. On his trial for the murder of his girlfriend he was acquitted on the basis that her independent act in committing suicide was the cause of her death.

Mr. Grotjohn's acquittal caused the Minister of Justice to refer to this court the following questions: '(a) Whether encouraging, providing the means for or helping a man or woman to commit suicide was a crime? And (b) If so, what crime?'

The judgment dealt at length with the question whether suicide or attempted suicide was a crime and concluded that they were not. It then said that this did not mean that the first question posed to the court had to be answered in the negative. A person who encouraged, provided the means for or assisted a suicide to commit suicide was concerned with the life of that person and their criminal liability had to be determined in accordance with the ordinary principles of our criminal law. In both *Grotjohn* and *Gordon* the actions of the accused had formed part of the factual complex leading up to the death of the deceased. The trial courts had proceeded on the footing that the independent actions of the deceased had interrupted the causal chain between the accused's actions and the deceased's death in each case. While the correctness of those findings in each case was not questioned, as it did not fall within the compass of the questions and the records of the trials were not before the court, Steyn C.J. said that:

> 'I would not subscribe to a general proposition that the final "voluntary and independent" act of the suicide must always result in the acquittal of the accused, without reservation in regard to the independence of that act.' (My translation.)

Steyn C.J. went on to explain that the fact that the immediate cause of the suicide's death is the act of suicide, does not necessarily interrupt the chain of causation between the conduct of the accused person and that person's death, so as to free the accused from criminal liability. In other words, not every subsequent event that leads to a particular consequence is to be viewed as a *novus actus interveniens* (an intervening cause). To have that effect the intervening cause must be a completely independent action ('n volkome onafhanklike handeling') in the sense of being separate from and unconnected to the earlier conduct.

In a lengthy passage that requires careful consideration Steyn C.J. went on to say that:

> 'Where the [deceased's] act formed a calculated part of the chain of events that the [accused] set in train, an event that he foresaw as a possibility *and desired to bring about in order to achieve his goal, or was something on which he could rely to bring about the desired result,* intention would also not be lacking, and it would be contrary to accepted legal principles and every sense of justice to permit [the accused] to shelter behind the [deceased's] act as a subsequent intervening act. That it [suicide] is not a crime does not make a difference. So too, I consider that it is obvious that the suicide's final act, although it may be his own independent act and the immediate cause of his death, is not necessarily a completely independent act in the abovementioned sense, and that its non-criminality is rarely relevant to the causative impact of the actions or conduct of the person who encouraged, helped or enabled the deceased to commit suicide. It is reasonably conceivable that the intended action or conduct [by the accused] may be an immediate contributory cause of the final deed ... *The conclusion can hardly be avoided that he who provides the desired or necessary means for an intended suicide, has a causative role therein if suicide is committed; and if he does that willingly and knowingly, with the requisite intention of putting an end to the life of the person who wishes*

> *to commit suicide, he is guilty of murder even though the final act is performed by the non-criminal hand of the deceased, because he [the accused] has then unlawfully and intentionally complicit in ending the life of another.* If the act is not completed then he is likewise guilty of attempted murder.' (My translation and emphasis. The insertions are made for the sake of clarity.) ...

There is little difficulty in applying these principles to a case such as *Grotjohn.* If a man hands his wife a loaded gun and invites her to shoot herself, adding that she is a burden to him, it would be legitimate to draw the inference that he intended that she should kill herself and that this was his intention in providing her with the means to do so. That is what the court held in very similar circumstances in *Hibbert.* But it is, to say the least, debatable how to apply these principles to a failed suicide pact or the case of a medical practitioner who reluctantly and at the insistence of a dying patient provides the means for them to commit suicide, while counselling them against doing so.

This court was extremely careful in *Grotjohn* to say no more than that it was not an automatic conclusion from the fact that the final act in the chain of events was that of the suicide, that a person who encouraged, provided the means or assisted the suicide in that act, would commit no crime. It recognised the possibility that they might be guilty of murder if their actions were performed with criminal intent and there was no break in the chain of causation between their actions and the ultimate death of the suicide, or culpable homicide if their actions were merely negligent. Every case was to be decided in accordance with basic principles and on its own peculiar facts. That much is apparent from the final answers given to the questions posed to this court, which were: 'As will appear from the aforegoing the answer to the questions posed is to be found in the applicable principles of our criminal law. The first question cannot be answered with a simple "yes" or "no". Whether a person who encourages, assists or enables another to commit suicide commits an offence will depend on the facts of the particular case. With an eye on the cases that gave rise to these questions it is necessary to place in the foreground that the mere fact that the final act was the suicide's own, independent, non-criminal act, will not without more result in that person not being guilty of a crime. The answer to the second question depends entirely on the factual circumstances. After consideration thereof the crime may be murder, attempted murder or culpable homicide.'

Steyn C.J. was not dealing with the kind of case that is before us. He said that the correctness of the findings in *Gordon* and *Grotjohn* were not questions that he would enter upon. It is true that certain academic commentators have viewed the judgment as incompatible with the results of those cases and suggested that they must be taken to have been overruled. But that is not a reason for assuming how the judgment is to be applied in relation to circumstances that not only were not before the court, but so far as can be discerned from the judgment were not within its contemplation. The first question posed to the court was not answered with a simple yes or no. That demonstrates that the court did not decide that a criminal offence is committed whenever a person encourages, helps or enables someone to commit suicide or to attempt to do so. Whether they will depends on the facts of the case and issues of intention (mens rea), unlawfulness and causation. It follows that it cannot be said that in the current state of our law PAS is in all circumstances unlawful. The [lower court] judge's statement to that effect went too far.

A court confronted with a case of PAS would have to consider how the principles articulated in *Grotjohn* should be applied and adapted to the present day. The facts of the particular case of PAS would have to be considered. The background would be markedly different, given changes in medical circumstances in the nearly fifty years that have passed since that judgment was delivered. The court would also have to pay particular heed to the requirements of s 39(2) of the Constitution, which requires that in the development of the common law the court must strive to give effect to the nature purport and objects of the Bill of Rights. Assistance could profitably be sought from the approach to causation in this type of situation in other jurisdictions. Whether and to what extent it would determine that PAS was unlawful is unforeseeable. Only at that stage would the question arise whether the criminal law involved an infringement of a right in the Bill of Rights.

Assuming that a matter reached the stage where the court thought that a development of the common law was required in relation to PAS, it would then have to decide whether that should take the form of a different view of causation, or of intention (mens rea), or of unlawfulness. The possibility of a special defence for medical practitioners or carers would arise and have to be explored. All of this is absent from the judgment in the court below and generally speaking from the arguments presented in this court. There is also a complete absence of evidence on these issues.

* * *

The next question that was not considered by the high court was the issue of justification in terms of s 36 of the Constitution. All the foreign jurisprudence to which I have referred [in portions of the opinion omitted from this excerpt] makes it clear that the state has a legitimate interest in imposing constraints on the application of PAE, PAS and other forms of aiding and abetting suicide. The facts of *Grotjohn, Hibbert* and *Robinson* illuminate why that is also necessary in South Africa. Some constraint is plainly reasonable and justifiable in an open and democratic society based on human dignity, equality and freedom. The question is what? And that requires a court to consider the nature of any right that is infringed by the present state of the law; the importance and purpose of the limitation; its nature and extent; the relation between the limitation and its purpose and less restrictive means to achieve that purpose.

In considering that last issue, it should be borne in mind that it was only on the question of overbreadth that the Supreme Court of Canada held in *Carter* that the criminalisation of aiding and abetting suicide unjustifiably infringed a protected right. Whether a South African court faced with the same issue would arrive at the same conclusion would need to be determined in the light of the very different circumstances in this country; the availability of medical care and especially palliative care; the wide diversity of our society in its cultures and belief systems; our sense of the need to protect the poor, the weak and the vulnerable and the value attached to providing such protection. The high court's too ready adoption of the reasoning in *Carter* ignored the very different context in which that case was decided.

Lastly, a consideration and determination of these issues without any live dispute existing would raise the issue of remedy. Would the appropriate remedy be declaratory? Should there be a development of the common law crimes of murder and culpable homicide and if so to what extent and how should that be defined? Assuming the basis for any judgment was a finding that a constitutionally protected right had been infringed, would the more appropriate remedy be that adopted by the Canadian Supreme Court of a declaration of incompatibility joined with a suspension of the order to enable parliament to remedy the deficiency? That would be an extremely important possibility bearing in mind that on issues of this nature, raising complex questions of the public interest, the nature of any regulations that should attach to permitted PAE or PAS and the supervisory regime that should accompany any relaxation of the law, the legislature is the proper engine for legal development ...

[The court went on to argue that the factual record on which the lower court had based its opinion was incomplete.]

Finally under this head I mention one further concern. South Africa is a very different country facing very different challenges from countries such as Canada, Switzerland, the Netherlands, Belgium and Luxembourg, and states such as Oregon, Washington, California, Vermont and Colorado in the United States. Those countries and states have sophisticated health care systems and extensive palliative care networks. Comparatively speaking they are wealthy. South Africa is not. Our health care system faces significant challenges dealing with everyday cases. Voluntary organisations and private medical practitioners largely provide palliative care. It is not widely available to the majority of people. Regulatory enforcement in many fields is under pressure or completely lacking. Our population is diverse and there are substantial disparities of wealth and resources. Before a court could be satisfied that the acknowledged risks attendant upon permitting PAE or PAS could be guarded against by way of regulation, as is the case in other countries, it would need to be satisfied that a proper regulatory framework was, or could be put, in place and that the framework would not be a pious hope designed in a bureaucrat or idealist's office, but one the functional operations of which had been tested and not found wanting.

The different challenges facing this country emerge from the affidavit of Ms. Mayeza, tendered by the HPCSA. She is a palliative care social worker employed at Chris Hani Baragwanath Academic Hospital, Soweto and has specialised in the treatment of people with HIV/AIDS and TB. This constitutes about 40 to 45 per cent of her caseload, with a similar proportion suffering from cancer and cancer-related conditions. Ms. Mayeza drew attention to the fact that, among the communities that she serves, the life of aged and infirm members is valued and they are usually cared for within the family and the broader community. The attitude towards life is communitarian and it is treated as a gift to be preserved. Suicide is alien to this culture.

She suggested that in these communities permitting PAE and PAS posed a real threat given their socio-economic circumstances.

A court addressing these issues needs to be aware of differing cultural values and attitudes within our diverse population. It needs to consider the impact of its decision beyond our affluent suburbs into our crowded townships, our informal settlements and in the vast rural areas that make up South Africa. It is in that context that it must determine whether its decision will further undercut the foundational value of the right to life or be supportive of it. The notion of a dignified death must be informed by a rounded view of society, not confined to a restricted section of it. This was not done in this case and could not have been done because of the inadequacies of the evidence and the haste with which it was decided ...

Notes

1. The South African court, like its Canadian counterpart, cited foreign experiences extensively when coming to its conclusion about whether there is a right to aid in dying, but came to the opposite conclusion. Consider how the *Carter* and *Estate Stransham-Ford* cases adopt very different framings of the question in the opinions—as an exercise of a constitutional right to protect the dignity of an individual against interventions of the state in the former and as the state's ordinary exercise of the criminal law as applied to a new fact pattern in the latter. Moreover, one is more focused in constitutional law making, while the other in common law development of the criminal code. To what extent do you think these two "frames" responsible for the different conclusions the courts reach? Does one approach seem fairer than the other in considering the matter, or is the choice of frame purely a strategic results-oriented choice?

2. The *Estate Stransham-Ford* case explicitly considers case law involving a non-medicalized assisted suicide—through a rifle shot. To what extent should courts and legislatures considering permitting aid in dying also consider such methods in their deliberation? Many have a visceral reaction to this means of ending life they do not have to taking a drug to cause death. Are there valid distinctions based on the method used to end life? Why should doctors/medical professionals have a privileged role in providing aid in dying? While there are administrative and regulatory reasons to privilege doctors, are there ethical or other legal reasons to allow doctors to monopolize aid in dying?

3. The South Africa court cites the country's level of economic development and cultural values as reasons to deny a right to aid in dying. How relevant should these factors be to the legal and ethical issues related to patient autonomy and human dignity? Are these values universal?

4. In 1997, Colombia's constitutional court ruled that injection was legally permissible. However, doctors would not act on the ruling because of a separate law that remained on the books that punished mercy killings. In 2015, however, the

Colombian ministry of health adopted regulations to put the law into practice. Does the fact that Colombia is a predominantly Catholic country, with much lower GDP than Canada, Belgium, or the Netherlands, matter for the legal analysis? Does the country's religious affiliation affect the way you think about the answer to the question above about economic development and culture?

4. Japan

Although most countries view the withdrawal of treatment as more acceptable and less radical than euthanasia, the Japanese case that follows both accepts a physician's direct, active aid in ending a patient's life, in principle, and takes a very conservative view (by Western standards) of withdrawal of treatment.

Tōkai University Hospital—Euthanasia Case

Judgment of Yokohama District Court, March 28, 1995, 1530 *Hanrei Jihō* 28 (Japan v. Tokunaga), (Tōkai University Hospital euthanasia case)
Translated and edited by Robert B Leflar

[Translator's note: This case was the first case in Japan in which a physician was prosecuted for an act of euthanasia. The patient, Mr. Katsuhara, age 57, was terminally ill with bone marrow cancer. He was hospitalized in Tōkai University Hospital at the end of 1990. His three physicians were Dr. Nozaki, Dr. Noguchi, and the defendant, Dr. Tokunaga.]

Facts

Dr. Nozaki, the original attending physician, informed the patient's son and wife that the patient, Mr. Katsuhara, had untreatable bone marrow cancer. The son strongly requested that his father not be informed of the cancer diagnosis; so the patient was told there was an "insufficiency of bone marrow function."

The patient's condition worsened in late March 1991. The defendant, Dr. Tokunaga, was told by Drs. Nozaki and Noguchi about Mr. Katsuhara's condition and prognosis, and about the family's request that the patient not be informed of his diagnosis. On April 5, the patient began vomiting blood, and on April 8 a plasma exchange was commenced. [There follows a day-by-day account, somewhat excerpted, of his last illness.]

April 9: The patient was scarcely conscious, and could respond only to simple commands. At 9 am his wife and son said to Dr. Noguchi: "The patient didn't sleep at all last night. He is complaining of pain from the Foley catheter. He's suffering so much we can't watch. We want the plasma exchange stopped. Take out the I.V. and the Foley catheter, and stop all treatment. The patient understands what's happening. This is an incurable illness, there's no point in treating it any more; please don't keep him suffering."

Dr. Noguchi told Dr. Tokunaga of this request by the family to cease treatment; Dr. Noguchi also presented it to the senior physician on his rounds. But the family withdrew the request later after hearing an explanation from the senior physician.

April 10: The patient could not respond when spoken to, but his condition had stabilized. At 6:30 pm the wife and son asked Dr. Noguchi again to stop treatment and to discontinue the I.V. and catheter. Despite his attempts at persuading them to continue treatment, they tenaciously refused to acquiesce. After an hour of his persuasion, though, they finally acquiesced in the continuation of treatment. But at 9 pm Mrs. Katsuhara called Dr. Noguchi at home, angry that his promise that sedative drugs would not be injected had been broken. Dr. Noguchi was at a loss to respond to the family; he lost confidence in his ability to relate to them.

April 11: * * * 9 am: Dr. Noguchi told the defendant of the family's request to cease treatment, and of the angry phone conversation the previous evening. Drs. Noguchi, Nozaki and Tokunaga conferred, and decided that Dr. Noguchi would henceforth be in the background, and Dr. Tokunaga would deal with the family. They also agreed that the plasma exchange, which carried some risk, would be discontinued.

Defendant, thinking the family's attitude might be changed a little, met with the wife at 9:30, saying: "It's a critical situation. But as a physician, as long as there's any possibility [of cure], of course we'll keep treating the patient. I believe there's some hope, so I'll continue treatment. So please grit it out with me. If we stopped all treatment, you'd regret it afterward."

The son said, "When the time comes, let him face death naturally. Withdraw the I.V. and the catheter." Dr. Tokunaga responded: "*Even when the patient is facing death, I believe a physician must not cease treatment. So I must refuse your request. It's the physician's job to continue treatment right up to the end.*" (Emphasis by the court)

But the son said, "Don't make my father suffer. When death is near, don't use meaningless treatment. I want him to be able to face death easily, without pain." Dr. Tokunaga responded, "Well anyway, we won't use CPR at the end." But Tokunaga was wondering, how much does this patient really mean to his family?

April 12: The patient's condition worsened; lung inflammation had set in. Antibiotics were started and a breathing tube put in. The patient's level of consciousness slipped further, and he had difficulty breathing.

* * *

The son and wife spent the night at the hospital. The son brought a photo of the patient's oldest daughter (his sister); the patient showed no response. The son, thinking that he had lied to his father about his disease and given him false hope of an impossible cure, was filled with regret.

* * *

April 13: The patient declined through the day. Breathing was more difficult; consciousness declined to level 6 (no reaction to painful stimuli); cyanosis of the fingers with light pressure.

The son said, "My mother and I can't take this any more. Stop all treatment; liberate him from this suffering and let him die naturally; even if death comes a little sooner, it's all right." Later that morning, the wife happened to meet Dr. Nozaki in the corridor.

"I've been with him without sleeping for a week now, and I'm tired," she exclaimed. "If it's incurable, stop the treatments. I'm going to say this to Dr. Tokunaga too."

About 10 am, the son and wife said to a nurse, "You've done everything you can do. We want you to take him off the I.V. and the Foley catheter." Dr. Tokunaga, hearing this, came in about 11. The family told him: "You've done everything you can. We want you to take him off the I.V. and the catheter. We want to take him home quickly. We can't stand to see him suffer like this any more. We want you to let him be comfortable. We've thought about this and decided."

Dr. Tokunaga said, "Taking him off the I.V. means stopping nutrition and hydration, and that would shorten his life. Wouldn't that be too selfish, to let him die? I can't do that. As a doctor I'm going to fight it to the end."

Defendant on the one hand as a doctor believed he couldn't stop treatment. On the other hand, he understood the family's feeling that with death only a day or two away, advancing that death by removing the I.V. and Foley catheter that the patient seemed to dislike and permitting him to die naturally, probably wouldn't contravene the patient's own wishes. All these things flitted through the doctor's mind. [Translator's comment: The judge is exercising a good deal of creativity in setting out these facts.]

So Dr. Tokunaga finally reached the conclusion that removing the life-sustaining treatment and speeding up the patient's death would be acceptable, and he answered the family: "All right. I understand." He went back to the nurse station, and said to Head Nurse Itō, "I've been told by the family that they want all treatment stopped. I've tried over and over to persuade them otherwise, but they won't listen. So we'll stop all treatment, and remove the I.V. and Foley catheter." Hearing this, Nurse Itō said, "Let me try to talk with them." She did so, but to no avail.

At 11:20 am defendant Tokunaga told a nurse to stop all treatment, and wrote the order in the chart. About 1:30 pm, the nurse disconnected all the equipment.

The son thought that the father would die naturally as though in his sleep that night. He stayed in the hospital room with him. But the father's breathing became more labored still, weighing on the son's mind. (The wife, at the son's suggestion, had gone home in the afternoon to rest.)

About 2 pm, Dr. Nozaki came by and was surprised to find the I.V. and catheter out. Thinking that Dr. Tokunaga, to whom he had turned over the patient's care, had given in to the family's requests, he called out to Dr. Tokunaga at the nurse station, "I see you've stopped the I.V." Dr. Tokunaga responded: "I tried to persuade them, but they wouldn't listen, so I stopped it." Dr. Nozaki, acquiescing, then left for a conference in Kyoto.

About 3 pm, Dr. Tokunaga checked the patient. The breathing tube was in, and the EKG monitor was attached. The patient's level of consciousness was Level 6: no reaction to pain stimuli, no consciousness. He thought the patient probably would die that day or the next. At about 4 pm, he met Dr. Mishima of the same department and rank as he; he told Mishima that he had stopped treatment. Mishima replied, "That ought to shut the family up."

The son, seeing his father apparently suffering with heavy breathing and wanting him to die quietly as though in his sleep, called Dr. Tokunaga to the room about 5 pm. "He's suffering. I want you to take out the breathing tube." Dr. Tokunaga replied, "I can't do that. There's a danger that his tongue will block his throat and he'll stop breathing." The son renewed the request. Dr. Tokunaga thought, it's all right with the son if his father dies. I've already agreed to his request to disconnect the I.V. and catheter. So at 5:45 pm, he took out the breathing tube.

The patient's labored breathing continued. About 6 pm the son called Dr. Tokunaga to the bedside again. "I can't stand to listen to his breathing, and see him suffering like this. Please put him to rest. Please let me take him home quickly." Dr. Tokunaga, thinking that at least he could quiet the father's breathing, said "I understand." He went back to the nurse station, considering what drug would suppress this labored breathing.

He decided on Horizon, an analgesic with the side effect of suppressing breathing, knowing the drug might hasten the patient's death. He had Nurse Kadogawa prepare twice the usual dose: 4 ml. At 6:15 he injected it into the patient's left arm. The son silently watched him from the bedside.

After watching for nearly an hour after this injection, the son, seeing that his father's labored breathing continued unchanged, called loudly for Dr. Tokunaga: "He's still breathing. I want to take him home quickly." Dr. Tokunaga went back to the nurse station, filled a syringe himself with double the normal dose of the drug Sereneisu, and at about 7 pm injected it into the patient's left arm. (Sereneisu also has the side effect of suppressing breathing.)

The son, after watching the injection, asked "How long will it take?" Dr. Tokunaga replied: "His heart's really strong. Maybe an hour or two."

After the Sereneisu injection, Dr. Tokunaga, seeking to forestall any more requests from the son, called him out of the hospital room. "You're asking me to kill him with these drugs. Well, the law doesn't allow it, and as a physician I can't do it." The son just listened silently.

The son, seeing the father unchanged after the second injection, suspected Dr. Tokunaga of trying to fool him with meaningless injections. He paged Dr. Tokunaga, who was in his car to get some dinner outside the hospital. Dr. Tokunaga turned and came back without getting dinner. The son confronted him at the nurse station angrily. "What are you up to, doctor? He's still breathing! I want to take him home before this day is over."

Dr. Tokunaga felt that he could not escape from the unusually persistent demands of the son. He went into the nurse station without answering, worried about what to do. He felt as though as much as he tried to refuse the son's requests, he couldn't keep doing so forever. He was physically and mentally exhausted. Finally he decided to do the son's bidding, and make the patient die.

He decided to use a drug that would make the patient's heart stop. Looking in the bookcase at the nurse station, he saw in a drug compendium that Wasoran, used for circulatory conditions, had the side effect of transient heart stoppage. He decided to use it. But that alone might not kill the patient immediately. So he decided to add KCl (potassium chloride), which causes damage to the heart's electrical function, to the mix.

Usually potassium chloride is diluted and given patients intravenously. But Dr. Tokunaga decided to inject it in undiluted form. He asked Nurse Miyoko Takanishi if they had potassium chloride and Wasoran available. She said "There's some potassium chloride, but no Wasoran." But she knew about his trying the other two drugs, and she acceded to his request. She wrote up an order for Wasoran to the hospital pharmacy, and gave it to Dr. Tokunaga. He got it from the pharmacy.

Dr. Tokunaga put 5 ml of Wasoran—twice the usual dose—into a syringe. He put 20 ml of potassium chloride in another. He went to the patient's room. The patient was breathing laboriously. The son watched him silently.

Facts Constituting the Crime

The defendant, on April 13, 1991 at about 8:35 pm, in Isehara City, Kanagawa-ken, at Tōkai University Affiliated Hospital, 6th floor Room 14, injected the patient first with Wasoran; upon seeing that had no effect, he injected 20 ml of undiluted potassium chloride into the patient's left arm. Nurse Kadogawa immediately noticed an abnormality on the heart monitor and shouted, "There's a ventricular narrowing." But Dr. Tokunaga kept on with the injection. He confirmed the patient's heart stoppage on the monitor, checking for lack of a heartbeat and pulse. He said to the son "It's over." At about 8:46 pm, the patient died of heart stoppage caused by an acute high level of potassium in the blood.

Judgment of the Court

Part I. Introduction

[The court makes general observations about medical progress, euthanasia, and how this case forces us to define the legal limits; what's important about the case; the consequences of the decision.]

Part II. Requirements for Cessation of Treatment

Death must be unavoidable; the patient must be in the last stages of an incurable disease with no prospect of recovery. The cessation of treatment originates in the patient's right of self-determination and the limit of a physician's duty in cases of medical futility. This is not to recognize the patient's right to die as such, or right to choose death. It simply recognizes a right to choose the method or process of facing death. This is to prevent us from viewing death too lightly. It is desirable that more than one physician make the judgment that recovery is impossible. Also, if the treatment in question is one that has only a small influence on the patient's continued life, it should be easier to terminate the treatment than if it ties in directly with the patient's death—in which latter case the patient should be actually facing death before the treatment is terminated.

It is necessary for the patient to have made an expression of intent that treatment cease, and that that intent [not be revoked] at the time of the cessation of treatment. It goes without saying that it is most desirable for the patient himself to have clearly expressed that intention. The expression of intention should be based on the patient's own accurate knowledge of his disease, nature of treatment, and prognosis. For this reason the importance of informing the patient of his diagnosis and of informed consent is indicated.

However, in the great majority of cases, patients will be unable to express their intention about cessation of treatment at the time the decision must be made. Most Japanese today, we expect, would want meaningless treatment stopped, and we can expect that in future, living wills will become more prevalent. But we must consider whether substituted consent [lit. "inferred intent"—*suiteiteki ishi*] should be recognized.

If there is a prior expression of will by the patient, whether written or oral, it is powerful proof—if near in time. But if remote in time, or vague, then the case should be treated like situations where no expression of will by the patient exists. Where no reliable expression of the patient's intent exists, it is best to rely on the family to state the patient's "inferred intent." Better this, than digging into fragmentary evidence of what the patient might have said in passing. The family is likely to know the patient's character, values, and view of human existence. The family, like the patient, should be given accurate information about the patient's condition, nature of treatment, prognosis, etc. To judge the family's ability to speak for the patient, it is necessary for the physician to know about the patient's relationship to his family, how close they are, and so forth.

The treatments that may be terminated include drugs, chemical treatment, artificial respiration, blood transfusion, nutrition and hydration—both measures for treatment of disease and life support measures. However, what treatments should be stopped, and when, are medical judgments about when the treatments are meaningless.

Part III. Requirements for Euthanasia

Conditions for active euthanasia by a physician:

a. Physical pain difficult to bear.
b. The time of unavoidable death is drawing near.
c. Methods of eliminating or easing physical pain are exhausted, and no substitute means remain.
d. There is a clear expression of intent to accept the shortening of life.

Conditions for cessation of treatment: An expression of intent by family members who can infer the patient's will, will suffice. [Moreover, cessation must be medically appropriate.]

Defendant's acts here did not meet the conditions allowing either "cessation of treatment" or "active euthanasia."

The patient had bone marrow cancer. A doctor at Tōkai University Hospital received a request from the patient's son to "put him to rest," saying "I want to take him home quickly" [i.e., as a corpse].

A distinction must be made between physical suffering (whether existing or probable in the future), which can serve as a justification for active euthanasia, and mental suffering, which cannot. Judging mental suffering is too subjective; we could start to view death too lightly.

Active euthanasia is permitted as long as death is imminent. But if it is not, "indirect euthanasia" [*kansetsu-teki anrakushi*], in the sense of pain relief treatment with the possibility of hastening death, can be used.

The idea of allowing euthanasia is based in part on the concept of patient autonomy: the patient must choose whether to undergo suffering or shorten life. So an indication of the patient's will is essential. Whether a clear indication of the patient's will is required, or whether merely an inference of the patient's intent will suffice, depends on the method of euthanasia.

[The court sets out three types of euthanasia:

Passive (*shōkyokuteki*): the cessation of life-prolonging treatment, a non-deliberate (*fusakui*) act

Indirect (*kansetsuteki*): giving pain relief treatment with the possibility of hastening death

Active (*sekkyokuteki*): treatment deliberately inviting death in order to free the patient from suffering]

The permissibility of euthanasia differs according to which of the three types is in question.

The permissibility of passive euthanasia is to be judged merely as a matter of whether it is medically appropriate to cease treatment. Indirect euthanasia is permitted in accordance with the principle of patient autonomy. An inference of the patient's intent will suffice; and this can be inferred from the family's expression of intent. Active euthanasia is permissible only when all means of removing or easing pain have been exhausted, and no other alternate methods exist. Then as the Nagoya High Court said in its December 22, 1962 judgment (Hanrei Jihō 324:1): "It must be performed by a physician."

Active euthanasia is based on the principles of emergency refuge [*kinky ū hinan*] and patients' self-determination; so it is permissible only with a clear expression of intent by the patient. Passive euthanasia is permissible only if the patient is in an incurable state, nearing death, with no prospect of recovery. Some evidence of the patient's intent is required for passive euthanasia. Clear evidence of the patient's will at the time of the decision to cease treatment is desirable. It should be based on continuing consideration and accurate information concerning prognosis, accurately understood.

However, clear evidence of the patient's will is not necessary for cessation of treatment. Passive euthanasia is also allowed based on inferences from the patient's own previous expression of will, or from the family's statement of intent. Still, to recognize that the family is properly inferring the patient's will, the family must know the patient's character and values, and must have full and accurate information on the nature of the disease, treatment, and prognosis. Moreover, the physician assessing the family's expression of will must be in a position to know both the patient's own thoughts and position concerning his disease and treatment, and the level of the patient's relationship with his family.

The conditions justifying active [or indirect] euthanasia were not met here. The fatal injection was not for the purpose of relieving physical pain, since at that time the patient was not suffering; and since the patient had never been told he was suffering from cancer, there was no clear statement available as to the patient's own intent.

Part IV. Evaluation of Defendant's Specific Acts

Removal of I.V., Foley Catheter & Breathing Tube: Both Dr. Tokunaga and Dr. Nozaki judged that the patient, as of April 13, 1991, had only a day or two to live. Other physicians said the same; even with aggressive treatment, the patient could at most have survived 4–5 days. So objectively, the patient's condition was at the stage appropriate for consideration of termination of treatment.

As for the expression of the patient's will, this patient had not been informed of his diagnosis, and had not received an accurate explanation of his condition and prognosis. At the time of decision, he was incapable of expressing his will. So we must determine whether the family could properly speak for the patient. Both the wife and son had lived with the patient for many years, and knew his character, values, and outlook on life. They kept insisting on cessation of treatment over several days. We can conclude that they were capable of expressing the patient's inferred intent. However, the family were not properly informed of the patient's inability to feel pain. On April 13, when they asked that the I.V. and Foley catheter be discontinued, they were not told that he had no response to painful stimuli. So their request cannot be considered to be properly grounded, inferred expressions of the patient's intent.

This defendant had only known the family for a short time—less than two weeks—at the time he became attending physician for this patient. There is doubt whether he really understood their position. He was not in a position to judge whether their decisions were a proper expression of the patient's intent. The patient's intent was neither expressed nor could be inferred from the family. Therefore the withdrawal of the I.V., etc. was not permitted by law.

2. The Injections of Horizon and Sereneisu

Not being premised either on the patient's own expression of intention nor on the patient's inferred intent stated by a properly informed family, these injections do not fall within the permitted indirect euthanasia.

3. The Injections of Wasoran and Potassium Chloride

Since the patient was feeling no pain at the time, the prerequisite for legal active euthanasia—intractable physical pain—was not met. Nor was there a finding that alternative measures were not available. Neither did the patient give express consent. The conditions for legally permissible active euthanasia were not fulfilled. Defendant pleaded that the son was an "instigator." But the court considered the doctor's higher status and position, and rejected the argument.

Reasons for Punishment

[The court concluded these illegal acts undercut trust in medicine, and speculated that doctors might start shortening the lives of patients who are not facing immediate death.]

Even though the hospital at which defendant was employed has high standards, its system for end-of-life care was deficient. The "team concept" did not function well, because of the shuffling around of staff.

The family's influence on end-of-life decisions is great. This doctor's training and experience in dealing with such situations was poor. [The court gave reasons for leniency with the punishment: e.g. the family does not hold bad feelings toward the defendant.]

Sentence: Two years, suspended. [The sentence was not appealed.]

Note

The Tokai University case has been influential among legal and medical scholars and practitioners. In one other case, the same court generally followed the Tokai University court's analytical framework, also holding a physician criminally liable for his part in bringing about a terminally ill patient's death. *Judgment of Yokohama District Court,* March 25, 2005, 1909 Hanrei Jiho 130.

However, the decision has not ended debate on the subject in Japan: it was just a district court case, most of the court's analytical framework was not necessary to the decision in the case, and there are few subsequent court decisions raising similar issues. Thus, the court's analytical framework lacks authoritative support and, absent authoritative guidance and fearing criminal liability, many physicians simply refuse families' requests to remove life support from comatose terminal patients. Other physicians will halt medications but will not remove a respirator. Aiming at clarification of this controversial area, the health ministry named a blue-ribbon committee to propose authoritative guidelines for end-of-life care—or at least to propose procedures for making the decisions—that released its guidelines in 2007, but the situation has not much changed. (This note provided by Robert Leflar and Norio Higuchi.)

Chapter 4

The Rights of the Individual and the Interests of Society

A. Public Health Law: Legal Approaches to HIV/AIDS

The first three chapters of this book have dealt primarily with the rights of private patients and consumers in their relationships with professionals, institutions, or the government in matters pertaining to health care. The law also plays a role in protecting the health of the public. The topic of public health law is the subject of this final chapter.

Public health law came into its own in the late 19th century, as the law was used as a tool to impede the spread of infectious diseases, promote sanitation, protect workers from threats to their health and safety, and defend the public from unsafe food or drugs. Public health law has evolved over the last century to tackle other health promotion and prevention concerns. Recently, public health law in the United States has grappled with the opioid crisis and its implications for other diseases, such as the spread of HIV via used syringes. See Melissa Vallejo, Note, Safer Bathrooms in Syringe Exchange Programs: Injecting Progress into the Harm Reduction Movement, 118 *Colum. L. Rev.* 1185 (2018).

One of the greatest challenges to confront public health law in recent decades has been the spread of HIV/AIDS. HIV/AIDS emerged in the 1980s, at a time when the developed nations had become quite complacent about infectious diseases. The disease emerged quite suddenly; seemed to be incurable and invariably fatal; and appeared initially in marginalized groups such as homosexuals, intravenous drug users, and prostitutes. For all of these reasons, there was in some countries a push to adopt laws that would treat HIV/AIDS differently than other infectious diseases. In particular there was a tendency on the part of some policy-makers to argue for the use of traditional public health tools such as screening, quarantine, and contact tracing, rather than more modern approaches of education and persuasion. To this day, HIV-positive people face many restrictions, including those that limit the resources of public health initiatives like prohibitions on blood or organ donation. See Erica Pauline Spiro, A Lift on the Statutory Prohibitions Against HIV-Positive Organ Donation, 10 *Drexel L. Rev.* 535 (2018); Neiloy Sircar, Good Public Health Policy, Better Public Health Law: Blood Donation, Individual Risk Assessments, & Lifting the Deferral for Men Who Have Sex with Men, 73 *Food & Drug L.J.* 103 (2018). These restrictions raise important questions about the balance between protecting public health and preserving individual rights. See James J. Misrahi, The CDC's Communicable Disease Regulations: Striking the Balance between Public Health & Individual Rights, 67 *Emory L.J.* 463 (2018); cf. Lawrence O. Gostin, Katharina E. Ó Cathaoir, Lurching from Complacency to Panic in the Fight Against Dangerous Microbes: a Blueprint for a Common Secure Future, 67 *Emory L.J.* 337 (2018).

Beyond the nuances of HIV prevention policy, HIV's emergence presented a truly global public health crisis that led to unprecedented worldwide coordination. The United Nations combats the spread of HIV/AIDS via a program called "UNAIDS" run through the Global AIDS Response Progress Reporting program. Some commentators observe that UNAIDS represents a unique level of transnational cooperation—one necessitated by HIV/AIDS. See Gabrielle Goldstein, Christopher Ansell, Experimentalist Governance in Global Public Health: the Case of UNAIDS, 35 *Ariz. J. Int'l & Comp. L.* 219 (2018). The following excerpt discusses the contrasting approaches taken by various European jurisdictions to the HIV/AIDS crisis:

John A. Harrington, *AIDS, Public Health and the Law: A Case of Structural Coupling?*

European J. Health Law, vol. 6, pp. 213, 213–26 (1999)

1. Introduction

AIDS has been a focus of health care policy and medical law in Europe for almost two decades now. In its early years AIDS represented the greatest challenge to public health since the pre-World War II era when tuberculosis was prevalent. The sense of panic or crisis which affected policy makers as well as the general public was caused not primarily by the numbers of persons affected, but by the potential for huge and rapid spread of the disease in the population. The risk of future catastrophe, even more than the reality of present disaster, was the significant object of public policy. It was this future orientation which marked AIDS out as typically a public health issue: that is, measures proposed and measures taken were preventive in purpose and design. Given the passing of time it is now appropriate to speak of a history of AIDS in Europe. This history is at least partly one of public health responses to the disease. A history, that is, of competing predictions, proposals and measures implemented to combat the spread of AIDS.

Each model of disease control envisaged a very specific, but variable role for the law. The imposition of legal sanctions for disapproved behaviour, the application of coercive control to high risk groups and the availability of legal remedies for infected persons were all thus significantly dependent upon differing public health understandings. An examination of the history of AIDS can therefore be expected to reveal the varying incidence and intensity of links between public health medicine and the law. It can, in other words, demonstrate a positive correlation between specific medical theories and recommendations on the one hand, and specific legal change on the other.

* * *

2. Public Health—"Old and New"

Although public health and other medical experts, often liaising with gay activists and other interest groups, were at the heart of policy making on AIDS across Europe, there was no unanimity in their recommendations. Science does not necessarily give an unambiguous, clear-cut message to policy makers, and the case of AIDS illustrates the scope for conflicting signals from experts. These distinct responses to HIV/AIDS may be related to what has been termed the "old" and the "new" public health. * * *

The old public health evolved in the nineteenth century as a response to the spread of infectious disease. Epidemics of cholera, typhus, tuberculosis and scarlet fever had devastating effects in the massively expanded industrial cities of Europe. * * * As the century progressed, scientific breakthroughs, such as those of Louis Pasteur and Robert Koch, showed that prevalent diseases were very frequently caused by the transmission of viruses from person to person and that this process of infection was intensified by the social conditions [of the time]. In the absence of effective vaccines for most conditions and before the development of "miracle" drugs such as penicillin, the chief recommendation of epidemiologists and other public health specialists was that in each case the chain of infection should be broken, thus stopping the spread of the disease. To achieve this local and state health authorities implemented programmes of quarantine, isolation, testing and compulsory treatment on the outbreak of infectious disease in their areas. * * * Importantly, these measures were cast in legal form: they empowered officials acting on the advice of doctors to impose drastic restrictions upon the freedom of movement of individuals and upon economic activity in affected areas.

With the abatement of the great epidemics, these powers, though remaining in force, were used more and more infrequently. Their coercive approach was displaced in orthodox public health medicine in response to changing patterns of morbidity and mortality in Europe, especially after the Second World War. This "new" public health sought to combat much more prevalent conditions such as cancer, heart disease and obesity with strategies of persuasion, education and behaviour modification. * * * The obvious distinction with the major nineteenth century illnesses was that none of the more recently occurring conditions is contagious. The issue of whether and how to break chains of infection did not arise. Neither, therefore, did the question of whether to reactivate the inherited corpus of draconian health legislation. All this was to change with the advent of AIDS in the early 1980s.

3. Policy Responses to HIV/AIDS

Soon after the diagnosis of the first cases of AIDS, epidemiological studies indicated a concentration of cases among two main social groups: homosexual men and intravenous drug users. Subsequently it became clear that members of other groups could also be infected. In 1983–4 French and American scientists, working independently of each other, demonstrated that the immune weakness, which lead ultimately to the complex of illness known as "full-blown" AIDS, was caused by the so-called Human Immunodeficiency Virus (HIV). Further studies showed that the virus is passed from person to person by certain, rather limited forms of human contact, in particular by the exchange of body fluids such as blood, semen and breastmilk. Although the main aetiological questions were settled, two outstanding issues remained: the fact that AIDS was an incurable condition leading to the death of almost all those infected with HIV; and, in the light of this, the question of how to stop or at least slow the spread of the virus in the population. * * *

Two main approaches to the control of AIDS were recommended, one non-coercive and broadly in line with the new public health, the other coercive and in line with the old public health. In essence the non-coercive strategy sought to mobilize infected persons and the general public to change their behaviour in order to reduce the spread of infection. As the United Kingdom Chief Medical Officer put it in 1986, "[i]n the absence of a vaccine or effective anti-viral agent, public education to help people avoid risky sexual behaviour and drug abuse is the mainstay of a policy for controlling the spread of infection." Consequently a strong message was conveyed that the use of condoms in sexual intercourse and of sterile equipment in intravenous drug-taking was the best means of protecting oneself and others. These education campaigns were essentially based upon the utilitarian assumption that, once the risks of certain behaviours were explained to them, individuals would act rationally in their own best interests.

There is a further, less immediate sense in which general education campaigns were intended to reduce the spread of AIDS. It was widely recognized that those groups at highest risk of infection had suffered from discrimination before the advent of AIDS solely by reason of their choice of lifestyle. Activists and public health specialists repeatedly emphasized that the new association of these stigmatized lifestyles with a fatal, incurable disease would further distance high risk groups from both the wider society and the state medical system. Without these contacts behaviour modification among those most at risk of being infected and of infecting others would be very difficult to achieve. Thus, homosexual men, drug users and prostitutes were intended to understand public health campaigns in a further indirect sense: as indicating a tolerant and inclusive attitude on the part of the authorities, and as creating a less hostile attitude toward them among the heterosexual and non-drug taking population. This distinctive approach to public health is sometimes formulated as "the AIDS-paradox": only by protecting at risk persons from discrimination and coercion could the state protect the interests of the uninfected majority of the population. In other words to respect the human rights of persons immediately affected by the epidemic was at the same time to promote the health of all. AIDS was, therefore, constructed in these campaigns as a "national" problem, a condition which could and did affect everyone. Gay groups in particular met with a largely positive response on initiating contact with and making proposals for action to national health authorities. Partly pro-active, partly co-opted, they were used by the medical establishment to organize information campaigns as well as practical help for their constituencies.

As has been noted, the coercive response to HIV/AIDS was typically founded upon older notions of public health medicine outlined above. In particular it remained true to the initial epidemiological emphasis upon high risk groups, as opposed to high risk activities. * * * On the basis of this methodology, homosexuals, drug users and prostitutes, were defined as being outside and "other than" the largely unaffected heterosexual population. The task of medicine and law was, therefore, to protect the "majority" by preventing the epidemic from crossing this notional divide. It is clear that this recommendation of public health was reciprocally linked with common moral and political responses to epidemics. Right-wing cultural critics promoted a view of AIDS as an inevitable consequence of, if not a punishment for, decadent forms of life. By contrast with the non-coercive approach, this model of disease prevention did not attribute to high risk groups the same self-interested rationality as that of the rest of the population. They were assumed instead to be typically irrational and heedless of the danger presented to themselves and others by their "hedonistic" pursuits. Consequently they could not be reached in the first instance by education, that is by rational persuasion. Neither were they seen as likely to respond to a more tolerant climate by modifying their behaviour. Control strategies were to be directed rather more at the bodies than the minds of infected or potentially infected persons, identified by their status as members of high risk groups. It was thus clear that, in attempting to break the chain of infection, the authorities would resort to techniques of surveillance, testing and isolation, i.e. legally sanctioned coercion. The only reflective response on the part of targeted groups and individuals contemplated was one of fear. * * *

The chief examples of the non-coercive strategy in Western Europe are provided by the United Kingdom and all but one of the German federal states; those of the coercive strategy by the German state of Bavaria and Sweden. * * *

4. The Non-Coercive Approach

4.1 United Kingdom

United Kingdom governmental policy on AIDS was shaped by a high degree of agreement between ministers, public health specialists and representatives of affected groups. Challenges to the overridingly non-coercive policy adopted came most frequently not from rival schools of public health, but from social conservatives on the right wing of the political spectrum. More than a policy, non-coercion became a culture which spread, admittedly not without local resistance, from political and professional elites to volunteer and health service workers involved in treating and counselling people with HIV. The latter group was significantly comprised of doctors and nurses. * * *

In Britain the main legislation relating to contagious diseases is the Public Health (Control of Diseases) Act 1984, a consolidation of measures which date from the Victorian era. It provides local authorities with powers to deal with certain listed conditions. These include the classic targets of nineteenth century public health: cholera, plague, tuberculosis, small pox, scarlet fever, etc. Most, though not all, of these conditions are notifiable under s. 11 of the Act, i.e. a doctor encountering them in a patient must inform the local authority or face criminal sanction. Further permissible measures include detention and isolation of sufferers or suspected sufferers, compulsory examination and testing, prohibition of employment and upon the use of public facilities such as buses, libraries and swimming pools. At the beginning of the epidemic there was pressure in Britain to make AIDS and HIV notifiable conditions, but this was successfully resisted. (The AIDS (Control) Act 1987 does provide for the collection of data on the prevalence of the disease in the United Kingdom, but this is done on an anonymous basis.) Admittedly, AIDS was added to the list of infectious conditions for which some of the other, aforementioned coercive measures might be taken. Local authorities and medical practitioners, therefore, still have the power to adopt an authoritarian approach to persons with AIDS. However, the liberal policy consensus prevailed. It was generally accepted that "AIDS" within the terms of the Act does not include the condition of being asymptomatically infected with HIV. This restricts the applicability of coercive measures in the case of an individual sufferer to the last year or so of their lives when they are in any case usually subject to treatment (and therefore supervision) in hospital. Furthermore even in relation to AIDS itself the powers provided were used only once: a patient being subjected to compulsory detention in Manchester in 1985.

One of the most controversial issues in this area, throughout Europe, and indeed elsewhere, has been that of non-voluntary testing for HIV (whether against the express wishes of the patient or secretly, without their consent). Since 1990 blood taken from patients at ante-natal and genito-urinary medicine clinics in Britain has been tested for HIV. Test results are "anonymized" and the data obtained are used solely for epidemiological purposes. * * *

Even though anonymized testing continues to be carried out, academic constructions of the relevant law have had a restraining effect upon policy makers and medical professionals alike. In 1988, for example, the British Medical Association was forced to overturn a resolution of its annual representative meeting to the effect that unconsented to testing for HIV be left entirely to the discretion of the individual doctor. Legal advice indicated that action in accordance with the resolution would be in breach of civil and possibly criminal law. Furthermore a series of guidelines on ethically permissible testing was issued in 1987 by United Kingdom General Medical Council (GMC), the profession's own disciplinary body. These stated that secret testing was only allowed, as a matter of professional ethics, where it was necessary to avert a clear and immediate danger to others, in particular health care workers carrying out risky procedures on a patient. * * *

The approach of the medical and governmental authorities to the testing of health care workers has been similarly non-coercive. Admittedly there have been frequent outbursts of panic regarding HIV-infected doctors and nurses in Britain and tracing of patients has been conducted in several cases. The authorities have, however, forgone recourse to compulsory screening of hospital staff. Furthermore, there has in the recent past been only a single prosecution of a health worker in connection with infectious disease. Instead of a widespread use of the criminal law, regulation has again been left to the GMC. Its 1987 guidelines also contained ethical advice directed to practitioners who are or might be infected with HIV or other contagious diseases. This embodies a voluntary approach: advising doctors who suspect that they might be carrying the virus to come forward for testing and, if found to be HIV positive, to desist from working in situations where they pose a risk to their patients.

Closely linked to testing is the generally recognized obligation of confidentiality. Again the law in England on this issue is unclear. In the case of *X v Y*, it was held that no exception was available to allow publication of an identified doctor's HIV positive status by the press. * * * Rose J noted that:

> Confidentiality is of paramount importance to [HIV-infected] patients including doctors ... If it is breached, or if patients have grounds for believing that it may be or has been breached they will be reluctant to come forward for and to continue treatment and, in particular, counselling. If the actual or apprehended breach is to the press that reluctance is likely to be very great. If treatment is not provided or continued the individual will be deprived of its benefit and the public are likely to suffer from an increase in the rate of spread of the disease. The preservation of confidentiality is therefore in the public interest.

In this respect, his judgement is clearly based upon the public health consensus already outlined.

* * *

4.2 Germany

As in the United Kingdom, the central issue in the German debate on HIV/AIDS was whether a coercive, legally backed campaign should be waged against the disease, or whether a non-coercive, voluntaristic approach should be taken. The main German legislation in this area is the Federal Law on Contagious Diseases. This is rather similar to the British Public Health (Control of Diseases) Act 1984 in the conditions it is aimed at and in the powers which it confers upon health officials. It is important to note that the requirement of notification under para. 3 of the Law is limited to a list of seventeen specific conditions. Discussion and commentary in Germany focused *inter alia* on whether legislation should be passed to include HIV and AIDS in this list. The authorities in all the federal states apart from Bavaria, agreed that they would not be so included. As in the United Kingdom, however, a system of anonymous collection of data on the incidence of HIV/AIDS was put in place under the Laboratory Notification Ordinance 1987. A declaration issued by their Health Ministers together with Federal Minister for Youth, Family and Health testifies to a general policy consensus in Germany similar to that which emerged in the United Kingdom. It accepted that:

> the availability of voluntary testing, advice and social assistance in various forms would be more effective in controlling the disease than the introduction of a legal duty of notification under the infectious disease legislation. The transmission of disease by way of sexual contact cannot be subject to control by the state. The state cannot take away the highly personal responsibility of

each citizen for his or her own sexual behaviour and therefore cannot ensure absolute protection in this regard.

By contrast with the requirement of notification, the other powers under the Federal Law on Contagious Diseases are not limited to specifically enumerated conditions. For these purposes, para. 1 of the Law defines as "contagious diseases" those which are caused by pathogenic agents capable of being transmitted from one human being to another. Whether a disease or condition comes within para. 1 is, therefore, a matter of interpretation. In so far as it does, para. 34 of the Law allows the following measures to be taken: compulsory testing, exclusion from employment, quarantining and supervision by the authorities. * * * In their declaration, however, the health ministers considered that the powers contained in para. 34 would rarely be needed, if at all, owing to the manner in which HIV is transmitted and the ease with which individuals can protect themselves. In addition, because such measures would severely abrogate the fundamental, constitutionally guaranteed rights of persons with HIV or AIDS they would come under scrutiny in accordance with the general administrative and constitutional law requirement of proportionality. Academic commentary largely took the view that coercive measures taken under para. 34 would not withstand such scrutiny, especially given their relative inefficacy as means of reducing the spread of HIV.

Instead, in implementation of a non-coercive programme, federal and state authorities have spent sums in excess of DM 150 million on information and education campaigns since 1987. A special commission of the Federal Lower Chamber of Parliament on AIDS reported in 1990 that the chief aim of this campaign was and should be: 1) to inform the public; 2) to encourage responsible, self-protective behaviour; 3) to reduce irrational anxiety; 4) to promote solidarity with the victims of AIDS; and 5) to counter discrimination against high risk groups. A nationwide confidential telephone counselling service was established. An important dimension of the AIDS campaign in Germany, with parallels in the United Kingdom, has been the encouragement and financial support given to voluntary and self-help organizations active in the field. These groups, largely federated under the umbrella of the Deutsche AIDS-Hilfe eV, include gay groups, prostitute organizations and others active in providing social and health services and in political campaigning. * * *

A certain amount of "wild" or speculative testing was carried out, particularly in hospitals, in the early years of the epidemic in Germany. This has become much less frequent in the light of both the public health consensus outlined above, and an increased awareness of how medical professionals can protect themselves. The latter especially has led to a restrictive interpretation of the relevant law, as in the United Kingdom. There is no dispute that an AIDS test, carried out against the express wishes of a patient, would give rise to criminal liability for invasion of bodily integrity under para. 223 of the German Criminal Code. The issue of implied consent, particularly where the patient presents for a general check-up, has been more controversial. Concern has been expressed that consent might be too easily implied due to the wide variety of symptoms associated with AIDS, e.g. tuberculosis. It has even been suggested that membership of a high risk group would be sufficient to justify testing were this ground recognized. Given the individual's constitutionally guaranteed right to self-determination, it has been argued strongly that consent to the carrying out of secret tests is not readily to be implied even where the patient has not openly ruled them out. * * * Finally it should be noted that breach of medical confidentiality is a criminal offence in Germany, under para. 203 I 1 of the Criminal Code, albeit with some exceptions. The sharing of information between members of a health care team is viewed as de minimis for instance. In addition it maybe permissible to make disclosure of a patient's HIV status to a third party at risk of infection under the defence of emergency. In each case, however, the rights to life and bodily integrity of the third party must be balanced with the rights to privacy and self-determination of the patient and with the general interest in maintaining the confidentiality of the doctor-patient relationship. * * *

* * *

5. The Coercive Approach

5.1. Bavaria

By contrast with the German Federal government and all the other states, Bavaria implemented a coercive programme of measures to prevent the spread of HIV/AIDS in its population. In essence it understood itself to be subject to a constitutional obligation to take such measures for the protection of its citizens' health. In a 1987 decision, however, the Federal Constitutional Court rejected the claim of a plaintiff who had been infected with contaminated blood that there was such a constitutional imperative. The Court agreed with his contention that the authorities were obliged to respond to the epidemic; but it held that judgments as to the broad policy of such campaigns as well as their fine detail were not appropriate to the judicial function. Decisions about timing, method and expenditure were contingent upon ever changing empirical data, more readily available to the legislative and executive organs of government. Only if the Federal Health Ministry had been completely inactive could the Court issue a declaration compelling legislative or other measures. As has already been seen, this was not the case.

In a piece written in 1988 Peter Gauweiler, the Interior Minister responsible for introducing and implementing the Bavarian Catalogue of Measures for the combat of AIDS, outlined the three public health principles on which it was based. These were: 1) the earlier and more intensive the intervention against the epidemic the better; 2) sources of infection must be dealt with without exception; 3) suitable measures must be taken to break the chain of infection. These clearly represented a prioritization of the dangerousness approach over that focused upon voluntarism and personal autonomy. Instead of education and information aimed in the first instance at the general population and seeking to persuade them, as rational agents to alter their behaviour, emphasis was laid upon identifying high risk groups and more or less coercing them to act in the interests of general well-being. The Catalogue of Measures was legally based for the greater part upon the powers contained in the Federal Law on Contagious Diseases. In the first six months of its implementation in Bavaria 1047 individuals were investigated by the authorities of whom 492 were tested for HIV. In three instances the blood had to be obtained by application of direct physical force. Police raids were carried out on sauna clubs and other establishments known to be frequented by homosexual men. Many were shut down. More generally the grant of residence permits in Bavaria to nationals of certain, non-EC countries, is made conditional upon their testing negative for HIV. Prostitutes and intravenous drug users are classified as "suspected infectious" within the Federal Law on Contagious Diseases and are subjected to routine testing. In the case of registered prostitutes this means every quarter. They are then granted a certificate of good health for the "reassurance" of their customers. Those testing positive are forbidden to continue with their work. All prostitutes are under an obligation, breach of which is punishable, to ensure condom use. Normally a positive test result leads to an obligation to notify sexual partners and medical authorities. The individual concerned can also be supervised by the Bavarian health authorities and there is also provision for the quarantining of the uncooperative, or "AIDS-desperados" as Minister Gauweiler labelled them. A challenge to compulsory testing was rejected by the Bavarian Administrative Court. Inevitably these measures, among the most coercive in Europe, provoked fierce criticism from activists and academic commentators. It was noted that the Bavarian authorities had applied the Federal Law on Contagious Diseases in this draconian and controversial manner merely on the basis of an administrative decree. Such measures should instead have been sanctioned by legislation, preferably at federal level. In practice, it soon became clear that the measures adopted were highly inefficient relative to the cost of their implementation. There is, for instance, some anecdotal evidence that members of high-risk groups were driven underground and therefore out of reach of counselling and therapy. Munich prostitutes, for example, were reported to have sought medical treatment in the city of Ulm which lies just over the border from Bavaria, so to speak, in the neighbouring state of Baden-Wuerttemberg. It should be remarked that, over a decade after their enactment, many of the powers contained in the Catalogue of Measures, though still "on the books" are no longer enforced.

5.2 Sweden

A coercive AIDS policy was also adopted in Sweden, a country long known for its distinctive mix of social democracy and state paternalism. Under an order of 1985, the Communicable Diseases Law (No. 231) of 1968 was amended to include infection with HIV among the venereal diseases in respect of which measures under the law could be taken. The latter include: registration of infected people; contact tracing; and isolation of a patient in hospital when they are believed by their physician not to be following instructions necessary to stop the spread of the disease. Anyone who believes that they have been exposed to infection must report this to a physician and must facilitate contact tracing. In addition the National Board of Health and Welfare promulgated regulations regarding the behaviour of HIV positive individuals. The latter must seek regular medical examinations, inform all sexual partners about their HIV status, and inform physicians and dentists of any condition for which they are being treated. If the patient fails, or is suspected of failing to comply with these norms of behaviour, the doctor must inform the local contagious diseases officer. On investigation of the patient's case, including inspection of all relevant files, the officer may engage the support of social workers and the police in order to enforce compliance. Although there has been a certain amount of flexibility on the part of the authorities in using these powers, there is no doubting the coercive thrust of Swedish AIDS policy. One power under the Communicable Diseases Law which has been deployed is that of isolation. Use of this measure has been criticized from the non-coercive public health perspective as "arbitrarily cruel, astronomically dear, and epidemiologically inefficient." 1987 saw a parliamentary decision forcibly to shut down gay saunas and bathhouses. Admittedly, in Sweden a vigorous educational campaign was waged to inform people of how to protect themselves against infection with HIV. However, moralistic advertising always went hand in hand with the ultimate and very real threat of coercive sanctions.

* * *

Notes

1. The United States has by and large embraced the non-coercive approach to AIDS prevention, although some states have adopted elements of more coercive approaches. In particular, laws requiring reporting of AIDS/HIV infection are quite common, and contact tracing is required in some states. Compulsory testing is rare, and state laws protecting confidentiality are generally quite strict. There are some cases, however, recognizing an obligation on the part of HIV-infected health care employees to notify their patients. Also the laws of some states authorize disclosure of HIV tests under some circumstances, for example to emergency care workers or corrections officers who have been exposed to blood.

The approach to HIV in the West has also shifted over time. As medical technology advanced, in the reality of treatment and the public consciousness of most high-income countries HIV has been transformed from a fatal disease to a chronic condition. These changes have been reflected in the Obama administration's approach to the disease. In its 2015 National HIV/AIDS Strategy report, the Obama administration focused its goals primarily on increasing healthcare access for those with the disease rather than developing new treatments. Moreover, the prevention of the disease has been aided by the introduction of pre-exposure prophylaxis (PrEP), which is typically administered to those at a high-risk of contracting the disease. For the full HIV/AIDS strategy, see National HIV/AIDS Strategy for the United States (2015).

2. At the beginning of the twenty-first century, HIV/AIDS is having its most devastating impact on Africa. The fact that Africa lacks the health resources available in North America and Europe for combating this epidemic makes the effect of the epidemic all the more disastrous. African nations are, however, adopting laws to address this crisis. The approach that various nations take depends to some extent on which of the multitude of legal traditions found within Africa is dominant in a particular

nation. The following excerpt discusses the various approaches African countries are taking:

Maya Berinzon, *Copy and Paste: Transplanting International HIV/AIDS Model Laws into African Countries*

23 Cardozo J. Int'l & Comp. L. 295, 296–297, 308–313 (2015)

HIV/AIDS is prevalent throughout large parts of Sub-Saharan Africa. Over thirty million people are currently HIV positive, and AIDS has killed twenty-five million since 1981. As a result, many means have been used to try and curb the spread of the illness. One such attempt allows physicians to disclose the seropositive (HIV-positive) status of patients to sexual partners and spouses. This is done to encourage behavioral change in their partners, to prevent further transmission of the disease, and to encourage treatment adherence.

This duty to disclose comes in a variety of forms from country to country throughout the world. Africa is the world's second largest continent, with thousands of ethnic groups, and over 2,000 languages, making it one of the most diverse regions on earth. This diversity would lead one to expect a large variance in laws curtailing a physician's duty to disclose HIV/AIDS status. While there is some variety across existing legislation, there has been a meaningful push to encourage states to adopt legislation in line with a model law created by the United Nations. As a result, laws on this issue in Africa are surprisingly homogenous. Since HIV/AIDS has only been of major concern since the 1980s, at which point most African nations were no longer under the control of a colonial state, this conformity is somewhat surprising. Both the UN Model Law and one created in West Africa are part of a trend of model legislation based on perceived universal best practices.

* * *

1. Countries with an Affirmative Duty to Disclose Only on the Part of the HIV-Positive Person

Out of the thirty-eight countries studied, four countries have imposed an affirmative duty only on patients to disclose their seropositive status to their sexual partners. In determining that a country fits into this category, I disregarded regulations that allowed doctor disclosure in the cases of an inability to consent (such as in the case of minors) or legal mandate to do so. In these situations, the purpose of disclosure is not for a doctor to prevent onward transmission, but as a part of the rules governing legal guardians and public health records. The remaining countries have relied heavily on the right to privacy as the dominant of the two rights weighed.

For example, Tanzania has a very strict law preventing the disclosure of HIV status by doctors to spouses or sexual partners, which makes any practitioner who does so liable to pay a fine of "not less than five hundred thousand shillings or to imprisonment for a term of not less than six months or to both." Zimbabwe also has a law that only places a burden on the HIV-positive person to disclose his or her status to sexual partners. This is in large part due to the contents of the Medical Practitioners-Professional Conduct-Regulations. There is a general impression that there is a lack of trust between patients and medical personnel, and therefore greater confidentiality is required to establish trust in this relationship. In Djibouti, the violation of this confidentiality is seen as a violation of the principle of dignity. While Djibouti law specifically mentions that family and friends should receive information to help support a seropositive person, there is an unequivocal and clear directive to allow the HIV-positive person to make the final decision about whether or not to disclose. Art. 12 of the same law allows disclosure after a seropositive person's death unless they expressed that they did not want their status to be disclosed. Read together, Djibouti's laws point to the consistent prioritization of an individual's desires. How to balance those desires against the protection of partners is a choice, but one that should be, and was, decided by a national legislature.

Many of these countries still use their laws as a mechanism to prevent the onward transmission of HIV through criminalization of the transmission. The laws often criminalize the individual only when the onward transmission is intentional.

2. Countries That Conditionally Allow Physicians to Disclose HIV Status

Most countries in Africa that allow a health professional to disclose HIV status do not make this notification requirement an affirmative duty. Instead, they give health professionals a generous amount of discretion. Nonetheless, these professionals are able to disclose this information if it goes against the will of the person who is HIV-positive. Of the countries examined, twenty-four give health professionals some discretion in deciding when to disclose an HIV positive person's status.

One reason not to allow a doctor to disclose one's HIV status to others is that the resulting stress can hasten the onset of AIDS. This was the argument made in a case before a South African Court, which upheld that a doctor should not disclose HIV status. Furthermore,

> [I]n the long run, preservation of confidentiality is the only way of securing public health; otherwise doctors will be discredited as a source of education, for future individual patients will not come forward if doctors are going to squeal on them. Consequently, confidentiality is vital to secure public as well as private health, for unless those infected come forward they cannot be counseled and self-treatment does not provide the best care [...].

Nonetheless, disclosure to partners is allowed in South Africa at the health practitioner's discretion.

This type of allowance is also permitted, according to the HIV laws in some African countries. One such law is the one created in Benin, which, in Article 4, prevents health care professionals from disclosing a person's HIV status in any situation. This can be breached, however, according to Article 6, which allows physicians to disclose the status of patients in the case of extreme necessity or in the case of an HIV positive person whose behavior may endanger the health of others. What is included in the category of an 'extreme necessity' is not explained. Including more specificity in their law, Kenya allows a medical practitioner to disclose someone's seropositive status to any sexual contact if the person is aware of being infected and has not "taken all reasonable measures and precautions to prevent the transmission of HIV to others" or has not informed "any sexual contact or person with whom needles are shared" that they are HIV positive or if the seropositive person requested that a medical practitioner inform or counsel a sexual contact.

One interesting example of a country that allows physicians to disclose in certain instances is Lesotho, which states that counselors can disclose HIV-status to partners when it occurs in the presence of the patient. This restricts the allowances for a health practitioner slightly, but still provides some flexibility.

The countries that follow the N'Djamena model law allow doctors to disclose the status of a person after six weeks have passed. Countries that follow the model law in N'Djamena may suffer because of legislation that is overly broad because it requires disclosure regardless of whether there is a significant risk of transmission. Several countries have nonetheless used the N'Djamena law as a model. For example, Burkina Faso has included this six-week stipulation in its Law on Reproductive Health in 2005.

Some of the countries that follow this trend to conditionally allow health practitioners to disclose serostatus replicate the model guidelines set out by the UNAIDS and OCHCR in their International Guidelines on HIV/AIDS and Human Rights. For example, in Malawi, the section of the law on "Beneficial Disclosure" is almost identical to the UNAIDS provision, except it skips the sections detailing that the counseling has failed to achieve the appropriate behavioral changes (ii) and the one that details that the identity of the HIV-positive person be concealed if possible (vi). Namibia's law is nearly identical to the one created in Malawi, and leaves out the same points (ii and vi) from the UNAIDS guidelines.

Furthermore, some countries have laws that are nearly identical, but use language that isn't in either model law. For example, Kenya and Sierra Leone have laws that are identical in language. Both laws outline that "a medical practitioner who is responsible for the treatment of a person and who becomes aware that the person has not, after reasonable opportunity to do so" complied with the obligation to take the necessary precautions to prevent the knowing or reckless infection of another, may "inform any sexual partner of that person, or the HIV status of that person."

Largely, however, it seems that many countries in Africa are developing laws that fit the national context. For example, in South Africa, there is no specific law that regulates when a doctor is allowed to disclose HIV status, but it fits within the greater legal framework. The Bill of Rights enshrined within the South African Constitution promotes equality, dignity and privacy. It is within the framework of this and other laws, such as the National Health Act of 2003 and the Promotion of Equality and Prevention of Unfair Discrimination Act of 2000 that doctors are supposed to act. It seems then that countries are finding diverse ways to create allowances for doctors to disclose a patient's HIV-positive status.

3. Countries that Create a Duty for Seropositive People and Physicians to Disclose HIV Status

Most countries do not oblige medical professionals to disclose HIV status to sexual partners. In fact, only one country has language that does create such an obligation. This country is Burundi, which mandates that physicians disclose the HIV/AIDS status of seropositive people to spouses if the person is psychologically incapable of, or opposed to, revealing this information. This is interesting, as it creates an affirmative duty on the part of the physician. There are notable problems with such a strict construction. It does not let the physician, or other health-care provider, take into consideration whether someone has been subject to violence or abuse from partners, what the relationship or likelihood of transmission is, and other important factors that would likely affect the effectiveness of disclosure. Furthermore, there is no mention in the law of the repercussions for doctors who choose not to disclose.

Another country, Guinea, forced doctor disclosure under a 2005 law, which was amended in 2009. While the old law was quite restrictive, the new law is inconsistent and incoherent. The new Article 23 allows conditional disclosure by a health professional if six criteria are all met. These include having the health professional clearly inform the HIV-positive person that disclosure will occur and also that the seropositive person is dead, unconscious or unable to give consent. These two criteria are clearly contradictory, essentially making it impossible for doctors to ever disclose HIV status. While we have seen that some countries do not allow for doctors to disclose, this was likely not the intention of this particular law.

* * *

Notes

1. HIV continues to take a devastating toll on Africa. Conditions have continued to be difficult in Africa. In 2016, Africa had 29 million people living with HIV, including 1.4 million new cases. The disease also claimed the lives of nearly 1 million people that year. See 2017 United Nations UNAIDS Databook, available for download at http://www.unaids.org/en/resources/documents/2017/2017_data_book.

2. Among the most controversial legal issues in recent years relating to AIDS in the developing world has been that of restrictions on access to patented anti-retroviral drugs under the International Trade Laws. The Trade Related Aspects of Intellectual Property Rights (TRIPS) agreement obligates members of the World Trade Organization to respect intellectual property rights, including patents for pharmaceutical products and processes. TRIPS limits the ability of developing nations to manufacture or import generic copies of patented drugs under compulsory licenses or without the permission of patent holders. TRIPS gave pharmaceutical companies the power to insist on prices for patented drugs that would have made them unaffordable for developing countries, but after embarrassing trade disputes, the WTO adopted the

Doha Declaration in 2001 recognizing the need for flexibility on this issue to permit WTO members to protect the public health of their people. This topic is beyond the scope of this book, but for an introduction to the issues see, Frederick M.Abbott, The WTO Medicines Decision: World Pharmaceutical Trade and the Protection of Public Health, 99 *Am. J. Int. L.* 317 (2005); Kevin Outterson, Pharmaceutical Arbitrage: Balancing Access and Innovation in International Prescription Drug Markets, 5 *Yale J. Health Pol'y, L. & Ethics* 193 (2005); and M. Gregg Bloche and Elizabeth R. Jungman, Health Policy and the WTO, 31 *J. L. Med. & Ethics* 529 (2003). Access to AIDS medications has also raised constitutional human rights issues in a number of countries, including South Africa and Venezuela, see Chapter 1 for a discussion of these issues.

3. At the international level the United Nation's World Health Organization has responsibility for public health issues. Though the WHO has legal competency, it has historically relied on education and assistance rather than on legal mandates. However, in the wake of the West African Ebola epidemic, some scholars argue that the WHO should be empowered to take on a more active role in enforcing global public health law. See Lawrence O. Gostin and Eric Friedman, A Retrospective and Prospective Analysis of the West African Ebola Virus Disease Epidemic: Robust National Health Systems at the Foundation and an Empowered WHO at the Apex, 385 *Lancet* 1902 (2015); Lawrence O. Gostin et al., The Global Health Law Trilogy: Toward a Safer, Healthier, Fairer World, *The Lancet Online* (May 15, 2017); Lawrence O. Gostin and Ana Sumei Ayala, Global Health Security in an Era of Explosive Pandemic Potential, 9 J. *Nat. Sec. L. & Pol'y* (2017).

4. African nations are rich in the diversity of their legal systems. Many inherited a common law or civil law system from the colonial powers, while others have adopted Muslim or socialist law. Traditional customary law is also usually present. Often the civil or common law affects a relatively small proportion of the population, with local disputes being settled through customary law and alternative dispute resolution fora. In this context, the existence of a statute directing or proscribing a certain form of behavior may not necessarily have a direct and immediate effect on conduct, though this is, of course, true in Western countries as well.

B. Public Health Law and Infectious Disease Emergencies: SARS and Ebola

Despite huge advances in public health, the twenty-first century has seen the outbreak of several global epidemics, chief among them Severe Acute Respiratory Syndrome (SARS) and Ebola. SARS and Ebola each posed public health emergencies, though both the underlying diseases and the public health responses for each were quite different. We discuss SARS then Ebola in these materials, but first it is helpful to understand a little bit more about the specifics of each.

It is not fully understood how exactly SARS spread. "In general, the disease starts with a high fever, accompanied by headaches, body aches, and mild respiratory symptoms. Most patients develop pneumonia, and some cases require mechanical ventilation. SARS spreads through respiratory droplets produced by an infected person when he or she coughs or sneezes or through physical contact. Thus, a person is vulnerable to the disease when engaging in a close person-to-person contact, such as kissing or embracing, and sharing eating or drinking utensils. Talking with a SARS patient within three feet can also be dangerous." Chenglin Liu, Regulating SARS in China: Law as an Antidote?, 4 *Wash. U. Global Stud. Rev.* 81, 82 (2005). SARS was thus perceived during the 2003 outbreak as posing a more general risk of infection through random contact; it also manifests itself very quickly, allowing more rapid containment of an epidemic through isolating infected persons. The rate of mortality from SARS is lower than that of AIDS or Ebola (probably 8% to 15%), although it is much higher among the elderly than among young people. On the other hand, when death comes from SARS it comes much more rapidly, limiting the spread of the disease.

Ebola presented quite different challenges. The disease "is a severe hemorrhagic fever caused by an RNA virus in the filovrius family. Signs and symptoms of Ebola—which appear anywhere from 2 to 21 days after exposure—include fever, headache, diarrhea, vomiting, muscle pain, stomach pain, and unexplained bleeding or bruising. EVD is associated with a case fatality rate between 30% and 90%.... Outbreaks are thought to originate from an animal reservoir, most likely a fruit bat, although that linkage has not been confirmed. Person-to-person infection occurs through direct contact with infected bodily fluids—usually blood, feces, or vomit. As a result, most cases occur in individuals who provide direct patient care, such as family members or clinicians." Emily A. Largent, EBOLA and FDA: Reviewing the Response to the 2014 Outbreak, to Find Lessons for the Future, 3 *J.L. & Biosciences* 489, 491–92 (2016). In other words, unlike SARS, the disease was *not* airborne, but was far more deadly, with the 2014 outbreak resulting in a reported case fatality rate as high as 55%. Part of the challenge of containment had to do with the sometimes-long window of time before any symptoms presented themselves. The global panic that ensued was often fueled by sensationalist media coverage, and sluggish global responses allowed the disease to spread rapidly through West Africa (and even, in isolated instances, to the United States).

SARS was first identified late in 2002 in a province in southern China. Over the course of 2003, over eight thousand people were diagnosed with the disease, and 774 died as a result; the disease also caused about $18 billion in direct economic loss. Partially to blame for the disease's rapid spread was the Chinese government's desire to keep the first instances of it secret from the public, and downplay the disease's severity once it became known, which delayed public response. The two readings that follow address both China's public health response to the SARS epidemic, and that of other countries to which SARS spread, focusing on legal approaches

Chenglin Liu, *Regulating SARS in China: Law as an Antidote?*

4 Wash. U. Global Stud. Rev. 81, 93–98, 100–01, 103–09, 115–17 (2005)

The SARS outbreak presented two options [to the Chinese government]: keep quiet and handle the crisis behind closed doors, or take an open and transparent approach. In the past, national emergencies, such as earthquakes, floods, and mining accidents, were handled quietly by the government. Some scholars have referred to this as a "black box" approach, under which the public becomes aware of the situation only after the government has emerged victorious over the catastrophe. * * *

In attempting to balance between economic loss and public health and safety, the new government chose to emphasize public health.* * * Choosing a transparent approach required the government to forego economic gains and even suffer losses. For a nation accustomed to the "black box" approach, openly dealing with the SARS epidemic was a milestone. The new approach proved a tremendous success. The new government earned a reputation as a people-loving government that candidly addresses the serious social issues left over from the economic boom of the 1990s. * * *

The SARS campaign took place from April 20 until June 24, 2003, during which time two major pieces of legislation were enacted: (1) Regulations on Dealing with the Outbreak of Public Health Emergencies (Regulations), which was enacted by the State Council on May 9, 2003 and took effect on May 12, 2003, and (2) Measures on the Prevention and Treatment of Infectious Atypical Pneumonia (Measures), which was promulgated by the Ministry of Health and took effect on May 12, 2003. In addition, The Laws of the People's Republic of China on the Prevention and Treatment of Infectious Diseases (PTID), which was originally passed by the NPC Standing Committee in 1989, was republished on April 26, 2003 by the State Council. In summary, these laws and regulations addressed three issues: emergency information reporting, treatment, and prevention.

* * *

* * * To disseminate information effectively, the new laws specifically delineate when to report, how to report, to whom the original report should go, and how the department receiving a report should deal with the information.

Article 19 of the Regulations specifies that the Health Department of the State Council shall be in charge of establishing an emergency reporting system. Not more than nine hours may elapse from discovery to the reporting of a case to the State Council, the highest authority. * * *

First, according to article 19, if a public health emergency occurs a provincial government that has received epidemic information has one hour to report it to the Health Department of the State Council. The law also requires the Health Department to report to the State Council when an emergency is of a significant danger to the public.

Second, article 20 requires medical institutions that have a confirmed or suspected case of SARS promptly report this to the local county government. After receiving the report, the local government and its health department must forward it to higher levels of the government. This transfer of information should not take more than two hours.

* * *

While reporting relevant information is important, it is only the first step toward establishing a transparent system. If information stops at a higher level, the system ceases to function. The flow of information should be vertical toward governments at higher levels and horizontal toward related departments, neighboring regions, and the public.

* * *

Lawmakers were aware of the problems caused by the lack of horizontal flow of information in the beginning of the outbreak. Article 23 of the Regulations requires the State Council to promptly release information to other related departments including hospitals and health departments of the Army. The provision also stipulates that the Head Official of any province experiencing an epidemic should inform neighboring provinces or regions of the outbreak.

However, article 23 is difficult to implement in practice. Under the centralized system, emphasis is placed more on vertical subordination of the local governments to the Central Government, rather than on cooperation between local governments at the same level. * * * Thus, it should not be surprising that, during the SARS outbreak, the spread of the virus was largely attributable to a lack of cooperation and coordination among various regions.

A system of making information public is described in article 25. The Central Government must inform the public of any epidemic information that provincial level governments report. The local government may then be authorized by the Central Government to publicly announce possible outbreaks independently. Article 25 states that the "announcement should be up-to-date, accurate, and comprehensive." However, article 25 does not provide guidance on interpreting the phrase "up-to-date, accurate, and comprehensive." It is thus unclear how soon the public should be informed after an epidemic is reported to the Central Government.* * * In practice, article 25 gives the Central Government vast discretion in deciding whether or when to release information about an epidemic that was reported from lower governments or health departments. * * *

In the Regulations, the lawmakers embedded an important provision for protecting whistleblowers. Article 24 provides that any unit or individual has the right to report an outbreak of an epidemic to the relevant government department, which in turn must conduct a thorough investigation of the situation. The unit or individual who has informed the government of an outbreak should be rewarded.

While the law provides that the informers should be rewarded, it does not specify or refer to punishment for retaliation by the local government. The major concern for most people is how to go about life after revealing the government's failure. Informers who continue to live under the same authority will be under constant pressure from the local government. Therefore, even with the rights conferred by the Regulations, most potential informers will likely choose to stay silent in the face of government irregularities.

Although the law allows an individual to report a local government's failure to the government at higher levels, it does not specify whether the individual enjoys the right to release related information to the media. According to a notice issued by the Health Department in 1989 that is still in force, no unit or individual may release and announce epidemic information to foreign media or publish unannounced epidemic information without the authorization of the Health Department.

Without adequate sanctions on those who impede the flow of information, the reporting system would not be effective. Article 22 states that any unit or individual should not conceal, delay, or falsely report emergency information, or direct others to do so. The sanctions are set forth in article 45 of the Regulations, which also states that the head of the department is required to take all responsibility for a failure to report. These penalties range from demotion to a lower administrative rank to removal from one's administrative position, depending on the seriousness of the concealment. The article also leaves the door open for criminal charges against the leader of a department if late reporting causes a massive spread of the disease. * * *

* * *

Before the new laws were enacted, health departments issued a number of guidelines to hospitals on the treatment and prevention of SARS. These guidelines were issued in great haste and produced mixed results. Nevertheless, these guidelines shaped many of the relevant provisions of the new laws on SARS. * * *

To deflect social attention away from SARS, especially during the congressional session, the Health Ministry required all SARS patients to be treated at the hospitals where they were admitted. This method was referred to as the "absorb" method. Officials hoped that hospitals could treat SARS cases and eliminate the disease without causing public panic like that in Guangzhou. The "absorb" method was consistent with the "black box" approach.

The "absorb" requirement was a complete failure. Hospitals not only failed to provide proper care to SARS patients, but the hospitals themselves became a source of infection.* * *

* * *

The catastrophe in the People's Hospital and other hospitals caused health officials to revisit the so-called "absorb" method. Based on the experience in Guangdong, some experts proposed designating a few hospitals with good medical facilities as SARS-designated hospitals suitable for treating infectious diseases. These designated hospitals played an important role in lowering the cross-infection rate at the start of the outbreak; however, the sharp increase of SARS patients soon caused these hospitals to be overwhelmed. The government decided to construct a specialized SARS hospital in a suburb of Beijing. This new hospital, containing 1,000 beds, was built in only seven days and accepted the first group of patients on May 1, 2003. By the time the last patients were discharged less than two months later, the new hospital had admitted 680 patients, of whom only eight died of SARS. As a result, the new hospital substantially reduced the pressure that hospitals in the urban areas faced.

* * *

The new laws also specify that hospitals should provide free treatment to SARS patients who cannot afford medical expenses. In some reported cases, hospitals refused or delayed admission to SARS patients. * * *

Refusing to accept SARS patients jeopardizes the patient's health and safety and puts the public at a higher risk because the disease is extremely infectious. Citing the law on infectious disease, the Health Ministry issued an urgent notice on April 22, 2003 that required all hospitals to accept SARS patients without exception. * * *

The government encountered enormous challenges in implementing the above rules. There are several reasons that hospitals were reluctant to admit SARS patients. First, they were afraid that the spread of the virus would put doctors, nurses, and patients in great danger because medical workers were among the very first victims of the outbreak. Second, after the economic reform in the 1980s, hospitals were pushed into market reliance. Many of the hospitals heavily relied on the revenue coming from patients. High cross-infection rates would hurt a hospital's reputation, thus reducing the volume of patient visits. Third, SARS treatment could be extremely expensive, costing hospitals up to RMB 100,000 ($12,000) per patient. To conform to the laws, hospitals had to cover the costs for patients without health insurance. * * *

To solve the financial pressure facing both patients and hospitals, the Ministry of Finance allocated RMB 2 billion ($242 million) for SARS prevention and treatment, a considerable portion of which was used for covering the treatment of the uninsured SARS patients. * * *

* * *

As the SARS situation worsened, many migrant workers in Beijing began to flee the city and return to their hometowns. In some cases, migrant workers escaped mandatory quarantine in Beijing and took a train home. * * *

The wave of migration was of great concern to the government because these migrant workers could bring the virus back to their home provinces. These workers usually came from poor rural regions where medical networks barely existed. Though SARS has no cure, high quality medical care plays an important role in treating the complications resulting from a SARS infection. If workers set off an epidemic back home, the consequences would be unimaginable.

* * *

In the meantime, local governments took measures to monitor the returning migrant workers closely to keep the virus out of their regions. Screening measures included setting up checkpoints at local train stations and bus stops, and imposing quarantine on all the returnees for two weeks.

Also, to reduce the danger of spreading SARS to those migrant workers' hometowns, the government required all the companies that employed migrant workers to comply strictly with the so-called "three-local principles": First, the prevention work for healthy workers must be carried out locally. Second, epidemiological observation of the workers in close contact with SARS patients must be conducted locally. Third, confirmed cases must be treated locally. If any company failed to do so, various sanctions would be imposed.

* * *

On May 5, 2003, Li Song was arrested on charges of obstructing the prevention of infectious disease and treatment, and endangering public security through dangerous means, in violation of the Criminal Law.* * *

Li's case was regarded as the first in which the government resorted to criminal sanctions in order to impose compulsory quarantine on a SARS patient. It was widely believed that Li's case directly led to the promulgation of the interpretation of the relevant articles of the Criminal Law regarding public safety jointly issued by the Supreme People's Court and Supreme People's Procuratorate (Interpretation). According to this Interpretation, those who cause death or serious injury by deliberately spreading the virus can be sentenced to a fixed prison term ranging from ten years to life imprisonment. They may even face the death penalty.

* * *

On April 12, 2003, the Transportation Ministry, Railroad Ministry, Airline Bureau, Health Ministry, and Finance Ministry jointly issued a notice requiring that their related departments take measures to prevent SARS from spreading through public transportation, including trains, boats, long distance buses, and airplanes. This notice required that "stay stations" be set up in the cities where transportation stations are located to provide a place where SARS patients or suspected cases found on the carriers can be accepted. To establish the "stay stations", the local government was to provide financial aid, technical support and the necessary equipment. Once a SARS patient (or suspected patient) was discovered on public transportation, the responsible head of the carrier was required to promptly contact the next closest "stay station" and arrange a drop-off for those patients to receive medical observation, quarantine, and treatment. All "stay stations" were obligated to accept these patients. The carrier was also to take measures necessary to enhance air circulation, and trace and record the identities of persons who have been in close contact with SARS patients. The notice also authorized the departments of transportation to persuade persons showing SARS symptoms not to use public transportation.

* * *

On August 28, 2004, the eleventh session of the Tenth NPC passed sweeping amendments to the PTID. [Law of the People's Republic of China on the Prevention and Treatment of Infectious Diseases]. * * *

Third, the new law emphasizes the government's role in coping with future epidemics. The law requires that infectious disease prevention be a part of the government's social and economic development plan. The purpose of adding this article is to show that epidemic prevention is an integral and permanent part of the government's regular responsibilities. Under the new law, the various levels of government are required to establish and maintain a functional epidemic surveillance system and routinely evaluate the epidemic situation in their respective regions. The central government is required to provide financial assistance to inner regions where the economy lags far behind, and provide adequate training to the medical personnel there to increase the capability of those regions to handle sudden epidemics. The law also requires hospitals to accept infectious disease patients and provide free treatment to those who can not afford their medical expenses.

Fourth, the new law strikes a balance between the protection of the rights of individuals and the public interest. To protect patients' privacy, the new law prohibits hospitals from releasing patients' medical records. * * * In order to increase cooperation from patients, the new law requires that patients be continuously paid by their employers during quarantine or isolation. On the other hand, the new law provides stricter rules on quarantine and isolation. For example, under the previous law, suspected carriers of Class A diseases were only subject to epidemiological observation at appointed facilities. The new law provides that suspect patients be placed in isolation, which is more restrictive.

* * *

Although SARS began in China, it quickly spread to other countries. A discussion of the responses of those countries follows.

Jason W. Sapsin, Lawrence O. Gostin, Jon S. Vernick, Scott Burris & Stephen P. Teret, *SARS and International Legal Preparedness*

77 Temp. L. Rev. 155, 157–164, 165, 167–68 (2004)

SARS' public health characteristics motivated authorities' choices of disease control strategies which, in nations governed under the rule of law, depend on effective legal systems. These included: (1) the novelty of the disease, resulting in the absence of rapid diagnostic tests to confirm infection and the current lack of a vaccine; (2) an unusual pattern of comparatively low viral shedding during the initial phase of the illness, posing further obstacles to the swift development of adequate diagnostic tools; (3) SARS' subclinical or atypical presentation in some patients; (4) the lack of effective treatment; (5) the disease's relative severity (an approximate overall case fatality rate of fourteen to fifteen percent); and (6) its mode of transmission, including the phenomenon of superspreading events. Each of these characteristics provided incentives to use nonmedical control strategies such as mandatory examination and testing, quarantine, and isolation. In the absence of effective therapy or a vaccine, health authorities' ability to control infectious disease necessarily depends upon preventing transmission by appropriately restricting the movement of exposed or infected people. Lack of adequate diagnostics limits public health authorities' ability to control transmission by impeding identification of mildly symptomatic or asymptomatic carriers and promotes reliance on contact history. Some SARS cases with atypical presentations or lacking history of direct contact with known SARS patients went undiagnosed and became "hidden reservoirs of infection on the wards of health-care facilities or in the community." To address this threat, some public health authorities chose to employ aggressive, legally based surveillance and quarantine measures. Researchers and clinicians also recommended exercising precautions in all cases of undifferentiated respiratory conditions, including isolation of health care workers and household contacts of cases.

SARS also appeared vulnerable to control measures such as quarantine and isolation: officials initially believed it to be transmitted through personal contact, possibly by air and also by fomites. In addition, "superspreading" events, by increasing the perceived risk resulting from failures to contain all cases, likely created greater incentives to implement aggressive control strategies. Five probable SARS patients in Singapore were each linked to events resulting in the apparent infection of ten or more health care workers, family or social contacts, or unrelated hospital visitors, accounting for 103 of the 205 probable SARS cases. Finally, effective isolation and quarantine become more difficult as cases accumulate, so public health authorities may more aggressively apply quarantine and isolation for a disease like SARS on the principle that "stringent measures implemented early in the course of the epidemic prevent the need for more stringent measures as the epidemic spreads."

The recommendations of the World Health Organization ("WHO") for the control of SARS provided a backdrop for national efforts * * *. By March 26th, 2003, however, governments had begun independently introducing more stringent personal control measures than those recommended by WHO—an indication both of the challenge of effectively unifying international action, and of some authorities' willingness and perceived need to implement mandatory personal control measures. In the process, many governments examined and revised their disease control laws. * * *

Singapore's public health response included important legal components. Authorities declared SARS a notifiable disease under the Infectious Disease Act ("IDA") on March 17th, allowing mandatory examination, treatment, medical information exchange, health care provider/institutional cooperation, use of facilities, quarantine, and isolation for SARS. The IDA was officially invoked for SARS on March 24th (quarantining contacts and closing hospitals to visitors two weeks before the WHO recommendation). By March 25th, approximately 740 people were in home quarantine under the IDA (with fines for noncompliance). They were legally required, among other things, to restrict visitors and maintain visitor registries; to respond immediately to health department communications; and to keep children under eighteen years of age at home. Private sector nurses and physicians were temporarily restricted from working in more than one medical facility. Further, in contrast to some other countries, Singapore concentrated all SARS patients into one facility and ultimately achieved containment more rapidly.

On April 24th, Singapore amended the IDA to: require persons with possibly infectious diseases to report to designated treatment centers; prohibit SARS contacts from going to public places; enforce home quarantine with electronic tagging and forced detention; and allow the quarantine and destruction of SARS-contaminated property. Section 21A of the Act imposed the affirmative obligation to avoid exposing others (outside immediate family) on any person knowing, or having reason to suspect, that he was a case, carrier or contact of SARS. To mitigate the effects of its aggressive containment strategy, Singapore provided economic assistance to people and businesses affected by home quarantine orders through a "Home Quarantine Order Allowance Scheme". While officials from Singapore's Ministry of Health maintained that broad surveillance, rapid and effective contact tracing, and early enforced quarantine were crucial in containing SARS, their actions were built upon a strong foundation of accessible, high-quality health and social services. * * *

Hong Kong's control measures also initiated the use and review of public health law. Like Singapore, Hong Kong added SARS to its disease control statutes (March 27th, 2003) and notified physicians that SARS was reportable. On April 15th, in order to establish a legal basis for further disease control measures, Hong Kong authorities amended the Prevention of the Spread of Infectious Diseases Regulations to allow health officers to prevent travelers from leaving the region; to permit authorized persons to measure travelers' body temperatures; and to examine travelers for SARS. At least one subsequent analysis of public health approaches in Hong Kong suggests that reductions in time from symptom onset to hospitalization, population contact rate, and incidence of nosocomial infection were jointly significant in bringing the epidemic under control. * * *

Toronto's SARS outbreak was the largest outside of Asia and carried economic effects estimated at one billion Canadian dollars in gross domestic product for 2003. * * *

The legal components of Canada's response included the closure of hospitals, the declaration of a public health emergency, the compulsory quarantine of recalcitrant citizens, and the imposition of mandatory self-quarantine. Canada's Quarantine Act and Regulations were amended to list SARS in the schedule of diseases; authorize detention of travelers with suspected SARS for up to twenty days; allow national quarantine officers to compel air carriers to distribute SARS information and questionnaires on flights; and require aircraft to report en route illnesses and deaths at Canadian airports. Health is a joint responsibility of the Canadian Federal and Provincial governments, and federal responses included lending personnel and equipment, coordinating strategy to boost the health workforce, screening travelers at borders, making employment insurance benefits available for quarantined citizens, and arranging tax relief for affected individuals.

Canada also provides an example of WHO's difficulty in coordinating health policies across independent, but inter-dependent, regions. Canada officially challenged WHO's April 23rd Toronto travel advisory and promised at least ten million Canadian dollars to promote Toronto as a safe destination. Even as late as May 2nd, a WHO official noted the failure to receive "good, fast information from Canada," further stating that "[c]ountries are not very good about reporting new cases, even the United States."

The United States' federal government has authority over public health measures at national borders and in matters affecting interstate transmission of disease, but assumes direction of states' internal health affairs only under extraordinary circumstances. * * * By April 2003, the United States' Centers for Disease Control and Prevention ("U.S. CDC") had deployed more than 40 public health professionals and scientists worldwide and assigned more than 400 staff members to SARS; as of June 18th, 2003, the United had 334 suspected and 75 probable cases of SARS.

SARS provoked at least one significant change in the United States' national legal structure for disease control. Early in the worldwide outbreak, federal authorities found themselves legally powerless to detain a noncompliant traveler from China and so federal regulations were amended in order to address failures to cooperate with SARS control measures. While the amendment brought SARS within the scope of "national" legislation (section 361(b) of the Public Health Service Act) it could not, however, redress the decentralization of public health authority across the United States. State and local authorities continued to be able to withhold or delay SARS reports to the federal government. Also, at least through the middle of April 2003, U.S. CDC relied on state and local health department resources to develop the necessary methods for actively monitoring exposed persons. But facing a smaller outbreak than those of other countries, policymakers in the United States generally avoided using compulsory personal control measures for disease containment and such powers were used infrequently. Only five aircraft arriving from SARS-affected regions were sequestered, and quarantine and isolation tended to be voluntary or quasi-voluntary, although there were some cases of compulsory confinement.

Overall, SARS quarantine and isolation events illustrate both general compliance with public health measures and the difficulties posed by even a relatively few, noncompliant individuals. Officials in Ontario prosecuted at least one recalcitrant individual and threatened unknown numbers of others with forced confinement. Ontario's Commissioner of Public Security perceived noncompliance as the greatest threat to controlling SARS. By April 19th, however, Toronto health officials had pursued legal measures against only fifteen people. Singapore enacted penalties for quarantine violation, utilized its Security Services and electronic, in-home cameras, and arrested at least one man violating a home quarantine order. Violations of quarantine led to calls in Hong Kong for stricter enforcement of orders with implementation of fines and detentions. In comparison, Taiwan apparently suffered serious difficulties in obtaining public cooperation, including citizens' refusal to register with local health authorities before traveling; large scale failures to cooperate with epidemiological contact tracing; mass disobedience of quarantine orders; and hospital concealment of SARS cases. The United States did not implement widespread quarantine. However, polling studies forecast U.S. voluntary quarantine noncompliance rates ranging from eight percent to twenty-five percent. Given the wide range of population responses internationally, the risk and consequences of noncompliance must also be considered when planning U.S. disease containment strategies.

* * *

Nationally effective health care and public health systems are crucial to effective disease control in modern societies.* * * Adequate preparation for widespread outbreaks of dangerous, communicable diseases necessarily is built on a foundation of accessible health care and competent, properly funded public health agencies regardless of the approach used. In societies such as the United States, which have chronically neglected public health infrastructures, this entails the swift expenditure of considerable public resources to overcome existing weaknesses in the nation's health system. Traditional U.S. market-based patterns of health care financing and delivery contribute heavily to this problem. Chronic underfunding of public hospitals and the lack of surge capacity to handle health emergencies are extensively documented and threaten U.S. public health preparedness. A recent study of urban U.S. hospitals concluded that while most had conducted basic planning and coordination activities for bioterrorism response (also relevant to a large-scale outbreak of a naturally occurring infectious disease such as SARS), "[m]ost hospitals, however, still lack equipment, medical stockpiles, and quarantine and isolation facilities for even a small scale response." Staffing shortages remain a major concern in public health departments, laboratories and hospitals across the country. * * *

* * *

Governing authorities in Singapore, Hong Kong, and Canada each furnished, to varying degrees, financial and material support to quarantined populations. Interestingly, in Beijing, China, it is reported that only some employers continued to pay salary to quarantined individuals (though all were provided food and medicine). Societies attempting to follow democratic principles and utilizing disease control measures such as quarantine and isolation must recognize the extraordinary responsibility necessarily undertaken by governments employing these measures. As acknowledged by the Canadian government, "[a]pplying the principle of reciprocity, society has a duty to provide support and other alternatives to those whose rights have been infringed under quarantine." Singapore, the Hong Kong Special Administrative Region, and Canada each recognized this duty. In nations which have only incompletely addressed this problem, quarantine and isolation regulations should legally require confined persons to be provided with: (1) safe, habitable, and medically appropriate housing during confinement, (2) necessary food, clothing, and medical care, (3) means of communication with family, friends, and personal representatives, (4) necessary social services (e.g., childcare and mental health services), (5) appropriate legal review; and (6) protection from adverse social and economic consequences, such as lost income or employment or insurance discrimination during confinement. * * *

1. As these excerpts suggest, Mainland China, Hong Kong, Singapore, Canada and the U.S. all adopted different strategies for coping with SARS. To what extent do you view these differences as the result of differences in their legal system versus historical contingency versus deeper cultural values? How does your answer affect how much lateral learning is possible in these areas?
2. Now that you have read about SARS and turn to excerpts on Ebola, consider the following question: what is the optimal mix of national versus international

public health law for dealing with infectious disease emergencies? How much does that question depend on the specifics of the diseases in question?

Hardly a decade after the SARS outbreak, Ebola struck West Africa, in the largest outbreak of the disease in history. Between 2013 and 2016, Ebola ravaged Liberia, Guinea, and Sierra Leone, with scattered outbreaks in Nigeria and Mali, resulting in about 28,000 suspected cases and approximately 11,000 deaths (although the WHO suspects these figures understate the epidemic). As SARS had done in Asia, Ebola revealed fissures not only in countries' abilities to successfully and ethically manage a rapidly spreading disease within their own borders, but also in the international health structures' capacity to actually impose order and cohesion on disease-control plans across states. The Ebola crisis also highlighted the very low numbers of health care workers available in the hardest hit countries *before* Ebola took its toll. This first excerpt provides a thorough discussion of the challenges brought to the fore in attempts to quarantine Ebola patients during the height of the crisis, which are likely to remain salient when it comes to combating any future pandemics.

Mark A. Rothstein, *From SARS to Ebola: Legal and Ethical Considerations for Modern Quarantine*

12 Ind. Health L. Rev. 227, 228, 250–51, 252–54, 254–57, 263–67, 267–68, 271–73, 273–76 (2015)

With the notable exceptions of the Severe Acute Respiratory Syndrome (SARS) outbreak in 2003 and the Ebola Virus Disease outbreak in 2014, quarantine has not been used on a large scale since the first half of the twentieth century. * * *

The use of quarantine is based on the assumption that asymptomatic individuals exposed to an infection are capable of transmitting the infection to others, perhaps as efficiently as symptomatic individuals. In addition to individual quarantine, area-wide quarantine may be an effective way of limiting the spread of the disease. The potential effectiveness of quarantine is related to the interval between exposure and the onset of illness. For infections with a short interval, such as the one to four days for influenza, there may be a narrower window to impose quarantine. For Ebola, with a two to twenty-one day incubation period, a longer quarantine has been used; indeed, the long quarantine period has been associated with many problems in Liberia and the United States.

* * *

During the Ebola epidemic, the government of Sierra Leone imposed an area-wide quarantine in about one-fourth of the country, affecting over one million people. Travelers were permitted to travel through quarantine zones only between the hours of 9 a.m. and 5 p.m., and they were warned not to get out of their vehicles while traveling through these areas. These restrictions came only a week after a three-day home quarantine of the entire country, in which 30,000 volunteers went house-to-house to educate the public about Ebola and remove the dead. President Ernest Bai

Koroma acknowledged that the new quarantine would "definitely pose great difficulties for our people," but he said there was little choice.

A poorly devised and implemented quarantine may cause great harm. In Sierra Leone, some villages set up informal "isolation centers," with citizens quarantining one another, "an incredibly dangerous ad hoc solution being performed without appropriate protection." Meanwhile, the lack of hospital beds, ambulances, and safe burial practices continued to spread infection. According to Anthony Banbury, head of the United Nations Mission for Ebola Emergency Response, up to one-half the deaths in Sierra Leone were caused by unsafe burial practices.

To be effective, a quarantine must be part of a scientifically compelling, overall strategy for battling the outbreak of infectious disease. For example, in Liberia the escalation in Ebola cases was largely due to the lack of hospital space, personal protective equipment, and strict infection control procedures in health care facilities. At the height of the epidemic, only eighteen percent of patients were being cared for in hospitals, well below the seventy percent the CDC estimated would be necessary to prevent cases from increasing. Because of a lack of functioning hospitals, most Ebola patients were cared for at home by relatives and friends who lacked training and infection control materials, thereby spreading the deadly infection to caregivers. The government provided little or no assistance. According to the son of one victim, "The only thing the government can do is come for the bodies. They are killing us."

Ebola has been an epidemic overwhelmingly affecting caregivers, both health care workers and family members of patients. According to a study of Ebola in Sierra Leone, the incidence of Ebola in health care workers was 103-fold higher than that of all other individuals in the country. This study further confirms that the necessity, effectiveness, and scientific rationale of any quarantine are closely related to the epidemiology of the disease outbreak.

* * *

[D]uring the early days of the Ebola epidemic in West Africa, some governments declared stay-at-home days for "reflection, education, and prayers" as a modest and noncoercive social distancing measure. Similarly, Guinea closed all schools and universities indefinitely. These measures were ineffective because they were not stringent enough and therefore not proportional to the threat. Later, when the epidemic worsened, some of the quarantine measures were overly aggressive and counterproductive to public health and humanitarian objectives. Public health officials need to strike the right balance in arriving at "proportionality"—and this is not easy to do.

When the initial Ebola cases spread to the United States, first in Dallas and then in New York City, public fears caused twenty-one states to impose a mandatory twenty-one-day quarantine of all health care workers returning to the United States after treating Ebola patients in West Africa. It is very unlikely that these low- to moderate-risk health care workers with "protected exposures" (i.e., they used personal protective equipment and strict infection control measures) needed to be in quarantine instead of self-monitoring. Even assuming some type of social distancing was prudent to prevent transmission of Ebola, imposing such a long period was not supported by the science. The mean incubation period for Ebola is eight to ten days, and very few people become symptomatic after fourteen days.

One consequence of states imposing twenty-one day quarantines was that essential health care workers were dissuaded from volunteering to serve in West Africa. Other important reasons for questioning these ad hoc state policies include possibly undermining the CDC's credibility and confusing the public by having different quarantine policies in each state. A universally applied twenty-one-day quarantine for all individuals who travelled to West Africa, including members of the armed forces who merely built health care facilities, was neither scientifically indicated nor proportional to the risk. Furthermore, such a long quarantine period increases the burdens on public officials to monitor compliance and to provide food, medicine, and other supportive services.

During the Ebola outbreak, the CDC did not initially recommend quarantine for asymptomatic contacts of Ebola patients whose only exposure to an Ebola patient occurred before the patient had symptoms and became contagious. The first quarantine order in the United States involving Ebola took place on October 2, 2014, when Texas health officials served a quarantine order on four close family members of the first Ebola case, Thomas Eric Duncan. The order required the family members to remain in their small apartment for an additional seventeen days (for a total of twenty-one days post exposure), and to comply with blood tests and other monitoring deemed necessary by public health officials. Subsequently, the CDC revised its recommendations to provide that all asymptomatic health care workers returning from West Africa should be regarded as having "some risk" of Ebola and therefore required "direct active monitoring" for twenty-one days, with possible additional restrictions on their right to travel freely to be determined on a case-by-case basis by local public health officials.

* * *

Quarantine requires substantial logistical support, although the amount of support depends on the size and scope of the quarantine as well as the resources in place at the start of the quarantine. In quarantine at home, food, medicine, and other supplies and services must be provided to people who are unable to leave their homes. Public health officials need to be able to monitor the individuals in quarantine, a communication system must be established to connect the individuals in quarantine with health care providers, and a transportation plan is needed to take individuals who become ill to a hospital or other health care facility as soon as possible. In addition, clothing, bedding, and other personal items used by a patient placed in isolation may need to be removed and safely disposed of to prevent the infection of others, including individuals placed in quarantine at the same location.

In monitoring the health status of the individuals in quarantine, public health officials need to strike a balance between public health and individual liberty. For example, in Singapore, during the SARS epidemic, all people quarantined at home were required to have a web camera connected at all times and to respond to random checks by the government to verify their presence at home. They also were required to check and record their temperatures twice a day, on camera if so directed. It is unlikely that such prescriptive and intrusive measures would be as well tolerated in the United States as they were in Singapore. Similarly, in the poor West African countries affected by Ebola, the use of a web camera is, obviously, out of the question.

Providing humane supportive services to individuals in quarantine is labor-intensive, but the available supply of service providers may be curtailed by illness, death, quarantine, or refusal to report to work. Providing humane supportive services is also more complicated in a pluralistic and heterogeneous society, such as the United States, than in more homogeneous Asian countries, such as those affected by SARS. Among the vulnerable populations that might be affected to a greater extent by quarantine are individuals with disabilities, elderly persons, pregnant women, children, prisoners, economically disadvantaged minorities, people with mental illness or mental retardation, and individuals with language barriers. Even beyond these groups, a broad quarantine is likely to involve large numbers of individuals with diverse lifestyles. For example, dietary restrictions based on religion, culture, and health conditions mean that a standard food package for home delivery will not be sufficient for diverse individuals in quarantine. Nongovernmental organizations, such as the Red Cross, and governmental social service agencies need to coordinate their efforts and consider the special needs of people in quarantine.

Other populations in quarantine raise additional logistical and policy challenges. If a home-based quarantine is adopted, alternate facilities will be needed for people without homes in the quarantine area, such as students, visitors, transients, and homeless people. Government officials will need to decide whether to ignore the lawbreaking status of undocumented aliens, criminal fugitives, and other individuals to encourage them to enter quarantine rather than possibly spread disease. Immunity from arrest and prosecution were among the measures adopted by Singapore during the SARS outbreak.

The quarantine of individuals addicted to illicit drugs poses another policy challenge. A simple admonition by public health officials or even a judicial order to stay at home is unlikely to be obeyed by individuals with a drug addiction, and home delivery of illicit drugs by the government is unlikely to take place for numerous political and logistical reasons. It would be lawful for police to arrest and jail suspected drug addicts for the duration of the quarantine period, but only after they violated a quarantine order.

The question of what measures are appropriate for the government to take when there is noncompliance with mandatory quarantine applies to all individuals. Once again, it is a matter of proportionality. In particular, guidelines need to be developed for law enforcement personnel who observe individuals violating quarantine. The options for police are to ignore, warn, fine, or arrest and re-quarantine lawbreakers. During the SARS epidemic, many police officers that lacked training in infection control and personal protective equipment were reluctant to have close contact with individuals who violated quarantine because they were concerned about their own health. In Singapore, anyone violating quarantine had an electric tag put on their leg so they could be monitored.

During the early days of the Ebola epidemic police initially failed to enforce quarantine provisions. More aggressive enforcement of the area-wide quarantine in the seaside slum of West Point, in Liberia's capital of Monrovia, led to a violent response. In Dallas, police were stationed outside the apartment where relatives of Thomas Eric Duncan were quarantined to ensure that they did not leave. Similarly, Kaci Wilcox, an asymptomatic nurse returning from West Africa who was placed in quarantine after a single elevated temperature reading, was under constant surveillance by state police when she left her home.

The financial effect on individuals in quarantine is also an important concern. During the SARS epidemic all of the affected countries realized that they needed to enact legislation prohibiting discrimination in employment against individuals in quarantine (and guaranteeing their reemployment) and to supply quarantined individuals with some form of income replacement. Without such protections many low-income and self-employed persons who were asymptomatic would feel compelled to violate quarantine and go to work. Unfortunately, few, if any, comparable legal protections currently exist in the United States, and it is questionable how rapidly such legislation could or would be enacted at either the federal or state level.

Providing humane supportive services is a government's moral obligation in a public health emergency. Individuals relinquish a degree of liberty in exchange for the government's actions to preserve public health. The provision of humane supportive services in a public health emergency furthers the ethical principles of beneficence, justice, respect for persons, and social solidarity. Furthermore, providing humane supportive services also reaffirms the importance of dignity and human rights during times of peril, thereby helping to preserve the social fabric of society that will emerge after the outbreak is contained. Internationally, the Siracusa Principles provide that when a state acts in an emergency it must still respect human dignity and freedom, such as by not acting arbitrarily or discriminatorily and using the least restrictive means. Similarly, the World Health Organization's (WHO) Global Alert and Response Guiding Principles for International Outbreak Alert and Response includes the following: "All Network responses will proceed with full respect for ethical standards, human rights, national and local laws, cultural sensitivities and traditions."

* * *

The public's willingness to comply with public health interventions to combat infectious disease outbreaks lessens the need for governmentally ordered coercive measures and enforcement actions directed at individuals who are noncompliant. Among other things, public support requires the government to act with transparency, due process, and fairness. The decision-making process used by public health officials and government leaders should be open, at least to the extent that the rationale for official action is clearly explained to the public. Decision makers should marshal the best available scientific evidence and expert opinion on the need for quarantine and then disclose the information in a timely and understandable manner. Good communication with the public may improve voluntary compliance and obviate the need for enforcement.

* * *

Predictably, during the Ebola epidemic, there were many incidents of irrational fear and discrimination. For example, in New Jersey, two students from Rwanda, which had no Ebola cases and is 2800 miles from the affected countries in West Africa, were told to stay home. Similarly, a third grader in Connecticut was barred from school because she had attended a family wedding in Nigeria, which the WHO had declared Ebola-free. In perhaps the most extreme example of irrational fear, a formerly thriving bridal shop in Akron, Ohio, went out of business because, after it was visited by a presymptomatic, Ebola-infected nurse from Dallas, it became known as "the Ebola store."

Panic, discrimination, and ostracism have not been limited to the United States. In Sierra Leone, the fortunate few who survived Ebola became literally "untouchable" in many communities. In addition, thousands of children who were orphaned by Ebola in Guinea, Liberia, and Sierra Leone were stigmatized or abandoned by members of their extended family due to irrational fear. According to the United Nations Children's Fund (UNICEF), there may be 10,000 Ebola orphans in West Africa, many of them languishing in group homes without prospects for adoption. Although there have been some efforts to provide support services and to reintegrate Ebola survivors into their communities, these efforts have been on a relatively small scale and their effectiveness has not been clearly established.

The final aspect of public justification involves the important relations among the government, the media (broadly defined), and the public. The 2009 H1N1 influenza epidemic provides an instructive case study, as it featured the convergence of a new presidential administration in Washington, a weak American economy, and a highly skeptical public whose fears and suspicions were stoked by cable news, social media, and a 24/7 news cycle. When the H1N1 influenza strain emerged in 2009, public health officials were quite concerned about a possible 1918–1919-type pandemic, inasmuch as the broad H1N1 influenza strain was the same. Yet, there were few hard facts or confident predictions available. In attempting to be candid and transparent, however, government admissions of uncertainty seemed to undermine public confidence rather than enhance it. "The result was to heighten public distrust and suspicion of both the government's credibility and its capacity to provide accurate information." Political party affiliation was closely associated not only with trust in the government's pronouncements, but with the likelihood of taking the H1N1 vaccine. Overall, although 80 to 90 million Americans received the vaccine, about 70 million doses went unused and had to be destroyed. In the future, public health officials should not only make the scientific case for public health action, but they must confront the reality that politicization of public health may undermine public support for any proposed action.

* * *

On August 24, 2014, the government of Liberia imposed an area quarantine or cordon sanitaire on the West Point section of the capital city, Monrovia. West Point, a "sprawling slum," is the home to 60,000 to 120,000 people, who live "crammed into crumbling shacks." The quarantine period of twenty-one days was intended to cover the incubation period for the virus. Unsurprisingly, the quarantine proved to be a disaster, and it was ended after ten turbulent days. The experience in Liberia serves as a case study of the need to apply the four ethical considerations discussed in the previous section of this article.

To begin with, it was highly questionable whether the first consideration, "necessity, effectiveness, and scientific rationale," was even remotely satisfied. Liberia's President, Ellen Johnson Sirleaf, who received the Nobel Peace Prize in 2011, reportedly rejected the recommendation of international experts and her own public health officials, and imposed the quarantine at the urging of the army. In theory, if the infection could be localized and contained, then it could "burn out" before spreading to the rest of Monrovia and beyond.

This rationale was unsupported by the conditions of the Ebola epidemic, however, as the virus was not localized in West Point. Furthermore, because people in West Point live so close together and formed angry crowds to protest the quarantine, the increase in close human contact actually increased the risk of transmission. At the start of the quarantine, Dr. Martin Cetron of the CDC commented that the quarantine "has a lot of potential to go poorly if it's not done with an ethical approach. Just letting the disease burn out and considering it [the deaths] the price of controlling it [Ebola]—we don't live in that era anymore." According to Gregory Hartl of the WHO, during a cordon sanitaire "human rights have to be respected."

Imposing a cordon sanitaire on such a heavily populated area also fails to satisfy the second consideration of "proportionality and least infringement." The Liberian government failed to use less drastic means of social distancing or other measures to enlist the support of residents in West Point or elsewhere in Liberia. Furthermore, with the twenty-one day period of infectivity, the confinement of such a large population in a small area was almost certain to cause hardship and panic.

The lack of "humane supportive services," the third ethical consideration, doomed the effort from the start. Almost immediately after the quarantine was imposed, essential goods, such as food and water, doubled in price. One resident remarked at the prospect of the twenty-one day quarantine, "I wouldn't die of Ebola but of hunger." Many residents worked outside of West Point, and they were left with no means of income. There were few health services available for the individuals with malaria and other diseases, and there was little or no medical surveillance to detect new Ebola cases and to isolate those individuals. Even before the quarantine order, highly infectious dead bodies remained in the streets for hours, sometimes days.

Perhaps the worst mistake of the cordon sanitaire was the lack of "public justification," the fourth essential ethical consideration. West Point was the site of an earlier riot in which residents raided an Ebola screening center, accusing the government of bringing sick people from all over Monrovia into their neighborhood. The lack of public health education was a major contributing factor to spreading the disease from the start of the Ebola outbreak, as many individuals did not understand how Ebola was transmitted and therefore failed to take steps for their own protection.

* * *

With both the temporal and geographical distance from the global health emergency that was the Ebola crisis of 2014, it is easier to spot errors and missed opportunities. But what did it look like "in the heat of the moment"? After all, that will be the context in which future public health lawyers will face the next crisis. As you read the next excerpt, as with SARS, consider how well domestic and international governments handled these problems.

Mark J. Siedner, Lawrence O. Gostin, Hilarie H. Cranmer & John D. Kraemer, *Strengthening the Detection of and Early Response to Public Health Emergencies: Lessons from the West African Ebola Epidemic*

12 PLoS Med. e1001804 (2015)

In March 2014, Guinea identified 49 cases of Ebola virus disease (EVD) and reported them to international health agencies. Nearly twelve months later, the epidemic, having exploded into neighboring Sierra Leone and Liberia, has reached over 22,000 cases and nearly 9,000 deaths. The toll on human life, impact on health infrastructure, diversion of funding from routine—but critical—priorities, and concentrated mortality among health care workers places the epidemic among the worst disease outbreaks in recent history.

After a delayed response, the World Health Organization (WHO) laid out a programmatic roadmap to mobilize financial support and human resources. In addition, for the first time in its history, the United Nations (UN) Security Council has authorized an emergency health mission, the UN Mission for Ebola Emergency Response, with assets typically committed to peacekeeping. The massive response that followed, involving multiple foreign governments, multinational partners, and regional ministries of health, has brought unprecedented resources to the West African region. Towards the end of 2014, the epidemic showed signs of coming under control, particularly in Guinea and Liberia. Compared to worst-case scenario estimates from earlier in the epidemic, this global response has likely saved many thousands of lives.

But while the international response has become an example of the great potential of the global public health community, it also revealed critical weaknesses. Had these same partners responded earlier and more effectively after the first signs of an uncharacteristic outbreak, it is likely that the number of lives lost, the impact on health infrastructure, and the magnitude of the eventual response could have been drastically diminished. It is incumbent upon the global public health community to identify gaps revealed during the early stages of the epidemic so that we improve our collective ability to detect and respond early to the inevitable next emerging disease. We offer lessons from the West African Ebola epidemic and propose solutions for future international health emergencies.

Location, Location, Location

Experts have observed that large-scale threats from EVD are limited primarily to countries with weak public health systems. The current epidemic has supported, if not confirmed, this observation. Previous EVD epidemics, almost all of which occurred in low-and-middle-income countries (LMICs) and predominantly in rural areas, have been controlled within 18 weeks, with the largest prior outbreak claiming less than 300 lives. In contrast, the current West African outbreak has now killed more people than all previous EVD outbreaks combined. Whereas WHO generally considers the health infrastructure of involved countries when assessing the risk of a potential public health emergency, this outbreak has revealed that a more granular consideration of risk will be of value. Guinea, Sierra Leone, and Liberia are all recovering from prolonged periods of civic unrest and suffering from decimated health systems with limited human resource capacity and thus demonstrate that all LMICs should not be considered the same. For example, Nigeria, another country broadly characterized as a LMIC, provides a clear illustration of how a functional, albeit limited, public health infrastructure can successfully bring an EVD outbreak under control. The country responded rapidly through efforts in public education, isolation, quarantine, contact tracing, and case identification to control an epidemic after only 20 cases and 8 deaths in a little over a month.

Consequently, when a disease of epidemic potential emerges, the international community should pay increased attention to the capacity of the local health system. For example, WHO could create and maintain a curated scoring system of LMICs to include standard measures of health infrastructure, including the availability and sufficiency of the health care work force, surveillance and laboratory capacity, and personal protection equipment availability and supply chains. Moreover, a careful analysis of factors that contributed to variations in epidemic severity might lead to identification of additional characteristics to include in a ranking system. For example, local burial practices, having had prior local experience with a similar outbreak, and urban versus rural environments appear to have contributed to variations in the severity of recent West African EVD epidemics. With a more precise risk stratification system, WHO and international partners could give expedited and focused attention to countries on the list that have a particularly weak health infrastructure. This would facilitate faster and stronger responses to both routine and extraordinary health threats, as well as help to target routine support for health systems strengthening.

Back to the Drawing Board

WHO primarily relies upon the revised 2005 International Health Regulations (IHR) to define a public health emergency of international concern (PHEIC), and to determine when such announcements should be made to alert the global community. To improve their predictive accuracy and effectiveness, WHO should reexamine the IHR's criteria for declaring a PHEIC following each major public health emergency. This strategy will enable WHO to incorporate the lessons learned from each event to guide future responses. Multiple characteristics of the West African EVD epidemic have revealed areas for potential improvement.

First, this outbreak exemplified the importance of an often neglected criterion in the IHR—i.e., paying particular attention to cases in which "external assistance [is] needed to detect, investigate, respond, and control" the incident. Although this criterion is included in the IHR as a consideration, it is subordinated to others, such as the present number of cases, which risks missing detection of threats before they reach epidemic proportions. This epidemic, in which the regional health infrastructure was quickly overwhelmed, taught us that a need for external assistance ought to become a primary condition for declaring a PHEIC. Doing so would assist struggling member states with weak health infrastructures in the crucial early stages of response.

Second, the IHR partially define a PHEIC as a disease outbreak that "constitutes a public health risk to other States through the international spread of disease," or poses a "significant risk of international travel or trade restrictions". By this definition, outbreaks must transcend a national border before they legitimately trigger an international response. From the standpoint of national sovereignty, this requirement is understandable. States retain authority to handle health threats purely within their territories. However, the current epidemic began in December 2013, months before it crossed borders into both Sierra Leone and Liberia. This realization should challenge us to reconsider whether national borders should have such clout in considerations of potential global health emergencies. At the very least, the risk of international spread—particularly to other countries with weak public health infrastructures—should be carefully examined to prevent epidemics from growing out of control.

A more modern approach to global public health should de-emphasize the a priori criterion of international spread. Modeling studies have demonstrated that, for pathogens with relatively short generation times, early cross-border coordination between nations is crucial when epidemic diseases arise in border regions. But even for diseases with relatively long generation times, as with the current EVD epidemic, waiting for cases to cross borders can result in disastrous delays. As such, removing the requirement that an outbreak be an "international threat"—or at minimum interpreting that criterion liberally—will decrease delays between reporting and response and allow much needed support to at-risk countries before epidemics have reached a tipping point.

Lastly, in hindsight this outbreak might have been defined as a public health emergency long before the WHO Director General (DG) declared it a PHEIC, and the delay probably exacerbated the slow global response to the outbreak. There are reasons not to prematurely declare a PHEIC. Doing so could damage already vulnerable political systems, lead to misallocation of scarce global health funding, and diminish the influence of the IHR. Additionally, a PHEIC declaration may inadvertently trigger harmful measures, such as border closings and travel bans, which can hinder the response to an epidemic. However, the current epidemic has taught us that delaying an announcement imperils lives and health systems and, in the long run, may do more economic harm, cost more response dollars, and undermine domestic political legitimacy much more than an early, errant PHEIC declaration.

Therefore, for high-consequence diseases of epidemic potential, a precautionary principle should take precedence. The WHO DG should be empowered to declare PHEICs early if criteria are met. In fact, the DG has broad discretion to determine when an outbreak constitutes a PHEIC. WHO should interpret this discretion to declare graduated PHEICs, ranging from high-consequence localized events (e.g., the current Ebola outbreak as of June 2014) to clear global threats (e.g., severe acute respiratory syndrome in 2003). It can then tailor its recommendations, as well as funding needs, as the scenario unfolds. In doing so, we could expect PHEIC announcements for outbreaks that never reach devastating proportions. A similar approach has been implemented in other domains—such as genocide prevention—in which a concerted international response is required to prevent urgent problems before they become catastrophic. In fact, the Emergency Response Framework, also published by WHO, which aims to grade and motivate responses to international emergencies, public health or otherwise, specifically includes a "no regrets" policy, stating that "it is better to err on the side of over-resourcing the critical functions rather than risk failure by under-resourcing." Although it garnered relatively less attention than the PHEIC announcement, WHO declared the 2014 West Africa EVD epidemic a Grade 3 International Emergency (the highest classification) on July 24, two weeks before the PHEIC was declared. Similar discretion for declaring a PHEIC might help prevent the next large epidemic from gaining such momentum before the international community responds appropriately.

Know (and Involve) Your Community

Overwhelmed and under-resourced, the affected countries have implemented drastic measures to control the epidemic, including hospital and school closures, local and national quarantines, and border closures. Not surprisingly, these measures have engendered widespread public distrust of health authorities. In contrast, prior successful responses to Ebola and other epidemics have prioritized early partnerships with local authorities, anthropologists, and civil society to establish buy-in from multiple stakeholders. This strategy helps ensure that the design and implementation of control measures are culturally appropriate. In hindsight, some of the negative fallout from decisions to use extraordinary measures might have been avoided had WHO, in partnership with local community leaders and public health experts, more assertively used their legitimacy to caution against the use of coercive measures without an evidence base.

When acting under emergency powers—and especially when using extraordinary control measures such as regional quarantines—governments should prioritize formation of community advisory bodies in the affected region. A rich institutional knowledge about best practices for community advisory boards exists from the research community and, in combination with recent experience gained through collaborations with community leaders during the current epidemic, can serve as the basis for much-needed guidelines for public health activities. Members should represent divergent interests and include religious leaders, community representatives, nongovernmental organizations (NGOs), and other stakeholders. The body should be briefed on the status of the threat and called on to offer recommendations on community desensitization, capacity building, and control measures. While national and local governments hold primary responsibility for creating community advisory bodies, international actors should provide support, including technical assistance for overstretched ministries as they weigh evidence about appropriate interventions.

Putting Money Where Our Mouths Are

Declaring a PHEIC is a critical early step to marshal an effective response. A PHEIC announcement alerts partners and should initiate a concerted, coordinated response. But a PHEIC is of little value without corresponding ammunition. For example, although the PHEIC was announced on August 6, six weeks passed between the declaration and the United States government's commitment of US$750 million and the planned deployment of 3,000 military personnel and 65 Public Health Service commissioned corps officers. In the interim, total cases of EVD increased from approximately 1,100 to over 6,500, and confirmed deaths more than tripled, from under 1,000 to approximately 3,000.

The steady march of the epidemic, not only before the PHEIC declaration but also long after it, reinforces the fact that global health preparedness is contingent on the immediate availability of funding and human resources to respond. This need can be fulfilled through the establishment of a global emergency fund and the formation of a corps of trained health workers that can be deployed rapidly to curb an outbreak, with expertise ranging from epidemic surveillance to supply chain management. An International Health Systems fund, through a sustained investment by global partners, would provide much needed preparedness in future cases of outbreaks in LMICs, where local resources are not capable of controlling epidemics.

In 2011, a WHO committee proposed the establishment of a US$100 million contingency fund for rapid response in a declared PHEIC. However, the commitment remains unfulfilled. Instead, the Organization has been forced to rely on mobilizing funding from member states and other partners, which inevitably delays a robust international response. Spurred by the current EVD epidemic, in January 2015 WHO's secretariat repeated calls for the creation of a rapid response fund, to be financed by member states, and WHO's executive board agreed to establish the fund. Yet, the onus remains on WHO and the international community to follow through with this request even after the present emergency has faded and ensure this call to action does not meet a similar fate as previous attempts.

There Is No Substitute for Prevention

Arguably the greatest lesson to emerge from the Ebola virus epidemic is that both national ministries and the global public health community were caught off guard and unprepared. In addition to the many thousands of lives taken from both Ebola infections and interrupted access to routine health services, billions of dollars that could have otherwise been used for development and health systems strengthening were allocated to direct the Ebola response. The deleterious impact on local economies is equally staggering. The World Bank predicts that the three most affected countries will lose US$1.6 billion in economic growth in 2015, corresponding to an average gross domestic product (GDP) loss of 12% across the three countries. In Sierra Leone, a loss of nearly 20% of the GDP is projected. All this resulted from a disease that is relatively easy to control in settings with established health systems. Had a disease like SARS, with airborne transmission and a high case-fatality rate emerged in a similar location, the fallout could have been far worse.

What can be done today to prepare for the unavoidable public health threats of tomorrow? In the long term, it will be essential to build more robust health systems. Beyond public health emergencies, strong health systems will improve the health and wellbeing of the population in LMICs by delivering a range of essential services. The IHR currently mandate that technical support—surveillance, epidemiology, and laboratory and other core capacities—be provided by high-income countries to low-income countries to build capacity to survey and respond to outbreaks and that a detailed international framework exist for defining and assessing these capacities. However, although this is a central component of the obligations borne by countries for collective health security, capacity building support to low-income countries has long been underfunded. As a result, most countries in sub-Saharan Africa continue to suffer from weak systems for disaster preparedness and emergency response.

To ensure a truly robust response to global health hazards, states must abide by their IHR obligations to build core public health capabilities in regions of need. Human resources capacity building, laboratory infrastructure, and epidemiologic surveillance expertise are all urgently needed in West Africa and beyond. These inputs should be routinely assessed through a demonstrated capability to deploy resources successfully and in a timely fashion to respond to emergencies. Moreover, such investments clearly will have secondary benefits for routine health services in the areas they are employed. While successful implementation of these elements of the IHR will require substantial resource expenditures by high-resource countries, it is a legal and moral duty to which wealthy countries bound themselves when joining the IHR. The EVD epidemic has brought broad realization that health systems strengthening will be crucial to realize the benefits of a global community protected against international infectious disease threats. A positive legacy of the otherwise disastrous EVD outbreak should be a global community with renewed commitment to the establishment of a capable emergency response infrastructure.

* * *

The materials above highlight several important legal and ethical questions raised by the Ebola outbreak of 2014. One potent potential tool both for citizens and aid workers was experimental drugs. Such drugs may hold benefit, but they also have not yet undergone extensive human subjects testing (a topic discussed later in this Chapter) nor approval. In the thick of the Ebola crisis, there was also the additional ethical problem that the drugs were in short supply. Given this uncertainty and scarcity, who should get them? Do countries have an obligation to offer them to one another, or can they justly reserve them for their own citizens? Or conversely, can poor, dying citizens give meaningful consent to a potentially dangerous clinical trial? Ebola will likely not be the last time more affluent countries like the United States will have to ask themselves these questions—consider the excerpt below.

James G. Hodge, Jr., et al., *Law, Medicine, and Public Health Preparedness: The Case of Ebola*

130 Pub. Health. Rep. 167, 168 (2015)

Evaluating novel and relatively untested vaccines and therapeutics is challenging when nearly every intervention for Ebola is experimental. Successful patient outcomes may be equally attributable to supportive care as to any therapeutic drugs or specific interventions. Conducting randomized trials of potentially beneficial vaccines and medications is limited by a lack of prospective participants in developed countries and difficulty controlling for inconsistent, supportive care. Few Ebola patients would likely turn away available experimental therapies or care techniques when facing significant risks of mortality. Organizing a human clinical trial for a drug that few have received is problematic ethically when risks and benefits of participation cannot even be well described. Garnering truly informed consent from patients is complicated by the real threat of death.

* * *

It takes millions of dollars to produce experimental drugs such as ZMapp. Even if sufficient doses were available and affordable for a handful of patients in the U.S., tens of thousands of people in West Africa would be left untreated, which is patently inequitable. The current distribution of prior and existing Ebola treatments to citizens of first-world nations heightens sensitivities to the injustices underlying access to care.

* * *

Emily A. Largent, *EBOLA and FDA: Reviewing the Response to the 2014 Outbreak, to Find Lessons for the Future*

3 J.L. & Biosciences 489, 499–501 (2016)

When the 2014 EVD outbreak began, several Ebola-specific drugs and vaccines were already under development. The most promising of these—most prominently, perhaps, ZMapp, a combination of three different monoclonal antibodies, developed by Mapp Biopharmaceutical Inc.—'all [had] roots in programs run by the Department of Defense'. Yet, Dr. Luciana Borio of FDA noted at the time that

> [t]he experimental vaccines and treatments in development are in the earliest investigational stages and have not been fully tested for safety or efficacy. Only small amounts of some experimental products have been manufactured for testing, which means few courses, if any, are available.

In addition to these investigational Ebola-specific vaccines and treatments, there was also interest in repurposing FDA-approved drugs—that is, drugs previously approved by the FDA for other indications—as treatments for EVD. Repurposing is the process by which a drug that is patented and FDA-approved for treating one disease is further developed for the purpose of treating another disease. Drugs could also be used 'off-label'. Off-label use is the prescribing of a drug or biological agent for a treatment regimen not specified in the FDA-approved labeling or package insert.

* * *

[A]t the onset of the 2014 EVD outbreak—the deadliest on record—the standard of care for hemorrhagic fevers, including EVD, had not progressed appreciably beyond supportive care since the 1950s. Due, however, to investments made by the U.S. Department of Defense and others, several candidate vaccines and treatments were in the works. Given the relative dearth of treatment options and a case fatality rate reported to be between 53% and 60%, calls were made for the use of experimental interventions in the field. In late August 2014, for instance, a panel convened by WHO concluded that an ethical imperative existed 'to offer the available experimental interventions that have shown promising results in the laboratory and in relevant animal models to patients and people at high risk of developing [Ebola]' as long as ethical criteria guided the provision of such interventions.

Using experimental interventions—particularly in the midst of an outbreak difficult to bring under control for the host of social, political, and economic reasons discussed in Section I above—poses practical and ethical challenges. A challenge of particular relevance to FDA—and therefore a focus of this article—is that of gathering high-quality evidence to prove that a novel drug or vaccine is both safe and effective when used in humans. Before a vaccine or drug can be approved by FDA for marketing, it must be rigorously evaluated for quality, safety, and efficacy.

Given the history of investment by the U.S. Department of Defense in Ebola-related interventions, specifically those that were thought in 2014 to be most promising, and the likely role of the U.S. government as an eventual buyer of these interventions, calls to use experimental interventions in the field directly implicated FDA. Although Ebola is not endemic in the United States, if an intervention will be stockpiled and/or used by the American military, as Ebola drugs and vaccines likely would be, 'all critical functions in the development and acquisition ... lead to and through FDA'.

Additionally, although national regulatory authority (NRA) officials in any Ebola-affected country are ultimately responsible for determining whether an MCM for Ebola should be approved for use within the nation's borders,

> [a]pproval from a stringent regulatory authority such as the US [FDA] ... can expedite another country's NRA review, given that such approval signifies to international medical and regulatory communities that the data have been thoroughly examined and ... meet[] performance and manufacturing standards.

Drug and vaccine manufacturers therefore had several clear incentives to work with FDA in the West African outbreak despite FDA's geographic remove.

Lastly, in addition to putting pressure on countries to tend to their citizens, the Ebola outbreak served as something of a stress test for the WHO's ability to handle a global epidemic convincingly and fairly. The following is a critique of the WHO's approach to handling the epidemic.

J. Benton Heath, *Global Emergency Power in the Age of Ebola*

57 Harv. Int'l L. J. 1, 26–27, 28, 29–30, 32–33, 35 (2016)

The tension between knowledge and decision ... emerges in potentially debilitating ways when the WHO exercises its emergency power. The International Health Regulations authorize the WHO Director-General to declare a state of emergency, to take emergency measures, and to identify the relevant categories of decision makers. With respect to each dimension of this power, the treaty rules provide nothing close to a step-by-step guide for reaching decisions. In high-profile responses to swine flu and Ebola, the WHO has attempted to fill the gap between knowledge and decision through various improvised tactics. These included adopting a stance of deference to other actors, employing a detailed, rule-bound decision-making framework, and attempting to depoliticize the role of the WHO's expert advisers. These improvisations often proved pathological, bringing to light inconsistencies between the WHO's role as an expert body and its power to make wide-ranging political decisions, and threatening to produce policy that could be justified from neither perspective. The WHO's experience in this respect highlights fundamental challenges facing global emergency governors.

* * *

The overriding criticism of the 2014 Ebola outbreak was that the WHO was slow to wake up to its severity. Médecins Sans Frontières warned of a massive Ebola outbreak of "unprecedented" scale as early as March 2014, but the WHO continually downplayed the matter and did not activate its international emergency powers for months.

* * *

In normative terms, the organization's strategy during the spring of 2014 was one of deference to regional and local authorities. For much of that time, the organization purportedly allowed its regional office in Africa to take the leadership role, with some support from the organization's global outbreak network of experts. It also stressed the primary responsibility of states to determine the urgency of public health threats in their own territory.

* * *

As the outbreak escalated, the justification for the WHO's decision-making structure began to crumble, and headquarters had to search for a reason to withdraw its deference and take action. It found its justification in what seemed to be a strict, rule-bound interpretation of its emergency authority. On July 20, 2014, as political pressure on the WHO ratcheted upward, an airline passenger from Liberia brought Ebola to Lagos, marking the first time the virus was known to cross international borders by air travel. The WHO treated this event as a paradigm shift, which converted the disease from a problem affecting an isolated geographical region spread across three countries into an international incident justifying an exercise of global emergency power. Now that someone with Ebola managed to get on an international flight, it was suggested, the situation justified global emergency power—the International Health Regulations, after all, are concerned with the international spread of disease.

This justification was paper thin, and it did little if anything to quell international criticism of the WHO's delayed response. First, there is no legal requirement that cross-border transmission take place before a public health emergency is declared; there need only be a risk associated with the international spread of disease. Second, it was undisputable that the disease had already spread across at least three countries and that further spread by air travel was only a matter of time. It did little to redeem the WHO to suggest that a single regional flight to Lagos marked the difference between an international health emergency and a localized event.

This rule-bound solution to the failure of the WHO's earlier deference strategy compounds the perception that the WHO's approach to its own emergency power is unprincipled and undisciplined. In the abstract, of course, there might be good reasons to delegate downward in the management of emergencies. A principle of institutional subsidiarity, for example, might provide that regional and local authorities take the lead, unless and until their capacities are proven to be overwhelmed. The decision to activate the WHO's global emergency powers, then, would be premised on an assessment of the operational and informational capacities of local offices and local governments. The trouble is that the WHO, at present, appears to lack both the normative vocabulary and the institutional architecture to make potentially contentious decisions about the capacities of local governments, and it therefore has had to fall back on legalistic triggers and ad hoc rules. Accordingly, the Director-General's decision to assert some control, although welcomed by most observers, appears just as unprincipled and unscientific as the decision to accord deference to the local authorities and regional bureaucracy in the first place.

* * *

The WHO's initial response to this problem highlighted the contradictions of imposing a rule-bound system on an expert-driven response. It could have acknowledged the inappropriateness of the pandemic plan for the current outbreak and simply changed tack. Instead, as the WHO was escalating its response, it began quietly removing references to "severity" from its pandemic-related materials. It published a new pandemic plan, which omitted any reference to severity, and it began deleting language on its website that associated a pandemic with "enormous numbers of deaths and illness." These maneuvers would recast a pandemic as a technical term, divorced from any meaning it might have in popular usage. The WHO thus placed itself in the uncomfortable position of insisting, no matter how silly it sounded, that swine flu was a "mild" pandemic.

With this move, the WHO brought to the surface the incoherence in its own efforts to navigate the conflicting demands of science and politics. From a political perspective, the shifting descriptions of a pandemic undermined any claims that the organization might have to clarity, to predictability, and to the rote, umpire-like application of rules. Instead, the shifting rules gave the impression of an ad hoc, improvised response conducted with a minimum amount of transparency. At the same time, the WHO struggled to justify its move from a public-health perspective: if the original pandemic plan's decision-making criteria were inappropriate to swine flu, then surely their policy prescriptions also were not designed with swine flu in mind. If that was the case, then why not simply change the criteria to fit the new disease? Why not change other elements of the plan, or ditch the plan altogether?

The failure of the pandemic plan was a microcosm for the pathologies of emergency power. The exercise of emergency authority cannot be organized according to precise, prearranged sets of rules; the very nature of catastrophe demands improvisation and flexibility. But, once the rules appear to be malleable, it becomes clear that the governor who purports to be applying the rules is actually making policy. For an expert body like the WHO secretariat, the rules provided valuable political cover, giving a sense that policy was both automatic and transparent, taking place according to a plan vetted by scientists and public health experts worldwide. With that cover stripped away, it becomes clear that the organization exercises discretion in ways that could have a broad range of social, political, and economic effects. The identity of the decision maker, then, becomes a key political issue.

* * *

In the recent Ebola response, the WHO took very small, cautious steps toward broadening its perspectives. For the first time since the entry into force of the IHR, the Director-General appointed a bioethicist to the Emergency Committee as an "adviser." The recognition that bioethics, which addresses deeply contested matters of political and moral commitment, plays a substantial role in the WHO's emergency response may constitute a step toward staffing decisions that acknowledge the broader implications of the WHO's activities.

* * *

Each of the vignettes in the foregoing section saw the WHO struggling with the gap between knowledge and decision. In the case of Ebola, the WHO sought to avoid this gap by purporting to delegate decision making downward, only to be confronted with a pathological institutional structure. In the case of swine flu, the WHO streamlined emergency policy using a clear set of rules, but circumstances undermined the foundation for these criteria. And, as Part III.C noted, the WHO will continue struggling to define the boundaries of what kinds of expertise is "relevant" for emergency response. Is relevance determined by the core competencies of WHO medical and scientific staff, or is it determined by the broad political consequences of the organization's activities? The law provides no clear answer to these questions, and the WHO has taken a different approach in each successive emergency response.

Notes

1. For more on SARS, see also Jacques deLisle, Atypical Pneumonia and Ambivalent Law and Politics: SARS and the Response to SARS in China, 77 *Temp. L. Rev.* 193 (2004); and Lawrence Gostin, Ronald Bayer, & Amy Fairchild, Ethical and Legal Challenges Posed by Severe Acute Respiratory Syndrome: Implications for the Control of Severe Infectious Disease Threats, 290 *JAMA* 3229 (2003). And for more on Ebola, see, for example, Gillian K. Steel Fisher, Robert J. Blendon & Narayani Lasala-Blanco, Ebola in the United States—Public Reactions and Implications, 373 *N. Eng. J. Med.* 789 (2015).

2. As you saw in the final Ebola excerpt, international law and international organizations play a more significant role in responding to infectious diseases than they do in most other areas of health law. Among the most important authorities here are the International Health Regulations (IHR) adopted by the World Health Assembly in 2005. The goal of the IHR, which was revised in 2005 to replace regulations that had been in place for half a century, was to balance the right of states to protect the health of their residents with the goal of minimizing interference with international trade, while also protecting human rights. Unlike the old Regulations, which applied only to a short list of traditional infectious diseases, the IHR apply comprehensively to infectious diseases and also to disease-causing hazardous substances and the intentional or negligent release of harmful biological, chemical, or radioactive agents. The IHR require states to develop surveillance and response capacities, and to report public health emergencies of international concern to the World Health Organization. The IHR obligates governments to incorporate human rights principles respecting rights to privacy and informed consent, and specifically limits the ways in which governments can limit international traffic. See, describing the IHR, David Fidler and Lawrence Gostin, The New International Health Regulations: An Historic Development for International Law and Public Health. 34 *J. L. Med. & Ethics* 85 (2006). But as we have seen, this is still not a perfect system. Even as the WHO is empowered by the IHR to determine if international public health emergencies exist and to issue temporary, non-binding recommendations for addressing emergencies, its decision to do so or not to is still subject to political pressure and can lack moral authority.

3. The past half century has been marked by a growing influence of globalization, and in particular with a concern that national public health measures not unduly restrain international trade. The General Agreement on Tariffs and Trade (GATT), the Agreement on the Application of Sanitary and Phytosanitary Measures (SPS), and the Agreement on Technical Barriers to Trade all limit the ability of World Trade Organization member states to unnecessarily limit international trade for public health reasons. GATT's Article XX(b) permits measures "necessary to protect human, animal and plant life or health" if they are not applied in a discriminatory or arbitrary fashion. The SPS also permits sanitary controls, but they must be based on scientific risk as-

sessment. The General Agreement on Trade in Services is also leading to the deregulation of the international flow of health services. Finally, regional agreements impose separate, perhaps greater, limitations on the ability of signatory states to limit trade in health care goods and services for public health reasons. See Jason Sapsin, et al., International Trade Law and Public Health Advocacy, 31 *J. L. Med. & Ethics* 546 (2003): David Fidler, Emerging Trends in International Law Concerning Global Infectious Disease Control, 9 *Emerging Infections Diseases* 285 (2003).

4. Consider the case of Kaci Hickox, an American nurse who traveled to Sierra Leone at the height of the Ebola epidemic with Doctors Without Borders. Her return home coincided with the first diagnosis of Ebola on U.S. soil—in a doctor returning from Guinea—causing widespread panic and leading authorities to detain Hickox on her arrival at Newark Airport. She presented no symptoms of the disease (though over the course of her detention she developed a low fever, which she attributed to her frustration), but was nonetheless transported via ambulance to a New Jersey hospital, where she was quarantined for three days, even after a test for the virus came back negative. Once New Jersey agreed to let her leave, they escorted her to her Maine home, where she was ordered to remain at home under observation for about a week and a half. Hickox eventually teamed up with the ACLU to sue for violation of her Fourth and Fourteenth Amendment rights; she ended up settling with the State of New Jersey on the condition that the State change its quarantine policy. Her story became a flashpoint for those on each side of the Ebola debate: Was this woman a Good Samaritan wronged by a needless and overzealous crackdown? Or was her insistence on being free to move around selfish in light of the huge risks the disease posed? Does the abundance of civil-rights lawsuits in the United States indicate anything about the general likelihood of success any future quarantine plan might hold? For more on Hickox, see Jennifer Jolly-Ryan, Balancing Interests and Risk of Error: What Quarantine Process Is Due After Ebolamania, 96 *Neb. L. Rev.* 100, 104–109 (2017); Marc Santora, *New Jersey Accepts Rights for People in Quarantine to End Ebola Suit*, N.Y. Times (July 27, 2017).

5. From 2015–16 the Americas saw an outbreak in the Zika virus—a disease that, while often mild for the infected party, could be transmitted from an infected pregnant woman to her unborn child, leading to microcephaly and other birth defects. Unlike the diseases discussed in this section, Zika is spread (other than between mother and fetus) by mosquito, not by human contact; this did not, however, stop the CDC from issuing travel guidance to and from affected areas. *See, e.g.*, Ernest Tambo et al., Ethical, Legal, and Societal Considerations on Zika Virus Epidemics Complications in Scaling-Up Prevention and Control Strategies, 12 Philosophy, Ethics, and Humanities in Medicine (2017). But in addition to raising questions about travel restrictions, which we faced above, it also raised a host of its own questions specifically tied to the regulation of reproduction. In Brazil, for example, the government recommended that woman delay pregnancy until the virus was under control. Critics challenged the recommendation for both restricting a fundamental human right (bodily autonomy), *see* Beatriz Galli & Christine Ricardo, Using a Human Rights Accountability Framework to Respond to Zika, *Blog, Health & Human Rights J.* (May 2016), https://www.hhr

journal.org/2016/05/using-a-human-rights-accountability-framework-to-respond-to-zika/, and for failing to take account of poor women's inability to delay pregnancy, *see* Johanna Bond, Zika, Feminism, and the Failures of Health Policy, 73 Wash. & Lee L. Rev. Online 841 (2017). But more broadly, national responses like Brazil's prompt normative questions about when—and how—a government can or should attempt to govern its citizens' reproductive decisions and rights, as well as how that decision interacts with sex, race, and class in disparate ways.

C. Public Health Law: Tobacco Regulation

While AIDS and SARS post obvious threats to the public health as infectious diseases, tobacco and other dangerous products such as asbestos or pesticides pose a public health threat of a different sort. They are also subject to legal regulation. Tobacco provides a fascinating subject for comparative study because of the conflict that it poses between the rights of individuals to enjoy their private pleasures and the rights of others to be free from the annoyance (and, as has become increasingly obvious, the health hazards) of breathing the smoke of others. It also poses a conflict between the right of the state to intervene paternalistically to restrict the use of substances that are dangerous and addictive and the autonomy of individuals to risk destruction of their health if they choose to do so. These challenges take on particular cultural valences in different countries, as will become clear in the discussion of various countries' approaches below. Moreover, the rise of e-cigarettes and vaping has created a host of new challenges and prompted creative regulations to tackle this new problem. Finally, the regulation of tobacco has very important financial implications, both at home and for international trade. On the one hand, tobacco is heavily taxed and is thus an important source of revenue in most countries; indeed, in some countries it is sold through a lucrative public monopoly. On the other, public health insurance programs bear a heavy cost for paying for the diseases tobacco causes (although tobacco also causes early death and thus may free public pension programs from considerable expense).

The most recent legislation enacted in the United States on the topic of smoking is the Family Smoking Prevention and Tobacco Control Act (FSPTCA), which President Obama signed into law in 2009. Below is a high-level overview of the history of U.S. tobacco regulation, as well as the goals of the new law.

Roseann B. Termini, *The "Why" of Tobacco Products Regulation*

Food and Drug Law: Federal Regulation of Drugs, Biologics, Medical Devices, Foods, Dietary Supplements, Personal Care, Veterinary and Tobacco Products vol. 12, 481–491, 497, 504, 509–511 (2019)

Introduction

Admittedly, smoking has plagued the United States for generations; however, it was not until the past several years that this issue received more serious scrutiny.

The United States Food and Drug Administration (FDA) determined that over 1,300 people die each day in the United States due to smoking and over 8.6 million Americans have chronic illnesses linked to smoking. According to the Centers for Disease Control (CDC) in the United States, cigarette smoking is responsible for more than 480,000 deaths annually, including more than 41,000 deaths resulting from secondhand smoke exposure. Based on CDC statistics, every day about 2000 youth start smoking their first cigarette and 300 youth become day-to-day smokers.[1] This means that using current rates of smoking among youth, 5.6 million Americans younger than 18 years of age are expected to die prematurely from a smoking-related illness. This denotes about one in every 13 Americans aged 17 years or younger who are alive today. FDA regulates tobacco products by utilization of a public health standard. The Center for Tobacco Products (CTP) within FDA regulates tobacco products with a single focused mission; that is, to diminish tobacco related deaths and diseases. Since its existence, the CTP has maintained a critical focus of prevention of youth smoking. Further, the marketing to and use of e-nicotine products by teens has escalated.

The United States Supreme Court decision of *Food and Drug Administration et al., v. Brown and Williamson Tobacco Corp. et al.* spurred the impetus for the Family Smoking Prevention and Tobacco Control Act (FSPTCA or Tobacco Control Act). The Supreme Court, in *Brown*, held that FDA lacked the requisite authority to regulate tobacco products. FDA asserted jurisdiction over tobacco products based on the Food, Drug and Cosmetic Act (FDCA) definitions of "drug" and "device." Nearly ten years after the *United States v. Brown* decision, Congress provided FDA with explicit legal authority or jurisdiction to regulate tobacco products. To that end, on June 22, 2009, Former President Obama signed the FSPTCA or Tobacco Control Act. This historic legislation conferred FDA with the authority to regulate tobacco products. The FSPTCA amended the FDCA and other federal laws by permitting FDA regulatory authority over the manufacture, marketing, and distribution of all tobacco products. Initially, this included cigarettes, cigarette tobacco, roll-your-own tobacco, and smokeless tobacco. In 2016, FDA issued what are known as "deeming regulations" to include regulation of electronic nicotine delivery systems (ENDS), popularly known as e-cigarettes, as well as other covered tobacco products such as cigars. Covered tobacco product means any tobacco product deemed subject to the Federal Food, Drug, and Cosmetic Act in accordance with 21 CFR. § 1100.2.

---

1. https://www.cdc.gov/tobacco/data_statistics/fact_sheets/youth_data/tobacco_use/index.htm. Previously, according to the 50 years of Progress Report issued in 2014, 3,200 youth started smoking their initial cigarette and 2,100 youth become day-to-day smokers. *See* The Health Consequences of Smoking—50 Years of Progress: A Report of the Surgeon General. Atlanta: U.S. Department of Health and Human Services, Centers for Disease Control and Prevention, National Center for Chronic Disease Prevention and Health Promotion, Office on Smoking and Health, 2014 (last accessed Oct. 11, 2018); https://www.cdc.gov/tobacco/data_statistics/fact_sheets/fast_facts/index.htm (last accessed April 24, 2019); https://www.ftc.gov/system/files/documents/reports/federal-trade-commission-cigarette-report-2016-federal-trade-commission-smokeless-tobacco-report/ftc_cigarette_report_for_2016_0.pdf (last accessed April 24, 2019).

The FSPTCA requires large graphic warnings on cigarette cartons that describe the health consequences of smoking; however, this was met with resistance. Finally in 2018, FDA was ordered to redraft the graphic warnings. See: *The American Academy of Pediatrics et al. v. United States Food and Drug Administration,* 1:16-cv-11985, (D. C. Mass. 2016); MEMORANDUM AND ORDER GRANTING INJUNCTIVE RELIEF (March 5, 2019); Proposed Rule for Publication in the *Federal Register* by August 15, 2019 and the Final Rule for Publication in the *Federal Register* by March 15, 2020. *https://www.tobaccocontrollaws.org/files/live/litigation/2631/US_American%20Academy%20of%20Pediatrics.pdf* (last accessed April 24, 2019).

The use of ENDS by youth has [] escalated to an epidemic. To that end, former FDA Commissioner Gottlieb announced in 2018 a further crackdown by initiating age restricted sales of ENDS and online heightened age verification of flavored tobacco products. Further, ongoing concern remains about menthol flavored cigarettes and the public health impact. Finally, the tobacco industry spends billions of dollars on cigarette and smokeless tobacco advertising. In 2016 alone, approximately $26 million daily was spent on marketing of cigarettes and smokeless tobacco. Finally, the economic costs are astounding with over $300,000 billion a year with a breakdown of nearly $170,000 billion in medical care and $156 billion in lost productivity.

***Impetus for Congressional Action in Enacting the Family Smoking Prevention and Tobacco Control Act—Food and Drug Administration, et al. v. Brown & Williamson Tobacco Corp. et al.* 529 U.S. 120 (2000)**

The FSPTCA or Tobacco Control Act, as detailed above, became law on June 22, 2009. Several factors contributed to the impetus of the FSPTCA such as the rise of youth smoking, death associated with smoking and as mentioned, the United States Supreme Court decision in *Food and Drug Administration et al., v. Brown and Williamson Tobacco Corp. et al.* 529 U.S. 120 (2000). As indicated above, the United States Supreme Court, in *Brown,* held that FDA lacked the authority to regulate tobacco products. Although the district court agreed with FDA in the decision of *Coyne Beam, Inc. v. Food and Drug Administration*, the court of appeals in *Brown and Williamson Tobacco Corp. v. Food and Drug Administration* reversed. The United States Supreme Court affirmed the court of appeals decision.

The Supreme Court held that FDA lacked jurisdiction over tobacco products because the measure lacked the requisite Congressional intent required to execute the regulatory framework. The Supreme Court denied FDA jurisdiction over tobacco products due to fundamental conflicts and inconsistencies in prior actions by FDA and prior Congressional inaction. Despite the strong showing of compatible existing regulatory provisions and evidence of the danger of nicotine addiction, the Court determined that FDA lacked jurisdiction over tobacco products. Subsequently, Congress provided FDA with explicit legal authority or jurisdiction to regulate tobacco products.

The FSPTCA consists of several titles. Title I is of significance because it expressly confers jurisdiction to regulate tobacco to the FDA by amending the Federal Food, Drug and Cosmetic Act of 1938. The provisions of Title I (Authority of the FDA) are codified in Title 21 (Food and Drugs), Chapter 9 (Federal Food, Drug and Cosmetic Act), Subchapter IX (Tobacco Products) of the United States Coded. Title II relates to the labeling of cigarette and smokeless tobacco packages, as well as requiring tobacco product manufacturers to disclose information about the composition of their products. The provisions of Title II (Tobacco Product Warnings; Constituent and Smoke Constituent Disclosure) amends the Federal Cigarette Labeling and Advertising Act and is codified in Title 15 (Commerce and Trade), Chapter 36 (Cigarette Labeling and Advertising) of the United States Code Annotated. Title III relates to the trade of illicit tobacco products within and outside the United States. The provisions of Title III (Prevention of Illicit Trade in Tobacco Products) are also codified in the Federal Food, Drug and Cosmetic Act in Title 21 (Food and Drugs), Chapter 9 (Federal Food, Drug and Cosmetic Act), Subchapter IX (Tobacco Products) of the United States Code.

United States Food and Drug Administration Center for Tobacco Products

Although the FSPTCA or Tobacco Control Act provides FDA with regulatory authority over the manufacture, marketing, and distribution of tobacco products, FDA cannot ban tobacco. In fact, the FSPTCA specifically prohibits FDA from banning an entire category of tobacco products, such as cigarettes. Implementing the FSPTCA involves a recognition of the complexity in terms of the role tobacco has played in the American economy and culture. That aforesaid, FDA must execute its responsibilities in complete recognition of the indisputable facts about tobacco use. Succinctly stated, it is an addictive product and has profound health effects on users and on the public health of our nation. FDA's regulatory role for drugs and medical devices is normally based on a safety and efficacy standard. The FSPTCA established a new standard; that is, to regulate tobacco products based on a public health and population health standard. To that end, the FDA Center for Tobacco Products (CTP) regulates tobacco products.

CTP Priorities, Goals and Accomplishments

The CTP priorities center on these goals: Implementation of restrictions to reduce and prevent youth from using cigarettes and smokeless tobacco; encourage adults who use tobacco to quit; reduce product harms and addictiveness; develop a science based product regulation to reduce the toll of tobacco-related disease, disability and death; use of a public health regulatory standard; tobacco product testing; provide accurate information on the contents of tobacco products ingredients; restriction of advertising and promotion; evaluation of whether a tobacco product can be marketed as a modified risk product; compliance training programs for retailers; establishment of tobacco product performance standards; and use of regulatory enforcement tools to assure adherence to the FSPTCA mandates. Accomplishments include the following:

- Issued Final Rule—Clarification of When Products Made or Derived From Tobacco Are Regulated as Drugs, Devices, or Combination Products; Amendments to Regulations Regarding "Intended Uses" (2017); *https://www.gpo.gov/fdsys/pkg/FR-2017-01-09/pdf/2016-31950.pdf.* **NOTE: Final rule only partially implemented;**

- Extended authority to regulation in "deeming" all tobacco products, including E-Cigarettes, Cigars, and Hookah (2016);
- Issued warning letters to cigarette manufacturers asserting "additive free" or "natural claims" (2016);
- Focused on efforts to curb marketing of electronic nicotine delivery systems to youth (2018);
- Use of Investigational Tobacco Products—Draft Guidance *https://www.fda.gov/TobaccoProducts/Labeling/RulesRegulationsGuidance/ucm463951.htm?source=govdelivery&utm_medium=email&utm_source=govdelivery*;
- Released Final Rule Restricting the Sales and Distribution of Cigarettes and Smokeless Tobacco Products to Children and Adolescents (effective June 22, 2010);
- No sales: *to youth under 18, cigarette packs with fewer than 20 cigarettes; vending machines, self-service displays or other impersonal methods of sale except under very limited circumstances*; No sale or distribution of hats, tee shirts or similar items with tobacco brand names, logos or selling messages;
- No distribution: of free cigarette samples and smokeless tobacco product restriction; of hats, tee shirts or similar items with tobacco brand names, logos or selling messages;
- No tobacco brand name sponsorship of athletic, musical or other social events and of teams and entries in those events;
- Implemented and enforced the Flavored Cigarette Ban in the FSPTCA for certain fruit and candy characterizing flavors;
- Mandated tobacco industry registration;
- Required tobacco company submission of ingredient listing;
- Issued Guidance on Registration and Product Listing;
- Prohibition: Misleading Marketing Terms "Light," "Low," and "Mild" (June 22, 2010); and
- Issued strategic initiatives for the youth epidemic of electronic nicotine delivery systems (ENDS).

Deeming Regulations and Covered Tobacco Product

The deeming regulations extended the authority of FDA to include the regulation of ENDS (such as e-cigarettes and vape pens), all cigars, hookah (waterpipe) tobacco, pipe tobacco and nicotine gels. See: 81 FR 28973 prohibits the sale of "covered tobacco products" to individuals under the age of 18 and requires the display of health warnings on cigarette tobacco, roll-your own tobacco, and covered tobacco product packages and in advertisements.

Covered tobacco product—means any tobacco product deemed to be subject to the Federal Food, Drug, and Cosmetic Act under 21 C. F.R.§ 1100.2, of this chapter (i.e., subchapter K), but excludes any component or part that is not made or derived from tobacco (parts 1140, 1143)

Sec. 1100.2 Requirements.

Cigarettes, cigarette tobacco, roll-your-own tobacco, smokeless tobacco are subject to chapter IX of the Federal Food, Drug, and Cosmetic Act and its implementing regulations. FDA has deemed all other tobacco products, except accessories of such other tobacco products, subject to chapter IX of the Federal Food, Drug, and Cosmetic Act and its implementing regulations.

Enforcement Emphasis

The CTP established the Office of Compliance and Enforcement (OCE); however, enforcement is limited as FDA's regulatory authority is dictated by the FSPTCP. Therefore, enforcement efforts must adhere to the mandates of the FSPTCA. In addition to warning letters, CTP has filed actions for civil monetary penalties mainly for sales to minors. A Civil Money Penalty (CMP) Complaint is used to initiate an administrative legal action against a retailer that can result in the imposition of a fine, termed a Civil Money Penalty. As an example of enforcement efforts, FDA filed well over 100 civil legal actions. Enforcement focuses on violations of the following: *Sales to minors; Flavored cigarette sales; Advertising/promotion/marketing restrictions (e.g., Describing the tobacco product as "light," "mild," or "low" or claiming that the product is safer or less harmful without an FDA order in effect; distributing t-shirts or other novelty items with brand name of a cigarette or smokeless tobacco product; and event sponsorship in the brand name of a cigarette or smokeless tobacco product); Free samples; Vending machines in prohibited areas/self-service display/direct access to cigarette or smokeless tobacco; and Sale of cigarettes in packs of less than 20.*[2]

Moving Forward to Address Critical Issues

There are myriad matters concerning tobacco products regulation by the United States Food and Drug Administration. This article provided an overview of tobacco products including the FSPTC or Tobacco Control Act. Yet, issues persist such as undue delay in terms of reissuing graphic warnings for cigarettes and the lengthy legal battles for instance with the language used in court ordered corrective statements. See: *United States, et al.*, v. *Philip Morris USA, Inc., et al.*, *Brown & Williamson Tobacco Corp.*, directly and as successor by merger to *American Tobacco Company, et al.*, 855 F.3d 321, No. 16-5101 Consolidated with 16-5127 (April 25, 2017).

Further, when enacted, the FSTCA focused on traditional cigarettes and was silent on other tobacco products such as cigars, pipe tobacco and electronic nicotine delivery systems such as e-cigarettes. To overcome the lack of inclusion in the predicate law, that is, the FSPTCA, deeming regulations were enacted. Despite the deeming regulations, the use of tobacco products including vaping and e-cigarettes has escalated to epidemic proportions among youth. Hopefully, the FDA strides in alleviating the

2. CTP issued a Compliance and Enforcement Report that details both compliance and enforcement actions from enactment of the FSPTCA in 2009 through Sept. 30, 2013. Total violations: 18,960. The majority of violations focused on selling tobacco products to a minor and failure to verify age; http://www.fda.gov/downloads/TobaccoProducts/GuidanceComplianceRegulatoryInformation/UCM396614.pdf (last accessed April 24, 2019).

rise in the use of e-delivery products by middle school and high school students will remain and provide a measurable impact.

William Tilburg, Kathleen Hoke & Melissa Sager, *FDA Regulation of Electronic Nicotine Delivery Systems and the "Deeming" Rule: What's Left for States?*

20 J. Health Care L. & Pol'y 27, 28–29, 56–63 (2017)

Smoking has been the leading cause of preventable death in the United States for many decades. This list of diseases and other negative health consequences caused by smoking is extensive; exposure to secondhand smoke creates similar health outcomes. As a result, medical and public health professionals are naturally concerned about the marketing of any product that emulates smoking yet are eager to offer smokers truly effective tools for cessation. This is why the electronic cigarette creates a conundrum for those working to reduce smoking and improve public health. Is this new product as bad as its namesake? Or is it a safe, viable method to achieve cessation?

As researchers embarked on the time-consuming and expensive process of determining the health effects and cessation potential of electronic cigarettes—now better term[ed] electronic nicotine delivery systems or ENDS—the product exploded in the marketplace. No longer a quirky, expensive mystery device sold at mall kiosks, ENDS are becoming ubiquitous, available in cheap disposable versions and elaborate, pricey, reusable devices with high-tech options. The liquid nicotine market has likewise developed rapidly to offer consumers virtually any flavor imaginable and a variety of nicotine levels. Specialty vape shops now pepper communities. ENDS are advertised in the same media venues as cigarettes—magazines and point-of-sale—and where cigarette promotion is forbidden—television and radio. Celebrities have touted the benefits of ENDS on network television and been seen using the product at major entertainment events. ENDS are used indoors in places where smoking has long been prohibited. Vaping consumers ardently supports ENDS, both as cessation devices and as a product offering the same enjoyment as cigarettes with much reduced risk or negative health outcomes. Within this frenzy, research moves forward as best possible.

Little is known about the long-term health effects and public health impact of ENDS. Preliminary research raises concerns, particularly to a public health community still waging a decades-long battle against the original cigarette. Policymakers and public health officials are stymied, having to take action and engage in public education with a modest amount of research. Caution has prevailed to some extent at the federal level; the FDA promulgated a regulation deeming ENDS tobacco products subject to the Family Smoking Prevention and Tobacco Control Act ("Tobacco Control Act") and the agency's regulatory power. Effective August 8, 2016, the FDA regulations impose requirements and restrictions on ENDS, some relatively minor and others far more significant. The impact of the regulation cannot yet be measured and we fully anticipate that FDA will issue additional provisions and guidance related to ENDS. Researchers will have to wait to determine the full impact of the federal regulation of ENDS. In the meantime, federal law gives wide room for state and local jurisdictions to do more.

* * *

In 2007, ENDS manufacturers Smoking Everywhere and NJOY began importing inventory into the United States and marketing their products for "smoking pleasure." Although designed to resemble traditional cigarettes, these cig-alike products do not burn or contain tobacco. In fact, NJOY's promotional materials emphasized "it's NOT a real cigarette, there is NO real smoke, flame, tar, or tobacco," and promised to "deliver the nicotine hit that smokers crave." In October 2008, FDA denied entry to a shipment of Smoking Everywhere products from China because they appeared to be an "unapproved drug-device combination product." Shortly thereafter, FDA denied entry to a shipment of NJOY products on the same grounds. In response, Smoking Everywhere filed suit in the U.S. District Court for the District of Columbia, and NJOY joined as an intervenor-plaintiff. The ENDS manufacturers sought a preliminary injunction barring FDA from regulating their products under the drug/device provisions of the FDCA. They argued that *Brown & Williamson* applies equally to electronic cigarettes as to conventional cigarettes because the nicotine in electronic cigarettes is derived from tobacco, and that FDA lacks authority under the FDCA to regulate their products as customarily marketed. FDA countered that the Supreme Court decision did not extend to electronic cigarettes, which do not contain tobacco and are not subject to the federal statutes the *Brown & Williamson* Court relied upon in finding that Congress has not intended to give regulatory power over tobacco products to FDA. The injunction was granted by the District Court and FDA appealed.

[FDA's authority to regulate was decided in] *Sottera v. Food and Drug Admin.* [where the agency made] three main arguments: (1) electronic cigarettes are combination drug devices under the provisions of the FDCA, (2) the reasoning of *Brown & Williamson* does not apply to electronic cigarettes, and (3) the Tobacco Control Act does not restrict FDA's preexisting authority under the FDCA to regulate electronic cigarettes as drug-delivery devices. First, FDA argued that unlike traditional cigarettes, the agency had regulated nicotine products under the FDCA, without challenge, for at least two decades. For instance, the agency regulated "Favor Smokeless Cigarettes," a product virtually identical to ENDS, under its FDCA authority beginning in the mid-1980s. FDA advised Favor that the product was "a nicotine delivery system intended to satisfy a nicotine dependence and to affect the structure and one or more functions of the body" and therefore an unapproved new drug. FDA likewise had long used its drug-device authority to regulate nicotine hand gels, lollipops, lip balms, and water. All of these similar products were regulated as drug-devices under the FDCA, and FDA argued that the electronic cigarettes sold by NJOY and Smoking Everywhere were likewise subject to the Act's provisions.

Second, the *Brown & Williamson* Court gleaned from a handful of federal statutes that Congress had reserved tobacco authority for itself and did not intend for FDA to regulate cigarettes. In *Sottera*, FDA argued that *Brown & Williamson* did not apply to electronic cigarettes because, unlike conventional cigarettes, electronic cigarettes were not subject to any of the federal statutes cited in the Supreme Court case as Congress's intent to preclude FDA oversight in the area of tobacco control.... Third, FDA argued that the newly enacted Tobacco Control Act did not limit its ability to regulate electronic cigarettes or other drug-device products under the FDCA. While the Tobacco Control Act granted FDA new authority over any product derived from tobacco, the statute expressly excluded any drug, device or combination product regulated under the FDCA. According to FDA, since electronic cigarettes "fit" the drug-device statutory definition FDA was authorized to regulate these products under its preexisting FDCA authority.

NJOY opposed FDA's action on nearly identical grounds as the cigarette manufacturers in *Brown & Williamson*. The company argued that (1) electronic cigarettes are tobacco products and (2) the FDCA does not grant FDA authority to regulate tobacco products absent therapeutic claims (i.e. as customarily marketed). First, the Tobacco Control Act defines "tobacco product" as "any product made or derived from tobacco," which even FDA conceded encompasses electronic cigarettes like those sold by NJOY that contain nicotine derived from tobacco. Second, NJOY asserted that in passing the Tobacco Control Act Congress ratified the *Brown & Williamson* decision that FDA lacked jurisdiction over tobacco products under the FDCA. Given that Congress enacted specific legislation to regulate "any product made or derived from tobacco," the company argued that their products, which are derived from tobacco, could only be regulated under the Tobacco Control Act.

In its decision the Court of Appeals admitted that *Brown & Williamson* was not "crystal clear," but ultimately sided with NJOY holding that electronic cigarettes fit into the definition of "tobacco product" under the Tobacco Control Act and Congress did not intend for tobacco products to be regulated as drug/devices absent a therapeutic claim. Rather than appeal the decision, FDA elected to regulate NJOY and other ENDS products under its tobacco control authority through the "deeming rule" process outlined in the Tobacco Control Act.

* * *

The Tobacco Control Act grants FDA immediate authority to regulate cigarettes, cigarette tobacco, smokeless tobacco, and roll-your-own tobacco, and contains specific prohibitions on the advertising and sale of these products. The Act does not expressly regulate other tobacco products such as cigars, pipe tobacco, hookah, or ENDS, but FDA may promulgate regulations governing any product derived from tobacco. In order to extend agency oversight to include other tobacco products such as ENDS, FDA must first issue regulations "deeming" the product as subject to its tobacco regulatory authority. Once deemed, the agency may regulate the manufacturing, distribution, marketing, and sale of any tobacco product.

On April 25, 2014, nearly five years after the Tobacco Control Act was enacted, FDA published the proposed Deeming Rule in the *Federal Register*. The proposed rule extended agency jurisdiction to all other present and future products derived from tobacco, specifically including ENDS, cigars, pipe tobacco, nicotine gels, waterpipe/hookah tobacco, and dissolvable tobacco products. More than 135,000 comments were filed in response to the draft rule. FDA reviewed each submission, as required by statute, prior to submitting the final rule to the White House Office of Management and Budget (OMB) for approval. OMB approval resulted in the removal of several proposed regulations including the banning of flavors and premarket approval for ENDS. The final rule was published more than two years later, on May 10, 2016, with an effective date of August 8, 2016, although many provisions governing ENDS manufacturers have later effective dates.

The Deeming Rule is a foundational rule that authorizes FDA to regulate all products derived from tobacco. The rule also triggers specific requirements and restrictions for tobacco manufacturers and retailers. All newly deemed tobacco product manufacturers must register with the FDA and report product and ingredient listings; only market new products after FDA review; not make reduced risk claims without scientific data and FDA approval; not distribute free samples; and pay user fees. In addition, retailers may not sell tobacco products to individuals under 18 years of age and must check ID for anyone appearing to be under 27 years of age; vending machine sales are prohibited except in adult-only facilities.

In the Deeming Rule, FDA also clarified that all ENDS products are subject to the Tobacco Control Act and that most provisions regulating cigarettes, smokeless tobacco, and roll-your-own tobacco will extend to these products, including premarket approval. Under the Act, manufacturers of new tobacco products must secure FDA authorization prior to marketing their product. The agency will consider several factors in determining whether a product is new and therefore subject to the premarket approval process, but the most important is whether a "substantially equivalent" tobacco product was commercially available on or before February 15, 2007. This issue is critical for ENDS manufacturers because there is uncertainty as to whether any electronic devices containing liquid nicotine were on the U.S. market by this date. Without a substantially equivalent product, ENDS manufacturers must undergo the lengthy, costly, and uncertain premarket tobacco application process.

... Several lawsuits have been filed challenging FDA's decision to subject ENDS to the premarket approval process. In addition, Congress could step-in and alter the substantial equivalence date to accommodate ENDS manufacturers or otherwise exempt the devices from premarket approval. The regulatory landscape post-deeming remains uncertain for ENDS, but the devices are expected to stay on the market until FDA and the industry determine the appropriate pathway to regulation.

FDA can and will adopt additional rules in the future regulating the newly deemed tobacco products, including ENDS. These rules could restrict ingredients or limit concentrations, restrict online sales, ban flavored products or self-service displays (both of which currently apply to cigarettes), or limit advertising and promotion. The Deeming Rule represents the beginning, not the end, of ENDS regulation. FDA may enact, and is expected to pursue, a wide variety of provisions not specified in the Deeming Rule in order to protect public health.

With this background on U.S. regulation of tobacco, you can consider how other legal systems have handled similar issues. As you read, consider where there are reasons unique to these countries that either helps or hinders their efforts to crack down on smoking?

Leslie Zellers, *Global Tobacco Control: What the U.S. Can Learn from Other Countries*

Tobacco Control Legal Consortium (2013)

In 2005, the world's first public health treaty—the Framework Convention on Tobacco Control (FCTC)—was adopted. The FCTC was negotiated under the World Health Organization (WHO) and to date more than 170 countries have become parties. Although the United States signed the treaty in 2004, it has never ratified the FCTC and is not bound by its terms. The FCTC provides an internationally coordinated response to the tobacco epidemic and includes more than a dozen articles specifying both demand reduction and supply reduction strategies such as creating smoke-free places, requiring prominent health warnings on tobacco packages, and increasing tobacco taxes to reduce consumption. Although this publication references the Framework Convention's provisions when relevant, it is not limited to strategies required by the FCTC.

* * *

The following ten tobacco control strategies include four of the World Health Organization's package of six proven tobacco control demand reduction strategies known as MPOWER: Monitor tobacco use and prevention policies; Protect people from tobacco smoke; Offer help to quit tobacco use; Warn about the dangers of tobacco; Enforce bans on tobacco advertising, promotion, and sponsorship; and Raise taxes on tobacco.

* * *

As part of the 2009 Family Smoking Prevention and Tobacco Control Act ("Tobacco Control Act"), the United States finally mandated that graphic health warnings replace the U.S. Surgeon General's textual warnings, which had appeared on tobacco packages since 1984. Unfortunately, due to a series of court challenges, these graphic warnings have yet to be implemented. The U.S. can learn from the experiences of other countries that require graphic health warnings that are larger and indeed more graphic than those originally proposed by the U.S. Food and Drug Administration.

Article 11 of the FCTC requires that package health warnings cover at least 30% (and preferably 50% or more), on average, of the package's front and back. The use of pictures is optional. However, the WHO considers the most effective graphic warnings to cover at least 50% of the principal display area of the pack, to include seven specific warning criteria, and to prohibit the use of deceitful terms.

* * *

The number of countries adopting picture-based health warnings for tobacco packages is rising rapidly, with approximately 50 countries mandating pictorial warnings. According to the WHO, as of 2010, 19 countries (representing 15% of the world's population), meet the best practices for graphic health warnings, including the United States, even though the U.S. has not yet implemented these graphic warnings. People in high- and middle-income countries are more likely to be protected by strong warning labels.

Currently, Uruguay has the largest overall warning requirements, with 80% of the packaging covered. Australia requires 75% of the front of the pack and 90% of the back covered (resulting in an 82.5% coverage). Thailand is set to increase the size of its graphic warnings to 85% of packs in late 2013. Sri Lanka is also planning to implement 80% warnings, pending regulations. Canada, which was the first country in the world to require color package warnings, has strengthened its law from 50% to 75% coverage of the pack.

Some countries, such as Argentina and Canada, require a toll-free number for smoking cessation help along with the color package warnings. Ecuador's new pictorial health warnings law also requires information about toxic emissions on 70% of a one-side panel. A number of websites reproduce actual pictorial graphic warnings. Thailand's are particularly explicit.

* * *

Large pictorial health warnings have a broad reach and have been shown to be effective in communicating the risks of tobacco use to smokers and non-smokers. Data from a variety of studies found that more smokers reported getting information about the risks of smoking from cigarette packages than from any other source except television. Picture-based warnings are especially important in developing countries where there are higher rates of illiteracy and low literacy.

Additionally, effective warnings have been associated with reduced tobacco consumption, an increased likelihood of quitting, increased use of cessation services, and long-term abstinence among former smokers. Large graphic warnings also may discourage youth from smoking. For example, a study of Singapore's graphic health warnings found that, because of the warnings, 28% of the smokers surveyed reported smoking fewer cigarettes; 14% said that they tried to avoid smoking in front of children; and 8% said that they smoked less at home. To be effective, warnings should be large, feature graphic images (such as depictions of disease), and be rotated. Text warnings, such as those currently used by the United States, are significantly less effective than large warnings with pictures.

* * *

Even in countries with large graphic warnings, the industry continues to have influence through its brand imagery on the package. The next step in reducing the impact of the tobacco package itself is to remove tobacco logos, brands, and colors from the packaging, leaving only a "plain" package with the name of the product (brand) and the health warnings.

* * *

The first country to adopt plain packaging requirements was Australia, whose law took effect December 1, 2012. New Zealand has announced its intention to follow

Australia by introducing a similar law, although it will delay implementation until Australia's legal issues are resolved (see below). Ireland has announced it will become the first European Union country to tackle the issue. France, India, South Africa, the United Kingdom, and the European Union are also considering stricter packaging laws for tobacco products.

* * *

Article 13 of the FCTC requires parties to undertake a "comprehensive ban of all tobacco advertising, promotion, and sponsorship." The theme for the 2013 World No Tobacco Day was to ban tobacco advertising, promotion, and sponsorship. Enforcing bans on advertising, promotion, and sponsorship is part of the WHO's MPOWER package of six proven policies (the "E" standing for Enforce).

* * *

As of 2010, 19 countries with 425 million people, representing 6% of the world's population, had comprehensive laws to fully prevent tobacco industry marketing tactics. An additional 101 countries prohibit national television, radio and print tobacco advertising, as well as some but not all other forms of direct and/or indirect advertising. Only 7 of the 19 countries with comprehensive advertising prohibitions were rated as having "complete" enforcement.

The WHO best practice is to prohibit all forms of "direct" and "indirect" advertising. Direct advertising is defined by the WHO as advertising on national television and radio; local magazine and newspapers; billboards and outdoor advertising; and point of sale. Indirect advertising is defined by the WHO as the free distribution of tobacco products in the mail or through other means; promotional discounts; non-tobacco goods and services identified with tobacco brand names (brand extension); brand names of nontobacco products used for tobacco products; appearance of tobacco products in television and/or films; and sponsored events.

Other strong laws (which include prohibiting some but not all indirect advertising) can be found in Australia, Singapore, New Zealand, and most of Western Europe. In comparison, the U.S. was rated at the lowest level, indicating the complete absence of a ban or a ban that does not cover national television, radio, and print media.

In 2008, Panama became the first country in the Americas to prohibit all advertising, promotion and sponsorship of tobacco products. The law completely prohibits all forms of direct or indirect tobacco advertising and promotion, including product placement in television and movies, and promotional price discounting.

Turkey has a law prohibiting nearly all tobacco advertising, promotion and sponsorship. The law contains a few exceptions, such as for internet sales by authorized dealers and for point-of-sale advertising which cannot be seen or accessed by minors. In 2012, Turkey amended its laws to limit "brand stretching" (where a tobacco brand is connected with a non-tobacco product) and "brand sharing" (where a non-tobacco product brand is connected with a tobacco product.)

The WHO considers sponsorship of events by tobacco companies to be a form of indirect advertising. A European Union directive prohibited the display of tobacco advertising in motor racing and other sports in 2005. Despite this directive, Marlboro has continued to sponsor a Formula 1 team, using red colors and barcode designs to evoke its brand. Tobacco sponsorship remains a problem at other events. In Indonesia, tobacco control advocates enlisted the media as active partners creating negative publicity, which helped tobacco sponsorship to be withdrawn for concerts by singers such as Alicia Keys and Kelly Clarkson.

When tobacco sponsorship of sports and other events is prohibited, tobacco companies often still participate in corporate social responsibility (CSR) programs to promote their organizations. CSR campaigns can take the form of scholarships, donations to nonprofits, or event sponsorship in the corporate versus the brand name. Article 5.3 of the FCTC encourages countries to regulate CSR campaigns and some countries have done so. For example, Mauritius and Namibia have prohibited tobacco industry CSR campaigns by law. Other countries, like Vietnam, have restricted CSR activities to certain causes, such as hunger eradication, poverty reduction, and the prevention and control of natural disasters. Vietnam's law also prohibits publicizing these campaign contributions in the media.

* * *

Article 13 of the FCTC includes point-of-sale promotion among its best practices on advertising bans, including prohibitions of all tobacco advertising, promotion, and sponsorship at the point of sale, as well as the display of tobacco products at the point of sale.

* * *

More than 50 countries completely prohibit advertising at the point of sale, including Ireland, New Zealand, Norway, Spain, Thailand, Turkey, and Venezuela. In Norway, retailers may place a sign saying that tobacco products are sold on the premises. New Zealand allows for a single price list.

Countries such as Australia, Brazil, and Canada partially limit tobacco promotions at the point of sale. For example, a number of states in Australia prohibit point-of-sale advertising and limit the display of tobacco packs to no more than one packet of each product line. Some countries, such as Canada and Ireland, prohibit the advertising and promotion of tobacco products except in stores that sell tobacco only and/or don't allow minors.

Fewer than 10 countries have passed laws to prohibit visible pack displays. Ireland's display prohibition includes the label, container, wrapper or package used for the product. Thailand prohibits tobacco product displays at the point of sale except for duty-free shops for people leaving the country.

* * *

There is no safe level of exposure to secondhand tobacco smoke. More than 600,000 people die each year due to exposure from secondhand smoke. When smoke-free areas are created, levels of smoke exposure are more than 90% lower than in areas where smoking is permitted.

Article 8 of the FCTC requires parties to adopt and implement measures to provide "protection from exposure to tobacco smoke in indoor workplaces, public transport, indoor public places and, as appropriate, other public places." Protecting people from tobacco smoke is also one of the WHO's set of six proven tobacco control policies known as MPOWER (the "P" stands for Protect People from Tobacco Smoke).

* * *

According to the WHO, 31 countries have comprehensive smoke-free laws as of 2010, which it defines as all public places completely smoke-free or at least 90% of the population covered by complete state or local smoke-free laws. Visitors and residents of these countries can enjoy smoke-free bars, restaurants, and pubs. Of these 31 countries, 10 have been rated as having "complete" enforcement. Although the U.S. has many strong state and local smokefree laws, as a country the U.S. is ranked in the lowest category with only two or more public places required by law to be smoke-free out of eight categories: health-care facilities; universities; educational facilities other than universities; government facilities; indoor offices and workplaces; restaurants or facilities that serve mostly food; pubs and bars or facilities that serve mostly beverages; and public transport. Other countries with the same ranking include Sweden and Belize. In contrast, Canada is rated as having a comprehensive smoke-free law.

Many of the completely smoke-free countries are in Europe although Latin America has recently had a great deal of success in adopting comprehensive smoke-free laws. In 2004, Ireland was the first country to require smoke-free indoor workplaces, including restaurants, bars, and pubs. Norway and New Zealand followed shortly thereafter with similar laws. In Africa, Uganda and Niger also have comprehensive smoke-free laws. Uruguay was the first Latin American country to pass a law requiring all public places to become smoke-free. The 2006 Uruguay law prohibits smoking in public places and workplaces, including restaurants, bars, and casinos.

Some countries are going beyond traditional smoke-free laws to accommodate recent trends. For example, Turkey has recently prohibited the smoking of hookah in public places.

* * *

Raising the price of tobacco products through tobacco tax increases is one of the most effective tobacco control strategies. An increase in tobacco prices encourages existing smokers to quit or cut down and deters youth from beginning smoking. Higher taxes also increase government revenue, which can be devoted to tobacco control efforts as is done in several U.S. states, such as California.

Raising tobacco taxes is part of Article 6 of the FCTC and is one of the WHO's MPOWER package of six proven policies (the "R" stands for Raise Taxes on Tobacco). The WHO recommends that at least 75% of the retail price of tobacco products come from excise taxes. The World Bank recommends that countries should attain tax rates of at least two-thirds to four-fifths of the retail price of tobacco products.

Best practices in tobacco taxes include: a simple tax structure (rather than imposing different rates based on price or product characteristics), increasing taxes regularly to keep up with inflation and purchasing power, and earmarking a portion of tobacco tax revenues to support public health or tobacco control efforts.

* * *

As of 2010, 26 countries and one territory met the WHO best practices for tobacco taxation, with a tax representing 75% or more of the retail price. For reference, the tax rate in the U.S. is currently 45% of retail price. (This represents only the federal tobacco tax; state tobacco taxes increase this rate.) Many countries have demonstrated success in increasing government revenue and decreasing tobacco use through tax increases. For example:

- Between 1992 and 2011, the price of cigarettes in the United Kingdom increased more than 200%. During the same period, cigarette sales declined 51% and government revenue from tobacco taxes increased 44%. Adult smoking prevalence dropped from 27% in 2000 to 20% in 2010.
- Between 2005 and 2011, the price of cigarettes in Turkey increased by 195%. During the same period, cigarette sales dropped by 15.5% and government revenue increased by 124%. Between 2005 and 2011, revenue from tobacco taxes increased by 124%, even as sales declined.
- In Thailand, tax increases between 1994 and 2007 raised cigarette excise taxes from 60% to 80% of wholesale price, increasing tax revenue from 20,002 million THB in 1994 to 41,528 million THB in 2007 even as consumption decreased.

Some countries use a portion of tobacco taxes to fund public health efforts. For example, a comprehensive tobacco control law in Vietnam created a tobacco control fund as of May 1, 2013. The fund is financed by a 1% levy on the pre-tax excise price of tobacco products; the levy increases in future years. In Thailand, a 2% tax surcharge is devoted to the Thai Health Promotion Foundation, which supports a variety of health promotion programs.

* * *

Some countries have taken a comprehensive approach to tobacco control, adopting multiple effective tobacco control strategies in a single law or in multiple laws over time. The U.S. Centers for Disease Control and Prevention recommends a comprehensive approach to tobacco control, including smoke-free policies, increasing the price of tobacco products, promoting cessation, and limiting minors' access to tobacco. The most comprehensive law passed in the U.S.—the Tobacco Control Act—does not address smoke-free areas.

* * *

A number of countries have adopted and effectively implemented comprehensive tobacco control laws either as individual laws or as a package of laws adopted over time. Six of those countries are highlighted here.

Uruguay: Uruguay has implemented a series of strong measures to reduce tobacco use, including a comprehensive law requiring smoke-free workplaces and public places, which extends to casinos; a prohibition of tobacco advertising, promotion, and sponsorships (except at the point of sale); and a number of tobacco tax increases (taxes currently make up 72% of the retail price of cigarettes). In 2010, Uruguay implemented the world's largest graphic warning labels, which cover 80 percent of the front and back of cigarette packs. Uruguay also prohibited deceptive cigarette labels such as "light" and "low-tar" and became the first country to limit each cigarette brand to a one-pack design.

Thailand: Thailand's law requires smoke-free public places and workplaces with two exemptions: designated smoking areas in international airports and in areas where food and drink is not served for non-air-conditioned facilities serving food and/or drink. Thailand has one of the strongest tobacco marketing laws, including a prohibition of point of-sale-advertising. Both Thailand's smoke-free and advertising laws are strongly enforced. Thailand was an early adopter of graphic health warnings, which are now required on 55% of the front and back of each cigarette package. The tax rate for cigarettes represents 69% of the retail price. The Thai government has announced that it will prohibit the sale of tobacco products to people under 20 years old and prohibit the addition of flavors to cigarettes.

Turkey: Since July 2009 Turkey has outlawed smoking in all cafes, cafeterias, restaurants and bars, and strongly enforces these laws. Turkey has a law prohibiting all tobacco advertisement, promotion and sponsorship. Combined picture and text warnings are required on smoked tobacco products. Turkey has increased its tobacco tax, which is now 78% of the retail price of cigarettes.

Ireland: Ireland was the first country to require smoke-free indoor workplaces and public places, including restaurants, bars, and pubs. Ireland also prohibits advertising and promotion of tobacco products with a few limited exceptions, such as point-of-sale advertising at shops that sell only tobacco. Ireland plans to adopt plain packaging. Compliance with smoke-free and advertising laws is high. Graphic health warnings are required as of February 2013. Tobacco is taxed at 79% of the retail price.

Panama: Panama prohibits smoking in all indoor public places, indoor workplaces, and public transport as well as outdoor sports venues. Panama also has a law prohibiting all forms of tobacco advertising, promotion, and sponsorship, including point-of-sale advertising and pack displays. Enforcement of smoke-free and advertising laws is high. Graphic health warnings must cover 50% of the pack.

New Zealand: Smoking is prohibited in indoor workplaces and public places, with a few exceptions. There is a near comprehensive law prohibiting tobacco advertising and promotion, as well as the display of all tobacco products at points of sale. Both the smoke-free laws and the advertising restrictions have a high level of compliance. Graphic warnings are required on 60% of the principal display areas and the sale of smokeless tobacco products is prohibited.

* * *

Many countries are also regulating the content of tobacco products or at least requiring disclosure of the content. Because of nicotine's addictiveness, researchers support reducing nicotine levels in tobacco products for public health goals. In the U.S., the Food and Drug Administration has the authority to regulate the nicotine levels of tobacco products under the Tobacco Control Act, although the agency has yet to take action.

Articles 9 and 10 of the FCTC address the regulation of the contents and disclosures of tobacco products. These articles require parties to adopt laws or regulations to test the contents and emissions of tobacco products and to disclose the results of the tests on a regular basis. Mandatory reporting for all nicotine and tobacco products should include design components (such as filter ventilation level and paper porosity), tobacco constituents, emissions for combustible products, as well as measures of abuse liability.

A related idea is to prohibit the sale of certain types of tobacco or nicotine products. The U.S. Tobacco Control Act prohibits the use of flavoring in cigarettes but it contains exceptions for menthol and for the use of flavors in other tobacco products such as little cigars and smokeless tobacco.

One of the world leaders in tobacco product regulation is Canada, which requires periodic emissions testing and emissions disclosure based on all characteristics of the tobacco product. Significantly, the Canadian regime requires a more intensive testing regimen than the ISO smoking machine testing protocol (which is not recognized as valid by the WHO since it can be manipulated by tobacco companies).

The European Union sets maximum limits for tar, nicotine, and carbon monoxide yields of cigarettes. This information must be disseminated to consumers, in part by listing the maximum yields for cigarettes on at least 10% of the surface area of the pack. Additionally, the European Union Directive requires the tobacco industry to report annually on the ingredients used in its products.

Singapore and Australia also set limits on tar and nicotine yields. Other countries, such as Canada, Brazil, and Venezuela, require tobacco companies to measure and report cigarette emissions data. Seychelles and Mexico require the tobacco industry to submit information to the government on ingredients and emissions, measures of constituents, etc.

As a related public health strategy, some countries have outlawed the sale of certain types of tobacco or nicotine products. For example, Brazil and Chile made history recently by prohibiting the use of menthol and other flavorings in tobacco products. (Brazil's law is on hold pending resolution of a tobacco industry lawsuit.) New Zealand prohibits the sale of smokeless tobacco. The European Union outlaws the sale of certain forms of smokeless tobacco, such as snus (with an exception for Sweden) and it plans to prohibit the use of menthol and other flavorings in cigarettes.

A number of countries are taking steps to address the proliferation of e-cigarettes. Brazil and Singapore outlaw the sale of e-cigarettes altogether. France is planning to prohibit their use in public places and the U.K. has announced its intention to regulate e-cigarettes as non-prescription medicine, similar to nicotine gum and patches. The European Union plans to classify certain e-cigarettes as medicinal products requiring approval prior to marketing. In the U.S., the FDA has the authority to regulate e-cigarettes as tobacco products but it has yet to do so.

In what is believed to be a world first, a court in India issued an historic order stating that chemical nicotine is a poisonous substance and cannot be used in the two states affected by the ruling. The decision applies to chemical nicotine, which is added to products such as hookah, as opposed to naturally occurring nicotine in tobacco leaves.

Unsurprisingly, aggressive stances towards tobacco regulation are not universally popular. One of the strategies that many countries have used to limit tobacco use is to control tobacco advertising. This has been contentious in the World Trade Organization, which recently heard a dispute between Indonesia and Australia. Indonesia, along with several other countries (and Philip Morris, a multibillion dollar international tobacco company), sued Australia in the WTO, alleging that Australia's plain-packaging laws violated its international obligations under the Technical Barriers to Trade (TBT) Agreement, the General Agreement on Tariffs and Trades (GATT), and the Agreement on Trade-Related Investment Measures (TRIMS). As you read the decision below, ask yourself how we ought to balance one country's economic well-being with another country's domestic public health policies. Did the panel give adequate weight to Australia's health objectives? Too much weight?

Panel Report, *Australia—Certain Measures Concerning Trademarks, Geographical Indications and Other Plain Packaging Requirements Applicable to Tobacco Products and Packaging*

WTO Doc. WT/DS435/R, WT/DS441/R, WT/DS458/R, WT/DS467/R
(adopted June 28, 2018)

2.1 The measures at issue in these proceedings are the following:

a) the *Tobacco Plain Packaging Act 2011* (Cth)164 (TPP Act);

b) the *Tobacco Plain Packaging Regulations 2011* (Cth), as amended by the *Tobacco Plain Packaging Amendment Regulation 2012 (No. 1)* (Cth) (TPP Regulations); and

c) the *Trade Marks Amendment (Tobacco Plain Packaging) Act 2011* (Cth) (TMA Act).

* * *

2.5. The Panel will hereafter use the term "TPP measures" to refer to these instruments taken together.

* * *

2.6. The legislative process that led to the adoption of the TPP measures started in 2008 with the establishment of the National Preventative Health Taskforce (NPHT). The NPHT was responsible for developing a "National Preventive Health Strategy", to "provide a blueprint for tackling the burden of chronic disease currently caused by obesity, tobacco, and excessive consumption of alcohol". A Tobacco Working Group (TWG) was also created. The NPHT published in 2009 a discussion paper, accompanied by a Technical Report by the TWG that recommended a range of measures.

2.7. In September 2009, the NPHT released its final report, entitled *Australia: The Healthiest Country by 2020—National Preventative Health Strategy—The Roadmap for Action*. With respect to tobacco control, this report identified 11 "key action areas": "Make tobacco products significantly more expensive"; "Increase the frequency, reach and intensity of social marketing campaigns"; "End all remaining forms of advertising and promotion of tobacco products" (which included a specific "action" to "Eliminate promotion of tobacco products through design of packaging"); "Eliminate exposure to second-hand smoke in public places"; "Regulate manufacturing and further regulate packaging and supply of tobacco products"; "Ensure all smokers in contact with health services are encouraged and supported to quit ..."; "boost efforts to reduce smoking and exposure to passive smoking among Indigenous Australians"; "Boost efforts to discourage smoking among people in other highly disadvantaged groups"; "Assist parents and educators to discourage tobacco use and protect young people from second-hand smoke"; "Ensure that the public, media, politicians and other opinion leaders remain aware of the need for sustained and vigorous action to discourage tobacco use"; and "Ensure Implementation and measure progress against and towards targets".

2.8. On 29 April 2010, the Australian Government announced four measures to "deliver on [the] recommendations of the [NPHT]", which it identified as a tobacco excise increase of 25%; legislation requiring that "all cigarettes ... be sold in plain packaging by 1 July 2012"; restrictions on Australian internet advertising of tobacco products; and extra expenditure on anti-smoking campaigns. In May 2010, the Australian Government released a response to the NPHT final report, in which it elaborated on these four measures.

2.9. On 7 April 2011, the Australian Government released an Exposure Draft of the Tobacco Plain Packaging Bill 2011 (Cth) (TPP Bill) for public consultations, which lasted until 6 June 2011.182 The TPP Bill and Trade Marks Amendment (Tobacco Plain Packaging) Bill 2011 (Cth) (TMA Bill) were passed by the Parliament in November 2011 and received Royal Assent on 1 December 2011, thus becoming, respectively, the TPP Act and the TMA Act.184 The TPP Regulations were adopted on 7 December 2011 and amended on 8 March 2012.185 As indicated above186, taken together, the TPP Act, the TMA Act and the TPP Regulations form the TPP measures at issue in these disputes.

* * *

2.20. Section 18(1) of the TPP Act provides that the outer and inner surfaces of the retail packaging of all tobacco products must not have any "decorative ridges, embossing, bulges or other irregularities of shape or texture, or any other embellishments" (other than as permitted by the TPP Regulations). Additionally, "any glues or other adhesives used in manufacturing the packaging must be transparent and not coloured". The TPP Regulations set out other specifications for the physical features of tobacco packaging for retail sale211, including requirements for cigarette packs, cigarette cartons, cigar tubes, and any other type of packaging.

2.21. Cigarette packs and cigarette cartons must be rigid and made only of cardboard. When closed, each outer surface of the pack or carton must be rectangular, and the surfaces of the pack or carton must meet at a 90-degree angle. All edges of the pack or carton must be rigid, straight, and not rounded, bevelled, or otherwise shaped or embellished (unless permitted by the TPP Regulations). The dimensions of cigarette packs are determined by the TPP Regulations.

2.22. The opening of a cigarette pack must be a flip-top lid. The inside lip of the cigarette pack must have straight edges, other than the corners which may be rounded, and neither the lip nor the edges of the lip may be rounded, bevelled or otherwise shaped or embellished. Any lining in the pack must be made only of foil backed with paper (unless prescribed by the TPP Regulations).

* * *

2.23. Section 19 of the TPP Act sets out additional requirements for all outer and inner surfaces of certain retail packaging of tobacco products....

* * *

2.24. Section 20 of the TPP Act prohibits the appearance of trademarks and marks anywhere on the retail packaging of tobacco products, with the exception of the brand name, business or company name, variant name, the relevant legislative requirements, and other trademarks and marks permitted by the TPP Regulations....

2.25. Section 21 of the TPP Act, operating together with the TPP Regulations, prescribes the requirements for the manner in which the brand, business, company or variant names for tobacco products may appear on the retail packaging of a tobacco product....

* * *

2.27. With respect to cigar tubes, a brand, business or company name, or variant name, may only appear once, across a single line only, and must not obscure any relevant legislative requirement ...

2.28. Brand, business or company names or variant names may appear on other retail packaging across one line only on each of the front and back outer surfaces (and no others), in the same orientation as, and not above, the health warnings on the surface, and must not obscure any relevant legislative requirement. Variant names on such packages must appear parallel to, in the same orientation as, and immediately below the brand, business or company name.

* * *

7.15. Article 2.2 of the TBT Agreement provides that:

> Members shall ensure that technical regulations are not prepared, adopted or applied with a view to or with the effect of creating unnecessary obstacles to international trade. For this purpose, technical regulations shall not be more trade-restrictive than necessary to fulfil a legitimate objective, taking

> account of the risks non-fulfilment would create. Such legitimate objectives are, *inter alia*: national security requirements; the prevention of deceptive practices; protection of human health or safety, animal or plant life or health, or the environment. In assessing such risks, relevant elements of consideration are, *inter alia*: available scientific and technical information, related processing technology or intended end-uses of products.

7.16. Honduras, the Dominican Republic, Cuba and Indonesia claim that the TPP measures are inconsistent with Article 2.2 because they are "more trade-restrictive than necessary to fulfil a legitimate objective" within the meaning of Article 2.2. Australia considers that some aspects of the TPP measures should not be reviewed under Article 2.2 of the TBT Agreement and, to the extent that they do fall within the purview of this provision, it considers that the complainants have not made a *prima facie* case that they are inconsistent with Article 2.2.

* * *

7.21. Australia accepts that the "physical requirements" under the TPP measures are technical regulations within the scope of the TBT Agreement but expresses "significant concerns" with the "systemic implications" of the complainants' contention that the "trademark requirements" under the TPP measures can also be reviewed under the TBT Agreement. It argues that the TBT Agreement addresses technical regulations and does not, on its face, appear to be concerned with the exploitation of IP. Australia considers that, should the Panel take the view that requirements affecting the use of trademarks can be "technical regulations" within the scope of the TBT Agreement, Article 20 of the TRIPS Agreement would remain "the applicable provision in respect of the trademark requirements imposed by the tobacco plain packaging measure", to the exclusion of Article 2.2 in respect of those requirements.

7.22. Australia further argues that the TPP measures are "in accordance with relevant international standards" for tobacco plain packaging and therefore must be, by virtue of the second sentence of Article 2.5, rebuttably presumed not to be more trade-restrictive than necessary: a presumption, it claims, the complainants did not rebut. As a consequence, Australia claims, the Panel "need not proceed any further with its analysis of the complainants' claims under Article 2.2".

7.23. Australia argues that the complainants have failed to establish that the TPP measures are "trade-restrictive" at all. As a result, even if the Panel concludes that the presumption under Article 2.5 is inapplicable, Australia submits that any further relational analysis with respect to the substance of the claim under Article 2.2 would not be required to examine the inconsistency of the TPP measures, as the complainants have failed to establish a *prima facie* case that they are inconsistent with Article 2.2.

* * *

7.26. We recall that Article 2.2 of the TBT Agreement provides that:

> Members shall ensure that technical regulations are not prepared, adopted or applied with a view to or with the effect of creating unnecessary obstacles to international trade. For this purpose, technical regulations shall not be

> more trade-restrictive than necessary to fulfil a legitimate objective, taking account of the risks non-fulfilment would create. Such legitimate objectives are, *inter alia*: national security requirements; the prevention of deceptive practices; protection of human health or safety, animal or plant life or health, or the environment. In assessing such risks, relevant elements of consideration are, *inter alia*: available scientific and technical information, related processing technology or intended end-uses of products.

7.27. It is undisputed that, in accordance with the applicable rules on burden of proof, the burden of establishing that the TPP measures are inconsistent with Article 2.2 rests on the complainants ...

7.28. Article 2.2 applies to measures that are "technical regulations" within the meaning of the TBT Agreement....

7.30. As described by the Appellate Body, an assessment of whether a technical regulation is "more trade-restrictive than necessary" within the meaning of Article 2.2 involves a number of considerations:

> In sum, we consider that an assessment of whether a technical regulation is "more trade-restrictive than necessary" within the meaning of Article 2.2 of the *TBT Agreement* involves an evaluation of a number of factors. A panel should begin by considering factors that include: (i) the degree of contribution made by the measure to the legitimate objective at issue; (ii) the trade-restrictiveness of the measure; and (iii) the nature of the risks at issue and the gravity of consequences that would arise from non-fulfilment of the objective(s) pursued by the Member through the measure. In most cases, a comparison of the challenged measure and possible alternative measures should be undertaken. In particular, it may be relevant for the purpose of this comparison to consider whether the proposed alternative is less trade restrictive, whether it would make an equivalent contribution to the relevant legitimate objective, taking account of the risks non-fulfilment would create, and whether it is reasonably available.

7.31. An assessment of the consistency of a technical regulation with Article 2.2 thus involves in the first instance a "relational analysis"of three factors:

> i. the degree of contribution made by the measure to the legitimate objective at issue;
>
> ii. the trade-restrictiveness of the measure; and
>
> iii. the nature of the risks at issue and the gravity of consequences that would arise from non-fulfilment of the objective(s) pursued by the Member through the measure.

* * *

7.104. Further, the TBT Agreement needs to be interpreted in light of its preambular objective that "no country should be prevented from taking measures necessary ... for the protection of human ... life or health". By virtue of the same preambular paragraph, this prerogative of Members is "subject to the requirement that [such measures] are not applied in a manner which would constitute a ... disguised restriction on international trade, and are otherwise in accordance with the provisions of th[e TBT] Agreement". Likewise, in setting forth that "Members may, in formulating or amending their laws and regulations, adopt measures necessary to protect public health", Article 8.1 of the TRIPS Agreement makes this conditional on "such measures [being] consistent with the provisions of th[e TRIPS] Agreement".

7.105. Taken in context, therefore, Article 2.2 of the TBT Agreement and Article 20 of the TRIPS Agreement may each be assumed to reflect a certain balance between at least three dimensions: (i) the objective of reducing and avoiding trade barriers; (ii) the possibility of adopting measures for legitimate public policy purposes, including public health; and (iii) the imperative of complying with applicable requirements under the relevant provisions of each agreement. The requirements under these two provisions may thus be seen as complementary rather than contradictory.

* * *

7.140. Turning to the measures at issue, as set out in section 2.1.2, the requirements in the TPP Act and the TPP Regulations, operating in conjunction with other legislative requirements that are not challenged in these proceedings (such as those relating to GHWs), have the cumulative effect of requiring that tobacco products (including their retail packaging) appear in a standardized manner. ... The elements of the TPP measures that prescribe that tobacco products (including their retail packaging) appear in this uniform manner, taken together, constitute the integral and essential aspects of the TPP Act and TPP Regulations. We thus give particular weight to these elements in assessing whether the TPP measures lay down one or more product characteristics.

* * *

7.142. Accordingly, we find that in laying down the requirements for the appearance of tobacco products in this way, the TPP Act and the TPP Regulations, operating together, lay down product characteristics for tobacco products.

7.143. As described in section 2.1.2.3, the TPP Act and the TPP Regulations also set out detailed requirements for the retail *packaging* of tobacco products. Specifically, the "tobacco product requirements" set out in Part 2, Chapter 2 of the TPP Act, and elaborated in the TPP Regulations, govern the packaging of tobacco products. According to the Simplified Outline of Chapter 2704, Part 2 of Chapter 2 "specifies requirements for the retail packaging and appearance of tobacco products", including, in respect of packaging, "the physical features of retail packaging", "the colour and finish of retail packaging", "marks on retail packaging (including a prohibition on trade marks generally appearing on retail packaging)", "wrappers", "retail packaging after retail sale". Accordingly, we find that the TPP Act and the TPP Regulations, operating together, lay down product characteristics by regulating the packaging of tobacco products.

* * *

7.213. In these proceedings, it is undisputed that the objective of the TPP measures relates to public health protection and more specifically to the protection of public health in relation to the use of tobacco products in Australia.

7.214. However, the parties articulate the particular objective pursued by Australia through the TPP measures somewhat differently. As described above, the complainants define the objective pursued by Australia with specific reference to the improvement of public health "by reducing smoking prevalence". Australia considers that a focus exclusively on smoking prevalence would "ignore the causal pathway through which the measures will contribute to their objective". As described above, Australia considers that the objective of the measures, properly defined, is to "reduc[e] smoking rates in Australia by reducing the appeal of tobacco products, increasing the effectiveness of graphic health warnings, and reducing the ability of packages to mislead consumers about the harms of smoking". In the complainants' view, these three aspects constitute "mechanisms" in the operation of the measures, i.e. the means through which the general objectives identified in the TPP Act are intended to be carried out, and cannot properly be characterized as "objectives" of the TPP measures within the meaning of article 2.2 of the TBT Agreement.

7.215. In light of the diverging descriptions by the parties of the objective of the TPP measures, we next consider further how exactly it should be characterized....

* * *

7.246. [We conclude] that the objective pursued by Australia through the TPP measures is the protection of human health, and more precisely the improvement of public health by reducing the use of, and exposure to, tobacco products.

7.247. The "protection of human health or safety" is one of the "legitimate objectives" explicitly identified in Article 2.2. We note in this respect that, in the context of Article XX(b) of the GATT 1994, the preservation of human life and health through the elimination or reduction of well-known and life-threatening health risks (in that instance, as caused by asbestos fibers) was considered to be a value "both vital and important in the highest degree".

7.248. It is undisputed, in these proceedings, that tobacco use and exposure to tobacco smoke cause death and disease, and that the protection of human health from such risks is thus a legitimate public health objective within the meaning of Article 2.2 of the TBT Agreement.

7.249. We also note Honduras's observation that it has itself implemented comprehensive tobacco regulation measures and shares Australia's goal of "reducing smoking prevalence and tobacco consumption". The Dominican Republic considers "the improvement of public health by reducing smoking prevalence" to be a legitimate objective within the meaning of Article 2.2. Cuba also accepts that the objective of reducing smoking prevalence is an entirely legitimate objective and that tobacco consumption and exposure to tobacco smoke cause death and disability. Indonesia also does not dispute that measures to reduce smoking prevalence protect public health and does not challenge the legitimacy of the objective pursued by Australia's TPP measures.

7.250. We further note that "curbing and preventing youth smoking" has already been recognized as a "legitimate health objective" in the context of the TBT Agreement and that the Appellate Body has also, in the context of applying the TBT Agreement, already recognized "the importance of Members' efforts in the World Health Organization on tobacco control". As described above, the "spread of the tobacco epidemic" as "a global problem with serious consequences for public health", and "the devastating worldwide health ... consequences of tobacco consumption and exposure to tobacco smoke" have been expressly recognized by the FCTC. As also described above, the very objective of the FCTC, an international convention with 180 parties (the vast majority of which are also WTO Members), is to provide "a framework for tobacco control measures to be implemented by the Parties at the national, regional and international levels in order to reduce continually and substantially the prevalence of tobacco use and exposure to tobacco smoke".

7.251. It is clear, in light of the above, that the improvement of public health by reducing the use of, and exposure to, tobacco products is a "legitimate objective" within the meaning of Article 2.2 of the TBT Agreement.

* * *

7.419. Having determined that the objective pursued by the TPP measures is to improve public health by reducing the use of, and exposure to, tobacco products and that this is a legitimate objective within the meaning of Article 2.2 of the TBT Agreement, we must now conduct a relational analysis of different factors, including the degree to which the TPP measures contribute to this objective, the extent to which they are trade-restrictive, and the nature of the risks of non-fulfilment of the objective pursued and the gravity of the consequences that would arise from such non-fulfilment.

7.420. We note that no particular order is *a priori* required in all cases in considering the three aforementioned factors of the "relational analysis". However, in the circumstances of this case, we find it appropriate to consider first the degree of contribution of the TPP measures to their objective, to the extent that there may be a correlation between the extent to which the measures contribute to this objective and their trade-restrictiveness. In this respect, without prejudice to our later analysis of this question, we note Australia's observation that the TPP measures will result in a limiting effect on overall trade in tobacco products because "(i) the measure will reduce the use of tobacco products (by discouraging uptake and relapse and encouraging quitting); and (ii) since imports will soon represent the entirety of Australia's tobacco product market, with domestic production being phased out, a reduction in the use of tobacco products will necessarily limit overall trade in tobacco products".

* * *

7.422. These various factors will inform our further assessment, as relevant, of whether the complainants have shown that there are *less* trade-restrictive alternative measures reasonably available to Australia, that would achieve an equivalent contribution to its objective, such that the TPP measures would be *more* trade-restrictive than necessary within the meaning of Article 2.2.

* * *

7.450. Australia responds that, by removing "one of the last remaining frontiers for tobacco advertising in Australia" through the introduction of tobacco plain packaging, it "sought to sever the link between tobacco product packaging and tobacco smoking behaviour, particularly for youth". As acknowledged by the tobacco industry, and evidenced in marketing and public health science, left unregulated, tobacco product packaging can perform the same function as other forms of marketing and promotion, including advertising, especially in a dark market like Australia. Branding, packaging innovation, and design elements influence consumer behaviour by producing positive perceptions of the brand and tobacco products. Youth can be motivated to begin smoking by tobacco packaging that communicates that the brand will fulfil important psychological needs, which outweigh any consideration of the potential risks. Similarly, branded packaging can serve as a cue for maintaining tobacco use for smokers and those who have quit but are at risk of relapse. Packaging thus functions as a form of advertising which influences initiation, cessation, and relapse behaviours, thereby increasing overall demand for tobacco products.

7.451. Australia argues that "TPP fulfils its objectives" by way of a "mediational" model, or "causal chain", whereby the TPP measures improve public health by impacting the three mechanisms identified in the TPP Act. There is "strong empirical evidence" that each of the mechanisms will contribute to Australia's overall objective of protecting human health. Namely, plain packaging decreases the appeal of tobacco products by (i) reducing the attractiveness of tobacco packaging; (ii) reducing positive perceptions of taste; and (iii) reducing positive perceptions of smokers. Plain packaging also increases the effectiveness of health warnings by minimizing distractions of pack design and elements that suppress risk perception, as indicated by studies demonstrating (a) increases in visual attention paid to the warnings; and (b) increases in health warning recall and perceptions about the warnings' believability and seriousness. Both directly and via each mechanism, the TPP measures affect consumer intentions and behaviour with respect to smoking.

7.452. Australia adds that the evidence supporting tobacco plain packaging is extensive, comprehensive, and reliable, and the complainants' critiques fail to consider its "overwhelming weight" and "convergent nature". The complainants instead exaggerate the studies' limitations and ignore their strengths, among other errors. The most appropriate approach to discerning the effects of the TPP measures in the early stages of its introduction was to rely upon experiments and surveys which consider drivers of choice, attitudes and, ultimately, the elicitation of behavioural intentions, one of the strongest predictors of future behaviour. The complainants' dismissal of this evidence is mistaken, as non-behavioural variables are commonly relied on in consumer, psychology, and marketing research journals and textbooks, and are considered strong predictors of behaviour in tobacco control. Further, empirical evidence demonstrates the effect of the TPP measures on smoking-related behaviour, as the complainants necessarily concede as a consequence of their argument that the TPP measures have reduced consumers' willingness to pay for certain tobacco products.

7.453. The principal basis on which the complainants argue that the TPP measures are not capable of contributing to their objective is their contention that the quantitative evidence does not indicate discernible reductions in smoking prevalence and tobacco consumption in Australia. The complainants have failed to establish that tobacco plain packaging will increase tobacco consumption, or that prevalence and consumption have not declined since the introduction of tobacco plain packaging. Australia considers the complainants' empirical post-implementation evidence on prevalence and consumption to be fundamentally flawed, and submits that the post-implementation data indicates that the TPP measures have resulted in discernible reductions in prevalence and consumption.

* * *

7.1129. Australia argues that "none of the complainants have discharged [their] burden in relation to their four overarching claims of trade-restrictiveness", which Australia characterizes as being that the TPP measures are trade-restrictive because of their alleged effects on brand differentiation and downtrading; that the TPP measures are trade-restrictive because they raise barriers to entry for the Australian tobacco market; that the TPP measures are trade-restrictive because they result in increased compliance costs; and that the TPP measures are trade-restrictive because the mandatory requirements they impose operate as a condition for the importation of tobacco products into Australia.

* * *

7.1163. As described above, the complainants generally argue that the TPP measures restrict their competitive opportunities by affecting the ability of tobacco manufacturers to distinguish their products, and compete on the Australian market, on the basis of brands, thereby "eliminating competitive opportunities" and, in Indonesia's words, "fundamentally restructur[ing] the competitive conditions of the Australian cigarette market".

* * *

7.1255. On the basis of the foregoing, we conclude that the TPP measures are trade-restrictive, insofar as, by reducing the use of tobacco products, they reduce the volume of imported tobacco products on the Australian market, and thereby have a "limiting effect" on trade. We also conclude that, while it is plausible that the measures may also, over time, affect the overall value of tobacco imports, the evidence before us does not show this to have been the case to date. We are also not persuaded that the complainants have demonstrated that the TPP measures impose conditions on the sale of tobacco products in Australia or compliance costs of such magnitude that they would amount to a limiting effect on trade.

* * *

7.1324. As observed above, whether a technical regulation is "*more* trade-restrictive than necessary" within the meaning of the second sentence of Article 2.2 of the TBT Agreement, and thereby creates an "unnecessary obstacle[] to international trade" within the meaning of the first sentence, may be established on the basis of a "comparative analysis" of the challenged measure and possible alternative measures that may be reasonably available *and* less trade-restrictive than the challenged measure, taking account of the risks non-fulfilment would create.

7.1325. Having determined above that the TPP measures contribute to their objective and are also trade-restrictive, we now consider whether, as the complainants argue, certain *less* trade-restrictive alternative measures would be reasonably available to Australia to achieve an equivalent contribution to its objective, taking account of the risks that non-fulfilment of the objective would create.

* * *

[The panel went on to conclude that none of the proposed alternative measures, such as increased taxation alone, would serve as adequate substitutes or would be, in effect, any less trade-restrictive.]

* * *

7.1725. In our assessment of the complainants' claims under Article 2.2 of the TBT Agreement, we reached the following conclusions in respect of the various relevant factors:

a. The objective of the TPP measures is to improve public health by reducing the use of, and exposure to, tobacco products.

b. The TPP measures are apt to, and do, make a meaningful contribution to this objective;

c. The TPP measures are trade-restrictive, to the extent that they result in a reduction in the total volume of imports; and

d. The nature of the risks that would arise from the non-fulfilment of Australia's objective is that public health would not be improved, as the use of, or exposure to, tobacco products, would not be reduced, and the consequences of such use, and exposure, are particularly grave.

7.1726. We have also considered each of the four alternative measures proposed by the complainants, and determined, in respect of each of these, that the complainants have not demonstrated that it would constitute a less trade-restrictive alternative measure that would make an equivalent contribution to Australia's objective, as a substitute for the TPP measures.

* * *

7.1729. Specifically, we are mindful that the TPP measures are, by their design, not intended to operate as a stand-alone policy, but rather were implemented as part of "a comprehensive suite of reforms to reduce smoking and its harmful effects" in Australia. In our view, taking due account of this broader regulatory context of the TPP measures is essential to our understanding of their degree of contribution to Australia's objective. We have thus given due weight in our analysis to the fact that the TPP measures operate in conjunction with a number of other wide-ranging tobacco control measures.

* * *

7.1731. The fact that a proposed alternative measure need not contribute to the objective to a degree that is identical to the measure at issue does not, in our view, imply that, where the concern being addressed is of a multifaceted nature and legitimately involves a multidimensional response, one aspect of a comprehensive strategy could be substituted for another, where this would leave unaddressed the aspect of the problem that the challenged measures seek to address. We have found that, in the particular context of tobacco control and the regulatory efforts of Australia to improve public health by reducing the use of, and exposure to, tobacco products, none of the alternatives proposed by complainants would contribute to Australia's objective to an equivalent degree as the TPP measures, taking into account the risks non-fulfilment of the objective would create and the actual contribution made by the challenged measures as well as the principle reflected in the sixth recital of the TBT Agreement, that no Member should be prevented from pursuing legitimate objectives "at the levels it considers appropriate".

7.1732. Overall, on the basis of the above, we conclude that the complainants have not demonstrated that the TPP measures are more trade-restrictive than necessary to fulfil a legitimate objective, within the meaning of Article 2.2 of the TBT Agreement.

* * *

In addition to the international dimension, advertising restrictions also create freedom of expression problems at home. When reading the following case from the Canadian Supreme Court, pay attention to the way it relies on legal materials from other legal systems as well.

RJR-MacDonald Inc. v. Canada

[1995] 3 S.C.R. 199, 127 D.L.R. (4th) 1
Supreme Court of Canada (1995)

* * *

The following is the judgment delivered by *McLachlin J.*:

At issue in these cases is the validity of the *Tobacco Products Control Act*, S.C. 1988, c. 20 (the "Act"), a law which imposes a ban on all advertising of tobacco products in the Canadian media and requires tobacco manufacturers to print unattributed health warnings on the packages of all tobacco products [i.e. warnings not attributed to a government official or agency].

* * *

The second issue is whether the ban and warning requirements violate the *Canadian Charter of Rights and Freedoms*. The *Charter* guarantees free expression, a guarantee which has been held to extend to commercial speech such as advertising * * *. [T]he prohibition on advertising and promotion of tobacco products constitutes a violation of the right to free expression * * * I take the view that s. 9 of the Act, which requires tobacco manufacturers to place an unattributed health warning on tobacco packages, also infringes the right of free expression. * * *

The only remaining question is whether these infringements of the right of free expression are saved under s. 1 of the *Charter*, as being reasonable and "demonstrably justified in a free and democratic society". * * * I share the trial judge's view that the Attorney General of Canada has failed to establish justification under s. 1 for ss. 4, 8 and 9 of the Act, those provisions which impose a total advertising ban, prohibit trade mark usage on articles other than tobacco products and mandate the use of unattributed health warnings on tobacco packaging.

* * * The ultimate issue [under section 1] is whether the infringement is reasonable and "demonstrably justified in a free and democratic society". The jurisprudence laying down the dual considerations of importance of objective and proportionality between the good which may be achieved by the law and the infringement of rights it works, may be seen as articulating the factors which must be considered in determining whether a law that violates constitutional rights is nevertheless "reasonable" and "demonstrably justified". If the objective of a law which limits constitutional rights lacks sufficient importance, the infringement cannot be reasonable or justified. Similarly, if the good which may be achieved by the law pales beside the seriousness of the infringement of rights which it works, that law cannot be considered reasonable or justified. * * *

First, to be saved under s. 1 the party defending the law (here the Attorney General of Canada) must show that the law which violates the right or freedom guaranteed by the *Charter* is "reasonable". In other words, the infringing measure must be justifiable by the processes of reason and rationality. The question is not whether the measure is popular or accords with the current public opinion polls. The question is rather whether it can be justified by application of the processes of reason. * * *.

Second, to meet its burden under s. 1 of the *Charter*, the state must show that the violative law is "demonstrably justified". The choice of the word "demonstrably" is critical. The process is not one of mere intuition, nor is it one of deference to Parliament's choice. It is a process of *demonstration*. * * *

The bottom line is this. While remaining sensitive to the social and political context of the impugned law and allowing for difficulties of proof inherent in that context, the courts must nevertheless insist that before the state can override constitutional rights, there be a reasoned demonstration of the good which the law may achieve in relation to the seriousness of the infringement. * * *

The factors generally relevant to determining whether a violative law is reasonable and demonstrably justified in a free and democratic society remain those set out in *Oakes*. The first requirement is that the objective of the law limiting the *Charter* right or freedom must be of sufficient importance to warrant overriding it. The second is that the means chosen to achieve the objective must be proportional to the objective and the effect of the law—proportionate, in short, to the good which it may produce. Three matters are considered in determining proportionality: the measures chosen must be rationally connected to the objective; they must impair the guaranteed right or freedom as little as reasonably possible (minimal impairment); and there must be overall proportionality between the deleterious effects of the measures and the salutary effects of the law.

* * *

The question at this stage is whether the objective of the infringing measure is sufficiently important to be capable in principle of justifying a limitation on the rights and freedoms guaranteed by the constitution. Given the importance of the *Charter* guarantees, this is not easily done. To meet the test, the objective must be one of pressing and substantial importance.

* * * The objective of the advertising ban and trade mark usage restrictions must be to prevent people in Canada from being persuaded by advertising and promotion to use tobacco products. The objective of the mandatory package warning must be to discourage people who see the package from tobacco use. Both constitute important objectives, although the significance of the targeted decrease in consumption is reduced by the government's estimate that despite the ban, 65 percent of the Canadian magazine market will contain tobacco advertisements, given that the ban applies only to Canadian media and not to imported publications.

* * * The critical question is not the evil tobacco works generally in our society, but the evil which the legislation addresses.

While the limited objective of reducing tobacco-associated health risks by reducing advertising-related consumption and providing warnings of dangers is less significant than the broad objective of protecting Canadians generally from the risks associated with tobacco use, it nevertheless constitutes an objective of sufficient importance to justify overriding the right of free expression guaranteed by the *Charter*. Even a small reduction in tobacco use may work a significant benefit to the health of Canadians and justify a properly proportioned limitation of right of free expression.

* * *

As a first step in the proportionality analysis, the government must demonstrate that the infringements of the right of free expression worked by the law are rationally connected to the legislative goal of reducing tobacco consumption. * * *

The trial judge in the cases at bar found that the government had not established a rational connection between the advertising ban and unattributed warnings and a reduction in tobacco use in the first, scientific sense. The only direct or scientific evidence offered of the link between advertising bans and smoking reduction consisted of a report of the New Zealand Toxic Substances Board entitled *Health or Tobacco: An End to Tobacco Advertising and Promotion* (1989), which reviewed the effect of advertising restrictions in 33 countries and concluded that there was a correlation between the degree of restrictions imposed in each country and decline in tobacco use. * * * The trial judge, after lengthy consideration, rejected this evidence. The report was found to contain serious methodological errors which rendered it "for all intents and purposes devoid of any probative value". * * *

The question is whether this evidence establishes that it is reasonable or logical to conclude that there is a causal link between tobacco advertising and unattributed health warnings and tobacco use. * * * Why would tobacco companies spend great sums on advertising if not to increase the consumption of tobacco, it asks?

To this the tobacco companies reply that their advertising is directed not at increasing the size of the total market but at obtaining a larger share of the existing market. The evidence indicates that one of the thrusts of the advertising programs of tobacco companies is securing a larger market share, but there is also evidence suggesting that advertising is used to increase the total market. * * *

On the other hand, there does not appear to be any causal connection between the objective of decreasing tobacco consumption and the absolute prohibition on the use of a tobacco trade mark on articles other than tobacco products which is mandated by s. 8 of the Act. * * * I find that s. 8 of the Act fails the rational connection test.

As the second step in the proportionality analysis, the government must show that the measures at issue impair the right of free expression as little as reasonably possible in order to achieve the legislative objective. * * *

* * *

I turn first to the prohibition on advertising contained in s. 4 of the Act. It is, as has been observed, complete. It bans all forms of advertising of Canadian tobacco products while explicitly exempting all foreign advertising of non-Canadian products which are sold in Canada. * * * Smoking is a legal activity yet consumers are deprived of an important means of learning about product availability to suit their preferences and to compare brand content with an aim to reducing the risk to their health.

* * * A full prohibition will only be constitutionally acceptable under the minimal impairment stage of the analysis where the government can show that only a full prohibition will enable it to achieve its objective. Where, as here, no evidence is adduced to show that a partial ban would be less effective than a total ban, the justification required by s. 1 to save the violation of free speech is not established.

* * * The government had before it a variety of less intrusive measures when it enacted the total ban on advertising, including: a partial ban which would allow information and brand preference advertising; a ban on lifestyle advertising only; measures such as those in Quebec's *Consumer Protection Act*, R.S.Q., c. P-40.1, to prohibit advertising aimed at children and adolescents; and labelling requirements only. * * *

* * * The government presented no evidence in defence of the total ban, no evidence comparing its effects to less invasive bans.

* * *

I have found ss. 4, 8 and 9 of the *Tobacco Products Control Act* constitute unjustified infringements on free expression. These provisions spearhead the scheme under the Act and cannot be severed cleanly from other provisions dealing with promotion and trade mark usage, ss. 5 and 6. I would consequently hold that ss. 4, 5, 6, 8, and 9 are inconsistent with the *Charter* and hence are of no force or effect by reason of s. 52 of the *Constitution Act, 1982.*

The reasons of La Forest, L'Heureux-Dube and Gonthier JJ. were delivered by *La Forest J.* (dissenting) [In the original the dissent precedes the majority opinion. The dissenting justices set out at length and in detail evidence from Canadian and international sources documenting the health hazards of tobacco].

* * *

It must be kept in mind that the very nature of tobacco consumption makes government action problematic. Many scientists agree that the nicotine found in tobacco is a powerfully addictive drug. * * * Given the addictive nature of tobacco products, and the fact that over one-third of Canadians smoke, it is clear that a legislative prohibition on the sale and use of tobacco products would be highly impractical. Indeed a prohibition on the manufacture and sale of tobacco products would likely lead many smokers to resort to alternative, and illegal, sources of supply. As legislators in this country discovered earlier in the century, the prohibition of a social drug such as tobacco or alcohol leads almost inevitably to an increase in smuggling and crime.

However, the mere fact that it is not practical or realistic to implement a prohibition on the use or manufacture of tobacco products does not mean that Parliament cannot, or should not, resort to other intermediate policy options. * * * If we are stopping short of actually banning the sale of this hazardous product, what steps are we prepared to take to cut down on its use over the next number of years? Certainly, a ban on tobacco advertising is one strategy which is supportable in the move to cut down on the consumption of tobacco.

* * *

While it is clear that cigarette sales cannot be banned at this time, it is equally clear that the production, distribution and sale of cigarettes should no longer be considered in the same light as the production, distribution and sale of other products. It seems reasonable to introduce whatever steps are feasible to progressively eliminate the promotion of cigarette sales and preparations should be made to assist growers and others affected by reductions in cigarette sales. It is also desirable to increase educational efforts to discourage cigarette smoking and to expand activities to make cigarette smoking less hazardous for those who continue to smoke.

* * *

* * * [I]t is difficult to believe that Canadian tobacco companies would spend over 75 million dollars every year on advertising if they did not know that advertising increases the consumption of their product. In response to this observation, the appellants insist that their advertising is directed solely toward preserving and expanding brand loyalty among smokers, and not toward expanding the tobacco market by inducing non-smokers to start. In my view, the appellants' claim is untenable for two principal reasons. First, brand loyalty alone will not, and logically cannot, maintain the profit levels of these companies if the overall number of smokers declines. A proportionate piece of a smaller pie is still a smaller piece. * * *

Second, even if this Court were to accept the appellants' brand loyalty argument, the appellants have not adequately addressed the further problem that even commercials targeted solely at brand loyalty may also serve as inducements for smokers not to quit. The government's concern with the health effects of tobacco can quite reasonably extend not only to potential smokers who are considering starting, but also to current smokers who would prefer to quit but cannot.

* * *

However, it is not necessary to rely solely upon common sense to reach this conclusion because there was, in any event, sufficient evidence adduced at trial to bear out the rational connection between advertising and consumption. * * *

* * *

Perhaps the most compelling evidence concerning the connection between advertising and consumption can be found in the internal marketing documents prepared by the tobacco manufacturers themselves. Although the appellants steadfastly argue that their marketing efforts are directed solely at maintaining and expanding brand loyalty among adult smokers, these documents show otherwise. In particular, the following general conclusions can be drawn from these documents: the tobacco companies are concerned about a shrinking tobacco market and recognize that an "advocacy thrust" is necessary to maintain the size of the overall market; the companies understand that, in order to maintain the overall numbers of smokers, they must reassure current smokers and make their product attractive to the young and to nonsmokers; they also recognize that advertising is critical to maintaining the size of the market because it serves to reinforce the social acceptability of smoking by identifying it with glamour, affluence, youthfulness and vitality.

* * *

The internal marketing documents introduced at trial strongly suggest that the tobacco companies perceive advertising to be a cornerstone of their strategy to reassure current smokers and expand the market by attracting new smokers, primarily among the young. * * *

* * *

Taking into account the legislative context, it is my view that the measures adopted under the Act satisfy the *Oakes* minimal impairment requirement. It must be kept in mind that the infringed right at issue in these cases is the right of tobacco corporations to advertise the only legal product sold in Canada which, when used precisely as directed, harms and often kills those who use it. As I discussed above, I have no doubt that Parliament could validly have employed the criminal law power to prohibit the manufacture and sale of tobacco products, and that such a prohibition would have been fully justifiable under the *Charter*. There is no right to sell harmful products in Canada, nor should there be. Thus, in choosing to prohibit solely the advertisement of tobacco products, it is clear that Parliament in fact adopted a relatively *unintrusive* legislative approach to the control of tobacco products. Indeed, the scope of conduct prohibited under the Act is narrow. * * * The prohibition under this Act serves only to prevent these companies from employing sophisticated marketing and social psychology techniques to induce consumers to purchase their products. * * *

* * *

The reasonableness of Parliament's decision to prohibit tobacco advertising has been amply borne out by parallel developments in the international community before and after the passage of the Act. It is of great significance, in my view, that over 20 democratic nations have, in recent years, adopted complete prohibitions on tobacco advertising similar to those adopted under the Act, including Australia, New Zealand, Norway, Finland and France. It is also of significance that the constitutionality of full advertising prohibitions have been upheld by the French *Conseil constitutionnel* to be constitutionally valid and by American courts. The decisions of the American courts, which have traditionally been jealous guardians of the right to freedom of expression, are particularly instructive in this context because they demonstrate that the adoption of a full prohibition upon tobacco advertising is perceived as neither novel nor radical in other democratic nations. * * *

* * *

Notes

1. Following its defeat in this case, the Canadian government in 1997 reenacted advertising legislation aimed at lifestyle rather than brand-name advertising. In litigation challenging this legislation, it introduced evidence totalling nearly 10,000 pages of transcript and 988 exhibits, a step it had not taken in the first round of litigation. Challenges to the new legislation were rejected. Currently Canada has one the most restrictive approaches to tobacco of any country in the world, including very high (by U.S. standards) excise taxes, which it supplemented in 2018 with the Tobacco and Vaping Products Act, yet another set of restrictive regulations. But neither Canada nor any other country has had successful tobacco class action cases like those in the United States. See Jeff Berryman, Canadian Reflections on the Tobacco Wars: Some Unintended Consequences of Mass Tort Litigation, 53 *Int. & Comp. L. Q.* 579 (2004). See also Jeffrey S. Quinn, Does Mass Product Tort Litigation Facilitate or Hinder Social Legislative Reform? A Comparative Study of Tobacco Regulation, 9 *Rutgers J.L. & Pub. Pol'y* 106 (2012); Andrei Sirabionian, Why Tobacco Litigation has not Been Successful in the United Kingdom: A Comparative Analysis of Tobacco Litigation in the United States and the United Kingdom, 25 *Nw.J. Int'l L. & Bus.* 485 (2005).

2. Canada cited a number of American cases in striking down the advertising legislation. How do you think the First Amendment should interact with tobacco regulation? After the FSPTCA, numerous scholars lamented the Act's encroachment on individual liberty, invoking the commercial speech doctrine to argue for the restrictions' unconstitutionality. *See, e.g.*, Richard J. Bonnie, The Impending Collision Be-

tween First Amendment Protection for Commercial Speech and the Public Health: The Case of Tobacco Control, 29 *J.L. & Pol.* 599 (2014); Arlen W. Langvardt, Tobacco Advertising and the First Amendment: Striking the Right Balance, 5 *Wm. & Mary Bus. L. Rev.* 331 (2014); Nathan Cortez, Do Graphic Tobacco Warnings Violate the First Amendment?, 64 *Hastings L.J.* 1467 (2013). The D.C. Circuit in 2012 struck down an FDA rule requiring graphic images like the ones required in Australia on the grounds that it violated the First Amendment's commercial speech doctrine, *R.J. Reynolds Tobacco Co. v. FDA*, 696 F.3d 1205 (D.C. Cir. 2012), but two years later upheld USDA regulations, conceding that disclosure of "purely factual" information did not violate the commercial speech doctrine, *Am. Meat Inst. v. USDA*, 760 F.3d 18 (D.C. Cir. 2014). To what extent will upholding these regulations require re-conceiving First Amendment protections in the United States? Does it require some kind of proportionality as-of-yet foreign to the First Amendment?

3. In 2000, the European Court of Justice struck down the EU Tobacco Advertising Directive, which banned tobacco television advertising and sponsorship. Case C-376/98, *Federal Republic of Germany v. Parliament and Council*, 2000 E.C.R. I-8419. It did so primarily for federalism reasons. The Court held that the primary goal of the legislation was to protect public health, and that the EU had not jurisdiction over public health, which was the province of the separate states, and that television advertising was primarily local, and thus free trade was not involved. The ECJ, on the other hand, upheld the EU Tobacco Products Directive, which regulated tar, nicotine, and carbon monoxide and label warnings regarding these toxins and prohibited the use of terms like "mild" or "light" for tobacco products. Case 491/01, *The Queen v. Sec'y of State for Health ex parte British American Tobacco (Investments) Ltd.*, 2002 E.C.R. I-11453. The Court held that the Directive was legitimately aimed at trade. The EU subsequently adopted an advertising ban covering print media, the internet, radio and international sporting events, Directive 2003/33/EC, which the Court of Justice upheld. Case C-380/03, *Germany v. Parliament and Council*, 2006 E.C.R. I-11631. The Court noted, "[W]hilst the principle of freedom of expression is expressly recognized by Article 10 of the ECR and constitutes one of the fundamental pillars of a democratic society, ... freedom of expression may also be subject to certain limitations justified by objectives in the public interest." *Id.* ¶ 154. The EU has updated its directives to address e-cigarettes, as well. Directive 2014/14/EU.

4. Tobacco use is clearly on the decline in the world's wealthy countries. Tobacco use among males age 15 and over in the United States declined from 52% in 1965 to 26% in 1999 to 19.5% in 2015, in the U.K. from 61% in 1960 to 28% in 1998 to 19.9% in 2015. Even in Japan, it has declined from 81% in 1960 to 33.7% in 2015. See, World Health Organization, *Global Health Observatory Data Repository*, http://apps.who.int/gho/data/view.main.1805?lang=en/. To what is this decline attributable? Legal regulation? Cultural changes? Public health education? In much of the developing world, on the other hand, smoking rates are high and rising. All ten of the countries with the highest combined rates of male and female smoking

are now in Eastern Europe, Asia, and Africa. Indeed, western tobacco companies are making up much of the profits they have lost in the West in the developing world. What, if any, legal response to this issue is appropriate? What are we to make of the rise of e-cigarettes? Are they a useful tool in helping smokers quit real cigarettes, or are they likely to chip away at the hard-won social stigma against cigarette usage?

D. Research Involving Human Subjects

Biomedical research represents another context in which the rights of the individual and the interests of society may conflict. Biomedical research is essential if the scientific development of medicine is to continue, and valid research is sometimes only possible if human "guinea pigs" are available. But even before the Nuremberg trials exposed the horrors that resulted from unethical human experimentation in Nazi Germany, research involving human subjects had already resulted in abuses of the rights of research subjects elsewhere as well.

Biomedical research is regulated first and foremost at the national level. Research is often funded by governments, which in turn take responsibility for protecting research subjects. In the United States, for example, the Common Rule (46 C.F.R. part 46) governs research funded by the federal government. Drugs and medical devices developed through research must also be approved by national governments before they can be sold. These authorities usually require that research relied on in developing the drugs meet certain standards of conduct. Food and Drug Administration Regulations in the United States, for example, impose requirements similar to the federal common rule. (See 21 C.F.R. Parts 50 and 56. A summary of recent changes to the Common Rule, particularly relevant to the handling of biospecimens, is included below.)

Increasingly, however, research takes place on an international scale. Drug and device manufacturers are not satisfied to market in only a single country, but want to sell to the entire world. They also do not want to have to conduct separate drug trials for every approving authority, but rather want to carry out their research once, and then have it accepted everywhere. The European Union has already established the European Medicines Agency (EMA), which offers a centralized procedure to achieve authorization of medicines in Europe. Beyond this, the International Council for Harmonisation of Technical Requirements for Pharmaceuticals for Human Use (ICH), a swiss non-profit, attempts to harmonize pharmaceutical regulations in some of the world's largest markets (including the United States, Europe, and Japan, so that a manufacturer has one set of regulations with which to comply. See Shona Walter & Katerina Mitkidis, The Risk Assessment of Pharmaceuticals in the Environment: Eu and Us Regulatory Approach, 9 *Eur. J. Risk Reg.* 527 (2018).

Though regulation of biomedical research is only now being harmonized, international statements on research ethics have long been available. Among the earliest of these was the Nuremberg Code itself, which begins "The voluntary consent of the human subject is absolutely essential." Such consent could only be obtained after the research subject is fully informed about the nature and risks of the experiment. See George J. Annas and Michael A. Grodin, *The Nazi Doctors and the Nuremberg Code* (1992).

The Nuremberg Code, with its emphasis on the protection of patients, has been largely eclipsed as an international reference point by the World Medical Association's Declaration of Helsinki, first promulgated in 1964, and revised several times since. Though the Declaration is in fact the statement of a professional association, and not law in any sense, it is widely regarded throughout the world as a foundational document of research ethics.

World Medical Association, *Declaration of Helsinki, Ethical Principles for Medical Research Involving Human Subjects*

Adopted by the 18th WMA General Assembly, Helsinki, Finland, June 1964, as revised 1975, 1983, 1989, 1996,2000, 2002, 2004, 2008, 2013

Preamble

1. The World Medical Association (WMA) has developed the Declaration of Helsinki as a statement of ethical principles for medical research involving human subjects, including research on identifiable human material and data.

The Declaration is intended to be read as a whole and each of its constituent paragraphs should be applied with consideration of all other relevant paragraphs.

2. Consistent with the mandate of the WMA, the Declaration is addressed primarily to physicians. The WMA encourages others who are involved in medical research involving human subjects to adopt these principles.

General Principles

3. The Declaration of Geneva of the WMA binds the physician with the words, "The health of my patient will be my first consideration," and the International Code of Medical Ethics declares that, "A physician shall act in the patient's best interest when providing medical care."

4. It is the duty of the physician to promote and safeguard the health, well-being and rights of patients, including those who are involved in medical research. The physician's knowledge and conscience are dedicated to the fulfilment of this duty.

5. Medical progress is based on research that ultimately must include studies involving human subjects.

6. The primary purpose of medical research involving human subjects is to understand the causes, development and effects of diseases and improve preventive, diagnostic

and therapeutic interventions (methods, procedures and treatments). Even the best proven interventions must be evaluated continually through research for their safety, effectiveness, efficiency, accessibility and quality.

7. Medical research is subject to ethical standards that promote and ensure respect for all human subjects and protect their health and rights.

8. While the primary purpose of medical research is to generate new knowledge, this goal can never take precedence over the rights and interests of individual research subjects.

9. It is the duty of physicians who are involved in medical research to protect the life, health, dignity, integrity, right to self-determination, privacy, and confidentiality of personal information of research subjects. The responsibility for the protection of research subjects must always rest with the physician or other health care professionals and never with the research subjects, even though they have given consent.

10. Physicians must consider the ethical, legal and regulatory norms and standards for research involving human subjects in their own countries as well as applicable international norms and standards. No national or international ethical, legal or regulatory requirement should reduce or eliminate any of the protections for research subjects set forth in this Declaration.

11. Medical research should be conducted in a manner that minimises possible harm to the environment.

12. Medical research involving human subjects must be conducted only by individuals with the appropriate ethics and scientific education, training and qualifications. Research on patients or healthy volunteers requires the supervision of a competent and appropriately qualified physician or other health care professional.

13. Groups that are underrepresented in medical research should be provided appropriate access to participation in research.

14. Physicians who combine medical research with medical care should involve their patients in research only to the extent that this is justified by its potential preventive, diagnostic or therapeutic value and if the physician has good reason to believe that participation in the research study will not adversely affect the health of the patients who serve as research subjects.

15. Appropriate compensation and treatment for subjects who are harmed as a result of participating in research must be ensured.

Risks, Burdens, and Benefits

16. In medical practice and in medical research, most interventions involve risks and burdens.

Medical research involving human subjects may only be conducted if the importance of the objective outweighs the risks and burdens to the research subjects.

17. All medical research involving human subjects must be preceded by careful assessment of predictable risks and burdens to the individuals and groups involved in

the research in comparison with foreseeable benefits to them and to other individuals or groups affected by the condition under investigation.

Measures to minimise the risks must be implemented. The risks must be continuously monitored, assessed and documented by the researcher.

18. Physicians may not be involved in a research study involving human subjects unless they are confident that the risks have been adequately assessed and can be satisfactorily managed.

When the risks are found to outweigh the potential benefits or when there is conclusive proof of definitive outcomes, physicians must assess whether to continue, modify or immediately stop the study.

Vulnerable Groups and Individuals

19. Some groups and individuals are particularly vulnerable and may have an increased likelihood of being wronged or of incurring additional harm.

All vulnerable groups and individuals should receive specifically considered protection.

20. Medical research with a vulnerable group is only justified if the research is responsive to the health needs or priorities of this group and the research cannot be carried out in a non-vulnerable group. In addition, this group should stand to benefit from the knowledge, practices or interventions that result from the research.

21. Medical research involving human subjects must conform to generally accepted scientific principles, be based on a thorough knowledge of the scientific literature, other relevant sources of information, and adequate laboratory and, as appropriate, animal experimentation. The welfare of animals used for research must be respected.

22. The design and performance of each research study involving human subjects must be clearly described and justified in a research protocol.

The protocol should contain a statement of the ethical considerations involved and should indicate how the principles in this Declaration have been addressed. The protocol should include information regarding funding, sponsors, institutional affiliations, potential conflicts of interest, incentives for subjects and information regarding provisions for treating and/or compensating subjects who are harmed as a consequence of participation in the research study.

In clinical trials, the protocol must also describe appropriate arrangements for post-trial provisions.

Research Ethics Committees

23. The research protocol must be submitted for consideration, comment, guidance and approval to the concerned research ethics committee before the study begins. This committee must be transparent in its functioning, must be independent of the researcher, the sponsor and any other undue influence and must be duly qualified. It must take into consideration the laws and regulations of the country or countries in which the research is to be performed as well as applicable international norms and standards but these must not be allowed to reduce or eliminate any of the protections for research subjects set forth in this Declaration.

The committee must have the right to monitor ongoing studies. The researcher must provide monitoring information to the committee, especially information about any serious adverse events. No amendment to the protocol may be made without consideration and approval by the committee. After the end of the study, the researchers must submit a final report to the committee containing a summary of the study's findings and conclusions.

Privacy and Confidentiality

24. Every precaution must be taken to protect the privacy of research subjects and the confidentiality of their personal information.

Informed Consent

25. Participation by individuals capable of giving informed consent as subjects in medical research must be voluntary. Although it may be appropriate to consult family members or community leaders, no individual capable of giving informed consent may be enrolled in a research study unless he or she freely agrees.

26. In medical research involving human subjects capable of giving informed consent, each potential subject must be adequately informed of the aims, methods, sources of funding, any possible conflicts of interest, institutional affiliations of the researcher, the anticipated benefits and potential risks of the study and the discomfort it may entail, post-study provisions and any other relevant aspects of the study. The potential subject must be informed of the right to refuse to participate in the study or to withdraw consent to participate at any time without reprisal. Special attention should be given to the specific information needs of individual potential subjects as well as to the methods used to deliver the information.

After ensuring that the potential subject has understood the information, the physician or another appropriately qualified individual must then seek the potential subject's freely-given informed consent, preferably in writing. If the consent cannot be expressed in writing, the non-written consent must be formally documented and witnessed.

All medical research subjects should be given the option of being informed about the general outcome and results of the study.

27. When seeking informed consent for participation in a research study the physician must be particularly cautious if the potential subject is in a dependent relationship with the physician or may consent under duress. In such situations the informed consent must be sought by an appropriately qualified individual who is completely independent of this relationship.

28. For a potential research subject who is incapable of giving informed consent, the physician must seek informed consent from the legally authorised representative. These individuals must not be included in a research study that has no likelihood of benefit for them unless it is intended to promote the health of the group represented by the potential subject, the research cannot instead be performed with persons capable of providing informed consent, and the research entails only minimal risk and minimal burden.

29. When a potential research subject who is deemed incapable of giving informed consent is able to give assent to decisions about participation in research, the physician must seek that assent in addition to the consent of the legally authorised representative. The potential subject's dissent should be respected.

30. Research involving subjects who are physically or mentally incapable of giving consent, for example, unconscious patients, may be done only if the physical or mental condition that prevents giving informed consent is a necessary characteristic of the research group. In such circumstances the physician must seek informed consent from the legally authorised representative. If no such representative is available and if the research cannot be delayed, the study may proceed without informed consent provided that the specific reasons for involving subjects with a condition that renders them unable to give informed consent have been stated in the research protocol and the study has been approved by a research ethics committee. Consent to remain in the research must be obtained as soon as possible from the subject or a legally authorised representative.

31. The physician must fully inform the patient which aspects of their care are related to the research. The refusal of a patient to participate in a study or the patient's decision to withdraw from the study must never adversely affect the patient-physician relationship.

32. For medical research using identifiable human material or data, such as research on material or data contained in biobanks or similar repositories, physicians must seek informed consent for its collection, storage and/or reuse. There may be exceptional situations where consent would be impossible or impracticable to obtain for such research. In such situations the research may be done only after consideration and approval of a research ethics committee.

Use of Placebo

33. The benefits, risks, burdens and effectiveness of a new intervention must be tested against those of the best proven intervention(s), except in the following circumstances:

Where no proven intervention exists, the use of placebo, or no intervention, is acceptable; or

Where for compelling and scientifically sound methodological reasons the use of any intervention less effective than the best proven one, the use of placebo, or no intervention is necessary to determine the efficacy or safety of an intervention and the patients who receive any intervention less effective than the best proven one, placebo, or no intervention will not be subject to additional risks of serious or irreversible harm as a result of not receiving the best proven intervention.

Extreme care must be taken to avoid abuse of this option.

Post-Trial Provisions

34. In advance of a clinical trial, sponsors, researchers and host country governments should make provisions for post-trial access for all participants who still need an intervention identified as beneficial in the trial. This information must also be disclosed to participants during the informed consent process.

Research Registration and Publication and Dissemination of Results

35. Every research study involving human subjects must be registered in a publicly accessible database before recruitment of the first subject.

36. Researchers, authors, sponsors, editors and publishers all have ethical obligations with regard to the publication and dissemination of the results of research. Researchers have a duty to make publicly available the results of their research on human subjects and are accountable for the completeness and accuracy of their reports. All parties should adhere to accepted guidelines for ethical reporting. Negative and inconclusive as well as positive results must be published or otherwise made publicly available. Sources of funding, institutional affiliations and conflicts of interest must be declared in the publication. Reports of research not in accordance with the principles of this Declaration should not be accepted for publication.

Unproven Interventions in Clinical Practice

37. In the treatment of an individual patient, where proven interventions do not exist or other known interventions have been ineffective, the physician, after seeking expert advice, with informed consent from the patient or a legally authorised representative, may use an unproven intervention if in the physician's judgement it offers hope of saving life, re-establishing health or alleviating suffering. This intervention should subsequently be made the object of research, designed to evaluate its safety and efficacy. In all cases, new information must be recorded and, where appropriate, made publicly available.

* * *

Note

The Helsinki Declaration has been roundly criticized as having "endorsed shifting the focus of protection of the human subjects in medical research from the protection of human rights through informed consent to the protection of patient welfare through physician responsibility," and as having "attempted to undermine the primacy of subject consent in the Nuremberg Code and displace it with the paternalistic values of the traditional doctor-patient relationship." George J. Annas & Michael A. Grodin, Medical Ethics and Human Rights: Legacies of Nuremberg, 3 *Hofstra L. & Pol'y Symp.* 111, 116 (1999). Do you read the Declaration in this way?

Another important statement on research ethics is the European Convention on Human Rights and Biomedicine. This document, promulgated by the Council of Europe (again, not to be confused with the European Union), is binding upon signatories, though to date many European nations (including Germany and the United Kingdom) have not signed it. How does it resemble and differ from the Helsinki declaration? Is it more or less protective of research subjects? Consider this as you read the Convention and the most relevant of its Additional Protocols below.

European Convention on Human Rights and Biomedicine, Oviedo, 1997

Council of Europe, Convention for the Protection of Human Rights and Dignity of the Human Being with Regard to the Application of Biology and Medicine

Chapter I—General provisions

1. Parties to this Convention shall protect the dignity and identity of all human beings and guarantee everyone, without discrimination, respect for their integrity and other rights and fundamental freedoms with regard to the application of biology and medicine.

Each Party shall take in its internal law the necessary measures to give effect to the provisions of this Convention.

2. The interests and welfare of the human being shall prevail over the sole interest of society or science.

3. Parties, taking into account health needs and available resources, shall take appropriate measures with a view to providing, within their jurisdiction, equitable access to health care of appropriate quality.

* * *

Chapter II—Consent

5. An intervention in the health field may only be carried out after the person concerned has given free and informed consent to it.

This person shall beforehand be given appropriate information as to the purpose and nature of the intervention as well as on its consequences and risks.

The person concerned may freely withdraw consent at any time.

6. (1) Subject to Articles 17 and 20 below, an intervention may only be carried out on a person who does not have the capacity to consent, for his or her direct benefit.

(2) Where, according to law, a minor does not have the capacity to consent to an intervention, the intervention may only be carried out with the authorisation of his or her representative or an authority or a person or body provided for by law.

The opinion of the minor shall be taken into consideration as an increasingly determining factor in proportion to his or her age and degree of maturity.

(3) Where, according to law, an adult does not have the capacity to consent to an intervention because of a mental disability, a disease or for similar reasons, the intervention may only be carried out with the authorisation of his or her representative or an authority or a person or body provided for by law.

The individual concerned shall as far as possible take part in the authorisation procedure....

7. Subject to protective conditions prescribed by law, including supervisory, control and appeal procedures, a person who has a mental disorder of a serious nature may

be subjected, without his or her consent, to an intervention aimed at treating his or her mental disorder only where, without such treatment, serious harm is likely to result to his or her health.

8. The previously expressed wishes relating to a medical intervention by a patient who is not, at the time of the intervention, in a state to express his or her wishes shall be taken into account.

* * *

Chapter III—Private life and right to information

10. (1) Everyone has the right to respect for private life in relation to information about his or her health.

(2) Everyone is entitled to know any information collected about his or her health. However, the wishes of individuals not to be so informed shall be observed.

(3) In exceptional cases, restrictions may be placed by law on the exercise of the rights contained in paragraph 2 in the interests of the patient.

Chapter IV—Human genome

* * *

13. An intervention seeking to modify the human genome may only be undertaken for preventive, diagnostic or therapeutic purposes and only if its aim is not to introduce any modification in the genome of any descendants.

14. The use of techniques of medically assisted procreation shall not be allowed for the purpose of choosing a future child's sex, except where serious hereditary sex-related disease is to be avoided.

* * *

Chapter V—Scientific research

15. Scientific research in the field of biology and medicine shall be carried out freely, subject to the provisions of this Convention and the other legal provisions ensuring the protection of the human being.

16. Research on a person may only be undertaken if all the following conditions are met:

i. there is no alternative of comparable effectiveness to research on humans;

ii. the risks which may be incurred by that person are not disproportionate to the potential benefits of the research;

iii. the research project has been approved by the competent body after independent examination of its scientific merit, including assessment of the importance of the aim of the research, and multidisciplinary review of its ethical acceptability;

iv. the persons undergoing research have been informed of their rights and the safeguards prescribed by law for their protection;

v. the necessary consent as provided for under Article 5 has been given expressly, specifically and is documented. Such consent may be freely withdrawn at any time.

17.(1)Research on a person without the capacity to consent as stipulated in Article 5 may be undertaken only if all the following conditions are met:

i. the conditions laid down in Article 16, sub-paragraphs i to iv, are fulfilled;

ii. the results of the research have the potential to produce real and direct benefit to his or her health;

iii. research of comparable effectiveness cannot be carried out on individuals capable of giving consent;

iv. the necessary authorisation provided for under Article 6 has been given specifically and in writing; and

v. the person concerned does not object.

(2) Exceptionally and under the protective conditions prescribed by law, where the research has not the potential to produce results of direct benefit to the health of the person concerned, such research may be authorised subject to the conditions laid down in paragraph 1, sub-paragraphs i, iii, iv and v above, and to the following additional conditions:

i. the research has the aim of contributing, through significant improvement in the scientific understanding of the individual's condition, disease or disorder, to the ultimate attainment of results capable of conferring benefit to the person concerned or to other persons in the same age category or afflicted with the same disease or disorder or having the same condition.

ii. the research entails only minimal risk and minimal burden for the individual concerned.

18.(1) Where the law allows research on embryos *in vitro*, it shall ensure adequate protection of the embryo.

(2) The creation of human embryos for research purposes is prohibited.

* * *

Additional Protocol to the Convention on Human Rights and Biomedicine Concerning Biomedical Research, 2005

Council of Europe, Convention for the Protection of Human Rights and Dignity of the Human Being with Regard to the Application of Biology and Medicine

* * *

Chapter II—General provisions

3. The interests and welfare of the human being participating in research shall prevail over the sole interest of society or science.

4. Research shall be carried out freely, subject to the provisions of this Protocol and the other legal provisions ensuring the protection of the human being.

5. Research on human beings may only be undertaken if there is no alternative of comparable effectiveness.

6. (1) Research shall not involve risks and burdens to the human being disproportionate to its potential benefits.

(2) In addition, where the research does not have the potential to produce results of direct benefit to the health of the research participant, such research may only be undertaken if the research entails no more than acceptable risk and acceptable burden for the research participant. This shall be without prejudice to the provision contained in Article 15 paragraph 2, sub-paragraph ii for the protection of persons not able to consent to research.

7. Research may only be undertaken if the research project has been approved by the competent body after independent examination of its scientific merit, including assessment of the importance of the aim of research, and multidisciplinary review of its ethical acceptability.

8. Any research must be scientifically justified, meet generally accepted criteria of scientific quality and be carried out in accordance with relevant professional obligations and standards under the supervision of an appropriately qualified researcher.

Chapter III—Ethics committee

9. (1) Every research project shall be submitted for independent examination of its ethical acceptability to an ethics committee. Such projects shall be submitted to independent examination in each State in which any research activity is to take place.

(2) The purpose of the multidisciplinary examination of the ethical acceptability of the research project shall be to protect the dignity, rights, safety and well-being of research participants. The assessment of the ethical acceptability shall draw on an appropriate range of expertise and experience adequately reflecting professional and lay views.

(3) The ethics committee shall produce an opinion containing reasons for its conclusion.

10. (1) Parties to this Protocol shall take measures to assure the independence of the ethics committee. That body shall not be subject to undue external influences.

(2) Members of the ethics committee shall declare all circumstances that might lead to a conflict of interest. Should such conflicts arise, those involved shall not participate in that review.

11. (1) All information which is necessary for the ethical assessment of the research project shall be given in written form to the ethics committee.

(2) In particular, information on items contained in the appendix to this Protocol shall be provided, in so far as it is relevant for the research project. The appendix may be amended by the Committee set up by Article 32 of the Convention by a two-thirds majority of the votes cast.

12. The ethics committee must be satisfied that no undue influence, including that of a financial nature, will be exerted on persons to participate in research. In this respect, particular attention must be given to vulnerable or dependent persons.

Chapter IV—Information and consent

13. (1) The persons being asked to participate in a research project shall be given adequate information in a comprehensible form. This information shall be documented.

(2) The information shall cover the purpose, the overall plan and the possible risks and benefits of the research project, and include the opinion of the ethics committee. Before being asked to consent to participate in a research project, the persons concerned shall be specifically informed, according to the nature and purpose of the research:

i. of the nature, extent and duration of the procedures involved, in particular, details of any burden imposed by the research project;

ii. of available preventive, diagnostic and therapeutic procedures;

iii. of the arrangements for responding to adverse events or the concerns of research participants;

iv. of arrangements to ensure respect for private life and ensure the confidentiality of personal data;

v. of arrangements for access to information relevant to the participant arising from the research and to its overall results;

vi. of the arrangements for fair compensation in the case of damage;

vii. of any foreseen potential further uses, including commercial uses, of the research results, data or biological materials;

viii. of the source of funding of the research project.

(3) In addition, the persons being asked to participate in a research project shall be informed of the rights and safeguards prescribed by law for their protection, and specifically of their right to refuse consent or to withdraw consent at any time without being subject to any form of discrimination, in particular regarding the right to medical care.

14. (1) No research on a person may be carried out, subject to the provisions of both Chapter V and Article 19, without the informed, free, express, specific and documented consent of the person. Such consent may be freely withdrawn by the person at any phase of the research.

(2) Refusal to give consent or the withdrawal of consent to participation in research shall not lead to any form of discrimination against the person concerned, in particular regarding the right to medical care.

(3) Where the capacity of the person to give informed consent is in doubt, arrangements shall be in place to verify whether or not the person has such capacity.

Chapter V—Protection of persons not able to consent to research

15.(1) Research on a person without the capacity to consent to research may be undertaken only if all the following specific conditions are met:

i. the results of the research have the potential to produce real and direct benefit to his or her health;

ii. research of comparable effectiveness cannot be carried out on individuals capable of giving consent;

iii. the person undergoing research has been informed of his or her rights and the safeguards prescribed by law for his or her protection, unless this person is not in a state to receive the information;

iv. the necessary authorisation has been given specifically and in writing by the legal representative or an authority, person or body provided for by law, and after having received the information required by Article 16, taking into account the person's previously expressed wishes or objections. An adult not able to consent shall as far as possible take part in the authorisation procedure. The opinion of a minor shall be taken into consideration as an increasingly determining factor in proportion to age and degree of maturity;

v. the person concerned does not object.

(2) Exceptionally and under the protective conditions prescribed by law, where the research has not the potential to produce results of direct benefit to the health of the person concerned, such research may be authorised subject to the conditions laid down in paragraph 1, sub-paragraphs ii, iii, iv, and v above, and to the following additional conditions:

i. the research has the aim of contributing, through significant improvement in the scientific understanding of the individual's condition, disease or disorder, to the ultimate attainment of results capable of conferring benefit to the person concerned or to other persons in the same age category or afflicted with the same disease or disorder or having the same condition;

ii. the research entails only minimal risk and minimal burden for the individual concerned; and any consideration of additional potential benefits of the research shall not be used to justify an increased level of risk or burden.

(3) Objection to participation, refusal to give authorisation or the withdrawal of authorisation to participate in research shall not lead to any form of discrimination against the person concerned, in particular regarding the right to medical care.

16. (1) Those being asked to authorise participation of a person in a research project shall be given adequate information in a comprehensible form. This information shall be documented.

(2) The information shall cover the purpose, the overall plan and the possible risks and benefits of the research project, and include the opinion of the ethics committee. They shall further be informed of the rights and safeguards prescribed by law for the protection of those not able to consent to research and specifically of the right to refuse or to withdraw authorisation at any time, without the person concerned being subject to any form of discrimination, in particular regarding the right to medical care. They shall be specifically informed according to the nature and purpose of the research of the items of information listed in Article 13.

(3) The information shall also be provided to the individual concerned, unless this person is not in a state to receive the information.

17. (1) For the purposes of this Protocol it is deemed that the research bears a minimal risk if, having regard to the nature and scale of the intervention, it is to be expected that it will result, at the most, in a very slight and temporary negative impact on the health of the person concerned.

(2) It is deemed that it bears a minimal burden if it is to be expected that the discomfort will be, at the most, temporary and very slight for the person concerned. In assessing the burden for an individual, a person enjoying the special confidence of the person concerned shall assess the burden where appropriate.

Chapter VI—Specific situations

18. (1) Research on a pregnant woman which does not have the potential to produce results of direct benefit to her health, or to that of her embryo, foetus or child after birth, may only be undertaken if the following additional conditions are met:

i. the research has the aim of contributing to the ultimate attainment of results capable of conferring benefit to other women in relation to reproduction or to other embryos, foetuses or children;

ii. research of comparable effectiveness cannot be carried out on women who are not pregnant;

iii. the research entails only minimal risk and minimal burden.

(2) Where research is undertaken on a breastfeeding woman, particular care shall be taken to avoid any adverse impact on the health of the child.

19. (1) The law shall determine whether, and under which protective additional conditions, research in emergency situations may take place when:

i. a person is not in a state to give consent, and

ii. because of the urgency of the situation, it is impossible to obtain in a sufficiently timely manner, authorisation from his or her representative or an authority or a person or body which would in the absence of an emergency situation be called upon to give authorisation.

(2) The law shall include the following specific conditions:

i. research of comparable effectiveness cannot be carried out on persons in non-emergency situations;

ii. the research project may only be undertaken if it has been approved specifically for emergency situations by the competent body;

iii. any relevant previously expressed objections of the person known to the researcher shall be respected;

iv. where the research has not the potential to produce results of direct benefit to the health of the person concerned, it has the aim of contributing, through significant improvement in the scientific understanding of the individual's condition, disease or disorder, to the ultimate attainment of results capable of conferring benefit to the person concerned or to other persons in the same category or afflicted with the same disease or disorder or having the same condition, and entails only minimal risk and minimal burden.

(3) Persons participating in the emergency research project or, if applicable, their representatives shall be provided with all the relevant information concerning their participation in the research project as soon as possible. Consent or authorisation for continued participation shall be requested as soon as reasonably possible.

20. Where the law allows research on persons deprived of liberty, such persons may participate in a research project in which the results do not have the potential to produce direct benefit to their health only if the following additional conditions are met:

i. research of comparable effectiveness cannot be carried out without the participation of persons deprived of liberty;

ii. the research has the aim of contributing to the ultimate attainment of results capable of conferring benefit to persons deprived of liberty;

iii. the research entails only minimal risk and minimal burden.

Chapter VII—Safety and supervision

21. (1) All reasonable measures shall be taken to ensure safety and to minimise risk and burden for the research participants.

(2) Research may only be carried out under the supervision of a clinical professional who possesses the necessary qualifications and experience.

22. (1) The researcher shall take all necessary steps to assess the state of health of human beings prior to their inclusion in research, to ensure that those at increased risk in relation to participation in a specific project be excluded.

(2) Where research is undertaken on persons in the reproductive stage of their lives, particular consideration shall be given to the possible adverse impact on a current or future pregnancy and the health of an embryo, foetus or child.

23. (1) Research shall not delay nor deprive participants of medically necessary preventive, diagnostic or therapeutic procedures.

(2) In research associated with prevention, diagnosis or treatment, participants assigned to control groups shall be assured of proven methods of prevention, diagnosis or treatment.

(3) The use of placebo is permissible where there are no methods of proven effectiveness, or where withdrawal or withholding of such methods does not present an unacceptable risk or burden.

24. (1) Parties to this Protocol shall take measures to ensure that the research project is re-examined if this is justified in the light of scientific developments or events arising in the course of the research.

(2) The purpose of the re-examination is to establish whether:

i. the research needs to be discontinued or if changes to the research project are necessary for the research to continue;

ii. research participants, or if applicable their representatives, need to be informed of the developments or events;

iii. additional consent or authorisation for participation is required.

(3) Any new information relevant to their participation shall be conveyed to the research participants, or, if applicable, to their representatives, in a timely manner.

(4) The competent body shall be informed of the reasons for any premature termination of a research project. The interests and welfare of the human being participating in research shall prevail over the sole interest of society or science.

Chapter VIII—Confidentiality and right to information

25. (1) Any information of a personal nature collected during biomedical research shall be considered as confidential and treated according to the rules relating to the protection of private life.

(2) The law shall protect against inappropriate disclosure of any other information related to a research project that has been submitted to an ethics committee in compliance with this Protocol.

26. (1) Research participants shall be entitled to know any information collected on their health in conformity with the provisions of Article 10 of the Convention.

(2) Other personal information collected for a research project will be accessible to them in conformity with the law on the protection of individuals with regard to processing of personal data.

27. If research gives rise to information of relevance to the current or future health or quality of life of research participants, this information must be offered to them. That shall be done within a framework of health care or counselling. In communication of such information, due care must be taken in order to protect confidentiality and to respect any wish of a participant not to receive such information.

28. (1) On completion of the research, a report or summary shall be submitted to the ethics committee or the competent body.

(2) The conclusions of the research shall be made available to participants in reasonable time, on request.

(3) The researcher shall take appropriate measures to make public the results of research in reasonable time.

Chapter IX—Research in states not parties to this Protocol

29. Sponsors or researchers within the jurisdiction of a Party to this Protocol that plan to undertake or direct a research project in a State not party to this Protocol shall ensure that, without prejudice to the provisions applicable in that State, the research project complies with the principles on which the provisions of this Protocol are based. Where necessary, the Party shall take appropriate measures to that end.

Chapter X—Infringement of the provisions of the Protocol

30. The Parties shall provide appropriate judicial protection to prevent or to put a stop to an unlawful infringement of the rights or principles set forth in this Protocol at short notice.

31. The person who has suffered damage as a result of participation in research shall be entitled to fair compensation according to the conditions and procedures prescribed by law.

32. Parties shall provide for appropriate sanctions to be applied in the event of infringement of the provisions contained in this Protocol.

* * *

Notes

1. The convention has several additional Protocols, covering more specific topics such as human cloning, organ transplant, and genetic testing for health purposes.

2. Another important statement of research ethics is the International Guidelines for Biomedical Research Involving Human Subjects, published by the World Health Organization and the Council for International Organizations of Medical Sciences, usually referred to as the CIOMS Guidelines. These Guidelines focus particularly on research carried out in low-resource settings. The 2016 version of the Guidelines It can be found on the CIOMS website, https://cioms.ch/shop/product/international-ethical-guidelines-for-health-related-research-involving-humans/.

3. As discussed above, in the U.S. the main research ethics guidelines comes from the Common Rule (46 C.F.R. part 46) and largely similar requirements of the Food and Drug Administration Regulations (See 21 C.F.R. Parts 50 and 56). The Common Rule was recently revised in the U.S. One of the precipitating events was the public attention directed to the case of Henrietta Lacks, an African-American woman who died of cancer in 1951. It was revealed by journalist Rebecca Skloot that Ms. Lacks' cell samples were extracted for research without her knowledge or consent (arguably in keeping with then prevalent research ethics practices) and used to create the HeLa cell line. This cell line was used very widely in biomedical research around the country, including commercial medical activities. Ms. Lack's family finally became aware of the cell line in the 1970s. Rebecca Skloot, *The Immortal Life of Henrietta Lacks* (2011). There was an additional controversy in 2013 when researchers published information about the genome of HeLa cells, raising concerns for Ms. Lacks' living relatives. Kathy L. Hudson & Francis S. Collins, Family Matters, 500 *Nature* 141 (2013). The result was a several year effort at altering the Common Rule (including changes not related to biospecimens) that at the time of this writing have only recently gone into effect. The changes are summarized in the following excerpt announcing the new rule:

Federal Policy for the Protection of Human Subjects

82 Fed. Reg. 7149 (2017)

Purpose of the Regulatory Action

Individuals who are the subjects of research may be asked to contribute their time and assume risk to advance the research enterprise, which benefits society at large. U.S. federal regulations governing the protection of human subjects in research have been in existence for more than three decades. The Department of Health, Education, and Welfare first published regulations for the protection of human subjects in 1974, and the Department of Health and Human Services (HHS) revised them in the early 1980s. During the 1980s, HHS began a process that eventually led to the adoption of a revised version of the regulations by 15 U.S. federal departments and agencies in 1991. The purpose of this effort was to promote uniformity, understanding, and compliance with human subject protections as well as to create a uniform body of regulations across federal departments and agencies (subpart A of 45 Code of Federal Regulations [CFR] part 46), often referred to as the "Common Rule" or "Protection of Human Subjects Regulations." Those regulations were last amended in 2005, and have remained unchanged until the issuance of this final rule.

Since the Common Rule was promulgated, the volume and landscape of research involving human subjects have changed considerably. Research with human subjects has grown in scale and become more diverse. Examples of developments include: an expansion in the number and types of clinical trials, as well as observational studies and cohort studies; a diversification of the types of social and behavioral research being used in human subjects research; increased use of sophisticated analytic techniques to study human biospecimens; and the growing use of electronic health data and other digital records to enable very large datasets to be rapidly analyzed and combined in novel ways. Yet these developments have not been accompanied by major change in the human subjects research oversight system, which has remained largely unaltered over the past two decades.

[The history of the revision process is omitted here]

* * *

The final rule is designed to more thoroughly address the broader types of research conducted or otherwise supported by all of the Common Rule departments and agencies such as behavioral and social science research. It also benefits from continuing efforts to harmonize human subjects policies across federal departments and agencies.

Summary of the Major Changes in the Final Rule

The final rule differs in important ways from the [proposed rule]. Most significantly, several proposals are not being adopted:

- The final rule does not adopt the proposal to require that research involving nonidentified biospecimens be subject to the Common Rule, and that consent would need to be obtained in order to conduct such research....

- The final rule does not expand the policy to cover clinical trials that are not federally funded....
- The final rule does not include the proposed standardized privacy safeguards for identifiable private information and identifiable biospecimens. Aspects of proposals that relied on those safeguards have been modified or are not being adopted.
- The final rule does not adopt the most restrictive proposed criteria for obtaining a waiver of the consent requirements relating to research with identifiable biospecimens.

The final rule makes the following significant changes to the Common Rule:

- Establishes new requirements regarding the information that must be given to prospective research subjects as part of the informed consent process.
- Allows the use of broad consent (i.e., seeking prospective consent to unspecified future research) from a subject for storage, maintenance, and secondary research use of identifiable private information and identifiable biospecimens. Broad consent will be an optional alternative that an investigator may choose instead of, for example, conducting the research on nonidentified information and nonidentified biospecimens, having an institutional review board (IRB) waive the requirement for informed consent, or obtaining consent for a specific study.
- Establishes new exempt categories of research based on their risk profile. Under some of the new categories, exempt research would be required to undergo limited IRB review to ensure that there are adequate privacy safeguards for identifiable private information and identifiable biospecimens.
- Creates a requirement for U.S.-based institutions engaged in cooperative research to use a single IRB for that portion of the research that takes place within the United States, with certain exceptions. This requirement becomes effective 3 years after publication of the final rule.
- Removes the requirement to conduct continuing review of ongoing research for studies that undergo expedited review and for studies that have completed study interventions and are merely analyzing study data or involve only observational follow up in conjunction with standard clinical care.

Other minor changes have been to improve the rule and for purposes of clarity and accuracy....

* * *

The Changing Nature of Research

This final rule recognizes that in the past two decades a paradigm shift has occurred in how research is conducted. Evolving technologies—including imaging, mobile technologies, and the growth in computing power—have changed the scale and nature of information collected in many disciplines. Computer scientists, engineers, and social scientists are developing techniques to integrate different types of data so they can be combined, mined, analyzed, and shared. The advent of sophisticated computer software programs, the Internet, and mobile technology has created new areas of research activity, particularly within the social and behavioral sciences. In biomedical science, the Human Genome Project laid the foundation for precision medicine and promoted an environment of data sharing and innovation in analytics and technology, and drew attention to the need for policies that support a changing research landscape. New technologies, including genomic sequencing, have quickly led to exponential growth in the data to which investigators have access. The sheer volume of data that can be generated in research, the ease with which it can be shared, and the ways in which it can be used to identify individuals were simply not possible, or even imaginable, when the Common Rule was first adopted.

Research settings are also shifting. Although much biomedical research continues to be conducted in academic medical centers, more research is being conducted in clinical care settings, thus combining research and medical data. Biospecimen repositories and large databases have made it easier to do research on existing (stored) biospecimens and data. Clinical research networks connected through electronic health records have developed methods for extracting clinical data for research purposes and are working toward integration of research data into electronic health records in a meaningful way. The scientific community recognizes the value of data sharing and open-source resources and understands that pooling intellectual resources and capitalizing on efficient uses of data and technology represent the best ways to advance knowledge.

At the same time, the level of public engagement in the research enterprise has changed. More people want to play an active role in research, particularly related to health.

As technology evolves, so does the nature of the risks and benefits of participating in certain types of research. Many studies do not involve interaction with research subjects, but instead involve secondary analysis of data or biospecimens. Risks related to these types of research studies are largely informational, not physical; that is, harms could result primarily from the inappropriate disclosure of information and not from the research interventions themselves. Nonetheless, those harms can be significant.

Because of these shifts in science, technology, and public engagement and expectations, a wide range of stakeholders have raised concerns about the limitations of the existing regulatory framework, arguing for a re-evaluation of how the fundamental principles of the 1979 Belmont Report that underlie the Common Rule—respect for persons, beneficence, and justice—are applied in practice to the myriad new contexts in which U.S. research is conducted in the 21st century. The changes that are being implemented in the final rule continue to be shaped by those principles.

* * *

The research that grounds the development of new drugs necessarily requires the use of human subjects. This research thus raises important ethical issues, indeed human rights issues. Research is increasingly taking place on an international basis as large, multicenter, trials become more common. Though there are international expressions of principle that address these issues, most notably the Revised Declaration of Helsinki on Research Involving Human Subjects, research, including international research, is also addressed by substantive regulations governing research at the national level. These regulatory instruments reflect different approaches to the ethical issues grounding human subjects research.

* * *

Notes

1. As the excerpts from the Common Rule revision as well as the other research ethics codes discussed in this Chapter recognize, research is increasingly being carried out on a global basis. Particularly problematic has been research in developing countries. On occasion there has been suspicion that research has been carried out in these countries to avoid the strict oversight imposed in developed nations. On other occasions, however, research has been conducted in developing nations because the products or procedures being developed are allegedly of value to the populations of these nations. When research is carried out, however, on populations with radically different cultures there are ample opportunities for misunderstanding. Where research is carried out on illiterate, or poor, or socially marginalized populations, there are also ample opportunities for exploitation. The following reading discusses these issues.

Solomon R. Benatar, *Towards Progress in Resolving Dilemmas in International Research Ethics*

Journal of Law, Medicine and Ethics, vol. 32, pp. 574, 574–75, 579–81 Winter 2004

* * *

In her recent review of agreements and controversies in international research ethics, Ruth Macklin has concluded that, despite seeming agreement on several issues, many different viewpoints persist. In her view it is unlikely that these will be resolved easily. I begin by listing the issues on which Macklin notes broad agreement, followed by a brief reference to the nature of remaining controversies (in italics).

• Research must be responsive to the needs of people in the community being studied. *How are decisions taken about what research to undertake in developing countries and how are these prioritized?*

• Research is needed on diseases that occur frequently in poor countries, especially when these cause high morbidity and mortality. *What sorts of study designs are acceptable? Can placebos be used and what comparative arms should be included?*

• It is unethical to exploit the vulnerable. *What specifically does it mean not to exploit people?*

• It is unacceptable to lower the ethical standards for research in developing countries. *What is the standard of care that should apply in research in developing countries? How is this defined and justified?*

* * * Researchers largely share a common scientific world-view and have a primary, if not exclusive interest in advancing knowledge. Underprivileged and deprived research subjects within traditional cultures tend to share a non-scientific world-view and have a predominant, and often even exclusive interest in receiving care for their illnesses. Although these differences in how people view medical research and access to health care lie along a spectrum and there may be much that is shared, the extent of such differences is not trivial and they are of practical importance in developing ethical policies for research. * * *

Anthropologists and social scientists have been critical of modern bioethics on the grounds that it is based on Western moral philosophy and western biomedical perspectives. An additional criticism is that bioethics is applied within a theoretical framework that emphasizes the application of scientifically rigorous medical care to people who are sufficiently autonomous to make self-interested decisions about themselves in a context of minimal social connectedness. Such a highly reductionist and individualistic approach takes insufficient consideration of the social and cultural context of illness or associated ethical dilemmas, isolates bioethical issues from spiritual perspectives and neglects the dynamic nature of relationships between individuals, their families and their community.

Some critics of modern bioethics favor a more embracing communitarian conception of the individual that acknowledges and values closer links with other people. As an example, the African notion of a person values links with the past (ancestors), the present (family and community), and with other animate beings within a "web of relations" that has been labeled as an "Eco-bio-communitarian perspective." Within this more embracing context of many traditional cultures, illness represents more than mechanical dysfunction, and understanding and dealing with illness requires an explanatory model with greater attention to the influence of external social interactions, luck, fate and magico-religious considerations.

These two views of people, within social relationships defined in a polarized manner either as individualistic or communitarian along a single dimension, have generated much debate in relation to cross-cultural research ethics. Some insist that the individualistic approach is the best universal model and that it must be rigorously applied in the research context. Others argue that this is a "particular rationality" about human life, one that is attractive in its abstract form but lacks resemblance to the real world in which people live. In addition it is argued that more attention should be paid to complex notions of social relationships, and in particular to potential exploitation of vulnerable subjects.

* * *

How are decisions taken about what research to undertake in developing countries and how are these prioritized?

In keeping with an approach that acknowledges that there are different forms of social relations and that understanding these and working with them offers greater prospects for resolving conflicting views the following could be advised. First, clinical trials in developing countries should be relevant to the health needs of the host country. Second, the design and conduct of trials should involve members of the host country in participatory partnerships of an emancipating nature. Third, prior evaluation should be made of whether study findings can, and will, be incorporated into local health care systems. These processes, involving dialogue and collaboration from the earliest stages of research design, are in a sense analogous to the idea of democratic deliberation, and could assist in explicating and justifying priorities in particular contexts.

What sorts of study designs are acceptable? Can placebos be used and what comparative arms should be included?

In my view it will not be possible to resolve the current debate about the use of placebos unless the different motives and world-views of those who argue for differing regulations regarding their use are considered. In addition, while general statements can be made about the use of placebos in research, their valid use in every conceivable setting cannot be deduced simply from a few sentences in research ethics guidelines. If we accept that abstract universal principles are valid; if we consider local factors to be relevant to the application of universal principles; and if we value the process of moral reasoning, then we must agree that in order to determine whether or not a placebo arm is justified, then careful consideration is required of potential harms and benefits in relation to studies designed to ask and answer specific questions in specific contexts. In those situations where morally valid reasons can be mounted for placebo-controlled trials, and where such studies are designed specifically for the benefit of local populations rather than as surrogates for acquiring information for wealthy countries (for example studies of "me too" drugs, the use of a placebo may be justified on rational grounds. The proviso is that utilitarian calculations for the benefit of whole groups of people (and with their agreement) should be constrained by the need to prevent harm to individuals, and to avoid the use of placebo when this may result in unnecessary suffering, avoidable injuries or death. Each study in which a placebo arm is anticipated should thus be considered on its merits, rather than precluded or allowed entirely on the basis of a bluntly designed clause in a declaration. Considerations of context are required aspects of moral reasoning in the application of universal principles in specific situations, and taking relevant moral factors into consideration does not entail moral relativism.

A simple definition of exploitation in the research context would include the following:

• Taking advantage of power differentials to do what researchers want to do and in any way they wish without consideration of the harms that may be perceived by research participants.

• Using research subjects as a means to achieving the ends of researchers (advancing knowledge) when the benefits of the research will not be fairly available to research participants and their communities.

• Undertaking studies in which minimal benefits accrue to participants and large benefits, especially financial, may accrue in the long term to research sponsors, thus failing to ensure fair balance of benefits and burdens to sponsors/researchers and research participants in the longer term.

• Denying participants post-trial use of therapies identified as beneficial in the trial in environments where such treatments would not otherwise be available.

To avoid exploitation priority should be given to trials that will provide useful knowledge for the host country, the balance of benefits and burdens should be fairly distributed and the benefits of research should be seen to flow into health care settings. Efforts should also be made to ensure that existing disparities are not entrenched by deflecting local human or material resources away from healthcare systems in host countries towards research.

What is the standard of care? How is this defined and how can it be justified?

The idea of a global universally applicable ethical framework for the standard of care in international research would be inclusive of at least the following features:

• Conducting research with the same respect for the dignity of all subjects wherever they are in the world—as reflected in treating them as ends in their own right and not using them merely to acquire knowledge that could be of benefit to others.

• Obtaining meaningful informed consent by structuring the process of obtaining consent within the linguistic and cultural framework of research subjects. Providing care for other diseases concomitantly afflicting research subjects for which treatment would not otherwise be available in impoverished settings and in this way enhancing the potential for community benefit to flow from research.

• The avoidance of exploitation as indicated above.

It has been further argued that such a globally reasoned universal standard of care can be translated into feasible local practices (reasoned contextual universalism). This would require the shaping an acceptable standard of care for a particular study through a deliberative scholarly process (not merely political haggling) among researchers and the community of research participants within respectful partnerships. Making progress on a continuous basis through successive research projects in local contexts could in this way improve health care and move the standard of care in research towards the reasoned global universal level.

Attempts to resolve the vexed question of the "standard of care" for research in developing countries by utilizing arguments totally within a single world-view are unlikely to convince those who have a different perspective on social relations and how these should influence social policy in research. Making progress towards narrowing the differences identified by Macklin requires giving due moral weight to morally significant contextual considerations, including the values of research participants, where these are not harmful and do not infringe on the physical and emotional integrity of others.

With regard to justification for a broader overall standard of care, several arguments have been offered. These include moral arguments that embrace concerns not to do harm, to do good and to be fair. There should be respect for harmless practices within other cultures, while rejecting those that infringe human rights. There should also be sensitivity to the adverse invasive social impact of itinerant researchers from developed countries. Strategically it can also be argued that an improved standard of care could enhance participation in research and the achievement of research goals. Not least, an operational argument can be mounted in support of the idea that research coupled to improved standards of care facilitates improvements in the delivery of health care. As the goal of medical research is to improve health care there should be greater support for encouraging closer links between research and its application at sites where the research is being undertaken. These justifications and examples of how they have been applied in practice have been described in detail elsewhere.

While dual standards of care will ensue from implementing a broader standard of care in poor countries, this is an inevitable aspect of progress. Inability to achieve immediate equity should not be an impediment to making improvements that could spread more widely with time and effort. It could be argued that it is more unethical to be satisfied with existing low or non-existent standards than to create dual standards as part of a progressive means of improving care. Of course a higher standard of care will be an inducement. But inducements are only morally wrong if they result in participants taking risks with their health and lives. What is wrong with an inducement that enables access to otherwise unavailable care and continues after the trial is over? Inability to achieve immediate equity should not be an impediment to achieving progressive reductions in inequity.

* * *

Making * * * progress will require new paradigms of thinking. Firstly, it must be acknowledged that research does not take place in a vacuum but rather in a world with wide disparities in which much research on vulnerable people has never been applied for their benefit. Secondly, researchers should increasingly view continuation of current patterns of exploitative research as ethically unacceptable. Thirdly, the need to link moral progress to scientific progress should become a high priority. Progress could be made towards such goals by coupling research to improvements in health through a broader conception of the standard of care and by linking research to development through partnerships and strategic alliances that could promote sustainability.

Notes

1. Perhaps the most famous incidents involving research in developing countries were the HIV transmission trials carried out in a number of nations in the mid-1990s. See, discussing these, Symposium, 88 *Am. J. Pub. Health* 548ff, including articles by Ruth Fadin and Nancy Kass, Isabelle De Zoysa, et al., Quarraisha Abdool Karim, et al., George Annas and Michael Grodin, Salim S. Abdool Karim, and Ronald Bayer. Among many other articles on vertical transmission HIV trials, see, criticizing the tests, M. Angell, The Ethics of Clinical Research in the Third World, 337 *New Eng. J. Med.* 847 (1997) and P. Lurie and S. Wolfe, Unethical Trials of Interventions to Reduce the Perinatal Transmission of the Human Immunodeficiency Virus in De-

veloping Countries, 337 *New Eng. J. Med.* 853 (1997); and, defending the trials, H. Varmus and D. Satcher, Ethical Complexities of Conducting Research in Developing Countries, 337 *New Eng. J. Med.* 1000 (1997). Among the other articles discussing this controversy, see, Symposium, HIV Research in Developing Countries, 12 *Bioethics* 286 (1998); Symposium, A World of Research Subjects, 28 *Hastings Ctr. Rep.*, November/December 1998 at 25; and H. Varmus & D. Satcher, *The Conduct of Clinical Trials of Maternal-Infant Transmission of HIV Supported by the United States Department of Health and Human Services in Developing Countries, http://www.nih.gov/news/mathiv/mathiv.htm*. See also, generally, Ruth Macklin, *Double Standards in Medical Research in Developing Countries* (2004); and, specifically on the question of compensating victims of such trials, Charles Weijer, Guy J. LeBlanc, The Balm of Gilead: Is the Provision of Treatment to Those Who Seroconvert in HIV Prevention Trials a Matter of Moral Obligation or Moral Negotiations? 34 *J. L. Med. & Ethics* 793 (2006).

2. Among the many issues raised by research in developing countries is whether international Guidelines like the Declaration of Helsinki or the CIOMS Guidelines should govern research in radically different cultures. One particular issue, for example, is whether the notion of informed consent endorsed by these guidelines is in fact an artifact of Western notions of autonomous individuality, and thus inappropriate for cultures where the concept of individuality is much weaker, and where, perhaps it might be more culturally sensitive to seek consent from a subject's family or social group. Opponents of this position defend these ethical guidelines as universal, and suggest that varying these principles to fit different cultures might result in "ethical apartheid." See, espousing a principle of "ethical pluralism," Nicolas A. Christakis, The Distinction Between Ethical Pluralism and Ethical Relativism: Implications for the Conduct of Transcultural Clinical Research, and arguing for ethical universalism, Medical Research and the Principle of Respect for Persons in Non-Western Culture, both in *The Ethics of Research Involving Human Subjects: Facing the 21st Century* (Harold Y. Vanderpool, ed., 1996).

Index